The Analytic Tradition in Philosophy

The Analytic Tradition in Philosophy

VOLUME 1
THE FOUNDING GIANTS

•SCOTT SOAMES•

PRINCETON UNIVERSITY PRESS
PRINCETON AND OXFORD

Copyright © 2014 by Princeton University Press
Published by Princeton University Press, 41 William Street,
Princeton, New Jersey 08540
In the United Kingdom: Princeton University Press, 6 Oxford Street,
Woodstock, Oxfordshire OX20 1TW
press.princeton.edu
All Rights Reserved
ISBN 978-0-691-16002-3
British Library Cataloging-in-Publication Data is available
This book has been composed in Baskerville 10 Pro and John Sans
Printed on acid-free paper. ∞
Printed in the United States of America
10 9 8 7 6 5 4 3 2 1

FOR MARTHA, BRIAN, AND GREG

CONTENTS

∞᠙᠙ᕫ

Acknowledgments   ix

Preface   xi

PART ONE: FREGE

CHAPTER 1
Foundations of Logic, Language, and Mathematics   3

CHAPTER 2
Critical Challenges   60

PART TWO: G. E. MOORE

CHAPTER 3
Becoming G. E. Moore   133

CHAPTER 4
Goodness and the Foundations of Ethics   172

CHAPTER 5
Truth, Skepticism, Perception, and Knowledge   206

CHAPTER 6
The Mixed Legacy and Lost Opportunities of Moore's Ethics   242

PART THREE: RUSSELL

CHAPTER 7
Early Russell: Logic, Philosophy, and *The Principles of Mathematics*   263

CHAPTER 8
Russell's Theory of Descriptions: "On Denoting"   328

CHAPTER 9
Truth, Falsity, and Judgment   413

CHAPTER 10
Russell's Logicism   473

CHAPTER 11
Our Knowledge of the External World   535

CHAPTER 12
The Philosophy of Logical Atomism   568

Looking Ahead   631

References   633

Index   647

ACKNOWLEDGMENTS

I am grateful to my colleague, Gabriel Uzquiano, for reading and making many helpful comments on chapters 1, 2, 7, and 10. Thanks also to my former disseration students Geoff Georgi and Brian Bowman for spotting many errors in their reading of the entire manuscript. Special credit goes to the two referees provided by the Princeton University Press, whose extraordinary insight and erudition greatly improved the manuscript, not least of which by identifying important omissions and pointing me in directions that allowed me to correct them in some cases and compensate for them in others. I also appreciate the useful feedback from the graduate students in Philosophy 500 at USC in the fall semesters of 2011 and 2012.

PREFACE

❦

This is the first of a new multivolume work on the analytic tradition in
philosophy in which I plan to discuss major milestones in the subject
extending from the late nineteenth century to the end of the twentieth
century. Naturally, not all important pieces of the enormous volume of
work done in this period will find their way into these volumes. However,
my aim is to include a great deal. All the topics treated in the two volumes
of my earlier work *Philosophical Analysis in the Twentieth Century* will be
discussed here, plus much more. The issues presented will be pursued at
greater length, in more detail, and, I hope, at a higher level of philosophical sophistication. Whereas the previous volumes grew out of lectures at
Princeton intended for advanced undergraduates and beginning graduate
students, these volumes will be more demanding.

The goal is to tell a coherent (though complicated) story of where the
tradition has been, and where it appears to be heading. As before, this
requires identifying major insights and achievements, and distinguishing
them from major errors or disappointments. Although I have more space
to devote to historical influence and context, my chief focus will continue
to be on the explication and evaluation of arguments—lots of them. Inevitably, some discussions will be contentious. Philosophical histories of the
sort I am attempting to write are also works of philosophy. In my case,
this means arguing with the greats in the process of learning from them.
Make no mistake; the real philosophical progress that has occurred since
the early days of the analytic tradition has put us in a better position to
discern the errors and limitations to which even our greatest forebears
were prone. However, it has not exhausted the rich store of insights to be
gleaned from their work and from which we may hope to make still more
progress. Those who did so much to make us who we are, are still our contemporaries in what amounts to a common quest.

This first volume covers the initial phase of the analytic tradition, prior
to the English publication of Wittgenstein's *Tractatus Logico-Philosophicus*
in 1922. My discussion focuses on the period from Frege's *Begriffsschrift* in
1879 through Russell's *The Philosophy of Logical Atomism* in 1918. In addition to works that appeared within this time frame, I also discuss Moore's
1925 "A Defense of Common Sense," and his 1939 "Proof of an External
World"—both of which articulated positions for which he was already well
known prior to the publication of the *Tractatus*. The major milestones of
this first phase of analytic philosophy on which I concentrate are:

(i) the extraordinary development of symbolic logic pioneered by Frege and Russell;

(ii) their ground-breaking transformation of the philosophy of mathematics;

(iii) the use of the concepts and methods developed in their logico-mathematical investigations to lay the foundations for systematic investigations of language;

(iv) Russell's relentless attempts, between 1905 and 1918, to use his method of logical and linguistic analysis to attack traditional problems of epistemology and metaphysics, and to establish such analysis as the chief methodological tool by which philosophy advances;

(v) the revolt of Moore and Russell against the systems of Kantian- and Hegelian- inspired Idealism that dominated British philosophy at the end of the nineteenth and the beginning of the twentieth century, as well as their resistance to the American Pragmatism of their time;

(vi) Moore's agenda-setting metaethical views that framed debate in the subject for nearly half a century; and

(vii) Moore's vigorous commonsense priorities in epistemology, the effects of which continue to influence philosophy down to the present day.

By the end of this initial analytic period, logic, language, and mathematics had become central topics of philosophical inquiry in a way never before seen. But although logic and language were increasingly viewed as important for broad areas of philosophy, they did not yet define it. The three great philosophers of this period did not hold revolutionary views about the nature of philosophy itself. Although Frege differed sharply with Kant about logic, arithmetic, and the analytic-synthetic distinction, he had great respect for Kant's view of the synthetic apriority of geometry and much of the Kantian conception of mind that went with it. Moore's view of the nature of philosophy—which he makes clear in his 1910–11 lectures later published as *Some Main Problems of Philosophy*—were traditional; philosophy's job was to tell us what kinds of things there are, how they are related to one another, what we can know, how knowledge is achieved, and what is of greatest intrinsic value. What Moore added to this familiar picture was a way of proceeding that led to principled skepticism about the power of philosophy to establish highly revisionary views about any of these things. Russell was more ambitious. He too wished to provide answers to ancient questions about the nature of reality and our ability to know it. However, far from being skeptical about the possibility of arriving at novel and far-reading answers, he believed that the powerful methods of logical and linguistic analysis could be used to establish a stunningly revisionary epistemological and metaphysical system rivaling the great philosophical systems of the past.

All of this was about to change with the publication of the *Tractatus* in 1922. Though the system of logical atomism developed there had much in common with Russell's 1918 system, Wittgenstein's focus and underlying view of philosophy were very different from Russell's. Whereas Wittgenstein's ideas represented a decisive "linguistic turn" in the philosophy of his time and the decades thereafter, Russell's approach came to appear dated. This perception, though to some extent justified by the extravagant metaphysics elaborated in *The Philosophy of Logical Atomism*, was not entirely fair to him—since in the last few pages of that work he articulated an attractive and forward-looking view. There, he characterized philosophy as the leading edge of science, pushing inquiry into areas beyond the reach of reliable established methods, and gradually working issues into a shape fit for scientific investigation and the attainment of genuine knowledge. Looking back today, we may not only sympathize with that view, but also recognize the justification for it that had already been provided by the birth of modern logic, the impressive work being done in the foundations of mathematics, and the early steps taken in the struggle to develop a science of language.

This volume tells that story and more—from Frege, through Moore, to the logical atomism of Russell. The first two chapters on Frege, which compose nearly a quarter of the volume, are entirely new. Chapter 1 explicates his powerful system of logic, his seminal analysis of quantification, his domestication of the mathematical notion of a function for use in semantics, his distinction between sense and reference, his critical philosophy of mathematics and positive account of number presented in *The Foundations of Arithmetic,* and his strategies for proving the axioms of arithmetic from those of logic, plus his definitions of arithmetical primitives from logical ones. Chapter 2 critically evaluates his treatments of existence, generality, quantification, propositions (thoughts), the analysis of the attitudes, his hierarchy of indirect sense and reference, the problems raised by names, anaphora, and quantifying-in, the strengths and weaknesses of Fregean treatments of time, tense, and indexicality, the philosophical foundations of his logicist reduction, and the devastating blow dealt to it by Russell's paradox.

At this point, the story moves to Moore. Chapter 3, which is also entirely new, recounts the journey from his youthful Idealism through his early "metaphysical realism" to his more mature analytic perspective. Particularly interesting, in part because of their influence on the young Russell, are his views on truth and propositions. What is most significant, however, is his remarkably prescient analysis of perception based on an incipient philosophy of mind that anticipates much in contemporary "intentionalist" theories. This chapter is followed by discussions in chapters 4, 5, and 6 of Moore's celebrated ethical and metaethical views, his defense of common sense, and his proof of an external world. These chapters are reworked versions of the material in the first four chapters of volume 1 of *Philosophical Analysis in the Twentieth Century*—expanded to include a new section in chapter 4 discussing the influence of Sidgwick and Russell on *Principia Ethica* and a new section in chapter 5 on the material in *Some*

Main Problems of Philosophy. In addition, there is substantial new material incorporating modern perspectives on Moore in chapters 5 and 6 on his "Proof of an External World" and his analysis of 'good'.

The chapters on Moore are followed by six chapters on Russell, which make up more than half the book. After introducing the reader to the young Russell's engagement and growing struggles with his Idealist predecessors, chapter 7 takes up some of his early mathematical views, their relation to those of Cantor and Frege, the philosophical logic of his 1903 *Principles of Mathematics*, his struggles with propositions and denoting complexes, and his philosophical development between 1903 and his discovery of the celebrated theory of descriptions in 1905. Like chapters 1, 2, and 3, this chapter is also entirely new. Chapter 8 is an exhaustive explication and critical evaluation of "On Denoting." In it material from chapter 5 of volume 1 of *Philosophical Analysis in the Twentieth Century* is reorganized and integrated into an expansive discussion of all major points in that classic article. Special attention is paid to the famous "Gray's Elegy" argument, which, though ignored and misunderstood for a century, was regarded by Russell as the centerpiece of the work. Although this fascinating argument fails in the end, I argue that much of its persuasive power came from an all-too-common conception of propositions shared by Russell that must be replaced in order to put the issues raised by the argument to rest. The chapter closes with assessments and refinements of Russell's theory of descriptions from the perspective of contemporary philosophy of language and mind, emphasizing the differences and similarities between his theoretical projects and ours.

Chapter 9, also entirely new, begins with Russell's, and Moore's, critiques of Idealists' theories of Truth and Reality. It is here that the second half of the story begun in chapter 7, of the metamorphosis of the young and impressionable mathematics and philosophy student into the Bertrand Russell we know today, is completed. This is followed by a substantial discussion of Russell's (and Moore's) telling critique of American Pragmatism, which was then emerging as a rival heir to the throne previously occupied by Absolute Idealism. The remainder of the chapter focuses on Russell's problem with propositions as bearers of truth and falsity, and his eventual replacement of them by his multiple relation theory of judgment. The difficulty at bottom was, I argue, his misdiagnosis of the problem of the unity of the proposition, and hence his failure to solve it. It was this that led to his ingenious, though ultimately ill-fated, reanalysis of belief and other "propositional" attitudes. After explaining his multiple relation theory and its manifold shortcomings, I identify an extraordinary Russellian insight which, I argue, could have been used to solve the problem that defeated him, and thereby rehabilitate propositions. Capitalizing on this insight, I use it to sketch a promising conception of propositions capable of solving many problems with them, past and present, while shedding much needed light on the difficulties in chapter

8 arising from Russell's startling impossibility argument against Fregean treatments of definite descriptions as singular terms. The chapter closes with a brief chronicle of Russell's later struggles over the dying multiple relation theory.

Chapters 10, 11, and 12 are massively reworked and greatly expanded versions of chapters 6, 7, and 8 of volume 1 of *Philosophical Analysis in the Twentieth Century.* Chapter 10 explains the philosophy behind Russell's reduction of arithmetic to logic, and sketches the logical techniques used to accomplish it. The chapter begins by comparing the Fregean and Russellian strategies for the reduction, indicating why trading Frege's concept-extensions for a hierarchy of Fregean concepts (thereby blocking paradox) won't work. The idea of a developing hierarchy of classes on which paradox-blocking type restrictions are directly stated is then broached, along with a warning about the need to guarantee that we won't run out of classes in constructing it. This is followed by an explanation of what theoretical reduction is, and a much simplified reconstruction of Russell's reduction of arithmetic to logic using *a first-order system of logic combined with a type-theoretical conception of classes* as the reducing theory. The need to justify the otherwise problematic restrictions in the type-hierarchy is explained, along with worries about the Axiom of Infinity to which Russell was driven. This leads to a discussion of the philosophical significance of the reduction in which I review his changed and more mature conception of that significance—according to which the goal of *justifying* mathematics by removing doubts about its absolute, a priori certainty is replaced by the goal of *explaining* why mathematical statements are true, and how they could, in principle, come to be known. I then move to a more complicated reconstruction of the reduction, in which the earlier first-order theory of logic-cum–set theory (to which arithmetic is reduced) is traded for a *second-order system* that looks more like a theory that might rightly claim the title "pure logic." Though the packaging is closer to Russell's own, and the propriety of characterizing the reducing system as *logic* is less questionable, the essential philosophical issues are the same as before.

The chapter closes with an extended critical discussion of Russell's infamous no-class theory—according to which classes are *logical fictions,* and so not really required by the reduction. The points at issue are not, primarily, the technicalities of the reduction, but their interpretation. Although the higher-order quantifiers Russell uses are said to range over *propositional functions*—from which characteristic functions of classes can easily be constructed when the "functions" so labeled are taken to be *genuine functions from objects to propositions*—Russell had given up such functions when he gave up propositions. In *Principia Mathematica,* he still uses the old terminology, while identifying "propositional functions" with formulas. After noting the challenge this poses for the quantification he employs, and for the significance of his reduction, I examine an interpretation offered

by Greg Landini and Kevin Klement. According to them the quantification in *Principia Mathematica* (and later works) is substitutional, rather
than objectual. On this interpretation, the type-restrictions used in the
reduction seem to fall out automatically, without need of further justifying explanation, and the entire construction is, astonishingly, seen as free
of ontological commitment to classes, objective Fregean concepts (characteristic functions of classes), and nonlinguistic propositional functions of
the sort that Russell had previously embraced.

Despite the attractiveness of these ideas to Russell, I argue that this
interpretation cannot be maintained. Although he did seem to have some
thoughts of a substitutional sort, they were, understandably, not thoroughly worked out, and, unfortunately, run together with other, earlier,
thoughts with which they were inconsistent. What is worse, if a consistent
and well-worked-out substitutional construal were imposed on *Principia*
and later works, the result would undermine Russell's logicist reduction
of mathematics to logic, while also wreaking havoc with central tenets of
his broader philosophical logic. The best interpretation is one that preserves Russell's genuine insights and builds upon them. When it comes to
Principia this is one in which the quantification is objectual, and hence ontologically committing, and the theory of types is Ramsey's simple theory,
rather than the baroque ramified theory of the *Principia* (which required
the questionable Axiom of Reducibility). This, as I note in the chapter, is
the interpretation that was historically most influential, becoming pretty
standard among philosophers and logicians who followed Russell. The
chapter closes with a very brief discussion relating these points to Russell's *vicious circle* principle, and his view of semantic and other paradoxes.

In chapters 11 and 12, I explore Russell's attempt in *Our Knowledge of
the External World* and *The Philosophy of Logical Atomism* to transfer leading
ideas behind his logicist reduction to traditional problems of epistemology and metaphysics. His reduction of numbers to classes, followed by
his purported elimination of classes themselves, was taken to explain how
we could legitimately know, or come to know, something approximating
what we use mathematical statements to report, without assuming epistemic access to abstract objects of which we have no clear conception.
Similarly, his analysis of material objects as logical constructions out of
one's own sense data plus those of other agents, and his later analysis of
agents themselves as logical constructions out of the objects of immediate sensation, were designed to explain how we can legitimately know
something approximating what we ordinarily use empirical statements to
report, without relying on unverifiable assumptions about metaphysically
suspect substances standing behind the appearances. Roughly put, the
idea in the mathematical case was (i) to use definitions of arithmetical
primitives to translate arithmetical statements into purely logical ones,
(ii) to prove those statements from purely logical axioms, and (iii) to perform similar tasks reducing theorems of higher mathematics to those of

arithmetic, and thereby to those of logic. Transferring this idea to the empirical case meant (a) thinking of both agent and material-object statements as being translatable into statements about the properties of momentary objects of immediate sensation, and the relations in which they stand to one another, and (b) showing how they are verified or falsified by immediate perceptual reports.

In the end, the parallel between the two cases was more imagined than real. Whereas in the mathematical case Russell stated precise definitions yielding definite translations in (i) and rigorous proofs in (ii) of the translations of arithmetical theorems, in the empirical case no precise definitions were ever stated, no definite translations ever provided, and no methods giving verdicts of verification or falsification were ever articulated. Although Russell was aware of this, he did not appear to be bothered by it. It was enough, he seemed to think, to sketch the leading ideas in a way that made it plausible to think that the task could, in principle, be completed. In my critical comments in chapters 11 and 12 I explain why I think he was mistaken in this.

Nevertheless, I believe Russell's attempt to have been an important one. It is not just that the errors in constructing his system are instructive, though they are. Nor is it simply that having a clear conception of his version of logical atomism to compare and contrast with Wittgenstein's celebrated system in the *Tractatus* sheds light on the latter, though it does. Rather, the conception of reality that Russell aspires to in *The Philosophy of Logical Atomism* is one of the great empiricist systems of metaphysics, having a good deal in common with Carnap's in the *Aufbau*. Seen in this light, Russell's is one of philosophy's recurrent and seemingly irrepressible attempts to make sense of reality as a whole—one of the last before the fabled "linguistic turn," and also one that may usefully be compared to David Lewis's attempt at something similar more than a half century later, after the linguistic turn had run its course.

Part 1

· FREGE ·

CHAPTER 1

∽᠑ᡅ᠑᠍ᢒᢀ

Foundations of Logic, Language, and Mathematics

1. Overview
2. The Language of Logic and Mathematics
3. Sense, Reference, Compositionality, and Hierarchy
4. Frege's Logic
5. Frege's Philosophy of Mathematics
   5.1. Critique of Naturalism, Formalism, and Psychologism
   5.2. Critique of Kant
   5.3. Frege's Definition of Number
      5.3.1. Numerical Statements Are about Concepts
      5.3.2. But Numbers Are Objects
      5.3.3. Objects and Identity
      5.3.4. The Number of F's, Zero, Successor, and the Numerals
      5.3.5. The Natural Numbers
6. The Logicist Reduction
   6.1. The Axioms of Logic and Arithmetic
   6.2. Informal Proofs of the Arithmetical Axioms
   6.3. Arithmetical Operations
   6.4. Further Issues

1. OVERVIEW

The German philosopher-logician Gottlob Frege was born in 1848, graduated with a PhD in Mathematics from the University of Gottingen in 1873, and earned his Habilitation in Mathematics from the University of Jena in 1874, where he taught for 43 years until his retirement in 1917, after which he continued to write on issues in philosophical logic and the philosophy of mathematics until his death in 1925. While he is now recognized as one of the greatest philosophical logicians, philosophers of mathematics, and philosophers of language of all time, his seminal achievements in these areas initially elicited little interest from his contemporaries in mathematics. Though he did attract the attention of, and have an important influence on, four young men—Bertrand Russell,

Edmund Husserl, Rudolf Carnap, and Ludwig Wittgenstein—who were to become giants in twentieth-century philosophy, it took several decades after his death before the true importance of his contributions became widely recognized.

Frege's main goal in philosophy was to ground the certainty and objectivity of mathematics in the fundamental laws of logic, and to distinguish both logic and mathematics from empirical science in general, and from the psychology of human reasoning in particular. His pursuit of this goal can be divided into four interrelated stages. The first was his development of a new system of symbolic logic, vastly extending the power of previous systems, and capable of formalizing the notion of proof in mathematics. This stage culminated in his publication of the *Begriffsschrift* (*Concept Script*) in 1879. The second stage was the articulation of a systematic philosophy of mathematics, emphasizing (i) the objective nature of mathematical truths, (ii) the grounds for certain, a priori knowledge of them, (iii) the definition of number, (iv) a strategy for deriving the axioms of arithmetic from the laws of logic plus analytical definitions of basic arithmetical concepts, and (v) the prospect of extending the strategy to higher mathematics through the definition and analysis of real, and complex, numbers. After the virtual neglect of the *Begriffsschrift* by his contemporaries—due in part to its forbidding technicality and idiosyncratic symbolism—Frege presented the second stage of his project in remarkably accessible, and largely informal, terms in *Die Grundlagen der Arithmetik* (*The Foundations of Arithmetic*), published in 1884. In addition to being among the greatest treatises in the philosophy of mathematics ever written, this work is one of the best examples of the clarity, precision, and illuminating insight to which work in the analytic tradition has come to aspire. The third stage of the project is presented in a series of ground-breaking articles, starting in the early 1890s and continuing at irregular intervals throughout the rest of his life. These articles include, most prominently, "Funktion und Begriff" ("Function and Concept") in 1891, "Über Begriff und Gegenstand" ("On Concept and Object") in 1892, "Über Sinn und Bedeutung" ("On Sense and Reference") in 1892, and "Der Gedanke" ("Thought") in 1918. In addition to elucidating the fundamental semantic ideas needed to understand and precisely characterize the language of logic and mathematics, this series of articles contains important insights about how to extend those ideas to natural languages like English and German, thereby providing the basis for the systematic study of language, thought, and meaning. The final stage of Frege's grand project is presented in his treatise *Grundgesetze der Arithmetik* (*Basic Laws of Arithmetic*), volumes 1 and 2, published in 1893 and 1903 respectively. In these volumes, Frege meticulously and systematically endeavors to derive arithmetic from logic together with definitions of arithmetical concepts in purely logical terms. Although, as we shall see, his attempt was not entirely successful, the project has proven to be extraordinarily fruitful.

The discussion in this chapter will not strictly follow the chronological development of Frege's thought. Instead, I will begin with his language of logic and mathematics, which provides the starting point for developing his general views of language, meaning, and thought, and the fundamental notions—truth, reference, sense, functions, concepts, and objects—in terms of which they are to be understood. With these in place, I will turn to a discussion of the philosophical ideas about mathematics that drive his reduction of arithmetic to logic, along with a simplified account of the reduction itself. The next chapter will be devoted to critical discussions of Frege's most important views, including the interaction between his philosophy of language and his philosophy of mathematics. In what follows I refer to Frege's works under their English titles—with the exception of the *Begriffsschrift,* the awkwardness of the English translation of which is prohibitive.

2. THE LANGUAGE OF LOGIC AND MATHEMATICS

I begin with the specification of a simple logical language which, though presented in a more convenient symbolism than the one Frege used, is a direct descendant of his. The first step is to specify how the formulas and sentences of the language are constructed from the vocabulary of the language. After that, we will turn to Fregean principles for understanding the language.

THE SYMBOLIC LANGUAGE L_F

Vocabulary

Names of objects: $a, b, c, \ldots$

Function signs: $f(\,), g(\,), h(\,), f'(\,,\,), g'(\,,\,) h'(\,,\,,\,), \ldots$. These stand for functions from objects to objects. Function signs are sorted into 1-place, 2-place, $\ldots$, and n-place. One-place function signs combine with a single name (or other term) to form a complex term, 2-place function signs combine with a pair of names (or other terms) to form a complex term, and so on. Standardly, the terms follow the function sign, but in the case of some 2-place function signs—like '+' and '×' for addition and multiplication—the function symbol is placed between the terms.

Predicate signs: $(\,) = (\,), P(\,), Q(\,,\,), R(\,,\,,\,) \ldots$ Predicate signs are sorted into 1-place, 2-place, etc. An n-place predicate sign combines with n terms to form a formula.

Terms

Individual variables (ranging over objects) are terms: $x, y, z, x', y', z', \ldots$

Names of objects are terms: $a, b, c, \ldots$

Expressions in which an n-place function sign is combined with n terms are terms: e.g., if a and b are terms, f and h are 1-place function signs, and g is a 2-place function sign, then ⌜f(a)⌝, ⌜g(a,b)⌝, ⌜h(f(a))⌝, and ⌜g(a,f(b))⌝ are terms.

Definite descriptions are terms: If Φv is a formula containing the variable v, then ⌜the v Φv⌝ is a term.

Nothing else is a term.

Formulas

An atomic formula is the combination of an n-place predicate sign with n terms. Standardly the terms follow the predicate sign, but in the case of some 2-place predicate signs—like '( ) = ( )' for identity—the terms are allowed to flank predicate sign.

Other (non-atomic) formulas

If Φ and Ψ are formulas, so are ⌜~Φ⌝, ⌜(Φ ∨ Ψ)⌝, ⌜(Φ & Ψ)⌝, ⌜(Φ → Ψ)⌝ and ⌜(Φ ⟷ Ψ)⌝ . If v is a variable and Φ(v) is a formula containing an occurrence of v, ⌜∀v Φ(v)⌝ and ⌜∃v Φ(v)⌝ are also formulas. (Parentheses can be dropped when no ambiguity results.)

⌜~Φ⌝, which is read or pronounced ⌜not Φ⌝, is the negation of Φ; ⌜(Φ ∨ Ψ)⌝, read or pronounced ⌜either Φ or Ψ⌝, is the disjunction of Φ and Ψ; ⌜(Φ & Ψ)⌝, read or pronounced ⌜Φ and Ψ⌝, is the conjunction of Φ and Ψ; ⌜(Φ → Ψ)⌝, read or pronounced ⌜if Φ, then Ψ⌝, is a conditional the antecedent of which is Φ and the consequent of which is Ψ; ⌜(Φ ⟷ Ψ)⌝, read or pronounced ⌜Φ if and only if Ψ⌝, is a biconditional connecting Φ and Ψ; ⌜∀v Φ(v)⌝, read or pronounced ⌜for all v Φ(v)⌝, is a universal generalization of Φ(v); and ⌜∃v Φ(v)⌝, which is read or pronounced ⌜at least one v is such that Φ(v)⌝, is an existential generalization of Φ(v). ∀v and ∃v are called "quantifiers."

Sentences

A sentence is a formula that contains no free occurrences of variables. An occurrence of a variable is free iff it is not bound.

An occurrence of a variable in a formula is bound iff it is within the scope of a quantifier, or the definite description operator, using that variable.

The scope of an occurrence of a quantifier ∀v and ∃v, or of the definite description operator, *the v*, is the quantifier, or description operator, together with the (smallest complete) formula immediately following it. For example, ∀x (Fx → Gx) and ∃x (Fx & Hx) are each sentences, since both occurrences of 'x' in the formula attached to the quantifier are within the scope of the quantifier. Note, in these sentences, that (i) *Fx* does not *immediately* follow the quantifiers because '(' intervenes, and

(ii) *(Fx* is not a *complete* formula because it contains '(' without an accompanying ')'. By contrast, *(∀x Fx → Gx)* and *(∀x (Fx & Hx) → Gx)* are not sentences because the occurrence of 'x' following 'G' is free in each case. The generalization to 'the x' is straightforward.

Frege's representational view of language provides the general framework for interpreting L_F. On this view, the central semantic feature of language is its use in representing the world. For a sentence S to be meaningful is for S to represent the world as being a certain way—which is to impose conditions the world must satisfy if it is to be the way S represents it to be. Since S is true iff (i.e., if and only if) the world is the way S represents it to be, these are the *truth conditions* of S. To sincerely accept, or assertively utter, S is, very roughly, to believe, or assert, that these conditions are met. Since the truth conditions of a sentence depend on its grammatical structure plus the representational contents of its parts, interpreting a language involves showing how the truth conditions of its sentences are determined by their structure together with the representational contributions of the words and phrases that make them up. There may be more to understanding a language than this—even a simple logical language like L_F constructed for formalizing mathematics and science—but achieving a compositional understanding of truth conditions is surely a central part of what is involved.

With this in mind, we apply Fregean principles to L_F. Names and other singular terms designate objects; sentences are true or false; function signs refer to functions that assign objects to the n-tuples that are their arguments; and predicates designate concepts—which are assignments of truth values to objects (i.e., functions from objects to truth values). A term that consists of an n-place function sign f together with n argument expressions designates the object that the function designated by f assigns as value to the n-tuple of referents of the argument expressions. Similarly, a sentence that consists of an n-place predicate P plus n names is true iff the names designate objects $o_1, \ldots, o_n$ and the concept designated by P assigns these n objects (taken together) the value "the True," or truth. According to Frege, concepts are also designated by truth-functional operators. The negation operator '~' designates a function from falsity to truth (and from truth to falsity), reflecting the fact that the negation of a sentence is true (false) iff the sentence negated is false (true); the operator '&' for conjunction designates a function that assigns truth to the pair consisting of truth followed by truth (and assigns falsity to every other pair), reflecting the fact that a conjunction is true iff both conjuncts are; the disjunction operator '∨' designates a function that assigns truth to any pair of arguments one of which is truth, reflecting the fact that a disjunction is true iff at least one of its disjuncts is. The operator '→' used to form what are called *material conditionals* designates the function that assigns falsity to the pair of arguments the first of which is truth and the second of which is falsity—capturing the fact that a material conditional $\ulcorner\Phi \rightarrow \Psi\urcorner$ is false whenever its antecedent Φ is true and its consequent Ψ is false. The material conditional, employed in the Fregean logical language, is true on every other assignment of truth values to Φ and Ψ. Finally, the biconditional operator '$\longleftrightarrow$' designates a function that assigns truth to the pairs of <truth, truth> and <falsity, falsity>, while assigning falsity to the other two pairs, thereby ensuring that $\ulcorner\Phi \longleftrightarrow \Psi\urcorner$ is equivalent to $\ulcorner(\Phi \rightarrow \Psi)$ & $(\Psi \rightarrow \Phi)\urcorner$.

Despite Frege's use of the term 'concept'—which sounds as if it stands for an idea or other mental construct—concepts, in the sense he uses the term, are no more mental than the people, places, or other objects that are the referents of proper names. Just as different people who use the name 'Boston' to refer to the city in Massachusetts may have different images of, or ideas about, it, so the predicate 'is a city' may bring different images or ideas to the minds of different people who predicate it of Boston. For Frege, understanding the predicate involves knowing that it designates a concept that assigns truth to an object o iff o is a city, which, in effect, amounts to knowing that to *say of* o "it's a city" is to say something true just in case o is a city. The truth or falsity of such a statement depends on objective features of o to which the function designated by 'is a city' is sensitive. Thus, Frege takes concepts to be genuine constituents of mind-independent reality.

This example brings out a related feature of Frege's view. Just as predicates and function signs are different kinds of linguistic expressions than names, and other (singular) terms, so, Frege thinks, concepts and other functions are different kinds of things than objects. On the linguistic side, Frege begins with two grammatical categories of what he calls "saturated expressions." These are sentences and (singular) terms—all of which he, idiosyncratically, calls "Names."[1] What he calls "Names" are said to refer to objects, including sentences that are said to refer to truth values "the True" and "the False." In addition, there are different types of "unsaturated expressions"—each of which is thought of as containing one or more gaps, to be filled by expressions of various types in order to produce a "saturated expression"—i.e., a singular term or a sentence. An n-place predicate, for example, is an expression that combines with n terms to form a sentence. For Frege, these include not only those that are called simple "predicate signs" in the specification of the language above, but also compound expressions that result from removing n terms from a sentence, no matter how complex.

---

[1] The singular terms in L_F include ordinary names, definite descriptions $\ulcorner$the v Φv$\urcorner$ and expressions formed by combining an n-place function sign with n terms. In the next section I will explain why Frege came to view sentences as designating truth values in much the way that singular terms designate their referents—and so as being a kind of "Name." For now, however, I mostly ignore this complication.

For example, starting with the sentence 'Cb & Lbm', stating that Boston is a city and Boston is in Massachusetts, we may provide analyses that break it into parts in several different, but *equivalent*, ways. It may be analyzed (i) as the conjunction of a sentence formed by combining the one-place predicate 'C( )'—designating the concept that assigns the value the True to an object iff that object is a city—with the name 'b', and another sentence formed by combining the two-place predicate L(,)—designating the concept that assigns the True to a pair iff the first is located at the second—with the names 'b', and 'm'; (ii) as a sentence that results from combining the one-place predicate 'C( ) & Lbm'—designating the concept that assigns the True to an object iff it is a city and Boston is located in Massachusetts—with the name 'b'; (iii) as a sentence that results from combining the one-place predicate 'C(_) & L(_,m)'—designating the function that assigns the True to an object iff it is a city located in Massachusetts—with the name 'b'; (iv) as a sentence that results from combining the one-place predicate 'Cb & L(b,)'—designating the concept that assigns the True to an object iff the object is a place, Boston is a city, and Boston is located at that place; (v) as a sentence that results from combining the two-place predicate 'Cb & L(,)'—designating the concept that assigns a pair of objects the value the True iff Boston is a city and the second object is a place at which the first is located—with the names 'b' and 'm'; and (vi) as a sentence that results from combining the two-place predicate 'C(_) & L (_,)'—designating a concept that assigns the True to a pair of objects iff the first is a city and the second is a place at which it is located—with the names 'b' and 'm'.[2]

The fact that concepts are referents of predicates (themselves regarded as "unsaturated" expressions requiring completion), plus the fact that there is no explaining what concepts are except as intermediaries that assign truth values to objects, led Frege to distinguish concepts from objects, taking them to be "incomplete" or "unsaturated" in some manner thought to parallel the way in which predicates are supposed to be incomplete. The same conclusion is drawn for (i) concepts designated by truth-functional operators, the *arguments* (along with the values) of which are truth values, and (ii) functions designated by function signs that combine with (singular) terms to form complex (singular) terms, the *values* of which are ordinary objects (rather than truth values). As we shall see, these distinctions don't preclude some higher-order functions (and concepts) from taking other functions (or concepts) as arguments. There are such higher-order functions/concepts, which take lower-order functions/concepts as arguments. Corresponding to these function-argument combinations are sentences, or singular terms, formed from expressions each of which designate concepts, or functions, rather than (what Frege calls) "objects."

---

[2] Underlining in clauses (iii) and (vi) indicates that the empty positions are linked, and so to be filled by the same Name.

Examples include sentences containing quantifiers, or the definite description operator. Consider the sentence ⌜∃x Φx⌝, where Φx is a formula (no matter how complex) in which 'x' and only 'x' occurs free. To say that only 'x' occurs free in Φx is to say that Φx counts as a one-place predicate for Frege, since it is an expression which, when combined with a name 'a' (in the sense of replacing the free occurrences of 'x' with 'a'), would form a sentence.[3] Thus, Φx designates a concept that assigns the True or the False to an object as argument (corresponding to whether the sentence that would result from replacing free occurrences of 'x' with a name of the object would be true or false). It is this concept, C_Φ, that combines with the referent of the quantifier to determine a truth value. Given this much, one can easily see what Frege's treatment of the quantifier '∃x' had to be. On his analysis, it designates the second-order concept, $C_\exists$, which takes a first-order concept C as argument and assigns it the True iff C assigns truth to some object or objects (at least one). Thus, ⌜∃x Φx⌝ is true iff there is at least one (existing) object o such that *the concept designated by Φx assigns o the value the True* iff *o "satisfies" the formula Φx* iff *replacing occurrences of 'x' in Φx with a name n for o would result in a true sentence.* By the same token, '∀x' designates the second-order concept, $C_\forall$, which takes a first-order concept C as argument and assigns it the True iff C assigns the True to every object. Thus, ⌜∀x Φx⌝ is true iff every object o is such that *the concept designated by Φx assigns o the value the True* iff *o "satisfies" the formula Φx* iff *replacing occurrences of 'x' in Φx with a name n for o would result in a true sentence.* This is Frege's breakthrough insight—creating the foundation of the new logic of quantification—into how quantificational sentences are to be understood.

His treatment of the definite description operator, 'the x', is a variant on this theme. In specifying our symbolic language, we noted that 'the x' combines with a formula Φx to form a compound singular term (a Fregean "Name") ⌜the x Φx⌝ (called "a definite description"). On Frege's analysis, the definite description operator designates the second-order function (not concept), F_{the}, which takes a first-order concept C as argument and assigns it an object o as value iff C assigns the True to o, and only to o. What should be said in the event that no object o satisfies this condition will be a topic for later. For now, we simply note that the description ⌜the x Φx⌝ is a singular term (Fregean Name) that designates o if *the concept designated by Φx assigns o, and only o, the value the True*—i.e., if *o, and only o, "satisfies" the formula Φx*, which, in turn, will hold if *o, and only o, is such that replacing occurrences of 'x' in Φx with a name n for o would result in a true sentence.*

Taken together, the above principles constitute the core of a Fregean interpretation of the language L_F. Though conceptually quite simple, the general framework is powerful, flexible, and extendable to languages of much greater complexity, including ordinary spoken languages like

---

[3] The variable, in effect, marks the gap—as well as linking related gaps—in the predicate.

English and German. However, as we shall see in the next section, there are further central elements of Frege's framework that remain to be put on the table.

3. SENSE, REFERENCE, COMPOSITIONALITY, AND HIERARCHY

So far, we have ignored an entire dimension of meaning—namely, what Frege calls "sense." He introduced his conception of sense in the first few paragraphs of "On Sense and Reference" with an argument involving identity sentences containing names or definite descriptions. Although the argument was a powerful and influential one, its focus on the identity relation—which holds only between an object and itself—introduced unnecessary complications, and spawned confusions, separable from the main point at issue. For that reason, I will present the idea behind Frege's argument in a different way, reserving a critical discussion of his own formulation of the argument until chapter 2. The argument here is based on a famous problem known as "Frege's puzzle," which involves explaining why substituting one term for another in a sentence sometimes changes meaning, even though the two terms refer to the same thing. The argument takes English sentences (1–3) to be obvious examples of such cases. (The same points could have been made using examples drawn from L_F.)

1a. The brightest heavenly body visible in the early evening sky (at certain times and places) is the same size as the brightest heavenly body visible in the morning sky just before dawn (at certain times and places).
  b. The brightest heavenly body visible in the early evening sky (at certain times and places) is the same size as the brightest heavenly body visible in the early evening sky (at certain times and places).
2a. Hesperus is the same size as the brightest heavenly body visible in the morning sky just before dawn (at certain times and places).
  b. Hesperus is the same size as Hesperus.
3a. Hesperus is the same size as Phosphorus.
  b. Phosphorus is the same size as Phosphorus.

The contention that the (a)/(b) sentences in these examples differ in meaning is supported by three facts. First, one can understand both sentences, and so know what they mean, without taking them to mean the same thing, or even to agree in truth value. For example, understanding the sentences is consistent with taking the (b) sentences to be true and the (a) sentences to be false. Second, one who assertively utters (a) would typically be deemed to say, or convey, something different from, and more informative than, what one would say, or convey, by assertively uttering (b). Third, one would standardly use the (a) and (b) sentences in ascriptions ⌜A believes that S⌝, in which (a) and (b) take the place of S, to report what one took to be different beliefs. If these three points are sufficient for the (a) and (b) sentences to differ in meaning, then principles T1 and T2 cannot be jointly maintained.

T1. The meaning of a name or a definite description is the object to which it refers.

T2. The meaning of a sentence S (or other compound expression E) is a function of its grammatical structure plus the meanings of its parts; hence, substituting an expression β for an expression α in S (or E) will result in a new sentence (or compound expression) the meaning of which does not differ from that of S (or E), provided that α and β do not differ in meaning.

Although Frege takes both ordinary names and definite descriptions to be singular terms the referents of which are objects, he rejects T1. For him, the meaning of a name is not its bearer, and the meaning of a definite description is not what it denotes. Instead, meaning—or in his terminology, *sense*—is what determines reference. It is the mode by which the referent of a term is presented to one who understands it. This sense, or *mode of presentation,* is a condition, grasped by one who understands the term, satisfaction of which by an object is necessary and sufficient for that object to be the referent of the term. For example, the sense of the description 'the oldest living American veteran of World War II' is a complex condition satisfaction of which requires one both to have been an American soldier in World War II, and to be older than any other such soldier. Although different terms with the same sense must have the same referent, terms designating the same referent may differ in sense, which explains the difference in meaning between the (a) and (b) in sentences (1) and (2). The explanation is expanded to (3) by Frege's contention that, like definite descriptions, ordinary proper names have senses that determine, but are distinct from, their referents.

The case of proper names is complicated by his admission that it is common for different speakers to use the same name to refer to the same thing, even though they may associate different senses with it. Frege's examples suggest that he regards the sense of a name n, as used by a speaker s at a time t, to be a reference-determining condition that could, in principle, be expressed by a description.[4] On this view, n as used by s at t refers to o iff o is the unique object that satisfies the descriptive condition associated with n by s at t. When there is no such object, n is meaningful, but refers to nothing. Although Frege thinks that pains should be taken to avoid such reference failures in a "perfect" language constructed for logic, mathematics, and science, he seems to regard such failures in ordinary speech as tolerable nuisances with limited practical effects. (Comparable points hold for meaningful definite descriptions that fail to designate any object.) In the case of a proper name n, the meaning, for a speaker (at a

---

[4] See Frege (1892b), p. 153, including footnote B; also, Frege (1918a), pp. 332–33, both in Frege (1997).

time), of a sentence containing n is the same as that of the corresponding sentence in which the reference-determining description the speaker implicitly associates with n (at the time) is substituted for n. Thus, for Frege, (3a) and (3b) differ in meaning for any speaker who associates the two names with different descriptive modes of presentation.

Although we have followed Frege in using examples involving names and descriptions of ordinary objects—like 'Hesperus' and 'the brightest heavenly body visible in the early evening'—to motivate his distinction between the sense and referent of a term, the distinction is meant to apply to all singular terms. Thus, it should not be surprising that other, quite different, examples—such as those in (4)—could have been used to motivate the distinction.

4a. $6^4 > 1295$
  b. $1296 > 1295$

The same can be said about these examples as was said about (1–3)—namely that the contention that they differ in meaning is supported by three facts. First, one can understand them, and so know what they mean, without taking them to mean the same thing, or even agree in truth value. Hence, understanding them is consistent with taking (4b) to be true and (4a) to be false. Second, one who assertively utters (4a) would typically be deemed to say, or convey, something different from, and more informative than, what one would say, or convey, by assertively uttering (4b). Third, one would standardly use (4a) and (4b) in ascriptions ⌜A believes that S⌝, in which they take the place of S, to report what one took to be different beliefs. If these observations justify a distinction between the Fregean senses and referents of the names and definite descriptions occurring in (1–3), then they also justify such a distinction for '6^4' and '1296'.

This is true, *even though (4a), (4b), and the identity '$6^4 > 1295$' are a priori truths of arithmetic that qualify as "analytic" for Frege.* This means that the two expressions '6^4' and '1296' can have different Fregean senses despite the fact that it is possible for one who understands both to reason a priori from knowledge *that for all x '6^4' refers to x iff x = 6^4 and for all y '1296' refers to y iff y = 1296* to the conclusion *that '6^4' and '1296' refer to the same thing.* This is not a criticism of Frege's notion of sense, which corresponds quite well in this respect to standard conceptions of linguistic meaning. However, it is also not without consequence for his overall philosophical view, which includes not only his philosophy of language but also his philosophy of logic and mathematics. Since his views about language evolved in the service of his goal of illuminating mathematics and logic, it is an important question, usefully emphasized in Beaney (1996), how well the notion of sense that emerges from his linguistic investigations in "On Sense and Reference" and related essays advances his central project of providing an analysis of number that reduces arithmetic to logic. This is something to keep an eye on as we proceed.

With this in mind, we return to Frege's puzzle, in which he uses the compositionality principle T2 for senses of sentences and other compound expressions, to reject a purely referential conception of meaning. T2 is paralleled by the compositionality of reference principle, T3, for terms, plus Frege's thesis T4 about sentences.

T3. The referent of a compound term E is a function of its grammatical structure, plus the referents of its parts. Substitution of one coreferential term for another in E (e.g., substitution of '5³' for '125' in 'the successor of 125') results in a new compound term ('the successor of 5³') the referent of which is the same as that of E. Moreover, if one term in E fails to refer, then E does too (e.g., 'the successor of the largest prime').

T4. The truth or falsity of a sentence is a function of its structure, plus the referents of its parts. Substitution of one coreferential term for another in a sentence S results in a new sentence with the same truth value as S. For example, the sentences in the following pairs are either both true, or both false.

The author of the *Begriffsschrift* was widely acclaimed during his time.
The author of "On Sense and Reference" was widely acclaimed during his time.
The probe penetrated the atmosphere of Hesperus.
The probe penetrated the atmosphere of Phosphorus.
$2^{10} > 6^4$
$1024 > 1296$

As before, I use examples drawn from English. However, perhaps surprisingly, Frege would insist that T3 and T4 hold (along with T2) not just for some terms and sentences of some languages, but for all languages. To be sure, T3 and T4 are already incorporated into our semantic interpretation of L_F. Since the language was constructed by us, we were free to set things up so as to make this so. Following Frege, we defined the truth value of an atomic sentence of L_F consisting of an n-place predicate sign Θ plus n terms to be the value assigned by the concept designated by Θ to the n-tuple of objects that are referents of the terms. Hence if $\ulcorner\Theta\ t_1...t_n\urcorner$ is true (false), then the result of substituting coreferential terms for any, or all, of $t_1...t_n$ must also be true (false). We also followed Frege in defining the referent of a compound term of L_F consisting of an n-place function sign ϕ plus n terms to be the object assigned by the function designated by ϕ to the n-tuple of objects that are referents of the terms. Hence if o is the referent of $\ulcorner\phi(t_1...t_n)\urcorner$, then o is also the referent of any compound term that results from substituting coreferential terms for any, or all, of $t_1...t_n$. Finally, we defined the operators that combine with sentences Φ and Ψ to form larger sentences as designating functions from truth values to truth values, thereby ensuring that if T4 holds for Φ and Ψ, it will hold for the compound sentences constructed from them using the operators. These points generalize to ensure that T3 and T4 are true of the sentences and terms of L_F.

However, it is one thing to construct a fruitful formal language for logic and mathematics that conforms to these principles, and quite another to show that natural languages like English and German do, or—even more strongly—that all possible languages (perhaps with a certain minimal expressive power) do. It certainly *seems* possible (i) that a language might contain a function sign designating a function that assigns a value to an n-tuple of arguments, one or more of which is the sense, rather than the referent, of the term supplying the argument, or (ii) that the language might contain a two-place predicate Θ occurring in a sentence ⌜α Θ's β⌝ designating a concept that maps the referent o of α plus the sense s of β onto the value the True (or the False), depending on the relationship between o and s, or (iii) that the language might have a sentential operator O designating a concept that maps the sense, rather than the truth value, of S onto the truth value of the complex sentence ⌜O(S)⌝. Languages that allow these possibilities will violate T3, T4, or both. Thus, when L is a naturally spoken language—not devised with the purpose of conforming to these and other principles—it would seem to be an empirical question whether the principles are true of L. This question will be examined in chapter 2. For now, we take T3 and T4 for granted.

T5 is a corollary of T4, which is also worth noting.

> T5. If one term in a sentence S fails to refer, then S lacks a truth value (is neither true nor false). Examples include:
> The present king of France is (isn't) wise.
> The largest prime number is (isn't) odd.

Truth value gaps of the sort illustrated here will arise in any language that both allows some singular terms that fail to refer and incorporates the Fregean semantic principles illustrated by L_F. In any such language, the truth value of a sentence consisting of a predicate Θ plus a term α is the truth value assigned to the referent of α by the concept designated by Θ—which is a function from objects to truth values. Since there is no argument for the function to apply to when α fails to refer, the sentence has no truth value. This is significant for Frege's account of negation, since when S lacks a truth value, there is no argument on which the truth function designated by the negation operator can operate—so the negation of S must also be truth valueless. The analysis generalizes to many-place predicates and truth-functional connectives. Reference failure anywhere in a sentence results in its truth valuelessness. Such sentences aren't epistemically neutral. Since the norms governing belief and assertion require truth, asserting or believing something that isn't true is incorrect no matter whether the thing asserted or believed is false or truth valueless. Thus, for Frege, there is something wrong about asserting or believing that either the present king of France is wise or he isn't, or that the largest prime number is odd or it isn't.

All of the sentences we have looked at so far share an important characteristic: in every case, the truth value of the sentence depends on the referents of its parts. *Noticing this, Frege subsumed T4 and T5 under T3 by holding that sentences refer to truth values—the True and the False—which he took to be objects of a certain kind.* On this picture, the referent (truth value) of a sentence is compositionally determined by the referents of its parts, while its meaning (the thought it expresses) is *composed* of the meanings of its parts. Just as the sentence

5. The author of the *Begriffsschrift* was German.

consists of a subject phrase and a predicate, so (ignoring tense) the sense of the sentence—which Frege calls the *thought* it expresses—consists of the sense of the subject (which determines an object o as referent iff o, and only o, wrote the *Begriffsschrift*), and the sense of the predicate (which determines as referent the function that assigns the True to an individual iff that individual was German, and otherwise assigns the False).[5] As for the structure of thoughts, he says:

> If, then, we look upon thoughts as composed of simple parts, and take these, in turn, to correspond to the simple parts of sentences, we can understand how a few parts of sentences can go to make up a great multitude of sentences, to which, in turn, there correspond a great multitude of Thoughts.[6]

The idea, of course, is that the structure of thoughts mirrors the structure of the sentences that express them. Just as a sentence has a grammatical unity that comes from combining (complete/saturated) nominal expressions that stand for objects with an (incomplete/unsaturated) predicate expression that stands for a concept to form a grammatically unified structure that is more than a mere list, so, Frege thinks, the thought expressed by a sentence has a representational unity that comes from combining complete/saturated senses (which are modes of presentation of objects) with an incomplete/unsaturated sense (which is a mode of presentation of a concept) to form an intentional unity that represents things as being a certain way—and so is capable of being true or false, depending on whether the things in question are, in reality, as the thought represents them to be.[7]

---

[5] Frege explicitly extends his sense and reference distinction to predicates in the first page of Frege (1892d), "Comments on Sense and Reference." The same considerations apply to function signs generally. See Currie (1982), pp. 86–87, for discussion.

[6] "Compound Thoughts," published in 1923, translated and reprinted in Geach (1977), pp. 55–77, at page 55.

[7] The parallel between the structure of sentences and that of the thoughts they express is here illustrated with simple sentences and thoughts. However, it also holds for complex sentences and thoughts of all types—including, for example, sentences in which an incomplete/unsaturated predicate expression (standing for a concept) combines with an incomplete/unsaturated quantifier expression (standing for a higher-level concept) to form a grammatical unity. The thoughts expressed by such sentences are unities in which the incompleteness of the sense that determines the higher-level concept complements the incompleteness of the sense that determines the lower-level concept in just the way needed for

The relationship between the Fregean sense of a predicate and its referent parallels the relationship between the sense of a name or description and its referent. The sense of an expression is always distinct from, and a mode of presentation of, the referent of the expression. This gives us a clue about the identity conditions for concepts, and functions generally. One possible way of conceiving of functions allows them to differ, even if, given the way the world actually is, they assign precisely the same values to precisely the same objects—provided that they do so on the basis of different criteria. On this conception, ϕ might assign the True to an individual in virtue of the individual's being a human being (while assigning the False to everything else in virtue of their not being human beings), and ψ might assign the True to an individual in virtue of the individual's being a rational animal (while assigning the False to everything else in virtue of their not being both rational and an animal). If all and only human beings happen to be rational animals, then, on this conception of functions, ϕ and ψ will assign the same values to the same actual arguments, even though they are different functions—as shown by the fact that they *would have assigned* different values to certain objects if, for example, a nonhuman species of rational animal had evolved. However, Frege didn't think of functions in this way—and, given his insistence that the sense of a predicate, or other functional expression, is always distinct from its referent, he had no need to individuate concepts, or other functions, so finely. Instead, he took concepts in particular, and functions in general, to be identical iff they in fact assign the same values to the same arguments.[8]

Being a Platonic realist about senses, Frege accepted the truism that there is such a thing as *the* meaning of 'is German', and that different speakers who understand the predicate know that it has that meaning. For him, senses, including the thoughts expressed by sentences, are public objects available to different thinkers. There is, for example, one thought—*that the square of the hypotenuse of a right triangle is equal to the sum of the squares of the remaining sides*—that is believed by all who believe the Pythagorean theorem. It is this that is preserved in translation, and this that is believed or asserted by agents who sincerely accept, or assertively utter, a sentence synonymous with the one used to state the theorem. For Frege, thoughts and their constituents are abstract objects, imperceptible to the senses, that are grasped by the intellect. These are the timeless contents in relation to which our use of language is to be understood.

a representational unity to be formed. The rule, for Frege, is that grammatical unities all require at least one incomplete/unsaturated expression, while representational unities all require at least one incomplete/unsaturated sense. Frege's views of this—which are responses to what has come to be known as "the problem of the unity of the proposition"—will be critically discussed in chapter 2. The evolving responses of G. E. Moore and Bertrand Russell to the same problem will be explained and discussed in chapters 3, 7, and 9.

[8] Frege makes this clear in "Comments on Sense and Reference." See, in particular, Frege (1997), p. 173.

We have seen that the Fregean sense of a singular term is a mode of presentation of its referent, which is an object, while the Fregean sense of a predicate is a mode of presentation of its referent, which is a concept. Something similar can be said about the Fregean sense of a sentence. Since he took the referent of a sentence to be a truth value, he took its sense—the thought it expresses—to be a mode of presentation of the True or the False. Although the analogy is not perfect, the relationship between the sense and referent of a sentence is something like the relationship between the sense and reference of a definite description. Just as the sense of a definite description may be taken to be a condition the unique satisfaction of which by an object is sufficient for that object to be the referent of the term, so a thought expressed by a sentence may be taken to be a condition the satisfaction of which by the world as a whole is sufficient for the sentence to refer to the True. The strain in the analogy comes when one considers what happens when no object uniquely satisfies a description, as opposed to what happens when the world as a whole doesn't "satisfy" the thought expressed by a sentence. In the former case, the description is naturally said to lack a referent, while in the latter case Frege takes the referent of the sentence to be a different object—the False. However, even here the analogy is not entirely off the mark, as is evidenced by his lament that reference failure is a *defect* in natural language to be *remedied* in formal work by *supplying* an arbitrary stipulated referent in cases in which the conventional reference-determining condition fails to be satisfied. Perhaps reference to the False should be understood along similar lines.

This brings us to a more important complication. Frege recognized that, given the compositionality of reference principle T3, he had to qualify his view that sentences refer to truth values. While taking the principle to unproblematically apply to many sentences, he recognized that it doesn't apply to *occurrences of sentences* as content clauses in attitude ascriptions ⌜A asserted/ believed/ . . . that S⌝. Suppose, for example, that (6a) is true, and so refers to the True.

6a. Jones believes that $2 + 3 = 5$.

Since '$2 + 3 = 5$' is true, substituting another true sentence—'Frege was German'—for it ought, by T3, to give us another true statement, (6b), of what John believes.

6b. Jones believes that Frege was German.

But this is absurd. An agent can believe one truth (or falsehood) without believing every truth (or falsehood). Thus, if the truth values of attitude ascriptions are functions of their grammatical structure, plus the referents of their parts, then the complement clauses of such ascriptions must, if they refer at all, refer to something other than the truth values of the sentences occurring there.

Frege's solution to this problem is illustrated by (7), in which the putative object of belief is indicated by the italicized noun phrase.

7. Jones believes *the thought expressed at the top of page 91.*

Since the phrase is not a sentence, its sense is not a thought. Thus, what is said to be believed—which is itself a thought—must be the referent of the noun phrase that provides the argument of 'believe', rather than its sense. This result is generalized in T6.

> T6. The thing said to be believed in an attitude ascription ⌜A believes E⌝ (or similar indirect discourse report) is what the occurrence of E in the ascription (or report) refers to.

Possible values of 'E' include ⌜the thought/proposition/claim that S⌝, ⌜that S⌝, and S. In these cases what is said to be believed is the thought that S expresses. If T6 is correct, this thought is the *referent* of occurrences of S, ⌜that S⌝, and ⌜the thought/proposition/claim that S⌝ in attitude ascriptions (or other indirect discourse reports). So, in an effort to preserve his basic tenets—that meaning is *always* distinct from reference, and that the referent of a compound is *always* compositionally determined from the referents of its parts—Frege was led to T7.

> T7. An occurrence of a sentence S embedded in an attitude ascription (indirect discourse report) refers not to its truth value, but to the thought S expresses when it isn't embedded. In these cases, an occurrence of S refers to S's ordinary sense. Unembedded occurrences of S refer to the ordinary referent of S—i.e., its truth value.

Here, Frege takes not expressions but their *occurrences* to be semantically fundamental. Unembedded occurrences express "ordinary senses," which determine "ordinary referents." Singly embedded occurrences, like those in the complement clauses in (6a) and (6b), express the "indirect senses" of expressions, which are modes of presentation that determine their ordinary senses as "indirect referents."[9] The process is repeated in (8).

8. Mary imagines that John believes that *the author of the Begriffsschrift was German.*

The occurrences in (8) of the words in

9. John believes *that the author of the Begriffsschrift was German*

refer to the senses that occurrences of those words carry when (9) is not embedded—i.e., to the ordinary senses of 'John' and 'believes', plus the indirect senses of the words in the italicized clause. In order to do this, occurrences of 'John' and 'believe' in (8) must *express* their indirect senses (which are, of course, distinct from the ordinary senses they determine as indirect referents), while occurrences in (8) of the words in the italicized clause must *express* doubly indirect senses, which determine, but

---

[9] Because they aren't embedded, occurrences of italicized words in (7) have their ordinary, not, indirect referents.

are distinct from, the singly indirect senses that are their doubly indirect referents. And so on, *ad infinitum*. Thus, Frege ends up attributing to each meaningful unit in the language an infinite hierarchy of distinct senses and referents.

But if this is so, how is the language learnable? Someone who understands 'the author was German' when it occurs in ordinary contexts doesn't require further instruction when encountering it for the first time in an attitude ascription. How, given the hierarchy, can that be? If s is the ordinary sense of an expression E, there will be infinitely many senses that determine s, and so are potential candidates for being the indirect sense of E. How, short of further instruction, could a language learner figure out which was *the* indirect sense of E? Different versions of this question have been raised by a number of philosophers from Bertrand Russell to Donald Davidson.[10] These, in turn, have provoked an interesting neo-Fregean answer, to be taken up in chapter 2.

4. FREGE'S LOGIC

The logic invented in the *Begriffsschrift* is the modern *predicate calculus*, which is the result of combining the truth-functional logic of the *propositional calculus*—familiar, in one form or another, from the Stoics onward—with a powerful new account of quantification ('all' and 'some') supplanting the long-standing, but far more limited, syllogistic logic dating back to Aristotle. The key to Frege's achievement was his decision to trade in the traditional subject/predicate distinction of syllogistic logic for a clarified and vastly expanded version of the function/argument distinction from mathematics, ingeniously extended to quantification in the manner illustrated by the semantics for L_F in the previous sections. [11]

A system of logic, in Frege's modern sense, consists of a formal language of the sort illustrated by L_F, plus a proof procedure, which, in his case, is put in the form of a small set of axioms drawn from the language, plus a small number of rules of inference. A proof in the system is a finite sequence of lines, each of which is an axiom or a formula obtainable from earlier lines by the inference rules. His fundamental idea is that whether or not something counts as a proof in such a system must, in principle, be decidable merely by inspecting the formula on each line, and determining

[10] One version of the question is raised by a central argument in Russell's "On Denoting." This will be discussed in chapter 8. Another version is what stands behind Davidson's notion of "semantic innocence" presented in his "On Saying That." This version of the question will be addressed in chapter 2.

[11] Informative discussions of the relationship of Frege's system to syllogistic logic, as well to the logical contributions of Leibniz, Boole, and De Morgan, can be found in Kneale and Kneale (1962) and Beaney (1996). The former also usefully compares Frege's contribution to that of his contemporary, Charles Sanders Peirce.

(i) whether it is an axiom, and (ii) whether, if it isn't, it bears the required structural relation to earlier lines in order for it to be obtainable from those lines by the rules. For this reason, the axioms themselves must constitute an effectively decidable set—i.e., there must be a purely mechanical procedure capable of deciding, in every case, whether a formula is one of the axioms. Similarly, rules of inference—like *modus ponens*, which allows one to infer B on a line in a proof iff earlier lines include both A and ⌜A → B⌝—must be stated in such a way that the question of whether one formula is obtainable from earlier ones is effectively decidable in the same sense. When these requirements are met, the question of whether or not something counts as a proof in the system can always be uncontroversially resolved—thereby forestalling the need to prove that something is a proof.[12]

Questions can, of course, be raised about the status of the axioms, and about whether the rules of inference successfully transmit that status to formulas provable from them. Formal systems of logic in the modern sense, which employ fundamental notions not available, or at least not explicit, in Frege's time, characterize some sentences (of the languages of those

---

[12] For Frege, the chief factor motivating these requirements was a perceived practical need in the foundations of mathematics for a logical system powerful enough to eliminate avoidable error and uncertainty by formalizing proof in mathematics. Speaking about this on p. 1 of *The Foundations of Arithmetic,* he says:

> After deserting for a time the old Euclidean standards of rigor, mathematics is now returning to them, and even making efforts to go beyond them. In arithmetic . . . it has been the tradition to reason less strictly than in geometry. . . . The discovery of higher analysis only served to confirm this tendency; for considerable, almost insuperable, difficulties stood in the way of any rigorous treatment of these subjects. . . . Later developments, however, have shown more and more clearly that in mathematics a mere moral conviction, supported by a mass of applications, is not good enough. Proof is now demanded of many things that formerly passed as self-evident. Again and again the limits to the validity of a proposition have been in this way established for the first time. The concepts of function, of continuity, of limit and infinity have been shown to stand in need of sharper definition. Negative and irrational numbers, which had long since been admitted into science, have had to submit to a closer scrutiny of their credentials. In all directions these same ideals can be seen at work—rigor of proof, precise delimitation of extent of validity, and as a means to this, sharp definition of concepts.

As Frege points out in section III of the preface of the *Begriffsschrift* (Frege 1997, p. 48), the pursuit of these goals required a precise formal language, or "concept script," in the service of a formal proof procedure of the sort discussed above.

> So that nothing intuitive could intrude here unnoticed, everything had to depend on the chain of reasoning being free of gaps. In striving to fulfill this requirement in the strictest way, I found an obstacle in the inadequacy of the language. . . . Out of this need came the idea of the present "concept script." It is intended to serve primarily to test in the most reliable way the validity of a chain of inference and reveal every presupposition that tends to slip in unnoticed, so that its origin can be investigated. The expression of anything that is without significance for logical inference has therefore been eschewed.

systems) as *logically true*, and some sentences as being *logical consequences* of others. To understand what this means, one must understand the difference between two classes of symbols. Certain expressions are singled out as "logical vocabulary," the rest are called "nonlogical." For example, the logical vocabulary of L_F consists of the quantifiers '∀' and '∃', the definite description operator 'the', and the truth functional connectives '&', 'v', '~', '→', and '↔'. The identity predicate '='—which can be treated either as logical or nonlogical, depending on the aims of the system—will here be regarded as a logical symbol. A sentence in the language is said to be *logically true* iff it is true and would remain so (i) no matter what (nonempty) domain of objects its quantifiers were taken to range over, and (ii) no matter how its nonlogical vocabulary was interpreted to apply (or not apply) to those objects (i.e., no matter which objects in the domain its names refer to, no matter which objects its predicates, other than '=', apply to, and no matter which functions from things in the domain to things in the domain its function signs designate).

Although this way of thinking about logical truths wasn't itself made the subject of precise meta-mathematical investigation until Alfred Tarski formalized the notion of a model, or interpretation, of a formalized language in the 1930s, the foundations of Tarski's idea were, I think, implicit in Frege.[13] Using the idea of a model, we say that S is a logical truth iff S is true in all models/interpretations of the language, and that Q is a logical consequence of a sentence (or set of sentences) P iff every model/interpretation that makes P (or the sentences in P) true also makes Q true. Since only the interpretation of the logical vocabulary remains fixed across models, this fits the implicit Fregean ideas (i) that the logical truths, and our knowledge of them, are, in principle, independent of special truths that are unique to any particular domain, and (ii) that when Q is a logical consequence of P, what is required by one who knows P in order to come to know Q on that basis is not further specialized knowledge of the subject matter of P and Q.[14]

With this, we return to proof in a logical system. In addition to *consistency*, which requires that one's proof procedure not enable one to derive

---

[13] Tarski's work will be discussed in volume 2.

[14] According to Frege, the truths of logic (as well as those of arithmetic) are entirely general, and do not depend on any special subject matter. This suggests that any sentence that counts as a logical truth should remain such no matter how its names, function signs, and predicates are interpreted—and, one would think, no matter what domain of objects the quantifiers are chosen to range over (though this may be less than transparent). Since a model is just a formalization of the idea of such an interpretation, it should not be seen as foreign to Frege, even though he lacked any such explicit notion. Of course, this picture also depends on taking definitions, which play the central role in his reduction of arithmetic to logic, as themselves counting as "logical truths." This is at variance with the Tarskian tradition. Perhaps it would be best to characterize Fregean logical truth as consisting of all sentences that can be turned into more standard logical truths by substitution on the basis of correct definitions. In other words, the logical and the analytic are merged.

contradictions (defined as sentences false in all models) from the axioms of the system, there are three natural demands one might place on a formal proof procedure. The maximal demand is that there should be a *decision procedure* which, given any sentence S of the language of the system, will always decide correctly (in a finite number of steps) whether S is, or is not, a logical truth. The only logical system we will be concerned with that satisfies this demand is the propositional calculus—which consists solely of atomic sentences, plus compound sentences constructed from them using only the truth-functional connectives. A sentence S of this system is a logical truth iff S is a tautology—i.e., a sentence that comes out true no matter what truth values are assigned to the (finitely many) atomic sentences from which it is constructed. That there is a decision procedure for tautology is evident from "the truth-table method"—which consists of writing down every possible assignment of truth values to the atomic sentences from which S is constructed, and then determining the truth value of each compound clause in S, relative to each such assignment—starting with the simplest and working one's way up to more complex clauses, and finally to S itself—by consulting the function from truth values to truth values designated by the connective used to form each clause. If, at the end of this process, no assignment of truth values to the atomic sentences makes S false, then S is a logical truth; otherwise it isn't.

Since the method always terminates, an answer is always reached. Hence it is a decision procedure. However, employing it, when the number of atomic sentences in S gets large, can be quite laborious. Hence authors of logic texts sometimes formulate a small number of axioms drawn from the language of the system and one or two rules of inference, from which all the tautologies can be derived. Frege's axiomatic proof procedure for the propositional calculus in the *Begriffsschrift* is particularly simple and elegant—more so, he argued, than those of some of his illustrious predecessors, like George Boole.[15] However, apart from such modest improvements, this well-trodden ground is not where he made his revolutionary advance.

Once we move beyond the propositional calculus, the maximal demand—for a decision procedure—is too strong for most interesting systems of logic, though the minimal demand—that every sentence provable from the axioms be true in all models, and hence be a genuine logical truth—is within the reach of any system of logic worthy of the name. Systems meeting this requirement (including Frege's version of the predicate calculus) are called *sound*. The most interesting, and modestly ambitious,

---

[15] Frege's system of the propositional calculus takes just two connectives ('~' and '→') as primitive, defining the others from these. There are two rules of inference, *modus ponens* and substitution, plus six axioms. He argues—in Frege (1880–81) and (1882)—that his system is superior to, and more explanatory than, Boole's formalization, due to its fewer axioms and primitives—a point discussed in Beaney (1996).

demand to be placed on such systems goes beyond this in requiring the specified proof procedure to provide a formal proof (from the axioms) of every logical truth. A logical system that satisfies this demand is called *complete*.

Here the facts are more complex, and require us to distinguish *the first-order predicate calculus* from *the second-order predicate calculus*. The language L_F that I have used to illustrate Frege's ideas is a first-order language—which means that the only quantifiers it employs are those that combine with *individual variables* (a type of singular term), and range over objects. However, this is just a fragment of Frege's total system, which qualifies as a version of the second-order calculus by virtue of allowing quantifiers to combine with predicate and function variables that range over concepts and functions. Still, the first-order fragment is a significant part of his system. Although the metatheorem that there are complete proof procedures for the first-order predicate calculus wasn't established until Kurt Gödel did so in his doctoral dissertation in 1929 (which is repeated in more succinct form in Gödel 1930), Frege's proof procedure for the first-order fragment of his logical system is, in fact, complete. What he didn't, and couldn't, know is that no higher-order version of the predicate calculus of the sort he offered can be both sound and complete—which is a corollary of Gödel (1931).[16]

To convert the first-order language L_F into second-order language L_{F+} we add new n-place predicate variables—$\mathscr{P}$, $\mathscr{Q}$, $\mathscr{R}$, etc.—for arbitrary n, and/or new n-place function variables—f, g, h, etc. (Frege has both.) Syntactically the predicate variables combine with (singular) terms to form atomic formulas, and the function variables combine with terms or other function symbols to form (singular) terms. These new variables require the addition of new rules for forming quantified formulas that parallel those for the first-order quantifiers. When $\Phi(\mathscr{P})$ is a formula containing the predicate variable $\mathscr{P}$, $\ulcorner\forall\mathscr{P}\Phi(\mathscr{P})\urcorner$ is a formula that is a universal generalization of $\Phi(\mathscr{P})$, and $\ulcorner\exists\mathscr{P}\Phi(\mathscr{P})\urcorner$ is a formula that is an existential generalization of $\Phi(\mathscr{P})$. Similarly, when $\Phi(f)$ is a formula containing the function variable f, $\ulcorner\forall f\Phi(f)\urcorner$ is a formula that is a universal generalization

---

[16] In addition to being complete, first-order logic is also *compact*—in the sense that every inconsistent set of first-order sentences (i.e., every set the members of which are not jointly true in any model) has a finite subset that is inconsistent. By contrast, second-order logic is neither complete nor compact. The reason that logical truth is not decidable in complete systems of first-order logic is that although each such truth can be proven in finitely many steps, there is no upper bound on the number of steps required in searching for a proof of an arbitrary sentence. We know that if S is a logical truth, we will ultimately find a proof, and if S isn't a logical truth, we will never find a proof that it is. What we don't, and can't, know in the general case is whether, after determining that there is no proof with n, or fewer, steps, there is proof with more than n steps waiting to be found. Hence, although the proof procedure is an effective positive test for logical truth, no end point can, in general, be established for failure, which means that we have no effective negative test for logical truth, and hence no decision procedure.

of $\Phi(/)$, while $\ulcorner \exists/\Phi(/)\urcorner$ is a formula that is an existential generalization of $\Phi(/)$. (Free and bound occurrences of variables are determined exactly as before.)

In Frege's system, predicate variables are, of course, used to quantify over concepts, while function variables are used to quantify over (other) functions. Thus, the semantics for the higher-order quantifiers parallels the semantics of the first-order quantifiers.

Existential Quantification

1st-Order: '$\exists$x' designates the 2nd-level concept C_2, which takes a 1st-level concept C as argument and assigns it the value the True iff C assigns this value to at least one *object*. So $\ulcorner \exists$x Φx$\urcorner$ is true iff there is at least one *object* o such that the concept designated by Φx assigns o the value the True iff o "satisfies" the formula Φx iff replacing occurrences of 'x' in Φx with a *name* n for o would result in a true sentence. Example: '$\exists$x (Number x & Even x & Prime x)' is true iff at least one object falls under the concept *being a number that is both even and prime* iff there is something of which it is true that it is an even prime number.

2nd-Order: '$\exists\mathscr{P}$' designates the 3rd-level concept C_3, which takes a 2nd-level concept C_2 as argument and assigns it the value the True iff C_2 assigns this value to at least one 1st-level *concept*. So $\ulcorner \exists\mathscr{P}\Phi(\mathscr{P})\urcorner$ is true iff there is at least one 1st-level concept C such that the 2nd-level concept designated by $\Phi(\mathscr{P})$ assigns C the value the True iff C "satisfies" the formula $\Phi(\mathscr{P})$ iff replacing occurrences of '$\mathscr{P}$' in $\Phi(\mathscr{P})$ with a *predicate* designating C would result in a true sentence. Example: '$\exists\mathscr{P}(\mathscr{P}$Aristotle & $\mathscr{P}$Plato & ~$\mathscr{P}$ Pericles)' is true iff at least one 1st-level concept falls under the 2nd-level concept *being something under which Plato and Aristotle but not Pericles fall* iff there is something that is true of both Plato and Aristotle but not Pericles.

2nd-Order: '$\exists/$' designates the higher-level concept C_3, which takes a concept C_2 as argument and assigns it the value the True iff C_2 assigns this value to at least one 1st-level *function*. So $\ulcorner \exists/\Phi(/)\urcorner$ is true iff there is at least one 1st-level function F such that the 2nd-level concept designated by $\Phi(/)$ assigns F the value the True iff F "satisfies" the formula $\Phi(/)$ iff replacing occurrences of '/' in $\Phi(/)$ with an expression designating F would result in a true sentence. Example: '$\exists/[\forall$x$\forall$y ((Ax & Ay & x ≠ y) → (B/(x) & B/(y)

&$/(x) \neq /(y)))$]' is true iff at least one function from objects to objects falls under the concept *being something that maps every A onto a distinct B* iff it is possible to put all of the A's into 1-1 correspondence with some of the Bs.

The rules for the corresponding types of universal quantification are exactly analogous.

However, Frege's system doesn't stop here. For all finite n, his system allows n[th]-order quantification over concepts/functions of level n − 1.For example, call any first-level concepts A and B *equal* iff the objects falling under each can be put in one-to-one correspondence with the objects falling under the other—in the sense that all the A's can be put into one-to-one correspondence with some of the B's (as spelled out in the final example of second-order quantification above), and all the B's can be put in one-to-one correspondence with some of the A's (as spelled out by interchanging 'A' and 'B' in the example). In Frege's system, this two-place predicate—'( ) is equal to ( )'—will syntactically combine with a pair of *first-order predicates* to form an atomic formula, e.g., 'A is equal to B'. The new predicate will designate *a second-level concept* that maps a pair of first-level concepts onto the True iff the objects falling under each can be exhaustively paired off 1 to 1 with the objects falling under the other. Next we ascend the quantificational hierarchy by replacing the equality predicate with a two-place, *second-level predicate variable* $\mathcal{R}^2$ that ranges over *second-level concepts*. This gives us the formula 'A $\mathcal{R}^2$ B' that designates the third-level concept C_3 that assigns the value the True to any two-place, second-level concept C_2 that assigns the True to the pair of first-level concepts A and B. The existential quantifier '$\exists \mathcal{R}^2$'will then designate a fourth-level concept C_4 that takes a third-level concept as argument and assigns it the value the True iff that concept assigns this value to *at least one two-place, second-level concept*. This means that the quantified sentence '$\exists \mathcal{R}^2$[A $\mathcal{R}^2$ B]' that results from attaching the quantifier to the formula 'A $\mathcal{R}^2$ B' is true iff the fourth-level concept designated by the quantifier assigns the True to the third-level concept C_3 designated by the formula (which assigns the value the True to any two-place, second-level concept C_2 that assigns the True to the pair of first-level concepts A and B). Thus, the quantified sentence will be true iff *there is at least one second-level concept that is true of the first-level concepts A and B*. This is an example of *third-order quantification, which is quantification over second-level concepts*. (The "order level of the quantification" comes from the level of the concept that is the argument of the higher-level concept designated by the quantifier.)

Although it is worth knowing how this higher-order system works for each n, the system itself is complicated. Fortunately, our purposes don't require close examination of the higher reaches of the system. However, the differences between first- and second-order quantification can't be ignored. As mentioned above, while it is an important Gödelian metatheorem that the first-order predicate calculus has sound and complete formalizations, it is an equally important Gödelian metatheorem that no sound formalization of the second-order calculus can be complete. If a given proof procedure for the second-order calculus is sound, then (i) although every sentence provable from its axioms will be a logical truth, there will be many logical truths (sentences true in all models) that are not provable from the axioms, and (ii) although every sentence Q derivable in the system from a set of sentences P will be a logical consequence of P (in the model-theoretic sense), there will be many logical consequences of P that are not derivable in the system.

This failure of *logical truth* and *logical consequence* to be fully formalizable would have surprised Frege, and—I believe—deeply troubled him. A central goal of his construction of a fully explicit and precise "concept script," accompanied by a clearly understood semantics, plus a rigorous proof procedure, was to formalize proof in mathematics in a way that would allow one to eliminate all appeal to fallible intuition, uncheckable insight, or unacknowledged presupposition in demonstrating the results of mathematical discovery. His system of the first-order predicate calculus can be said to have achieved this goal for a large and important range of cases. However, we now know that the goal is not fully realizable in the sense of providing a system capable of proving all second-order logical truths.

The significance of this result for his goal of reducing arithmetic, and with it much higher mathematics, to logic is not entirely straightforward. As we will see, the axioms of arithmetic to be reduced are, with one exception, capable of being stated by first-order sentences, all of which can be derived by a version of Frege's system of logic plus definitions. The one exception is the principle of mathematical induction, which, informally put, states that if (i) the number zero has a property, and (ii) whenever a natural number has a property, the successor of that number also has the property, then (iii) every natural number has the property. There are two well-known ways of formalizing this principle. The first formulation—used in first-order theories of arithmetic—is an *axiom schema,* adoption of which counts as adopting each of its infinitely many instances as an arithmetical axiom.

The First-Order Axiom Schema of Mathematical Induction

$$[F(0) \mathbin{\&} \forall x\, (NNx \to (Fx \to \exists y\, (Sxy \mathbin{\&} Fy)))]$$
$$\to \forall x\, (NNx \to Fx)$$

Here 'NN', 'S', and '0' are, respectively, the primitive arithmetical predicate true of all natural numbers, the primitive arithmetical predicate true of all pairs the second of which is the successor of the first, and the arithmetical name of the number zero. Instances of the schema are obtained by replacing 'F' with any first-level formula of the language of arithmetic in which 'x' (and only 'x') occurs free, and replacing 'F(0)' with the sentence of the language that results from replacing all free occurrences of 'x' in the formula that replaces 'F' with occurrences of '0'. Informally, each instance of this axiom says *that if zero "is so-and-so," and if whenever a natural number "is so-and-so" its successor is too, then every natural number "is so-and-so"*— where the range of the "so-and-so's" is the class of Fregean concepts designated by formulas of the language of arithmetic with one free variable.

The second formulation of the principle of mathematical induction—used in second-order theories of arithmetic—is a universally quantified second-order sentence of the language of second-order arithmetic.

The Second-Order Axiom of Mathematical Induction

$$\forall \mathscr{P}\,[[\mathscr{P}(0)\ \&\ \forall x\,(NNx \rightarrow (\mathscr{P}x \rightarrow \exists y\,(Sxy\ \&\ \mathscr{P}y)))] \rightarrow \forall x\,(NNx \rightarrow \mathscr{P}x)]$$

Here, '$\mathscr{P}$' is a predicate variable ranging over all first-level Fregean concepts—i.e., all functions assigning truth values to individuals in the domain of the first-order quantifiers. The axiom tells us that any such concept true of zero, and true of the successor of a natural number whenever it is true of the natural number itself, is true of all natural numbers.

The difference between these two is that the second-order sentence is stronger than the collection of the infinitely many instances of the first-order axiom schema. The reason for this is that there are more Fregean concepts assigning truth values to natural numbers than there are such concepts *that are designated by the formulas of first-order arithmetical theories.* The basis for this claim will be explained in chapter 7, which will include a discussion of Bertrand Russell's reaction to Georg Cantor's proof that *the power set* of any set s (which is the set of all subsets of s) is larger than s—in the sense that although the members of s can always be exhaustively paired off 1 to 1 with a proper subset of the members of its power set, the members of its power set cannot be so paired off with the members of s. For now, it is enough to note (i) that the set of formulas (in which only 'x' occurs free) of the language of first-order arithmetic can be exhaustively paired off with the set of natural numbers—which means that the set of Fregean concepts designated by those formulas is the same size as the set of natural numbers; and (ii) that since there is an exact correspondence between an arbitrary set s and the Fregean concept that assigns the True to all and only members of s, the set of Fregean concepts that assign truth values to the natural numbers is the same size as the power set of the set of natural numbers. It follows from (i) and (ii) plus Cantor's result that the set of Fregean concepts that assign truth values to the natural numbers is larger than the set of such concepts that are designated by the formulas of first-order arithmetical theories. Hence the second-order axiom of mathematical induction is stronger (more inclusive) than the set of instances of the first-order axiom schema of mathematical induction.

The effect of this on formal theories of arithmetic is striking. Let T be a theory consisting of a formal language L_T plus a decidable set of axioms drawn from L_T. Let the theorems of T be all and only the logical consequences of the axioms of T. Call the theory L_T-complete iff for every sentence S of L_T either S or its negation is a theorem of T. (Note, this is a different notion of completeness than that which applies to systems of logic.) Since we are strongly inclined, at least pre-theoretically, to think that every sentence S in the language L_A of arithmetic is either true or false, and also that the negation of S is true iff S is false, we are strongly inclined to think that for every sentence S in L_A, either S or the negation of S is true. This means that in order for a theory to capture all arithmetical truths it must be L_A-complete. However, it is a fact, deriving ultimately from Gödel (1931), that *every consistent axiomatizable theory of first-order arithmetic (employing the axiom schema of mathematical induction) is incomplete in this sense.* Thus, no axiomatizable first-order theory is capable of capturing all and only the arithmetical truths. Interestingly, this result does not carry over to second-order arithmetic. So, if we substitute the second-order axiom of mathematical induction for the first-order schema, we get a theory that is L_A-complete. The cost, of course, is that although (i) this second-order theory can in fact be *derived* from (a modest reconstruction of) Frege's logic plus his definition of arithmetical concepts in logical terms (using the proof procedure provided by the system), and (ii) every arithmetical truth is in fact a *logical consequence* of the arithmetical theory derived from the logic, (iii) not every arithmetical truth can be *derived* from (a suitably modified version of) Frege's logical axioms by the proof procedure, because second-order logical consequence is not fully formalizable.

These striking metalogical results—proved years after Frege's death—are now settled facts. What is not conclusively settled is their philosophical significance—including their significance for his philosophical project of grounding the certainty, objectivity, and a priori knowability of mathematics in the fundamental laws of logic. In order to approach this issue, we must delve further into his philosophical views of logic and mathematics, and how they influenced his attempted reduction of the latter to the former.

Although there is no denying that Frege was one of the chief architects of our contemporary, essentially mathematical, understanding of symbolic logic, he was also an ambitious philosophical epistemologist whose views about logic were strongly tied to its role in justifying knowledge.[17] As is well known, he was fond of characterizing the goal of logic as the discovery of the laws of truth, in something like the way in which the aim of physics is the discovery of the laws of heat, or light.[18] But what are these laws? Not, as he correctly and repeatedly insisted, the psychological laws by which we think and reason. Rather, he contended, they are laws by which reasoning is justified.[19] A good statement of this view is found in a draft, written sometime between 1879 and 1891, of a logic text that never appeared.

> Logic is concerned only with those grounds of judgment which are truths. To make a judgment because we are cognizant of other truths as providing a justification for it is known as inferring. There are laws governing this kind of justification, and to set up these laws of valid inference is the goal of logic.[20]

Although the first statement in this passage is a bit misleading, the general import of Frege's position is clear. A fundamental goal of logic—perhaps its fundamental goal—is to lay down laws of truth preservation. We now know that truth preservation and the preservation of justification do not always coincide. However, they often do, which seems to be what Frege had in mind. To be sure, the logical laws of truth preservation will also relate false premises to conclusions derived from them, but since no genuine knowledge is thereby achieved, that is not where the interest and value of logic is to be found.[21] Rather, it is its role in extending and justifying our knowledge that provides logic with its *raison d'être*.

This is the perspective from which Frege's program of reducing arithmetic and (much of) the rest of mathematics must be viewed. Commenting in 1896 on the ambitious program initiated in the *Begriffsschrift*, he says:

> I became aware of the need for a *Begriffsschrift* when I was looking for the fundamental principles or axioms upon which the whole of mathematics rests. Only after this question is answered can it be hoped to trace successfully the springs of knowledge upon which this science thrives.[22]

The thought here is that finding the principles on which mathematics rests—by constructing logically valid proofs, in the manner of the *Begriffsschrift*, of the propositions of mathematics from those principles—will show how to arrive at justified knowledge of mathematics from antecedent

---

[17] Frege's deep concern with the epistemological role of logic is rightly emphasized by Gregory Currie. See, in particular, chapters 1 and 4 of Currie (1982).

[18] See, for example, Frege (1918a), p. 325, and Frege (1897), p. 128.

[19] Frege (1918a), p. 326 of Frege (1997).

[20] Frege (1879–91), p. 3.

[21] Frege's recognition that in *formulating* the laws of logic connecting premises and conclusions we have no interest in the truth of the premises is made explicit in Frege (1906), p. 175, where he says, "The task of logic is to set up laws according to which a judgment is justified by others, irrespective of whether they themselves are true." However, the value of this task is to be found in its employment on known truths to extend our knowledge.

[22] Translated in Frege (1969), p. 1.

knowledge of the underlying principles. Of course, the strength of the justification thereby transferred will depend on the strength of the principles from which the mathematical truths are derived. Where might the strongest justification be found? About this, Frege is unequivocal. The strongest justification is provided by deriving a proposition from the fundamental laws of logic. Thus, he says in the *Begriffsschrift*,

> The firmest proof is obviously the purely logical, which, prescinding from the particularity of things, is based solely on *the laws on which all knowledge rests*. Accordingly, we divide all truths that require justification into two kinds: those whose proof can be given purely logically and those whose proof must be grounded on empirical facts.[23]

These fundamental laws "on which all knowledge rests" are not just any statements that turn out to be true in all models; nor are they just any rules for "inferring" one statement from others that turn out to be truth preserving no matter what the model. Rather, they are the foundational laws of a logical system—its axioms and rules of inference—from which other, non-obvious logical truths can be formally derived, and other, derived or secondary, rules of inference can be constructed. How are these foundational laws and principles known to be true (or truth preserving)? Frege briefly addresses this question in the introduction to volume 1 of *The Basic Laws of Arithmetic*.

> Now the question of why and with what right we acknowledge a logical law to be true, logic can only answer by reducing it to another logical law. Where that is not possible, logic can give no answer. Leaving aside logic, we may say: we are forced to make judgments by our nature and external circumstances; and if we make judgments, we cannot reject this law—of identity, for example; we must recognize it if we are not to throw our thought into confusion and in the end renounce judgment altogether. I do not wish to either dispute or endorse this view and only remark that what we have here is not a logical implication. What is given is not a ground [reason] for [something's] being true, but of our holding [it] as true.[24]

The picture of justification suggested here is foundational. Some logical principles are justified by deriving them from other, more fundamental ones. The process of justification ends with the most basic logical laws, which are self-evidently true, and knowable without any further justifying reason. In addition to being self-evident, Frege takes these fundamental laws to be the most pragmatically significant general truths underlying all of our reasoning. It is because he understands them to have this status, while also taking arithmetic to be derivable from them, that he claims, in *The Foundations of Arithmetic,* that the same is true of "the fundamental propositions of the science of number," holding that "we have only to

[23] Sec. 3 of the Preface, p. 48, my emphasis.
[24] Preface, sec. 17, p. 204.

deny any one of them and complete confusion ensues. *Even to think at all seems no longer possible."*[25]

This is the epistemological bedrock on which stands Frege's project of establishing the a priori certainty of mathematics by reducing it to logic. In the end, he simply presupposes that logic itself is both certain and knowable a priori. Having no doubt that this is so, he recognizes that there are limits to how far we can go in explaining why it is. Regarding justification, he thinks that all there is to say about the most fundamental laws of logic is that they are self-evident; hence they neither need, nor are susceptible to, justification by anything more certain than they are. For those who find this position less than fully satisfying, I recommend holding off judgment until we have had a chance, in volume 2, to see how hard it is to advance beyond it—by examining the difficulties encountered by Rudolf Carnap's view that the truths of logic, and all other a priori truths, can be known to be true simply by understanding them, because their truth is guaranteed by their meaning alone.

Whether or not Frege's epistemological position is ultimately correct, some suitably qualified version of it may have some merit—especially if one emphasizes the generality and indispensability of at least some logical laws, gestured at in his remarks in *The Basic Laws of Arithmetic*.[26] It is a characteristic of logical laws that their domain is universal, and so not dependent on any special subject matter. To the extent that they are indeed, indispensable, they apply to, and are needed in, all domains of thought. Consequently, to reduce a mathematical theory to such laws is to ground it in principles needed for reasoning in every domain, and hence to render it immune from special skeptical doubts arising from any specific domain. Although a showing of the indispensability of certain logical "laws" for the thought of beings like us would not guarantee their correctness—or even add to our justification for taking them to be such—it might at least render such laws, plus that which can be formally derived from them, resistant to the kind of *reasoned refutation* that itself must presuppose the very logical principles it seeks to undermine. In this way, a showing of indispensability might provide as secure a bulwark against the sincere arguments of actual skeptics about logic and mathematics as one might reasonably hope for.

Nevertheless, it is important not to let one's epistemological goals become too expansive. The incompleteness of first-order theories of arithmetic, plus the incompleteness (in a related sense) of systems of second-order logic—and hence the unformalizability of second-order

---

[25] *The Foundations of Arithmetic* (Frege 1950), sec. 14, p. 21.

[26] The modern proliferation of alternatives to classical logic makes it unreasonable to suppose that all of its principles are indispensable to our thought. Nor would it be easy to precisely identify some restricted core that was indispensable in the required sense. However, it is also not obvious (to me) that there is nothing to this line of thought, or that no significant sort of justification could be made to emerge from it.

logical consequence—means that, if the language of arithmetic is indeed bivalent, then any hope of providing justifying knowledge of all arithmetical truths by deriving them from the fundamental laws of logic must be given up in favor of something weaker. How much of the heavily epistemological motivation of Frege's grand project can be salvaged is, at this point, an open question. One factor to bear in mind as we proceed to his proposed reduction of arithmetic to logic is the extremely high epistemic bar that Frege sets for the self-evidence and indispensability of any logical axiom needed for the reduction. This, as we will see, is an important source of potential difficulties.

Finally, epistemology aside, there are other perspectives from which one can view Frege's attempted reduction of arithmetic, and (much) of higher mathematics, from logic. For example, one may think one understands what makes propositions about ordinary middle-sized objects, like houses, true because one knows what houses are, and what it is for them to have one or another property, while at the same time being puzzled about what makes arithmetical, or other mathematical, propositions true, because one has no idea what numbers—e.g., 7 or 0—are, and what it is for them to have properties. It is not inconceivable that a reduction of higher mathematics to arithmetic, and arithmetic to logic, might effectively dispel this sort of metaphysical puzzlement, even if not all of Frege's epistemological goals for the reduction can be fulfilled.

5. FREGE'S PHILOSOPHY OF MATHEMATICS

5.1. Critique of Naturalism, Formalism, and Psychologism

Though the significance of Frege's philosophy of mathematics extends beyond the epistemological, both his positive views and his criticisms of those of others are, as Gregory Currie contends, driven in large part by his epistemology.[27] For Frege, our knowledge of mathematics is certain—as well as not being dependent on, or refutable by, experience in the way in which empirical propositions always are. For this reason, the laws of arithmetic cannot be high-level empirical generalizations supported by induction from past experience. The target of repeated attacks in Frege's 1884 *The Foundations of Arithmetic,* the view that they are such generalizations was prominently defended by John Stuart Mill in *A System of Logic.* The flavor of Mill's views about arithmetic is illustrated by the following passage from that work.

> What renders arithmetic the type of deductive science is the fortunate applicability to it of a law so comprehensive as "The sums of equals are equals":

[27] Currie (1982).

or (to express the same principle in less familiar but more characteristic language), "Whatever is made up of parts, is made up of the parts of those parts." This truth, *obvious to the senses in all cases which can be fairly referred to their decision*, and so general as to be co-extensive with nature itself, being true of all sorts of phenomena (for all admit to being numbered), must be considered an *inductive truth*, or law of nature, of the highest order. And every arithmetical operation is an application of this law, or of other laws deduced from it. *This is our warrant for all calculations. We believe that five and two are equal to seven, on the evidence of this inductive law, combined with the definitions of those numbers.*[28]

The most fundamental of Frege's many criticisms of this view is that it mistakes the *application* of arithmetic to experience for *inductive dependence* of arithmetic on experience. Consider, for example, the claim that a collection of seven things can (always) be conceptually divided into a collection of five and a collection of two (which we may take to be an obvious corollary of the arithmetical claim that $7 = 5 + 2$). Properly understood, this is true, and knowable a priori. However, to understand it in this way—which Frege insists is how we really do understand it—one must not confuse it, as Mill seemingly does, with the claim that whenever one can discern seven parts that exhaustively make up some physical whole, it is always possible to physically break up that whole, without loss, into something exhaustively made up of five of those parts, plus something else exhaustively made up of two of them. Frege criticizes this view as suffering from the problems (i–iii):[29]

(i) The things to which arithmetical claims apply aren't limited to physical things; events, ideas, concepts, thoughts, lines, points, and sets can all be numbered, even if they don't exist in space or time, and/or there is no physical operation of breaking them up.

(ii) Even when physical objects are involved, the truth of an arithmetical claim doesn't depend on assumptions about what we can perceive or imagine, or the parts we can *discern* in them.

(iii) If o is a physical object that consists of seven non-overlapping parts, whether or not it is possible to physically break up o, without loss, into one thing exhaustively made up of five of the parts and another non-overlapping thing made up of the other two, is an empirical claim which we cannot know with the certainty that attaches to an arithmetical claim, and which may turn out to be false for non-arithmetical reasons.

For Frege, these problems point in the same direction. Rather than being something on which the truth of the purely arithmetical proposition that

---

[28] Mill (1843), book III, chapter 24, sec. 5, p. 401, my emphasis.
[29] These criticisms of Mill, along with others, can be found in sections 7–10 of *The Foundations of Arithmetic*, Frege (1950).

$7 = 5 + 2$ epistemically depends, the truth of the empirical proposition *that the seven coins on the table are made up of five coins belonging to Mary and two belonging to John* epistemically depends, in part, on the truth of the arithmetical proposition. Indeed, the content of the empirical claim is the conjunction of the empirical propositions *that the number of coins on the table that are Mary's = 5* and *that the number of coins on the table that are John's = 2* with the a priori truth *that $7 = 5 + 2$.*

This point is buttressed by an interesting argument about induction thought of not as a psychological process by which general beliefs arise from particular beliefs—but rather as a theory of when, and to what degree, experience provides evidence for an empirical claim by making the truth of the latter more probable than it otherwise would have been. Frege says:

> The procedure of induction, we may surmise, can itself be justified only by means of general propositions of arithmetic—unless we understand by induction a mere process of habituation, in which case it has of course absolutely no power whatever of leading to the discovery of truth. The procedure of the sciences, with its objective standards, will at times find a high probability established by a single confirmatory instance, while at others it will dismiss a thousand as almost worthless; whereas our habits are determined by the number and strength of the impressions we receive and by subjective circumstances, which have no sort of right at all to influence our judgment. *Induction [then, properly understood,] must base itself on the theory of probability,* since it can never render a proposition more than probable. *But how probability theory could possibly be developed without presupposing arithmetical laws is beyond comprehension.*[30]

The point, I take it, is that revising our assessment of the probable truth of a putatively empirical proposition in light of empirical evidence presupposes calculations, which are themselves arithmetical, or dependent on underlying claims that are. If this is right, then any claim that certain propositions are rendered probable by our evidence will presuppose arithmetic, which must already have been justified (if the probability claim is). Thus, Mill's claim that *arithmetic* is inductively justified (made probable) by experience itself requires that arithmetic be independently justified. Since this means that the ultimate grounding for arithmetic can't be empirical, it undermines his position.

In addition to this fundamental flaw in Mill's, and—Frege would say—any, empiricist view of arithmetic, he locates other shortcomings in Mill that any acceptable view must overcome. Although the passage from Mill adverts to specific arithmetical results, and talks about some laws being *deducible* from others, he doesn't offer any significant deductions, he does little to identify what numbers are, and he fails to show how their arithmetical properties could possibility be deduced from, or explicated by,

---

[30] Ibid., pp. 16–17, my emphasis; bracketed insert added by the translator, J. L. Austin.

empirical facts. One foray he does make into the identification of individual numbers with particular objects concerns the number three, which he
says is defined by the equation '2 + 1 = 3'. Though he takes this statement
to be a definition, he also takes it—somehow—to state an empirical fact.
The fact in question is that there exist groups of physical objects we perceive to be spatially arranged as follows:

They can be separated into two parts that look like this.[31]

Frege has a bit of fun with this, noting (i) that lots of things that aren't,
or can't be, perceived can be numbered, (ii) that some groups of things are
"nailed down," in the sense that they don't allow physical rearrangement,
(iii) that how things appear to us, if they appear at all, has nothing to do
with number, (iv) that very large numbers exist without our ever having
encountered groups with the requisite number of discriminable parts, and
(v) that it is hard to fit the number zero into Mill's simplistic scheme.

To this we may add a further point, based on Frege's insistence in other
contexts, that '3' and 'the number three' are singular terms that denote
a unique object—*the one and only* number three. Mill slurs over this, adding to the first illustration above the idea that "we term all such parcels
Threes." Our question, however, is, "What is *the* number three?" Surely no
one group of three things is a better candidate than any other for being
this number, which, by definition, is *the* number that follows two. Is Mill
telling us that there are many number threes? If not, what is he telling us?
The same questions arise here.

> The fact asserted in the definition of a number is a physical fact. *Each of the
> numbers* [he should have said "numerals"] two, three, four, &c., denotes phys-
> ical *phenomena* [note the plural], and connotes a physical property of those
> phenomena. Two, for instance denotes *all pairs of things, and twelve all dozens
> of things*, connoting what makes them pairs or dozens; and that which makes
> them so is something physical.[32]

In and of itself, this point may seem to be a small one. Instead of in-
timating something seemingly incoherent—that each collection of three
things is *the* number three, and hence that the numeral, '3', standing for
that number, denotes each three-membered collection—couldn't Mill have

[31] Mill (1843), Book II, chapter 6, sec. 2, p. 169 (all references to the Longmans 1961 edition).
[32] Ibid., Book III, chapter 24, sec. 5, pp. 399–400.

said that the number three is the property of being a three-membered collection, or that it is the collection of all three-membered collections, either of which is something coherent and closer to what Frege has in mind? Perhaps. But the real issues here are larger. The features of Mill's position that he finds most attractive, and that are most distinctive to him—namely, the supposed inductive dependence of arithmetical truths on empirical evidence, and the avoidance of abstract objects (not existing in space or time) in favor of physical objects and properties—cause serious problems, while adding nothing to the explanation of what numbers really are, and how arithmetical truths are justified.

For Frege, the way to discover what numbers are, and how statements about them are justified, is first, to determine what we pre-theoretically know about them, and second, to frame definitions of each number, and of the class of natural numbers as a whole, in a way that allows the definitions to be combined with other background knowledge to deduce what we pre-theoretically know. How, for example, should 2, 3, 5, and addition be defined so that facts like (11) can be deduced from the definitions, plus our knowledge of logic and facts like (10)?

10. $\exists x \exists y$ (x is a black book on my desk & y is a black book on my desk & $x \neq y$ & $\forall z$ (z is a black book on my desk $\rightarrow z = x \lor z = y$)) & $\exists x \exists y \exists z$ (x is a blue book on my desk & y is a blue book on my desk & z is a blue book on my desk & $x \neq y$ & $x \neq z$ & $y \neq z$ & $\forall z^*$ (z^* is a black book on my desk $\rightarrow z^* = x \lor z^* = y \lor z^* = z$)) & $\forall x \forall y$ ((x is a black book & y is a blue book) $\rightarrow x \neq y$)

11a. The number of black books on my desk = 2 and the number of blue books on my desk = 3, so there are 5 books on my desk.

  b. There are 2 black books on my desk, and 3 blue books on my desk, so there are 5 books on my desk.

More generally, how might a proper understanding of what natural numbers and arithmetical operations are be used to derive our purely arithmetical knowledge, plus its empirical applications, from the laws of logic, supplemented when necessary with relevant empirical facts? This, for Frege, is the most important question that a philosophical theory of number must answer.

His most fundamental objections to Mill—and to others he criticizes—are (i) that they generally don't even attempt to answer this fundamental question, and (ii) that what they do say only gets in the way of a proper answer. Mill's repeated emphasis on the *physical* properties of *physical* things being numbered is a case in point. This was attractive to him, and other naturalistically minded philosophers, as a way of avoiding commitment to non-spatiotemporal "logical" or "mathematical" objects, which can easily seem problematic. However, the wish to avoid potentially troubling commitments is no excuse for refusing to answer the fundamental Fregean question. Worse, even when the things being numbered are physical, as in the example about the books on my desk, the fact that they are physical, and have physical properties, plays no role in getting from (10) to (11). To that extent, Mill offers no real theory of number at all. At best, his remarks about the relevance of our sense experience of physical things to statements about number are elaborate warm-ups for a pitch that never comes—except for cases in which the things numbered are not physical, or not experienced, and taking his remarks seriously *prevents* any pitch from being made.

This is the context in which Frege's remarks about the importance of the ordering of the natural numbers to our understanding of them, and the inability of induction from experience to shed light on what follows from this ordering, should be understood.

> It is in their nature to be arranged in a fixed, definite order of precedence; and each one is formed in its own special way and has its own unique peculiarities, which are specially prominent in the cases of 0, 1, and 2. Elsewhere when we establish by induction a proposition about a species, we are ordinarily in possession already, merely from the definition of the concept of the species, of a whole series of its common properties. *But with the numbers we have difficulty in finding even a single common property which has not actually to be first proved common. . . .* The numbers are literally created, and determined *in their whole natures,* by the process of continually increasing by one. Now, this can only mean that from the way in which a number, say 8, is generated through increasing by one *all its properties can be deduced. But this is in principle to grant that the properties of numbers follow from their definitions, and to open up the possibility that we might prove the general laws of numbers from the method of generation which is common to them all, while deducing the special properties of the individual numbers from the special way in which, through the process of continually increasing by one, each one is formed.*[33]

Here we have the ultimate critique of the view that arithmetic inductively depends on experience for justification. It doesn't because if we understand what the natural numbers are, and discover their proper definitions, we will see that the purely arithmetical propositions about them are logically derivable from those definitions, leaving nothing for induction to justify. Of course, at this stage of the *Foundations of Arithmetic*, Frege was not in a position to demonstrate this. However the burden of most of the rest of that work is to lay the foundations for just such a proof, to be executed in *The Basic Laws of Arithmetic*.

Mill's inductivism is, of course, not the only form of naturalism to which Frege objected. Another variant of the view, psychologism, holds that the laws of logic are natural laws that describe human reasoning, while natural numbers are ideas in the minds of agents. Although the general lessons extracted from the critique of Mill apply with equal force against

[33] Frege (1950), pp. 15–16, my emphasis.

psychologism, Frege gives further objections to psychologism. The locus of his attack is the discussion in sections 26 and 27 of *The Foundations of Arithmetic*, and sections xiv–xxv of the preface to *The Basic Laws of Arithmetic*, where he makes the following points:

(i) There may be natural laws describing the thinking processes of all human beings—past, present, and future—but we don't, at present, know what they are. Whatever their content may turn out to be, though, they will be high-level generalizations subject to falsification by future experience, the justification of which must come from experience. By contrast, the laws of logic (and arithmetic) are readily identifiable, known to be true, and incapable of falsification by experience. Thus, it would, as Frege says, "be strange if the most exact of all the sciences had to seek support from psychology, which is still feeling its way none too surely."[34]

(ii) The reason for the contrast between the (still unknown) natural laws of human psychology and the (well known) laws of logic is that they are laws in different senses. Whereas the former provide descriptive, perhaps causal, accounts of human reasoning, the latter are laws of truth preservation that underlie the way in which knowledge claims may be justified. The application of these laws to human reasoning is derivative and indirect. To the extent that one aims at truth, validly deriving a logical consequence from a set of premises is correct—in the sense of being guaranteed to produce a truth (if one's premises are jointly true), and of transferring one's justification to one's conclusion (if the conjunction of ones premises is justified).[35]

(iii) If numbers were mental constructs, they would be ideas in the minds of agents. But, Frege thinks, one's ideas are private to oneself. From this, he draws three conclusions, each intended as a *reductio ad absurdum* of the claim that numbers are ideas in the mind. First, if numbers were ideas, then we could no longer speak of *the* number two, for example. Instead, "we should then have it might be many millions of twos on our hands. We should have to speak of my two and your two." Second, although there might be millions of twos, large numbers might not exist, since it would "be doubtful whether there existed the infinite number of numbers that we ordinarily suppose. 10^{10}, perhaps, might be only an empty symbol, and there might exist no idea at all, in any being whatever, to answer to that name." Finally, since (Frege thinks) the ideas

---

[34] Ibid., sec. 17, p. 38.

[35] This statement of what some call "the normativity of logic" is a bit weaker, and more explicitly qualified, than Frege's own statement of the view in sec. 15, p. 202, of *The Basic Laws of Arithmetic*: "That the logical laws should be guiding principles for thought in the attainment of truth is generally admitted at the outset; but it is only too easily forgotten. The ambiguity of the word 'law' is fatal here. In one sense it states what is, in the other it prescribes what should be. Only in the latter sense can the logical laws be called laws of thought, in laying down how one should think."

in one mind are inaccessible to others, for all we know, the numbers and arithmetical properties in one mind might be different from those in other minds, in which case arithmetic would be entirely subjective, rather than objective.[36]

The upshot of these remarks is that, for Frege, psychologism was less a coherent theory of the nature of logic and mathematics than a source of confusion that obscured, and didn't take seriously, the fundamental questions with which any genuine philosophical theory of these sciences must be concerned.

The same is true of his critique of the crude versions of formalism of his time that identified numbers with physical marks on paper—such as inscriptions of numerals.[37] Pointing out that this is a confusion—in fact, the same confusion as the all-too-common identification of functions from numbers to numbers with expressions (often formulas containing variables)—was an important prerequisite to clarifying the mathematical use of the notion of a function, and extending it to logic, the philosophy of mathematics, and philosophical semantics, where, thanks to Frege, it now plays central roles. This is the purpose of his 1891 article "On Function and Concept," the first few pages of which are devoted to dispelling crude formalist confusions of symbols with things signified. He says, in criticism,

Thus, e.g., the expression '$2x^3 + x$' would be a function of x, and '$2 \times 2^3 + 2$' would be a function of 2. This answer cannot satisfy us, for here no distinction is made between form and content, sign and thing signified. . . . Now what is the content of '$2 \times 2^3 + 2$'? The same thing as '18' or '3×6'. What is expressed in the equation '$2 \times 2^3 + 2 = 18$' is that the right-hand complex of signs has the same reference as the left-hand one. I must here combat the view that, e.g., $2 + 5$ and $3 + 4$ are equal but not the same. . . . Difference of sign cannot by itself be a sufficient ground for difference of the thing signified. The only reason why in our case the matter is less obvious is that the reference of the numeral 7 is not anything perceptible to the senses. . . . [T]his leads . . . to numerals being taken to be numbers. . . . [S]uch a conception . . . is untenable, for we cannot speak of any arithmetical properties of numbers whatsoever without going back to what the signs stand for. For example, *the property belonging to 1, of being the result of multiplying itself by itself, would be a mere myth; for no microscopal or chemical investigation . . . could ever detect this property in the possession of the innocent character we call . . . [numeral] one.* . . . The characters we call numerals have . . . physical and chemical properties depending on

[36] All these points, and the quoted passages, come from *The Foundations of Arithmetic* (Frege 1950), sec. 27, pp. 37–38.

[37] These views, attacked by Frege, are not to be confused with the much more sophisticated views of David Hilbert, for example, which were presented and attained a following toward the end of Frege's life, long after the publication of *The Foundations of Arithmetic* and the two volumes of *The Basic Laws of Arithmetic*.

the writing material. One could imagine the introduction some day of quite new numerals. . . . Nobody is seriously going to suppose that in this way we should get quite new numbers.[38]

As before, we see the primacy of Frege's central insight. The account of what numbers are should be such that from it (plus logic and background facts needed for empirical applications) we can deduce the properties they have that constitute our pre-philosophical knowledge of them. No matter what other difficulties or absurdities may plague physical, psychological, or formalistic conceptions of number—of which there are many—it is their failure to satisfy this central criterion that disqualifies them as viable philosophical theories.

5.2. Critique of Kant

Unlike the views criticized above, Kant's views of mathematics were taken quite seriously by Frege. He agreed with Kant that there is an important distinction between the analytic and the synthetic that cuts across the distinction between a priori truths (the justifications of which aren't dependent on experience) and a posteriori truths (which can be justified only by experience). According to Kant the "judgment" expressed by ⌜A is B⌝ is analytic iff the concept/property expressed by the predicate B is contained in the concept/property expressed by subject A, whereas a synthetic judgment is one in which the concept/property expressed by the predicate is not so contained, in which case the judgment adds something to the subject concept/property.[39] We may take Kant's "judgments" to correspond to Frege's thoughts, and his "concepts/properties" to roughly correspond to Frege's senses. A key point for Kant, and for Frege, is that judgments that count as analytic *in Kant's sense* are epistemologically trivial. Since they don't provide new information, they don't represent substantial increases in our knowledge. Thus, it is not surprising that Kant regarded both geometry and arithmetic to be examples of *the synthetic a priori*.

Although Frege agreed that the distinction between analytic and synthetic truths is both important and not coextensive with the distinction between the a priori and the a posteriori, he was critical of the assumption—implicit in Kant's formulation of the analytic/synthetic distinction—that all judgments are of subject-predicate form.[40] This was a natural assumption for Kant to make during a time in which the traditional Aristotelian logic of generality still held sway, while being clearly unacceptable to the man who showed us the logical and philosophical benefits to be gained from abandoning it. Once the assumption was abandoned, it was clear to

---

[38] "On Function and Concept," pp. 21–23 in Geach and Black (1970), my emphasis.
[39] See Immanuel Kant (1781, 1787), A6–7/B10.
[40] See Frege (1950), sec. 88, p. 100.

Frege that Kant's division of judgments into analytic and synthetic simply left out those that are not of subject-predicate form. Hence, the distinction had to be redrawn.

For Frege, an analytic truth is either a logical truth or a consequence of a set of logical truths plus one or more correct definitions of nonlogical notions. A synthetic truth is any truth that isn't analytic. Since he took logical truths to be a priori, while implicitly assuming that correct definitions are themselves a priori (and that logical consequences of a priori truths are always themselves a priori), Frege naturally regarded all analytic truths as a priori.[41] However, since he also realized that logical consequences of truths, each of which we already know, may be decidedly nontrivial, he recognized that analytic truths can sometimes be highly informative extensions of our knowledge. Thus, the informativeness of arithmetic and other branches of mathematics was, for Frege, no bar to their being analytic.

This was the backdrop for his view that arithmetic, and much else, is analytic. His agreement with Kant, whom he held in high regard, that Euclidean geometry is synthetic a priori is more surprising.[42]

> There is a remarkable difference between geometry and arithmetic in the manner in which they justify their principles. The elements of all geometrical constructions are intuitions, and geometry points to intuition as the source of all its axioms. Since the axioms of arithmetic have no intuitiveness, its principles cannot be derived from intuition.[43]

To understand this passage, one must understand what Frege, following Kant, means by "intuition." When he claims that the axioms of arithmetic "have no intuitiveness," he is not saying that they aren't self-evidently obvious. He is saying that their correctness isn't guaranteed by Kantian "intuitions," which are presentations of objects in perception, introspection, and imagination. For Kant space and time are categories imposed

---

[41] Though these assumptions are correct within the sphere in which Frege uses them, they are connected to more contentious and complex issues about the justification of definitions that will be examined in chapter 2.

[42] *Foundations of Arithmetic*, sec. 89 (Frege 1950, pp. 101–2):

> I have no wish to incur the reproach of picking petty quarrels with a genius to whom we must all look up with grateful awe; I feel bound, therefore, to call attention also to the extent of my agreement with him, which far exceeds any disagreement. . . . I consider Kant did great service in drawing the distinction between synthetic and analytic judgments. In calling the truths of geometry synthetic and a priori, he revealed their true nature. . . . If Kant was wrong about arithmetic, that does not seriously detract, in my opinion, from the value of his work. His point was, that there are such things as synthetic judgments a priori; whether they are to be found in geometry only, or in arithmetic as well, is of less importance.

[43] Frege (1874), at p. 50 of Angelelli (1967).

on our experience as forms in which things are presented to us. It is in the nature of our minds to perceive events as temporally ordered, and objects as arranged in Euclidean space. It is because no other experience of objects is possible, or even perceptually imaginable, that the truth of Euclidean geometry is guaranteed, a priori, to be true of the world *as we experience it*. Frege seems to have accepted this. But he didn't accept Kant's view that arithmetic is similarly guaranteed to be true by our temporal "intuitions"—i.e., by the way our minds must, of necessity, perceive events.

Two factors seem to have played a role in his divergence from Kant on this point.[44] First, whereas geometry applies only to things in space, our conception of which may be constituted by our "spatial intuitions," arithmetic is not limited to the temporal or the spatial, since everything whatsoever, including purely abstract objects, can be numbered.[45] Second, whereas in geometry Frege thinks we are able to see individual figures as representing all other perceptually identical figures, and hence to draw conclusions about the whole class from what we see to be true of the representing instance, the inherent peculiarities of each individual number don't allow us to use one to represent all the others.[46] For these reasons, he concludes, arithmetic can't be given the kind of Kantian grounding that Euclidean geometry can. Thus, a different grounding, in logic, is required.

Looking back on Frege today, the most difficult aspect of his view for us to fathom is not his idea that arithmetic is a priori in virtue of being analytic, but that geometry is also a priori, despite its being synthetic. Non-Euclidean geometries had been around for more than 50 years at the time of the *Begriffsschrift*. For decades some had speculated that they were more accurate depictions of physical space than Euclidean geometry, and in 1868 models of non-Euclidean systems were produced, demonstrating their consistency. Why, we now ask, did Frege think that Euclidean geometry is a priori? In section 14 of *The Foundations of Arithmetic*, he hints at an answer.

> Empirical propositions hold good of what is physically or psychologically actual, the truths of geometry govern *all that is spatially intuitable, whether actual or product of our fancy*. The wildest visions of delirium, the boldest inventions of legend and poetry . . . all these remain, so long as they remain *intuitable*, still subject to the axioms of geometry. *Conceptual thought alone can after a fashion shake off this yoke*, when it assumes, say, a space of four dimensions or

---

[44] See Currie (1982), pp. 34–37, for an illuminating discussion.

[45] "[T]he ideal as well as the real, concepts as well as objects, temporal as well as spatial entities, events as well as bodies, methods as well as theorems; even numbers can themselves be counted. . . . [T]he basic propositions on which arithmetic is based cannot apply merely to a limited area whose peculiarities they express in the way in which the axioms of geometry express the peculiarities of what is spatial; rather these basic propositions must extend to everything that can be thought." Frege (1885), pp. 141–42.

[46] See Frege (1950), sec. 13, pp. 19–20.

positive curvature. To study such conceptions is not useless by any means; but it is to leave the ground of *intuition* entirely behind. . . . For purposes of conceptual thought we can always assume the contrary of some one or other of the geometrical axioms, without involving ourself in any self-contradictions when we proceed to our deductions, *despite the conflict between our assumptions and our intuition.* The fact that this is possible shows that the axioms of geometry are independent of one another and the primitive laws of logic, and consequently are synthetic.[47]

Frege recognizes that non-Euclidean geometries are logically consistent, and hence that Euclidean geometry is synthetic, but he denies that our knowledge of it is empirical, and so neither certain nor a priori. Euclidean geometry can't be empirical because it applies to all genuinely conceivable—i.e., imaginable—space, as opposed merely to actual space. Like Kant, he took Euclidean geometry to be grounded in our spatial intuitions, which provide a priori certainty about space *as we experience it.* On this view, the physical space we experience *must be* as we imagine it to be. Euclidean geometry provides knowledge of this space. Although he grants that competing conceptions of space are conceptually coherent (in the narrow sense of being logically consistent) and so can be abstractly investigated, he doesn't take the idea that they could be true of space as it really is very seriously, presumably because he finds it hard to credit the thought that *space as it really is* could differ in fundamental respects from *space as we do, and must, experience it.*[48]

Our main concern is, of course, not with Frege's questionable views of geometry, but with his contrast between it and arithmetic, which is

---

[47] Ibid., pp. 20–21, my emphasis.
[48] Frege's attachment to Euclidean geometry is illustrated by the following passage from p. 169 of "On Euclidean Geometry," written between 1899 and 1906, published in Frege (1979).

If Euclidean geometry is true, then non-Euclidean geometry is false, and if non-Euclidean geometry is true then Euclidean geometry is false. . . . People at one time believed they practiced a science, which went by the name of alchemy; but when it was discovered that this alleged science was riddled with error, it was banished from among the sciences. . . . The question at the present time is whether Euclidean or non-Euclidean geometry should be struck off the role of the sciences and made to line up as a museum piece alongside alchemy and astrology as mummies. If one is content to have only phantoms hovering around one, there is no need to take the matter so seriously, but in science we are subject to the necessity of seeking after truth. There it is a case of either in or out! Well, is it Euclidean or non-Euclidean geometry that should get the sack? That is the question. Does one dare to treat Euclid's elements, which have exercised unquestioned sway for over 2000 years, as we have treated astrology? It is only if we do not dare to do this that we can put Euclid's axioms forward as propositions that are neither false nor doubtful. In that case, non-Euclidean geometry will have to be counted amongst the pseudo-sciences, to the study of which we still attach some slight importance, but only as historical curiosities.

emphasized in the lines immediately following, and completing, those of the passage just quoted.

> Can the same be said of the fundamental propositions of the science of number? *Here we have only to try denying any one of them, and complete confusion ensues. Even to think at all seems no longer possible.* The basis of arithmetic lies deeper, it seems, than that of any of the empirical sciences, and even than that of geometry. The truths of arithmetic govern all that is numerable. *This is the widest domain of all; for to it belongs not only the actual, not only the intuitable, but everything thinkable.* Should not the laws of number, then, be connected very intimately with the laws of thought?[49]

This is an echo of something we saw above in section 4, where we discussed Frege's idea that the fundamental laws of logic are both self-evident (and so not in need of or susceptible to any justification) and also essential norms of thought, which we are incapable of rejecting "if we are not to throw our thought to confusion and in the end renounce judgment altogether."[50] This is connected to their absolute generality, applying, as he takes them to do, not just to all that is plus all that could be visualized, but also to all that can be conceived or thought. For Frege, the reason that arithmetic shares this status with logic is that it is derivable from the combination of pure logic with the logical definitions of arithmetical terms. It is time to make good on this idea.

5.3. Frege's Definition of Number

5.3.1. NUMERICAL STATEMENTS ARE ABOUT CONCEPTS

In determining the sense and referents of numerical expressions, we can't appeal to mental images of numbers, or to objects we have in mind when we use such expressions. It is unlikely that we have definite images of any number, or group of objects, in mind when we use any numeral, and it is obvious that we don't have them in mind for every numerical expression we use. Thus, Frege concluded, we can't first determine what the numbers are, and then use this identifying knowledge to analyze numerical statements. But we do have a good sense of what we use such statements to say, or assert. Thus, he reasoned, the best strategy is to abstract a definition of number from the contents of these statements.

He starts down this road in section 46 of *The Foundations of Arithmetic* when he says:

> It should throw some light on the matter to consider number *in the context of a judgment* which brings out its basic use. While looking at one and the same external phenomenon, *I can say with equal truth* both "It is a copse"

---

[49] Frege (1950), sec. 17, p. 21.

[50] *The Basic Laws of Arithmetic*, vol. 1, Preface, sec. 17, in Frege (1997), p. 204.

and "It is five trees," or both "Here are four companies" and "Here are 500 men." Now what changes here from one judgment to the other is neither any individual object, nor the whole, the agglomeration of them, but rather *my terminology. But that is itself only a sign that one concept has been substituted for another. This suggests . . . that the content of a statement of number is an assertion about a concept.*[51]

By 'concept' Frege means neither a word, nor an agent's subjective idea or mental content associated with a word. Rather it is an objective entity denoted by a predicate—a function from objects to truth values. The idea, in a nutshell, is that the content of the statement we make when we say, e.g., that Jupiter has four moons, is that given by (12).

12. The number of entities falling under the concept *moon of Jupiter* = 4.

5.3.2. BUT NUMBERS ARE OBJECTS

Example (12) is an identity statement flanked by a pair of singular terms. Since the referents of such terms are objects, for Frege, this means that if the statement is true, then the terms 'the number of entities falling under the concept *moon of Jupiter*' and '4' must refer to the same object. What is this object? We haven't yet been told. After emphasizing this in section 56 of *The Foundations of Arithmetic*, in section 58 Frege considers the objection that, because nothing we can picture, or imagine, seems to be an apt candidate for this number, it is a mistake to suppose that numbers are objects at all—which he rejects on the grounds that there are many meaningful words that are not uniformly connected by speakers with specific images, or definite (subjective) ideas. The lesson he draws from this is what has come to be called his "Context Principle," stated in section 60.

> That we can form no idea of its [a number term's] content is therefore no reason for denying all meaning to a word, or for excluding it from our vocabulary. We are indeed only imposed on by the opposite view because we will, when asking for the meaning of a word, consider it in isolation, which leads us to accept an idea as the meaning. Accordingly, any word for which we can find no corresponding mental picture appears to have no content. But we ought always to keep before our eyes a complete proposition [sentence]. *Only in a proposition have the words really a meaning.* It may be that mental pictures float before us all the while, but these need not correspond to the logical elements in the judgment. *It is enough if the proposition taken as a whole has a sense; it is this that confers on its parts also its contents.*[52]

The Context Principle, expressed by the two italicized sentences, seems to be that (i) the notion of a sentence having a meaning (which Frege identifies with the claim it is used to assert or express) is explanatorily

---

[51] Frege (1950), p. 59, my emphasis.
[52] Ibid., p. 71, my emphasis.

primary, while (ii) what it is for a word or phrase to have a meaning is to be explained in terms of what it contributes to the meanings of sentences containing it. Somehow, in a manner not further clarified by Frege, this is supposed to disarm the objection that number words (including numerals) can't designate objects, because we can't—simply by understanding them—identify which objects they are supposed to designate.

But how, precisely, is the Context Principle supposed to do this? Perhaps the idea is that, given fixed meanings for sentences, we may employ one or more ways of abstracting word meanings from sentence meanings so as to see the latter as constituted by the former. In the case of number, this would mean (i) determining what numerical sentences mean (as used both in mathematics and ordinary life), and hence what senses/thoughts they express, (ii) constructing definitions of 'zero', 'successor', 'natural number', and other arithmetical notions, irrespective whether, when we consider the definitions in isolation, we can recognize the referents presented by the *definienda* as what we pre-theoretically had in mind, (iii) articulating principles for constructing senses of arithmetical sentences out of the senses assigned to their parts, and (iv) showing that the senses yielded by (ii) and (iii) are, in fact, those identified in (i). Of course, Frege doesn't exactly do this, in part because at the time he wrote *The Foundations of Arithmetic*, he hadn't yet developed his theory of the senses of expressions and sentences. However, that isn't the whole story, since—even given his later theory—it is far from clear that anyone could do the job.

Frege does, of course, provide the definitions alluded to in (ii), and use them to derive the axioms of arithmetic from (what he takes to be) axioms of logic. In so doing, he also provides convincing reasons to believe that his definitional counterparts of ordinary numerical sentences are (outside of hyper-intensional contexts like those provided by belief and other propositional attitude ascriptions) both necessarily and a priori equivalent in truth value to numerical statements we all, pre-theoretically, understand. Whether or not this is enough to justify the claim that he has *correctly and accurately defined* the relevant numerical notions is, perhaps, the most important question to ask about Frege's philosophical conception of his project. *If* we take the Context Principle as implicitly embodying the claim that such equivalence *is* sufficient to justify the correctness and accuracy of his analysis, then, as Currie points out, this enhanced understanding of the Principle will not only disarm the objection that prompted it, but also express the governing idea behind both Frege's own philosophical understanding of his project, and his criticism of other accounts of the nature of arithmetical claims.[53] Examining the contentious criterion of analytic success embodied in this enhanced understanding of the Context Principle is a matter for chapter 2. At this stage, nothing so far-reaching is needed. Since, by the time the Context Principle is stated

[53] See pp. 151–56 of Currie (1982).

in *The Foundations of Arithmetic*, Frege has already convincingly shown that many words we properly take to designate objects are not uniformly connected by speakers with specific images or definite subjective ideas, he is free to proceed with his definitions of number.

5.3.3. OBJECTS AND IDENTITY

Having disposed of the objection to taking numbers to be objects, even though we have no antecedent idea what they are, Frege takes up another objection in section 62.

> How, then, are numbers to be given to us, if we cannot have any ideas or [Kantian] intuitions [perceptions/apprehensions] of them? Since it is only in the context of a proposition [sentence] that words have any meaning, our problem becomes this: To define the sense of a proposition in which a number word occurs. That, obviously, leaves us still a very wide choice. But we have already settled that number words are to be understood as standing for self-subsistent objects [which can't be referents of predicates—p. 72]. *And that is enough to give us a class of propositions which must have a sense, namely those which express our recognition of a number as the same again. If we are to use the symbol a to signify an object, we must have a criterion for deciding in all cases whether b is the same as a, even if it is not always in our power to apply the criterion.* In our present case, we have to define the sense of the proposition 'the number which belongs to the concept F is the same as that which belongs to the concept G.'[54]

Here, Frege takes a good idea too far. Having used the occurrence of numerical expressions in identity statements as the basis for his claim that their referents—numbers—are objects, he can defend this position by providing a criterion for assigning truth values to identities like ⌜The number of entities falling under the concept F = the number falling under the concept G⌝ the results of which we recognize to be correct. This is precisely what he does in the sections immediately following the quoted passage in his discussion of a principle he attributes to David Hume. However, his *general* comments about the need for a criterion of identity *whenever* we use singular terms to refer to objects are highly contentious, and go far beyond the Humean principle he needs. In both empirical science and everyday life we often use singular terms for things without having any nontrivial criterion for distinguishing those things from all others. Think for example of oceans or mountain ranges. Surely there are such things, and singular terms referring to them—despite the fact that there is no non-question-begging criterion known to anyone that correctly and precisely specifies where one ocean (or mountain range) begins and another ends. By the same token, there is no known criterion the application of which (even by God) would distinguish all true identity statements involving oceans or mountain ranges from all false ones. The same is, of course, true

---

[54] Frege (1950), p. 73, my emphasis.

of many other things we use singular terms to designate. We will return to this point in our discussion in chapter 2 of Frege's notion of a logically perfect language. Here it is enough to note that his definition of number need not be made to depend on any such over-the-top *no entity without a criterion of identity* claim.

Hume's Principle, discussed in sections 64–66 of *The Foundations of Arithmetic*, is a way of understanding, and assigning intuitively correct truth values to, sentences ⌜the number of F's = the number of G's⌝ — without presupposing any prior understanding of numerical terms.[55] According to the principle, for all concepts F and G, the number belonging to F is identical with the number belonging to G iff the extension of F (the class of things falling under F) can be put in one-to-one correspondence with the extension of G. This simple and commonsensical idea gives correct results for all finite classes, while being extendable to infinite classes in a natural way. The number belonging to F is identical with the number belonging to G iff one can exhaust the class of things falling under F and the class of things falling under G by forming pairs the first of which is a member of the class of things falling under F and the second of which is a member of the class of things falling under G, where no member of either class occurs in more than one pair.

Lest one be concerned that numerical notions have been illicitly presupposed in this explanation, one-to-one correspondence may be defined as follows.

One-to-One Correspondence

For all concepts F and G, the extension of F (the class of things falling under F) is in one-to-one correspondence with the extension of G (the class of things falling under G) iff for some relation R, (i) for every object x such that Fx, there is an object y such that Gy & Rxy, and for every object z if Gz & Rxz, then z = y, and (ii) for every object y such that Gy, there is an object x such that Fx & Rxy, and for every object z if Fz & Rzy, then z = x.

Since this definition neither contains nor presupposes any arithmetical terms, the relation of one-to-one correspondence it defines can be used in Hume's Principle without presupposing the notion of number Frege aims to explicate. Some terminology may be helpful. When two extensions (classes) are in one-to-one correspondence, we will say they are *equinumerous*, and when the extensions of two concepts are equinumerous the

---

[55] In this sentence 'F' and 'G' are used as metalinguistic variables over predicates/formulas; in the rest of the paragraph, they are used as second-order variables ranging over Fregean concepts.

concepts will be called *equal*. With this understanding, Hume's Principle tells us that for all concepts F and G, the number belonging to F is identical with the number belonging to G iff F *equals* G iff the extension of F is *equinumerous* with the extension of G. So, when $\mathscr{F}$ and $\mathscr{G}$ are predicates (formulas) designating concepts F and G, respectively, ⌜the number of $\mathscr{F}$s = the number of $\mathscr{G}$s⌝ is true iff the extension of F is equinumerous with the extension of G.

Since this criterion assigns correct truth conditions to the target class of sentences, ⌜the number of $\mathscr{F}$s = the number of $\mathscr{G}$s⌝, without presupposing any antecedent understanding of number, it suits Frege's purposes. However, even though it correctly accounts for the truth of the sentence 'the number of fingers on my right hand = the number of fingers on my left hand', for example, it does not identify the object to which the singular terms flanking the identity sign refer. By the same token, it tells us nothing about the numeral '5', or sentences containing it, and leaves us in the dark about what the number 5, or any other number, is. These shortcomings are remedied by Frege's definition of number.

5.3.4. THE NUMBER OF F'S, ZERO, SUCCESSOR, AND THE NUMERALS

Frege's definition of number, from section 68, is: For any concept F, the number that belongs to F is the extension of the concept *equal to F*.[56] Let's unpack this. The extension of a concept is the class of entities that fall under it. For any concept F, the entities that fall under the concept *equal to F* are those the extensions of which are equinumerous with the extension of F. So, the number that belongs to F is the class of all and only those concepts the extensions of which are classes equinumerous with the class of things of which F is true. So, the number of fingers on my right hand is the class of all those concepts the extensions of which are classes equinumerous with the class of fingers on my right hand—it is the class of concepts that apply to five things, or, if we ignore the difference between concepts and the classes of things that fall under them, it is the class of all five-membered classes. Although we can see from the definition that this is so, we are, of course, not yet allowed to use a numeral like 'five', since no definitions have yet been given for the numerals. However, this is easily remedied.

We begin with Frege's definition of zero as the number that belongs to the concept *not identical with itself*. So, zero is the class of all and only those concepts the extensions of which can be put into one-to-one correspondence with the class of things that are not identical with themselves. Since there are no objects that are not identical with themselves, this means that zero is the class of concepts the extensions of which can be put into one-to-one correspondence with the empty class—i.e., the class with no members. So, zero is the class of concepts that don't apply to anything.

---

[56] In this section, I return to using 'F', 'G', etc. as variables. Here. 'F' is a variable over Fregean concepts.

Next we define the notion of n *directly following* (i.e., succeeding) m. According to Frege, n directly follows (succeeds) m iff for some concept F, and some object x falling under F, n is the number belonging to F, and m is the number belonging to the concept *falling under F but not identical with x*. When m is zero, this means that n directly follows (succeeds) zero iff for some concept F and object x falling under F, n is the number belonging to F, and zero—namely the class of concepts that don't apply to anything—is the number belonging to the concept *falling under F but not identical with x*. Since this concept doesn't apply to anything, n is a class of concepts each of which applies to some object x, and to nothing else. Assuming something I will say more about in section 6—namely that there is one and only one such class—we have identified *the unique object* that directly follows (succeeds) zero. In general, we define the successor of m as the unique object that directly follows (succeeds) m. As for numerals, '1' designates the successor of 0, '2' designates the successor of 1, etc. So, 0 is the class of concepts under which nothing falls, 1 is the class of concepts under which, for some x, x, and only x, falls, 2 is the class of concepts under which some nonidentical objects x and y, and only those objects, fall, and so on. From this it is transparent that 0 is the class of concepts that apply to nothing, 1 is the class that apply to exactly one thing, 2 is the class that apply to exactly two things, and—in general—n is the class of concepts that apply to exactly n things. Note, we do not presuppose an antecedent understanding of the numerals in deriving this result. Rather, the result is an automatic consequence of the Fregean definitions.

Two features speak to the naturalness of what Frege has done.

(i) Just as redness isn't identical with any red thing, but rather is something all red things have in common, so a particular number n is not identical with any collection of n things (or with any concept under which just those n things fall); rather it is something all concepts applying to n things have in common—membership in the number n.

(ii) Just as counting any collection of things consists in putting them in one-to-one correspondence with the numerals, starting with '1', used in the count, so such correspondence is the crucial notion in defining each of the numbers.

5.3.5. THE NATURAL NUMBERS

Having defined '0' and 'successor', plus individual numerals, the next step is to define what we mean by the "natural numbers," which constitute the domain of arithmetic. The simplest thought is that a natural number is something that is a member of every class that contains zero and is closed under successor (i.e., that contains the successor of x whenever it contains x). We can put this in terms of concepts by first defining *an inductive concept* as one that is true of zero and closed under successor (i.e., is true of the successor of x whenever it is true of x). A *natural number* is then one that falls under all inductive concepts. Although this is not identical to the definition Frege gave, it is equivalent to it. The virtue of the definition (and its Fregean equivalent) is that it makes it easy to prove *mathematical induction*. Since this is a crucial axiom of arithmetic, proving it from Frege's system of logic was a major step in his program. To see that mathematical induction must be true on the suggested definition, let F be any concept true of zero and closed under successor. Since F satisfies the definition of an inductive concept, and since, by definition, the natural numbers fall under every such concept, F is true of every natural number. Q.E.D.

Frege's own definition of natural number (and proof of mathematical induction) is given in the *Begriffsschrift,* published five years before *The Foundations of Arithmetic*. Though equivalent to the one just mentioned, it is based on related ideas that are independently worth knowing. We begin by noting the connection between the relations *parent* and *ancestor*: any parent of x is an ancestor of x, as is any parent of any ancestor of x. Because this condition holds for any x, the *ancestor* relation is called the *transitive closure* of the *parent* relation. We can put this more generally, using T to define what it is for a relation to be transitive and TC to define the transitive closure R_{TC} for arbitrary R.

T. $\forall x \forall y \forall z \, ((Rxy \,\&\, Ryz) \supset Rxz)$
TC. $\forall x \forall y \, (R_{TC}xy \text{ iff } \forall P \, [(\forall z \, (Rxz \supset Pz) \,\&\, \forall u \forall v \, ((Pu \,\&\, Ruv) \supset Pv)) \supset Py])$

Applying these to *parent* and *ancestor*, we see that the former isn't transitive, while the latter is, and that when *Rxy* is the relation *y is a parent of x*, $R_{TC}xy$ is the relation *y is an ancestor of x*. For (going left to right in TC) if y is an ancestor of x, then, for any concept P, y will fall under P, provided that (i) every parent of x falls under P, and (ii) any parent of someone who falls under P also falls under P; and (right to left in TC) if for any concept P whatsoever, y will fall under P provided that (i) every parent of x falls under P, and (ii) any parent of someone who falls under P also falls under P, then—given all this—y must be an ancestor of x. For this reason, the transitive closure of an intransitive relation R is often called *the ancestral of R*. It is this notion of the ancestral of a relation that Frege used in the *Begriffsschrift* to establish mathematical induction.

Let *Rxy* be the relation that holds between zero and its successor, and in general between any extension of a concept and its successor—using Frege's definition of successor (i.e., *directly follows*) given above. The ancestral of this relation is the relation *y follows x (in a series under successor)*, or, in other words, *y is greater than x*. We can then define the natural numbers as those objects (extensions of concepts) that are greater than or equal to zero. With this definition in mind, we return to mathematical induction, which states that if zero falls under a concept P that is closed under successor, then every natural number falls under P. To prove this we assume the antecedent—that zero falls under P and P is closed under successor—and show that every natural number must fall under P. Using the notation in TC, we express the antecedent as *P(0) & $\forall u \forall v((Pu \,\&\, Ruv) \supset Pv)$*, with *Rxy* as the successor relation *y directly follows x*. Since *greater than* is the ancestral, R_{TC}, of successor, R, TC tells us that everything greater than zero falls under P. Since, by definition, the natural numbers are zero plus everything greater than zero, it follows that every natural number falls under P. This is the import of Frege's theorem 81 in the *Begriffsschrift*. It is also the import of his discussion in sections 79–81 of *The Foundations of Arithmetic*, where (i) (in section 79) he repeats his definition of the ancestral—*y following in the φ-series after x*—of a relation φ, (ii) (in section 81) he takes the natural numbers to be zero plus those that *follow in the φ-series after* zero (where φ is the relation *directly following/successor*), and (iii) (in section 80) he comments that "Only by means of this definition of following in a series [i.e., the ancestral of the successor relation] is it possible to reduce the argument from n to (n + 1), which is peculiar to mathematics, to the general laws of logic."[57]

6. THE LOGICIST REDUCTION

The derivations of the axioms of arithmetic from what Frege took to be the basic laws of logic are carried out in daunting and meticulous detail in *The Basic Laws of Arithmetic*. No such exhaustive treatment will be given here. Instead, the leading ideas will be presented informally, but in enough detail to give the reader an idea of the strategies used to derive the crucial results.

6.1. The Axioms of Logic and Arithmetic

We begin with the system of logic Frege used. The first part of the system consists of axioms and inference rules for proving standard logical truths in the sense, recognized today, of formulas that come out true on all interpretations of their nonlogical symbols, and all choices of domains of quantification. As explained in section 4, Frege's system for proving such truths was as effective as any we now have. Since I won't here be constructing explicit formal proofs, there is no need to go into details of this aspect of either his, or equivalent, systems. However, something must be said of other "logical principles," implicit or explicit in Frege's system.

Since meaningful predicates/formulas denote concepts that determine which objects they are true of, the comprehension principle for concepts is taken for granted.

Concept Comprehension

For every stateable condition φ on things, there exists a concept C that is true of all and only those things that satisfy the condition $\exists C \, \forall y \, (Cy \longleftrightarrow \phi y)$.

[57] Frege (1950), p. 93.

A further principle explicates Frege's conception of what concepts are—namely, assignments of truth values to objects. As we saw in section 3, he took this to be all there is to concepts, and so took concepts that assign the same values to the same arguments to be identical—which is what *Concept Extensionality* tells us.

Concept Extensionality

Concepts P and Q are identical iff everything that falls under one falls under the other: $\forall P \forall Q$ (P = Q iff $\forall x$ (Px $\leftrightarrow$ Qx)).

Being inherent in his understanding of his symbolism, these two principles about concepts didn't require separate statement. But when it came to the derivation of the axioms of arithmetic, he did require a special "logical" axiom—numbered V in his system—that guarantees extensionality and comprehension for *extensions of concepts*—i.e., classes.

Axiom V

For all (first-level) concepts P and Q, the extension of P (the class of things falling under P) = the extension of Q (the class of things falling under Q) iff $\forall x$ (Px $\leftrightarrow$ Qx).

This gives us *comprehension for classes* since '$\forall P \forall x$ (Px $\leftrightarrow$ Px)' will always be true, which, by Axiom V, means that the class of things falling under P is identical with the class of things falling under P. Although this doesn't require the class to be nonempty, it does require there to be a class of all and only those things of which P is true. Of course, Axiom V also guarantees *extensionality for classes*—identifying classes with the same members. This special axiom is ubiquitous in Frege's proof of the axioms of arithmetic from those of logic.

Prior to Frege, a complete set of axioms for arithmetic had been given by the mathematician Richard Dedekind, who appears to have come up with it in 1888. Nevertheless, the resulting system is usually called *Peano arithmetic*, after Giuseppe Peano, who published an influential work (with a footnote to Dedekind) in 1889. The axioms can be given different formulations, depending on whether *successor* is stated as a totally defined function, or simply a two-place relation. In order to be as explicit as possible in indicating what must be proved from the logic, I have selected the latter option, which requires the presence of Axiom A2, which, together with A5, establishes that successor is a function defined on all natural numbers. With this proviso, the axioms of Peano arithmetic are:

A1　Zero isn't a successor of anything. $\sim \exists x \; Sx0$
A2　Nothing has more than one successor. $\forall x \forall y \forall z$ ((Sxy & Sxz) $\supset$ y = z)

A3   No two things have the same successor: $\forall x \forall y \forall z ((Sxy \& Szy) \supset x = z)$
A4   Zero is a natural number: NN0
A5   Every natural number has a successor: $\forall x (NNx \supset \exists y\, Sxy)$
A6   A successor of a natural number is a natural number: $\forall x \forall y ((NNx \,\&\, Sxy) \supset NNy)$
A7   Mathematical Induction: If zero falls under a concept, and a successor of something that falls under a concept always falls under the concept, then every natural number falls under the concept. $\forall P\, [(P0 \,\&\, \forall x \forall y ((Px \,\&\, Sxy) \supset Py)) \supset \forall x (NNx \supset Px)]$

6.2. Informal Proofs of the Arithmetical Axioms

We start with A1, which, given the definition of *successor*, states that there is no concept F and object x falling under F such that (i) zero is the number belonging to F, and (ii) there is a y that is the number belonging to the concept *falling under F but not identical with x*. The proof is trivial. Since zero is, by definition, the class (the existence and uniqueness of which is guaranteed by Axiom V) the only member of which is the concept under which nothing falls, the extension of that concept (the empty class) can't be put into one-to-one correspondence with the extension of any concept F under which something falls. So, zero can't be the number belonging to F.

Next consider A2. In order for x to have nonidentical successors y and z, there would have to be concepts F and G such that (i) y = the number belonging to F, z = the number belonging to G, and y ≠ z, and (ii) for some object o_F falling under F and some object o_G falling under G, x = the number belonging to the concept *falling under F but not identical with o_F* and x = the number belonging to the concept *falling under G but not identical with o_G*. This could be true only if the extensions of the concepts F and G could not be put into one-to-one correspondence, but the results of removing a single item from each could be put into such correspondence. Since this is impossible, A2 must be true. This shows that the successor relation is indeed a function.

A3 says that no two different things have the same successor. In order for two such things x and y to have the same successor z there must be concepts F and G and objects o_F and o_G such that (i) z = the number belonging to F = the number belonging to G, (ii) x = the number belonging to the concept *falling under F but not identical with o_F* and y = the number belonging to the concept *falling under G but not identical with o_G*, and (iii) x ≠ y. (i) tells us that the extensions of the concepts F and G can be put into one-to-one correspondence, while (ii) and (iii) tell us the extensions that result from removing a single item from each can't be put into such correspondence. Since this is impossible, A3 is true. Given A2, A3 tells us that successor is a 1-1 function.

A4 says that zero is a natural number, which, by Frege's official definition, means that zero falls under the concept *equals zero or follows zero in a series under successor.* Hence A4 is true by definition (plus Axiom V). Although A5 is more complicated, we can still see why it must be true. We start with zero, which is the number belonging to the concept *not identical with itself.* From Axiom V, we know that there is a class of all and only those things that are not identical with themselves. Since this class is empty, zero is the class of concepts the extensions of which are equinumerous with the empty class—i.e., the class of concepts under which nothing falls. Given his conception of concepts, this is the class the only member of which is the concept that assigns the False to every argument. Next, the successor of zero is, by definition, the number belonging to a concept F under which an object x falls, such that the concept *falling under F but not identical with x* is a member of zero. Can we be sure, on the basis of Frege's logic alone, that there is such a concept F and object x? Yes. We already have zero, and we know there is a concept *being identical with zero.* This plus Axiom V guarantees that there is a class that is the number belonging to this concept, and hence that there is a class of concepts the extensions of which are equinumerous with the class the only member of which is zero. This class of concepts under which exactly one thing falls is the successor of zero—i.e., the number 1. Since 1 *follows zero in the series under successor*, it satisfies the definition of being a natural number. Similar reasoning—this time using the concept *being identical with either with zero or 1*—establishes that 1 has a successor—the number 2—which is the class of concepts under which pairs of nonidential things, and nothing else, fall. Since 2 also follows zero in the series under successor, it is also a natural number. Similar results can, in this way, be established for each n. So, each instance of A5 is derivable using Frege's logic plus definitions. Although this isn't itself a proof of the universal generalization A5, Frege found a way of turning it into one. With this, we are assured that the successor function is totally defined on the natural numbers.

This brings us to A6, which, in the presence of A5, is trivial. For suppose that x is a natural number. Then, x is either zero or something that follows zero in the series under successor. A5 tells us that x has a successor y. But then y must follow zero in the series under successor—which, by the definition of *natural number*, guarantees that y is a natural number. As for A7, mathematical induction, we have already seen how Frege's definition of *natural number* guarantees its truth.

6.3. Arithmetical Operations

Frege's achievement was to show how to derive the axioms of Peano arithmetic from his system of logic. However, Peano arithmetic consists of more than a set of axioms characterizing the natural numbers. In addition, it also defines the arithmetical operations *addition* and *multiplication*. The definition of addition is as follows.

Definition of Addition

> For any natural numbers x and y, the result of adding zero to x is x; the result of adding the successor of y to x is the successor of the result of adding y to x.

In formulating this definition in symbols we use '$' to stand for the function that assigns a number its unique successor. This gives us

$$\forall x\, \forall y\, [(NNx\ \&\ NNy) \rightarrow (x + 0) = x\ \&\ (x + \$(y)) = \$(x + y)]$$

This kind of definition is called a *recursive*, or *inductive*, definition. It works by first specifying what it is to add zero to an arbitrary number x, and then specifying what it is to add the successor of a number y to a number x. So, we first determine the sum of zero and x to be x. Then we determine the sum of x and the successor of zero (namely 1) to be the successor of x. Applying the definition again, we determine the sum of x and the successor of 1 (namely 2) to be the successor of the successor of x. The process can be repeated to determine, for each number y, the result of adding y to x. Since x can be any number, the definition completely determines the sum of every pair of numbers, even though it does not have the familiar form of an explicit definition.

The way in which particular results are derived in Peano arithmetic is illustrated by the example: $3 + 2 = 5$.

(i) $\$(\$(\$(0))) + \$(\$(0)) = \$[\$(\$(\$(0))) + \$(0)]$
   from the definition of '+' together with A4 and A6, which guarantee that $\$(\$(\$(0)))$ and $\$(\$(0))$ are natural numbers

(ii) $\$(\$(\$(0))) + \$(0) = \$[\$(\$(\$(0))) + 0]$
   from the definition of '+', A4, and A6

(iii) $\$(\$(\$(0))) + \$(\$(0)) = \$(\$[\$(\$(\$(0))) + 0])$
   from substitution in (i) of equals for equals on the basis of (ii)

(iv) $\$(\$(\$(0))) + 0 = \$(\$(\$(0)))$
   from the definition of '+'

(v) $\$(\$(\$(0))) + \$(\$(0)) = \$(\$(\$(\$(\$(0)))))$
   from substitution in (iii) on the basis of (iv)

That is how the arithmetical system to be reduced to Fregean logic derives particular arithmetical results. To show that Frege's logical system allows the derivation of results such as these, involving addition, one must show that his logical axioms guarantee there is a (unique) function f that satisfies the pair of equations defining addition: $f(x,0) = x$ and $f(x,\$(y)) = \$(f(x,y))$—or, what comes to the same thing, that there is a (unique) three-place relation (concept) $Rxyz$ (intuitively, z *is a sum of x and y*) that satisfies the pair of formulas $Rx0z \longleftrightarrow z = x$ and $Rx\$(y)z \longleftrightarrow \exists v(Rxyv\ \&\ z = \$(v))$. Given the strength of the comprehension and extensionality principles generated by Frege's assumptions about concepts and their extensions, including Axiom V, this is not problematic.

As pointed out in Burgess (2005), once we have this, we can use mathematical induction to establish the associative law for addition—$(x + y) + z = x + (y + z)$—by (i) establishing associativity when z = 0, using the clause defining addition of zero, which gives us $(x + y) + 0 = x + y$, and $(y + 0) = y$, which, together, give us $(x + y) + 0 = x + (y + 0)$, and (ii) showing that associativity holds for the successor of z, provided that it holds for z, using the other clause of the definition of addition. Once this result is established, the commutative law of addition—that $x + y = y + x$—can be similarly proved, using mathematical induction.

Analogous results hold for multiplication, which is defined in a similar fashion (using '×' as the symbol for the multiplication function).

> Definition of Multiplication
>
> For any natural numbers x and y, the result of multiplying x times zero is zero, and the result of multiplying x times the successor of y is the sum of x and the result of multiplying x times y.

$$\forall x \, \forall y \, [(NNx \, \& \, NNy) \rightarrow ((x \times 0) = 0 \, \& \, x \times \$(y) = (x \times y) + x)]$$

This works the same way the definition for addition does. Thus, multiplication is defined in terms of repeated addition, which in turn is defined in terms of repeated application of the successor function. As before, there is no difficulty deriving the arithmetic results involving multiplication from Frege's logical system.

6.4. Further Issues

This completes the overview of Frege's reduction of arithmetic to logic, which was, of course, only one step in the grander project of reducing higher mathematics to logic. The next step was to reduce these advanced theories to arithmetic/logic by deriving their axioms from the axioms and definitions of arithmetic/logic plus definitions of the numbers—integers (including negative and positive), real (including rational and irrational), complex, and infinite—required by such theories. Although Frege had much to say about this, others contributed valuable and important work on this as well.

In 1903, when Frege was about to publish volume 2 of *The Basic Laws of Arithmetic,* the prospects for the success of the ambitious logicist project of showing mathematics to be an elaboration of pure logic seemed bright. However, daunting difficulties were to come. In the next chapter we will see that despite Frege's undeniable achievement, all was not well with the reduction of arithmetic to logic. As Bertrand Russell was to show—informing Frege in a letter in 1902, shortly before the publication of volume 2—there was a paradox lurking in Frege's crucial, and heavily utilized, Axiom V. Although Frege inserted a hastily constructed fix into the volume, which even Russell initially thought might allow him to avoid contradiction, it soon became clear that it wouldn't. This proved to be a heavy blow, altering the course of Frege's future work. However, it wasn't the end of the story. As we shall see in chapters 7 and 10, Russell drew his own conclusions from the paradox, using a conception of number much like Frege's to reduce arithmetic to a system of logic, complete with a way—albeit at significant cost—of avoiding the paradox. Much more recently, considerable work has been done within an avowedly Fregean framework to construct a paradox-free version of his derivation of arithmetic, and, in general, to provide a foundation sufficient for much or all of classical mathematics. The best, most exhaustive, and nuanced review and assessment of this work is found in Burgess (2005).[58]

[58] The basic idea behind the paradox-free treatment is to scrap Frege's Axiom V, with its overly strong comprehension principle for extensions of concepts (sets), and to make due with Hume's Principle (thought of as an implicit definition of natural number). Doing so changes the proofs needed for the derivation of arithmetic from logic, which still seems to go through. The question then becomes how much mathematics can be reduced to this primitive "logical base." Burgess's verdict is, "not enough."

CHAPTER 2

ᔿᕮᕮ

Critical Challenges

1. Existence and Generality
2. The Concept *Horse*, the Analysis of Quantification, and the Unity of the Proposition
3. Truth
4. Sense, Reference, and Identity
5. Platonism and Frege's Hierarchy
6. Nontransparent Thoughts: Names, Anaphora, and Quantifying-In
7. Time, Tense, and Indexicality
8. The Philosophical Foundations of Frege's Mathematical Project
9. Russell's Paradox: A Mathematical and Philosophical Threat to Logicism
10. Frege's Legacy

1. EXISTENCE AND GENERALITY

As explained in chapter 1, Frege's semantic analysis of quantification, both universal and existential, was a major advance that played a central role in his invention of modern logic. There are, however, some puzzles and confusions that are either inherent in, or have been associated with, the analysis. The first cluster of difficulties concerns the relationship between the notion of existence and what I will here call "the particular (as opposed to universal) quantifier," but which in fact is usually called "the existential quantifier," namely '∃'. As we have seen, Frege would formalize the English sentence (1a) as (1b), implicitly taking (1a) to be synonymous with (1c) and (1d).

    1a. There is a (at least one) square root of 4.
      b. ∃x (x is a square root of 4)
      c. There exists a (at least one) square root of 4.
      d. A (at least one) square root of 4 exists.

According to Frege, in asserting the thought expressed by these sentences, I say of the concept *square root of 4* that it is nonempty—i.e., that it assigns the True to at least one existing object. What is this second-level concept that is predicated of the first-level concept? Since my assertion makes an existence claim, Frege takes it to be the concept *existence*. In short, *existence* is a second-level concept expressed by '∃x'.

Frege says so in both "Concept and Object" and *The Foundations of Arithmetic.*

> I have called existence a property of a concept. How I mean this to be taken is best made clear by an example. In the sentence 'there is at least one square root of 4' we have an assertion, not about (say) the definite number 2, nor about −2, but about a concept *square root of 4*; viz. that it is not empty.[1]

> By properties which are asserted of a concept I naturally do not mean the characteristics which make up the concept. These latter are properties of the things which fall under the concept, not of the concept. Thus 'rectangular' is not a property of the concept 'rectangular triangle'; but the proposition that there exists no rectangular equilateral rectilinear triangle does state a property of the concept 'rectangular equilateral rectilinear triangle', it assigns to it the number nought. In this respect existence is analogous to number [in being a second-level concept]. Affirmation of existence is in fact nothing but denial of the number nought. *Because existence is a property of concepts the ontological argument for the existence of God breaks down.*[2]

There are three main mistakes either made, or suggested, here.[3] The first is that existence is the second-level concept expressed by the quantifier '∃x'. The second is that it is in the nature of that quantifier, and its natural language counterparts, to range only over existing things. The third, and the most infamous, mistake (though perhaps not the most pernicious) is expressed by the venerable canard "Existence is not a predicate," subscribed to not only by Frege, but also by Kant and Russell. We will take these in turn.

We know what the second-level concept expressed by the quantifier is; it is the concept *assigning the value the True* (or truth, if unlike Frege, you don't mind thinking of it as a property rather than an object) *to at least one argument.* If *existence* were identical with this concept, then the only things it could truly be predicated of would be functions. But surely, just as the concept *redness* can truly be predicated of something iff it is red, and the concept *being bigger than an ant* can be truly predicated of something iff it is bigger than an ant, so the concept *existence* can be truly predicated of something iff it exists. Thus, we get the absurd result that functions are the only things that exist. Since the culprit here is the identification

---

[1] Frege (1892a), pp. 187–88. On pp. 189–90 he also tells us that in saying that *so-and-so* is a property of x he is saying that x falls under the concept *so-and-so*. For Frege, talk of properties is talk of concepts.

[2] Frege (1950), sec. 53, pp. 64–65.

[3] I here overlook the exaggeration in the claim that an affirmation of the existence of (at least one) F is nothing but the denial that the number of F's is zero. Although the thoughts asserted by the affirmation and denial are indeed trivially equivalent, they are nonidentical senses of the sentences Frege has in mind. Fortunately, this doesn't seriously affect his point in the passage—and at the time he wrote it he had not yet developed his theory of sense.

of existence with the concept *assigning the True to at least one argument*, we reject that identification as being the confusion that it is.

This doesn't mean that Frege's analysis of '∃x' as a second-level concept is incorrect. However, it does lead to a question about that concept. Is it the concept *assigning The True to at least one object*, or is it the concept *assigning the True to at least one existing object*? Although many philosophers would accept the latter as the proper reading—while either rejecting the former outright (as an illegitimate quantificational reading), or, more likely, tacitly equating it with the later—such a position flies in the face of common sense. Consider, for example, the truth expressed by (2).

2. Socrates is dead, and so no longer exists.

Since (2) is true, 'Socrates' must refer to something of which the concepts *being dead* and *no longer existing* are true. But to say that 'Socrates' refers to something is just to say that, for some object x, 'Socrates' refers to x— which may be expressed '∃x ('Socrates' refers to x)'—and to say that the concepts *being dead* and *no longer existing* are true of something is just to say that, for some object x, the concepts are true of x—which may be expressed '∃x (x is dead & x no longer exists)'. Since the truth of these quantified claims requires the quantifier to range over things that don't (now) exist, the concept expressed by the quantifier is the concept *assigning the True to at least one object*; it is *not* the concept *assigning the True to at least one existing object*.[4]

An analogous point applies to Frege's analysis of the definite description operator 'the' given in chapter 1. According to Frege, the operator designates a second-level function that takes a first-level concept C_F as argument and assigns it an object o as value iff C_F *assigns the True to o and only o*. So ⌜the x Fx⌝ refers to the unique object to which C_F assigns the True (if C_F assigns the True to any object; otherwise it fails to refer). Should the condition governing the second-level function be the italicized clause given above, or should it be *'among all existing objects, C_F assigns the True to o and only o'*? Although many would either reject the first condition, or assimilate it to the second, the truth of (3) shows that this is incorrect.

3. The teacher of Plato (i.e., the individual who taught Plato) is dead, and so no longer exists.

These arguments show that there is nothing inherent in either the particular quantifier, '∃x', or the definite description operator, 'the', that restricts its domain to existing things. The same is true of the universal quantifier. This doesn't mean that these operators are *never* used with that understanding. They are. In fact, sometimes their domains are restricted

---

[4] These points extend to quantification over things that never have existed, but will, as well as to things that never have and never will exist, but could have existed. For discussion, see Salmon (1987), and Soames (2010a), pp. 30–32 and 128–29.

to a small subset of existing things, as when a father uses (4a) or (4b) to truly describe the situation at one of his children's overnight parties.

4a. Everyone is asleep.
  b. No one is still awake.

What these examples show is that natural language quantification is context sensitive—which, in Fregean terms, means that the specific second-level concepts they are used to designate vary from context to context depending on the intentions of speaker-hearers.

In Frege's defense, it must be said that his central concern was with quantification in the specially constructed languages of mathematics, where context sensitivity is deliberately avoided. Since, in addition, mathematical theories deal with things that, arguably, exist either eternally and necessarily (without temporal or modal qualification) or not at all, the issues raised by examples like (2) and (3) do not naturally arise for quantification in pure mathematics. The lesson of these examples is that care must be taken in applying Frege's powerful and highly versatile semantic framework to natural language, so that the special features of mathematics are not wrongly taken to be aspects of the framework's fundamental analysis of quantification and related notions.

This lesson applies not just to quantifiers and the description operator, but to concepts too. Whereas those of pure mathematics don't impose special temporal or modal existence conditions on the things they are true of, those of natural language do. Most can be true (at a time and world-state) only of things that exist (at that time and state). These include *being a human being, being a doctor, being employed by Macy's, being a dog owner, being located in North America, being a river, being a city, being more than 200 years old,* and, of course, *existing.* However, there are also concepts that can be true (at a time and world-state) only of things that don't exist (at that time and state). These include *being dead, being nonexistent,* and *being something of which these fossils are the only remains* as well as *being something I will build, or bring into being, in the future.* Others can be true (at a time and world-state) both of things that exist (at that time and state) and of things that don't. These include *being loved/admired/hated/feared/forgotten, being referred to/ talked about/surpassed/eclipsed,* and *being influential/inconsequential,* as well as *being something I could have built/seen/profited from* or *someone I could have known.* The variety here—of which I have given only a brief indication—is rich and worth exploring.[5] Once confusions about existence are overcome, there is no reason to suppose that Frege's system can't accommodate it.

This brings us to the oft-repeated and improperly expressed canard that "existence is not a predicate." Since existence is a concept and a predicate is a word or phrase, the slogan is wrongly expressed. This may be corrected either by saying "the English word 'exists' is not a predicate," which, as the books on English grammar tell us, is clearly false, or by

---

[5] See the works cited in the preceding note for further explanation.

saying "the concept *existence* is not designated by anything that functions semantically as a predicate"—or perhaps, even more cautiously, "the concept *existence* is not a first-level concept, and so does not apply to objects at all"—both of which are falsified by truths like (5a), the content of which may be formally represented along the lines of (5b) (which contains particular rather than existential quantifiers).

5a. Someone we have been talking about—namely Socrates/the teacher of Plato—is dead, and so doesn't exist, while someone else we have been talking about—namely Noam Chomsky (the famous MIT linguist) is still alive, and so does exist.

b. $\exists x \, \exists y$ ($x \neq y$ & we have been talking about x & we have been talking about y & x = Socrates [the teacher of Plato] & y = Noam Chomsky [the famous MIT linguist] & (x is dead & $\sim$ x exists) & (y is alive & y exists))

Since in this example, 'exists' functions semantically as a predicate of objects—designating a concept that assigns the False to Socrates and the True to Noam Chomsky, the concept *existence* is indeed designated by a predicate. It should also be noted that, even for Frege (who wrongly restricts '$\exists y$' to ranging over existing objects), the formula '$\exists y \, (y = x)$' is a predicate, designating a concept that assigns the True to objects iff they exist. Given his identity conditions for concepts, it is the only such concept, which is surely also designated by 'exists'. Whether or not the sense of 'exists' is the same as that of the formula is something we need not settle. Of course, none of this lends credibility to the ontological argument for the existence of God.[6]

Disposing of these confusions about existence doesn't threaten any fundamental aspect of Frege's system. However, there is a worry about his analysis of quantification as higher-order predication that strikes closer to home. Consider (6a) and (6b).

6a. Something is F.
b. Everything is F.

According to Frege, the thought expressed by (6a) is one in which the second-level concept *assigning the True to some object* is predicated of the concept *F*.[7] Thus, it would seem, the thought *that something is F* is the thought *that concept F assigns the True to some object*. We abbreviate this: the thought *that something is F* is the thought *that being F is true of something* (or, equivalently *that something falls under the concept F*). By the same reasoning, the thought expressed by (6b) is the thought *that being F is true of everything* (or, equivalently, *that everything falls under the concept F*). The truth conditions thereby ascribed to (6a,b) are correct, which is what Frege needs for his formal logic of quantification. However, combining

---

[6] See Salmon (1987) for discussion of the argument.
[7] In discussing this problem I will use 'F' as a schematic letter throughout.

this analysis with his theory of sense generates a puzzle about the structure of quantified thoughts.

We start with Fregean analysis FAQ of quantification.

> FAQ (i) The thought *that everything is F* is the thought that predicates *(the concept) being true of everything* of *(the concept) being F* (while not predicating anything further of anything). (ii) The constituents of this thought are (a) the sense of 'everything', which is also the sense of 'is true of everything', and (b) the sense of 'is F'.

Frege is explicit about (i). He is also committed to the thought *that everything is F* being composed of the sense of 'everything' and the sense of 'is F'. If the sense of 'everything' is *not* the sense of 'is true of everything' (used to state the analysis), then we have no clue what it is. Frege himself gives us reason to think that he does not intend to leave us in the dark, but rather does accept this identity of sense. For example, he speaks of the sentence 'There is at least one square root of 4' as making "an assertion about a concept, *square root of 4*; viz. *that it is not empty*."[8] Making the natural assumption that for *(the concept) square root of 4* to be nonempty is (by definition) for it to be *true of at least one thing*, we reach the conclusion that the thought *that there is at least one square root of 4* is the thought *that (the concept) square root of 4 is true of at least one thing*. By parity of reasoning, the thought *that everything is F* is the thought T6b.

> T6b. the thought that *being F* is true of everything (equivalently, the thought that everything falls under the concept F)

Obviously, this thought is also expressed by sentences (6b$_2$) and (6b$_2$').

> 6b$_2$. *Being F* is true of everything.
> 6b$_2$'. Everything falls under (the concept) *being* F.

So (6b), (6b$_2$), and (6b$_2$') express the same thought. However, since (6b$_2$) and (6b$_2$') also involve universal quantification one might think that Frege's analysis ought to apply directly to them, thereby identifying (T6b) with (T6b$_2$), and so on *ad infinitum*.

> T6b$_2$. the thought that *being an object that being F is true of* is true of everything (or that everything falls under the concept *falling under the concept being F*)

Are the thoughts produced in succeeding cycles in this process the same, or different? For each stage s of the process, both the thought generated at s, and the thought generated at s + 1, predicate *being true of everything* of a concept. In fact, they predicate this higher-level concept of *the same lower-level concept*. In (T6b), that concept is *being F*, which assigns the True to o iff o is F; in (T6b$_2$) it is *being an object that the concept being F is true of*

---

[8] "On Concept and Object," p. 49 in Geach and Black (1970).

(or *being an object that falls under the concept F)*, which assigns the True to the same things that *being F* does. So, by Frege's usual identity conditions for concepts, the concepts are identical.

If sameness of concepts predicated, plus sameness of that of which they are predicated, were sufficient for sameness of thoughts, then the above hierarchy would be harmless. But it is a cardinal feature of Frege's 1892 distinction between sense and reference, which identifies thoughts with *senses* of sentences and concepts with *referents* of predicates, that this criterion is *not* sufficient for sameness of thoughts. If it were, then any two logically equivalent formulas with only 'x' free (by which I mean any two such formulas that, for every model M, are true of precisely the same objects of M) would express the same Fregean senses. Since, for Frege, the structures of the senses of complex expressions parallel the semantically significant constituent structures of the expressions that express them, this can't be. In general when a sentence S, or complex expression E, contains a constituent that is (an occurrence of) a name, predicate, truth-functional operator, or quantifier, the sense of S or E may correctly be analyzed as containing the sense of that constituent.[9] Since logically equivalent sentences (and formulas) can vary enormously in their constituent structure—and since one who understands a pair of such sentences (or formulas) can often recognize that one is true (of a certain object), while not recognizing that the other is—such sentences (and formulas) must, by Frege's principles, have different senses.

These principles lead him to a very fine-grained individuation of thoughts, which he illustrates in the following passage from "Negation," published in 1918.

---

[9] See, for example, this passage from Frege's "Logic in Mathematics," written in 1914:

[O]ne cannot fail to recognize that the thought expressed by '5 = 2 + 3' is different from that expressed by the sentence '5 = 5', although the difference only consists in the fact that in the second sentence '5', which designates the same number as '2 + 3', takes the place of '2 + 3'. So the two signs are not equivalent from the point of view of the thought expressed, although they designate the very same number. Hence, I say that the signs '5' and '2 + 3' do indeed designate the same thing, but do not express the same sense. . . . It is remarkable what language can achieve. With a few sounds and combinations of sounds it is capable of expressing a huge number of thoughts, and, in particular, thoughts which have not hitherto been grasped or expressed by any man. How can it achieve so much? *By virtue of the fact that thoughts have parts out of which they are built up, so that the construction of the sentence out of parts of a sentence corresponds to the construction of a thought out of parts of a thought. And as we take a thought to be the sense of a sentence, so we may call a part of a thought the sense of that part of the sentence which corresponds to it."* (my emphasis, p. 225). Applying this to Frege's example, the thought *that 5 = 2 + 3* can be analyzed as containing constituent senses expressed by '2', '+', and '3', which go to make up the sense of '2 + 3', which is also a constituent of the thought. However, none of these is a constituent of the thought *that 5 = 5*.

Designations of thoughts with such a structure are got according to the pattern: *'the negation of the negation of A,'* where 'A' takes the place of the designation of a thought. Such a designation is to be regarded as directly composed of the parts *'the negation of __'* and *'the negation of A.'* But it may also be regarded as made up of the parts: *'the negation of the negation of __'* and *'A.'* . . . The two different ways of regarding the designation have answering to them two ways of regarding the structure of the thought designated.[10]

Frege is here concerned with thoughts expressed by sentences ⌜~~S⌝ involving double negation. The point he illustrates is that thoughts, especially those expressed by complex sentences, can often be correctly analyzed into parts in more than one way. In making this reasonable point, he takes it for granted that because ⌜~~S⌝ contains two occurrences of the negation sign, its sense (the thought it expresses) can be correctly analyzed into parts corresponding to one, or both, of those occurrences. Since— when the unnegated sentence S is itself simple, like 'It is red' (said pointing at a tomato)—Frege would *not* claim that the thought expressed by S can be analyzed into parts one of which is the negation of itself, he would, rightly, distinguish the thought expressed by S from the thought expressed by ⌜~~S⌝, even though the two sentences are easily recognizable as logically equivalent. This is confirmed in the last paragraph of the article.

If A is a thought not belonging to fiction, the negation of A likewise does not belong to fiction. In that case, of the two thoughts: A and the negation of A: there is always one and only one that is true. Likewise, of the two thoughts: the negation of A, and the negation of the negation of A: there is always one and only one that is true. In the first case, *neither* A *nor* the negation of the negation of A is true. In the second case, *both* A and the negation of the negation of A are true. Thus, *of the two thoughts:* A, and the negation of the negation of A: either *both* are true or *neither* is.[11]

Applying these ideas to the hierarchy illustrated by (T6b) and (T6b₂) generates an apparent problem. Whereas the thought (T6b) is correctly analyzable as made up of (a) the sense of 'assigns the True to every object' (i.e., the sense of the universal quantifier), and (b) the sense of *'being F'* (which is a mode of presentation of the concept F), the thought (T6b₂) is correctly analyzable as made up of (a) and (b₂) the sense of *'being an object that being F is true of'*—which is identical with the sense of *'being an object to which the concept being F assigns the True'*. Since these are ways of *exhaustively* dividing the respective thoughts into a pair of constituents, and since the analyses differ *only* in the second constituent, the thoughts can be identical only if (b) and (b₂) are. But (b) and (b₂) are *not identical*. Since the former is a mere a subconstituent of the latter (without, of

[10] Frege (1918b), p. 360.
[11] Ibid., p. 361, my emphasis.

course, being a mere subconstituent of itself), the usual Fregean principles of sense individuation lead to the conclusion that the thoughts (T6b) and (T6b$_2$) are *different*. Which, then, is *the thought* expressed by the unambiguous (6b)? Since Frege's analysis of quantification seems to lead to an infinite hierarchy of thoughts, each of which is characterized by his theory of sense as *distinct from* all the rest, while seemingly also being *identified with* all the rest by that analysis, we have a problem.

I believe this problem can be solved by distinguishing the sentence (6b$_2$)—which expresses the thought the analysis assigns to sentence (6b)—from sentence (6b), and *not* applying the analysis to (6b$_2$) . However, Frege never explicitly addressed the problem, and may not have been aware of any potential difficulty.[12] The nearest thing to a response to the puzzle that might reasonably be reconstructable from his explicit remarks comes from a section of "On Concept and Object" that will be discussed in section 2.[13] Here, it is worth focusing on how the problem arises. Our Fregean specification of the thought expressed by a sentence containing the universal quantifier—as saying of a concept that *it assigns the True to every object*—uses the very quantifier being analyzed. This makes it tempting to think that the analysis must then reapply to the sentence used to identify the proposition supposedly expressed by the initial sentence. It is precisely such reapplication that generates the difficulty. So if the analysis is to be accepted, one needs a way of understanding it that avoids the temptation to reapply it to its own output.

Once this is realized, it is natural to think that the solution might lie in restating the analysis in other terms. For example, one might maintain that sentences containing the quantifier say of concepts that they are *always true*, while taking *always true* to be primitive, and so not analyzable in terms of quantification. However, this is not very satisfying, since if one of the two notions—*everything* versus *a function's being always true*—stands in need of analysis in terms of the other, it might well seem to be the latter. A different variant on the idea uses existential (particular) quantification to analyze universal quantification, viewing sentences involving the latter as saying of concepts that *it is not the case that there is an object to which they assign the False*. There are two problems with this. First, it only postpones the evil day when the problematic hierarchy is regenerated,

---

[12] The solution is presented in Soames (2014a), "A Puzzle about the Frege/Russell Analysis of Quantification."

[13] The possible Fregean response is to deny that the thought *that everything is F* is the thought *that (the concept) being F is true of everything*—on the (incredible) ground that, despite appearances, the latter thought predicates a concept of an *object* rather than of another concept. This maneuver is an instance of the paradoxical Fregean doctrine that leads him to deny that the concept *horse* is a concept. I explain and criticize this doctrine in the next section. Here, I simply note that the maneuver for blocking the identification of the italicized propositions works by denying Frege's own analysis FAQ (i) of quantification, and so is unacceptable.

this time by an analysis of the existential quantifier. Second, although *in systems of logic* either quantifier can be defined, using negation, in terms of the other, *in semantic theories* incorporating Frege's fine-grained conception of thoughts, definitions of one quantifier in terms of the other are questionable. It seems simply untrue that the thought I contemplate when I understand a sentence S with a string of interspersed universal and existential quantifiers is the very same thought as the one I contemplate when I understand the more complex sentence gotten by substituting $\ulcorner \sim Qx \sim \urcorner$ for each occurrence in S of the quantifier to be "defined" in terms of the quantifier Qx.

This brings us to a more general point about the relationship between logic and semantics. Frege's analysis of quantification arose as part of the logical system in the *Begriffsschrift*, while his theory of sense arose from the semantic ideas presented in "On Sense and Reference." Although logic and semantics are clearly related, and although advances in one can shed light on the other, their aims are different, and sometimes pull in different directions. It is a commonplace in logic that all truth functions can be defined from a very small set of them (and ultimately from the single truth function of joint denial). Different systems select different subsets without any one choice being "right" and the rest "wrong." Similarly for definitions of one quantifier in terms of another. Logic is concerned with guaranteed truth, truth preservation, and equivalence (i.e., with logical truth, logical consequence, and logical equivalence). Given any choice of truth-functional (and quantificational) primitives, and definitions of the others in terms of these, the results concerning logical truth, consequence, and equivalence in one system are easily translatable into equivalent results of other systems. Because of this, it makes no real difference which choice one makes.[14] By contrast, the idea that it makes no semantic difference how the truth functions and quantifiers are treated, as long as the results are logically equivalent, is at odds with any conception of semantics which, like Frege's theory of sense, incorporates (i) the idea that the semantic contents of compound expressions typically contain, or encode, the semantic contents of the constituents of those expressions, (ii) the pivotal role played by the assertions sentences are used to make, and the beliefs they are used to express, in individuating their semantic contents, and (iii) the commonplace observation that sometimes logically equivalent sentences are used to assert different things, and express different beliefs.[15]

[14] In the *Begriffsschrift*, Frege's truth-functional primitives are negation and the material conditional; the universal quantifier is his quantificational primitive.

[15] Although the great bulk of Frege's writings on semantics supports this claim, there is one article, "Compound Thoughts," published in 1923, that may appear to be at odds with it. The thesis of the article is expressed in its very last sentence: "If one component of a mathematical compound thought is replaced by another thought having the same truth-value, then the resultant compound thought has the same truth-value as the original." This

Given all this, there will be some distinctions important to semantics that are irrelevant to logic (and vice versa). The puzzle posed by the problematic hierarchy is a potential worry for semantics, not for logic. There was, therefore, no reason for Frege to notice it in the *Begriffsschrift*. After the development of his theory of sense it did become noticeable, and noticed—if only obliquely—in "On Concept and Object"—to which we now turn.

2. THE CONCEPT *HORSE*, THE ANALYSIS OF QUANTIFICATION, AND THE UNITY OF THE PROPOSITION

In "On Concept and Object," Frege attempts to elucidate the distinction between concepts, which are the referents of predicates, and objects, which are the referents of "proper names"—a category that, for him, includes both sentences and compound singular terms, as well as linguistically simple proper names like 'Paris'. The distinction is based on the way in which senses of predicates must, he thinks, differ from those of "proper names." It is the need to distinguish these senses—i.e., the complete or "saturated" senses of proper names from the incomplete or "unsaturated" senses of predicates—that is supposed to lead to a corresponding distinction between objects and concepts. For Frege, these dichotomies are mutually exclusive. No concept is an object, and no unsaturated sense is complete.

Because an object is anything that can be the referent of a "proper name," the linguistic correlate of the doctrine that no concept is an object is the doctrine that no concept can be the referent of any such name. Since

---

substitution thesis applies to compound *thoughts*, not sentences, and indeed to the special subdomain of such thoughts that are needed in purely mathematical reasoning. The article proceeds by showing how the *senses* of negation and conjunction can be used to define the *senses* of all other truth-functional compoundings—just as the connectives '~' and '&' can be used to define all other truth-functional connectives. However, Frege insists, there is nothing special about these two, since there are five other forms of thought-compounding, in addition to conjunction, which, if taken as primitive, could be used, along with negation, to derive the others. In one sense, this is unobjectionable. Each of those choices would allow Frege to derive the quoted thesis. For mathematical purposes, it doesn't matter which choice we make. However, if our goal is to describe what speakers of some mathematical language actually understand its sentences to express, it is very likely that the six different choices for generating compound thoughts would not all be equally correct. On the contrary, the system of linguistically encoded compounding utilized by speakers might assign distinct but related senses to many, perhaps all, of the different connectives, without explicitly defining all from a limited subset. What is not mathematically parsimonious might well be a realistic account of the psychological attitudes of language users—which play a central role in determining the identity conditions of the thoughts assigned to sentences in semantics. It is, I suspect, because Frege was not much concerned with semantics in this humdrum descriptive sense, while being centrally focused on mathematics, that some of his remarks in "Compound Thoughts" appear, at least on the surface, to conflict with what, in most of his work, are his central semantic tenets.

⌐the concept F⌐ counts as a Fregean proper name, we are immediately led into paradox. The concept *horse* (designated by the description) is not a concept. How can that be? Frege addresses this problem as follows:

> It must indeed be recognized that here we are confronted by an awkwardness of language, which I admit cannot be avoided, if we say that the concept *horse* is not a concept, whereas, e.g., the city of Berlin is a city, and the volcano Vesuvius is a volcano. Language is here in a predicament that justifies the departure from custom. . . . In logical discussions one quite often needs to assert something about a concept, and to express this in the form usual for such assertions—viz., to make what is asserted of the concept into the content of the grammatical predicate. Consequently, one would expect that the reference of the grammatical subject would be the concept; *but the concept as such cannot play this part, in view of its predicative nature; it must first be . . . represented by an object.* We designate this object by prefixing the words 'the concept', e.g., 'The concept *man* is not empty.' Here the first three words are to be regarded as a proper name, *which can no more be used predicatively than 'Berlin' or 'Vesuvius.' When we say 'Jesus falls under the concept man,' then, setting aside the copula, the predicate is: 'someone falling under the concept man' and this means the same as 'a man.' But the phrase 'the concept man' is only part of this predicate.*[16]

He also says:

> We may say in brief, taking 'subject' and 'predicate' in the linguistic sense: A concept is the reference of a predicate; an object is something that can never be the whole reference of a predicate, but can be the reference of a subject. [17]

In these passages, we are told that the *referent* of an expression that can be used predicatively can't be the *referent* of a "proper name." We are also given two argument sketches based on examples (7–9), for a key lemma needed to establish that claim—namely, that the *sense* of an expression that can be used predicatively can't be the *sense* of a singular term.

    7. Jesus is a man.
    8. Jesus falls under the concept *man*.
    9. *Jesus is the concept *man*.

Argument 1

P1.   (7) and (8) mean the same thing, as do their predicates, 'a man' (ignoring the copula in (7)) and 'falls under the concept *man*'.

P2.   The singular term 'the concept *man*' doesn't mean the same thing as the predicate 'falls under the concept *man*', of which it is merely a part.

---

[16] Geach and Black (1970), pp. 46–47, my emphasis.
[17] Ibid., pp. 47–48.

C1.   So, 'the concept *man*' doesn't have the same *sense* as the predicate 'a man'.

C2.   More generally, no singular term has the same *sense* as any predicate.

Argument 2

P1.   If 'the concept *man*' in (9) meant the same as the predicate 'a man' in (7), then (9) would have a reading in which 'is' occurs as copula and (9) means the same as (7).

P2.   (9) has no such reading.

C1/C2. As before.

If these arguments were sound, then a stronger Fregean conclusion might also be forthcoming—namely that it is *impossible* for a predicate to have the same sense as a singular term. Even then, however, Frege's thesis

C3.   No singular term can refer to the referent of any predicate.

would remain to be established—since the claim that no expression in one class has the same sense as any expression in another class doesn't, by itself, entail that no expression in the first *refers* to the same thing as any expression in the second. Frege's argumentative route to C3 would, I suspect, invoke the idea that the function of a sense is exhausted by its role as a "mode of presentation" of a referent. Given this, one can rule out the possibility that C2 is true, but C3 is false. For, if that were so, then the sense of some singular term would determine the same referent as that of some predicate P, even though the two senses are both modes of presentations, albeit different ones. But if the role of sense is simply to present a referent—*without, in addition, encoding the semantic counterpart of the grammatical information about what in the sentence is predicated of what*—then there will be nothing to stop one from introducing a new singular term t (perhaps by stipulation) with the same sense as P. Since this violates C2, C2 plus the assumption that the function of a sense is exhausted by its role in presenting a referent gives us C3. In what follows, I will raise doubts about the route to C2, and thereby to the route to C3.

The tacit assumption behind P1 of Argument 2 is that the grammatical structure of a complex expression makes no significant contribution to its sense. The phrases 'a man' and 'the concept *man*' are instances of different grammatical categories. The category to which the former belongs allows it to be combined with the copula to form a predicate; the category to which the latter belongs, we may suppose, does not. Thus, (7) and (9) have different grammatical structures—one being well formed with 'is' as copula, and one not. If the rules assigning senses to sentences are sensitive not only to the senses of their parts, but also to their grammatical structures, then there is no reason to think that (7) and (9) must have the same sense, if their parts do. Since Frege says nothing to exclude this, P1 is unsupported, and Argument 2 is inconclusive.

Argument 1 is, arguably, worse. Intuitively, it seems possible for someone to assert or believe that Jesus is a man, without having studied philosophical logic, and so without asserting or believing anything about objects falling under concepts. Since thoughts are what one believes and asserts, this would mean that (7) and (8) don't express the same thought, and don't mean the same thing. The falsity of P1 also seems to follow from Frege's doctrine that the sense of a sentence is made up of the senses of its parts. On this view, the sense of (7) is a thought the constituents of which are the senses of the subject 'Jesus' and the predicate 'a man' (ignoring the copula), while the sense of (8) is made up of the senses of its subject 'Jesus', the grammatical object 'the concept *man*' and the predicate 'falls under'. Since the senses of (7) and (8) contain different constituents, and have different structures, the claim that the sentences have the same meaning is suspect. The point at issue here is the same as the one that leads to grief over the quantificational hierarchy in section 1. There, failing to notice the difference between a thought T and what his normal compositional principles would identify as a truth-conditionally equivalent but *distinct* higher-order thought T⁺, leads Frege to miss the fact that succeeding thoughts in the hierarchy can't be the same. Here, it leads him to miss the falsity of P1.

It must be admitted that Frege might take himself to have grounds for rebutting this objection. On one principle of thought individuation, often attributed to him, thoughts T1 and T2 are identical only if anyone who understood both a sentence S1 expressing T1 and a sentence S2 expressing T2 would accept S1 iff he or she would accept S2. Since an agent with no training in Frege's philosophical logic could not be expected to understand sentence (8), 'Jesus falls under the concept *man*', we can't use this principle of individuation to distinguish the thought expressed by (8) from the thought expressed by sentence (7), 'Jesus is a man'. But then, it might be maintained, we can't be sure that our untutored agent who accepts (7) doesn't thereby believe the proposition *that Jesus falls under the concept man.*

Although one can understand why the Fregean might find this counter-argument attractive, it doesn't, I think, provide an effective defense of Frege's identification of thoughts (7) and (8). For one thing, it relies on a transparency principle—that two sentences that express the same thought will be recognized as making the same or equivalent claims by anyone who understands them—that I will later argue to be false. For another, one can easily imagine a philosopher who understands Frege's semantics but rejects Fregean concepts altogether, and so understands both sentences (7) and (8) while taking the former to be true and the latter false. Finally, on Frege's own account one who entertains thought (7) must have a way of picking out, and so thinking about, both the man designated by 'Jesus' and the concept designated by 'a man'. But there is no reason to suppose that having these resources guarantees also having the cognitive resources needed to pick out, and so think about, the higher-level concept designated by 'falls under' that relates arbitrary first-level concepts to the objects to which they assign the True. Thus, it is reasonable to suppose that some agents capable of believing simple thoughts like (7) lack them, and so cannot believe the thought expressed by (8). For these reasons, the objection to Argument 1 stands.

Of course, the failure of the arguments for C2, and hence for C3, doesn't show that they are false. However, it does leave one without a compelling reason to accept them, which—seeing that they lead to paradox—is all to the good. We shouldn't, and philosophers normally don't, accept claims that lead to paradox. Why then does Frege? The answer is that he thinks that paradox is unavoidable.

> Somebody may think . . . that there is no need . . . to take account of . . . what I call a concept; that one might . . . regard an object's falling under a concept as a relation, in which the same thing could occur now as object, now as concept. . . . This may be done; but anybody who thinks the difficulty is avoided . . . is very much mistaken. . . . *For not all the parts of a thought can be complete; at least one must be 'unsaturated', or predicative; otherwise they would not hold together.* For example, the sense of 'the number 2' does not hold together with that of the expression 'the concept *prime number*' without a link. We apply such a link in the sentence 'the number 2 falls under the concept *prime number*'; it is contained in the words 'falls under,' which need to be completed . . . *and only because their sense is thus "unsaturated" are they capable of serving as this link.* I say that such words or phrases stand for a relation. We now get the same difficulty for the relation that we were trying to avoid for the concept. For the words 'the relation of an object to the concept it falls under' designates not a relation but an object; and *the three proper names 'the number 2', 'the concept prime number', 'the relation of an object to a concept it falls under', hold aloof from one another just as much as the first two do by themselves; however we put them together we get no sentence.*[18]

The thesis here is that every thought must contain an unsaturated sense (not expressed by any singular term). The argument is that since no sequence of singular terms makes a sentence, no structure of saturated senses of such terms makes a thought—because nothing in such a structure is predicated of anything else. But this is a non sequitur.

Consider a non-Fregean analysis of (10).

10. [$_S$ [$_N$ John] [$_{VP}$ is [$_{ADJ}$ human]]]

The copula is here regarded merely as part of grammatical structure—something needed to form a sentence, but not itself a sense-bearing unit. The thought expressed by (10) is taken to contain just two constituents: the sense of 'John', which presents the man John, and the sense of 'human', which presents the concept *being human*. Both may be referents of singular terms, and so qualify as "objects" in Frege's sense, provided that *something*

---

[18] Ibid., pp. 54–55, my emphasis.

about the thought indicates that the concept is *predicated* of the man. There is no need for this something to be a constituent of the thought. Rather, we may suppose, it is the structural relation in which the sense of 'human' stands to the sense of 'John' in the thought. The constituents of the sentence provide the constituents of the thought. The grammatical structure of the sentence provides the structure of the thought, which indicates what is predicated of what. Since Frege says nothing to rule this out, he fails to establish his doctrines C2 and C3, about incomplete senses and referents. Since rejecting these doctrines allows us to reject the absurdity, that the concept *horse* is not a concept, to which he is committed, we are well advised to do so.

This brings us back to his analysis of quantification, illustrated by (11a).

11a. There is at least one square root of 4.

Frege says that in this sentence "we have an assertion . . . about a concept, *square root of 4*; viz. that it is not empty."[19] However, this analysis is threatened by his incompleteness doctrine C3. The analysis of quantification tells us that (11a) asserts something about a concept. C3 tells us that since *the subject of this assertion* is a concept, it can't be the referent of a singular term. But this is self-refuting, since we have just made the concept the referent of the term, 'the subject of this assertion'. Note also Frege's identification of what is asserted—namely, "that it is not empty." If 'it' is here used as a Fregean proper name, then C3 compels him to deny that its referent is a concept, while his analysis of quantification requires him to say that it is one.

Here is the larger text in which Frege's self-refuting remark is embedded.

> In the sentence [(11a)] we have an assertion . . . about a concept, square root of 4; viz. that it is not empty. But if I express *the same thought* thus: 'The concept *square root of 4* is realized' then the first six words form the proper name of an object, and it is about this object that something is asserted. But notice carefully that what is asserted here is not the same thing as was asserted about the concept.[20]

In this passage, Frege says that the thought expressed by (11a) can be taken in two ways: (i) as asserting (i.e., predicating) of a certain concept that it's not empty; (ii) as asserting (predicating) of a certain object that it "is realized." Whatever the mysterious difference between *being nonempty* (predicated of the concept) and *being realized* (predicated of the object) is supposed to be, the doctrine is self-refuting. For Frege is committed to identifying the concept as the referent of the singular terms, 'the subject of the first assertion', and 'the referent of the phase 'square root of 4''.

---

[19] Ibid., p. 49. What is it for a concept "to be nonempty"? Presumably it is for there to be something to which it assigns the True.
[20] Ibid., p. 49, my emphasis.

The quoted passage continues in the same vein.

> Language has means of presenting now one, now another, part of the thought as the subject. It need not then surprise us that the same sentence may be conceived as an assertion about a concept and also as an assertion about an object; only we must observe that what is asserted is different. In the sentence [(11a)] it is impossible to replace the words 'square root of 4' by 'the concept *square root of 4*'; i.e., *the assertion that suits the concept does not suit the object.*[21]

Here Frege observes that whereas (11a) expresses a thought that can be used to make an assertion about a concept, (11b) cannot.

11b. *There is at least one the concept *square root of 4*.

For Frege, (11b) isn't well formed, because the sense of the quantifier requires completion by the sense of a predicate, rather than by that of a "proper name." As usual, he ignores the possibility that the ill-formedness of (11b) is a *grammatical* violation, and that the reason (11b) doesn't express a thought is that it lacks a grammatical structure the semantic significance of which is a way of *structuring* the senses of the quantifier and predicate that indicates that the higher-level concept presented by the former is to be *predicated* of the lower-level concept presented by the latter. Since Frege ignores this explanation, his observations don't show that his analysis, in terms of unsaturated senses, is correct.

He completes the passage as follows:

> Although our sentence [(11a)] does not present *the concept* as a subject, it asserts something about it [the concept]; it *[(11a)]* can be regarded as expressing the fact that a concept falls under a higher one.[22]

Here we get a third way of taking (11a)—as predicating of the concept designated by the predicate that it has the relational property *falling under* the higher-level concept designated by the quantifier. This, too, is incoherent, since it requires the subject of the assertion to be both a *concept* and the *object* indicated by the subject of (11c).

11c. The concept *square root of 4* falls under H. ('H' designates the higher-level concept.)

In sum, Frege's doctrines of unsaturatedness and incompleteness are neither established by his arguments, nor the solution to any coherent problem about the unity of thoughts.[23] In light of this, they can hardly be

---

[21] Ibid., p. 49, my emphasis.

[22] Ibid., p. 49, my emphasis.

[23] As we shall see in chapters 3, 7 and 9, there is, nevertheless, an important philosophical problem in the background of Frege's discussion that also worried Moore and Russell, though neither philosopher correctly identified it, let alone solved it. Further discussion in those chapters of "the unity of the proposition" will cast more light both on Frege's insights in dealing with the problem and his shortcomings.

relied on to defuse the problem of the hierarchy of apparently distinct thoughts generated by the most natural way of combining his analysis of quantification with his theory of sense.

3. TRUTH

Until now I have pretended that there are two mysterious objects, "the True" and "the False," that are "the truth values" of sentences. Instead of speaking of truth and falsity as properties of thoughts, I have, for the most part, followed Frege in speaking of them as objects that sentences refer to in virtue of the thoughts they express. This is unnatural. 'Is true' and 'is false' are predicates, and it is normal to speak of the contents of predicates as properties. Frege himself uses "property" in this sense when speaking informally, even though the work normally done by this word is divided between his official notions of "concept" and "unsaturated sense"—except when speaking of 'is true' and 'is false'. Instead of treating them like other predicates, he sometimes denies that they function logically as predicates, that they refer to concepts, or that they make any contributions to the thoughts expressed by sentences containing them.

> One might be tempted to regard the relation of the thought to the True not as that of sense to reference, but rather as that of subject to predicate. *One can indeed say: "The thought, that 5 is a prime number, is true." But closer examination shows that nothing more has been said than in the simple sentence '5 is a prime number.' The truth claim arises in each case from the form of the declarative sentence, and when the latter lacks its usual force, e.g., in the mouth of an actor upon the stage, even the sentence, 'The thought that 5 is a prime number is true' contains only a thought, and indeed the same thought as the simple '5 is a prime number.'* It follows that the relation of the thought to the True may not be compared with that of subject to predicate. Subject and predicate (understood in the logical sense) are indeed elements of thought; they stand on the same level for knowledge. By combining subject and predicate, one reaches only a thought, never passes from sense to reference, never from a thought to its truth value. . . . A truth value cannot be part of a thought, any more than, say, the Sun can, for it is not a sense but an object.[24]

Although there is, as we shall see, an important insight about truth here, there is also much that is mistaken, which must be cleared away before we can appreciate Frege's insight. Even if one accepts his view that "the True" is an object to which all true sentences refer, one can still define a genuine truth predicate: for all thoughts T, T *is true* iff T is a thought that determines the True (where *determination* holds between a sense s and entity x when expressing s determines that an expression refers to x). With

---

[24] "On Sense and Reference," in Geach and Black (1970), p. 64, my emphasis.

this definition, the thought (12a) will consist of the indirect sense of (12b) plus a mode of presentation of the concept *determines the True,* which is predicated of the thought expressed by (12b).

12a. The thought that 5 is a prime number is true.
  b. 5 is a prime number.

By contrast, the thought expressed by (12b) doesn't predicate anything of itself; rather, it predicates the concept *prime number* of 5. So the thoughts (12a) and (12b) are different, even though we know a priori that they are necessarily equivalent. Not only that, but the explanation of the effortless transition by which we pass from one of these thoughts to the other is readily explained. Anyone who understands the two sentences will know that the thought expressed by (12b) is the thought of which truth is predicated by the thought expressed by (12a). Hence, one immediately sees that in assertively uttering either sentence one asserts, and thereby commits oneself to, both thoughts. No wonder it seems as if no new information is added by an assertion of (12a) not already made available by an assertion of (12b). This is so even though the content of the truth predicate is by no means empty, as shown by its use in examples like "You can believe whatever he says, because what he asserts is always true."

Some Fregeans would not be happy with this argument, requiring as it does giving up the principle that *if anyone who understands two sentences will either accept both, reject both, or be undecided about both, then the two sentences must express the same thought.* There are, however, two things to say about this. First, the principle is obviously false, as is shown by pairs of sentences like the following: '1 = 1' and '2 = 2'; '3 = 3' and '3 = 3 ∨ 3 ≥ 3'; '0 < 1' and '~~0 < 1'. In each case anyone who understands both sentences will accept both, even though they express *different* thoughts. Second, as I pointed out in section 1 of this chapter, Frege himself distinguishes the thought expressed by S from the thought expressed by ⌜~~S⌝ (in Frege 1918b). If one assumes, as I believe he does, that anyone understanding both would accept or reject both, one must reject the principle of thought individuation here offered in his defense.

Returning to the italicized words in the passage cited above, we next ask "What does the example of the actor on the stage have to do with the question of whether the thought expressed by (12a) predicates truth of the proposition that 5 is a prime number (which is expressed by (12b))?" On the face of it, the obvious fact that an actor who utters (12a) or (12b) doesn't *assert* the thoughts these sentences express, and so isn't committed to their truth, seems to have little to do with Frege's contentious claim that the thought expressed by her words doesn't, *even in the case of (12a),* contain the sense of the truth predicate, and so doesn't predicate *being true* of anything. Certainly, there is no positive argument here for Frege's conclusion, any more than the fact that the actor's use of (12b) doesn't assert the thought it expresses, and so doesn't commit her to 5's being prime, provides an argument for the claim that the thought expressed by her words doesn't include the sense of the predicate 'is a prime number', and so doesn't predicate *being a prime number* of anything.

Perhaps, however, Frege was simply trying to use the contrast with the actor to make the defensible point that one who assertively utters (12b) is every bit as committed to the truth of thought (12b) as is one who assertively utters (12a). On this reading, his dialectical purpose in making this point is *to remove the temptation* to think that when calling a thought 'true' we are predicating anything of it. The problem, for Frege, is that there is much more than temptation behind the view he rejects, since, as I indicated above, we know independently of examples like (12) that 'is true' does function as a genuine predicate. The real temptation to be avoided is, I think, the one to which Frege succumbs after plausibly noting, "One can indeed say: 'The thought, that 5 is a prime number, is true.' But closer examination shows *that nothing more has been said* than in the simple sentence '5 is a prime number'" (my emphasis).

From this, Frege concludes that the two sentences express the same thought. The principle he tacitly relies on to support this inference is that *if assertive utterances of S and S′ standardly result in assertions of the same thoughts (when they result in assertions at all), then the two sentences (semantically) express the same thoughts.* This innocent-sounding principle fails because (i) when an assertive utterance of S asserts the thought (semantically) expressed by S, it also asserts thoughts that are obvious and relevant consequences of that thought, and (ii) the thoughts (semantically) expressed by S and ⌐the thought that S is true⌐ are trivially obvious consequences of each other. This is the lesson to be learned from Frege's otherwise unilluminating passage.

Later a positive argument will be given, based on an insightful observation from Frege's 1918 "Thought," to show that 'is true' does, in fact, function semantically as a predicate, and so contributes like other predicates to thoughts expressed by sentences containing it. Before doing that, however, it will be useful to dispose of the view that sentences have "truth values"—"the True" and "the False"—which are their referents. Although talk of "truth values" is now standard in philosophy, it is quite unnatural. We don't speak of "the gender values" of human beings—the Male and the Female—even though humans are either male or female; nor do we speak of "the color values" of objects—the Red, the Blue, and the Green—even though objects are red, or blue, or green, etc.

Why then do philosophers speak of "truth values"? For Frege, there is a reason: (12b) is true because the *function* designated by its predicate assigns *a certain value* to the *argument* designated by its subject. The conjunction of (12a) and (12b) is true because the *truth function* designated by 'and' assigns *that same value* to the *truth values* designated by its conjuncts. Frege's semantic analysis of logical and mathematical language was gotten by purifying the notion of a function found in the mathematics of his time, eliminating confusions of use and mention, and employing an extended version of that notion to give a compositional account of the truth conditions of sentences. There are other ways to give such an account, but Frege's unstinting reliance on the notions *function, argument,* and *value* naturally led to one value for all true, and a different value for all false, sentences. These "values" don't have to be seen as referents of sentences, but as long as one limits oneself to languages of logic and mathematics—which can easily be written so as to avoid reference failure—and as long as one focuses on the truth conditions of sentences, rather than the fine-grained linguistic acts, and mental states, of language users, there is no harm in taking all true sentences to refer to some designated object that, for mnemonic reasons, you call "the True," and all false ones to refer to something else you call "the False." However, this isn't deep philosophical truth; it is elegance and convenience in theorizing about an important, but limited, domain.

By contrast, when we turn our attention to speakers' use of language, the idea that sentences refer to "the True" or "the False" is a nonstarter. For Frege, senses (of Fregean "proper names") are ways that speakers' think of the referents of those terms. But it hardly seems that we are all thinking of the same thing whenever we believe something true. Rather, in believing different truths, we are often thinking of different things. If pressed, I suppose, a desperate philosopher might grant this, while claiming that in some other sense we are all thinking of one thing—*reality.* But, *in that sense,* we always thinking of reality, even when it isn't the way we take it to be; there is no second thing of which we are all thinking when we believe something false. In short, the idea of senses as modes of presentation by which speakers think of referents breaks down when applied to "truth values" as referents of sentences. This needn't be a worry if we drop the idea that sentences are Fregean "proper names" with the job of referring to "the True" or "the False." Once we do, other benefits follow. First, we are no longer forced to take truth-functional operators to be predicates of, or relations on, "truth values." For example, conjunction no longer needs to be seen as a two-place relation holding between a certain thing and itself—which is all to the good, since when using a conjunction, we don't conceive of ourselves as predicating such a relation of a pair of identicals. Second, we can explain why, in natural language, we have no quantificational variables occupying sentence positions that range only over truth and falsity.

We can also accommodate reference failure of some singular terms, and related phenomena, in natural languages, outside the straightjacket, (13), imposed by a strict Fregean analysis.

13. Let S be a sentence in which an n-place predicate P combines with n singular terms. (i) If one of those terms lacks a referent, or if the n-place function designated by P is undefined for the n-tuple of referents of the terms, then S lacks a truth value, and so is neither true nor false. (ii) If S

lacks a truth value, then any truth-functional compound (negation, conjunction, disjunction, material conditional, biconditional) of which S is a
component will itself lack a truth value, and so be neither true nor false.

Frege himself didn't worry about (13), not because it is a descriptively correct statement about failure of reference and lack of truth value in natural
language, but because natural language was not his primary concern. His
interest was in the languages of logic, mathematics, and science, from
which the "imperfections" of natural language can be eliminated to better
serve investigations in those areas. Once these languages have been made
optimal for such purposes, (13) becomes a nonissue.

Speaking of this in "On Sense and Reference," he says:

> This [the possibility of reference failure in natural language] arises from an
> imperfection of language from which even the symbolic language of math-
> ematical analysis is not altogether free; even there combinations of symbols
> can occur that seem to stand for something but have (at least so far) no ref-
> erence, e.g. divergent infinite series. This can be avoided, e.g., by means of a
> special stipulation that divergent infinite series shall stand for the number 0.
> *A logically perfect language [Begriffsschrift] should satisfy the conditions that every
> expression grammatically well constructed as a proper name out of signs already in-
> troduced shall in fact designate an object, and that no new sign shall be introduced as
> a proper name without being secured a reference.* The logic books contain warn-
> ings against logical mistakes arising from the ambiguity of expressions. I
> regard it no less pertinent a warning against apparent proper names having
> no reference. . . . It is by no means unimportant to eliminate the source of
> these mistakes, at least in science, once and for all.[25]

One logical problem with reference failure in a formal language is the
complication required in rules of proof in order to block the derivation
of falsehoods from truths when one infers $\ulcorner \exists x \ldots x \ldots \urcorner$ from $\ulcorner \ldots n \ldots \urcorner$, or
$\ulcorner \ldots n \ldots \urcorner$ from $\ulcorner \forall x \ldots x \ldots \urcorner$ in cases in which a name or other singular term
n fails to refer. Because of this, it is reasonable when possible, e.g., in
mathematics, to avoid the problem by setting up one's language so that
reference failure does not occur—just as it is reasonable to exclude ambiguity (which is rampant in natural language) when pursuing logical,
mathematical, or scientific investigations. Since Frege's main interest was
to provide optimal logical and linguistic frameworks for these investigations, it was reasonable for him to urge the stipulations he did.

If, however, one's goal is to *describe* the semantic structure of existing
languages, including natural languages, which have evolved to suit many
purposes beyond the narrowly logical, then there is no place for stipulation, and little point in remarks about what may be an imperfection
when considered only from one specialized point of view. Unfortunately,
some of Frege's discussions do not carefully distinguish stipulative from

---

[25] Geach and Black (1970), p. 70, my emphasis.

descriptive imperatives, or features of semantic frameworks sufficient, or even optimal, for specialized purposes from those that further all-purpose language use.

With this in mind, we return to (13), assuming, for the sake of argument, that some singular terms in natural languages fail to designate referents— Fregean definite descriptions like 'the largest prime number' or terms like '3 divided by 0' in which a function sign combines with two names. Let P be an n-place predicate designating an n-place function f_P from n-tuples of objects to truth values. If a non-designating term occurs as argument of P, f_P won't have an n-tuple on which to operate, and, on a Fregean analysis, no truth value will be assigned. The same result will be reached if, as we may further assume, there are predicates, e.g., 'is red', that designate functions that are undefined for some objects because the rules governing them don't provide definite results for borderline cases.[26] Frege's analysis of truth-functional connectives as designating functions from truth values to truth values extends these instances of (13)(i) to instances of (13)(ii).

This is problematic, leading as it does to the claim that, if reference failure occurs in (14a), and 'is red' is undefined for o in (14b), then (15a) and (15b) are neither true nor false.

14a. The king of France is in hiding.
   b. O is red (where it is indeterminate that o is red, since 'is red' is undefined for o).
15a. Either there is no king of France, or the king of France is in hiding.
   b. Either it is indeterminate that o is red, or o is red, or o isn't red.

In fact, (15a) and (15b) are clearly true; so, either (14a) and (14b) *are* true or false, or their failure to be so is *not* inherited by all truth-functional compounds in which they occur. From this we conclude either (i), or (ii), or both.

(i) The predicates in (14a,b) *don't* designate functions that map arbitrary referents of subject expressions onto values "the True" and "the False" such that the resulting sentences are true iff the value is "the True," and false iff the value is "the False."

(ii) The disjunction operator *doesn't* designate a function that maps arbitrary pairs consisting of the "truth values" of the disjuncts onto the values "the True" and "the False," such that the resulting disjunctions are true iff the value is "the True," and false iff the value is "the False."

Both options undermine the rationale for the doctrine that all true sentences designate "the True" and all false sentences designate "the False," which should be given up.

We now return to the central question of whether 'is true' functions semantically as a predicate, in which case its sense should be a constituent of

---

[26] See Soames (1999), chapter 7, (2003b), and (2009c).

thoughts expressed by sentences containing it, and those thoughts should be taken as predicating the concept truth of thoughts (as well, perhaps, as of sentences or utterances expressing them). The key Fregean insight to be brought to bear on this question is found in the following passage.

> We cannot recognize a property of a thing without at the same time finding the thought *this thing has this property* to be true. So, with every property of a thing there is tied up a property of a thought, namely truth. It is also worth noticing that the sentence 'I smell the scent of violets' has just the same content as the sentence 'It is true that I smell the scent of violets.' So it seems, then, that nothing is added to the thought by my ascribing to it the property truth. And yet is it not a great result when the scientist after much hesitation and laborious research can finally say 'My conjecture is true'? The meaning of the word 'true' seems to be altogether *sui generis*.[27]

Though Frege hasn't completely escaped from his former view that 'true' is semantically inert, and so doesn't not function logically as a predicate, by 1918 his view has advanced considerably. Here, he is willing to speak of truth as a property of thoughts, even if he does so with some uncertainty. In addition, he draws an important contrast between two linguistic environments in which the truth predicate may occur.

Environment 1: *It is true that S / The thought that S is true*
Environment 2: *My conjecture / everything John said / something Mary believes is true*

He observes that when we use the truth predicate in Environment 1—e.g., when we say ⌜it is true that S⌝—we don't seem to be adding anything significant to what we express with S alone. In support of this, we may note that an agent who assertively uttered either one could correctly be reported using either ⌜x said/asserted that S⌝ or ⌜x said/asserted that it is true that S⌝. Still, this doesn't show that the thoughts are identical. Although the fact about assertion is consistent with the view that any thought T is identical with *the thought that T is true*, it is also consistent with the view that the thoughts are different but trivially, and a priori, recognizable as equivalent (in which case explicitly committing oneself to one, by assertively uttering a sentence that expresses it, implicitly commits one to the truth of the other as well). It is interesting that though Frege says that S "has the same content as" ⌜it is true that S⌝, he doesn't say that the thoughts expressed are identical, or that 'true' doesn't function as a predicate. This is all to the good, since he also suggests that when the truth predicate is used in Environment 2, it does add something to the thought expressed by the sentence containing it—and so is not dispensable in the way it is in Environment 1. Though he doesn't elaborate on the nature of this contrast, it turns out to be significant. Type-2 environments

---

[27] "Thought," p. 328, in Frege (1997).

are important because they provide a reason for having a truth predicate of thoughts. Type-1 environments are important because they play a privileged role in explaining the meaning of that predicate.

First consider Environment 2, in which we predicate truth of a thought, or set of thoughts, we don't explicitly assert or display. For example, we might assert that everything John reported is true, on the basis of our knowledge of his character and intellect, even if we don't know what he reported, or believe the conjunction of all he, in fact, asserted. Similarly, we might claim that every thought or its negation is true, without having to produce an infinite list of disjunctions. In such cases, we use the truth predicate to say something we would not be able to say without it. By contrast, if we never wished to say of a thought that it is true without displaying it, as we do when we say ⌜It is true that S⌝ or ⌜The thought that S is true⌝, then we could get by reasonably well without a truth predicate, by saying S instead. In short, Environment 2 provides the truth predicate with its reason for being.

Environment 1, which involves the equivalences ⌜It is true that S iff S⌝ and ⌜The thought that S is true iff S⌝, is crucial in explaining what truth is. In explaining what it is for the thought that violets are flowers to be true, one can scarcely do better than point out that it is true iff violets are flowers. In explaining what it is for an arbitrary thought to be true, it seems to be enough to note that the same sort of explanation could be given in each case. To come to understand what truth is, it seems sufficient to learn that the thought that violets are flowers is true iff violets are flowers, the thought that the earth is round is true iff the earth is round, and so on. Although this isn't a definition, it sheds considerable light on the property. More generally, for any thought T, T and the thought that T is true are necessary and a priori consequences of one another; moreover, any warrant for asserting, denying, believing, doubting, or taking a variety of related attitudes toward T, or toward the thought that T is true, is warrant for taking that attitude toward the other.[28] Although Frege himself doesn't say anything this detailed or explicit, his insight in the quoted passage from "Thought" suggests that he was moving in this direction.

Nothing in this attractive line of reasoning dictates that truth is, or that it isn't, definable. Frege, however, was convinced that it is not. His argument, given in the first few pages of "Thought," starts as follows:

> Grammatically, the word 'true' looks like a word for a property. . . . We find truth predicated of pictures, ideas, sentences, and thoughts. . . . A picture is meant to represent something. (Even an idea is not called true in itself, but only with respect to an intention that the idea should correspond to something.) It might be supposed from this that truth consists in correspondence

---

[28] See Soames (2003a) for extended discussion.

of a picture to what it depicts. Now correspondence is a relation. But this goes against the use of the word 'true', which is not a relative term and contains no indication of anything else to which something is to correspond.[29]

The argument to this point is simple.

(i) Grammatically, 'true' is a predicate applied to individual things, and so it should stand for a property—truth—if it stands for anything at all.

(ii) Correspondence is a relation holding between a pair of things.

(iii) Since 'true' doesn't stand for a relation, truth isn't correspondence.

The point is general, applying not just to pictures, but to thoughts too. However, it has no force against correspondence theories. Such theories don't say that 'true' means 'corresponds to' or that the property *truth* is identical with the relation *corresponds to*. They say that truth is the relational property *corresponding to something* (different versions choose different things). Such theories may be correct or incorrect, but they are not guilty of an elementary category mistake.

After getting off to this unpromising start, Frege gives a general argument directed against all attempts to define truth in terms of correspondence, and, by implication, against every definition of truth whatsoever. He begins by noting that the truth of a thought can't involve *complete* correspondence because that would be identity, and according to the correspondence theory, a truth is supposed to be distinct from what it corresponds to. He goes on:

> But could we not maintain that there is truth when there is correspondence in a certain respect? But which respect? For in that case what ought we to do so as to decide whether something is true? We should have to inquire whether it is *true* that an idea and a reality, say, correspond in the specified respect. And then we should be confronted by a question of the same kind, and the game could begin again. So the attempted explanation of truth as correspondence breaks down. And any other attempt to define truth also breaks down. For in a definition certain characteristics would have to be specified. And in application to any particular case the question would always arise whether it were *true* that the characteristics were present. So we should be going round in a circle. So it seems likely that the content of the word 'true' is *sui generis* and indefinable.[30]

The argument suggested here can be reconstructed as a *reductio ad absurdum*.

P1.   Suppose that truth is definable: For any thought T, T is true iff T is D.

P2.   Then, to inquire (establish) whether T is true in any particular case, one must inquire (establish) whether T is D.

[29] Frege (1997), pp. 326–27.
[30] Frege (1997), p. 327.

P3. But, to inquire (establish) whether S is to inquire (establish) whether it is true that S, which is to inquire (establish) whether the thought that S is true.[31]

C. So, to inquire (establish) whether a thought T is true, one must inquire (establish) whether the thought *that T is D* is true, which in turn requires one to inquire (establish) whether the thought *that the thought that T is D is itself D* is true, and so on *ad infinitum.*

Since C is supposed to be absurd, P1 is supposed to be falsified. But it isn't. C is absurd only if judging whether something is so-and-so—e.g., whether T is D—requires a *prior* judgment that the thought *that something is so-and-so* is true—e.g., that the thought *that T is D* is true. However, the crucial premise P3 is false when understood in this way. To the extent that P3 is plausible, its content is simply that the thought *that T is true* is a trivially recognizable a priori, and necessary, consequence of T. Thus, one who establishes (or explicitly asserts) that T doesn't have to do anything else to implicitly establish (or implicitly assert) *that T is true.* But if that is all P3 gives us, then there is no absurdity in C, and no *reductio ad absurdum* of the claim that truth is definable.[32]

4. SENSE, REFERENCE, AND IDENTITY

It is a familiar fact in philosophy that a great thinker, responsible for a stunning advance, sees the way through a thicket of problems, but none too clearly. Undaunted, the philosopher moves ahead, showing us the way. Once on the path, ascending higher than ever before, we sometimes look back, with a better view of the terrain than our predecessor had. From there we can see how incomplete and insecure our guide's original vision must have been, a fact that only increases our admiration for the achievement. We have seen a bit of this already in Frege's insights about truth and quantification. The same is true of his distinction between sense and reference.

There is no more influential paper in the philosophy of language than "On Sense and Reference," and no section more studied than its opening pages, where the distinction is introduced. Strangely, it is not the only, or perhaps even the primary, focus of those pages. Instead, Frege begins with what he takes to be a problem about identity.

Equality [identity] gives rise to challenging questions which are not altogether easy to answer. Is it a relation? A relation between objects, or between names or signs of objects? In my *Begriffsschrift* I assumed the latter. The reasons which seem to favor this are the following: $a = a$ and $a = b$ are obviously

---

[31] P3 is a premise schema. Instances are obtained by substituting sentences for occurrences of 'S'.

[32] This argument is discussed in more detail on pp. 24–27 of Soames (1999).

statements of differing cognitive value; $a = a$ holds *a priori* and, according to Kant, is to be labeled analytic, while statements of the form $a = b$ often contain very valuable extensions of our knowledge and cannot always be established *a priori*. The discovery that the rising sun is not new every morning, but always the same, was one of the most fertile astronomical discoveries. Even today the identification of a small planet or a comet is not always a matter of course. Now if we were to regard equality as a relation between that which the names 'a' and 'b' designate, it would seem that $a = b$ could not differ from $a = a$ (provided $a = b$ is true). A relation would thereby be expressed between a thing and itself, and indeed one in which each thing stands to itself but to no other thing.[33]

Up to this point we have what seems to be a problem about the identity relation, leading to a *reductio ad absurdum* of the idea that it holds between objects. Frege speaks of sentences ⌜a = a⌝ and ⌜a = b⌝ in which a and b are singular terms (names, definite descriptions, or terms applying functions to arguments). In support of his claim that these sentences can differ in "cognitive value," even when ⌜a = b⌝ is true, he cites the analyticity and apriority of ⌜a = a⌝, to which he opposes the fact that ⌜a = b⌝ may contain "valuable extensions of our knowledge," adding that often ⌜a = b⌝ isn't a priori. In speaking of apriority, he must, given his view of thoughts as the things known, be taking a sentence to be a priori iff the thought it expresses can be known without empirical justification. Although his point about analyticity doesn't require thoughts as intermediaries, it is otiose. Analytic truths don't contrast with those that contain "valuable extensions of our knowledge"— since, as Frege insists, mathematics is both analytic and the source of many such extensions. Nor is apriority the key. Although true identity statements ⌜a = b⌝ in mathematics are a priori, they can also be highly informative, and so differ in "cognitive value" from ⌜a = a⌝. They are instances of Frege's puzzle, just as the more familiar empirical cases are.

As for "cognitive value," Frege seems to have two things in mind. First, he judges two sentences to differ in cognitive value iff an agent may believe one to be true without believing the other to be true, while understanding and attending to both. Second, he judges them to differ in cognitive value iff an agent may believe the thought T (semantically) expressed by one, without believing the thought T' expressed by the other, while entertaining both. For Frege, these criteria come to the same thing, because he takes the meaning of a sentence to be the thought it expresses, while also taking meaning to be transparent—in the sense that anyone who understands a pair of expressions will know both what they mean and whether they mean the same thing. Later, we will see that the transparency assumption is less obvious than it first seems. Once it is questioned, it is unclear that Frege's two criteria for difference in "cognitive value" are

---

[33] Frege (1992b), p. 56 in Geach and Black (1970).

equivalent, or that satisfaction of the first is an effective positive test for difference in linguistic meaning.[34]

However, these are, for us, complications. The question at hand is, how are we to understand the alleged *reductio* of the view that identity is a relation between objects? The first implicit premise on which the *reductio* depends seems to be R1.

R1. If identity were a relation between objects, then knowing *that n = m* or *that the so-and-so = the such-and-such* would be trivial (when the identity statement was true), since to know the identity statement it would be sufficient to know (i) that the identity relation holds of all and only objects and themselves, and (ii) what objects n and m, or *the so-and-so* and *the such-and-such,* are.

Given that the knowledge of (i) is trivial, one might invoke R2 in support of the alleged triviality of the knowledge of (ii).

R2. To entertain the proposition *that n = m*, one must know what the objects n and m are (ditto for *the so-and-so* and *the such-and-such*).

Speaking of sentences rather than thoughts, Currie hints at a view along these lines:

What do we have to know in order to know that 'a is taller than b' is true? First we need to know what objects a and b *are*, then we need to know what relation *is taller than* is, and finally we need to have some way of determining whether a is taller than b. But the case of identity is different. If we know what objects a and b are, and if we know what relation identity is, then we know already that a is identical with b. We do not need any way of determining it. This, then, is the sense in which the truth value of an identity statement can be determined *a priori*.[35]

Since identity claims are not so easily established, the argument concludes, identity is *not* a relation on objects.

Although the argument raises some tricky issues, it is easy to falsify R1 (and to put pressure on R2) by showing that even though knowledge of (i) and (ii) in R1 is *not* sufficient for knowledge *that the so-and-so = the such-and-such*, identity *is*, nevertheless, a relation on objects.[36] We begin with a special case involving definite descriptions. Looking up in the morning, I can entertain the thought I express by saying "The heavenly body that

---

[34] See Salmon (1984) for an excellent discussion of these points.

[35] See Currie (1982), p. 109.

[36] R2 clearly fails when descriptions are involved. A strong case can be made that R2 also fails when names are involved—but this brings up the complicated question of what *knowing what/which/whom* involves. See Boer and Lycan (1986) and Soames (1988). As for R1, it is arguable that there is a sense in which the proper name version of it is true, even if it does not lead to a *reductio* of the claim that identity is a relation on objects—because there is a sense in which knowledge of the proposition expressed by ⌜n = m⌝ is trivial. (This depends on taking a non-Fregean view of proper names.)

appears there [pointing and referring to Venus and the position it occupies] every morning at this time of year is either a planet or a star." I can also entertain the thought I express in the evening (at other times) by saying "The heavenly body that appears there [pointing at and referring to Venus and the position it occupies] every evening at this time of year is either a planet or a star." In so doing, I satisfy all requirements for entertaining the thoughts, including any there may be on knowing which objects are (a) *the heavenly body that appears in such-and-such place every morning at a certain time of year*, and (b) *the heavenly body that appears in such-and-such other place every evening at another time*. In this case, we can say something further—namely that there is a single object, Venus, of which I know both that it is the heavenly body that appears in a certain place every morning at a certain time of year, and that it is the heavenly body that appears in a certain other place at another time. So, there is no doubt that I satisfy whatever (if any) requirement there may be for entertaining the thought expressed by (16).

16. The heavenly body that appears in such-and-such position every morning at a certain time of year = the heavenly body that appears in such-and-such other position every evening at another time.

This doesn't guarantee that I know, or am in a position know, that the thought is true.

With this, we return to R1 and R2. Either we have a *reductio* of one or both of them, or we have a *reductio* of the idea that identity holds between objects. Note, there is nothing unique about the use of identity in R1 and R2. Replacing it with any other relation known a priori to be (universally) reflexive (i.e., to apply to any pair of an object and itself, even if it applies to other pairs too) allows one to reach the same conclusion by similar reasoning. More precisely, when R is such a relation, R1* and R2* are true if R1 and R2 are.

R1*. If R were a relation between objects, then knowing *that n R m* or *that the so-and-so R the such-and-such* would be trivial (when the singular terms designated the same thing), since to know the R-statement it would be sufficient to know (i) that R holds of every object and itself, and (ii) what objects *n* and *m*, or *the so-and-so* and *the such-and-such,* are.

R2*. To entertain the proposition *that n R m*, one must know what the objects *n* and *m* are (ditto for *the so-and-so* and *the such-and-such*).

So, if we have a *reductio* of the idea that identity is a relation on objects, then we have a *reductio* of the idea that there are any (universally) reflexive relations on objects.[37] For example, even though the definite descriptions in (17) are coreferential, I can't know the thought expressed by (17) to be true, just by being able to entertain it (and/or knowing what the relevant objects are).

---

[37] Here I use "reflexive relation" for "relation knowable a priori to be reflexive."

17. The heavenly body that appears in such-and-such position every morning at a certain time of year *is not larger than* the heavenly body that appears in such-and-such other position every evening at another time.

If the original argument appealing to R1/R2 were sound, then a similar argument appealing to R1* and R2* would show that the reflexive relation *not being larger than* isn't a relation on objects. And if it isn't, then surely, *being larger than* isn't a relation on objects either. The point can be extended. When F(x) and G(y) are formulas (with only 'x' and 'y' free, respectively) designating concepts that can be known a priori not to be satisfied by the same object, the concept designated by ⌜~[F(x) & G(y)]⌝ will be a relation that is knowable a priori to be (universally) reflexive. So, if R1 and R2 were correct, this concept would *not* be a relation on objects, in which case it is hard to see how the concept designated by ⌜F(x) & G(y)⌝ could be such a relation, *or even how the concepts designated by F(x) and G(y), could be defined on objects.* Since this threatens the idea that *any* concepts hold of objects, it is a *reductio* of R1 and R2.[38]

We can also falsify R3, which might naturally be thought to accompany R1. Here, we let F and G be arbitrary predicates that *can* apply to some of the same objects.

R3. If both identity and the relation designated by ⌜F(x) & G(y)⌝ are relations on objects, then when it is true that $n = m$ and also that *the so-and-so = the such-and-such*, (i) knowing *that F(n) & G(m)* or knowing *that F(the-so-and-so) & G (the such-and-such)*, plus (ii) knowing what objects n and m are, or knowing *what objects the so-and-so and the such-and-such are*, will together guarantee that one is in a position to infer *that something is both F and G.*

The arguments already given generalize to cases in which one knows the propositions expressed by (18a) and (18b), while also knowing "what the relevant objects are"—even though one is in no position to come to know the proposition expressed by (18c).[39]

18a. The heavenly body that appears in such-and-such position every morning at a certain time of year is F and the heavenly body that appears in so-and-so position every morning at another time is G.
  b. Phosphorus is F and Hesperus is G.
  c. ∃x [x is F and x is G].

---

[38] To repeat, the arguments given above falsify the descriptive version of R1. Of course, the descriptive version of R2 also fails. Whether or not the name versions of R1 and R2 also fail is more complicated, and depends, in the case of R2, on the analysis of *knowing what*.

[39] See Soames (1987) for discussion of this result. R3 is relevantly different from R1 in that even the name version of R3 can be decisively falsified. By contrast, some Millians take the name version of R1 to be true, even though it provides no *reductio* of the claim that identity is a relation on objects.

Thus, neither R1 nor R3 can be used to provide a *reductio ad absurdum* of the view that identity is a relation on objects. Contrary to the opening page of "On Sense and Reference," *the view that it is leads to no difficulty at all.*

There is a genuine problem here that has nothing to do with identity, or with relations in general, whether reflexive or not.[40] There are thoughts (semantically) expressed by ⌜a = a⌝ and ⌜a = b⌝ such that one can believe the former without believing the latter. This is an unremarkable instance of a more general point: there are formulas (predicates) F(x) and Fregean singular terms a and b such that one can believe the thought (semantically) expressed by the result F(a/x) of substituting a for all free occurrences of 'x' in F(x), without thereby believing the thought expressed by F(b/x). From this, plus the *reconstructed* Fregean argument in chapter 1, one may conclude that the meanings, or senses, of some terms are distinct from their referents. This is the argumentative route that contemporary philosophers take to the Fregean legacy; it is *not* the argument Frege gives.

Frege continues his argument where the supposed *reductio* of identity as a relation between objects leaves off.

> What is intended to be said by a = b seems to be that the signs or names 'a' and 'b' designate the same thing, so that those signs themselves would be under discussion; a relation between them would be asserted. But this relation would hold between the names or signs only in so far as they named or designated something. It would be mediated by the connexion of each of the two signs with the same designated thing. *But this is arbitrary.* Nobody can be forbidden to use any arbitrarily producible event or object as a sign for something. In that case the sentence a = b would *no longer refer to the subject matter,* but only to its mode of designation; *we would express no proper knowledge by its means.* But in many cases this is just what we want to do [to express proper knowledge of the subject matter]. *If the sign 'a' is distinguished from the sign 'b' only as object* (here by means of its shape), not as sign (i.e. not by the manner in which it designates something), the cognitive value of a = a becomes essentially equal to that of a = b, provided a = b is true. *A difference [in cognitive value] can arise only if the difference in the sign corresponds to a difference in the mode of presentation of that which is designated.*[41]

After dismissing identity as a relation between objects, Frege here turns to the view that it is a relation between expressions—i.e., that ⌜a = b⌝ says that symbol a is coreferential with symbol b, while ⌜a = a⌝ says that a is coreferential with a. Although these are different pieces of information, neither amounts to much, since *if all there is to know about symbols is their*

---

[40] Salmon (1984) gives arguments that Frege's puzzle has nothing special to do with identity. Fine (2007) recognizes this, but argues that relations are the key to Frege's puzzle. Soames (2012b) disputes this.

[41] "On Sense and Reference," pp. 56–57 in Geach and Black (1970), my emphasis.

orthographic shape, we learn nothing about the nonlinguistic subject matter they are used to talk about by being told that the shapes are coreferential. So, if knowledge of coreference is to provide useful information, *there must be more to know about symbols than their shapes; there must also be modes of presentation of the objects they designate.* Frege closes by illustrating what he means.

> Let a, b, c be lines connecting the vertices of a triangle with the midpoints of the opposite sides. The point of intersection of a and b is then the same as the point of intersection of b and c. So we have different designations for the same point, and these names ('point of intersection of a and b,' 'point of intersection of b and c') likewise indicate the mode of presentation; and *hence the statement contains actual knowledge.*[42]

He goes on to say that these modes of presentation are senses that determine reference. So, if you understand 'the point of intersection of a and b' and 'the point of intersection of b and c', then learning that they are coreferential (i.e., that *being a unique point at which a and b intersect* and *being a unique point at which b and c intersect* determine the same thing) will provide you with information about nonlinguistic subject matter.

One natural way of reading the argument in these pages is to see it as (i) trying to show that identity can't be a relation on objects, and hence that identity statements must say that the "proper names" in them are coreferential, (ii) arguing that this is tenable only if these terms have senses, and that knowing them to be coreferential involves knowing, of the senses, that they determine the same referent, and (iii) extending the sense-reference distinction to all "proper names," since each can occur in an identity claim.[43] On this reading, Frege doesn't abandon his earlier view that identity claims are metalinguistic; he attempts to make it tenable by replacing his former view that "names" merely stand for contents (referents) with the view that they also express senses.

In fleshing this out, it is helpful to look back at the *Begriffsschrift*.

> Elsewhere [i.e., outside of identity sentences], signs are mere proxies for their content [what they designate], and thus any phrase they occur in just expresses a relation between their various contents; but names at once appear *in propria persona* [as designating themselves] as soon as they are joined together by the symbol for equality of content; *for this signifies the circumstance of two names' having the same content [referent].* Thus, along with the introduction of a symbol for equality of content [reference], all symbols are necessarily

---

[42] Ibid., p. 57, my emphasis.

[43] Though not the standard interpretation, it is, arguably, the one that sticks closest to the text. It is defended in Thau and Caplan (2000), which discusses Frege's remarks *before and after* "On Sense and Reference," in which he speaks of identity sentences as expressing metalinguistic claims. This interpretation also finds some support in Stroll (1967), Dejnozka (1981, 1996), Currie (1982), and Morris (1984).

given a double meaning—the same symbols now stand for their own content, now for themselves.[44]

Here we see Frege's earlier view (i) that the "contents" of singular terms are what they designate, which they contribute to "contents" of larger expressions containing them, and (ii) that in identity sentences, terms flanking '=' refer to themselves, while '=' designates the two-place relation *having the same content* (referent). At this point, he notes a worry. Why, if the content of a name is its referent, do we need a second name with the same content? His answer involves a geometric example like the one given in "On Sense and Reference." Applied to the later example, it involves introducing a name n for the intersection of lines a and b and a name m for the intersection of b and c. Later, $\ulcorner n = m \urcorner$ is proven using the information associated with the introduction of the names. So, in addition to names, we have reference-determining conditions. He continues:

> To each of these two ways of determining it [the common referent] there answers a separate name. The need of a symbol for equality of content thus rests on the following fact: The same content can be fully determined in different ways; and *that*, in a particular case, *the same* content actually is given by *two ways of determining it*, is the content of the *judgment*. Before this judgment is made, we must supply, corresponding to the two ways of determination, two different names for the thing determined. The judgment needs to be expressed by means of a symbol for equality of content, joining the two names together. It is clear from this that different names for the same content are not always just a trivial matter of formulation; if they go along with different ways of determining the content, they are relevant to the essential nature of the case. In these circumstances the judgment as to equality of content is, in Kant's sense, synthetic [as it would not be if identity were a relation on objects and names only had referents].[45]

What is the change in view from the *Begriffsschrift* to "On Sense and Reference"? A case can be made (i) that the metalinguistic view of identity remained roughly intact, (ii) that Frege came to see that the information contained in *judgments* we use identity sentences to express should be included in their *meanings*, (iii) that the post-*Begriffsschrift* development of the view that sentences refer to truth values helped him to see that they must have another semantic value as well, and to realize that his earlier talk of "the content of a sentence" had been ambiguous between talk of their truth values and talk of the information they carry,[46] (iv) that recognizing the senses of sentences brought with it recognition of the senses of

[44] *Begriffsschrift*, section 8, "Equality of Content," pp. 10–11 of Geach and Black (1970), my emphasis.
[45] Ibid., 11–12.
[46] See "Letter to Husserl," 1891 in Frege (1997); "Function and Concept," in Frege (1997); Geach and Black (1970).

all "proper names," and (v) that it occurred to him that such senses would also solve "the identity problem," and that this problem would be a good vehicle for introducing the general notion of sense.

Whether Frege really maintained a version of the metalinguistic view, even after introducing his distinction between sense and reference, is a question of whether he remained confused about identity even after introducing the distinction, or whether he ceased being confused, but chose a misleading argument to introduce the distinction that was likely to confuse others. Since our concern is with his legacy rather than his psychology, we need not resolve this question. But we do need to clear up the confusion. It must be understood (i) why identity sentences are not metalinguistic (whether or not senses are involved), (ii) why they must express thoughts that predicate the identity relation of objects, rather than predicating another relation of expressions, concepts, or senses, and (iii) how such predication should be understood.

For (i) it is sufficient to note that since one who has no knowledge of English can believe the thought expressed by (19a) without believing the thought expressed by (19b), the thought expressed by the former is not the thought expressed by the latter.

19a. The heavenly body visible from place A at time B = the heavenly body visible from place C at time D.
  b. The expression 'the heavenly body visible from place A at time B' (which designates whatever is unique in being a heavenly body visible from A at B) refers to the same thing as the expression 'the heavenly body visible from place C at time D' (which designates whatever is unique in being a heavenly body visible from C at D).

If the parenthesized material in (19b) (expressing senses of the expressions) is deleted, then one can *also* believe the thought expressed by (19b) without believing the thought expressed by (19a). However, this is not necessary to distinguish the two thoughts, since whether or not the co-reference claim brings with it a grasp of the relevant senses, it certainly requires cognitive perspective on the expressions flanking the identity sign that believing the thought expressed by (19a) does not.

Next consider the difference between (19a) and (19c).

19c. The concept *being uniquely a heavenly body visible from A at B* is true of the same object as the concept *being uniquely a heavenly body visible from C at D*.

Though I think the same argument applies as before, it is not as obvious that it does, because agents capable of having sophisticated beliefs about concepts, as well as beliefs about objects, might—with some plausibility—be counted as believing the thought expressed by (19c) iff they believe the thought expressed by (19a). Still, it is unclear that all agents—including young children and intelligent animals—capable of believing an identity claim *about* objects are capable of believing the corresponding claim *about* concepts. Moreover, there is good reason to think the thoughts must be different. The thought expressed by (19c) seems to be the same as that expressed by (19c′).

19c′. The object of which *being uniquely a heavenly body visible from A at B* is true = the object of which *being uniquely a heavenly body fixable from C at T* is true.

Since this is itself a statement to which the analysis of identity claims about objects must apply, we generate a still higher thought, which the Fregean must distinguish from the thought expressed by (19c).

19c″. The concept *being uniquely an object of which the concept being uniquely a heavenly body visible from A at B is true* is true of the same object as the concept *being uniquely an object of which the concept being uniquely a heavenly body visible from C at D is true*.

The way to stop the generation of this absurd hierarchy is to distinguish the thoughts expressed by (19a) and (19c). The same reasoning applies to an analysis that claims that (19a) expresses a thought about the *senses* of the two descriptions (to the effect that they determine the same object). Beyond this, there is, of course, an overarching reason not to use Frege's puzzle as a pretext for adopting a special analysis of identity statements. Since the puzzle arises equally for any pair of sentences expressing different thoughts while differing only in the substitution of an occurrence of one singular term for an occurrence of another coreferential term, any attempt to resolve the puzzle by claiming that identity statements don't predicate relations of objects will lead to the absurd conclusion that no statements predicate either properties, or relations, of objects.

How, then, should we understand the thought expressed by (19a) as predicating identity of a pair of objects? The explanation can be generalized from the simpler example (20), where the descriptions pick out the same thing.

20a. The F is G.
b. The H is G.

On the Fregean analysis of definite descriptions, 'the' designates the function f_{the} that takes a concept C as argument and assigns o as value iff o is unique in being something of which C is true. Entertaining the thought expressed by (20a) involves (i) applying f_{the} to the concept *being F* and (ii) predicating the concept *being G* of the result. Entertaining the thought expressed by (20b) involves (iii) applying f_{the} to the concept *being H* and (iv) predicating the concept *being G* of the result. [47] These thoughts are different because (i) and (iii) are different, even though, in our example, they result in the same object. Requirement (i) involves thinking of *being F*, and hence having it in mind under a certain mode of presentation, while taking it as argument of f_{the}, whereas (iii) involves thinking of *being H*, and hence

[47] 'F', 'G', and 'H' are here used as schematic letters.

having it in mind under a different mode of presentation, while taking it as argument of f_{the}. So, although the same thing gets predicated of the same object, the manner in which this is done is different in the two cases, reflecting the different constituents of the two Fregean thoughts, and the designations they determine. Applying this idea to identities allows one to explain how the thoughts expressed by ⌜the F = the F⌝ and ⌜the F = the H⌝ can differ, even if they predicate the identity relation of the same objects.[48]

5. PLATONISM AND FREGE'S HIERARCHY

At the end of section 3, chapter 1, I noted that Frege's theory of indirect discourse generates a hierarchy starting with the customary sense of an expression E (carried by occurrences not embedded under any propositional attitude verb), continuing (when E is embedded under a single occurrence of such a verb) with E's indirect sense, which is a mode of presentation of E's customary sense, and leading, for each n, to E's nth-level indirect sense (carried by occurrences of E embedded under n occurrences of attitude verbs), which is a mode of presentation of E's $(n-1)^{th}$ sense. This led to a question: How is it possible to learn a language, if, for each of its expressions E, one must identify infinitely many different senses of E in order to understand all the sentences in which E occurs?

Although Fregeans have long had what they regard as a satisfactory answer to this question, recently—in Kripke (2008)—the answer has been put in a form that some have found more appealing. Consider the attitude ascriptions in (21).

21a. A believes that S.
  b. B knows that A believes that S.

On Kripke's version of the Fregean story, one who understands unembedded occurrences of S is thereby *acquainted* with its ordinary sense, OS. Given (21a), the agent focuses on OS, knowing that the function designated by 'believe' must operate on it. Since thinking about anything requires a way of presenting it, thinking about OS requires such a mode of presentation. This isn't a problem, Kripke suggests, since *acquaintance* with something always provides a way of thinking about it, which, in the case of OS, the agent must already have. This is the indirect sense IS of S, grasp of which allows the agent to understand (21a). What about (21b), in which S is embedded under a pair of such verbs? Since the agent has grasped the customary sense of (21a), he is already acquainted with IS. This acquaintance provides him with the doubly indirect sense of S, required for understanding (21b). Repeating the story for higher levels of

---

[48] For more on how predication is understood, see Soames (2010b, chap. 7) and (2014c and forthcoming).

the hierarchy, Kripke seems to contend, disarms the objection that Frege's analysis of indirect discourse can't be correct, since it leads to an infinite, unlearnable hierarchy of senses.

By itself, however, this story doesn't resolve all relevant worries. The meaning of (21a) doesn't change from agent to agent, depending on how they think of the common meaning OS they all ascribe to S. Nor does it change from time to time in which they consider (21a), due to changes in the modes of presentation by which they apprehend OS. Thus, what Frege needs is not *an* acquaintance-based way of thinking of OS for each agent and time, but *the* acquaintance-based way of so doing, the same for every agent and time. Kripke's story doesn't explain how this is guaranteed. In addition, if the story is to be adequate, the indirect sense of S at a given level n of the hierarchy must *rigidly* pick out the same $(n-1)^{th}$-level sense *at any counterfactual circumstance as it does at the actual circumstance.*

What does this mean? Consider the thought T *that the present chairman of the USC philosophy department grew up in Seattle.* This is true because, in the world as it actually is, I both grew up in Seattle and am now chairman of the USC department. Next consider a counterfactual circumstance C differing a bit from the way things actually are. Who would have had to grow up in Seattle, if C had been actual, in order to make T true? Whoever *would have been* chairman of the USC philosophy department, of course. Since there are circumstances in which, had they been actual, Jim Higginbotham would have been the present chairman, there are circumstances in which *his background*, rather than mine, determines the truth or falsity of T. To say this is to say that 'the present chairman of the USC philosophy department' isn't a *rigid designator*—in Fregean terms, its sense doesn't *rigidly* pick out anyone. Now apply this reasoning to the thought T', *that Mary believes that Frege was German.* According to Frege, for T' to be true, the indirect sense IS of 'Frege was German' must present a thought believed by Mary. For any possible counterfactual circumstance C, T' would have been true, had C been actual, iff had C been actual, IS would have picked out a certain thought believed by Mary. Which one? Is it the same thought, for every circumstance, or does the thought Mary must believe in order for T' to be true change from one circumstance to the next? Clearly, it doesn't change. So, the indirect sense required at each stage of the hierarchy must *rigidly* present the same lower-level sense at all circumstances. It is not obvious that Kripke's story guarantees this.

Can it be guaranteed? Acquaintance with people, institutions, and physical objects doesn't guarantee any such unique and rigid sense by means of which agents think of them. All these things can appear to us in different ways, and—since they all have many properties—sometimes we think of them in terms of one set of salient properties, and sometimes we think of them in terms of another set. Since we don't think about them in the same way every time, the Fregean modes of presentation by which we apprehend them vary from agent to agent, and time to time. Moreover, these modes of presentation typically don't pick out their objects rigidly—since no matter how such an object may appear, it is usually possible for other objects to appear that way. Nor is the point limited to the objects mentioned so far. Surely books, poems, plays, musical pieces, and the like—thought of as abstract objects we are acquainted with through their instances—can appear differently to us, perhaps in ways it would be possible for different things of this kind to appear. If the same is true of Fregean thoughts, then prospects for rendering his hierarchy harmless in the manner suggested by Kripke aren't good.

Although these considerations don't disprove Frege's theory, the problems they raise are, I think, ones that only an ambitious Platonist epistemology might address. Suppose it could somehow be shown that, unlike the objects we encounter in everyday life, the abstract senses of Frege's postulated "third realm" of being are cognitively transparent and beyond appearance—with essential natures fully and immediately graspable in the same way by every mind acquainted with them. Then the epistemic worries raised here about his hierarchy might be put to rest.[49] That, of course, is a tall order. It is not that Frege shies away from such an epistemology. Far from it. However, he provides very little detail, and so leaves us with what can only be regarded as mysterious.[50]

The alternative to resting so heavily on the promise of a comprehensible Platonic epistemology is to change the analysis of attitude ascriptions, so as not to generate the hierarchy. There are two ways to do this, each of which involves giving up one of Frege's sweeping generalizations. The first carves out exceptions to the Fregean principle that whenever we think about, or refer to, something, we do so by thinking about it in a certain way—which is the mode of presentation by which it is presented to us. The exceptions are cases in which we are acquainted with the sense of an expression we understand. When we are acquainted with such a denizen of the "third realm," the suggestion goes, our epistemic relationship with it is so immediate and secure that we don't need any mode of presentation to think of it. In these special cases, the constituent of the thought we are thinking is *not* something that represents something else, which our thought is about. Rather, the constituent of our thought *is* what the thought is about. For example, when I entertain the thought JBT, expressed by ⌐John believes that the F is G⌐, and thereby think about John and the thought T expressed by ⌐the F is G⌐, (i) I think about John by

---

[49] Kripke would, I think, recognize, and even emphasize, this aspect of Frege's thought. The view he attributes to Frege is that acquaintance with a certain very limited range of things, including senses, provides the agent with further senses that not only present those things, but "reveal" what they are. Though Kripke isn't explicit about what this amounts to, the parallel he draws with Russellian acquaintance (in his post-"On Denoting" period) suggests that the cognitive perspective achieved through this special acquaintance is guaranteed to be accurate regarding the existence and nature of the items in question.

[50] See his discussion in "Thought," in Frege (1997).

virtue of the fact that my thought contains, not John himself, but a mode of presentation that picks him out, but (ii) I think about T, not by virtue of there being any constituent T* of JBT, distinct from T, that picks out T, but rather by virtue of the fact that T itself is a constituent of JBT. On this view, championed in Yourgrau (1982) and (1986–87), there is no Fregean hierarchy of senses.

The difference between this view and the one extracted from Kripke involves a subtle point about the role played by acquaintance with a sense s. In Kripke's story, such acquaintance is meant to guarantee that the agent will always have immediate cognitive access to an indirect sense IS, distinct from s, that nevertheless picks out s *when the agent thinks about s and predicates concepts or relations of it* (as opposed to when the agent merely uses s to think about something else). In Yourgrau's story, acquaintance is meant to obviate the need for any distinct mode of presentation of s at all. As we shall see in our discussion of "On Denoting" in chapter 8, Russell's notion of acquaintance has important points of contact with the corresponding notions sketched, on Frege's behalf, by both Kripke and Yourgrau. However, whereas Yourgrau more or less makes Frege a Russellian on this point, thereby eliminating the hierarchy, Kripke tries to preserve the hierarchy, while bringing Frege close enough to Russell to neutralize it. Having spelled out the potential problems with Kripke's Frege, I will here simply mention that Yourgrau's Frege must find some way to distinguish those cases in which the role of a sense in a thought is— as it normally is for Frege—to represent that of which it is a mode of presentation (which the thought is thereby about) from those cases in which its role is simply to represent itself (which the thought is then supposed to be about). Without a clear account of this distinction—over which Russell labors mightily in his critique of Frege in "On Denoting"—the amalgam of Frege and Russell that eliminates the hierarchy remains mysterious. More on that in chapter 8.

This brings us to the second way of eliminating Frege's hierarchy of senses, which is to make exceptions to his generalization that the truth or falsity of a sentence S, and the referent of a compound term T, is *always* a function of its grammatical structure, plus the *referents* of occurrences in S, or T, of its constituent parts. The exceptions are cases in which the truth or falsity of S, or the referent of T, are functions of their syntactic structure plus the *senses and referents* of their parts. To recognize such cases is to recognize the existence of *nonextensional* operators, which designate (refer to) functions that take as arguments some semantic values of the expressions with which they combine *other than the referents of those expressions*. There are two natural options of this sort for attitude ascriptions ⌜A believes that S⌝. One option takes ⌜A believes that __⌝ to designate a function that maps *the sense* of S (the thought S expresses) onto truth iff the referent of A believes that sense (thought), and onto falsity otherwise. The second way of getting the same ultimate result is to take 'that' to designate a function that maps the *sense* of S onto itself, which is assigned as *referent* of ⌜that S⌝. Here, ⌜that S⌝ is treated as a compound referring expression the referent of which *is not* a function of the referents of its parts. On this option, 'believe' designates a function that maps the referents of A and ⌜that S⌝ onto truth or falsity depending on whether the former believes the latter. On both options, S and the expressions in S retain their ordinary sense and reference in attitude ascriptions, no hierarchy is generated, and sense and reference don't have to be relativized to occurrences of expressions in different linguistic environments.

6. NONTRANSPARENT THOUGHTS: NAMES, ANAPHORA, QUANTIFYING-IN

Let us continue with this nonextensional alternative to Frege's analysis of attitude ascriptions. On this analysis, the complement clause S and its constituents retain their ordinary sense and reference; it is just that what they contribute to the reference of ⌜that S⌝, and the truth or falsity of ⌜A believes that S⌝, are their senses, not referents. The analysis has advantages for dealing with anaphora and quantification.

22a. Mary believes that *Bill* is stupid, but *he* isn't.
   b. *Bill* fooled Mary into thinking that *he* wasn't Bill.

It is natural to take the sense and reference of these anaphoric occurrences of 'he' to be the same as that of their antecedent noun phrases. However, this is problematic for Frege's analysis of attitude ascriptions. In (22a), the Fregean indirect referent of the occurrence of the antecedent is its ordinary sense, and its indirect sense is a special way of thinking about that sense. Since the anaphoric occurrence of the pronoun occurs outside of indirect discourse, neither its referent nor its sense can be the same as that of the occurrence of its antecedent. As a result, Frege's hierarchy complicates this way of understanding anaphoric pronouns.

The nonextensional analysis avoids this complication. However, (22b) presents a further problem, since assigning the anaphoric occurrence of 'he' the same Fregean sense as 'Bill' would get the truth conditions wrong, while taking the referent, Bill himself, to be its sense isn't allowed.[51] For Frege, expressions always contribute *ways of thinking of their referents*, rather than the referents themselves, to the thoughts expressed by sentences. To admit a class of thoughts containing such referents would be an important change. Presumably, to believe such a thought would be to believe, of an object o, that it has the properties specified by the thought, *where having*

---

[51] The truth conditions would be wrong, because if the occurrence of 'he' expressed the Fregean sense of 'Bill', the truth of (22b) would require Mary to have believed the absurd Fregean proposition expressed by 'Bill isn't Bill'. (Remember, on the nonextensional analysis, there is no distinction between direct and indirect sense, or reference.)

this belief doesn't require thinking of o in one specific way. This opens the door to the possibility of believing *that o is F* by virtue of thinking of o in way 1, and believing the negation of that thought by thinking of o in way 2— while being unable to notice the inconsistency because nothing in these ways shows them to be ways of thinking of the same thing. Perhaps this is what is going on with Mary when (22b) is true. If so, however, it violates Frege's assumption that our thoughts, and the meanings of our words, are always transparent to us.

Although this assumption may seem natural, quantification into attitude ascriptions like (23a) constitutes a *prima facie* case against it.

> 23a. *There is a planet* (Venus), such that the ancients asserted, and believed, when they saw *it* in the morning, that *it* was visible only in the morning, and they asserted, and believed, when they saw *it* in the evening, that *it* was visible only in the evening.

Example (23a) is true, despite the fact that the ways the ancients thought of Venus, morning and evening, were different. To explain how this works, we begin with the italicized phrase, which is a quantifier binding occurrences of 'it' (functioning as a variable). On the standard analysis of quantification inherited from Frege, 'There is an x such that …x…' is true iff for some object o '…x…' is true when o is taken as referent of 'x'. Given this, we know that (23a) will be true iff for some object o, (23b) is true when o is assigned as referent of 'x', which, in turn, is true iff (23c) is true.

> 23b. The ancients asserted, and believed, when they saw x in the morning, that x was visible only in the morning, and they asserted, and believed, when they saw x in the evening, that x was visible only in the evening.
>
> c. The ancients asserted, and believed, the thought expressed by 'x is visible only in the morning' relative to an assignment of o to 'x'—when they saw o in the morning—and they asserted, and believed, the thought expressed by 'x is visible only in the evening' relative to an assignment of o to 'x'—when they saw o in the evening.

Next we invoke the idea of a thought expressed by a formula containing a free occurrence of a variable, relative to an assignment of an object as referent of the variable. Although Frege never considered this (since it doesn't come up in formalizing mathematics), there is a natural way of construing it. If we assume what seems natural in any case, that variables of quantification don't have senses, but may be assigned referents, we arrive at the non-Fregean result that a free occurrence of a variable in S contributes *its referent*, relative to an assignment, to the thought S expresses, relative to that assignment. We further hold that one can believe this thought iff one believes, of the object referred to, that it has the properties specified in the thought, *where this belief doesn't require thinking of the object in one specific way.*

On this analysis, (23a) is true iff (23b) is true, relative to the choice of Venus as referent of 'x', which, in turn, is true iff the ancients asserted and believed the thought p expressed by 'x is visible only in the morning' (relative to this choice), when they saw Venus in the morning, and they asserted and believed the thought q expressed by 'x is visible only in the evening' (relative to the same choice), when they saw Venus in the evening. Here, p is the non-Fregean thought containing Venus that attributes to it the property of being visible only in the morning, while q is the corresponding thought that attributes to it the property of being visible only in the evening. These thoughts—called *singular thoughts, or singular propositions*—differ from traditional Fregean thoughts in that believing them doesn't require thinking of what they are about (Venus) in one particular way. There are, of course, *some* constraints on how one must think of o in order to believe a singular proposition about it. It is not enough to think ⌜the F, whatever it may be, is visible . . .⌝ for absolutely any F that happens to pick out o. However, these constraints leave room for believing one thing about Venus *by virtue of thinking of it in one way*, and believing a different, inconsistent, thing about it *by virtue of thinking of it in another way*—without being able to notice the inconsistency because it is not transparent that the two ways of thinking about Venus are ways of thinking of the same thing. This is what (23a) correctly reports. In cases like this, we report agents' attitudes toward objects in a way that abstracts away from the precise manner in which they think about them.

This analysis is non-Fregean in recognizing a class of nontransparent thoughts, belief in which may involve different ways of thinking of something. However, there is also a broadly Fregean analysis of (23a) that doesn't have this feature. Following David Kaplan (1968–69), one may accept the usual analysis of both quantification and propositional attitude ascriptions that *don't* contain free occurrences of variables, while adding a *new* analysis of ascriptions that *do* contain such occurrences. The analysis claims that (24a) is equivalent to (24b), where '$^{mm}F(M)^{mm}$' names the transparent Fregean thought the constituents of which are the sense of F and the mode of presentation M.[52]

24a. John believes that Fx.
   b. There is a mode M of presentation such that M both determines, and puts John *en rapport* with, x, and John believes the Fregean thought $^{mm}F(M)^{mm}$.

On this analysis, (23a) is represented as (23d).

23d. *There is a planet* x (namely Venus), and a mode M of presentation, such that M determines, and puts the ancients *en rapport* with, x, and the ancients asserted, and believed, $^{mm}Visible\ only\ in\ the\ morning\ (M)^{mm}$ when they saw *x* in the morning, and there is a mode M' of presentation, such that M' determines, and puts the ancients *en rapport* with, x, and they

---

[52] (24b) reflects the fact that not all modes of presentation of an object o put an agent *en rapport* with o. These are, roughly, the ways of thinking of o mentioned in the final paragraph above of the non-Fregean analysis.

asserted, and believed, ^{mm}*Visible only in the evening* (M′)^{mm} when they saw x in the evening.

The maneuver works because the attitude ascriptions (even relative to an assignment of Venus to 'x') don't report the specific thoughts believed or asserted, morning or evening, but rather report agents as asserting and believing (in the morning) some unspecified member of a certain class of Fregean thoughts about Venus, while asserting and believing (in the evening) some unspecified member of a another class.[53]

Although this works pretty well as a formal exercise, certain worries cast doubt on its accuracy as an analysis of natural language. Imagine you are learning English, and are already familiar with quantification and attitude ascriptions. Up to now, however, you have never been exposed to quantifying-in to such an ascription, as in (25).

25. Don't look now, but there is a man standing just in front of us who Mary says/thinks is interested in her.

Will this be incomprehensible because it is a completely new language lesson, or will your antecedent mastery of quantification and attitude ascriptions allow you to interpret it? If the Frege-style analysis were correct, it ought to be a new, and perhaps challenging, lesson. I suspect it isn't (though I don't know this for a fact).

Another worry is posed by (26).

26. One of the defendants previously asserted that he was asleep at the time, which Mary challenged when she testified that he wasn't asleep.

On the non-Fregean analysis, this remark identifies a specific singular proposition asserted by Mary that directly contradicts a related singular proposition asserted by one of the defendants. *He asserted one thing; she asserted its negation.* By contrast, the Frege-style analysis merely places the thought Mary asserted in a large class of Fregean thoughts (without identifying the one really asserted), while placing the thought asserted by the defendant in another class (without identifying it), thereby leaving it open that the two thoughts actually asserted may be consistent. Since we would naturally understand (26) in the first way, this is a problem for the Fregean analysis.

The problem is part of a larger worry illustrated by (27).

27a. There is one proposition—namely that Richard Feynman was brilliant— that everyone who knew anything about him believed.

---

[53] It could be objected that (23d) is still inaccurate insofar as its truth requires all (relevant) ancients to have thought of Venus, when seen in the morning, under the same mode of presentation (and similarly for the evening). If this is a problem, it might be dealt with by treating 'the ancients' as a quantifier taking wider scope than the quantifications over modes of presentation. I put this complication aside for the moment, since the issues it raises will be dealt with in the examples that follow.

b. One well-known physicist, Richard Feynman, is such that there is one proposition—namely that he was brilliant—that everyone who knew anything about him believed.

Here we have a generalization about a class of agents the truth of which requires one proposition to be believed by all. Surely, (27a,b) may be true, even if, as seems likely, there is no single Fregean thought (with a single mode of presentation of Feynman) that everyone in the class believes (including childhood friends, colleagues, wives, physics students, and those who know him only as "a famous scientist"). This is both problematic for the Kaplan-style account of quantifying-in, and inconsistent with a Fregean analysis of ⌜A believes that S⌝ as reporting a relation between the referent of A and the transparent Fregean thought expressed by S.

Frege remarks on one component of this problem—namely that different people are likely to associate different senses with the same name—in several places, including the following passage from "Thought."[54]

> Dr. Gustav Lauben says, "I was wounded." Leo Peter hears this and remarks some days later, "Dr. Gustav Lauben was wounded." Does this sentence express the same thought as the one Dr. Lauben uttered himself? Suppose that Rudolph Lingens was present when Dr. Lauben spoke and now hears what is related by Leo Peter. *If the same thought was uttered by Dr. Lauben and Leo Peter, then Rudolph Lingens, who is fully master of the language and remembers what Dr. Lauben said in his presence, must know at once from Leo Peter's report that he is speaking of the same thing. But knowledge of the language is a special thing when proper names are involved.*[55]

He extends the passage by spelling out circumstances in which Leo Peter and Rudolph Lingens associate the same thought with "Dr. Gustav Lauben was wounded," but one which differs from that expressed by Dr. Lauben himself. This is already troubling, since, surely, if Mr. Peter were to report "Dr. Gustav Lauben told me a few days ago that he, Dr. Gustav Lauben, was wounded," his remark would be true, despite the fact that the

---

[54] See also "On Sense and Reference" (Geach and Black 1970, p. 58, my emphasis):

In the case of an actual proper name such as 'Aristotle' opinions as to the sense may differ. It might, for instance, be taken to be the following: the pupil of Plato and teacher of Alexander the Great. Anybody who does this will attach another sense to the sentence 'Aristotle was born in Stagira' than will a man who takes as the sense of the name: the teacher of Alexander the Great who was born in Stagira. *So long as the reference remains the same, such variations of sense may be tolerated, although they are to be avoided in the theoretical structure of a demonstrative science and ought not to occur in a perfect language.*

Note, the emphasis here is not on constructing a semantic theory that systematically describes ordinary language, but on what can be "tolerated" when using it, but must be avoided in serious science.

[55] "Thought," p. 332 in Frege (1997), my emphasis.

Fregean thought supposedly expressed by Dr. Lauben is, by hypothesis, different from the Fregean thought ascribed to him in Mr. Peter's report.

So far, we have different senses associated with the use of a name versus a use of the first-person singular pronoun. Frege continues the passage by sketching a scenario in which the same name is associated with different senses by different agents.

> Suppose further that Herbert Garner knows that Dr. Gustav Lauben was born on 13 September 1875 in N.N. and this is not true of anyone else; suppose, however, that he does not know where Dr. Lauben now lives nor indeed anything else about him. On the other hand, suppose Leo Peter does not know that Dr. Lauben was born on 13 September 1875 in N.N. Then as far as the proper name 'Dr. Gustav Lauben' is concerned, Herbert Garner and Leo Peter do not speak the same language, although they do designate the same man with this name; *for they do not know that they are doing so. Therefore Herbert Garner does not associate the same thought with the sentence "Dr. Gustav Lauben was wounded" as Leo Peter wants to express with it.*[56]

These passages illustrate the extent of the problem posed by attitude ascriptions like (27) for the bedrock Fregean assumption that all thoughts are transparent.

Although Frege didn't think of this strategy, a diehard Fregean might wish to respond by assimilating (27a,b) to (28).

28. There is a person (physicist) x, such that x = Richard Feynman and for everyone y who knows anything about x there is a mode M of presentation that both determines x and puts y *en rapport* with x such that y believes [mm]Brilliant (M)[mm].

But this has its own problems. First, the elaborate analysis risks assimilating virtually all normal attitude ascriptions—including (27a) which, on the face of it, doesn't involve quantifying-in—to what were initially supposed by the Fregean to be special cases of quantifying-in. Second, it makes the new lesson one (who already understands 'Richard Feynman

---

[56] Ibid., p. 333, my emphasis. The way Frege concludes this passage is revealing:

Accordingly, with a proper name, it is a matter of the way that the object so designated is presented. This may happen in different ways, and to every such way there corresponds a special sense of a sentence containing the proper name. The different thoughts thus obtained from the same sentences *correspond in truth-value*. . . Nevertheless the differences must be recognized. *So we must really stipulate that for every proper name there shall be just one associated manner of presentation of the object so designated.*

If Frege were really giving a descriptive semantic theory for natural language—instead of laying out principles for theoretical uses of language—"stipulating" would be out of place. Also, if semantics were the project, attitude ascriptions *differing in truth value*, due to different senses attached to the same name, would have to be considered.

was brilliant', 'believe', and 'assert') must master before interpreting attitude ascriptions with that complement clause even more difficult—since now one must be instructed on both ordinary quantification, and the special Frege-style twist involving clauses with free occurrences of variables, before comprehension can take place. Third, the analysis misses the apparent implication of (27a,b) that some one proposition was believed by all. Finally, it treats (29) in a way that reinforces the problems already found in its treatment of (26).

29. Mary's assertion that Feynman wasn't brilliant explicitly contradicts what everyone who knew anything about him believed, and many have asserted.

For these reasons, the use of names, attitude ascriptions, quantifying-in, and anaphora puts pressure on Frege's doctrine of transparent thoughts. This shouldn't be surprising. Although his general semantic framework was a brilliant innovation, the modifications needed to render it capable of providing a comprehensive description of natural language go far beyond his primary linguistic goal, which was the creation of a proper language for logic and mathematics, and the articulation of principles needed to understand it.

7. TIME, TENSE, AND INDEXICALITY

Similar concerns arise for Frege's views of tense and indexicals. For Frege, thoughts are true, or false, timelessly. Nevertheless, many sentences appear to express true thoughts on some occasions and false thoughts on others, without changing meaning. If this really is so, then the meanings of these sentences cannot be the thoughts they are used to express. In fact, Frege regarded such sentences as incomplete, requiring completion by a time—often the time of utterance—in order to express a thought.

> But are there not thoughts which are true today but false in six months' time? The thought, for example, that the tree there is covered with green leaves, will surely be false in six months' time. No, for it is not the same thought at all. The words 'this tree is covered with green leaves' are not sufficient by themselves for the utterance, the time of utterance is involved as well. Without the time-specification thus given we have not a complete thought, i.e. we have no thought at all. *Only a sentence with the time-specification filled out, a sentence complete in every respect, expresses a thought.* But this thought, if it is true, is true not only today or tomorrow but timelessly.[57]

This point about contextual completion is extended to other forms of completion for sentences containing indexicals, both temporal and otherwise.

---

[57] "Thought," p. 343 in Frege (1997), my emphasis.

If a time indication is conveyed by the present tense one must know when the sentence was uttered to grasp the thought correctly. *Therefore the time of utterance is part of the expression of the thought.* If someone wants to say today what he expressed yesterday using the word 'today', he will replace this word with 'yesterday'. Although the thought is the same its verbal expression must be different in order that the change of sense which would otherwise be affected by the differing times of utterance may be cancelled out. *The case is the same with words like 'here' and 'there'. In all such cases the mere wording, as it can be preserved in writing, is not the complete expression of the thought; the knowledge of certain conditions accompanying the utterance, which are used as means of expressing the thought, is needed for us to grasp the thought correctly.* Pointing the finger, hand gestures, glances may belong here too. The same utterances containing the word 'I' in the mouths of different men will express different thoughts of which some may be true, others false.[58]

For Frege, present tense sentences, and those containing indexicals, are incomplete. To express a thought they must be supplemented—sometimes by the time of utterance, sometimes by hand gestures or other demonstrations, and sometimes by the speaker. It is the combination of the grammatical sentence plus elements from the context of utterance that expresses a thought. It is as if times, demonstrations, or speakers, were added, as extra nonlinguistic constituents, to the words of sentences to yield *completed sentences*, the senses of which are always true, or always false.[59]

The challenge is to accommodate this while remaining faithful to Frege's central doctrines. Again, I turn to Kripke (2008) for an illuminating attempt to do so. On his suggested analysis, the words in (30a–c) express not thoughts, but senses determining concepts that map times t onto truth iff Scott is sick at t (for (30a)), sick on the day of t (for (30b)), or sick on the day before t (for (30c)).

30a. Scott Soames is sick (now).
  b. Scott Soames is sick today.
  c. Scott Soames was sick yesterday.

'Now', 'today', and 'yesterday' designate, respectively, the identity function on times, the function mapping times to days in which they occur, and the function mapping times to the day before they occur. In each case, one constituent of the *completed sentence* is the time u_t of utterance, which *refers to itself* by virtue of expressing an *acquaintance-based sense* that determines u_t. This sense is, of course, a constituent of the thought expressed by the completed sentence (along with a sense that determines the function denoted by 'now', 'today', or 'yesterday'). As a result, the thoughts expressed by the completed sentences are eternally true, or false,

---

[58] Ibid., p. 332, my emphasis.
[59] Salmon (2002) reconstructs Frege in this way.

depending on whether, in the case of (30a), u_t is a time at which I am sick, or, in the case of (30b), the day in which u_t occurs is one in which I am sick, or, in the case of (30c), the day before the one in which u_t occurs is a day in which I am sick.

This approach can be extended to (31).

31. I am sick (said by Scott at t).

Here, the words require two completions—a time and a speaker. On the occasion imagined, the *completed sentence* contains the time u_t of utterance and the compound constituent 'I'-plus-Scott. The former refers to itself by virtue of expressing a sense that determines u_t *that can be grasped only at* u_t,[60] while the latter refers to me by virtue of expressing a sense determining me that *only I am able to grasp,* due to the fact that I am acquainted with myself in a way that no one else is, or could be. As a result, the thought expressed by the completed sentence is a timeless truth, or falsehood, that *only I am able to entertain.*

This Frege-inspired account is partly true to Frege, and partly not. One part that is found in Frege is the privacy of first-person thoughts, discussed in "Thought."

> Now everyone is presented to himself in a special and primitive way, in which he is presented to no one else. So when Dr. Lauben has the thought that he was wounded [which he expresses to himself "I was wounded"], he will probably be basing it on this primitive way in which he is presented to himself. And only Dr. Lauben himself can grasp thoughts specified in this way.[61]

Two parts of the account *not* found in Frege are (i) the extension of the reasoning about first-person cases to sentences containing 'now', as well as to ordinary uses of the present tense that carry a time indication, and (ii) the descriptive definitions of other temporal indexicals in terms of the time of utterance. Point (i) involves the idea that (to paraphrase Frege on the first person) *every moment t is presented to us at t in a special and primitive way, in which it is not presented at any other time. So when, at t, we have the thought that we are hungry, or that we are hungry then* [which we express "we are hungry" or "we are hungry now"], *we will probably be basing it on this primitive way in which t is presented to us at t. And only at t can we grasp thoughts about t specified in this way, i.e. thoughts containing this special, acquaintance-based sense.* Point (ii) involves treating 'today' and 'yesterday' as designating functions the arguments of which are the times of utterance and the values of which are, respectively, *the day in which the utterance occurred,* and *the day before the utterance occurred.*

Not only does Frege *not* explicitly commit himself to points (i) and (ii), but a passage already cited from "Thought" points in a different direction.

---

[60] This condition also applies in the analysis of the sentences in (30).
[61] "Thought," p. 333 in Frege (1997).

If someone wants to say today what he expressed yesterday using the word 'today', he will replace this word with 'yesterday'. *Although the thought is the same its verbal expression must be different in order that the change of sense which would otherwise be affected by the differing times of utterance may be cancelled out.* The case is the same with words like 'here' and 'there'.[62]

According to this passage, one who accepts, or assertively utters, (30b) on day d, believes or asserts the very same thought as one who accepts, or assertively utters, (30c) on d + 1. But on Kripke's Frege-inspired analysis, this is not true, since the thoughts expressed by those sentences on the two days include distinct senses presenting different utterance times, as well as distinct senses presenting different functions from times to days. These thoughts are not just different; they can't be entertained at the same time, since *neither is capable of being entertained at any moment other than the moment it was expressed.*

Despite this, Frege's observation that, e.g., the thought expressed by (30b) on day d is the same as the thought expressed by (30c) on day d + 1 was not a silly mistake, but an important insight reflecting the way we normally report beliefs, assertions, and other propositional attitudes. Suppose, for example, that on Monday Mary assertively utters, "Scott is sick today." On Tuesday, John can *correctly* report "Mary said that Scott was sick yesterday." Under the standard assumption, endorsed by Frege, this report is correct only if the proposition expressed and asserted by Mary on Monday is the same as the one expressed by the complement clause of John's report on Tuesday.[63] What makes this case difficult for Frege is that Mary's cognitive perspective on the day, Monday, when she referred to it as "today" was, we may imagine, different from John's cognitive perspective when he referred to it a day later as "yesterday." Different and irrelevant. No matter what cognitive perspectives they had—even if they were confused about the dates, or days of the week—John's report will be correct iff it was made one day after Mary's utterance. Since uses of 'today' and 'yesterday' *always* refer, respectively, to the day of, or the day before, the utterance (no matter what dates speakers have in mind), John's report will be true iff the *referent* of his use of 'yesterday' was also the *referent* of Mary's use of 'today'. In short, our reporting practices suggest that the thoughts that utterances containing these words are used to assert must include nontransparent singular propositions that are identical because the referents of 'today' at d and 'yesterday' at d + 1 are identical (whether

[62] Ibid., p. 332, my emphasis.
[63] One way to (at least partly) accommodate Kripke's Frege-friendly analysis would be to recognize that assertive utterances often result in multiple assertions. (See chapter 7 of Soames (2010a).) In particular, Mary's utterance might plausibly be taken to assert *both* a thought that is entertainable only on day d and the non-Fregean singular thought involving d itself (the entertainment of which is not time-restricted). If John's assertive utterance were treated similarly, it might truly be taken to report that thought.

or not those utterances also express, or assert, thoughts that include Fregean senses for the days that are their referents, or for times of utterance that are then mapped onto those days).

The passage from Frege suggests that he takes his observation about 'yesterday' and 'today' to generalize, and it does. If utterances of ...*today*... and ...*yesterday*... on different days can express the same proposition, then the same is true of utterances of ...*I*... said by me, utterances of ...*you*... said addressing me, and utterances of ...*he*... said demonstrating me. One main reason we have indexicals in natural language is precisely to provide a way for the same thoughts to be expressed from different perspectives. This can be true only if those thoughts are nontransparent singular propositions, rather than transparent Fregean senses. Having gotten this far, we can easily comprehend how an utterance by Venus, speaking to her companion Mars, might assert something true (even though neither the way Venus thinks of herself, nor the way Mars does, could have been modes of presentation of Venus for the ancients).

32. The ancients asserted, and believed, when they saw me in the morning, that I was visible only in the morning, and they asserted, and believed, when they saw me in the evening, that I was visible only in the evening.

As this discussion shows, the correct analysis of indexicals must be at least partly non-Fregean. Frege himself was pulled in two directions without resolving the tension between them. On the one hand, he was wedded to the idea that thoughts are always epistemically transparent—which led him to private, first-person senses as constituents of incommunicable thoughts. On the other hand, he was sensitive to our practice of using indexicals to abstract away from specific cognitive perspectives in reporting attitudes, where nothing stronger than sameness of indexical reference is required. There is no good way of reconciling this reporting practice—plus the Fregean assumption that ⌜A Vs that S⌝ reports an attitude that the referent of A bears to the thought/proposition expressed by S—with the refusal to admit nontransparent thoughts/propositions. However, a limited *rapprochement* may well be possible if (i) nontransparent singular propositions are allowed as objects of (some) beliefs and assertions, (ii) some thoughts/propositions essentially involve private ways of thinking about oneself and time-restricted ways of thinking about a time t at t, and (iii) an explanation can be given of how believing or asserting the latter always brings with it belief and assertion of corresponding propositions of the former kind.

Although I believe that such a limited *rapprochement* is possible,[64] I doubt that the needed private, or present-time-restricted, propositions can be made to fit the expanded Fregean framework that Kripke sketches.

---

[64] See Soames (2014c and forthcoming).

One problem concerns the so-called acquaintance-based senses needed for each possible agent and each time. It is, I think, plausible that each agent A has a way of thinking about A that no one else could use to think about A, and that for each time t there is a way of thinking about t, when t is occurring, that we can't use to think about t at other times. But the Fregean picture sketched by Kripke requires much more. In addition, each acquaintance-based agent sense must differ from every other such agent sense, and each acquaintance-based time sense must differ from every other such time sense. Moreover, each of these senses must *rigidly* determine its referent in every possible circumstance. There is, I am afraid, no reason to think that these conditions are fulfilled.[65]

Imagine Rip Van Winkle dropping off to sleep and put into cryogenic stasis. Twenty years later he wakes up in exactly the same environment, feeling exactly the same way he did before dropping off, looking at the same things appearing in exactly the same way, and having just the same internal dialogue with himself as before. Unaware of having been asleep, he notices no change—since there has been no change in experience. Doubtless, if he thinks to himself, "It is just about noon on September 14, 2010"—exactly as he did a few seconds before falling asleep—the Fregean will take the new thought (which is timelessly false) to be different from the old thought (which is timelessly true). For Kripke's Fregean, this can only be so only if the acquaintance-based sense associated with use of the present tense has changed. But how can it have changed? Everything about Rip is qualitatively the same—every twinge, tingle, appearance, image, and the like, is as before. We may even suppose that he is molecule for molecule identical at the two times. In short, there is no change in cognitive perspective at all, which means there can be no change in Fregean sense. The acquaintance-based time senses required by Kripke's Fregean analysis do not exist.[66]

The same is true of the acquaintance-based agent senses the analysis requires, as an example from David Kaplan (1989) illustrates.[67] We are asked to imagine two unfortunate identical twins, Castor and Pollux, born ten minutes apart, who are separated and kept in scientifically controlled environments. As a result of astounding genetic and environmental engineering, every sound, sight, smell, touch, taste, or other experience had by one is accompanied by a qualitatively identical experience had by the other. In fact, they are molecule for molecule identical. Both have learned the same words, both utter the same sentences, and whenever one does, or says, anything, the other does, or says, the same (in the next room where he is confined). Each has been told he has a brother, and each thinks, "I am older than my brother," but only one of them is right. For the

[65] A more extended discussion of these points can be found in Soames (forthcoming).
[66] The example is based on one from Perry (1977).
[67] Kaplan (1989), p. 531.

Fregean, the two private agent-centered thoughts must differ because the two acquaintance-based agent senses must differ. But since the cognitive perspectives of Castor and Pollux don't differ at all, there can be no difference in the Fregean senses or thoughts they entertain. Hence, Kripke's Frege-inspired picture collapses.

If the Kripke version of Frege is incorrect, what then do first-person, and present-tense, thoughts amount to? Consider an agent A who understands and accepts *'He is in danger'* when looking at a reflection of someone—who is in fact A himself—in a store window, while not accepting *'I am in danger'*. It is plausible that A could use these two sentences to express the same nontransparent singular proposition. A believes this proposition because he accepts it when presented in the first way, even though he doesn't accept it when presented in the second way. To accept the proposition when presented by 'I am in danger' A must be in a special first-person cognitive state. The difference between "(immediate) first-person thought" and other thought isn't a difference in what might be called "third-person propositions" believed, but a difference in cognitive states by which they are believed.[68] For any agent A to think "in the (immediate) first-person way" that A is in danger is for A to "(immediately) self-ascribe" *being in danger*. This cognitive state is directly linked to one's motivational states—e.g., to the state *strongly wishing to avoid danger*—in a manner in which other ways of believing are not. Thus, the connection between thinking in the (immediate) first-person way that one is in danger and being motivated to act is direct, whereas the connection between believing this in other ways and being motivated to act is not. The crucial point, in comparing this view to the Fregean alternative, is that two agents—A and B—can be in *identical* cognitive states in which they (immediately) self-ascribe *being in danger,* by virtue of which they believe *different things*—namely, *that A is in danger* and *that B is*.[69]

How best to conceptualize this picture in cognitive and semantic theories is currently a contentious matter. On one approach, advocated in Perry (1977, 1979, 2006), the things believed and asserted are always third-person propositions, entertainable by anyone at any time. On this view, immediate first-person thought isn't a matter of coming to believe any special first-person, or present-tense, propositions; rather it is a matter of coming to believe ordinary propositions in a special first-person, present-tense way. The worries about this are that (i) in cases like the one just described, we are strongly inclined to describe A as lacking a certain belief that, when he at last comes to have it, he will correctly express by saying "Wow.

---

[68] Since the case is both first-person and present-tense, I combine the two strands into one, which I call "immediate first-person" thought. The strands are, of course, separable.

[69] Important relevant literature for understanding variants of the view just sketched includes David Kaplan (1989), David Lewis (1979), John Perry (1977, 1979, 2006), Nathan Salmon (1984), Soames (2014c and forthcoming), and Stalnaker (2006, 2008).

Although before I didn't, I now do *believe* that I am in danger"; and (ii) such first-person "bcliefs" seem to function like other beliefs in inference and explanation. The second approach, advocated in David Lewis (1979), holds that first-person self-ascription is genuine belief, but the thing believed is the property one ascribes to oneself, rather than a proposition. Here the worries include (i) that the view requires a tortuous reconstrual according to which the things believed are *always* properties (though of radically different sorts) and (ii) that it has the strange result that when I sincerely say "I will win" and you reply "No, I will win," it follows that if we were both expressing our sincere beliefs, then there is something we both believe—namely the thing we both asserted—even though we are diametrically at odds.[70] The third approach is suggested in Soames (2014c and forthcoming)—according to which first-person, present-tense beliefs are relations to genuine propositions that can be entertained only by oneself and only at the present time. The challenges for this approach are to develop a general account of propositions that explains (a) how this can be so, despite the fact that no constituents of simple propositions of this sort are, in principle, cognizable by only one person, or at only one time; (b) how beliefs in such private propositions can be straightforwardly reportable by others who can't entertain them; and (c) how one's beliefs and assertions of such propositions guarantee that one believes corresponding singular propositions of the usual sort. These points will be revisited in chapter 9.

For now, two final shortcomings of the Fregean treatment of indexicals should be noted. The first is that it can't plausibly be generalized to cover demonstrative uses of terms like 'he', 'she', 'this', and 'that'. Applying Kripke's treatment of 'today' or 'yesterday' to these expressions would require taking them to designate functions defined on some combination of speakers, times, and demonstrations provided by contexts of utterance. Suppose 'he' were taken to designate the function that assigns *the male to whom the speaker intends to refer* to the arguments—the speaker, the time of utterance, and the demonstration used. Nothing of this sort will work, since it is no part of the information carried by the proposition John asserts when he utters (33)

33. He [pointing at me] lives in North America.

that anyone is speaking, that anyone has been demonstrated, or that I am the one demonstrated. Rather, what is asserted is the singular proposition that predicates *living in North America* of me. This proposition is true, and would have been so in any possible circumstances in which I reside in North America—including those in which John never refers to me, but utters (33) in a qualitatively identical situation pointing at a European

[70] An updated version of Lewis's view of propositions as properties is defended by Jeff Speaks in chapter 5 of King, Soames, and Speaks (2014).

who merely looks like me. The best the Fregean might do is to add me, the person demonstrated, *as an element of the completed sentence.* But this is also problematic, since the strategy requires a Fregean sense expressed by me (in my unlikely role as a constituent of the completed sentence) that *both* rigidly presents me (and no one else) in every possible circumstance in which the thought could be considered for truth or falsity, and is used by the speaker, John, to single me out when he asserts the thought. Since it is most unlikely that there is any Fregean sense satisfying both conditions, the burden of proof is on the Fregean to show that there is.

The final shortcoming of my reconstruction of Kripke's Fregean proposal is that it fails to properly distinguish the context-sensitivity of tense operators—like the present tense—from the context-sensitivity of temporal indexicals—like 'now'. That reconstruction correctly accounts for the fact that the thoughts expressed by (33a,b) are either identical, or trivially equivalent.

33a. The person who occupies office 107 MHP lives in Santa Monica.
  b. The person who now occupies office 107 MHP lives in Santa Monica.

However, those expressed by (34a,b) clearly are not equivalent, since either could be true, when the other wasn't.

34a. In the future, it will be the case that the person who occupies office 107 MHP lives in Santa Monica.
  b. In the future, it will be the case that the person who now occupies office 107 MHP lives in Santa Monica.

Nothing in the Fregean account sketched above explains this, nor is there any indication that Frege ever noticed this important difference. However, as shown in Salmon (1989), it can be explained in a manner that combines some important elements of Frege's thought with the existence of non-transparent singular propositions.[71]

8. THE PHILOSOPHICAL FOUNDATIONS OF FREGE'S MATHEMATICAL PROJECT

Frege's motivations for reducing arithmetic to logic were a mixture of mathematical and philosophical concerns. On the mathematical side, arithmetic needed formalization. He conceived of his project before the formalization and dissemination of the now well-known Dedekind/Peano axioms of arithmetic, all of which can be seen to emerge, unheralded, in *The Foundations of Arithmetic.* Doing for arithmetic what Euclid did for geometry was certainly one of his goals. Accomplishing this task, he thought, required some conception of what the natural numbers are, which led him

---

[71] A very brief explanation of Salmon's main idea is presented in Soames (2010c).

to his elegant and celebrated conception of number. At this point, the idea of deriving the basic truths about numbers from the most fundamental truths of logic appeared to be a genuine and exciting possibility.

The point was not to derive arithmetic, and much of the rest of mathematics, from the different but related discipline of logic—which is close to our contemporary way of viewing the attempt. Rather, it was to derive large parts of mathematics from the most fundamental part of mathematics—i.e., deductive science—itself. Today's conception of logic—with its sharp separation between proof theory and model theory—was not Frege's. For him, logic was the study of the fundamental laws of truth preservation—which had epistemological, metaphysical, and semantic/linguistic components. On the epistemological side, he saw the laws of truth preservation as the normative principles governing rationally justified thought, by which we gain new knowledge by inference from known premises. On the metaphysical side, logic was also the study of a special domain of entities—most notably concepts (of various levels) and their extensions. Hence, when he saw that natural numbers could be seen as extensions of concepts he naturally came to think of them as "logical objects" too. On the semantic and more broadly linguistic side, his concerns drove him to discussions of the relationship between truth and assertion, sense and reference, and to a stunning analysis of the propositions expressed by quantificational sentences that goes well beyond the assignment of determinate truth conditions needed in what we now think of as logic proper. For him, logic encompassed much of what we now see as semantics, pragmatics, the epistemology of the a priori, and the metaphysics of mathematics. All of these played roles in his logicist reduction.

However, the epistemological motivation for the reduction was, I think, paramount. The aim was to remove every element of doubt concerning our knowledge of the truths of mathematics by showing them to be derivable, by self-evident steps, from correct definitions of mathematical notions in terms of purely logical concepts, plus self-evident principles of logic, known to be true a priori, with no need for further justification. Having looked in some detail at the strategy and techniques employed in the reduction, we can now address the epistemological goals driving the project. Were they achievable, and did Frege achieve them?

In addressing this question, I will, for the sake of argument, take certain aspects of his starting point for granted. Setting aside questions about his special Axiom V, which will be taken up in section 9, I will here suppose that the axioms of his logical system are self-evident and known a priori to be true. The rules of inference used in his formal proofs will also be assumed to be self-evidently truth preserving, and known a priori to be so. The focus of our epistemological questions will be on the definitions of arithmetical notions. If they are known, or knowable, a priori, then it seems that the arithmetical truths derivable from them plus the axioms of logic must also be. If they are also self-evident in Frege's strong sense, then any doubts concerning the justification of an arithmetical truth derivable with their help can satisfactorily be put to rest in the manner he envisioned.

How, then, did Frege justify his definitions? He could, one might think, have simply taken them to be true by stipulation. When one stipulates that one means M by a word w, the question of justification does not arise, since one is not reporting a preexisting fact, but signaling that when one uses w the thought one is to be understood as expressing is one to which w contributes M. So, if we understand Frege's definitions as stipulative, then, of course, the thoughts expressed by the arithmetical sentences he derives are known a priori, and justified in his very strong sense. In itself, however, this doesn't have the philosophical punch Frege was looking for, since the project is to show that the truths of *arithmetic* are known, or knowable, a priori, and capable of being given the desired justification. For Frege, *thoughts* are what is known. So when we speak of the truths of arithmetic being known, it must be the thoughts expressed by arithmetical sentences that are known. There is no suggestion in Frege that by *arithmetical truths* he means thoughts that only he, or those who have read his work, have come to associate with arithmetical sentences. No, he seems to mean the thoughts that everyone familiar with arithmetic has in mind. If so, his definitions of arithmetical notions can't be purely stipulative.

Although he seldom alluded to this question, he did discuss it once at some length, a decade after he completed his work on the reduction of arithmetic to logic. Writing first about stipulative definitions in logic and mathematics, he says:

> In constructing a system the same group of signs . . . may occur over and over again. This gives us reason for introducing a simple sign . . . with *the stipulation* that this simple sign is always to take the place of that group of signs. . . . Now when a simple sign is thus introduced to replace a group of signs, such a stipulation is a definition. *The simple sign thereby acquires a sense which is the same as that of the group of signs.* Definitions are not absolutely essential to a system. We could make do with the original group of signs. . . . A sign has a meaning once one has been bestowed upon it by definition, and the definition goes over into a sentence asserting an identity. *Of course the sentence is really only a tautology and does not add to our knowledge.* It contains a truth which is so self-evident that it appears devoid of content. . . . *In fact it is not possible to prove something new from a definition alone that would be unprovable without it. When something that looks like a definition really makes it possible to prove something which could not be proved before, then it is no mere definition but must conceal something which would have either to be proved as a theorem or accepted as an axiom.*[72]

---

[72] Frege (1914), pp. 207–10, my emphasis.

It is obvious from these remarks that the definitions that play a crucial role in the derivation of arithmetic from logic are not stipulative and are no mere abbreviations. Frege makes this evident with his remarks two pages later.

> We have a simple sign with a long established use. We believe that we can give a logical analysis of its sense, obtaining a complex expression which in our opinion has the same sense. . . . The sense of the complex expression must be yielded by the way it is put together. *That it agrees with the sense of the long established simple sign is not a matter of arbitrary stipulation, but can only be recognized by immediate insight.* No doubt we speak of definition in this case too. It might be called an "analytic definition" to distinguish it from the first case. . . . *In this second case there remains no room for an arbitrary stipulation, because the simple sign already has a sense.*[73]

It seems from this that Frege's ingenious definitions of arithmetical notions must have been intended to be "analytic definitions," in the sense sketched in the passage. But are they really? Can one tell *by immediate insight* that these "definitions" not only produce the desired mathematical results, but also *capture the senses* of the simple arithmetical expressions that have been used throughout the ages.[74] Although it would be nice to think that they do, it is hard to reconcile this idea with Frege's uncompromising commitment to the transparency of thought. What was it he said about this when discussing Dr. Lauben?

> Dr. Gustav Lauben says, "I was wounded." Leo Peter hears this and remarks some days later, "Dr. Gustav Lauben was wounded." Does this sentence express the same thought as the one Dr. Lauben uttered himself? Suppose that Rudolph Lingens was present when Dr. Lauben spoke and now hears what is related by Leo Peter. *If the same thought was uttered by Dr. Lauben and Leo Peter, then Rudolph Lingens, who is fully master of the language and remembers what Dr. Lauben said in his presence, must know at once from Leo Peter's report that he is speaking of the same thing.*[75]

With this in mind, suppose (i) that Dr. Lauben says, "There are two prime numbers greater than 7 but less than 17," (ii) that Leo Peter utters its long and complicated Fregean counterpart, about classes of concepts with equinumerous extensions, and (iii) that Rudolf Lingens hears both. If Frege is right about transparency, we must simply ask Mr. Lingens whether he "knows at once" from Leo Peter's remark that he is speaking of the same thing as Dr. Lauben. Unless Mr. Lingens has read the *Basic Laws of Arithmetic* in advance, there is little doubt that he won't. So, it seems, Frege must conclude the thoughts are different.

[73] Ibid., p. 210, my emphasis.
[74] Currie (1982), pp. 103–7, contains a good discussion of this issue.
[75] "Thought," p. 332 in Frege (1997), my emphasis.

In addition to being something he would not be very happy with, this result represents a fundamental conflict between Frege's philosophy of language and his philosophy of mathematics. Even if one puts aside the issue of transparency, his attractive conception of thoughts—as structured complexes the constituents of which are semantic contents of the constituents of sentences that express them—leads to great complexity in the thoughts expressed by the "translations" of arithmetical sentences into sentences of pure logic arising from Frege's "definitions." It is hard to justify taking simple arithmetical sentences to express those thoughts. Nor can Frege give up his structured conception in favor of a view that collapses all thoughts necessarily equivalent to one another into a single thought, thereby countenancing only one thought that is true necessarily. Since thoughts are, for Frege, the things known and believed, this would mean that whenever there is at least one sentence S such that ⌜A knows/ believes (the thought) that S⌝ is true, the ascription will remain true for all sentences necessarily equivalent to S. In addition to being wildly implausible,[76] such a view undermines Frege's project of justifying and explaining our a priori knowledge of arithmetic and higher mathematics by reducing them to logic. Since everyone already knows at least one necessary truth a priori (with the strongest possible justification), and all arithmetical truths are necessary, this view of thoughts would lead to the result that all arithmetical truths are already known a priori (with such justification)— thereby undermining the need for Frege's reduction.

Necessity (in the sense in which it is now commonly understood) did not play a significant role in Frege's philosophy, so the alternative just sketched (which was to gain adherents decades later) would not have occurred, or appealed, to him. However, a variant of the idea is worth mentioning. Instead of identifying thoughts expressed by necessarily equivalent sentences, one might identify thoughts expressed by analytically equivalent ones—i.e., where sentences are analytically equivalent iff each is a logical consequence of the other, plus definitions of the terms involved. However, this too is no help to Frege. Since reducing arithmetic and higher mathematics to logic brings with it the analytic equivalence of mathematical truths with logical truths, we get the absurd result that because these sentences express the same thought, mathematics doesn't extend the knowledge of anyone who already knows any analytic truth. Frege would never have stood for this. Nor would this identification of thoughts have solved the problem of showing the truths of arithmetic and higher mathematics to be logical consequences of fundamental logical truths plus *non-stipulative* definitions of mathematical notions *as commonly*

---

[76] Among other things, this view entails that if (i) believing a conjunction involves believing both conjuncts, and (ii) no one does, or could, simultaneously believe every thought, then (iii) no one does, or could, believe anything that is necessarily false. Since (i) and (ii) are true, while (iii) is false, the view is false. See Soames (1987) for discussion.

understood. Instead, the problem of establishing the credentials of his definitions, when understood as descriptive analyses rather than mere stipulations, is already present in characterizing mathematical truths as analytic, when these sentences are understood in the ordinary, non-stipulative way.

What can be said on Frege's behalf in addressing this problem? On the plus side, it is hard not to be impressed by the elegance and naturalness of his conception of the natural numbers, and the familiar arithmetical operations on them, as well as the obvious correspondence between counting the number of F's and explaining what the Fregean *number of F's* amounts to. On the negative side, it must be noted that, historically, his reduction of talk of numbers to talk of classes or sets was followed by other reductions that are equally effective in specifying correct truth conditions of arithmetical sentences—despite the fact that the set-theoretic constructions identified with the natural numbers, and with arithmetical operations on them, are different from, and incompatible with, those provided by Frege. Although each of these reductions is elegant and serviceable when considered on its own, it is hard to see how each could provide the, or even a, metaphysically correct identification of the number 7, for example—let alone how each could provide the, or even a, correct analysis of the meanings of arithmetical sentences, *as ordinarily understood.* It is conceivable that one of these reductions might be shown to be definitely superior to all others. However, no one has shown this yet, and it is not clear how, if at all, that could be done. In the absence of this, it is hard to justify taking any reduction, including Frege's, (i) to correctly identify the numbers, (ii) to show arithmetic, as ordinarily understood, to be analytic, (iii) to explain how it is that we know a priori the familiar arithmetical truths we all (pre-theoretically) take ourselves to know, or (iv) to provide the kind of maximally strong epistemic justification of the truths of arithmetic that Frege sought.[77]

Nevertheless, the philosophical picture is not entirely bleak. Let us grant that an agent who uses Frege's definitions stipulatively will know a priori the corresponding thought T the agent uses an arithmetical sentence S to express—provided that S is a consequence *that the agent has actually derived,* of the definitions plus Frege's fundamental logical truths. We further grant that for any arithmetical sentence S, and corresponding thought T the agent uses S to express, T will be *capable of being known a priori* provided that S is a *first-order* logical consequence of Frege's fundamental logical truths plus his definitions. Assuming his account of the justification of these logical truths plus the logical rules of inference, we may also grant that each such T will be *capable of being justified* in the strongest possible manner, from self-evident principles that both need no justification and are ineliminably presupposed by our reasoning about all subjects. All of this we grant, for the sake of argument. We will also put

---

[77] Benacerraf (1965) is the classic discussion of these points.

aside how, or even whether, we know ordinary arithmetical truths when understood in the normal way, prior to the reduction. From this perspective, our final assumption is that we *can* recognize, once the reduction is provided, that the thought expressed by any arithmetical sentence S, understood in the normal way, will be true iff the thought expressed by S, as understood by someone who uses Frege's definitions stipulatively, is true. Indeed, let us assume that we can recognize this to be so, simply by grasping the relevant thoughts, tracing how they are systematically correlated by Frege's analysis, and becoming correctly convinced—without appeal to empirical evidence for justification—that all such correlated thoughts will be true together, or false together.

Given all this, we can conclude that for any arithmetical sentence S, and thought T that S, *as ordinarily understood*, is used to express, (i) T will be *capable of being known a priori* provided that S is a *first-order* logical consequence of Frege's fundamental logical truths plus his definitions, and (ii) T can be given an epistemic justification as strong as our justification for believing that his analysis of number correlates the thoughts expressed by arithmetical sentences, as ordinarily understood, with those expressed by the same sentences, as stipulatively understood, *in a way that always matches truths with truths, and falsehoods with falsehoods*. These conclusions are not trivial, and one can understand how one who accepted Frege's assumptions about the apriority of logic would take them as constituting philosophical progress. *Given his assumptions, plus the observation that one can know a priori that his analysis of number is truth/falsity preserving, he will have shown that the relevant arithmetical truths are indeed knowable a priori, as well as capable of being justified by appropriately weighty considerations.* Whether that justification approaches—let alone exceeds—the justification we all had for accepting the Peano axioms *prior* to Frege's derivation of them from his laws of logic is, however, highly doubtful. So it remains questionable that the derivation puts arithmetical truths on a stronger epistemological footing than they were before. Nor have we settled how, or even whether, anyone had a priori knowledge of arithmetical truths prior to the reduction. Perhaps there are compelling stories to be told about all this. But if so, Frege didn't tell them.

9. RUSSELL'S PARADOX: A MATHEMATICAL AND PHILOSOPHICAL THREAT TO LOGICISM

Up to now, I have been discussing Frege's derivation of arithmetic from logic as if it were technically sound, even though some questions can be raised about the nature and extent of its philosophical significance. There is, however, a technical problem that made it unacceptable in its original form. The problem was discovered in 1902 by Bertrand Russell, who was then developing similar ideas about the relationship between logic and arithmetic (and mathematics in general). Russell, who had been thinking along lines very similar to Frege's, presented his ideas informally in *The Principles of Mathematics*, published in 1903 (much as Frege informally presented his analysis of number in *The Foundations of Arithmetic*). It is a mark of the lack of attention that Frege's work initially attracted that Russell didn't hear about it until he was far along on his project, and had, in effect, rediscovered much of the central thrust of Frege's analysis of the natural numbers. Like Frege, he conceived of numbers as classes (also called "sets"). For example, whereas for Frege (in *The Foundations of Arithmetic*) the number 2 is the class of *concepts* C *the extensions of which* contain an x and y such that (i) x ≠ y, and (ii) for all z, if z is a member of *the extension of* C, then z = x or z = y, for Russell concepts aren't mentioned; the number 2 is identified with the class of *classes* C such that (i) x ≠ y, and (ii) for all z, if z is a member of C, then z = x or z = y.

Another similarity was that both Frege and Russell recognized a universal set—i.e., the set of all objects, where sets themselves count as objects. (For Frege, this set is the extension of the first-level concept *being x such that x = x*.) However, Russell noticed a problem that arose in his study of Georg Cantor's proof that for any set s, the set of all subsets of s (often called the *power set* of s) is larger than s—in the sense that whereas s can obviously be put in one-to-one correspondence with a subset of the power set of s, *the power set of s cannot be put in one-to-one correspondence with any subset of s.* Cantor's proof, and Russell's adaptation of it to show that there is no universal set, will be presented in chapter 7. For now it is enough to note why this was a problem for Russell, which he came to see would be a problem for Frege as well.

At the time, Russell's logic could be represented as including an unrestricted axiom schema of comprehension for sets—Comp, for short—where 'ε' designates the relation between an entity x and a set of which x is a member.[78]

Comp: $\exists y \, \forall x \, (Fx \longleftrightarrow x \, \varepsilon \, y)$

Instances of this schema arise from replacing Fx with any formula of the language of Russell's logical system containing only the variable 'x' free. The underlying idea is that whatever formula replaces Fx, there must be a set of all and only those things that satisfy it—the set of things of which the formula is true. In some cases, this set will be empty. But that isn't a problem, since the empty set is (we may imagine) still a set. To think of this as a principle of logic is, in effect, to think that talk about an individual's being so-and-so is interchangeable with talk about it being in the set of things that are so-and-so.

Suppose, however, that we replace Fx with the formula '$\sim x \, \varepsilon \, x$'. Doing this gives us (35) as a logical axiom.

---

[78] Russell wouldn't have expressed comprehension as a first-order axiom schema employing a set-membership predicate, preferring instead a second-order formula as axiom. Nevertheless, he was committed to the schema Comp.

35. $\exists y \,\forall x \,(\sim x \,\varepsilon\, x \longleftrightarrow x \,\varepsilon\, y)$
   There is a set of all and only those things that are not members of themselves.

Let us introduce a new symbol 'R' as a name for this set. With this understanding, (36) must be true, if (35) is.

36. $\forall x \,(\sim x \,\varepsilon\, x \longleftrightarrow x \,\varepsilon\, R)$
   Everything is such that it is a member of R iff it is not a member of itself.

Since everything includes absolutely every thing, the claim made by (36) must include R. So, (37) must be true if (36) is.

37. $(\sim R \,\varepsilon\, R \longleftrightarrow R \,\varepsilon\, R)$
   R is a member of R iff R is not a member of R.

But (37) is a contradiction, and so cannot be true. Since (37) is a logical consequence of (35), which in turn is an instance of the axiom schema of comprehension, it follows that the principle cannot be included among the laws of any sound system of logic.

The fact that this is called "Russell's *paradox*" testifies to the initial plausibility of Comp, and to the puzzle of explaining why it goes wrong and how, since it is wrong, we should determine the existence conditions for sets instead. These were tasks to which Russell and others were to devote years of thought. With this problem in mind, he examined Frege's work in hope it might contain a solution. After discovering that it didn't, and that the contradiction in his logic also arose in Frege's, he wrote as follows to Frege on June 16, 1902:

> I have known your *Grundgesetze der Arithmetik* for a year and a half, but only now have I been able to find the time for the thorough study I intend to devote to your writings. I find myself in full accord with you on all main points. . . . On functions in particular (section 9 of your *Begriffsschrift*) I have been led independently to the same views even in detail. I have encountered a difficulty only on one point. You assert (p. 17) that a function could also constitute the indefinite element. This is what I used to believe, but this view now seems to me dubious because of the following contradiction: Let w be the predicate of being a predicate which cannot be predicated of itself. Can w be predicated of itself? From either answer follows its contradictory. We must therefore conclude that w is not a predicate. Likewise, there is no class (as a whole) of those classes which, as wholes, are not members of themselves. From this I conclude that under certain circumstances a definable set does not form a whole.[79]

Russell presents the problem in two forms: one involving "predicates"—which, for Frege, really should be concepts—and one involving classes. Only the second is a problem for Frege.

---

[79] From the excerpt of Russell's letter to Frege reproduced on p. 253 of Frege (1997).

The first form in which Russell presents the problem concerns the concept *being a concept that does not apply to itself (i.e., that does not assign truth to itself as argument)*. But, as Frege immediately recognized, this is not a problem for him. As we have seen, it is a fundamental tenet of his system that concepts are categorized by levels. At the first level, we have concepts the arguments of which are objects. Since no concept is an object, no first-level concept can apply to itself. Indeed, no claim—either that it does or that it doesn't—is expressible in Frege's system. Since second-level concepts take only first-level concepts as arguments, and since no second-level concept is a first-level concept, the result is repeated at the second level, and at every following level. Thus, there is no problematic "predicate"/ concept for Frege of the sort Russell imagined.

However, the second form of the problem does arise for Frege. Numbers, for Frege, are extensions of concepts, extensions are classes, and classes are objects. With this in mind, consider the first-level concept *being the extension of a concept under which it (the extension) does not fall*. Although this concept—call it C—cannot, meaningfully, be applied to itself, it can be so applied to its extension. If so applying it yields the value truth, then the extension of C does fall under C; if so applying it yields falsity, then the extension of C does not fall under C. Since for Frege, all concepts are defined for all arguments, one or the other result must hold. Suppose it is the latter—that the extension of C does not fall under C. Then the extension of C *is* the extension of a concept under which it does not fall. But if that is so, then C must assign truth to its extension as argument, which is just to say that the extension of C does fall under C. Since this contradicts our earlier supposition, we must conclude that, in fact, the extension of C *does* fall under C.

But now it follows that there must be *some concept*—call it C*—such that the extension of C = the extension of C* and the extension of C does not fall under C*, even though it does fall under C. Frege's Axiom V tells us this is impossible.

Axiom V

For all (first-level) concepts P and Q, the extension of P (the class of things falling under P) = the extension of Q (the class of things falling under Q) iff $\forall x \, (Px \longleftrightarrow Qx)$.

For if the extension of C = the extension of C* and P_C designates C and P_{C*} designates C*, then, by Axiom V, $\ulcorner \exists x \, (P_C x \, \& \sim P_{C*}x) \urcorner$ can't be true, which means that there is no object x such that C is true of x while C* isn't. Since the extension of C is an object, it can't be the case that C is true of it while C* isn't; so, the extension of C can't fall under C without falling under C*. Thus we have a contradiction. Nor should there be any doubt that Frege is committed to the existence of the extension of C. Since '$\forall P \forall x \, (Px \longleftrightarrow Px)$'

is always be true, '∀x (Px ⟷ Px)' will be true when 'P' designates C. So, by Axiom V, the extension of C = the extension of C. Although this doesn't tell us whether or not the class is empty, it does require there to be a class of all and only those things of which C is true. Since this gives us the contradiction, Frege's logical system is inconsistent.

Frege saw the point at once, immediately responding to Russell on June 22, 1902. In his letter, he dispels the worry over the version of the paradox involving "predicates" while seeing the import of the paradox, when stated in terms of classes, for his Axiom V. Here is an excerpt from the letter.[80]

Dear Colleague,

Your discovery of the contradiction has surprised me beyond words and, I should almost like to say, left me thunderstruck, because it has rocked the ground on which I meant to build arithmetic. It seems accordingly that the transformation of the generality of an equality [the right side of Axiom V] into an equality of value ranges [the left side of V] (section 9 of my *Grundgesetze*) is not always permissible, that my law V (section 20, p. 36) is false, and that my explanations in section 31 do not suffice to secure a *Bedeutung* [referent] for my combinations of signs in all cases. I must give some further thought to the matter. It is all the more serious as the collapse of my law V seems to undermine not only the foundations of my arithmetic, but the only possible foundations of arithmetic as such. And yet, I should think, it must be possible to set up conditions for the generality of an equality into an equality of value ranges so as to retain the essentials of my proofs. Your discovery is at any rate a very remarkable one, and it may perhaps lead to a great advance in logic, undesirable as it may seem at first sight. . . . The second volume of my *Grundgesetze* is to appear shortly. I shall have to give it an appendix where I will do justice to your discovery. If only I could find the right way of looking at it.

Unfortunately for Frege, he had very little time to prepare the needed appendix dealing with Russell's paradox. Though he did come up with what surely seemed even to him to be a hasty repair, he by no means underestimated the importance and difficulty of the problem. The appendix begins as follows:

Hardly anything more unfortunate can befall a scientific writer than to have one of the foundations of his edifice shaken after the work is finished. This was the position I was placed in by a letter of Mr. Bertrand Russell, just when

---

[80] Frege (1997), p. 254. See also pp. 128–33 of Currie (1982) for a useful discussion of the significance of the paradox for Frege's system, including, in particular, Theorem 1 of *The Basic Laws of Arithmetic*, which states, in effect, that every concept has an extension (class of things falling under it), as well as Frege's fallacious proof in section 31 that all names in the system have referents.

the printing of this volume was nearing its completion. It is a matter of my Axiom (V). I have never disguised from myself its lack of the self-evidence that belongs to the other axioms and that must properly be demanded of a logical law. And so in fact I indicated this weak point in the Preface to Volume I. . . . I should gladly have dispensed with this foundation if I had known of any substitute for it. And even now I do not see how arithmetic can be scientifically established; how numbers can be apprehended as logical objects, and brought under review; unless we are permitted—at least conditionally— to pass from a concept to its extension. *May I always speak of the extension of a concept—speak of a class?* And if not, how are the exceptional cases recognized? *Can we always infer from one concept's coinciding in extension with another concept that any object that falls under the one falls under the other likewise?*[81]

The repair of Axiom V he went on to give (surprisingly) answered "yes" to the first italicized question, and "no" to the second. Answering in this way has the effect of retaining the right-to-left half of Axiom V, while carving out a special exception for the left-to-right half. The idea is simple. One takes the extension of a (first-level) concept C to include all objects of which C is true, *except* the extension of C itself (so the extension of a concept is never a member of itself). This guarantees that when C and C* are true of the same objects, their extensions will be identical (which is the right-to-left half of Axiom V). However, it remains possible for the extensions of C and C* to be identical, even though C is true of their common extension, while C* is not. This is precisely what was ruled out by the left-to-right half of V, used above to demonstrate the inconsistency of Frege's system. This argument is blocked by Frege's revision V' of V.

> Axiom V'
>
> For all (first-level) concepts P and Q, the extension of P = the extension of Q iff for all x such that x ≠ the extension of P and x ≠ the extension of Q, (Px ⟷ Qx).

Consequences of V' include (i), which is the original right-to-left half of V, (ii), and (iii), which is the left-to-right half of V'.

> (i) For all (first-level) concepts P and Q, if ∀x (Px ⟷ Qx), then the extension of P = the extension of Q.
>
> (ii) For all (first-level) concepts P and Q, if, for all x such that x ≠ the extension of P and x ≠ the extension of Q, (Px ⟷ Qx), then the extension of P = the extension of Q.
>
> (iii) For all (first-level) concepts P and Q, if the extension of P = the extension of Q, then for all x ≠ the extension of P/Q, then (Px ⟷ Qx).

---

[81] Ibid., pp. 279–80, my emphasis.

However, removing one argumentative route to inconsistency is not enough. In addition to being far from self-evident in the sense that Frege requires to serve his ambitious epistemological goals, V′ leads to other devastating problems. As noted in Michael Dummett (1973), it blocks his former proof that every natural number has a successor, which he surely would have noticed had he had time prior to publication to check the proofs in which Axiom V plays a crucial role.[82] Worst of all, it doesn't save Frege's system from falsification by Russell's paradox. The key point, as shown in Quine (1955), is that V′ has the consequence that there is at most one object.[83] Although not itself a contradiction, this result is patently absurd, and would block any attempt to ground mathematics along Fregean lines. Nor is contradiction avoided in any case, since Frege's assumption that the True and the False are distinct objects is inconsistent with the consequence Quine showed to be derivable from Axiom V′.[84]

As pointed out in Burgess (2005), Quine's falsification of the system resulting from Frege's substitution of Axiom V′ for his original Axiom V relies on a comprehension principle Comp′ for sets that is slightly weaker than the principle Comp noted above in discussing Russell.[85]

Comp′ $\exists y\, \forall x\, ((Fx\ \&\ x \neq y) \longleftrightarrow x\ \varepsilon\ y)$

This tells us that for any concept F, there is a set (the extension of F) of all and only the things of which F is true, except that set itself (the extension of F), if it turns out that F is true of it. (On this conception, a concept is true of everything in what is called "its extension," but in some cases this doesn't exhaust the objects of which it is true.) This weakening of the set-theoretic comprehension principle is consistent with Axiom V′, sufficient to avoid commitment to the universal set, and enough to guarantee that no set is a member of itself. As a result, Russell's original reasoning is blocked.

However, something very like the original paradox can still be derived. In his original reasoning, Russell identified a formula which, by Comp, should guarantee the existence of the set of sets that are not members of themselves; he derived a contradiction by asking whether this set is

---

[82] Dummett (1973), at p. xxiii. In the penultimate paragraph of the Appendix, Frege (1997, p. 289) testifies to his rush: "It would here take us too far to follow out further the result of replacing (V) by (V′). We cannot but see that many propositions must have sub-clauses added; but we need scarcely fear that this will raise essential difficulties for the course of the proofs. Anyhow, all propositions discovered up to now will need to be checked through."

[83] Quine (1955).

[84] For further useful discussion, see Currie (1982), pp. 133–35.

[85] See Burgess (2005), p. 32. The discussion here is based on material found on his pp. 32–34. That material is an adaptation of an argument by Quine that Burgess characterizes (on p. 229) as "a refinement of Geach's reconstruction of an unpublished argument of Lesniewski."

a member of itself. However, one can equally well identify a formula which, by Comp, should guarantee the existence of a set SS of all single-membered sets that are not members of their unique member. From this, one can derive a contradiction by noting (i) that if $\{SS\} \, \varepsilon \, SS$, then, by the definition of SS, $\sim \{SS\} \, \varepsilon \, SS$, and (ii) if $\sim \{SS\} \, \varepsilon \, SS$, by definition, $\{SS\} \varepsilon \, SS$. Though this contradiction doesn't quite survive the change from Comp to Comp′, a different, and closely related, paradoxical result can be derived.

With this in mind, consider (38), where 'a' is a singular term for an arbitrary object.

38. $x = a$

If we let (38) play the role of 'F' in Comp, then the set y guaranteed by Comp to exist is the set the only member of which is a. However, if we let (38) play the role of 'F' in Comp′, then there are two possibilities for the set y that is guaranteed to exist: (i) if $a \neq y$, then y is the set the only member of which is a, (ii) if $a = y$, then y is empty, i.e., has no members. In either case, we will call y *a's singleton* and use '$\{a\}$' to designate it. Now notice that if b is an object distinct from a and (39) plays the role of 'F' in Comp′

39. $x = b$

then the set y_b guaranteed to exist—b's singleton—will be different from a's singleton. (This is obvious except when y_a and y_b are both empty, but that is impossible, since then we would have $a = y_a = y_b = b \neq a$.) More generally, distinct objects always have distinct singletons.

Next consider the set guaranteed to exist by letting (40) play the role of 'F' in Comp′.

40. $\exists z \, (x = \{z\} \, \& \sim x \, \varepsilon \, z)$

Intuitively, this is the set of singletons that are not members of their only members, though one must remember that in using Comp′ there are two possibilities—(i) and (ii) above—regarding precisely which things are the "singletons." Call this set, defined by (40) using Comp′, the set n_s—for "the set of normal singletons"—and consider its singleton $\{n_s\}$. Since distinct objects always have distinct singletons, we know that there is no other object z, distinct from n_s, such that $\{n_s\} = \{z\}$. We also know, from (i) above, that *if n_s has any members*, then $n_s \neq \{n_s\}$. We now ask, assuming that it does have members, "Is $\{n_s\}$ a member of n_s?" If $\{n_s\}$ is a member of n_s, then since n_s is, by definition, the set of singletons that are not members of their only member, it follows that $\{n_s\}$ is *not* a member of n_s. So we must conclude that $\{n_s\}$ is *not* a member of n_s. But this won't do either, since the definition of n_s guarantees that every singleton that is not a member of its only member *is* a member of n_s. Thus we have a contradiction *if n_s has any members*.

Next we show that if there are at least two objects, then *n_s will have a member*—which means that Frege's modified system entails the paradoxical, and falsifying, result that there can be only one object. Here we start with formulas (41) and (42), which, by Comp′, give us the empty set ∅, with no members, and the universal set V, which includes every object except V.

41. $x \neq x$
42. $x = x$

If there are at least two objects, then one of them must be a member of V, and so V must be distinct from ∅. This means that (i) above holds for {V}, in which case V ≠ {V}, and V ε {V}. The same reasoning gives us that {V} ≠ {{V}}, and {V} ε {{V}}. This gives us at least three objects—∅, V, and {V}—which means that the universal set V must have at least two members, and so V ≠ {{V}} (which has only one member). Since V is the only member of {V}, this means that {{V}} is *not* a member of {V}. *So, {{V}} is a singleton that is not a member of its only member.* Taking {{V}} as the value of 'x' and {V} as the value of 'z', this gives us a verifying instance of (40), which, together with Comp′, gives us the set n_s of "singletons that are not members of their only members."

40. $\exists z \, (x = \{z\} \, \& \sim x \, \varepsilon \, z)$

Is {{V}} a member of n_s or not? Letting (39) play the role of 'F' in Comp′,

Comp′ $\exists y \, \forall x \, ((Fx \, \& \, x \neq y) \longleftrightarrow x \, \varepsilon \, y)$

we see that if {{V}} ≠ n_s, then {{V}} ε n_s, *in which case n_s has a member*, and if {{V}} = n_s, then {V} is a member of n_s—since {V} ε {{V}}—*in which case n_s also has a member*. Having previously shown that the claim that n_s has a member is contradictory, we conclude that our provisional assumption that there are at least two objects is inconsistent with Frege's modified system in which Axiom V′ has replaced Axiom V, and Comp has given way to Comp′. Thus, Frege's rushed attempt to modify his original inconsistent system to avoid paradox fails.

Although no such demonstration appeared during Frege's lifetime, no one adopted his modified system, and it is evident that even he soon found it to be inadequate. As a result, the founder of modern logic largely dropped out of the next great stage of its development, abandoning his work on formal logic forever, and doing very little philosophical logic between 1903 and 1918.[86] He showed little or no interest in the development of set theory, and repudiated the idea that arithmetic could be derived from logic at all. Near the end of his life, he wondered whether geometry, itself synthetic and a priori due to its grounding in Kantian spatial intuition, might somehow provide the foundations of mathematics. However, he didn't write enough to get very far with this.[87] In short, the failure of his logicist project brought on by Russell's paradox was a severely discouraging blow from which he never recovered. In addition to presenting

[86] See Dummett (1973), pp. xxiii–xxv.
[87] See Currie (1982) pp. 135–38.

a mathematical difficulty for which he did not have an adequate solution, the paradox struck at the heart of his ambitious epistemology of logic as the indispensable, self-evidently obvious bedrock on which all knowledge of number is founded. This was the grand vision that could not be saved. It is not just that the repair of his original system was ad hoc and demonstratively defective. More profoundly, the centrality and severity of the problem cast doubt on the idea that any repair, even if technically adequate, could preserve his epistemological vision.[88]

Bertrand Russell fared rather differently. Continuing to work for years on the problem, he eventually lit on his influential theory of logical types, which though extremely complicated can be seen as the application to classes of Frege's hierarchy of concepts (whereby first-level concepts can take only objects as arguments, second-level concepts can take only first-level concepts as arguments, and so on). Applying this idea to classes, we get a hierarchy of classes. Since the members of a class are always on levels lower than the class itself, no class can be a member of itself. Since Russell's "logical system" builds this restriction into the notation, no formula of the system says of any class, either that it is, or that it isn't, a member of itself. That is, of course, a bit strange, since one would have thought that the end the system is designed to meet—namely assuring that no class is a member of itself—ought to be stateable. However, Russell had far-reaching things to say in response to this worry that were closely connected to his interesting, but also puzzling, idea that, in the end, classes are merely "logical fictions." Not surprisingly, the subject is complex and so must be put off until I discuss Russell's views of logic and mathematics in chapters 7 and 10.

One thing that need not be put off, but can instead properly be noted here, is Russell's admiration for Frege, of whom he and Alfred North Whitehead wrote in the preface to volume I of *Principia Mathematica*, "In all questions of logical analysis our chief debt is to Frege." Russell's admiration is also eloquently expressed in his letter of November 23, 1962 to Jean van Heijenoort, which says in part,

> As I think about acts of integrity and grace, I realize that there is nothing in my knowledge to compare to Frege's dedication to truth. His entire life's work was on the verge of completion, much of his work had been ignored to the benefit of men infinitely less capable, his second volume was about to be published, and upon finding that his fundamental assumption was in error, he responded with intellectual pleasure clearly submerging any feelings of personal disappointment. It was almost superhuman and a telling indication of that of which men are capable if their dedication is to creative work and knowledge instead of cruder efforts to dominate and be known.[89]

---

[88] See Currie (1982), pp. 190–91, for useful discussion.

[89] Bertrand Russell, letter to Professor van Heijenoort, published in Van Heijenoort (1967).

10. FREGE'S LEGACY

Focusing on the failure of Frege's hoped for reduction of mathematics to logic, and the downward trajectory of the last half of his career after such an impressive start, some may be more taken by the shadow cast by his failure than by the illumination provided by his early success. That would be a mistake. It is in the nature of philosophy for our imaginative reach to exceed our demonstrative grasp. There is an unmistakable tendency among our greatest thinkers to be guided by powerful and compelling visions that include elements that go beyond what they can demonstrate, or, in some cases, even rationally defend. Although this leads to more than its share of dashed hopes and failed expectations, it is doubtful that, were our greatest philosophers to have been less ambitious, they would have left us with the genuine fruits of philosophical progress we now enjoy. Frege's vision of the realms of logic, language, and mathematics is among the most compelling and original we have ever known—and also among the most fruitful. One of the greatest philosopher of mathematics of all time, he was, along with Gödel and Tarski, among those most responsible for the stunning development of modern symbolic logic—itself one of the paramount intellectual achievements of the past century and a quarter. Even though Frege sat out the development of set theory after the turn of the century, his reductionist project remained an important inspiration for the use of set theory as a foundation for mathematics, including the now standard reductions of arithmetic to set theory. In the study of language and the information it carries, we still have a long way to go. However, it was Frege whose compositional theories of sense and reference put us on the path, and it is still Frege—along with Russell, Tarski, Carnap, Kripke, Montague, and Kaplan—to whom we look for key elements of our scientific framework for studying both natural and artificial languages. Centuries from now, when our descendants reap the benefits of the knowledge flowing from their advanced science of language and information, they will remember Frege as one of the giants who made it possible.

Part 2

· G. E. MOORE ·

CHAPTER 3

❧❧❧

Becoming G. E. Moore

1. Philosophical Career
2. Freedom: Moore's Idealist Critique of Kant
3. Truth, Propositions, and Judgment: Moore's "Realist" Critique of Bradley
4. Metaphysical Realism: Objects, Concepts, and Analysis
5. Moore's Analytical Critique of McTaggart's Version of Absolute Idealism
6. The Refutation of Idealism

1. PHILOSOPHICAL CAREER

George Edward Moore was born in 1873 in a suburb of London. He entered Cambridge University in 1892 as a classical scholar. At the end of his first year he met Bertrand Russell, two years his senior, who encouraged him to study philosophy, which he did with great success. His teachers at Cambridge included one of the chief proponents of Absolute Idealism in Britain, J.M.E. McTaggart, and one of Idealism's important critics, the leading ethicist Henry Sidgwick. Of the two, Moore was most drawn to McTaggart, who temporarily converted him to Absolute Idealism and made him an admirer of the world's then leading exponent of it, F. H. Bradley. Though Moore and McTaggart continued to hold each other in high esteem until the death of the latter in 1925, Moore's early infatuation with idealist ethics and metaphysics didn't last much beyond his dissertation, "The Metaphysical Basis of Ethics," submitted, unsuccessfully, in a Trinity College Fellowship competition in 1897. By the next year, in which he won a fellowship with a revised and expanded version of the earlier dissertation, he was becoming more critical.[1] His movement away from the philosophical idealism of his youth continued with a series of publications produced during his six years on fellowship at Trinity. These include "Freedom" (Moore 1898),[2] "The Nature of Judgment" (1899),[3] "Mr. McTaggart's Studies in Hegelian Cosmology" (1901–2), "Truth and Falsity" (1902a),

---

[1] A discussion of this period is found in chapter 1 of Baldwin (1990).
[2] This was written in 1897.
[3] Written in 1898.

"Change" (1902b), "Relative and Absolute" (1902c),[4] "The Refutation of Idealism" (1903a), and "Kant's Idealism" (1903–4). By 1903, he had left idealism behind in ethics and metaphysics, adopted his own distinctive nonnaturalism in ethics and extreme realism in metaphysics, and planted the seeds of what was to later to evolve into a "common sense" brand of realism in metaphysics and epistemology, both of which were to have a profound influence on the philosophers of his day, and after.

His fame dramatically increased with the publication of *Principia Ethica* in 1903. Absent from Cambridge between 1904 and 1911, he accepted a university lectureship in Moral Science in 1911. In 1921 he succeeded one of his old teachers, G. F. Stout, as editor of the prestigious journal *Mind*, and in 1925 he succeeded another of his teachers, James Ward, as Professor of Philosophy at Cambridge, a position he held until his retirement in 1939. By that time he was widely regarded, along with Bertrand Russell and Ludwig Wittgenstein, as one of the three founding fathers of the analytic tradition in philosophy (Frege still being known to only a relative few), as well as one of the most important philosophers of the previous half century. After retiring, he held visiting lectureships at different American universities in 1940–44, and oversaw the publication in 1953, under the title *Some Main Problems of Philosophy*, of a series of lectures given in London in 1910–11, as well as a collection of nine previously published and two unpublished papers in 1958 under the title *Philosophical Papers*. A month after penning a short preface to this volume, he died in October of 1958 at the age of 85.

2. FREEDOM: MOORE'S IDEALISTIC CRITIQUE OF KANT

Moore's early idealism centered on Kant's arguments in the *Critique of Pure Reason* that space and time, being infinite, cannot be real, but are instead imposed on experience by our minds. This led the young Moore to distinguish the natural world—thought of as the totality of mere appearances in space and time—from timeless, unchanging Reality as it is in itself. Arguing in Moore (1898) that appearances are not constituents of Reality, he maintains that "the world as a whole is an impossible conception" when thought of in the ordinary way, as a totality of things in space and time.[5] Here, the man who was to become the great defender of "the Common Sense view of the world" repudiates common sense in the manner characteristic of much Idealist philosophy, while enthusiastically endorsing the view that time is unreal. Knowing the later work for which he would became famous, one would not suspect this. In fact, it would appear, from Moore's misdescription in his 1942 autobiographical essay of his introduction to the view that

---

[4] The last three, which appeared in 1902, were written in 1899.
[5] Moore (1898), p. 195.

time is unreal, that himself may have forgotten the extent of his early attachment to Idealism. In that essay he writes:

> Russell had invited me to tea in his rooms to meet McTaggart; and McTaggart, in the course of the conversation, had been led to express his well-known view that Time is unreal. This must have seemed to me then (as it still does) a perfectly monstrous proposition, and I did my best to argue against it.[6]

The argument in Moore (1898) is a partial endorsement of Kant coupled with criticism from an idealist direction. The target is Kant's discussion of human freedom, which, Kant argues, must be real if morality is to make sense, but which, he acknowledges, is difficult to accommodate given (i) that all actions, choices, and deliberations occur in time, and (ii) that every temporally occurring event has a temporal cause that necessitates it. The problem emphasized by Moore is that while (i) seems undeniable and (ii) is a fundamental Kantian thesis (with which Moore agrees),[7] they lead to the view that any choice an agent makes is one the agent could not have failed to make, which seems to be inconsistent with the sense in which Kant took us to be free.

The orthodox Kantian answer to this problem hinges on what the idealist Moore calls the difference between appearance and reality. On this view, everything in time is a mere (phenomenal) appearance of a (noumenal) reality. Though an appearance has phenomenal causes, it also has a noumenal ground that is (non-causally) responsible for it. The noumenal reality, in the case of a human agent, is the transcendental self, the essence of which is rationality. It is the activity of this being that appears in time as the empirical self, which is a collection of psychic states and events standing in causally necessary relations to each other and to other, external appearances. So viewed, the agent must *appear* to be causally determined. However, since we are really transcendental selves, the ultimate nature of which we cannot know, this verdict is inconclusive. We cannot know our (transcendental) selves to be free, because our categories of understanding are limited to empirical appearances. But we do know that we can't be moral agents if we are not. Kant's solution is to *postulate* that we are free.

Moore's chief objection is that this "solution" is no solution at all. Its proponent does not dispute that all actions, choices, and deliberations occur in time, that every temporally occurring event has a temporal cause that necessitates it, and that transcendental realities standing behind all appearances are unchanging and timeless. How could they not be, since time is "unreal" and temporal succession only makes sense when applied to phenomenal appearances? According to Moore, the proper conclusion for the true Kantian to draw is that our transcendental selves are not capable of *free action* or *free choice*—not because they aren't *free* in

---

[6] Moore (1942), pp. 13–14.
[7] Moore (1898), p. 188.

Kant's special nontemporal sense, but because they aren't capable of *action*, *choice*, or *deliberation* in the normal sense in which these are temporal events or processes. To be sure, everything in the world of appearance is what it is because of the Reality of which it is an appearance. But constituents of Reality don't *do* anything. Thus, Moore concludes, true Kantian freedom, Transcendental Freedom, is simply the role of Reality in shaping the world of appearance.

The flavor of this astonishing view is illustrated by the following passage.

> What then, if Kant is a Determinist, does he mean by that Freedom, the reality of which he asserts? The answer to this question is, I think, to be found in his discussion of Transcendental Freedom, as an Idea of Reason, in the *Critique of Pure Reason*. The result of this discussion seems to me to be that Transcendental Freedom, as an Idea of Reason, is the relation in which the world *as it really is* stands to events *as we know them. It is the relation of Reality to Appearance.* This relation necessarily appears to us as the logical relation of reason to consequent. The reason is free cause of its consequence. But . . . Transcendental Freedom is by this aspect of its nature absolutely distinguished from *empirical causality* and from *human volition*, as it appears in psychology. . . . This "free causality," therefore, is not causality in the ordinary sense; and there may well seem a good case for the contention that it is not free either, *on the ground that freedom has an essential reference to human volition.* Kant's conclusion at the end of the *Critique of Pure Reason* should have been that Transcendental Freedom was not merely possible but actual. But this independence of the proof of "Freedom" from the Categorical Imperative, would seem to justify a suspicion that this "Freedom" is not freedom, since its connexion with human action is by that independence certainly lessened. And, indeed, it must be admitted that there is no longer any reason for connecting the "Intelligible Character" [i.e., Noumenal Reality] with the psychological character which distinguishes one individual from another. *The "Intelligible Character" is the one sufficient reason of all phenomena, whether processes of inanimate nature, or human actions.* It is not proved that it is individualized in a multiplicity of souls; and it is certain that in any case it is the same in each. Our doctrine will not enable us to decide between a Monadism and a Monism, but it shows that if there be Monads, they will be identical in so far as each exemplifies the "Intelligible Character" [i.e., Reality].[8]

---

[8] Ibid., pp. 182–83, my emphasis. See also pp. 194–98, 201. Note also the following (p. 203):

My conclusion then is this: That 'will' [the locus of freedom in Kant] is only a special form of natural causality, or rather, a natural causal process, where the cause is of one definite sort. It is a special form of natural causality, just as explosion of gunpowder by a match is one special form of natural causality, and explosion of dynamite by concussion is another. And, that on which I wish to insist, is that voluntary action, of whatever sort, whether autonomous or heteronomous, exhibits "freedom," in the sense which I have hitherto explained as essential to Kant's notion, no more and no less than gunpowder explosions or any other natural process whatever.

The charitable thing to say about this position is that there is indeed a serious problem with Kant's view of freedom, when combined with his major epistemological and metaphysical views. As for Moore's judgment about what in Kant to retain, and what to reject, as well as his judgment about what one's final view should be, it is evident that after the passage of a relatively short period of time his later self did not think very highly of his earlier views.

3. TRUTH, PROPOSITIONS, AND JUDGMENT: MOORE'S "REALIST" CRITIQUE OF BRADLEY

Just as Moore (1898) was a critique of Kant for not being true enough to his transcendental-idealist principles on the subject of freedom, so Moore (1899) is a critique of the Absolute Idealist F. H. Bradley for backsliding when discussing truth, falsity, and the nature of judgment. The focus of the critique is given in the opening paragraph.

> "Truth and falsehood," says Mr. Bradley (*Logic*, p. 2), "depend on the relation of our ideas to reality." And he immediately goes on to explain that, in this statement, "ideas" must not be understood to mean mere "states of my mind." The ideas, he says, on the relation of which to reality truth depends, are "*mere ideas, signs of an existence other than themselves*," and this aspect of them must not be confused either with their existence in my mind or with their particular character as so existent, which may be called their content. For logic, at least, he says, "all ideas are signs" (p. 5); and "A sign is any fact that has a meaning," while "meaning consists of a part of the content (original or acquired) cut off, fixed by the mind, and considered apart from the existence of the sign" (p. 4).[9]

Moore's main criticism is that Bradley should have realized (i) that the bearers of truth and falsity are propositions, which are not in the mind in any significant sense, (ii) that the constituents of propositions are concepts, not ideas or mental contents abstracted from ideas, and (iii) that truth is simple and unanalyzable, and so is neither a relation nor the relational property *corresponding to reality*. Like the positive theses advanced in Moore (1898), those advanced here are intertwined with implausible doctrines about which Moore is clearly confused. But unlike Moore (1898), which at best makes a critical point about Kant, Moore (1899) contains insights that are worth taking seriously, and that were taken to be so by the young Bertrand Russell, who adopted views of truth and propositions in line with Moore's, which continue to influence philosophers today.

For Russell and Moore, propositions are bearers of truth and falsity, as well as being *what we know or believe* when we know or believe anything.

---

[9] Moore (1899), p. 176.

Clearly, there is something the agent knows or believes when the report ⌜A knows/believes that S⌝ is true—something identified by the sentential clause ⌜that S⌝. What is it? Is it the sentence S? Not likely, since people who speak different languages can know or believe the same thing, as, in some cases, can agents who speak no language at all. The point is strengthened by the observation that just as one can know or believe that so-and-so, one can also hope, imagine, or desire that so-and-so. An all-purpose object of the attitudes is needed for an analysis of ascriptions ⌜A v's that S⌝ that sees them as reporting relations—knowing, believing, imagining, etc.— between an agent and what the agent v's (knows, believes, imagines, etc.). The best candidates for objects of such attitudes are not sentences, but (roughly put) their meanings. Just as a meaningful declarative sentence S is a complex the constituents of which are words and phrases, so the meaning of S (the proposition it expresses) is a complex the constituents of which are meanings of S's constituents. This analysis requires there to be propositions and propositional constituents which, though independent of language, are available as sentence and expression meanings. Providing a defensible conception of such things is a challenge different theorists face in different ways. Challenges aside, the main outlines of this view were endorsed by Frege (of whom Moore was then unaware), and shared by Russell from 1900 to 1910. Even today, it continues to be endorsed, in one form or another, by many philosophers. For the most part, Moore simply takes it for granted in "The Nature of Judgment," trying to fill in gaps in the picture, and draw out further consequences.

His first main point is that propositions and their constituents are not subjective, mind-dependent, or the result of psychological abstraction from ideas in our minds, as suggested by empiricists such as Locke, Hume, or Mill. Moore criticizes Bradley for not being consistent on this point, sometimes seeming to recognize it, while at other times falling away. He should, Moore thinks, have recognized that propositions are complex *concepts* the constituents of which are *concepts*, where "the nature of a concept, as a *genus per se*, [is] irreducible to anything else . . . [moreover] the concept is not a mental fact, nor any part of a mental fact."[10] For Moore, concepts, e.g., truth, redness, and existence, are timeless, unchanging, abstract objects—properties to be predicated of things. What are they predicated of, e.g., when I say, pointing at a rose, "This is red"? Moore's answer seems to be that such things are combinations or "conjunctions" of concepts—an ambitious and strikingly implausible metaphysical view added to his general conception of propositions. On this view, the proposition I express is true or not depending on whether the rose at which I am pointing does, or does not, include redness among its constituent "parts."

Having come this far, Moore considers what he takes to be a tempting view, namely that "the truth of a proposition depends on its relation to

---

[10] Ibid., 178–79.

reality; that *any proposition is true which consists of a combination of concepts that is actually to be found among existents."*[11] Though he rejects this thesis, his reasons in "The Nature of Judgment" are not compelling. One such reason, given on page 180, depends on the interaction of the contentious italicized formulation of the dependence-on-reality thesis with two aspects of his idiosyncratic metaphysics: (i) that since *being red* is one of the concepts (properties) that make up some existing things (while *being a chimera* is not), the thesis that a concept, or combination of concepts, is true if "found among existents" would absurdly count *being red* as true (and *being a chimera* as false), and (ii) that since, for Moore, abstract objects like numbers are said to subsist, or "have being," but not to exist, the thesis would fail to count the proposition that $2 + 2 = 4$ as true.

Although it is clear that (i) and (ii) are insufficient to reject the claim that "the truth of a proposition depends on its relation to reality," what Moore had in mind requires some explanation. For him, all possible objects of thought—including things that can be thought (truly or falsely) not to exist—*subsist*, or "have being." For example, *there are* both roses in my garden and chimeras I have dreamed about. Both are constituents of reality that are not ideas in my mind. Existing things are located in time, while merely subsisting things are not. For the (one and only) red rose in my garden to exist is for the simple, unanalyzable property *existence* to be one of the concepts of which that rose is a combination, while for the (one and only) chimera I dreamt of last night not to exist (but merely to have being) is for existence not to be so included in the combination of concepts that is that chimera. This is the strange, even paradoxical, metaphysics in the background of Moore's argumentative use of (i) and (ii).

Since a similar metaphysics plays a large role in the thought of the early Bertrand Russell, I will delay discussion of its absurdity, and the lessons to be drawn from it, until chapters 7 and 8. Here it is enough to note, going back to (i), that for a concept or combination of concepts to be "found among the existents" is for it to occur as a constituent of some combination of concepts that also includes *existence* as a constituent. So, Moore reasons, if it were enough for a concept or combination of concepts to be true that it be "found among the existents," the existence of my red rose would guarantee that the concept *being red* is true. Since he rightly rejects the idea that such a concept is the sort of thing to be true, he rejects the proposed definition—though this is hardly enough to refute the thesis that the truth of a proposition depends on its relation to reality.

Having gone down this road, Moore attempts to specify why a proposition can be true, whereas a mere concept like *being red* cannot. Reminding us that a proposition is a "synthesis" of concepts standing in a certain relation to one another, he takes the truth or falsity of a proposition to depend on the kind of relation that the constituents of the proposition stand in to

[11] Ibid., 179–80, my emphasis.

one another. Since *being red* is not similarly composed of concepts stand-ing in relation to one another—let alone any relation on which truth and falsity depend—it is not the sort of thing to be true or false. Regarding the truth or falsity of propositions, Moore says:

> A proposition is constituted by any number of concepts, together with a spe-cific relation between them; and according to the nature of this relation the proposition may be either true or false. What kind of relation makes a prop-osition true, what false, cannot be further defined, but must be immediately recognized.[12]

The doctrine is a difficult one. Lest it seem utterly baffling, think of the true proposition *that o is red* as being a complex in which the constituent, redness, of the proposition bears the complex relation *being predicated of and instantiated by* to the constituent o of the proposition, whereas the false proposition *that o' is red* is a complex in which *redness* bears only the relation *being predicated of* to o'. Here, the relation that distinguishes truth from falsity is instantiation, which, it is plausible to suppose, "can-not be further defined." Now add the Moorean idea that the objects o and o' are just complexes of the concepts they instantiate. As for the thought that the crucial relation on which truth or falsity depend must be "immediately recognized," I suppose we can say this too for the prop-osition expressed by "This is red"—so long as we don't take Moore to be claiming that we can always immediately recognize the truth or falsity of a proposition, which he surely didn't intend. Though I cannot claim this to be exactly what he had in mind, it seems to be roughly what his view demands.

One of the more questionable features of his view is that it might seem to require all truths to be necessary truths. For example, if the relation holding between o and *being red* in the proposition *that o is red* is both constitutive of that proposition and that which determines its truth, then it would seem that the proposition could never exist, or even subsist, with-out being true. However, it is unlikely that Moore would, in 1899, have taken this to be an objection, since later in the article he explicitly main-tains that all truths are necessary truths. (See below.)

At this stage, Moore took existence to be a concept like any other; for o to exist, he thought, was for o to instantiate existence, which is for exis-tence to be one of o's constituents. Since it is quite plausible that existence is a concept, there is nothing newly objectionable in this that wasn't pres-ent already. However, Moore does add something new when he says:

> It is not denied that this [existence] is a particularly important concept. . . . It is only maintained that existence is logically subordinate to truth; that truth

---

[12] Ibid., 180.

cannot be defined by a reference to existence, but existence [can be defined] only by a reference to truth.[13]

In the context of the foregoing discussion, this comes out of the blue. Why think that existence, more than any other concept, is "logically subordinate" to truth, or that truth can't be defined in terms of it, but it can be defined by reference to truth? Moore's explanation doesn't help.

> When I say "This paper exists," I must require that this proposition be true. If it is not true, it is unimportant, and I can have no interest in it. But if it is true, it means only that the concepts, which are combined in specific relations in the concept of this paper, are also combined in a specific manner with the concept of existence. . . . All that exists is thus composed of concepts necessarily related to one another in specific manners and likewise to the concept of existence.[14]

Although Moore appears to think he is saying something deep and important here, there is nothing in this that couldn't, on his view, equally be said about concepts other than existence—and nothing that shows either that truth cannot be defined, or that all other concepts are "logically subordinate" to it.

His discussion continues with an ambiguous remark that is meant to seal the objection to defining truth as correspondence.

> It is similarly impossible that truth should depend on a relation to existents or to an existent, since the proposition by which it [truth? an existent?] is so defined must itself be true, and the truth of this can certainly not be established, without a vicious circle, by exhibiting its dependence on an existent.[15]

The ambiguity concerns the antecedent of 'it' in the above passage. If it is 'truth', then we have no genuine refutation of the thesis that the truth of a proposition depends on its relation to reality both because the thesis need not be a definition, and because, even if it is, the argument that truth is indefinable would simply be a version of the argument of Frege (1918a) shown to be fallacious in section 3 of chapter 2. If, on the other hand, the antecedent of 'it' is 'an existent', then Moore's point is that truth can't be defined in terms of a relation to an existent thing or fact, because characterizing (defining) the thing or fact as *existent* itself presupposes the *truth* of the proposition that it exists. However, this is also no refutation of the thesis in Moore's sights, since despite his previous contention, he has utterly failed to show that existence, or existents, presuppose truth.

Writing on truth a short time later in an article that would appear in 1902, he comes up with a more interesting argument.

---

[13] Ibid., 180.
[14] Ibid., 180–81.
[15] Ibid., 181.

It is commonly supposed that the truth of a proposition consists in some relation which it bears to reality; and falsehood in the absence of this relation. The
relation in question is generally called "correspondence" or "agreement"; and
it seems to be generally conceived as one of partial similarity to something
else, and hence it is essential to the theory that a truth should differ in some
specific way from the reality, in relation to which its truth is to consist. . . . It is
the impossibility of finding any such difference between a truth and the reality
to which it is supposed to correspond which refutes the theory.[16]

This argument, to which Russell also once subscribed, is (i) that for propositional truth to consist in a relation to reality is for the truth of an arbitrary *proposition that A is F* to consist in its correspondence to *the fact that
A is F*. However, once we distinguish propositions both from the words
used to express them, and from the acts, ideas, or mental states of agents
who believe them, there is no difference between a true proposition and
the fact to which it is supposed to correspond. As Moore says, "once it is
definitely recognized that the proposition is . . . not a belief or form of
words, but an *object* of a belief [the thing believed], it seems plain that a
truth differs in no respect from the reality to which it was supposed merely
to correspond."[17]

On this view, truth is neither correspondence nor coherence, but a simple, unanalyzable property of propositions. Although there are both true
and false propositions, only the true ones are facts. This denial of truth
as correspondence is consistent with the observation that the proposition
that some roses are red is true iff some roses are red, and so on for propositions in general. It is also consistent with the claim that for every proposition p, the proposition that p is true is both a priori and necessarily
equivalent to p, and indeed that any warrant in believing, disbelieving,
asserting, or denying one is warrant for taking the same attitude toward
the other. Thus, the view is consistent with the observation that typically
we come to know that p is true by coming to know p. Although Moore
wasn't explicit about this, and may not even have implicitly recognized it,
he didn't deny it.

By 1911, however, he had come to disavow the views about truth and
propositions he held between 1899 and 1902. In a lecture that later became chapter 14 of *Some Main Problems of Philosophy*, he describes his
earlier view as follows.

It is a theory which I myself formerly held, and which certainly has the advantage that it is very simple. It is simply this. It adopts the supposition that
in the case of every belief, true or false, there is a proposition which is what
is believed, and which certainly is. But the difference between a true and a
false belief, it says, consists simply in this, that where the belief is true the

[16] Moore (1902a), p. 717.
[17] Ibid., p. 717.

proposition, which is believed, besides the fact that it *is* or "has being," also has another simple unanalyzable property which may be called "truth" . . . which is possessed by some propositions and not by others. The propositions which don't possess it, and which therefore we call false, *are* or "have being"— just as much as those which *do*; only they just have *not* got this additional property of being "true."[18]

This is the view we have sketched. Moore criticizes it by saying that *a fact*

> does not, if you think about it, seem to consist merely in the possession of some simple property by a proposition—that is to say, by something which has being equally whether the belief is true or false. For instance, the fact that lions really do exist does not seem to consist in the possession of some simple property by the proposition which we believe, when we believe that they exist, even if we grant that there is such a thing as this proposition. *The relation of the proposition to the fact doesn't seem to consist simply in the fact that the proposition is a constituent of the fact—one of the elements of which it is composed.*[19]

This is a blunder. The theory criticized here is not the one described in the previous passage, or espoused in either Moore (1899) or Moore (1902a). As pointed out in Richard Cartwright (1987a), the theory under attack identified the fact that lions exist with the true proposition that lions exist, not with the proposition *the proposition that lions exist is true*.[20] The latter identification, which the early Moore did not endorse, would be the same as the former identification, which he did, only if the proposition that lions exist were identical with the proposition that predicates truth of it, i.e., only if the proposition were a subconstituent of itself, which is absurd. In light of their trivial equivalence, it is easy to confuse p with the proposition that p is true, and it is conceivable that Moore did. It is also conceivable that one who took an entity to be "a combination of concepts" (presumably of properties truly predicated of it), as the young Moore did, might fail to see how p and the proposition that p is true could differ. But no matter the source of confusion, Moore's 1911 critique is no good.

As Cartwright further points out, there is a different, and more respectable, criticism that Moore had in mind. Here is Cartwright's take on it.

> So let us suppose again that Brown believes that there are subways in Boston; and let us assume, in keeping with the early Moore-Russell theory, that this implies that there is something—namely, the proposition that there are subways in Boston—that Brown believes. Now, Brown's belief happens to be true; but of course, it is crucial to the theory that even had it been false it would have had that same proposition as its object. What someone believes, what the object of his belief is, cannot depend on the truth value of his belief.

---

[18] Moore (1953), p. 284.
[19] Ibid., p. 286, my emphasis.
[20] Richard Cartwright (1987a).

Hence the proposition Brown believes, the proposition that there are sub-ways in Boston, would have been present in the universe—there really would have been such a proposition—even if Brown's belief had been false. But con-sider the *fact* that there are subways in Boston. Since Brown's belief is true, there certainly is such a fact. But had his belief been false, there surely would not have been. *This fact, which, as things stand, certainly is present in the universe, would have been missing from the universe had Brown's belief been false.* Thus, there is something true of the proposition that there are subways in Boston which is not true of the fact that there are subways in Boston. The proposition would have been in the universe even if Brown's belief had been false, but not so the fact. Hence the proposition is not identical with the fact.[21]

Although this Moorean argument is pronounced "entirely cogent," in Ayer (1971), Cartwright rightly notes that it is question begging.[22] For how is the italicized claim in the above passage to be established? According to the theory being criticized, the fact that there are subways in Boston is the true proposition that there are. However, if that proposition had been false, then something which *is* true, and hence *is* the fact that there are subways in Boston, *would not have been* true, and so *would not have been* the fact that there are subways in Boston—i.e., a thing that *is* a fact *would have been a constituent of the universe without being a fact*. Unless one can show that this is impossible—perhaps because *being a fact* is a property that anything that has it couldn't have lacked—Moore's early theory will remain intact.[23]

Can one give such an argument? Although Moore didn't do so explicitly, the conception of facts he and Russell were operating under in 1911 allows for such an argument, which he probably had in mind. Consider the facts that Jupiter is round and that Jupiter is larger than Venus. Moore and Rus-sell would have referred to these as *Jupiter's being round*, and *Jupiter's being larger than Venus*. These in turn would have been taken to be complexes consisting, in the first case, of Jupiter and the property *being round*, and, in the second case, of Jupiter, Venus, and *being larger than*. In both cases, the constituents of the facts were taken to be "held together" by the property or relation applying to (or being instantiated by) the other constituents. The fact that Jupiter is larger than Venus is Jupiter's and Venus's instantiat-ing *larger than*, while the fact that Jupiter is round is Jupiter's instantiating *roundness*. On this view, the universe contains not just Jupiter and Venus, or even just Jupiter, Venus, *being round*, and *being larger than*, but also *Jupiter's being round*, and *Jupiter's being larger than Venus*. It is, of course, far

---

[21] Ibid., p. 77, my emphasis.

[22] Ayer (1971), p. 211.

[23] As noted above, the theory in Moore (1899) did take truth to be an essential property of anything that has it. However, this is not maintained in (1902a), where the argument against truth as correspondence, and in favor of truth as simple and undefinable, does not depend on it. It is also no part of Moore's 1911 critique of propositions.

from obvious that there really are facts in this sense, let alone that there is one for each true proposition.[24] However, on the view that there are, it is very natural to take *being a fact* to be a property which anything that has it couldn't have lacked. For surely, if there is such a thing as Jupiter's (really) standing in the *larger than* relation to Venus, then it could not have been a constituent of the universe if Jupiter hadn't been larger than Venus. Since the proposition that Jupiter is larger than Venus doesn't have this property, it can't be identical with the fact—which was Moore's point in 1911.

When he came to adopt this view of facts, he could not continue to maintain his (1902) identification of them with true propositions. However, Moore was not thereby required to fundamentally alter his earlier view of truth as an unanalyzable property of propositions. Although the new view of facts is inconsistent with his earlier argument that truth can't be correspondence with facts, it doesn't require him to hold that the truth of a proposition really does consist in its correspondence to a fact that makes it true. Perhaps the best example of a philosopher with a robust commitment to facts in the above sense, who does *not* define truth to be correspondence to a fact, is Wittgenstein, who opens *Tractatus Logico-Philosophicus* with the lines "The world is all that is the case. The world is the totality of facts, not things."[25]

Nevertheless, Wittgenstein held that there are true propositions that don't correspond to any facts. One such case is the negation of a proposition p, the truth of which consists of the fact that p *doesn't* correspond to any fact. Obviously, one who takes this position can't define the truth of a proposition as its correspondence with the facts.[26]

Thus, Moore could have continued to maintain that truth is simple and unanalyzable. He could also have continued to accept propositions in the sense that he did in Moore (1902a). Instead, he gave them up. Like Russell at the same time, he could not continue to believe that there are false propositions, in part because by this time he was running together nominalized clauses like *Jupiter's being larger than Venus*—which he took to designate facts in the above sense—with ordinary 'that' clauses, like *that Jupiter is larger than Venus*, which often do not. Although he could well imagine a universe containing Jupiter, Venus, and *larger than* in which Jupiter was not larger than Venus, and hence in which Jupiter's being larger than Venus—also known as the fact that Jupiter is larger than Venus— wasn't a constituent, he couldn't imagine the proposition that Jupiter is larger than Venus being a constituent of such a universe.

---

[24] For doubts, see Merricks (2007) and Soames (2008a).

[25] Wittgenstein (1922), p. 29. Citations will be to the 1999 edition published by Dover.

[26] This point must be tempered by the observation that although there is a sense in which Wittgenstein can be said to have accepted the existence of propositions, they are very different sorts of things (much more like interpreted sentences) than Moorean or Russellian propositions.

This problem is a version of the same difficulty that led Frege to maintain that every proposition must contain an unsaturated sense to "hold it together" as a unified object of thought capable of representing the world as being one way rather than another. Often dubbed "the problem of the unity of the proposition," this is one of the most long-standing, and persistently misunderstood, problems of philosophical logic. In section 2 of chapter 2, I argued that Frege's distinction between saturated and unsaturated senses—the former designating objects, which are complete, and the latter designating concepts, which are not—was ill-motivated and self-refuting. In chapters 7 and 9, I will examine Russell's diagnosis of the problem, his failed initial attempt to solve it, and his insightful but unsuccessful later attempt to use his multiple relation theory of judgment to avoid it, and dispose of propositions altogether.

The problem, at base, is that although propositions are complex entities, they are not mere collections of unrelated constituents. The proposition that Jupiter is larger than Venus is not the set consisting of its three constituents—not only because if it were, it would be identical with the proposition that Venus is larger than Jupiter, which it isn't, but more fundamentally because the proposition *represents* Jupiter as being larger than Venus, whereas a mere set of things doesn't represent anything. The same can be said of the ordered triple <Jupiter, Venus, *being larger than*>, the nested ordered pair <<Jupiter, Venus> *being larger than*>, and the nested set of sets {{{Jupiter}, {Jupiter, Venus}}, {{{Jupiter}, {Jupiter, Venus}}, *being larger than*}}. We could, of course, develop artificial systems pairing propositions one-to-one with ordered n-tuples, nested ordered n-tuples, or nested sets of sets—properly distinguishing, in each case, the construction paired with the proposition that Jupiter is larger than Venus from the construction paired with the proposition that Venus is larger than Jupiter (and similarly for other propositions). However, no such system would justify identifying propositions with such constructions. Unlike propositions, ordered n-tuples, nested ordered n-tuples, and nested sets of sets aren't *about* anything; they don't *represent* anything as being one way or another, and so can't be true or false. Although we could adopt conventions *endowing* them with representational content, this wouldn't do the job either. The propositions for which the early Moore was looking were not things to be given meanings. They were the meanings—objective, mind-independent contents—we give to sentences and other things. This is what he struggled with in Moore (1899, 1902a) and of which he despaired in 1911.

Facts were, by this time, another matter. Though conceived to be complex mind-independent entities that are genuine constituents of reality, they were not taken to be meanings, or to be representational. Nor was there any problem of "the unity of the fact." The fact that Jupiter is larger than Venus isn't a collection of unrelated constituents because, the story went, its constituents are unified by Jupiter's actually standing in the relation *being larger than* to Venus. So, by 1911, Moore thought that facts could be substituted for his old conception of true propositions, and that false propositions were a bad idea to begin with. Russell's struggles in *The Principles of Mathematics* (1903a) parallel those of the early Moore, while his chapter "Truth and Falsehood" in *The Problems of Philosophy* (1912) takes this reasoning a step further by developing a new analysis of belief (and other attitudes), including a new proposal about what the bearers of truth and falsity really are.

4. METAPHYSICAL REALISM: OBJECTS, CONCEPTS, AND ANALYSIS

Having dealt with truth and propositions in "The Nature of Judgment," Moore outlines his broader metaphysics.

> It seems necessary, then, to regard the world as formed of concepts. These are the only objects of knowledge. They cannot be regarded fundamentally as abstractions either from things or from ideas; since both alike can, if anything is to be true of them, be composed of nothing but concepts. A thing becomes intelligible first when it is analysed into its constituent concepts.[27]

This is Moore's startling "realist" conception of reality, in which things are merely collections of concepts (properties). Although he was later to leave it behind, his conception of the *analysis* of something as identifying, and breaking it up into, its constituent concepts survives in his most celebrated work, *Principia Ethica*, which appeared in 1903.

He continues:

> The opposition of concepts to existence disappears, since an existent [thing] is seen to be nothing but a concept or complex of concepts standing in a unique relation to the concept of existence. Even the description of an existent [thing] as a proposition (a true existential proposition) seems to lose its strangeness, when it is remembered that a proposition is here to be understood, not as anything subjective—an assertion or affirmation of something— but as the combination of concepts which is affirmed.[28]

Let's try this. My office lamp exists, and so is an existent, which means, for Moore, that it is a combination of concepts standing in a certain relation to the concept *existence*. In addition, he seems to imply, there is nothing strange about describing the lamp as a true existential proposition—I suppose, the proposition that my office lamp exists. In implying that this isn't strange he is, I take it, inviting us to think that my lamp just *is* that

---

[27] Moore (1899), p. 182.

[28] Ibid., pp. 182–83. See also Baldwin (1990) p. 41, which cites a letter written by Moore at the time: "I have arrived at a perfectly staggering doctrine. . . . An existent is nothing but a proposition: nothing *is* but concepts. There is my philosophy."

true proposition. However, this is very strange, and also untrue. For, whereas the proposition is true, the lamp isn't, and whereas I believe the proposition, I don't believe the lamp. Moreover, the proposition that the lamp exists will continue to exist long after the lamp itself does.[29] Conversely, whereas the lamp is connected to an electrical socket, and because of that provides light when switched on, the existential proposition isn't connected to the socket, never provides light, and is never switched on. What's more, I have seen the lamp, touched it, and once knocked it to the floor, nearly breaking it, but I haven't seen, touched, or nearly broken the existential proposition. For all these reasons, the lamp is not the proposition.

It is unlikely that Moore would have agreed. He says:

> It now appears that perception is to be regarded philosophically as the cognition of an existential proposition; and it is thus apparent how it can furnish a basis for inference, which uniformly exhibits the connexion between propositions.[30]

This isn't entirely off base. As I argue in Soames (2010b), seeing an object o as red, for example, is a form of cognition in which an agent predicates redness of o. Thus, the agent's visual experience represents o as red—which means that visual perception involves bearing cognitive attitudes toward propositions (properly conceived). But these are *not* what one sees. The proposition that o is red may be true, and implicitly cognized in perception, but it isn't red. Incredibly, Moore seems to have missed this.

What could he have been thinking? Consider the italicized phrase in his remark (two passages back) that "an existent [thing] is seen to be nothing but *a concept or complex of concepts standing in a unique relation to the concept of existence*." Since propositions are complexes of concepts, and since *existence* is one of the concepts that make up the proposition that my office lamp exists, the proposition does stand in an intimate relation to the concept *existence*. What about the lamp itself? If, as Moore maintains, an object is nothing more than a collection of its properties, then an existing object, like my lamp, must be a collection of properties that includes *existence* as a constituent. This, I think, is the perspective from which he takes it not to be strange to describe my office lamp as being the very same thing as the proposition that my lamp exists. Both are collections of properties of which *existence* is a constituent. The view is, of course, transparently absurd, not least because Moore would, I think, take my office lamp to be a proper constituent, but not the whole of, the proposition that it exists.

This point aside, the view would be absurd in any case. I dwell on it here in order to emphasize a future contrast. Within a decade or so, Moore would mature into a philosopher arguably unequaled in the history of

---

[29] See Soames (2014c and forthcoming) for an explanation.
[30] Ibid., p. 183.

the subject in his effectiveness in teaching a simple but powerful lesson. We know that philosophy is, perhaps more than any other theoretical enterprise, rife with obscurity, confusion, and uncertain speculation. Hence, when its attempts at grandeur lead to theses inconsistent with the most obvious of our pre-philosophical certainties, this is usually a better sign that the philosopher has gone astray than it is an indication that we have finally pierced the veil of appearance to grasp the nature of Reality. Understanding Moore's idealist and "metaphysical realist" phases helps us realize that his later lesson was not the naïve reaction of an innocent to the sophisticated but questionable ways of his elders; rather, it was the response of one who was himself vulnerable to the very temptations he later worked so hard to resist.[31]

5. MOORE'S ANALYTICAL CRITIQUE OF MCTAGGART'S VERSION OF ABSOLUTE IDEALISM

Moore's movement away from Absolute Idealism was a quarrel that encompassed both the Absolute part and the Idealist part. A characteristic feature of Absolute Idealism is its denial of contingency. Reality (which is ultimately spiritual) is said to be an interconnected whole, every part of which is non-contingently related to every other. Though this thesis isn't explicitly (or consistently) addressed in Moore (1899), there is a hint of Moore's dissatisfaction with it in his emphasis on the independence of concepts from any mind or minds that cognize them.

> Concepts are possible objects of thought; but that is no definition of them. It merely states that they may come into relation with a thinker; and in order that they *may* do anything, they must already *be* something. It is indifferent to their nature whether anybody thinks them or not. They are incapable of

---

[31] The second half of "The Nature of Judgment" is even stranger than the first. There Moore is concerned to improve on Kant's way of distinguishing a priori from empirical truths. For Moore, surprisingly, the distinction does not involve necessity, since, he argues, all truths are necessarily true (p. 89). Though the argument is obscure, Gilbert Ryle (1970) may have caught part of the main idea: *since the truth or falsity of a proposition doesn't depend on any potentially contingent correspondence with the world, it must depend solely on the connections inherent in the proposition itself, which, being conceptual, must not be contingent.* With necessity unavailable to enforce Kant's distinction, Moore concludes that it can only be understood as separating propositions containing concepts that can exist in time (i.e., be properties of things that so exist), and propositions not containing such concepts. This, of course, makes for a very strange distinction, since it seems to have nothing to do with how the two classes of propositions are known. However, on p. 191 Moore claims that no existential, and presumably no empirical, proposition, is "indubitable." Since he seems to hold that propositions of pure mathematics (which do not contain "empirical" concepts) can be indubitable, there is, perhaps, an epistemological distinction here. However, his discussion of this is neither clear, nor persuasive, nor plausible. See Baldwin (1990), pp. 55–61, for informative exposition.

change; and the relation into which they enter with the knowing subject implies no action or reaction.[32]

This seems to suggest that although concepts can be apprehended by minds, it is not essential that they should be, in which case any concept that happens to be so apprehended would have been no different had it not been. Since this implicitly denies the necessary and essential connection between concepts and the subjects that apprehend them, it is *prima facie* inconsistent with Absolute Idealism. However, Moore may not have been of one mind about this when he wrote the piece in 1898, since he concludes at the end of it that all truths are necessary truths. Nevertheless, the passage is a hint that Moore was moving away from Bradley and McTaggart. The movement continued later in 1899 when Moore wrote two entries, "Change" and "Relative and Absolute," which were to appear in Baldwin's Dictionary in 1902. In these short pieces he accepts the reality of space and time (and hence of constituents of reality that change over time), and denies that all relations between real things are essential, or necessary.

His criticism of Absolute Idealism came to maturity in "Mr. McTaggart's 'Studies in Hegelian Cosmology,'" which appeared in 1901. No longer criticizing the Idealism of his day from within, Moore here shows himself as the relentless, analytically meticulous, and even censorious critic of unconstrained philosophical speculation for which he was to become so widely known. Not without affection for the man in the crosshairs, or entirely without sympathy for the views under attack, he writes,

> This book possesses a combination of merits, which is as rare as it is valuable. Mr. McTaggart attempts to prove to us directly that the whole universe is of a certain kind; and he defines with most unusual clearness both what his conclusion is and what are the premises and arguments by which he holds it to be proved. Theology may give us conclusions even more definite and more capable of appealing to the imagination; but this advantage can only be obtained at the expense either of despicable reasoning or of fundamental assumptions, which are wholly arbitrary and accepted on authority. Philosophers, again, may reason well from self-evident premises; but they can rarely reach a conclusion more definite than that the world is "rational and righteous," and in proportion as their conclusions are important, the evidence for them is apt to be obscure. Mr. McTaggart's reasoning is inferior to none in ability; his fundamental premises are not arbitrary; his conclusions are definite; and he leaves us in no doubt as to the precise nature of the evidence which he has to offer for them. I know of no philosophical work which combines these merits in an equal degree."[33]

There is, I think, no reason to doubt the sincerity of Moore's praise. He does value not only McTaggart's clarity and definiteness, but also his

---

[32] Moore (1899), p. 179.
[33] Moore (1901–2), p. 177.

admirable attempt to answer "the most important of all philosophical questions—the question of what exists other than, or in addition to, the things which form the object of our everyday experience"—to assess our place in the universe, to speak to our longing for immortality, and to identify the ethical goal of all existence.[34] Moore himself had been drawn to philosophy in part by such concerns, which he believed should be taken seriously. Precisely for this reason, philosophical reasoning had to be held to the highest standards—standards which, he was coming to believe, such grand ambitions were unlikely to satisfy. Thus, though we may be startled by its directness, we are scarcely surprised by Moore's verdict when, less than a third of the way through the paper, he delivers this assessment of McTaggart's defense of the central proposition of his cosmology, "that the universe consists solely of conscious persons."

> It is plain, then, that he has given us no reason to believe his first proposition; and yet his attempt to establish it must be allowed to have the highest philosophic merit. It has the merit of being an excellent *reductio ad absurdum* of all attempts to construct what Mr. McTaggart would call an "Idealism," i.e., any philosophy which maintains that the universe is wholly "spiritual" and perfectly good. It is qualified to perform this useful service by the fact that, whereas its arguments are quite as good as any that are commonly offered, they and their premises are stated in so exceptionally clear a form that their complete impotence may be easily exposed.[35]

The positive view in defense of which McTaggart offered his arguments is one in which Reality is a complete, eternal, and morally perfect totality of immortal, but finite, persons (including us) non-contingently related by love to one another. This community of spiritual persons is not to be identified with a supreme person, God; there is no such person, and time and matter are merely appearances. McTaggart takes it to have been proven by Hegel that Reality is *in* each of its parts, while still being the whole of which they are merely parts. How, Moore wonders, can a whole be in (part of?) something that is merely a sub-part of the whole? McTaggart's example is the whole constituted by two people each of whom is conscious not only of himself/herself, but also of the other person. As Moore puts it,

> McTaggart's theory is, that when I know my friend, he is simultaneously both inside and outside my mind: this, he [McTaggart] thinks, is the relation in which consciousness always stands to its object. It is owing to this that a universe of conscious selves, each of which knew all about the others . . . would be a whole which not only contained all its parts, but was itself contained in each of them.[36]

[34] Moore (1899), p. 178.
[35] Ibid., p. 188.
[36] Ibid., p. 185.

Moore, who regards it to be contradictory to claim that a whole is a part of one of its sub-parts, takes the opportunity to explore what it is to be conscious of something. McTaggart is criticized for equivocating between the friend and the image, or idea, of the friend—which is sufficient to undermine his explanation of the Hegelian doctrine that the whole of Reality is present in each of its parts. Putting this equivocation aside, Moore notes that we don't take a mirror to be conscious because the friend may be outside the mirror, while he (or his image) is also "in the mirror"—so whatever relation between consciousness and its object McTaggart may be trying to get at is not sufficient to characterize what consciousness is. Finally, Moore makes a larger point—which he will elaborate at great length in Moore (1903a).

> In fact that what I am conscious of *must* be inside my mind is a mere traditional assumption for which there are no reasons. . . . It is commonly supposed, as it was by Berkeley, to be obvious to direct inspection that what I know is always in my mind; whereas the only thing which really is thus obvious, is that my consciousness of the thing is so. The history of philosophy exhibits a uniform inability to distinguish between that of which I am conscious and my consciousness of it—an inability which has found a monument in the word "idea" which regularly stands for both.[37]

Moore next turns to McTaggart's discussion of human immortality, which, he argues, comes to grief over the latter's equivocal commitment to his professed doctrine that time is unreal. Since time is unreal, Reality—i.e., both the persons and the Absolute Totality they make up—are officially supposed to be timeless and unchanging. Like the natural numbers, their existence is entirely outside of time. However, it is also pretty pallid, and not what we are interested in when wondering about our own immortality. What we want to know is whether we will live forever after death, and if so, what that existence will be like. Implicitly recognizing this, McTaggart, as Moore persuasively reads him, characterizes the value of the immortality for which he argues as that of an indefinite prolongation of our existence in time. The upshot is a kind of bait and switch. When arguing for immortality, McTaggart supposes himself to establish a static, unchanging, and timeless existence. When taking what is so established to be something of great value that fulfills our hopes, he repeatedly describes it as a continuation and improvement of our temporal lives.

This contradiction is not isolated, but implicit in many Idealist discussions purporting to establish that time as unreal. Is this doctrine supposed to mean that among the things there are, some—the very best and hence most deserving of the honorific "Real"—are timeless and unchanging, while others—much worse and mere appearances of the Real—are temporal, and so subject to change and even passing away? Or does it mean

---

[37] Ibid., p. 187.

that absolutely everything is timeless and unchanging, even though some of these things (wrongly) appear to us to change? Neither alternative is in the least probable, a point that may temporarily be obscured, but not changed, by vacillating between them.

Moore ties these points about time and value together in a general critique of the metaphysical ethics of Absolute Idealism.

> "All change in time," he [McTaggart] says . . . "must be taken as ultimately determined by the end of developing as a series the full content of the timeless reality." . . . He seems to assume as a certainty "that every addition to the series of temporal events must make that series a more complete manifestation of the timeless reality." Now we understand that the timeless reality itself is absolutely perfect, and therefore that no manifestation whatever can constitute any addition to the perfection of the universe; and this being so, it is plain that a more complete manifestation . . . is not one whit better absolutely than any other. Yet we can only understand . . . [McTaggart] as meaning that a complete manifestation of the timeless reality is demanded by the *perfection* of the universe. . . . It is, in fact, impossible for any philosophy which . . . distinguishes between a perfect timeless Reality and its manifestations or Appearance in time, consistently to ascribe any value whatever to the existence of anything in time; and that for two cogent reasons: (1) that it must maintain that nothing does really exist in time, and (2) that it cannot hold that the existence of anything in time can make any difference whatever to the perfection of the universe. Even if it allowed that things really existed in time, it could not allow any real value to such existence . . . its whole Ethics must consist in ascribing a value, which they cannot have, to things which do not exist.[38]

Think of it this way. If Reality is as the Absolute Idealists tell us—timeless, perfect, and all there is—then in addition to there being no action, there is nothing wanting, and so no scope for ethics; moreover, since the whole of this perfect Reality is supposed to be fully present in each of its parts, each part must be equally perfect as it is. On the other hand, if in addition to Reality—which is timeless and perfect—there are unreal things called "appearances," then since they can have no effect on Reality, or its value, presumably they can't have any *real* value either. Again there is no scope for ethics. For ethics to gain purchase, one or more central theses of Absolute Idealism must be given up. Perhaps Reality isn't timeless or perfect, but can be improved by our actions. Yes, Moore thought, but then we are not Absolute Idealists anymore.[39]

---

[38] Ibid., 194–95.

[39] Moore elaborates a similar critique in section 68 of *Principia Ethica*.
The last third of Moore's essay on McTaggart is an illuminating discussion of the light thrown on personal identity by our concern for our future selves. Asking, on page 201, "What is it which we really desire when we desire the continuance of our personal identity?" Moore criticizes McTaggart's theory, which (a) rejects memory as providing the criterion, and (b) substitutes for it causal dependence of later experiences on earlier ones. On page

6. THE REFUTATION OF IDEALISM

Moore's 1903 paper "The Refutation of Idealism" is a flawed but brilliant and underappreciated gem. The only one of his papers published before 1905 included in later collections of his work, it is also one about which he later expressed doubt. Throwing cold water on earlier work and expressing dismay over what he would later regard to be his "mistakes" was typical of Moore. However, his misgivings in 1922 about reprinting this paper were stronger. Pronouncing it "very confused," and embodying "a good many down-right mistakes," he justifies reprinting it only because it had been so influential.[40] It had been that, influencing Russell and the broader analytic tradition in turning away from British Idealism. But there is more to the paper than criticism. In it we see the beginnings of what was then a new analytic way of doing philosophy, accompanied by positive views in metaphysics, epistemology, and the philosophy of mind. Taken seriously then, it contains much worth reexamining now, despite containing some serious errors. Fortunately, most are instructive, and valuable for that. Beyond that, we see Moore beginning to emerge as the philosopher that history was to come to know so well—a relentless critic bent on dispelling confusion over large philosophical issues by separating questions previously run together, articulating overlooked distinctions, and exposing the weakest link in a chain of argument. As with many of his later critical attacks, his argument here is not a refutation in the sense of a proof of the negation of the thesis under attack. Rather, it is a radical undermining of support for a speculative view, which throws on his opponent a burden of proof made heavier by Moore's recitation of the extent of its conflicts with what we all *prima facie* take ourselves to know.

The article begins:

> Modern Idealism, if it asserts any general conclusion about the universe at all, asserts that it is *spiritual*. There are two points about this assertion to which

206, Moore gestures at the beginnings of what may be a more promising view: "What gives meaning to 'self' for us is that which distinguishes our *present* self from any conceivable simultaneous existent, however like us it may be; and we value the states causally connected with our present self, not because they are so connected, but because they are states of that which thus distinguishes our present self; it is this which we mean when we call them *our* past and future." Two pages later, he adds, "The only sense in which we use personal identity with 'much meaning'—the only sense in which we much desire it—is that in which what is meant by the past or future self has the same relation to the present self, as the present self has to itself." If I were developing this point, I would add that the relation in question is simply identity, that personal identity is therefore primitive, and that there is no reductive, noncircular criterion to be had. But this isn't exactly, or all of, what Moore says. He seems to be emphasizing that the consciousness the present self has of itself is connected to the consciousness the present self has of the past self (through memory) and the consciousness the future self will have of the present and past selves (through memory). Moore goes on to make several interesting observations without, I think, arriving at a determinative, or clearly formulated, final view. See Baldwin (1990), pp. 53–54, for further discussion.

[40] Moore (1922a), p. viii of the 1968 reprinting. All citations will be to that edition.

I wish to call attention . . . (1) that the universe is very different indeed from what it seems, and (2) that it has quite a large number of properties which it does not seem to have. Chairs and tables and mountains *seem* to be very different from us; but when the whole universe is declared to be spiritual, it is certainly meant to assert that they are far more like us than we think. . . . When the whole universe is declared to be spiritual, it is meant not only that it is in some sense *conscious,* but that it has what we recognize in ourselves as the *higher* forms of consciousness. That it is intelligent; that it is purposeful; that it is not mechanical; all these different things are commonly asserted of it. In general, it may be said, this phrase "reality is spiritual" excites and expresses the belief that the *whole* universe possesses *all the qualities* the possession of which is held to make us so superior to things which seem to be inanimate.[41]

It is hard to read this description of the position to be "refuted" without a sense of incredulity. Moore deliberately emphasizes how far his target is from, and at variance with, what we pre-philosophically think. But he doesn't dismiss the view for its pretensions; he takes it at its word. The very reason that the view under attack was seen by many to be so significant, informative, and even potentially life-changing (as philosophy often has been wont to be) is because the picture it paints of the world is so different from our ordinary one. Moore does, however, have a subtext: any view as revisionary as that had better be supported by powerful arguments.

Against this background, he spends the next several pages deflating expectations. He will produce no argument that Idealism is false. In fact, he doesn't believe that it is possible to *disprove* any of its central theses. Instead, he will examine one premise of one argument, which, as far as he can discern, all Idealists consider necessary to establish their view. His aim is to remove this link in their argumentative chain—not by proving the premise false, but by showing that the reasons for taking it to be true are based on confusions which, when removed, leave no basis for accepting it. The end result, Moore claims, will show that "Idealists have *no reason whatever* for their conclusion."[42]

His reconstruction of what he takes to be the Idealist's master argument begins with the principle that *esse* is *percipi*—to be is to be perceived (or at any rate experienced). He summarizes the argument as proceeding as follows.

If *esse* is *percipi*, this is at once equivalent to saying that whatever is, is experienced: and this again is equivalent, in a sense, to saying that whatever is, is something mental. But this is not the sense in which the Idealist *conclusion* must maintain that Reality is *mental*. The Idealist *conclusion* is that *esse* is *percipere* [to perceive or to experience]; and hence, whether *esse* be *percipi* or not, a further and different discussion is needed to show whether or not it is also *percipere*. And again, even if *esse* be *percipere*, we need a vast quantity

[41] Moore (1903a) pp. 1–2. All citations will be to the reprinted version in Moore (1922a).
[42] Ibid., p. 3.

of further argument to show that what has *esse* has also those higher mental qualities which are denoted by spiritual.[43]

The target of Moore's attack is the first premise, that *esse* is *percipi*. He contends "that every argument ever used to show that reality is spiritual has inferred this . . . from '*esse* is *percipere*' as one of its premises; and that this again has never been pretended to be proved except by use of the premise that *esse* is *percipi*."[44] He notes that this premise is taken to be a necessary, conceptual truth. This leads naturally to the idea that it is analytic, in that the property *to be experienced*, expressed by its predicate, '*percipi*', is contained in, and so is part of the analysis of, the property *being real*, expressed by its subject, '*esse*'. Since his discussion of this idea is somewhat confused, or at least confusing, I will try to straighten out what is at issue.[45]

He begins by noting that, for the Idealist, *being experienced* can't be the whole meaning of '*esse*', since otherwise '*Esse* is *percipi*' would be (equivalent to) a mere tautology, '*Esse* is *esse*', which it isn't. (Although the triviality claim implicit here could be disputed, we let it pass.) Hence, he reasons, the Idealist must hold that '*esse*' expresses a complex concept consisting of some concept X plus *being experienced*. Even so, he observes, the mere analyticity of the claim that whatever is both X and experienced is also experienced—supposedly expressed by '*Esse* is *percipi*'—is incapable of doing serious argumentative work. What the Idealist needs, either instead of this analysis or in addition to it, is the claim that, necessarily, whatever is X is experienced. Not wishing to muddy the waters, Moore doesn't try to specify what X is. One won't go wrong, however, by taking it to be *existence*, as ordinarily understood (by everyone except some Idealists)— namely, as not containing *being experienced* as a constituent. If it could be shown by philosophical argument that, in fact, anything that exists in this sense must also be experienced, then Idealists would have the argument they need to move us from our ordinary conception of the world to theirs.

Moore summarizes the point by saying that Idealists need the proposition that *esse* is *percipi* (understood as *X is percipi*) to be a *synthetic a priori and necessary truth*. He then initiates the next stage of his argument:

> And I may say at once that, understood as such, it cannot be refuted. If the Idealist chooses to assert that it is merely a self-evident truth, I have only to say that it does not appear to me to be so. But I believe that no Idealist ever has maintained it to be so. . . . They do not perceive that *Esse* is *percipi* must, if true, be *merely* a self-evident synthetic truth; they either identify with it or give as a reason for it another proposition which must be false because it is self-contradictory.[46]

[43] Ibid., p. 6.
[44] Ibid., p. 6.
[45] The discussion occurs on pp. 10 and 11.
[46] Ibid., pp. 11–12.

Though there will be an important point to salvage from this passage, there is also serious confusion stemming, in part, from Moore's uncritical use of the undefined notions *analytic* and *synthetic*. It will be instructive to start off by assuming that whatever he had tacitly in mind was more or less extensionally equivalent to (i–vii) for the range of cases under discussion.

   (i) A sentence S is analytic iff S is a logical truth or can be turned into one by putting synonyms for synonyms. Equivalently, S is analytic iff S is a logical consequence of a logical truth L plus definitions of one or more of the terms in S or L.

  (ii) S is a logical truth iff S is true in all models—i.e., iff S comes out true no matter what the domain of quantification is taken to be, and no matter how the nonlogical vocabulary of S is interpreted over that domain.

 (iii) A proposition P is analytic iff it is expressed by a sentence that is logically true. Since it is assumed that synonymous sentences, including those that differ only in the substitution of synonyms for synonyms, express the same proposition, this is equivalent to saying that P is analytic iff it is expressed by an analytic sentence.

  (iv) A true sentence that is not analytic is synthetic; similarly for propositions.

   (v) An *analysis* of a concept C into a cluster C* of concepts implicitly provides a *definition* of a word or phrase expressing C in terms of words expressing concepts in C*. Although in some cases there may be no words expressing concepts into which a complex concept is analyzable, new vocabulary can always be introduced for this purpose if necessary.

  (vi) Synonymous (interdefinable) sentences and expressions are trivially recognizable to be equivalent. The meanings of synonymous expressions, and the propositions expressed by synonymous sentences, are transparently recognizable as identical.

 (vii) There is an effectively decidable set of logically true sentences that are both epistemically self-evident and such that every logically true sentence is a logical consequence of them. Also, when a sentence S is a logical consequence of an effectively decidable set of sentences S*, there is a proof of S from a finite subset of S* each step of which is self-evidently obvious.

(viii) There is an effectively decidable set of analytically true propositions that are both epistemically self-evident and such that every analytically true proposition can be proven from them by a finite number of self-evidently obvious steps.

One upshot of this set of principles is that philosophical theses that are analytic truths should be hard to come by. For if a sentence or proposition is analytic, it must be provable from self-evident principles by self-evident steps—using only the tools of definition, analysis, and logical inference. However, it is hard to believe that important, disputed philosophical theses will be resolvable in this way. Surely, Moore never discovered any. If one further believes, as he seems to, that the truths of philosophy are conceptually necessary, then adherence to something extensionally equivalent to (i–viii) should lead one to expect them to be synthetic, necessary, and a priori—just as he insists that Idealists must take *'Esse* is *percipi'* to be. If establishable at all, such propositions must either be self-evidently obvious, provable by self-evidently obvious steps from other self-evidently obvious synthetic necessary a priori truths, or establishable by some other means. Moore rightly dismisses the idea that it is self-evidently obvious that *esse* is *percipi*. Although he doesn't consider the possibility of deriving that *esse* is *percipi* by self-evident steps from other self-evident synthetic necessary a priori truths, it must be admitted that the likelihood of doing this is small. In itself, however, this is not very serious, since, surely, the great mass of philosophical truths must fall in this category. But then, the fact that, if true, *'Esse* is *percipi'* does so as well doesn't tell us much, and cannot constitute a serious criticism. One of Moore's important errors, in this paper and beyond, is that he doesn't recognize this.

But this isn't the end of the matter. Despite his methodological overreach, and concomitant inability to show that Idealists will never find a way to make their case, he does have important things to say. He remarks:

> Idealists, we have seen, must assert that whatever is experienced, is *necessarily* so. And this doctrine they commonly express by saying that "the object of experience is inconceivable apart from the subject." I have hitherto been concerned with pointing out what meaning this assertion must have, if it is to be an important truth [i.e., it must be understood to be an instance of the synthetic necessary a priori]. I now propose to show that it may have an important meaning, which must be false, because it is self-contradictory. . . .
> What I suggest then is that Idealists hold the particular doctrine in question, concerning the relation of subject and object in experience, because they think it is an analytic truth in this restricted sense that it is proved by the law of contradiction alone.[47]

There are three points to notice. First, Moore seems to adopt what he takes to be the traditional definition of an analytic truth as one the denial of which is inconceivable because it is self-contradictory. This can be defended by noting that when S is a logical truth, $\ulcorner \sim S \urcorner$ is logically equivalent to $\ulcorner S \mathbin{\&} \sim S \urcorner$, which in turn is a denial of what is often called "the law of noncontradiction," $\sim(A \mathbin{\&} \sim A)$.[48] This, I think, is what Moore has in mind in reporting Idealists as supposing that their understanding of *'Esse* is *percipi'* "can be proved by the law of contradiction."[49] Second,

---

[47] Ibid., pp. 12–13.

[48] 'A' is here used as a schematic letter. Understood in this way the schema asserts each of its instances.

[49] This talk of what can be proved from what, based on an observation about what is a logical consequence of what, is, of course, unfortunate for mixing up the proof theory of logic with its model theory (for which Moore himself can't really be faulted). But in the present case this is no matter. The important point is that an analytic truth is one that is

he identifies the Idealists' reason for accepting '*Esse* is *percipi*' as the belief that it is analytic. Third, he has already argued that this belief is false. If he is right, this undermines the Idealists' master argument, *as they understood it,* by undermining their support for its first premise.

Now he goes further, suggesting that their belief is contradictory. Why? His answer involves an excursus into the philosophy of perception.

> I am suggesting that the Idealist maintains that object and subject are necessarily connected, mainly because he fails to see that they are *distinct*. . . . When he thinks of "yellow" and when he thinks of the "sensation of yellow," he fails to see that there is anything whatever in the latter which is not in the former. This being so, to deny that yellow [the thing experienced] can ever *be* apart from the sensation of yellow [the experiencing of it] is merely to deny that yellow can ever be other than it is; since yellow and the sensation of yellow are absolutely identical. *To assert that yellow is necessarily an object of experience is to assert that yellow is necessarily yellow*—a purely identical proposition, and therefore proved by the law of contradiction alone.[50]

Here we have an interesting diagnosis of a significant philosophical error. Since what I see when I see something yellow is *not* my experience of seeing it, anyone who failed to distinguish the two would be making an error, one which *might* be the source of the more general error of thinking that *esse* is *percipi*. Whether or not some, all, or none of those criticized by Moore really did commit these errors is beyond my brief. However, it is still puzzling why he took anyone who did so to hold a *self-contradictory* belief.

He continues the passage.

> Of course the proposition [that yellow is necessarily an object of experience, or that yellow = the sensation of yellow] also implies that experience is, after all, something distinct from yellow—*else there would be no reason for insisting that yellow is a sensation*: and that the argument thus both affirms and denies that yellow and [the] sensation of yellow are distinct, is what sufficiently refutes it.[51]

Moore is confused; nothing the Idealist asserts or implicitly assumes entails anything contradictory. Let us grant, what Moore seems to suppose, namely that the proposition the Idealist asserts—*that yellow is necessarily an object of experience*—is either identical with or equivalent to the proposition that *that necessarily yellow = the sensation of yellow*. Next suppose (i) that asserting *that necessarily A = B* only makes sense as a way of ruling out (what

---

synonymous with, and hence expresses the same proposition as, a logical truth. Hence the denial of an analytic truth is synonymous with, and expresses the same proposition as, a sentence logically equivalent to a contradiction. In this broad sense, an analytic truth is one the denial of which is self-contradictory. If this is what Moore assumes, there is nothing to which to object.

[50] Ibid., pp. 13–14, my emphasis.
[51] Ibid., p. 14, my emphasis.

one takes to be) *the genuine possibility that A ≠ B,* and (ii) *that If A = B, then it is no more possible that A ≠ B than it is possible that A ≠ A*—and so *if it is possible that A ≠ B, then A ≠ B.*[52] One who believed all this would take the Idealist's *insistence* that yellow = the sensation of yellow, as indicating that the Idealist "both affirms and denies that yellow and [the] sensation of yellow are distinct," which is very close to what Moore does. It differs from Moore's own way of putting the point in that the latter wrongly suggests that the Idealist's alleged inconsistency is alone attributable to the proposition the Idealist asserts, rather than to the Idealist's asserting of that proposition. But the real problem here is more serious. Although there may be interpretations of *necessity/possibility* on which (i) is true, and other interpretations on which (ii) is true, there is no (relevant) interpretation on which both are.

Having explained the source of Moore's error in terms of the interaction of identity, necessity, and possibility, it may be helpful to go over essentially the same ground using explicitly logical and semantic notions. When a and b are different singular terms (names, definite descriptions, or compound function/argument terms) ⌜a ≠ b⌝ is not, when true, a logical truth, and ⌜a = b⌝ is not, when false, logically equivalent to a contradiction.[53] So, 'Yellow ≠ the sensation of yellow' is *not* analytic in the sense I have characterized, and 'Yellow = the sensation of yellow' is *not* self-contradictory; similarly for the propositions these sentences express. Of course, ⌜a = a⌝ is a logical truth and its negation is self-contradictory (in our broad sense), but ⌜a = b⌝ isn't a logical truth (when true) and its negation isn't contradictory.[54] Since in some cases ⌜a = b⌝ expresses the same proposition as ⌜a = a⌝, sometimes the *proposition* it expresses is analytic. However, this doesn't affect the passage; neither 'Yellow = the sensation of yellow' nor the proposition it expresses is the "self-contradictory" negation of an analytic truth (in the sense here defined). So, there is no (logical) contradiction in the controversial identity that the Idealist asserts. *No such proposition* "[logically] implies that experience is, after all, something distinct from yellow," and *no argument* attributed to the Idealist "both affirms and denies that yellow and [the] sensation of yellow are distinct."

Might there, nevertheless, be a contradiction in what the Idealist believes, or implicitly commits himself to? Suppose one thought (i) that *all true* identity statements ⌜a = b⌝ express the same propositions as the corresponding statements ⌜a = a⌝, (ii) that because of this an utterance of the former can be no more informative than an utterance of the latter, and (iii)

---

[52] 'A' and 'B' are here used as schematic placeholders for singular terms (i.e., names, function-argument compounds, or definite descriptions).

[53] There are exceptions to this broad claim when one or more of the terms are definite descriptions—e.g., when b = ⌜the x: x = c & x ≠ a⌝—but none of these are relevant to Moore's example.

[54] Again, definite descriptions make for exceptions, as when b = ⌜the x: x = a⌝. These are irrelevant for Moore's example.

that one who *insists* on using the informative ⌜a = b⌝ rather than the uninformative ⌜a = a⌝ must therefore *implicitly* recognize both its falsity and the truth of the proposition expressed by its negation ⌜a ≠ b⌝. Then one could conclude that the Idealist implicitly believes, and commits himself to, a proposition that contradicts the one he asserts. The problem, of course, is that this not so; as shown in chapters 1 and 2, (i), (ii), and (iii) are false. In short, no matter how Moore's passage is elucidated, it does not show the Idealist's position to be contradictory.

Fortunately, Moore does not need to show that the Idealist's position is contradictory. If he is right that Idealists identify yellow with the sensation of it, and take *esse* to be *percipi* for this reason, then his criticism will hold—since the experience of yellow *is* different from that of which it is an experience. Moore realizes that some Idealists admit there to be a distinction between the two, while fudging the point by claiming that the two form "an organic unity" and so can't be considered apart from one another. He is understandably suspicious.

> A distinction is asserted; but it is *also* asserted that the things distinguished form an "organic unity." But forming such a unity, it is held, each would not be what it is *apart from its relation to the other*. Hence to consider either by itself is to make an *illegitimate abstraction*. The recognition that there are "organic unities" and "illegitimate abstractions" in this sense is regarded as one of the chief conquests of modern philosophy. . . . An abstraction is illegitimate, when and only when we attempt to assert of *a part*—of something abstracted—that which is true only of the *whole* to which it belongs. . . . The principle is used to assert that certain abstractions are *in all cases* illegitimate; that whenever you try to assert *anything whatever* of that which is *part* of an organic whole, what you assert can only be true of the whole. And this principle, so far from being a useful truth, is necessarily false.[55]

The principle Moore cites is, of course, false, and if those he criticizes in fact relied on it, they certainly were in error. While it is hard to be sure that he correctly diagnosed the source of their errors, it is even harder to believe that their confidence in overturning our fundamental commonsense convictions was matched by an ability to clearly identify cogent reasons for doing so. The burden of proof required to establish the impossibility of anything's existing without being experienced is high. The difficulty of Moore's struggle to unearth such justifying reasons in the work of those he criticizes is some evidence that they didn't exist.

This is the backdrop for the second half of the article, in which he advances an ambitious view about the relation between a thought, perception, or other conscious experience, and its object—that which is thought, perceived, or experienced. Though the view involves some surprising elements, which may themselves require some modest departures

---

[55] Moore (1903a), p. 15.

from common sense, it is an interesting one. Here is Moore's initial statement of it.

> We have then in every sensation two distinct elements, one which I call con-
> sciousness, and another which I call the object of consciousness. This must
> be so if the sensation of blue and the sensation of green, though different in
> one respect, are alike in another: blue is one object of sensation and green is
> another, and consciousness, which both sensations have in common, is dif-
> ferent from either.[56]

Having distinguished the color one is conscious of both from one's consciousness of it, and from consciousness in general, he asks whether it can
exist independently of being perceived. He rightly finds it *conceivable* that
it should, and quickly concludes that its unperceived existence is genuinely possible. Unfortunately, he doesn't seem to notice the gap between
the two claims.

> For we can and must conceive the existence of blue as something quite dis-
> tinct from the existence of the sensation. We can and must conceive that blue
> might exist and yet the sensation of blue not exist. For my own part I not
> only conceive this, but conceive [i.e., believe] it to be true. Either therefore
> this terrific assertion of inconceivability [by Idealists] means what is false and
> self-contradictory or else it means only that *as a matter of fact* blue never can
> exist unless the sensation of it does.[57]

The first three sentences of the passage run together the truth that blue ≠
the sensation of blue with the yet unestablished claim that it is possible for
the former to exist without the latter. The final sentence perpetuates the
error. The emphasis on "as a matter of fact" seems designed to signal that
since the evident *conceivability* of blue existing unperceived establishes
the genuine *possibility* of its so existing, the claim that it can't exist unperceived can only be understood as the claim that, as a contingent matter
of fact, blue never has, or will, exist unperceived. If so, then his argument
is only as good as the implicit assumption that conceivability entails possibility, a principle rendered problematic at best and obsolete at worst by
Saul Kripke's recognition of the necessary a posteriori.[58] Moore is right
that the claim that blue can't or doesn't exist unperceived isn't analytic,
but nothing he says demonstrates that it isn't necessary.

This is unfortunate because he didn't have to go overboard. When I look
at my blue 1971 Volvo I see blue.[59] Like Moore, I not only can conceive

---

[56] Ibid., p. 17.

[57] Ibid., p. 19.

[58] For a post-Kripkean account of the relationship between conceivability and possibility,
see Soames (2006b) and chapter 9 of Soames (2009c).

[59] Here and throughout I follow Moore in using locutions like 'I see blue'. Though
Moore's use may be metaphysically loaded—where the blue that is seen is an *instance* of the
universal blue (see Baldwin (1990), pp. 45–50)—I will use such locutions in the sense of 'I

of it existing when no one is looking, I firmly believe—in fact know—that it does. How do I know? Perhaps the fact that I can conceive it existing unperceived provides *prima facie* reason to believe that it does, which will be conclusive if I have no defeating, or contrary, evidence—which I don't. Perhaps the fact that the blue that I see is the color of my car, which is the kind of thing that can, and does, exist unperceived, adds to my justified confidence about the persistence of unperceived blue. There is, of course, a philosophical problem of explaining how I know what I know. Some philosopher might doubt that I *know* that blue can and does exist unperceived, or even that it *does*, or *could*, so exist. Moore's Idealists do both. What he doesn't clearly state at this stage of his career is that he doesn't have to *prove* them wrong—by coming up with an argument even they must accept—in order to vindicate his "Common Sense view." The burden of proof is on them to justify their denial of the obvious. If they do provide a putative justification, he or I will have to challenge it, or give up our view. *In this case, though, no such putative justification has been offered.* Since the burden of proof is on them, Moore is free to elaborate his alternative.

The example of seeing my Volvo invites a response—that the sense in which my car can be seen (as blue) is derivative from the primary sense in which the objects of perception are our own "ideas" or impressions. These are, the response continues, what, properly speaking, are *directly seen* to be blue or not. By contrast, cars—if there be such things—are only perceived in the indirect sense of standing in a certain relation R to car-ideas; for a car to be blue is for it to have the power to produce ideas in us that are directly seen as blue. A philosopher who takes this line may respond to my example by admitting that it is possible for the blue surface of my car to exist unseen [in the alleged secondary senses of 'blue' and 'see'], while insisting that it is impossible for any *idea* that I *directly* see to be blue to exist at a time when it is not perceived.

Though I find this theory of perception to be implausible, and sharply at odds with what we pre-theoretically think, it has a venerable history in philosophy, which would continue to win adherents long after Moore's "Refutation." What is striking about the second half of his paper is not that it offers any real refutation of this theory, or even any very sustained attack, but that it begins to sketch a plausible alternative that would be developed by others nearly a century later. Here is one insightful passage.

> [T]he most striking results both of Idealism and of Agnosticism are only obtained by identifying blue with the sensation of blue: that *esse* is held to be identical with *percipi*, solely because what is experienced is held to be identical

---

see something blue', or—better—as 'I see something *as blue,* or *as being blue'.* The difference is that the former doesn't specify whether what I see looks blue to me. While the latter settles this, it doesn't specify whether what I see really is blue. In the example of my Volvo, it both is and looks blue, so I won't worry about the difference. The same will be true for other examples, unless otherwise indicated.

with the experience of it. . . . [T]hat my opinion is plausible, I will now offer two pieces of evidence. The first is that language offers us no means of referring to such objects as "blue" and "green" and "sweet," except by calling them sensations. . . . And similarly we have no natural means of referring to such objects as "causality" or "likeness" or "identity," except by calling them "ideas" or "notions" or "conceptions." But it is hardly likely that if philosophers had clearly distinguished . . . between a sensation or an idea and what I have called its object, there should have been no separate name for the latter. They have always used the same name for these two different "things" . . . and hence there is some probability that they have supposed these "things" . . . to be . . . one and the same. . . . [S]econdly . . . when we refer to introspection and try to discover what the sensation of blue is, it is very easy to suppose that we have before us only a single term. The term "blue" is easy enough to distinguish, but the other element which I have called "consciousness"—that which the sensation of blue has in common with the sensation of green—is extremely difficult to fix . . . it seems . . . to be transparent—we look through it and see nothing but the blue.[60]

What good reason is there for supposing that whenever I have a sensation of blue, the thing I see is a mind-dependent thing the existence of which is contingent on its being experienced (by me)? "None," says Moore. The temptation to think otherwise comes from confusing the experience or sensation—thought of as a cognitive act or event—with that of which it is an experience.

What about cases in which something looks blue, even though it really isn't, or worse, cases of hallucination in which one seemingly has a sensation of blue despite the fact that nothing in one's environment even looks blue? Surely, it will be objected, what one sees in such cases are mind-dependent things that couldn't exist unperceived. Though Moore doesn't here address this objection, there is a three-part response available to him. First, when something in one's environment looks blue but isn't, the thing one sees *as blue* may continue to exist unperceived, which was all that was legitimately meant by his talk of seeing blue. Second, in hallucination one may have a cognitive experience very like the experience one has when seeing something blue; nevertheless, it is not a case of seeing anything as blue, since nothing whatsoever is appearing blue to one. No matter how much the experience resembles one of genuinely seeing something, it is not a case of seeing anything. Thus, the question of whether what one perceives could exist unperceived doesn't come up. Third, one's pseudo-perceptual experience may, despite this, have a propositional content related to that of an ordinary perception. When one sees an object o as blue, one's visual experience represents o as being blue, which means that one bears a certain attitude to the proposition that o is blue. Although the

[60] Ibid., pp. 19–20.

proposition isn't what one sees—what one sees is o—one is in a cognitive state of predicating *being blue* of o, which is what it is to entertain the proposition that o is blue.[61] In the hallucination case, one is not entertaining that proposition, or any other singular proposition, though one may be entertaining the proposition that *something here (in front of one) is blue.*

Of course, much more would have to be said to justify analyzing perceiving, imagining, believing, or in some other way cognizing, something as consisting of a certain kind of thing, on the one hand, and a cognitive attitude toward that thing on the other—where, in general, the thing could exist without being the object of the attitude. Moore didn't articulate any well-worked-out view of this kind. However, views of this sort can be worked out from a starting point very like his. For example, contemporary versions of what is often called "Intentionalism"—discussed in Byrne (2001)—hold that perceptual and cognitive states or experiences are all, at bottom, bearers of representational content. They are, or involve, relations to propositions, where propositions themselves may be taken to be mind-independent entities, constructed from, or intimately connected to, worldly objects and properties. Though proponents of such views may be able to accommodate internally perceived ideas or images, typically they find no motivation for such private objects of perception.

Here, it is useful to compare the last Moorean passage cited—about the confused use of the term 'idea' or 'sensation' to stand both for a certain kind of experience and for that of which it is supposed to be an experience—with parallel comments made by Byrne about a confusion engendered by two uses of the word 'pain'. Byrne's remarks occur in the course of defending the idea that pain—the alleged paradigm of a phenomenal thing "felt" or "experienced" that could not exist unexperienced—is really just the experience itself—a kind of perception (of hurt or damage)—rather than the thing experienced. Like Moore, Byrne notes the inconsistent ways in which the word 'pain' is commonly used as a source of resistance to this analysis.

> Although [Thomas] Reid thought the vulgar innocent of confusion, the evidence is very much against them. I have been following Reid in taking a "sensation" to be an experience, and that sometimes does correspond to ordinary usage: as Reid says, there is no difference between the sensation and the feeling of it; they are one and the same thing. However, we often think of sensations as being the objects of experiences, not the experiences themselves: "I feel an odd sensation in my elbow/a churning sensation in my stomach/ a painful sensation in my toe." Specific sensation words are no better off. On the one hand: "Pain is a feeling. Surely that is uncontroversial. To have pain and to feel pain are one and the same." On the other hand: pain is not

---

[61] To predicate *being blue* of o is not to judge o to be blue, but to consider o's being blue. For more on predication, and its relation to judging, believing, knowing, and asserting see Soames (2010b; 2014c; forthcoming).

a feeling—one's feeling of the pain in the toe is a mental event, and so is in the head, or in the mind, while the pain felt is (presumably) in the toe. If the distinction between pains-as-experiences and pains-as-objects-of-experiences was explicitly recognized then it would be evident that there was some question about whether pains-as-objects exist, or are as they seem to be. But almost everyone appears to be convinced that the question makes no sense at all: there are no illusions of pain—phantom limb pain is pain![62]

In short, there is a promising, and quite general, analysis of cognitive states for which Moore is groping—partially successfully and partially not—in "The Refutation of Idealism." He articulates his basic idea by saying that "In every sensation or idea we must distinguish two elements, (1) the "object," or that in which one differs from another; and (2) 'consciousness,' or that which all have in common—that which makes them sensations or mental facts."[63]

Although this distinction between a cognitive act or attitude and its object is very natural, there is something a bit contentious about how Moore draws it. Having correctly distinguished the sensation (perception, experience) of x from x, he characterizes that which the sensation (perception, experience) of x has in common with the sensation (perception, experience) of y, simply as "consciousness." This encourages the idea that the "object" of the experience is *no part of consciousness at all*, and so is utterly mind-independent. Being such, there is no reason to think that its existence requires being perceived or experienced. This is how Moore, perhaps rightly, seems to think of the matter. However, his discussion moves too quickly.

Whatever one thinks of its plausibility, there is room for the view that the sensation of blue consists of one's perception of a blue mental particular or "image." Think of one's "self" as analogous to a homunculus in the theater of the mind watching a parade of images produced on an internal screen by one's nervous system. The proponent of the analogy could admit what Moore belabors—namely, that the sensation of blue (the perception of a blue image) isn't itself blue—while continuing to insist that the object of the sensation—the blue image in one's mental theater—is itself a constituent of one's mind, and so can't exist unexperienced. Why this should be so—why we should think that the image on the mental screen would cease to exist if the occupant of the theater should direct his attention elsewhere—might, I suppose, remain unexplained. Of course, the whole idea of explaining perception by positing a homunculus is absurd. Since no one wants a homunculus within a homunculus, the perception of the original homunculus presumably would have to be explained as Moore would explain our ordinary perception—namely as consisting

---

[62] Ibid., p. 229.
[63] Moore (1903a), p. 20 of Moore (1922a).

of a perceptual act the object of which is independent of the cognitive activity of the perceiver. Why then posit a mental theater in the first place?

Proponents of the view that what we directly see are mental images—which have precisely the properties they appear to have and which can't exist unperceived—do not, of course, literally invoke a homunculus in such a theater. However, they face similar explanatory problems. Why is it that, according to them, what we *directly* see is a mental image rather than an external thing? The idea, I think, is roughly this: since what we really see is how things appear (to us), what we really see are *appearances*—images of things, rather than the things themselves. But how is this justified? When we see something, it does appear to us in a certain way, and so our visual experience represents it as being that way. However, recognizing this provides no support for the claim that *what we see* is an image. In everyday life, talk of seeing images or appearances is shorthand for talk of how things visually appear. The problem comes when (some) philosophers turn things back to front, by taking the things directly seen to be appearances, and analyzing talk of how things appear to be in terms of talk about how appearances really are. Once the switch is made, it will seem obvious that the appearances we directly perceive have precisely the properties they seem to have. That is just what it is to be an appearance. Moreover, when they don't appear to have any properties—because we are not perceiving them—they won't have any properties—because they don't exist. This conclusion, which Moore works so hard to resist, follows naturally enough, *if one starts with the idea that we see appearances*.

The problem is that there is no good reason to start there. Since the ordinary, default view is that what is seen, heard, touched, tasted, or smelled is independent of us, abandoning it in favor of the view that the only things we ever perceive are our own mental constructions requires powerful justification. In short, the burden of proof is on Moore's opponents. Of course, many philosophers who preceded Moore, and also many who followed, offered what they took to be good reasons—the most important of which will be dealt with in detail in later chapters (and volumes). In "The Refutation of Idealism," Moore was prescient both in opposing them, and in identifying some of the elements of a more satisfactory view. However, his attempts to confront the most defensible version of the views he was opposing were not as successful as they perhaps should have been.

For example, on pages 23 and 24 he runs together the view that what we see are mental images—mental particulars that may happen to be blue—with the view that our sensations *of blue*—i.e., cognitive acts of perceiving blue—are themselves blue. Since that latter is, if not patently absurd, at least grossly implausible, the former is, perhaps too quickly, placed in the same category. Here is Moore:

> We have it, then, as a universally received opinion that blue is related to the sensation or idea of blue, as its *content*, and that this view, if it is to be true,

must mean that blue is part of *what* is said to exist when we say that a sensation exists.[64]

The thought here is that for blue to be part of the "content" of a thing—e.g., a blue bead or a blue flower—is for the bead or the flower to be blue. So, on Moore's understanding of the views he is criticizing, the sensation is not just *of blue*, it is itself blue.[65] This leads him to suppose that these views *identify* a perception of blue with a blue thing perceived. This, he believes, is what philosophers have talked about when they have spoken of mental images (impressions). He continues describing what he takes to be their view:

> Any sensation or idea is a "*thing*," and what I have called its object is the quality of this thing. Such a "thing" is what we think of when we think of a *mental image*. A mental image is conceived as if it were related to that of which it is the image . . . in exactly the same way as the image in a looking-glass is related to that of which it is a reflection; in both cases there is an identity of content [i.e., they have the same visual properties], and the image in the looking-glass differs from that in the mind solely in respect of the fact that in the one case the other constituent of the image is "glass" and in the other case it is consciousness. [So in one case we have, I guess, *blue glass* while in the other we have *blue consciousness*.] If the image is of blue, it is not conceived that this "content" has any relation to the consciousness but what it has to the glass: it is conceived *merely* to be its *content* [i.e., to be one of its properties].[66]

He will shortly reject the idea that there are mental images of this sort, as well he should. But first he indicates the philosophical danger inherent in the position he will attack.

> And owing to the fact that sensations and ideas are all considered to be *wholes* of this description—things in the mind—the question: What do you know? is considered to be identical with the question: What reason have we for supposing that there are things outside the mind *corresponding* to these that are inside it?[67]

Having emphasized what is at stake, Moore at last delivers his conclusive rejection. Of course, a sensation *of blue* (the cognitive act of awareness of something being blue) is not that of which it is an awareness, and is not itself blue. Having tendentiously identified mental images (which many

---

[64] Ibid., p. 23.

[65] Moore is explicit about this on page 26, where he says: "I can now make plain what I meant by asserting . . . that blue is probably not part of the content of the sensation [of blue] at all. . . . [I meant] if it were true [that blue were part of the content of the sensation], then when the sensation of blue exists, there exists a *blue awareness*."

[66] Ibid., pp. 23–24.

[67] Ibid., p. 24.

philosophers have thought can be blue) with sensations *of blue*, he swiftly dispenses with mental images as that of which we are directly aware in perception or other cognitive acts.

> What I wish to point out is . . . that we have no reason for supposing that there are such things as mental images at all. . . . The true analysis of sensation or idea is as follows. . . . A sensation is, in reality, a case of 'knowing' or 'being aware of' or 'experiencing' something. When we know that the sensation of blue exists, the fact we know is that there exists an awareness of blue. And this awareness . . . has a perfectly distinct and unique relation to blue. . . . This relation is just that which we mean in every case by 'knowing.' To have in your mind 'knowledge' of blue, is *not* to have in your mind a 'thing' or 'image' of which blue is the content [i.e., a mental particular that is blue]. To be aware of the sensation of blue is *not* to be aware of a mental image—of a "thing" of which 'blue' and some other element are constituent parts in the same sense in which blue and glass are constituent parts of a blue bead. It is to be aware of an awareness of blue; awareness being used, in both cases, in exactly the same sense.[68]

I have no quarrel with the view here expressed, which seems to me to be brilliantly correct. My quarrel is that Moore has come by it too easily. The correct conclusion—that when we perceive (something) *as blue*, what we perceive is not a mental image—cannot be established simply by noting that no experiences *of blue* are themselves either blue, or the things experienced. Yet that is the only argument Moore gives. One of the very important possibilities he neglects was mentioned earlier. Some philosophers who speak of directly perceiving appearances or impressions of things would be perfectly content to grant that these objects of perception are distinct from all cognitive acts of being aware of them, even though both the acts and their objects are "parts of, or dependent on, our consciousness," and so mental. As I have indicated, I don't think these philosophers have any good grounds for their implausible view. But in order to engage them, one must deal more directly with their convictions than Moore did.

It remains only to sum up the lessons Moore drew from his discussion. Relating his discussion of sensation to the Idealist metaphysics, he says:

> Idealists admit that some things really exist of which they are not aware: there are some things they hold, which are not inseparable aspects of *their* experience, even if they be inseparable aspects of some experience. . . . And what my analysis of sensation has been designed to show is, that whenever I have a mere sensation or idea, the fact is that I am then aware of something which is equally and in the same sense *not* an inseparable aspect of my experience. . . . There is, therefore, no question of how we are to "get outside

---

[68] Ibid., pp. 24–25.

the circle of our own ideas and sensations." Merely to have a sensation is already to *be* outside that circle.[69]

So, it would seem, Idealists must at least *understand* Moore's claim that the object of my sensation could exist independently of my experience. Could they afford to admit that it is correct, while continuing to hold that for that object to exist, it must be the object of another experience, of me or someone else? Moore doesn't think so, since he thinks such an admission would undermine any reason they might have for taking *esse* to be *percipi*.

> I think I am not mistaken in asserting that the reason why Idealists suppose that everything which *is* must be an inseparable aspect of some experience, is that they suppose some things, at least, to be inseparable aspects of *their* experience. . . . But if we never experience anything but what is *not* an inseparable aspect of *that* experience, how can we infer that anything whatever, let alone *everything*, is an inseparable aspect of *any* experience? How utterly unfounded the assumption "*esse* is *percipi*" appears in the clearest light.[70]

In addition to undermining a radically revisionary metaphysical view, Moore takes his analysis to provide positive support for our ordinary conception of the world.

> If . . . we clearly recognize . . . that peculiar relation which I have called "awareness of anything"; if we see *this* is involved equally in the analysis of *every* experience . . . if, further, we recognise that this awareness is . . . of such a nature that its object, when we are aware of it, is precisely what it would be, if we were not aware: then it becomes plain that the existence of a table in space is related to my experience of *it* in precisely the same way as the existence of my own experience is related to my experience of *that* . . . and if it is true that my experience can exist, even when I do not happen to be aware of its existence, we have exactly the same reason for supposing that the table can do so also. . . . I am as directly aware of the existence of material things in space as of my own sensations. . . . The question requiring to be asked about material things is thus not: What reason have we for supposing that anything exists *corresponding* to our sensations? but: What reason have we for supposing that material things do *not* exist, since *their* existence has precisely the same evidence as that of our sensations? . . . The only *reasonable* alternative to the admission that matter exists *as well as* spirit, is absolute Scepticism—that as likely as not *nothing* exists at all. All other suppositions . . . are, if we have no reason for believing in matter, as baseless as the grossest superstitions.[71]

Although the vaulting ambition of the conclusion with which Moore ends the article is unmistakable, we should resist the temptation to read his argument as "a proof of the existence of a (partly material) external

[69] Ibid., pp. 26–27.
[70] Ibid., 27–28.
[71] Ibid., pp. 29–30.

world" from the premise that sensations, and experiences, exist. For one thing, the premise that sensations exist is hardly trivial if (i) Moore is right that the object of a sensation can always exist unperceived, and (ii) in at least some hallucinations there is no such object. For another thing, Moore didn't do much to establish the correctness of the analysis of perception and other forms of cognitive awareness that he so interestingly and provocatively articulated. Moreover, any attempt to do so would, I suspect, find it necessary to invoke, or take for granted, the existence of the very external world one was attempting to "prove."

For these reasons, Moore should, I think, be seen as engaged in a different project—namely as sketching an account of perception, and other forms of awareness, that both fits comfortably within our commonsense conception of the world, and allows us to specify, from within that perspective, the conclusive evidence we have that supports its central tenets. The fact that skeptics, or philosophers with other agendas, will not allow us our starting points, and cannot be led to them by self-evident steps from premises they already accept, does not undermine our claim to know them to be true, or defeat our explanation of how we know them. The contribution toward which Moore is groping is not one that provides an argument that must persuade any rational skeptic or revisionary metaphysician. Rather, it is one that articulates our largely pre-philosophical worldview in a way that offers the skeptic, or metaphysician, few, if any, materials to build a case against us. When this is accomplished, we will be in position to turn the tables on our commonsense-defying opponent by demanding a justification of *his* premises that provides *us* with a reason for accepting them. This, I think, was the heart of the program of the great epistemologist G. E. Moore. In "The Refutation of Idealism" we see him take his first major step in becoming that epistemologist.

∽⊖∾

CHAPTER 4

Goodness and the Foundations of Ethics

1. Moore's Main Theses about Goodness and Rightness
2. The Argument that *Good* Is Indefinable
   2.1. Definability and the Analytic/Synthetic Distinction
   2.2. Simple, Indefinable Properties: Being Good and Being Yellow
   2.3. The Open-Question Argument
3. The Role of the Indefinability Thesis in Moore's Argument for T1
   3.1. The Argument
   3.2. Interpretation 1
   3.3. Interpretation 2
4. Can Moore's Argument Be Repaired? Why Definability Is Not the Issue
5. Self-Evidence: The Tension in Moore's View
6. Moore's Flawed Conception of Justification in Ethics
7. Historical Note: The Influence of Sidgwick and Russell on *Principia Ethica*

1. MOORE'S MAIN THESES ABOUT GOODNESS AND RIGHTNESS

Moore's 1903 *Principia Ethica* was to become one of the philosophical classics of the twentieth century.[1] In the preface, he distinguishes two kinds of ethical questions.

A. What kinds of things ought to exist for their own sakes?
                are good in themselves?
                have intrinsic value?
B. What kinds of actions ought we to perform?
                are right?
                are duties?

He takes the different versions of A to be equivalent. The same is true of the B questions, with the exception of a slight difference between what he means by calling an action our *duty*, or one that *we ought to perform*, on the one hand, and what he means by calling it *right*. For Moore, there is no difference between duties and acts we ought to perform. Every such act is right. However, it is sometimes possible for our duty to be to perform

[1] Moore (1903b); all citations will be to the 1993 revised edition.

either one or the other of two different acts. In such cases both acts are right, though neither is, itself, a duty (or one we ought to perform). But for this exception, Moore takes the different versions of B to be equivalent.

Corresponding to these two kinds of questions are two kinds of ethical statements—those purporting to answer A-questions and those purporting to answer B-questions. Purported partial answers to A-questions are:

The apprehension of beauty is (intrinsically) good.[2]
Knowledge is (intrinsically) good.
Friendship is (intrinsically) good.

Purported partial answers to questions of type B are:

Keeping one's promises is right.
Telling the truth is right.
Helping others is right.

In the preface, Moore announces two theses about A-statements and B-statements.[3]

T1. If the conclusion of an argument is an A-statement, but none of its premises are, then the premises do not entail the conclusion, and their truth provides no evidence for, or any compelling reason to believe, it.

T2. If the conclusion of an argument is a B-statement, then the premises entail the conclusion only if they include both an A-statement and a "causal statement" (or another B-statement).

Thesis 2 expresses Moore's commitment to *consequentialism*—the view that the rightness of an action is wholly determined by the goodness or badness of its consequences. In other words, the rightness of an action is simply a matter of the goodness of the states of affairs it brings about.

The classical *utilitarianism* of Bentham and Mill is a theory of this kind.

1a. An act is right iff it produces more good consequences than any alternative act open to the agent.
 b. Happiness and happiness alone is good.
 c. Therefore, an act is right iff it produces more happiness than any alternative act open to the agent.

The first premise here is common to all consequentialist theories, expressing an idea in keeping with T2. The second premise is a statement of type A. Different versions of consequentialism result from taking different

---

[2] In discussing Moore, I will (unless otherwise indicated) use 'good' to mean *good in itself*, or *good as an end*, rather than *good as a means to some end*.

[3] In articulating these theses, Moore is putting aside technical niceties, and painting with a broad brush. For example, a statement containing a predicate distinct from, but defined in terms of, 'good' might entail an A-statement without itself being an A-statement. Moore is implicitly excluding such cases.

A-statements to play the role of (1b). For Moore, principles of type A provide the foundation of all ethical judgments. Hence, they are the ones with which he is most concerned.

They are also the subject of his main thesis, T1, which was viewed as a bold and startling claim. Ordinarily, one would think that the claim that something is good can, at least sometimes, be supported by evidence and argument. In such cases, one is inclined to think, one may truly say that x is good *because* x is so-and-so—where the claim that *x is so-and-so* is not itself an explicitly evaluative claim, requiring still further defense and justification. However, if T1 is correct, this natural idea is mistaken.

The main premise Moore uses to support T1 is thesis T3.

T3. *Good* is indefinable.

Moore thinks he can demonstrate the truth of T3. In addition, he thinks that once T3 is established, we will see that T1 must also be true. How so? One way of making the case is by adding a further thesis that he suggests at the end of section 5, chapter 1.[4]

T4. It is impossible to know what constitutes evidence for the proposition that something is good unless one knows the definition of *good*.

It might seem that if both T3 and T4 are true, then T1 must also be true. For suppose that *good* is indefinable. Then, since it has no definition, no one can know the definition of *good*. If, in addition, T4 is true, then no one can know what constitutes evidence that anything is good. This in turn suggests that there can be no evidence for the proposition that a particular thing is good, or any compelling reason to accept it. Hence, T1.

This seems, subject to certain clarifications, to have been Moore's view. The first clarification concerns his notion of definition, to which he devotes sections 6–8 of chapter 1. Immediately after asserting T4 in section 5, Moore devotes section 6 to discussing what he does, and doesn't, mean by a definition.

What, then, is good? How is good to be defined? Now it may be thought that this is a verbal question. . . . But this is not the sort of definition I am asking

---

[4] See also section 86, pp. 192–93. There, in commenting on why we need to settle what 'good' means by determining whether or not it is definable, Moore says:

[W]e can never know on what *evidence* an ethical proposition rests, until we know the nature of the notion which makes the proposition ethical. We cannot tell what is possible by way of proof, in favor of one judgment "That this or that is good," or against another judgment "That this or that is bad," until we have recognized what the nature of such propositions must always be. In fact, it follows from the meaning of 'good' and 'bad' [in particular that they are indefinable], that such propositions are all of them, in Kant's phrase, "synthetic": that they must rest in the end upon some proposition which must simply be accepted or rejected, which cannot be logically be deduced from any other proposition.

for. . . . I should, indeed, be foolish, if I tried to use it [namely the word 'good'] for something which it did not usually denote. . . . I shall, therefore, use the word in the sense in which I think it is ordinarily used. . . . [But] [m]y business is solely with that object or idea, which I hold, rightly or wrongly, that the word is generally used to stand for. What I want to discover is the nature of that object or idea.[5]

As should be clear, Moore's secondary concern with the definition of a word—in this case 'good'—is entirely derivative from his primary concern with the "object or idea" it denotes, by which he means the *concept* or *property* the word contributes to propositions expressed by sentences containing it.

What then is it for a concept to be definable, or indefinable? Moore illustrates what he means in section 7.

My point is that 'good' is a simple notion, just as 'yellow' is a simple notion. . . . Definitions of the kind that I was asking for, definitions which describe the real nature of the object or notion [i.e., of the concept] denoted by the word . . . are only possible when the object or notion [concept] is something complex. You can give a definition of a horse [i.e., of the concept *horse*] because a horse has many different properties and qualities, all of which you can enumerate. But when you have enumerated them all, when you have reduced a horse to his simplest terms [i.e., to the simplest concepts/properties that make up anything that is a horse], then you can no longer define those terms [concepts]. . . . And so it is with all objects [concepts] . . . which we are able to define: they are all complex; all composed of parts [simpler concepts], which may themselves . . . be capable of similar definition, but which must in the end be reducible to simplest parts [concepts], which can no longer be defined. But yellow and good, we say, are not complex: they are notions of that simple kind, out of which definitions are composed and with which the power of further defining ceases.[6]

In section 8, he sums up as follows:

When we say, as Webster says, "The definition of horse is 'a hoofed quadruped of the genus Equus,'" we may mean three different things. (1) We may mean merely: "When I say 'horse,' you are to understand that I am talking about a hoofed quadruped of the genus Equus." . . . (2) We may mean, as Webster ought to mean: "When most English people say 'horse,' they mean a hoofed quadruped of the genus Equus." . . . But (3) we may, when we define horse, mean . . . that a certain object [concept] . . . is composed in a certain manner: that it [really anything falling under it] has four legs a head, a heart, a liver, etc., etc., all of them arranged in definite relations to one another. It is in this sense that I deny good to be definable. I say that it [the concept

---

[5] Ibid., p. 58.
[6] Ibid., pp. 59–60.

good] is not composed of any parts [concepts], which we can substitute for it in our minds when we are thinking of it. We might think just as clearly and correctly about a horse [or about horses in general], if we thought of all its parts and their arrangement [or of all the simple concepts in terms of which the concept *horse* is analyzed, and how they are related to one another in the analysis] instead of thinking of the whole . . . but there is nothing whatsoever which we could so substitute for good: and that is what I mean, when I say that good is indefinable.[7]

Although these remarks about definition are not entirely coherent, we can, I think, put together a reasonable and coherent approximation of what Moore is looking for. He wants to know whether there is a definition of the word 'good' that gives an analysis of the concept, or property, that we use the word to express. He assumes that when P is any predicate, a definition of P is a definition (or analysis) of the property we use P to express—a definition expressed by a true sentence ⌜the property *being P* is the property *being D*⌝, where D is some word or phrase. For example, a definition of the word 'square' tells us that the property *being square* is the property *being rectangular with four equal sides*. On this view, the word 'square' is standardly used to express a complex property the constituents of which are *being rectangular* and *having four equal sides*. Since this property is also expressed by the phrase 'rectangular with four equal sides' the word 'square' means the same as this phrase, and one can be substituted for the other in any sentence without changing its meaning, or the proposition it expresses. In saying that *good* is indefinable, Moore is saying that the word 'good' cannot be given a definition in this sense; the property we use it to express is a simple, unanalyzable property that has no constituent properties whatsoever.

The second clarification needed to understand Moore's thesis T3 (that *good* is indefinable) involves distinguishing between knowing the meaning of the word 'good', on the one hand, and knowing its definition, on the other. If Moore is right that the property of being good is a simple, unanalyzable one, then the word 'good' has no definition in his sense, but it still has a meaning. Indeed its meaning simply is the indefinable property it expresses. So, even if no one can know the definition of 'good', one can know what 'good' means.

The third point of clarification (needed to understand T4) involves the relationship between knowing that something is good and having evidence that it is. For Moore, the statement that one can't know what is evidence for the claim that x is good does *not* entail that one can't know that x is good. On the contrary, he believes that some things are known without evidence—i.e., without inferring their truth, or even their probable truth, from other, more basic, claims. For example, he thinks we can

[7] Ibid., p. 60.

know that something is yellow, not by inferring the proposition that it is from more basic claims that provide evidence for it, but simply by looking at the thing under proper conditions. Similarly, he believes it possible to know that certain things are good simply by considering the question of their goodness, and properly distinguishing that question from others with which they might be confused.

Even with these necessary clarifications, Moore moves very quickly from indefinability (T3) to the impossibility of evidential support (T1), without spending much time on the alleged connection between the two. This is something we must examine in order to critically evaluate his view. But first we must understand Moore's argument for indefinability.

2. THE ARGUMENT THAT *GOOD* IS INDEFINABLE

2.1. Definability and the Analytic/Synthetic Distinction

As explained in section 6 of chapter 3, Moore seems to have understood the analytic/synthetic distinction along roughly Fregean lines. Using this distinction, we may classify his definitions as analytic equivalences. Although he didn't feel the need to precisely characterize what he meant by analyticity, he did devote part of chapter 1 to contrasting analytic with synthetic statements, and equivalences with generalities. He begins his discussion of the subject matter of ethics by indicating that when we say things like "Joe is a good man," or "I ought to keep my promise to Jane," we are making ethical statements. However, these statements are particular. We may become interested in ethics because we are interested in making particular evaluations like these; but we don't expect a philosopher to be concerned with each such judgment. Rather, Moore says, the philosopher is concerned with general ethical principles like (2a) and (2b).

2a. Pleasure is good.
  b. Pleasure and only pleasure is good.

The first of these statements is a *generality*. It says that all pleasure is good, while leaving open whether or not other things are too. The second statement is an *equivalence*. It says that pleasure is good, and furthermore nothing else is good.

The contrast between analytic and synthetic statements is illustrated in (3).

3a. For all x, if x is a U.S. senator, then x is a member of the U.S. Senate.
  b. For all x, if x is a U.S. senator representing California, then x is female.

Both of these statements are (now) true. But (3a) is a necessary truth that is knowable a priori, while (3b) is a contingent truth that is knowable only on the basis of empirical evidence. In addition, Moore would say that it is part of our concept of being a U.S. senator that anyone to which it applies is a member of the U.S. Senate. Indeed he would probably recognize 'is a U.S. senator' as synonymous with 'is a member of the U.S. Senate'. Thus, he would classify (3a) as analytic. By contrast, it is no part of our concept of being a U.S. senator representing California that x be female. Since it is possible for a California senator to be male, (3b) is a statement which, though true, could have been false. It is also one the truth of which cannot be known by reasoning and reflection alone, but rather requires empirical evidence. So, he would classify it as synthetic.

Analytic and synthetic equivalences are traditionally illustrated by (4).

4a. For all x, x is a human iff x is a rational animal.
 b. For all x, x is a human iff x is a featherless biped.

Although (4b) is (let us assume) true, it is contingent, and knowable only by appeal to empirical evidence. Thus, Moore would count it as synthetic, and the concepts *being human* and *being a featherless biped* would not be seen as necessarily equivalent. As for (4a), some philosophers are reputed to have held that it provides the definition of *being human*. They have thought it impossible to be human without being a rational animal, and vice versa; also, they have also thought that we somehow know this a priori just by thinking about the concepts involved. Although it seems highly doubtful that they are right, we at least have some idea of what they mean by claiming that (4b) is analytic. Other, more obvious, examples of analytic equivalences are (5a) and (5b).

5a. For all x, x is a square iff x is a rectangle with four equal sides.
 b. For all x, x is a brother of y iff x is a sibling of y and x is male.

In claiming *good* to be indefinable, Moore takes himself to be saying something from which it follows that (6) can't be turned into an analytic truth by filling the dots with a word or phrase expressing a complex property (not itself involving goodness).

6. For all x, x is good iff x is . . . .

Since he would also deny that 'good' stands for, and so is synonymous with, any term standing for a simple natural property like pleasure, he would also deny that (6) can be turned into an analytic truth by filling the dots with such a term—where a natural property is one that may properly figure in an empirical scientific theory, including psychology. However, he didn't take all statements of the form (6) to be false. In fact, he held that something along the lines of (7) is true.

7. For all x, x is good iff x is the contemplation of a beautiful object, or x is the enjoyment of human companionship.

What he insists is that no such truth is analytic—i.e., a sentence that expresses a truth that is necessary, knowable a priori, and capable of being seen to have the status of logical truth by conceptual analysis and/or the substitution of synonyms for synonyms.

A similar point holds for generalities involving goodness. According to Moore, no generality of the form (8) is analytic, when the dots are filled by a word or phrase expressing either a complex property (not itself containing goodness) or a simple natural property.

8. For all x, if x is . . . , then x is good.

He sums up these views at the end of section 6.

> If I am asked, "What is good?" my answer is that good is good, and that is the end of the matter. Or if I am asked "How is good to be defined?" my answer is that it cannot be defined, and that is all I have to say about it. But disappointing as these answers may appear, they are of the very last importance. To readers who are familiar with philosophic terminology, I can express their importance by saying that they amount to this: That propositions about the good are all of them synthetic and never analytic; and that is plainly no trivial matter. And the same thing may be expressed more popularly, by saying that, if I am right, then nobody can foist upon us such an axiom as that "Pleasure is the only good" or that "The good is the desired" on the pretence that this is "the very meaning of the word."[8]

It is this denial of the existence of analytic statements involving 'good' that leads Moore to think that no conclusion that something is good can be derived from premises not involving it. He does, however, think that some synthetic generalities involving goodness are true—e.g., he takes it to be true that human companionship is good.

2.2. Simple, Indefinable Properties: Being Good and Being Yellow

As we have seen, Moore maintains that premises that do not mention goodness can never even provide *evidence* that something is good. This point can be made clearer by considering an example involving the putatively simple property *being yellow*.

9a. Lemons are yellow.

One might, Moore observes, say this without saying that to be a lemon is the same thing as to be yellow. One might further hold that it is not a necessary feature of lemons that they are yellow, since there is nothing incoherent or impossible about a world in which lemons are orange. So, Moore would say, the statement that lemons are yellow is synthetic, which is analogous to his claim that (2a), about *good*, is synthetic.

A similar point can be made regarding equivalences.

---

[8] Ibid., pp. 58–59.

9b. For all x, x is yellow iff x reflects light waves of frequency n.

Although this equivalence is too simplistic to be strictly true, let us ignore technicalities and imagine that investigations into the physics of light established the truth of an equivalence of roughly this kind, for some specific n. Even then, Moore would deny that (9b) is analytic, or that the clause on the right gives the meaning of the one on the left. In support of these denials, he would point out that an ordinary person might know that something is yellow without having any idea about the frequencies of light waves. Thus, he would say, it is not part of our concept *being yellow* that anything that is yellow must reflect light waves of a certain frequency. Rather, we use one set of criteria to determine whether something is yellow—namely just looking at it—and another set of criteria to determine the frequency of the light waves it reflects. It is a matter of empirical discovery, not conceptual or philosophical reflection, that the two sets of criteria end up being satisfied by the same things. So, (9b), like (9a), is synthetic. Moore says the same sort of thing about equivalences involving 'good'. Although there are true statements of the form *x is good iff x is so-and-so*, none is a definition, and none is analytic. As he sees it, the reason that 'good' and 'yellow' are alike in this way is that *being good* and *being yellow* are simple, unanalyzable properties. They differ in that while we can tell that something is yellow by sense perception, we determine that something is good by intellectual intuition. This is a sign that *being yellow* is a natural property, while *being good* is nonnatural.

Given all this, we can better understand Moore's claim that the conclusion that something is good isn't entailed, or in any way supported, by premises that don't mention goodness. This is analogous to a claim that could be made about being yellow.

T1y. If the conclusion of an argument is a statement that something is yellow, but none of its premises are, then the premises do not entail the conclusion and their truth provides no evidence for, or any compelling reason to believe, it.

This claim has some plausibility. How, after all, does one typically establish that something is yellow? Not by argument, but by looking. There are, of course, cases in which an argument might be given. Presumably, however, Moore would maintain that none falsifies T1y. For example, consider the dialogue: Q. *What's in the box? Is it something yellow?* A: *It's a lemon.* C: *Then it is probably something yellow.* Here it might seem that the premise *It's a lemon* provides evidence for the conclusion *It's yellow*, and hence a reason for believing it.

I don't think Moore would regard this as a genuine counterexample to T1y. Rather, he would most likely reply, the argument relies on a suppressed premise, *All (most) lemons are yellow*, which itself depends ultimately on observation rather than argument. Once this premise is added to the dialogue, the argument's premises will contain a statement about what things are yellow, and so will cease to be a counterexample to T1y. Although it is debatable whether this is the right way to think about such examples, I suspect that Moore would say the same thing about the following case.

What color is that object at the blast sight?
It reflects light waves of frequency n.
Then, it must be yellow.

Supposing this argument to be sound, Moore would probably say that it is so only because it relies on a suppressed premise that has already been established—*Anything that reflects light waves of frequency n is yellow*. Perhaps examples like this made it seem to him all the more plausible that conclusions about what is yellow must ultimately rest on simple observations, rather than on demonstrative arguments the premises of which don't mention *being yellow*. In any case, Moore believed something similar regarding conclusions about goodness. The main difference is that we don't come to see that something is good in the same way we see that a thing is yellow. We see that something is yellow with our eyes. We come to see that something is good with our intellect—simply by clarifying what is before our minds.

2.3. The Open-Question Argument

So far I have concentrated on the content of Moore's conclusions T1 and T3. It is time to examine how he reaches his conclusions, beginning with the claim T3, that 'good' is indefinable. He gives his famous "open question" argument for this conclusion in section 13. He says that we can see that 'good' is indefinable, since no matter what definition is offered, it is always meaningful to ask of whatever satisfies the defining complex whether it is good. He illustrates this point by considering a sample definition.

G. For all x, x is good iff x is what we desire to desire.

Moore reasons that if G were a genuine definition, then not only would it be true, it would also give us the meaning of 'good'—in which case 'good' and the phrase 'what we desire to desire' would express the same property, and so mean the same thing. But he thinks that we can easily show that 'good' does not mean this by considering Q1.

Q1. Granted that x is what we desire to desire, is x good?

No matter what you might think the answer to this question is, Moore says, it is clear that the question is just as intelligible, and makes just as much sense, on reflection, as Q2.

Q2. Is x good?

But if 'good' and 'what we desire to desire' expressed the very same property, and so meant the same thing, then we could always substitute one of these expressions for the other in any sentence without changing the proposition, or question, it expresses. So, if G were a genuine definition, Q1 and Q3 would mean the same thing, and express the same question.

Q3. Granted that x is what we desire to desire, is x what we desire to desire?

But this is absurd; Q1 and Q3 don't mean the same thing, and the questions they express are different. Hence G does not define 'good'.

Moore's argument can be reconstructed as follows:

P1.　　If (a) ⌈For all x, x is good iff x is D⌉ is a definition of 'good', then 'good' expresses the same property as D, and the two expressions mean the same thing.

P2.　　If 'good' expresses the same property as D, and the two expressions mean the same thing, then the sentences (b) ⌈Granted that x is D, is x good?⌉ and (c) ⌈Granted that x is D, is x D?⌉ express the same self-answering question (i.e., (b) is on a par with (d) "Granted that x is a male sibling of y, is x a brother of y?" in that properly understanding these sentences, and reflecting on the propositions they express, should enable one to see that the answer to the questions is 'yes').

P3.　　There is no complex property (not itself containing goodness as a constituent), or simple natural property, p, and expression D, such that D expresses p, and (b) in P2 expresses the same self-answering question as (c); nor could we introduce such an expression D.

C1.　　Therefore, there is no definition of 'good' ⌈For all x, x is good iff x is D⌉ in which D expresses either a complex property, or a simple natural property.

C2.　　So, 'good' is indefinable, and must express a simple nonnatural property.[9]

The premises of this argument are intuitively plausible. P2 embodies the natural assumption that the meaning of a sentence (in these and other relevant cases) is a function of the meanings of its parts, while P1 is a reasonable statement of what we want from at least one significant kind of definition. Although not beyond question, these assumptions are attractive, and, for our purposes, may be accepted. Given this, our assessment of the argument depends on our assessment of P3.

Here it is helpful to articulate a principle that Moore may well have been relying on, though he doesn't make it explicit.

THE TRANSPARENCY OF MEANING

If expressions α and β mean the same thing (e.g., if two predicates express the same property), and if an agent x (fully) understands α and β, then x will be in a position to know (i) that they mean the same thing, and (ii) that any

---

[9] This last clause assumes (i) that if 'good' is meaningful, it expresses a property, and (ii) that if the property it expressed were complex, or if it were a simple natural property, we could find, or introduce, a word or phrase D expressing that property, such that ⌈For all x, x is good iff x is D⌉ would be a definition of 'good'. Although I will later call (i) into question, for now I will provisionally accept both (i) and (ii).

two sentences (of the sort under consideration) differing only in the substitution of one expression for the other will mean the same thing, and express the same proposition (in the case of declaratives) or question (in the case of interrogatives).

Moore seems to be tacitly relying on this, or some similar, principle when he takes it for granted that if D gave the meaning of 'good', then anyone who (fully) understood both could see by introspection that the interrogatives (b) and (c) of P2 expressed the same question.[10] Since it is plausible that we do (fully) understand 'good' and related expressions, and that we wouldn't judge the questions to be identical, he takes P3 to be true—as well he should, given that he accepts the transparency principle. As for the principle itself, the situation is more complicated. On the one hand, it has intuitive appeal, and was explicitly or implicitly accepted not only by Moore, but also by most analytic philosophers in the early to mid-twentieth century who dealt with substantial questions about meaning. On the other hand, important counterexamples to it have been found in recent decades—many involving proper names and natural kind predicates, understood in accordance with *direct reference theories* in semantics.[11] These counterexamples, though genuine and important in other contexts, are of only limited relevance to Moore's implicit reliance on the principle.[12] Thus, although the principle is, I think, ultimately incorrect, and so provides no basis for P3, the latter still remains plausible, and we need not, for this reason, challenge here Moore's conclusion that *good* is indefinable.

The appeal of this result may be enhanced by the existence of meaningful and widespread controversy about goodness among philosophers and others. The very fact that philosophers argue so persistently about questions like Q1 makes it unlikely that it should be as trivial as either of the questions (c) or (d) in P2. Regarding Q1, we can see how such controversy might arise by asking who the *we* is that is supposed to be doing the desiring. Does it include people like Hitler, Stalin, Mao, or Pol Pot? If so, then it is certainly not clear that what they desire to desire is good. If not, on what basis is it decided whom to include and whom to

[10] On p. 67 Moore speaks of our being able to find out things like this "by inspection."

[11] See chapters 3 and 10 of my *Beyond Rigidity* (Soames 2002).

[12] In my view, the only counterexamples to the principle involving natural kind predicates are those in which both α and β are simple terms (typically single words), like 'groundhog' and 'woodchuck'; when one term is simple (e.g., 'water') and the other is compound (e.g., 'substance molecules of which have two hydrogen atoms and one oxygen atom') the two expressions never mean the same thing. (See chapter 10 of Soames 2002; or, for an updated version of the view, Soames 2007a.) So, even if 'good' turned out to behave like a natural kind predicate, the corresponding result would ensure that it was indefinable by any expression D that expressed a complex property. This is not the end of the matter—there are further cases that could be considered in evaluating the principle. However, since there are other, more pressing problems with Moore's overall argument, there is no need to enter into such complications.

exclude? Difficulties like these suggest that Q1 has real force. Thus, Moore concludes that 'good' does not mean 'what we desire to desire'. It is not unreasonable to suppose that a similar defect could be found in every proposed philosophical definition of 'good', and hence that 'good' really is indefinable, in Moore's strict sense of definition.

3. THE ROLE OF THE INDEFINABILITY THESIS IN MOORE'S ARGUMENT FOR T1

The indefinability thesis, T3, is the first step in Moore's (implicit) argument for T1. That argument is reconstructed below, where we take D to be a word or phrase (excluding those themselves defined in terms of 'good') that stands for either a complex property or a simple natural property. S4 elaborates T1. (See Moore 1993, chapter 5, section 86.)

3.1. The Argument

S1. There is no relevant D such that ⌜For all x, x is good iff x is D⌝ is a definition of 'good'.

S2. There are no analytic equivalences, ⌜For all x, x is good iff x is D⌝, and no analytic generalities, ⌜If x is D, then x is good⌝, for any relevant D.

S3. There is no entailment of the statement (expressed by) ⌜α is good⌝ by the corresponding statement (expressed by) ⌜α is D⌝, for any relevant D.

S4. No statement (expressed by) ⌜α is D⌝, for any relevant D, provides any evidence for the conclusion (expressed by) ⌜α is good⌝, or any compelling reason to believe it. The claim that a particular thing is good can sometimes be derived from a general principle that states that all members of a certain class are good. But the fundamental principles of ethics—which state that all, or all and only, members of a certain class are good, and which provide the basis for justifying all other ethical claims—are self-evident propositions for which no justification is needed or possible; such propositions must simply be seen to be true.

3.2. Interpretation 1

Given Moore's very strict sense of what counts as a definition, his argument for the indefinability of 'good', and hence S1, is plausible. But there are serious questions about his move from there to S2–S4. First consider the transition to S2. Moore treats his argument that there is no definition of 'good' as if it were sufficient to establish that there are no analytic equivalences or generalities connecting goodness with the properties expressed by any relevant D. In light of this, it is striking that he devotes so little attention to *analyticity* and related notions central to his overall argument. The few occasions in *Principia Ethica* in which he talks about analyticity suggest that he takes analytic truths to be necessary truths the falsity of which is "inconceivable," and the negations of which are "contradictory." This fits with his discussion in "The Refutation of Idealism," which led to my conclusion in the previous chapter that he took analytic truths to be those that can be turned into logical truths by replacing synonyms with synonyms. When this conception of analyticity is combined with his restrictive conception of definition, and hence of what counts as synonymy, the analytic truths turn out to be a highly restricted subset of those that express propositions that are both necessary and knowable a priori. On this interpretation, the gap between S1 and S2 is minimized.

Unfortunately, the narrow conception of analyticity used to validate the move from S1 to S2 makes problems for the move from S2 to S3 and S4. To get to S3 one needs to say something about entailment. Moore tended to speak of this relation as being that of *logical implication*—a proposition p entails a proposition q iff p logically implies q—i.e., iff q is a logical consequence of p. However, by *logical implication* and *logical consequence*, he did not mean what is now meant by these notions in symbolic logic (the gist of which was explained in section 4 of chapter 1). For one thing, logical implication and logical consequence were, for Moore, relations between propositions or sets of propositions, whereas in logic they are relations between sentences or sets of sentences. Propositions are pieces of information that sentences encode, agents believe, and speakers assert—where different but synonymous sentences express (encode) the same proposition, and different propositions may be expressed (encoded) by different uses of the same sentence, if the sentence contains an indexical expression like 'I' or 'now'.[13]

Another point illustrating the difference between what Moore meant by *logical implication* and *logical consequence* and what these terms now mean is that whereas he regarded S3 as a momentous philosophical thesis, its counterpart S3$_1$, involving the modern notion of logical implication, is nothing more than a triviality.

> S3$_1$. For any relevant D, and name n, the sentence ⌜n is D⌝ does not logically imply ⌜n is good⌝.

S3$_1$ is a triviality because the mere fact that the word 'good' does not appear in D is enough to ensure that ⌜n is D⌝ does not logically imply ⌜n is good⌝. A simple example illustrates this point. In modern logic, the sentence 'The *object* is neither *round* nor *square*' logically implies the sentence 'The *object* isn't *round*' because any interpretation assigned to the italicized, nonlogical words in these sentences that made the first sentence true would make the second true as well. This is reflected by the fact that the result of uniformly replacing the italicized, nonlogical vocabulary

---

[13] In explicating Moore's ethical theses I will avoid sentences containing indexicals, and (unless otherwise indicated) I will set aside complications that can arise from different utterances of the same sentence expressing different propositions.

with other nonlogical words, while leaving the logical vocabulary intact, would never yield a pair of sentences in which the first was true and the second untrue. By this criterion the sentence 'A *square* is *inside* the *circle*' does not logically imply 'A *rectangle* is *inside* the *circle*', because the definition of logical implication doesn't constrain the words replacing 'square' and 'rectangle' to be related. Since Moore would insist that the proposition that a square is inside the circle *does* entail the proposition that a rectangle is inside the circle, the entailment relation in Moore's S3 cannot be logical implication in the modern sense.

At this point in the interpretation of Moore, one is pulled in two directions—one aimed at validating the move from S2 to S3, and one aimed at validating the move from S3 to S4. First the former. Recall our account of Moorean analyticity—a sentence is analytic iff it can be turned into a logical truth by putting synonyms for synonyms. (S is a logical truth iff S comes out true no matter how its nonlogical vocabulary is interpreted, and no matter which of its nonlogical expressions is uniformly replaced with other nonlogical expressions.) As explained in chapter 3, this definition of analyticity can be extended to propositions by defining a proposition to be analytic iff it is expressed by an analytic sentence. Entailment may then be defined in terms of analytic implication.

> Analytic Implication: Sentences
>
> A sentence, or set of sentences, S analytically implies a sentence R iff there is a sentence, or set of sentences, S' and a sentence R' that arise from S and R by replacing synonyms with synonyms, and S' logically implies R'.

> Entailment: Propositions
>
> A proposition (or set of propositions) p entails a proposition q iff there is a sentence (or set of sentences) S that expresses p (or, if p and S are sets, the sentences in S express the propositions in p) and there is a sentence R, such that R expresses q, and S analytically implies R.

On this account of entailment and analyticity, S3 follows unproblematically from S2.

However, these notions of entailment and analyticity are very restrictive. Analytic propositions are simply those expressed by formal logical truths, and the entailment relation holds only between propositions p and q expressed by sentences s_p and s_q, one of which logically implies the other (in the strict formal sense). Worse, the move from S3 to S4 becomes hopeless. In order to reach that conclusion, Moore must, at a minimum, rule out the possibility that for some relevant D, (10) expresses a necessary a priori truth that is validated by the kind of reasoning available in philosophy.

10. If α is D, then α is good.

If there is such a D, then the proposition P_G expressed by ⌜α is good⌝ will be an a priori, necessary, and philosophically validated consequence of the proposition P_D expressed by ⌜α is D⌝, in which case P_D might well constitute a proof of P_G, or at least a compelling reason for drawing that conclusion. Such a result would falsify Moore's most important meta-ethical thesis about goodness: namely that there can be no proofs of, or compelling arguments for, claims to the effect that something is, or isn't, good.

Moore's vulnerability is illustrated by the necessary, a priori, and self-evidently obvious examples in (11).

11a. For all x, if x *is chartreuse*, then *x is colored*.
  b. For all x, if x *is an automobile*, then *x is a vehicle*.
  c. For all x, if x *persuaded Jim to leave*, then x *communicated with Jim*.
  d. For all x, if x *intends to win*, then x *doesn't know that x won't win*.
  e. For all propositions p, if p *predicates being red of an object o, without predicating anything else of o, and without predicating anything of anything else*, then p *is true iff o is red*.

Although any of these will do, let us focus on (11a). Someone like Moore, who believed in the transparency of meaning, might even maintain that a competent speaker who knew the meanings of both 'chartreuse' and 'colored' would thereby realize that (11a) expresses a truth, and that anyone who entertained the proposition it expresses would be in a position to judge it to be true. This might be so despite the facts (i) that 'chartreuse' isn't *defined* in terms of 'colored'—since an individual might possess the determinate concept *being chartreuse*, without possessing the determinable concept *being colored* (under which anything chartreuse, magenta, crimson, etc. falls)—and (ii) that 'colored' isn't *defined* in terms of 'chartreuse'—since one can know what it is for something to be colored without knowing all the colors. Thus, it is plausible to suppose that we could establish that 'colored' can't be defined, in Moore's strict sense, using any relevant word or phrase D mentioning individual colors (and so isn't synonymous with any such D).

Combining this result with the definitions of analyticity and entailment mentioned above, we could get all the way to S3$_c$.

S3$_c$. For any relevant D, and name n, the statement expressed by ⌜n is D⌝ does not entail the statement expressed by ⌜n is colored⌝.

But now nothing interesting follows. The claim that something is chartreuse provides both evidence for, and compelling reason to believe, the claim that it is colored. In fact, one could *prove* or *establish* that a thing is colored by showing that it is chartreuse. Thus, the version of S4 involving the predicate 'colored' is false, even though S3$_C$ is true. Since the move from the one to the other is completely parallel to the original move from S3 to S4, involving 'good', S4 does not follow from S3. So, on this interpretation, Moore fails to establish his most important methodological conclusion.

3.3. Interpretation 2

Perhaps the problem lies in an unduly narrow conception of analyticity and entailment. Examples like (11) illustrate that two expressions can be conceptually connected even though neither is defined in terms of the other. Similarly, the proposition expressed by one sentence may be a necessary and a priori consequence of the proposition expressed by another, even though neither sentence is transformable into the other by putting synonyms for synonyms, and no chain of definitions relates the two. One might take this to indicate the need for notions of analyticity and entailment that recognize conceptual connections not grounded in definitions. Perhaps, using such notions, one could validate the move from S3 to S4 in Moore's argument. Let's try.

> Analytic Obviousness: Sentences and Propositions
>
> Let S be any sentence that is necessary, that expresses something knowable a priori, and that is so obvious that anyone who understands it is disposed to accept it, and anyone who entertains the proposition it expresses is inclined to judge it to be true. Call any such sentence, as well as the proposition it expresses, *analytically obvious*.

> Analytically Obvious Consequence: Sentences and Propositions
>
> A sentence R is an *analytically obvious consequence* of a (finite) set S of sentences iff the conditional sentence the consequent of which is R and the antecedent of which is the conjunction of the sentences in S is analytically obvious. A proposition q is an analytically obvious consequence of a (finite) set p of propositions iff there is some sentence R that expresses q and some set S_p of sentences that express the propositions in p, and R is an analytically obvious consequence of S_p.

I suspect Moore would have been willing to characterize the examples in (11) as analytically obvious, and (12b) as an analytically obvious consequence of (12a).[14]

---

[14] Although the above definitions, and the ones that follow, are improvements that allow one to recast Moore-like arguments for Moorean conclusions in their best light, they are

12a. n is chartreuse.
   b. n is colored.

Next we need the notion of a sentence or proposition that can be derived from other sentences or propositions by a series of analytically obvious steps.

Extended Analytic Consequence: Sentences and Propositions

A sentence R is an *extended analytic consequence* of a set S of sentences iff it is possible to construct a proof of R each line of which is either a member of S or an analytically obvious consequence of earlier lines in the proof. A proposition q is an extended analytic consequence of a set p of propositions iff some sentence R expresses q, and the members of some set S_p of sentences express the propositions in p, and R is an extended analytic consequence of S_p.

This leads to the notion of a sentence or proposition that is either analytically obvious, or an extended analytic consequence of other analytically obvious sentences or propositions.

Extended Analyticity: Sentences and Propositions

A sentence is *extendedly analytic* iff either it is analytically obvious, or it is an extended analytic consequence of some set of analytically obvious sentences. Extendedly analytic propositions are expressed by extendedly analytic sentences.

Finally, *extended entailment* among propositions is the converse of extended analytic consequence—p extendedly entails q just in case q is an extended analytic consequence of p.

Example (13) illustrates the difference between analytic obviousness and extended analyticity.

13. For all x, $x = 2^{11}$ iff $x = 2048$

---

almost certainly unacceptable in their present form. As Timothy Williamson has correctly observed, in Williamson (2008), there are few if any sentences—including paradigmatic examples of the form *if p, then p*—that everyone who understands is thereby inclined to accept, or judge to be true. Whether the conditions for analytic obviousness can be weakened so as to cover such cases, while excluding those Moore wishes to exclude and providing the basis for a philosophically useful conception of analyticity, is highly doubtful. However, this needn't trouble us here, since even the improved Moorean argument that uses them leads to a position that is very hard to sustain.

Notice that *2¹¹* is not a *synonym* for *2048*. One can understand what both of these expressions mean without knowing that 2^{11} is 2048. Thus, the question

14a. Granted that n = 2048, does n = 2^{11}?

is a genuine, non-self-answering question distinct from the question (14b).

14b. Granted that n = 2048, does n = 2048?

This shows that (13) is not a definition in Moore's strict sense. Nevertheless it is true. In fact, it is a necessary, a priori truth. It is not analytically obvious, since one can understand what the sentence means without realizing that it is true, and can entertain the proposition it expresses without being in a position to judge it to be true. However, it is, arguably, extendedly analytic, since it can be proved from obvious, self-evident premises by obvious, self-evident steps (where it is arguable that each step in the proof is either analytically obvious, or an analytically obvious consequence of previous steps).

The idea, of course, is that exponentiation can be reduced to repeated multiplication, which can be reduced to repeated addition, which can in turn be reduced to repeated application of the function that takes a natural number to its successor—all in such a way as to make each step in the proof of (13) either itself analytically obvious, or an analytically obvious consequence of earlier lines in the proof. This thought is supported by the fact that principles like those in (15), appealed to in such a proof, seem beyond rational dispute, in the sense that anyone who understands them can be expected to recognize their truth, if he pays careful attention and is not distracted.

15. 2^{11} = (2)(2)(2)(2)(2)(2)(2)(2)(2)(2)(2)
   (2)(2)(2)(2)(2)(2)(2)(2)(2)(2)(2) = [(2)(2)(2)(2)(2)(2)(2)(2)(2)(2)(2) +
      (2)(2)(2)(2)(2)(2)(2)(2)(2)(2)(2)]
   (2)(2)(2)(2)(2)(2)(2)(2)(2)(2)(2) = [(2)(2)(2)(2)(2)(2)(2)(2)(2)(2)(2) +
      (2)(2)(2)(2)(2)(2)(2)(2)(2)(2)]
   etc.
   2 + 2 = the successor of 2 + 1
   2 + 1 = the successor of 2 + 0
   2 + 0 = 2
   the successor of 2 = 3
   the successor of 3 = 4
   etc.

If this is right, then (13) may well be extendedly analytic, in which case the proposition expressed by (16a) will extendedly entail the proposition expressed by (16b).

16a. There are 2048 so-and-so's.
   b. There are 2^{11} so-and-so's.

Similar points hold for other mathematical statements. For example, the same argument could be given to support the claims that (17) is extendedly analytic and that the proposition expressed by (18a) extendedly entails the proposition expressed by (18b).

17. For all x, x is an equilateral triangle iff x is an equiangular triangle.
18a. That is an equilateral triangle.
  b. That is an equiangular triangle.

The extended entailment relation used in these claims is interesting for two reasons. First, if p extendedly entails q, then it is possible to prove, establish, or come to know q by deriving it from p, provided one can prove, establish, or come to know p, without first establishing q. Second, p can bear this relation to q, even though the connection between the two propositions is not initially evident, but may require considerable reasoning and analysis to discover. Thus, in a particular case it may be an important discovery to learn that p does, or does not, extendedly entail q.

With this in mind, suppose that analyticity in S2 and entailment in S3 of Moore's argument are defined as *extended analyticity* and *extended entailment*. Then, S3 would both follow from S2, and provide a reasonable basis for something approaching S4. If S2, and hence S3, could be established, it would follow that there could be no *proof* of the claim expressed by ⌜α is good⌝ from the premise expressed by ⌜α is D⌝, for any relevant D, each step of which was either itself analytically obvious (and hence undeniable) or an analytically obvious consequence of earlier steps (and hence undeniable given acceptance of those earlier steps). One can see how a philosopher might take this result to show that no proof of any claim to the effect that something is good is possible from premises not mentioning goodness. This, of course, is not quite Moore's S4, which maintains that the claim expressed by ⌜α is D⌝ never provides any *evidence* for the conclusion expressed by ⌜α is good⌝, or any compelling reason to believe it. But at least a step would have been taken in that direction.

However, this presupposes that S2 can be validly inferred from S1, when analyticity is given the expansive interpretation as extended analyticity. It cannot be. Moore's open-question argument establishes at most that 'good' is indefinable in his strict sense of definition. As we have already seen, a similar argument could be given that 'colored' is indefinable in this sense, despite the fact that generalities like (11a) may be extendedly analytic (if any sentences are). Thus, on this interpretation, Moore's overall argument fails to get beyond S1.

4. CAN MOORE'S ARGUMENT BE REPAIRED?
WHY DEFINABILITY IS NOT THE ISSUE

Yes, the argument can be repaired, but to repair it one must stop trying to derive conclusions about what does, or doesn't, entail or provide evidence for interesting claims about goodness from theses about the Moorean indefinability of 'good'. The lack of definitions of this sort, providing strict synonyms for 'good', is *not* the key point. Much more significant is the question of whether the claim expressed by ⌜α is good⌝ can be derived from the corresponding claim expressed by ⌜α is D⌝ by a series of steps each of which is obvious in the way in which the statements in (15), used in the proof of (13), are obvious. The fact that interesting, non-obvious mathematical truths like (13) and (17) can be derived by a series of such utterly obvious steps is what makes it possible for many mathematical truths to be not only interesting, and surprising, but also rationally certain. If one could show that interesting claims about goodness can *never* be derived in this way from premises not mentioning goodness, then one would have taken a significant step toward the kind of strong meta-ethical conclusion for which Moore was looking.

The best hope of doing this is to revise Moore's open-question argument as follows.

Expanded Open-Question Argument

P1. If ⌜For all x, if x is D, then x is good⌝ is analytically obvious, then the question (i) is a self-answering question on a par with (ii), (iii), and (iv).

   (i) ⌜Granted that α is D, is α good?⌝
   (ii) ⌜Granted that α is a male sibling of β, is α a sibling of β?⌝
   (iii) ⌜Granted that α is chartreuse, is α colored?⌝
   (iv) ⌜Granted that the successor of n = the successor of m, is it the case that n = m?⌝

In each case, the proposition corresponding to the question is an obvious necessary, and a priori, truth; anyone who truly understands the interrogative sentence, and entertains the question it expresses, is in a position to realize that the answer to it is 'yes'. Inability to see this would be evidence that one doesn't fully understand the sentence, or grasp the question.

P2. There is no complex, or simple natural, property P, and expression D, such that D expresses P, and the interrogative sentence (i) in P1 expresses a self-answering question on a par with (ii), (iii), or (iv).

C1. Thus, there is no analytically obvious generality ⌜For all x, if x is D then x is good⌝ in which D expresses either a complex p, or a simple natural, property.

C2. So, there is no extendedly analytic sentence ⌜For all x, if x is D then x is good⌝ in which D expresses either a complex, or a simple natural, property.

C1 follows from P1 and P2; C2 follows from C1; and S2 and S3 follow from C2 (when analyticity and entailment are taken to be extended analyticity and extended entailment, and the transparency of meaning is assumed). A weakened version of S4 that limits itself to the claim that theses about goodness cannot be *proven* from claims not mentioning goodness might plausibly be taken to be established on the basis of S3. Thus, the weight of Moore's overall argument now rests on P1 and P2.

Where does he stand on those premises? To answer this we must go back to his original open-question argument, the conclusion of which is that *being good* isn't a complex, or a simple natural, property. Moore argues for this by noting that the question expressed by ⌜Granted that α is D, is α good?⌝ is not the same as that expressed by ⌜Granted that α is D, is α D?⌝ or ⌜Granted that α is good, is α good?⌝ for any D that expresses either a complex, or a simple natural, property. Fair enough. But does he think that at least one of the questions expressed by ⌜Granted that α is D, is α good?⌝ and ⌜Granted that α is good, is α D?⌝ must be open?

That depends on what it means for a question to be "open." In the last sentence of section 13.1 of *Principia Ethica*, where he states the open-question argument, Moore says that the mere fact that "we understand very well what is meant by doubting" whether everything we desire to desire is good "shows that we have two different notions before our minds." The suggestion here is that whereas it is *unimaginable* that anyone might doubt whether everything that is good is good, or whether everything that we desire to desire is something we desire to desire, it is quite definitely *imaginable* that someone might doubt whether everything we desire to desire is good.[15] More generally, he seems to suggest that for any relevant D, it will always be imaginable that someone might doubt the proposition expressed by ⌜Everything that is D is good⌝.

Were 'good' truly definable, in the way that 'brother' is definable as 'male sibling' or 'square' is definable as 'rectangle with equal sides', Moore would take this not to be so. No one, he seems to think, could doubt what is expressed by 'Everything that is a square is a rectangle with equal sides', because that is just the proposition that everything that is a square is a square. Someone might, of course, be unsure whether the *sentence* 'Everything that is a square is a rectangle with equal sides' was true; presumably, however, Moore would maintain that this might happen only if the person was not a fully competent speaker of English, and failed to truly understand the sentence.

If this is right, then Moore may well have thought that for any relevant D, ⌜Granted that α is D, is α good?⌝ always expresses an open question,

---

[15] The idea that it is impossible or unimaginable to doubt that everything that is F is F (for any choice of 'F') is not nearly as clear-cut as it may first seem. For discussion see, chapter 3 of Soames (2002). Also see the *furze/gorse* example in Kripke (1979) and the *ketchup/catsup* example in Salmon (1989, 1990). Other relevant material can be found in Stephen Reiber (1992) and in sections III, IV, and IX of Soames (1986b).

in the sense that it is possible to understand the sentence, and entertain the question it expresses, without realizing that the answer to it is 'yes' (if indeed that is the answer). If Moore was correct in so thinking, then it is enough to establish P2, and, indirectly, C1 and C2. The only remaining issue is whether he would have accepted the (implicit) characterization of the interrogative sentences (ii), (iii), and (iv) of P1 as *not* expressing "open questions" in the sense in which (i) supposedly does. Although I believe he would have, I don't see the textual evidence in *Principia Ethica* as conclusively settling the matter. There is, however, some reason to think he would have been on board with these characterizations. He often speaks as if questions about goodness are substantial and open-ended in ways that trivial questions like those expressed by (ii), (iii), and (iv) are not. If there were no genuine contrast here, then his supposedly far-reaching conclusions S3 and S4 would vanish, or be drained of significance. Since he views them as of the highest importance, he would, I think, accept P1 and P2.

This, I believe, is the strongest reasonable reconstruction of Moore's argument for his main meta-ethical conclusion about goodness. This argument is a combination of the expanded version of the open-question argument, the weakened version of S4 that limits itself to ruling out *proofs* about goodness, plus the interpretation of steps S2 and S3 as involving extended analyticity and extended entailment (plus the transparency of meaning). There is, as I have indicated, some reason to think that Moore himself would have been willing to accept this reconstruction. In addition, it is clear that many philosophers who were influenced by him accepted something quite like it. However, as plausible as this position may have seemed to some, Moore didn't *establish* its correctness. In order to have done so, he would have had to show that there is a clear and definite contrast between questions like those expressed by (ii), (iii), and (iv) of P1, on the one hand, and questions about goodness expressed by (i) for all relevant D, on the other. This is something he neither did, nor seriously attempted. Moreover, the claim that there is such a contrast for all relevant D is not obvious. Thus, Moore's startling, and enormously influential, conclusion that one cannot establish by argument that something is good was itself insufficiently supported by argument. At best, we might regard it as an interesting, not altogether implausible, and historically influential conjecture.

5. SELF-EVIDENCE: THE TENSION IN MOORE'S VIEW

According to the Moorean conjecture, (i) for any relevant D, it is always possible to understand the sentence ⌜Things that are D are good⌝ without being inclined to accept it, and to entertain the proposition it expresses without being inclined to judge it to be true, and (ii) it is never possible to prove the claim expressed by ⌜α is good⌝ from a premise ⌜α is D⌝ by a series of steps that are so obvious that they cannot rationally be denied by anyone who carefully attends to those steps, understands the sentences that formulate them, and apprehends the propositions those sentences express. We may express this informally by saying that according to the Moorean conjecture, statements about goodness are never *analytically obvious*; nor are they *analytically provable* from statements not mentioning goodness. If one supposes that Moore really did accept this conjecture, one may be surprised to learn that he nevertheless believed that some very important propositions about goodness—including the most fundamental propositions of ethics—are self-evident.

Moore makes this clear in chapter 5 of *Principia Ethica*, when, in the course of summing up his earlier investigation of what 'good' means, he says:

> We cannot tell what is possible, by way of proof, in favor of one judgment that "This or that is good," or against another judgment "That this or that is bad," until we have recognized what the nature of such propositions must always be. In fact, it follows from the meaning of good and bad, that such propositions are all of them, in Kant's phrase, "synthetic": they all must rest in the end upon some proposition which must be simply accepted or rejected, which cannot be logically deduced from any other proposition. This result, which follows from our first investigation, may be otherwise expressed by saying that the fundamental principles of Ethics must be self-evident.[16]

For example, he takes (19) and (20) to be self-evident.

19. Pleasure is not the only (intrinsic) good.
20a. The appreciation of beautiful objects is (intrinsically) good.
  b. The pleasures of human companionship and interaction are (intrinsically) good.
  c. The appreciation of beautiful objects and the pleasures of human companionship and interaction are the only things that are (intrinsically) good.

(19) is declared by Moore to be self-evident in section 87. The examples in (20) are discussed in chapter 6, the main aim of which, Moore said,

> is to arrive at some positive answer to the fundamental question of Ethics—the question: "What things are goods or ends in themselves?" To this question we have hitherto obtained only a negative answer: the answer that pleasure is certainly not the *sole* good.[17]

Moore gives his positive answer in section 113.

[16] Moore (1903b), p. 193.
[17] Ibid., 233.

Indeed, once the meaning of the question is clearly understood, the answer to it, in its main outlines, appears to be so obvious, that it runs the risk of seeming to be a platitude. By far the most valuable things, which we know or can imagine, are certain states of consciousness, which may be roughly described as the pleasures of human intercourse and the enjoyment of beautiful objects. No one, probably, who has asked himself the question, has ever doubted that personal affection and the appreciation of what is beautiful in Art or Nature, are good in themselves; nor, if we consider strictly what things are worth having *purely for their own sakes*, does it appear probable that any one will think that anything else has *nearly* so great a value as the things that are included under these two heads. . . . What has *not* been recognized is that it is the ultimate and fundamental truth of Moral Philosophy. That it is only for the sake of these things—in order that as much of them as possible may at some time exist—that any one can be justified in performing any public or private duty; that they are the *raison d'être* of virtue; that it is they—these complex wholes *themselves*, and not any constituent or characteristic of them—that form the rational ultimate end of human action and the sole criterion of social progress: these appear to be truths which have been generally overlooked.[18]

My concern here is not with the truth or falsity of (19) and (20), but with the claim that they are self-evident. In characterizing them in this way, Moore is claiming (i) that they can be known to be true, (ii) that our belief in them is justified even though they cannot be deduced (logically or analytically) from other more basic known or justified propositions, (iii) that their justification does not rest in any way on propositions other than themselves, and (iv) that their truth is potentially obvious to us once we attend to them and carefully distinguish them from other propositions with which they might be confused. One might, of course, doubt whether the particular propositions Moore selects really are self-evident in this sense. I will return to that. First, it is important to address a question about the relationship between self-evident propositions, on the one hand, and those that are analytically obvious, on the other. How, if at all, do they differ?

For Moore, whether or not x has the nonnatural property of being good (in itself) is necessarily dependent on x's natural properties; it is impossible for two things x and y with exactly the same natural properties to be such that x is good (in itself) and y is not. Thus, Moore is committed to the view that a self-evident truth like (20b) is necessary, as well as being both potentially obvious and knowable a priori. How then does it differ from what we may take to be analytically obvious truths like (21a) and (21b), which are themselves necessary, knowable a priori, and potentially obvious?

21a. Red things are colored (i.e., for all x, if x is red, then x is colored).
   b. If a book has exactly 201 pages, then the number of pages in the book is the successor of 200.

---

[18] Ibid., pp. 237–38.

Is there some way in which these non-ethical truths are obvious that self-evident truths of ethics are not?

One passage from *Principia Ethica* that touches on this point occurs in section 87 (pp. 194–95). There Moore reviews his earlier attempt to persuade the reader of the untruth of the proposition that pleasure is the only good by showing that it contradicts other propositions that appear equally true. He emphasizes (i) that he has offered no *proof* of his claim that pleasure is not the only good, since that claim is self-evident and un-provable; he further emphasizes (ii) that while we are justified in holding that pleasure is not the only good, it is conceivable that we are wrong, and he says (iii) that though others have disagreed with him about the relationship between pleasure and goodness, this has typically been be-cause they have not understood what question was really at issue. Points (i) and (ii) lend some weight to the idea that, for Moore, questions about goodness are always substantial, open-ended, and not open to proof in the way that mathematical questions are. However, in elaborating (iii) he says something that emphasizes the similarity between ethical and mathe-matical questions. Anxious to show that the causes of disagreement about what is good in itself standardly involve a failure to make necessary dis-tinctions and to clearly understand the question at issue, he speculates that once the needed clarifications are made, *everyone* may agree about what is good. This leads him to compare ethics with mathematics.

> Though, therefore, we cannot prove that we are right [about (19)], yet we have reason to believe that everybody, unless he is mistaken as to what he thinks, will think the same as we. It is as with a sum in mathematics. If we find a gross and palpable error in the calculations, we are not surprised or troubled that the person who made this mistake has reached a different result from ours. We think he will admit that his result is wrong, if his mistake is pointed out to him. For instance if a man has to add up $5 + 7 + 9$, we should not won-der that he made the result to be 34, if he started by making $5 + 7 = 25$. And so in Ethics, if we find, as we did, that 'desirable' is confused with 'desired', or that 'end' is confused with 'means', we need not be disconcerted that those who have committed these mistakes do not agree with us. The only difference is that in Ethics, owing to the intricacy of its subject-matter, it is far more difficult to persuade anyone either that he has made a mistake or that that mistake affects his result.[19]

Here Moore seems to be suggesting that the most basic principles of eth-ics are, when truly understood, as obvious and self-evident as those of mathematics. But if so, how can these ethical principles *fail* to be analyti-cally obvious, if mathematical axioms are?

Whereas later philosophers would answer this question by backing away from Moorean self-evidence, and emphasizing what they took to be

[19] Ibid., p. 195.

the essentially motivating character of ethical principles, Moore neither took this position nor provided a clear answer to this question. It is possible that, if pressed, he would *not* have been willing to characterize the basic axioms of mathematics (apart from trivial and explicit definitions) as analytically obvious in the sense defined here. In that case, however, the basic truths of ethics and mathematics would be placed on a par, making it difficult to credit Moore's cautionary warnings about our inability to prove ethical claims, or to attach much philosophical significance to his conclusion that goodness is unanalyzable. Similar deflationary judgments would hold if he were to maintain that the most basic truths of *both* disciplines are analytically obvious.

On the other hand, it is possible that Moore thought that although the potential obviousness of self-evident ethical truths approaches that of mathematical axioms, the obviousness of the latter is tied to meaning and understanding in a way in which the obviousness of the former is not. Perhaps, unlike mathematical axioms, sentences expressing self-evident ethical truths can be fully understood, and the propositions they express apprehended, without one's being inclined to judge them true, even though thinking more about them, and distinguishing them from related propositions, can bring one to appreciate how obvious they really are. If so, then the potential for agreement in ethics may approach that of mathematics, even if the epistemological sources of agreement in the two domains are different. Such a position is not inconsistent, and it is one way of interpreting Moore. However, if he did believe something like this, he certainly didn't establish it, or do anything to make it clear. If this was his view, one would like to be told much more about what meaning and understanding amount to in a way that illuminates the alleged epistemological difference between mathematical axioms and self-evident ethical truths. One would also like to know why, if both are self-evident in their own ways, it makes a difference to philosophy that one bears a connection to meaning and understanding that the other does not.

6. MOORE'S FLAWED CONCEPTION OF JUSTIFICATION IN ETHICS

There is, as I see it, no resolution of these issues by Moore himself. He simply leaves us with a tension. On the one hand, he is sensitive to the facts that 'good' is difficult if not impossible to define, and that interesting claims about goodness seem, for whatever reason, to be resistant to proof. On the other hand, he tries to do justice to the further fact that we are accustomed to taking claims about goodness not only to be true or false, but also sometimes to be known. This fact is hard to explain unless some claims about goodness are self-evident. It was a strength of his philosophy that he was sensitive to these two sets of hard-to-reconcile facts, even though he failed to explain them, or to show how to plausibly bring them together. In subsequent volumes, I will discuss later philosophers who were strongly influenced by Moore's views on ethics. These philosophers were themselves sensitive to his tension. Most reaffirmed his indefinability and unprovability theses, while many resolved the tension by rejecting his view that fundamental ethical statements are self-evident, knowable, or even capable of being true or false. Thus, whether rightly or wrongly, it was his indefinability and unprovability theses that were historically most influential.

There is, however, a final point. As Sir David Ross, one of Moore's eminent successors in ethics, was later to make clear, the thesis that some ethical claims are self-evident is more plausible than it is often taken to be. One reason for this is that the examples Moore chose to illustrate his thesis are not the best candidates. Claims like those in (20) are too broad, far-reaching, and contentious to have this status. However, it was no accident that he chose the examples he did; his choices were driven by an implicit conception of ethical justification that led him in the wrong direction.

In thinking about such justification, Moore was, I believe, guided by three main ideas. First, some ethical claims are both true and capable of being known to be so; hence they must either be self-evident or be capable of being justified. Second, the process of justification always comes to an end with an appeal to certain ethical judgments that cannot themselves be justified, but rather must be accepted as self-evident. Third, ethical justification flows from the general to the particular. Ethical judgments about particular cases are justified by subsuming them under general moral principles. General principles are justified by appeal to still more general principles. For Moore, this process stops when one arrives at absolutely general, self-evident moral principles like (20c), which may be put in the form ⌜For all x, x is good iff x is D⌝. When he speaks of there being no reason or evidence for any ethical claims, he is thinking, in the first instance, that there is no reason or evidence supporting these fundamental principles upon which all ethical justification is based.

In my opinion, there is something right about this, but also something wrong. What is right, or at any rate quite plausible, is that all ethical justification must rest on principles that cannot themselves be justified by appealing to anything more basic. What is wrong, or at least oversimplified, is Moore's implicit conception of ethical justification as always involving the subsumption of specific ethical principles and judgments under more general ones. By contrast, I would suggest, if there are self-evident ethical truths at all, they are much more specific and circumscribed than the unrestricted generalities for which Moore was searching. Here are some candidates.[20]

---

[20] In formulating these, I put aside Moore's thesis of the primacy of goodness, according to which other ethical notions are defined in terms of goodness, and all ethical claims rest, at least in part, on claims about goodness.

22a. Any man who tortures children to death solely for the pleasure of watching them suffer and die is a bad man.

  b. An action that leads to widespread, avoidable suffering and the extinction of life is wrong.

  c. Any state of affairs in which every sentient being suffers alone in pain with no relief of any kind, followed by death, is bad.

  d. Harming others is *prima facie* wrong—i.e., wrong unless the action possesses right-making features that outweigh its *prima facie* wrongness.

  e. Keeping one's promises is *prima facie* right.

  f. A good man is concerned with the rights and the welfare of others.

  g. If one promises y that one will do x, then one has an obligation to do x, unless y releases one from the obligation.

Restricted generalizations like these are the platitudes that constitute our starting points in ethics. The central difficulty in ethics is that these essentially undisputed truths don't cover nearly all the cases for which evaluations must be made. Our problem is to systematize and extend these judgments by forming more encompassing generalizations, which may be justified by various factors—including issuing the right verdicts about what we antecedently take to be the self-evident cases, having independent plausibility themselves, and fitting well with our already accepted principles. If anything along these lines is correct, then the most encompassing and abstract generalizations in this area will not themselves be self-evident, but rather will be justified by how well they systematize a whole array of antecedently justified, but more limited, claims.

7. HISTORICAL NOTE: THE INFLUENCE OF SIDGWICK AND RUSSELL ON *PRINCIPIA ETHICA*

In March of 1904, six months after the publication of *Principia Ethica,* Bertrand Russell published a highly favorable review of his friend's book.[21] As undergraduates, he and Moore each took a course in the foundations of ethics taught by the great intuitionist, utilitarian philosopher Henry Sidgwick. Russell took the course in 1893–94. Deeply engaged with the topics Sidgwick presented, he wrote a series of papers for Sidgwick, plus a series of additional papers through 1899 developing the same topics further.[22] Many of these later papers were delivered at a secret and very select discussion club known as "the Apostles," of which Moore was, by then, a leading member. During these years, Moore and Russell were developing different but related lines of ethical and metaethical thought.

---

[21] Russell (1999).

[22] These are printed in Russell (1983), and reprinted as papers 3–12 in Russell (1999). See the introduction to the latter by Charles Pigden for informative commentary.

Moore was attempting to deepen and strengthen Sidgwick's thesis that *good* is indefinable with the goal of ensuring the autonomy of ethics from all naturalistic inquiry. By contrast, Russell was struggling to find a naturalistic definition of goodness capable of preserving the action-guiding character of judgments of goodness.[23]

Russell thought that any acceptable definition of goodness must be based on *what we desire*. But how should such a definition go? The story of his attempts to solve this problem is illuminatingly told by Charles Pigden in the editor's introduction to Russell (1999), as well as in Pigden (2007a, 2007b). As Pigden sees it, Russell's project was to find an analysis validating as many pre-theoretic desiderata such as (i–iv) as possible.

(i) Moral judgments, including those about what is and what is not good, should be true or false.

(ii) Those judgments about goodness should be liable to error.

(iii) There should be a conceptual connection between moral judgment and motivation. In many (though not necessarily all) cases, coming to believe that x is good must involve recognizing a reason to promote x.

(iv) It must be possible to desire the bad, and to have bad desires.

By 1897, Russell had found his analysis, which he presented in a paper "Is Ethics a Branch of Empirical Psychology?" read to the Apostles in February, with Moore in attendance.[24] According to Russell, for x to be good (in itself) is for x to be what we, or I, desire to desire (as an end, rather than a means). Absent equivocation about who is doing the desiring to desire—"me" or "we"—and hence who's *good* is being defined, the proposed analysis clearly satisfies conditions (i) and (iv). Though satisfaction of (ii) is less clear, it does seem to be *possible* to be mistaken in thinking that one desires, or that one desires to desire, x—if, for example, one doesn't know as much as one should about x, or if social pressure to conform to others' desires clouds one's judgment.

Condition (iii) may best be illustrated by an example. One thing I know I desire as an end in itself is the welfare of my children. So, coming to believe that something is necessary for their welfare will, other things being equal, provide me with a reason for promoting it. Do I desire to desire their welfare? I certainly don't desire *not* to desire their welfare (in the way that someone in the grip of unwanted temptation might desire not to desire something to which he is strongly attracted). But do I positively *desire* to have my first-order desire for the welfare of my children, or is my

---

[23] In his review of Moore's *Principia Ethica*, Russell says, "Sidgwick, who alone among Utilitarians, has recognised clearly that 'good' is indefinable, . . ." (Russell 1904b, and p. 100 in Russell 1999; the review was originally reprinted in Russell 1994). See section 14 of *Principia Ethica* as well, where Moore notes that Sidgwick correctly took 'good' to be indefinable.

[24] Russell's paper is published in Russell (1994) and reprinted in Russell (1999).

attitude toward that desire like my attitude toward my first-order desire
to eat pizza reasonably often—which is a desire I simply have, without
either desiring to have it or desiring not to have it? Reflecting on this, I
find myself thinking that if I lacked the second-order desire to desire the
welfare of my children, I would probably be less scrupulous about finding
opportunities to promote their welfare, and so I would be more likely to
miss chances to do so. I don't want that. So, yes, I suppose I do desire to
desire their welfare.

Thus, finding out that x is a component of the welfare of my children,
which is something that I desire to desire, will generally give me a reason to promote x, thereby satisfying condition (iii) above. There may, of
course, be other things that I desire to desire (and hence that count as
good for me on Russell's analysis), which I don't actually desire. I might,
for example, wish that I desired the welfare of all humankind, but find
that, in fact, I don't. If so, then the welfare of all humankind counts, on
Russell's analysis, as good for me, even though learning that something
increases the cumulative welfare of humankind doesn't motivate me to
promote it. Condition (iii) is not violated by this result, since, although
the required conceptual connection between moral judgment and motivation must explain the fact that *good (for me)*–judgments are often motivating, such judgments are not *always* required to be motivating. Not an
unwelcome result, I would say.[25]

Here is Russell's summary.

> An ethic which merely says: The good is the desired, leaves the good a prey to
> changing fancies. An ethics which says: The good is the satisfaction of desire,
> is open to all the objections to Hedonism: it chooses an aspect of the good, a
> mere result of desire, as the whole good. On the other hand, since we always
> do act from desire, an ethic which takes all desires as equally ultimate loses
> all criterion, all standard of judging action. . . . Now morality is exhibited
> only in action, and action springs only from desire. Therefore moral judg-
> ments must discriminate between desires. But since all contrast between ideal
> and actual rests on desire, since all goodness, all morality, rest on the contrast
> of ideal and actual, desire alone can supply the criterion among desires. The
> criterion must be supplied, therefore, by the criterion between ideal and ac-
> tual desires, by the contrast between desires we desire and desires we dislike.
> Whether we have them or not, for example, most of us desire a wish for the
> good of humanity, and dislike a craving for drink or morphia.[26]

I won't pause here over the problems with Russell's view, but will
instead mention something to be said for it that bears directly on our

---

[25] For a recent version of the *desire-to-desire* theory of goodness with consequences like
this one for the connection between value judgments and motivation, see Lewis (1989).

[26] Russell (1897b), at p. 78 of Russell (1999).

understanding of *Principia Ethica*. The key element involves an argument mentioned in the following passage of his review of Moore.

> Chapter II, on *Naturalistic Ethics*, discusses theories which hold that the only good things are certain natural objects, in so far as these theories are advocated as derivable from the very meaning of 'good'. It is shown that such theories always confuse 'good', in its correct and indefinable sense, with the sense which they assign to it by definition. For example, Evolutionist Ethics are apt to argue that 'good' means 'more evolved', *and on this to base practical recommendations. Yet if their contention were correct, no practical consequences could follow.* We ask: Why should I prefer this to that? And they reply: Because the more evolved is the better. *But if they were right in the reason they give for thinking so, they have only said that the more evolved is the more evolved, and this barren tautology can be no basis for action. The meaning of the two phrases cannot be the same, if it makes any difference whether we use one of them or the other; and applying this test, it is easy to see that 'more evolved' does not mean the same as 'better'.*[27]

Here, Russell rightly notes one aspect of Moore's critique of naturalistic ethics. Indeed, a variant of the argument Russell states here appears in section 11 of *Principia Ethica*, with further echoes in later sections. Of course, the conclusion of the argument also agrees with that of the open-question argument, which is presented in section 13.

Although one might be tempted to think that there is really only one argument for Moore's indefinability conclusion, in fact there are two, which can be teased apart. Calling the argument adverted to by Russell the *barren tautology argument*, Pigden (2007b) expresses it as follows.

P1.   For any naturalistic or metaphysical 'X', if 'good' meant 'X', then (i) 'X things are good' would be a barren tautology equivalent to (ii) 'X things are X' or 'Good things are good.'

P2.   For any naturalistic or metaphysical 'X', if 'X things are good' were a barren tautology, it would not provide a reason for action (i.e., a reason to pursue or promote X-ness).

C.   So, for any naturalistic or metaphysical 'X', either (i) 'X things are good' does *not* provide a reason for action, or 'good' does not mean 'X'.

The envisioned upshot is, of course, that since calling things good *does* provide a reason for action, we have a compelling argument that *'good' doesn't mean 'X'*, for relevant 'X'.

However, as Pigden points out, this final conclusion can be resisted. I would put it this way. First, we distinguish the claims made when we genuinely *call things good*—by saying things like (23a,b) (often with the

---

[27] Russell (1904b), at p. 100 of Russell (1999), my emphasis.

intention of guiding action)—from claims made when we attempt to give a definition of the form (24).

23a. These things are good.

  b. Pleasure, beauty, and human companionship are good.

24. For all z, z is good iff z is X.

Next, we find a naturalistic or metaphysical substitute Y for 'X' in (24) which, when substituted for 'good' in (23), preserves the usual action guiding force of (23a,b). Suppose we take Y to be 'what I/we desire to desire'. Then, Pigden contends, the result of substituting Y for 'X' in (24) ends up being Russell's (somewhat) plausible 1897 naturalistic definition of 'good', while the results of substituting Y for 'good' in (23a) and (23b) remain plausibly action guiding.

In short, a case can be made that the barren tautology argument is counter-exemplified by the *desire-to-desire* analysis of goodness, and hence the argument is insufficient to establish Moore's and Sidgwick's conclusion that 'good' is naturalistically indefinable. Since Sidgwick is generally credited with attempting to use the barren tautology argument to derive this conclusion, recognizing the argument's vulnerability to Russell's *desire-to-desire* analysis should motivate one who shared Sidgwick's goal to search for a different argument for the desired conclusion that is not vulnerable in this way. Moore's open-question argument is such an argument.

With this in mind, Pigden hypothesizes that Russell (1897b) motivated Moore to develop the open-question argument in 1903. Among the pieces of evidence supporting the hypothesis are:

(i) the fact that Moore explicitly selects the *desire-to-desire* analysis in presenting the open-question argument in section 13 of *Principia*.

(ii) the fact that Moore was familiar with Russell's paper, in which Russell explicitly addresses him in the final paragraph, saying, "that my conclusion is satisfactory, I do not pretend. If our brother Moore will give me an unexceptionable premise for his definition of the good, or even a hint of where to find one, I will retract."[28]

(iii) the fact that the last page of the (1897b) manuscript is marked by Russell's handwritten question "Shall we spell {Good/good}" to which Moore writes in reply "Good = good," echoing his famous remark in section 6 of *Principia*: "If I am asked 'What is good?' my answer is that good is good, and that is the end of the matter."

(iv) the fact that Russell—who was familiar with the barren tautology argument from Sidgwick—was not convinced in 1897 that it showed that all naturalistic analyses of 'good' were hopeless, but became convinced, presumably by Moore's open-question argument, by the time he wrote his 1904 review of *Principia Ethica*.

---

[28] Russell (1897b), at p. 78 of Russell (1999).

In light of all this, it is not unreasonable to think that Moore's goal in coming up with the open-question argument was, at least in part, to beat back the challenge of Russell (1897b). Whether or not this was indeed his goal, Russell was convinced in 1903 and remained so until 1913, after which he waivered between versions of emotivism and the error theory that he developed (without fanfare) on his own, decades before such views became widely known when championed by other authors.[29]

---

[29] The story is told in Pigden (2007a).

CHAPTER 5

⨳⨳⨳

Truth, Skepticism, Perception, and Knowledge

1. Moore's 1910–11 Lectures: *Some Main Problems of Philosophy*
   1.1. What Is Philosophy?
   1.2. Sense Data and Perception
   1.3. Worldly Knowledge: Moore contra Hume
2. Moore's 1925 Defense of Common Sense
3. Proof of an External World
   3.1. What Is to Be Proved and Why
      3.1.1. Roots of Skepticism and Attempts to Refute It
      3.1.2. External Objects vs. Objects Internal to, or Dependent on, Our Minds
   3.2. The Proof
   3.3. Does Moore's Argument Satisfy the Requirements for Being a Proof?
   3.4. Moore versus the Skeptic: What Is the Point of Moore's Proof?
4. Perception, Sense Data, and Analysis

1. MOORE'S 1910–11 LECTURES: *SOME MAIN PROBLEMS OF PHILOSOPHY*

1.1. What Is Philosophy?

The first chapter, "What Is Philosophy?," is an instructive indicator of the state of "analytic philosophy" in the first decade of the twentieth century. In it Moore discusses what he takes to be philosophy's most important questions, outlines alternative answers, and locates what later lectures will make clear to be the place occupied by his own position in this range of alternatives. Looking back a century later, two features leap from his text. First, the conception of philosophy in the mind of a founding father of what is often seen as a "revolutionary" new departure in philosophy remains thoroughly traditional. For Moore, the most important task of philosophy is to give a general description of the whole universe—by which he means an accounting of the kinds of things we know to be in it (material objects, human minds, etc.), the kinds of things which, though not known to be in it, may very well be (e.g., a divine mind or minds, human minds after death), and the relations holding among the different kinds of things (e.g., minds *attached* to bodies). Related to this metaphysical quest is the epistemological task of explaining how we know anything by specifying necessary and sufficient conditions for knowledge. Finally, Moore thinks, there are questions of value—the rightness or wrongness of actions, the goodness or badness of states of affairs, and even the value of the universe as a whole. In short, metaphysics, epistemology, and ethics (traditionally conceived) make up the unsurprising core of his conception of philosophy. Were we to supplement this sketch with the 1910 views of the two other major analytic figures of the day—Frege and Russell—logic, language, and mathematics would be added to Moore's main philosophical concerns. But the overall conception of philosophy wouldn't change much. In these early days of the analytic tradition some previously neglected philosophical topics have been given more prominence, but they haven't replaced traditional concerns, which continue to be addressed in new ways.

The second thing that leaps out of Moore's first lecture in the fall of 1910 is the respectful attention paid to what he characterizes as our (mostly pre-philosophical) commonsense conception of things. In the following passage, he indicates what he means by this conception, and lays out the role it will play for him.

> There are . . . certain views about the nature of the Universe, which are held, now-a-days, by almost everybody. They are so universally held that they may . . . fairly be called the views of Common Sense. I do not know that Common Sense can be said to have any views about the *whole* Universe. . . . But it has . . . very definite views to the effect that certain kinds of things certainly are in the Universe, and as to some of the ways which these kinds of things are related to one another . . . it seems to me that what is most amazing and most interesting about the views of many philosophers, is the way in which they go beyond, or positively contradict the views of Common Sense: they profess to know that there are in the Universe most important kinds of things, which Common Sense does not profess to know of, and also they profess to know that there are *not* in the Universe (or, at least, that, if there are, we do not know it), things of the existence of which Common Sense is most sure. . . . I wish, therefore, to begin by describing what I take to be the most important views of Common Sense: things which we all commonly assume to be true about the Universe, and which we are sure that we know to be true about it.[1]

Though he doesn't explicitly say so, Moore is here signaling that the most obvious and universal of our firmly held convictions constitute our starting point in philosophy. He is open to views that go beyond common sense by answering questions it leaves open. He is even willing to consider

---

[1] Moore (1953), p. 14.

views that contradict it. However, he gives the impression that those who contradict it face a very difficult task indeed.

Common sense is characterized as confident in the existence of (i) material objects including, for example, human and animal bodies, plants, stones, grains of sand and other inanimate things, manmade things, drops of water, rivers, oceans, mountain ranges, the earth, moon and stars, and (ii) nonmaterial minds and acts of consciousness. All of these things are taken to be *known* to exist, as is the purported fact that the things in (ii) are fundamentally different from those in (i) (despite the attachment of acts of consciousness to individual bodies, on which they are at least somewhat dependent). Material things are claimed to be known to be the sorts of things that are capable of existing unperceived, as well as being located in space—situated at various distances from one another, with the distance of the earth, for example, being "many millions of miles from the sun in one direction, and many more millions of miles distant from the pole star in another."[2] Like material things, minds and their conscious acts are claimed to be known to exist at one time or another, with some things of both kinds being known to exist now, but not in the past, as well as other things of both kinds being known to have existed in the past, but not now. All of this, common sense takes itself to know. Common sense further takes it to be probable that there was a time in which no acts of consciousness were associated with, or attached to, any material bodies on earth.

Although Moore goes into much more detail, it is clear enough from these examples that he recognizes our commonsense convictions to change over time, and not to be infallible. Common sense may be wrong, both about what it takes us to know, and about the nature of the things it takes us to know about. This is apparent in the case of our evolving knowledge of the earth, and its place in the universe. It is also apparent in our commonsense conviction, which we share with Moore, that what may have once been the commonsense conviction of our ancestors—namely, that much in nature, in addition to humans and animals, is conscious—is certainly not true. Where we may disagree with Moore is in finding it far from obvious that conscious mental states are not, in the end, a subspecies of the physical. Whatever may have been true of the common sense of his place and time, the common sense of ours leaves this question open.

Moore next uses the common sense worldview to organize his discussion of philosophical views that fall into one or more of the following categories: (i) those that add to common sense, without contradicting it, (ii) those that do contradict it by attempting to refute its claim to *know* what it does, and (iii) those that contradict it by *denying* the truth of propositions it claims to know, including those about the kinds of things that exist. Examples of (i) are views that posit one or more divine minds. Examples of

[2] Ibid., p. 17.

(ii) are those that claim that we don't know that material objects exist, as well as those that claim, often in addition to this, that no one knows that human minds other than his or her own exist. Examples of (iii) include those of idealists like Berkeley, who (Moore insists) deny the existence of matter, as well as other idealist philosophers who deny the existence of things existing in space and/or time.

One of the most interesting of Moore's observations about the third sort of view is framed in terms of the distinction between Appearance and Reality. Discussing a certain set of views of this sort, he says:

> [They] all . . . start by considering certain things which I call the Appearances of material objects. And I think I can easily explain what I mean by this. You all know that, if you look at a church steeple from a distance of a mile, it has a different appearance from that which it has, when you look at it from the distance of a hundred yards; it looks smaller and you do not see it in many details which you see when you are nearer. These different appearances which the same material objects may present . . . are very familiar to all of us: there certainly are such things in the Universe, as these things which I call Appearances of material objects. And there are two views about them, both of which might be held quite consistently with Common Sense, and between which . . . Common Sense does not pronounce. It might be held that some, at least, among them really are parts of [the surfaces of] the objects, of which they are appearances: really are situated in space, and really continue to exist, even when we are not conscious of them. But it might also be held, quite consistently with Common Sense, that *none* of these appearances are in space, and that they all exist only so long as they appear *to* someone.[3]

There are two points of interest here. First, Moore thinks that "there certainly are" such things as appearances we see. (Also those we touch, smell, hear, or taste?) Second, he thinks that common sense leaves it open both that these appearances might be mental images that exist only when perceived, and that they might be surfaces of material objects. But this is dubious, because it is dubious that we see *appearances* at all. It is, of course, obvious that things like church steeples can appear differently from different places, and also that we often see their surfaces. But when one sees a steeple that appears indistinct in color because it is a long way off, it isn't obvious that either one sees an indistinctly colored mental image in one's mind (which exists only while one sees it), or one sees an indistinctly colored part of the surface of the steeple, *which is the appearance of the steeple.* Which part of the surface would that be, anyway? Doesn't the surface itself *appear* indistinct in color? Surely we don't see the surface of the surface.

Moore is here being too philosophical for real common sense. What common sense tells us is that we see the church, its steeple, and the surface of the steeple. It also tells us that these may appear differently on different

3 Ibid., pp. 33–34.

occasions. It doesn't tell us that we see a certain kind of thing called "an appearance," the nature of which is for philosophers to discover. If someone claims we do see such appearances, it is up to that person to justify this addition to common sense—which Moore doesn't. It is hard not to see his discussion here as backsliding from the more promising account of perception and cognition toward which he seemed to be groping in "The Refutation of Idealism." There, it was suggested that perceptual experience (sensation) is always experience of something that could, in principle, exist without being experienced. Though highly promising, his 1903 discussion too quickly dismissed the alternative account of sensation as perception of private mental images (on the mistaken grounds that such an account rests solely on the absurd identification of an experience with that of which it is an experience). In 1910 he goes too far in the other direction, casting the internalist account of perception as the only reasonable alternative to the understandably undersubscribed view that the "appearances" we supposedly see are parts of the surfaces of objects that so appear.

He does, however, have a nice point about the use of the term "appearance" in some idealist views. After characterizing views that not only deny matter, but also claim that what common sense takes to be appearances of material objects are really appearances of conscious minds, none of which exist in space and so are not located anywhere, as "startling enough," he discusses those that reject time as well.[4]

> But there are other philosophers who have held views more startling still—who have held not only that space and material objects do not really exist, but also that time and our own conscious acts do not really exist either . . . What they *say* is that all these four kinds of things, material objects, space, our acts of consciousness and time, are Appearances. . . . [T]his proposition is ambiguous. . . . They might conceivably mean that these Appearances were just as real as the things of which they are appearances; by asserting that they are Appearances of something else, they might only mean to assert that there is in the Universe something else *besides*—something to which these things are related in the same sort of way in which the appearance of the church-tower . . . is related to the real church tower. . . . [I]f they did only mean this . . . they would merely be asserting that, in addition to the things which Common Sense believes to be in the Universe, there is *also* something else *beside* or *behind* these things. But it seems to me quite plain that they do not really mean this. They do mean to maintain that matter and space and our acts of consciousness and time are *not* real in the sense in which Common Sense believes them to be real, and in which they themselves believe that *something* else behind Appearances is real. . . . [W]hat they really mean is that these things are not real at all: that there are not really any such things in the Universe.[5]

4 Ibid., p. 35.
5 Ibid., pp. 35–36.

The views discussed are those that contradict common sense most thoroughly, and so require the most justification, though, as we saw in chapter 3, they are also views for which Moore thinks we have no justification. The valuable point here is his identification of a crucial ambiguity in idealists' talk about Appearance and Reality that makes them difficult to pin down. Of course, the disambiguation serves a larger, Moorean end. Once one sees that these views implicitly deny our own existence as conscious agents who think, deliberate, and act in time and space, one comes to see these views as clearly untenable—just as, in 1898 in his first published paper, Moore came to see Kantian freedom as untenable.

1.2. Sense Data and Perception

The second chapter in *Some Main Problems of Philosophy* discusses what we perceive. The context for the discussion is the larger question of how we know of the existence of material objects. The primary evidence, Moore quite naturally thinks, comes from sense perception—which leads him to the question of what we perceive, and—more specifically—what we see. He begins with a simple case. Holding an envelope in front of his class, he rightly insists that each student sees the same envelope. He also maintains that it looks different to each student depending upon where he is sitting. To someone in the back of the room it looks small, whereas to someone in the front it looks larger. To someone off to one side it looks elongated, whereas to someone directly in front of it, it looks less so. Even the colors seen by different students vary slightly, depending on the lighting, the strength of their eyes, and other factors. Moore expresses this by saying that a student in the front sees *a white patch*, rectangular in shape, that occupies a large part of his visual field, while someone in the back and to the side sees a smaller, slightly darker, and more elongated *patch*. But now, since the patch seen by someone in the front has different properties from the patch seen by someone in the back, the person in the front and the person in the back must see *two different patches*.

Moore then argues as follows:

P1. Each student sees a different patch.

P2. Each student sees the same envelope.

C. Therefore, at most one student sees a patch that is identical with the envelope seen by all the students.

Note that this argument has the same form as the following argument:

 (i) Each student has a different faculty advisor.
 (ii) Each student has the same philosophy teacher.
 (iii) Therefore at most one student has a faculty advisor who is identical with his philosophy teacher.

These arguments are logically valid; so if their premises are true, their conclusions must also be. Since Moore takes the truth of the premises of the first argument to be obvious, he is committed to the truth of its conclusion. In fact, he goes further, regarding it to be most implausible that only one student sees a patch identical with the envelope, while all the others see something else. Surely, it would be arbitrary to say this, since we have no criterion for picking out the lucky student. So, Moore concludes, it is most plausible to suppose that each student sees a patch distinct from the envelope they all see. He calls these patches, seen in perception, *sense data*. They are *directly seen*, while the envelope is seen only indirectly, by virtue of the direct perception of sense data.

What are sense data? Moore first considers that they may be parts of the material object seen (the envelope in this case).

> But it might be said: Of course, when we say that we all saw the envelope, we do not mean that we all saw the *whole* of it. I, for instance, only saw *this* side of it, whereas all of you saw *that* side. And generally, when we talk of seeing an object we only mean seeing some *part* of it. . . . Whenever we talk roughly of seeing any object . . . we only see [in a stricter sense of "see"] *a part of* it. And it might, therefore, be suggested that why we say we all saw this envelope, when we each, in fact, saw a different set of sense data, is because each of these *sets of sense data* [the patches] is, in fact, a *part* of the envelope.[6]

Moore finds this view dubious. If the different sense data (patches supposedly seen) are indeed all of slightly different colors, then, since the students see the same side of the envelope, that side has all those colors simultaneously. Ditto for the sizes, shapes, and other observational properties of the "patches" seen. Since it is hard to make good sense of this, Moore concludes that it is highly doubtful that sense data are surfaces of objects.

Having gotten into this fix by rashly supposing that if an envelope looks different to different agents, they must be seeing different *appearances* (which have the properties the envelope only appears to have), Moore has to find something other than the surface of the envelope to play the role of these "appearances." It is not surprising that he turns to mind-dependent things—mental images, in effect. Though he continues to harbor doubts, and so doesn't unequivocally subscribe to this view, he calls it "the accepted view," says that it is subscribed to by "an overwhelming majority of philosophers," and indicates that he thinks it "may very likely be true."[7]

It is helpful in characterizing this view to begin with certain unusual experiences that Moore does not discuss in this lecture, but does take up in other places.[8] One such case involves hallucinating a dagger. Imagine

---

[6] Ibid., p 47.
[7] Ibid., pp. 54–58.
[8] See, for example, Moore (1939), pp. 130–33.

yourself standing before a blank wall and hallucinating that there is a dagger before you. In describing the situation, there is a temptation to say that although you are not seeing a real dagger, and although no material object is looking to you like a dagger, nevertheless you are seeing something that has the visual characteristics of a dagger. Such an object/image—the thing that looks like a dagger but is not—if in fact you are seeing something that looks like a dagger, is what proponents of "the accepted view" call *a visual sense datum.*

Two other cases provide examples in which it is tempting to say that the sense datum one sees is not a material object. One involves afterimages, the other seeing double. If I close my eyes after staring directly at a bright light against a dark background, I have an experience that is naturally described as one of seeing a bright gold circle that gradually changes to blue in the middle of my visual field. Or, if I press my finger against the side of my eye so that I *see double* while looking at a pencil, it is natural to say that I see two images of the pencil. Since there is only one pencil before me, it seems that at least one of the images is not the pencil, or any other material object looking like a pencil. In the case of the afterimage it seems even more evident. If I saw a circle at all, then surely that circle wasn't a material object.

If, when things visually appear to me to have one or another (purely) perceptual property, I am seeing appearances (sense data) that have that property, then I should perceive them both in ordinary cases, like the one involving Moore's envelope, and in unusual cases involving hallucinations, afterimages, and double images. In lecture 2 of *Some Main Problems of Philosophy*, he identifies 1–3 as general characteristics attributed to sense data on the accepted view.

1. *For each, to be is to be perceived.* For example, when my afterimage fades away, we don't think that the circle I saw continues to exist somewhere unperceived. The same is true of the hallucinatory dagger, the double image, and the "patches" seen by Moore's students.

2. *Each is logically (conceptually) private.* It is impossible for sense data to be perceived by more than one person. Suppose two people both hallucinate rats running across the floor. One sincerely reports them as pink, the other reports them as white. We *wouldn't* say that one of the two must be misperceiving the hallucinatory rats that both see. We *would* say that their hallucinations are different. But if differing perceptual reports always lead to the conclusion that different hallucinatory objects are involved, then it seems reasonable to suppose that two people can't ever see the same hallucinatory objects. Similar reasoning applies to afterimages, double images, and to Moore's "patches."

3. *Sense data do not exist in any public space.* Your visual sense data are in your private visual space and mine are in mine. Thus, your sense data can never be in the same place as mine.

In addition to these three general characteristics, there was a fourth that proponents of the accepted view took to be a defining feature of sense data. Though Moore doesn't here articulate it as clearly or explicitly as the other three, much of his discussion tacitly relies on it—as when he assumes that because the envelope appears slightly different in color, size, and shape to different students, each sees a patch the color, size, and shape of which differs slightly from those seen by the others.

> 4. *For sense data there is no distinction between appearance and reality.* For them to seem to be so-and-so is for them to be so-and-so. Sense data such as hallucinatory objects, afterimages, and double images have all and only the observational properties they appear to have. If one person's hallucinatory rats seem pink, they are pink. If another's seem white, they are white. The patches "seen" by Moore's students have the colors, sizes, and shapes that the envelope, of which they are appearances, seems to have.

It is clear what is going on. Talk of hallucinations, afterimages, and the like is talk about how things appear. If, in these cases, one insists that one is always seeing *something*, it is natural to think that what one is seeing is *an appearance.* But then, the description of the appearance will match the description of how things appear.

While affording considerable deference to "the accepted view" of sense data, Moore continues to resist the characterization of sense data as *in the mind,* which, he suspects, is based on the confusion (exposed in "The Refutation of Idealism") of sensation as experience with sensation as that which is experienced. Though he is right to continue to make this distinction, his concessions to "the accepted view" eviscerate its philosophical significance. Thus, he admits, if the accepted view is correct, "then certainly nothing could well be more thoroughly dependent on my mind than they [the sense data I perceive] are."[9]

Moore is well aware that, having acquiesced in the accepted view, he needs to explain how (direct) perception of mind-dependent sense data could possibly provide knowledge of that of which they are allegedly appearances, or indeed of anything else.

> It is, therefore . . . very natural to suppose that all knowledge consists *merely* in the direct apprehension of sense-data and images. . . . But now observe what results if we combine this view with that view with regard to sense-data which I have called the accepted view. . . . It then follows that no one does in fact ever have before his mind anything at all except certain sense-data and images, which are quite private to himself, and which can never be before anyone else's mind. And the question then arises how any one of us can possibly know that there *is* anything else at all in the Universe except his own private sense-data and images; how he can possibly know, for instance,

---

[9] Moore (1953), p. 58.

that there are in the Universe, either the minds of other people, or material objects, or the sense-data and images of other people.[10]

Taking it for granted that no skeptical response to this question can be correct, he concludes that "There must, therefore, be some other ways of knowing of the existence of things besides the mere direct apprehension of sense-data and images."[11] While admitting that it is not easy to specify these other ways of knowing all that we commonly take ourselves to know, he closes the lecture by pointing out two ways of knowing of the existence of something other than the sense data of which we are directly aware. First, when one directly perceives a given sense datum, one may, by introspecting one's state of mind, also become directly aware of one's experience of that datum. Since the experience isn't identical with the datum, sense data are not the only things we can know to exist by being directly aware of them. Second, one can remember a sense datum one has experienced a moment ago. In such a case one has knowledge of something—the previously existing datum—of which one is not, at present, directly aware. Thus our knowledge is not limited to that of which we are presently directly aware. Of course, knowing the existence of material objects or other people cannot be assimilated to either of these two cases of knowledge. So, Moore's account of perception leaves him with the task of explaining how we can possibly have such knowledge. This is the subject of chapters 5 and 6 of *Some Main Problems of Philosophy*, "Hume's Theory," and "Hume's Theory Examined."

1.3. Worldly Knowledge: Moore contra Hume

Moore's chapters 5 and 6 confront the challenge to Moore's "Common Sense view" posed by the accepted view of sense data in combination with Hume's theory of knowledge. Putting aside a priori knowledge, this composite theory grants that one knows that what one (directly) apprehends (e.g., any present sense datum) exists, and also that one knows of what one remembers (directly) observing that it did exist. What about things one has never directly observed? Moore reports Hume as holding that one cannot know of the existence of such a thing A, unless one (somehow) knows of some thing B which one has so observed, that *it would not have existed*, unless A had existed (or was about to exist).[12] He illustrates Hume's claim with two nicely chosen examples: his own brain and the murder of Julius Caesar. Since the former is not directly observed, Moore knows of its existence only if he knows that had it not existed some of his sense data would not have existed. How, one wonders, would Hume's

---

[10] Ibid., p. 63.
[11] Ibid., p. 64.
[12] Ibid., p. 107.

Principle account for that? The case of Julius Caesar is even more per-plexing, since it hardly seems likely that the existence of any of Moore's sense data could be known to be dependent on the two-thousand-year-old murder.

How does one know that something of type B wouldn't have existed un-less something of type A had? The Humean answer is that one can know this only if (i) one has (directly) observed several cases of type B preceded (followed/accompanied) by something of type A, and (ii) one has never (directly) observed something of type B *not* to be so preceded (followed/accompanied). Moreover, one can never know that a thing of type B was *probably* preceded (followed/accompanied) by something of type A, unless (i) one has (directly) observed several cases of type B preceded (followed/accompanied) by something of type A, and (ii) more of the cases in which one has (directly) observed something of type B are cases in which one (directly) observed it to be so preceded (followed/accompanied) than are cases in which one (directly) observed it not to be so preceded (followed/accompanied). If this is what it takes for Moore to know that (some of) his sense data wouldn't have existed unless he had a brain, or unless Julius Caesar had been murdered, then clearly he doesn't know that he has a brain, or that Julius Caesar was murdered.

However, perhaps this isn't the Humean's last word on the matter. Hav-ing stated the rules just given, Moore notices what he thinks Hume would have regarded as an unintended consequence—namely that, according to them, no one can learn from *others* that one kind of thing is generally, or always, accompanied by another kind of thing, by learning that *others* have (directly) observed this to be so. Presumably, this result is something to be avoided. However, the fact that one doesn't directly observe the ex-periences of others makes it tricky to see how reports of their observations can provide one with evidence one can use. Moore expresses the basic idea as follows:

> If . . . I am to know that another person really has had any particular expe-riences, I must know that certain things which I *have* directly apprehended, would *not* have existed unless some other person had had the experiences in question. . . . I cannot ever learn it unless I have *myself* observed that when I hear or read certain words or directly apprehend other signs, then the state-ments conveyed by these words or signs are, as a general rule, true. And obviously this is a sort of thing which I could, conceivably, learn by my own experience in the way Hume lays down. If I hear statements made to the effect that I myself shall observe or have observed certain things, and if I constantly observe that, when I do hear such statements, made in a certain way . . . then I do really see or have really seen the things which the statements asserted that I had seen or should see, I might, in this way, upon Hume's own principles, arrive at the generalization that statements made in a certain way were as a general rule *true*. . . . I might apply it [this generalization] . . . to

statements which asserted the existence of things which I myself had never seen, and might thus come to know that other people really had experienced things which I had not experienced.[13]

As Moore intimates in the pages following this passage, the connection envisioned here is tenuous. I might (i) directly apprehend my own private "lip-moving-of-others" visual sense data, while (ii) directly apprehending similarly private "sounds-made-by-others" auditory sense data which I (iii) interpret as expressing propositions about the sense data I will directly apprehend (or have so apprehended), and (iv) come to find that more of these propositions turn out to be true than false. Still, how often do others make assertions about *my private sense data*? Even if I were convinced that they do regularly make true statements about my private mental life, this wouldn't tell me much. Perhaps I could come to know that what they tell me about it is *probably* true. However, since I know my own sense data quite well without their help, it is unlikely that I could learn much more about them in this way. What I need to know is that *certainly*, or at least *probably*, what they tell me about things I don't, and never could, directly apprehend is true. Well, I will never learn in this way that such propositions are *certainly* true. Since it is unclear the proposed amendment to Hume's principles will tell us that they are even *probably* true, it is unclear that it is of any real help.

Even this is too generous. Can the Humean legitimately interpret his private auditory sense data to be the result of attempts by others to *communicate* any identifiable messages to him? To do so, he must know that they exist, and that *the properties expressed* by the private auditory sense data they hear themselves "saying" (their symbols) match the properties expressed by his private symbols. But if others' familiarity with the property they use their version of 'red' to express is limited to its instances among their private sense data, while the Humean's familiarity with the property he uses his version of 'red' to express is limited to its instances among his private data, it is hard to see what basis he could have for believing that the property he uses 'red' to express is the same as the one they do. Don't we normally take ourselves to mean the same thing by an observation term like 'red' as what others do by checking for rough overall agreement in the objects to which we apply it? Surely, we would be in the dark if no such comparisons could ever be made. Since this is the position the Humean must take himself to be in, it is unclear that he can legitimately take the sounds he hears to be *testimony* of others, concerning what they think or know. This doesn't prevent him from interpreting, in his own way, the private auditory speech sounds he inexplicably hears accompanied by other inexplicable visual "lip-moving-of-others" sense data, and evaluating the truth or falsity of the propositions about his own sense data that he himself

[13] Ibid., pp. 115–16.

assigns to those sounds. But, as I have indicated, this doesn't tell him much about his own sense data that he doesn't already know.

Moore does not make this point, and even seems to grant, at least for the sake of argument, that one might be able to learn from others about their own private sense data, and, by extension, about what one's private sense data would be like in circumstances one has never encountered. However, he does emphasize that Humean rules will not provide knowledge of material objects. He brings this out with an example involving the bones in his hand, which he takes himself to know to exist. Since they are material objects, they are not—according to the accepted view—directly perceived by anyone, which means that Moore cannot, according to the suggested Humean rules, come to know of their existence by testimony. He generously grants that it is conceivable that he could learn from the testimony of others who, unlike him, have done what is called "dissecting a hand." In particular, he imagines, he might learn that, as a general rule, when they have had certain visual "ordinary-hand" experiences (as they call them) followed by visual and other (so-called) "dissecting-hand" experiences," these have been followed by (what they call) "white-bone" "skeleton-shaped" experiences. On this basis, he regards it as conceivable he could learn that if he were now to witness his hand being dissected, then he would come, in a few moments, to have white, skeleton-shaped visual sense data. He emphasizes, however, that this falls short of what he takes himself to know to exist *now* (when no dissecting is occurring), namely that certain things (bones)—*which are now white, now have a certain skeleton shape, and would be seen to be so if Moore were seeing them now*—exist now, even though they are not being perceived. Since, according "the accepted theory," anything he could directly see to be white, or to have a certain shape, are entities that *cannot exist unperceived*, there is, he thinks, no way for that theory, when combined with Hume's theory of knowledge, to accommodate what he takes himself to know.

He generalizes this point at the end of chapter 5, characterizing it as a line of reasoning common to proponents of the accepted theory of sense data plus Hume's theory of knowledge. According to that line of reasoning,

> what applies to the present existence of the skeleton of my hand, applies equally to the existence, past, present or future, of any material object whatsoever. I can never know that any material object even probably exists. The only things whose existence I can know of beyond what I myself have directly apprehended are (1) the past and future contents of my own mind, including both my acts of consciousness and also all the things I directly apprehend, and (2) the contents of the minds of other people, in the same sense.[14]

[14] Ibid., p. 123.

Though the possibility of knowing (2) on the basis of the principles in question is, in fact, extremely doubtful, Moore doesn't make an issue of it, concentrating instead on the denial that one can know of the existence of material objects.

His first point in chapter 6 is that those who deny that this characterization of what we know radically conflicts with what common sense takes us to know are wrong. Here Moore distinguishes two views, both incorrect, about what we all commonly take ourselves to know. According to one view, all we ever take ourselves to know beyond the things we are directly apprehending at the moment are things of types (1) and (2) above—the past and future contents of our own minds, and that of others. According to the second view, all we ever take ourselves to know are the things just mentioned plus the proposition that something, the nature of which we know nothing about, causes many of our sense data. Moore illustrates these views by spelling out what they say about his knowledge of a pencil he is holding. According to the first view, the sum total of this knowledge attributed to him by common sense is knowledge of (i) what private visual and tactile "pencil-like" sense data he is experiencing at the moment, (ii) what other private data of this type he would experience (at some later time) if certain conditions were fulfilled—e.g., if he were do what is called "looking at it from a different angle," "running his finger along its surface," or "cutting it in half to examine its interior," and (iii) what private sense data other people would experience if similar conditions were fulfilled. According to the second view, common sense would add that he also knows that something causes these private sense data, though he can't know what.

Moore's observation about these views is that what common sense takes us to know is quite different from what these views maintain.

> Now it seems to me quite plain that these views are utterly different from what we all commonly believe. . . . What we believe is that these sense-data which we now directly apprehend are signs of the existence of something which exists *now*, or at least did exist a moment ago—not merely of something which *would* exist, under conditions similar to what we have experienced in the past. And we believe . . . that this something . . . is not merely something which may or may not have shape or be situated in space. . . . We believe quite definitely that the sense data we now see are *signs* of the present or immediately past existence of something, which certainly has a cylindrical shape . . . and which certainly has an inside. I, for instance, claim to *know* that there does exist now, or did a moment ago, not only these sense-data . . . , but also something else which I am not directly apprehending. And I claim to know not merely that this something else is the *cause* of the sense-data which I am seeing or feeling: I claim to know that this cause is situated *here* . . . in some space. And moreover I claim to know [that it] has therefore some shape . . . [and] also roughly *what* its shape is. . . . I claim to know that the cause of the sense-data I am now directly apprehending is part of the surface of something which is

really roughly cylindrical; and that what is enclosed within this cylindrical surface is something different from what is here just outside it.[15]

The conclusion to be drawn is that the composite theory consisting of the accepted view of sense data plus the Humean account of knowledge really is inconsistent with common sense. As Moore puts it,

> those philosophers who argue, on the ground of Hume's principles, that nobody can ever know of the existence of any material object, are right so far as the first step of their argument is concerned. They are right in saying: *If Hume's principles are true, nobody can ever know of the existence of any material object—nobody can ever know that any even probably exists.*[16]

But are they right in the second step of their argument—that *since Hume's principles are true*, nobody can know that material objects even probably exist? Moore's answer, of course, is that they are not right; and the reason they aren't right is that the Humean theory they rely upon is false *because it conflicts with common sense*. He says:

> It seems to me that, in fact, there really is no stronger and better argument than the following. I *do* know that this pencil exists; but I could not know this if Hume's principles were true; *therefore*, Hume's principles, one or both of them, are false. I think this argument really is as strong and good a one as any that could be used: and I think it really is conclusive.[17]

Moore does not say that the argument is one that would *persuade* any philosophical defender of the Humean view. He says that it is *conclusive*. It is conclusive because (i) its conclusion really does follow from its premise, and (ii) its premises—including the premise that he (Moore) knows that the pencil exists—are themselves known to be true. Of course, the defender of the Humean view could produce an argument satisfying (i), the conclusion of which entailed the falsity of Moore's crucial premise. Such an argument would itself be conclusive *if its crucial premise were known to be true*—i.e., if the premise that the Humean theory (combined with "the accepted view" of sense data) is true were itself something we know. So how do we decide which of these two conflicting premises (if either) is known? Do we know that Moore knows (or we ourselves know) that this pencil exists, or do we know that the Humean theory of knowledge and perception is true?

Well, how do we know philosophical theories to be true, or untrue? Hume's isn't the only theory of knowledge that has ever been proposed, and surely we need some criteria for accepting one such theory rather than another. Isn't consistency with what we already know one such

[15] Ibid., p. 132.
[16] Ibid., p. 136
[17] Ibid., p. 136.

criterion—and don't we already know, before doing philosophy, that pencils exist? Moore thinks not only that we do, but also that such commonsense truths "are much more certain than any premise which could be used to prove that they are false; and also much more certain than any other premise which could be used to prove that they are true."[18] To put it in another way, at least some commonsense truths are not theses to be philosophically vindicated or repudiated; they are data against which philosophical theories are to be tested.

2. MOORE'S 1925 DEFENSE OF COMMON SENSE

Since *Some Main Problems of Philosophy* was not published until 1953, Moore's first full-scale published defense of his distinctive view of the role of "common sense" in philosophy is given in his famous paper, "A Defense of Common Sense."[19] There, he identifies the truths of common sense to be among those that all of us believe, and also feel certain that we know to be true. Examples of such propositions are given in (5):

5a. that he (Moore) had a human body which was born at a certain time in the past, which had existed continuously, at or near the surface of the earth, ever since birth, which had undergone changes, having started out small and grown larger over time, and which had coexisted with many other things having shape and size in three dimensions which it had been either in contact with, or located at various distances from, at different times;

b. that among those things his body had coexisted with were other living human bodies which themselves had been born in the past, had existed at or near the surface of the earth, had grown over time, and had been in contact with or located at various distances from other things, just as in (5a);

c. that the earth had existed for many years before his (Moore's) body was born; and for many of those years large numbers of human bodies had been alive on it, and many of them had died and ceased to exist before he (Moore) was born;

d. that he (Moore) was a human being who had had many experiences of different types—e.g., (i) he had perceived his own body and other things in his environment, including other human bodies; (ii) he had observed facts about the things he was perceiving such as the fact that one thing was nearer to his body at a certain time than another thing was; (iii) he had often been aware of other facts which he was not at the time

---

[18] Ibid., pp. 142–43.

[19] Moore (1925), reprinted in Moore (1958), pp. 32–59. (All page references will be to the 1962 Collier reprint edition.)

observing, including facts about his past; (iv) he had had expectations about his future; (v) he had had many beliefs, some true and some false; (vi) he had imagined many things that he didn't believe, and he had had dreams and feelings of various kinds;

e. that just as his (Moore's) body had been the body of a person (Moore himself) who had had the types of experiences in (5d), so many human bodies other than his had been the bodies of other persons who had had experiences of the same sort.

Finally, in addition to the truisms in (5) that Moore claimed to know, he claimed to know the following proposition about other human beings:

6. that very many human beings have known propositions about themselves and their bodies corresponding to the propositions indicated in (5) that he (Moore) claimed to know about himself and his body.

The propositions indicated by (5) and (6) constitute the core of what he calls the "Common Sense view of the world."[20] These propositions are the starting point for Moore, and, as such, cannot be overturned by philosophical argument. Part of his reason for specifying them in such a painstaking way was to make clear that he was *not* including every proposition that has commonly been believed at one or another time in history. For example, propositions about God, the origin of the universe, the shape of the earth, the limits of human knowledge, the difference between the sexes, and the inherent goodness or badness of human beings are *not* included in his "Common Sense" truisms—no matter how many people may believe them.

Although he didn't offer a precise explanation of what makes some commonly believed propositions, but not others, truths of common sense, his position was calculated to make the denial of common sense truths seem absurd. He recognized, of course, that the propositions in (5) aren't necessary truths, and that their denials aren't contradictory. However, it would have been hard for him to deny any of these propositions about himself, and hard for others to deny the propositions about themselves mentioned in (6). This is not to say that no philosophers have ever denied such propositions. Some have. However, Moore maintains, if any philosopher goes so far as to deny that there are any true propositions of the sort indicated in (5), and mentioned in (6), then the mere fact that the philosopher has done so refutes that denial. Assuming, as Moore does, that any philosopher is a human being who has lived on the earth, had experiences, and formed beliefs, we can be sure that if any philosopher has doubted anything, then some human being has done so, and so has existed, in which case many claims about that philosopher corresponding to the claims Moore makes about himself surely must be true. Moore expresses this

[20] Ibid.; see especially pp. 32–45.

point (in a somewhat exaggerated form) as follows: "the proposition that some propositions belonging to each of these classes are true is a proposition which has the peculiarity, that, if any philosopher has ever denied it, it follows from the fact that he has denied it, that he must have been wrong in denying it."[21]

But what about Moore's claim that he *knows* the propositions in (5) to be true, and his further, more general, claim (6)—that many other human beings *know* similar propositions about themselves to be true—which Moore also claims to know? Can these claims be denied? Certainly, the things claimed to be known aren't necessary truths, and their denials aren't contradictory. Some philosophers have denied that anyone truly knows any of these things, and this position is not obviously inconsistent or self-undermining. Such a philosopher might consistently conclude that though no one knows the things wrongly said in (6) to be known, these things may nevertheless turn out to be true after all. Though scarcely credible, this position is at least coherent. However, such a philosopher must be careful. For if she goes on confidently to assert, as some philosophers have, that claims such as the proposition that human beings live on the earth, which has existed for many years, are commonly believed, and constitute the core of the commonsense conception of the world, then she is flirting with contradiction. For one who confidently asserts this may be taken to be implicitly claiming to know that which she asserts—namely that certain things are commonly believed by human beings generally. But that means she is claiming to *know* that there are human beings who have had certain beliefs and experiences; and it is hard to see how she could do this without taking herself to *know* many of the same things Moore claimed to know in putting forward the propositions in (5). Finally, unless the philosopher thinks she is unique, she will be hard pressed to deny that others know such things too, in which case she will be on her way to accepting (6).

Moore advanced considerations like these in an attempt to persuade his audience that the Common Sense view of the world, as he understood it, should be regarded as so obviously correct as to be uncontentious. In this, he was quite persuasive. It is hard to imagine anyone sincerely and consistently denying the central contentions of his Common Sense view. Moore himself was convinced that no one ever had. He says:

> I am one of those philosophers who have held that the "Common Sense view of the world" is, in certain fundamental features, *wholly* true. But it must be remembered that, according to me, *all* philosophers, without exception, have agreed with me in holding this [i.e., they have all believed it to be true]: and that the real difference, which is commonly expressed in this way, is only a difference between those philosophers, who have *also* held views inconsistent

[21] Ibid., p. 40.

with these features in "the Common Sense view of the world," and those who have not.[22]

After all, Moore would point out, philosophers live lives like anyone else, in which they take for granted all the commonsense truths he does. This is evidenced as much in their profession of skepticism as in anything else. In propounding skeptical doctrines, they address their lectures to other men and women, publish books they know will be purchased and read, and passionately criticize the writings of others. In so doing, Moore would insist, they presuppose what their skeptical doctrines deny. If he is right, then his criticism of inconsistency is well taken. Many found it hard to disagree.

Despite its obviousness, Moore's view was in its own way ambitious. He not only claimed to know things other philosophers found problematic, he claimed to know them without directly answering traditional skeptical objections. In this, his position contrasts sharply with a different, more traditional, position that does *not* take pre-philosophical knowledge claims at face value, but rather assumes the role of an ultimate arbiter. Given the claims of the Common Sense view—e.g., that material objects are capable of existing unperceived, that there are other minds, or that perception is generally a reliable source of knowledge—the arbiter asks how we could possibly know them to be true. The question is taken as a challenge to *justify* our claims; if in the end we can't give *proofs* that satisfy the arbiter's demands, he is ready to conclude that we don't know these things at all. Worse, some philosophers have claimed to show our most deeply held commonsense convictions to be false. As explained in chapter 3, Moore began his days as a philosopher being quite sympathetic to then leading philosophers who held, among other things, that time is unreal (and so our ordinary belief that some things happen before other things is false), that all existence is spiritual (and so our view that there are material objects with no capacity for perceptual or other mental activity is false), and that only one all-encompassing being, the absolute, really exists (and so our ordinary conception of the world as consisting of many independent things is false). As chronicled, Moore addressed these views as a young man on their own terms, gradually become more critical, and ultimately freed himself from them. By 1925, he had long been puzzled about how philosophers who advocated such radically revisionist views could think themselves capable of so completely overturning our pre-philosophical convictions. From what source did they derive their alleged knowledge? How could they, by mere reflection, arrive at doctrines so certain that they could be used to refute our most fundamental pre-philosophical convictions?

For the mature Moore, conflicts between speculative philosophical principles and commonsense convictions force us to give up one or the other. It would be nice to be able to state some principle about how such choices

[22] Ibid., p. 44.

are to be made, while diagnosing what mistake one is guilty of if one decides against common sense (in the sorts of cases he has in mind). Is the Humean who denies that he can know that he is seeing, or touching, a pencil misusing, or misunderstanding, words like 'see', 'touch, 'pencil', and 'know'? Is he mistaking fallibility, which is the mere possibility of error, for unreliability, which is the lack of a reason to trust? Is he confusing the fact that one's perceptual experience would provide no evidence for an external world, if one had antecedent reason to think that its deliverances *were not* reports of such a world, with the fallacy that one's perceptions provide no evidence for an external world, if one doesn't already know there is one? One of the most frustrating things about Moore's epistemology is that he doesn't say much about this—leaving the needed explanations for later philosophers. Mostly he was content with the thought that one's confidence in a general philosophical principle could never be more secure than one's confidence in the bedrock convictions of common sense. Philosophers have no special knowledge prior to, and more reliable than, the strongest examples of commonsense knowledge. Consequently, no philosophical principle can be used to undermine such putative knowledge.

3. PROOF OF AN EXTERNAL WORLD

Moore revisits the subject of commonsense knowledge, and knowledge of the external world in particular, in his most well-known article in epistemology, "Proof of an External World."[23] The article, given as a lecture at the British Academy, appeared in 1939, the year he retired from Cambridge. Although one of his later works, its main ideas—touched on in his 1909 paper "Hume's Philosophy,"[24] developed further in his 1910–11 lectures that later appeared in *Some Main Problems of Philosophy*, and amplified in the "Defense of Common Sense," in 1925—had been fixtures of the philosophical world for 30 years. "Proof of an External World" is thus his final summing up of what may well have been (outside of ethics) his most important and influential contribution to philosophy.

3.1. What Is to Be Proved and Why

Moore begins the article with a quote from the preface to the second edition of Immanuel Kant's *Critique of Pure Reason*.

> It still remains a scandal to philosophy . . . that the existence of things outside of us . . . must be accepted merely on faith, and that, if anyone thinks good to doubt their existence, we are unable to counter his doubts by any satisfactory proof.

[23] Moore (1939), reprinted in Moore (1958). All page references will be to this work.
[24] Moore (1910), reprinted in Moore (1922a).

Moore points out that if this is a scandal to philosophy, then Kant must have taken it to be the job of philosophy to give a satisfactory proof of the existence of things outside of us, while believing such a proof to be possible. Kant was, of course, not alone in this; many philosophers since the great seventeenth-century philosopher René Descartes have taken this view. Moore sets himself the task of (i) finding out exactly what these philosophers have thought should be proved, and (ii) determining what sort of proof, if any, could be given for the desired conclusion. It is significant that he starts here. Why begin by focusing on a remark—with which everyone is familiar, and with which many thoroughly agree—that something is a *scandal,* if not to suggest that perhaps what has been thought to be a scandal really isn't? Perhaps when we look into what has previously seemed scandalous, we will find that it has only been thought to be so because we have misconceived something of fundamental importance to our inquiry. Though Moore doesn't say this, his opening leads his audience to expect such a message.

3.1.1. ROOTS OF SKEPTICISM AND ATTEMPTS TO REFUTE IT

It may be helpful for us to recall a bit of the legacy of Descartes, whose *Meditations* introduced a method of radical doubt. There he proposes to doubt, or at least suspend judgment on, everything he can imagine the slightest reason for doubting. He ends up doubting the existence of tables, chairs, other people, his own body—indeed everything except himself and, as he puts it, his thoughts. Although this might initially seem mad, his method was calculated to further his goal of grounding knowledge on a foundation of unquestionable certainty. With this in mind, he finds theoretical reasons for his doubts. He says he might be dreaming—he might always be in a long dream so that when he thinks he is seeing, hearing, touching, tasting, or smelling something, he is really experiencing nothing more than vivid dreams. He even considers the possibility that an evil demon might be causing him to have these dreams, and so deceiving him. This is like thinking that you may be in a coma all of your life, during which time a brilliant scientist has electrodes attached to your brain that cause you to have just the sensory and cognitive experiences you would have if you were leading a normal life.

By considering such scenarios, Descartes finds that the only things he can be completely certain of are that he thinks, that he exists, and that he has certain thoughts and experiences. His task is to reconstruct and justify, using only the materials available at this meager starting point, all, or nearly all, of what he originally took himself to know. In other words, his goal was to show that the structure of our ordinary, scientific (and theological) knowledge can be firmly grounded on an absolutely certain foundation. Not surprisingly, there were serious problems that prevented him from reaching this goal. In the end, he didn't succeed in getting much beyond his severely restricted starting point. From this an epistemological program was born—escaping from the skeptical position of Descartes's First Meditation. As a first approximation, Kant seems to be saying that it is a scandal to philosophy that no one has succeeded in refuting the Cartesian skeptic. Not that there really are any living, breathing skeptics to refute; it is hard to imagine anyone sincerely and consistently accepting the skeptic's incredible conclusions. Rather, Kant seems to be saying, it is a scandal that no one has completed the methodological program of refuting the Cartesian skeptic.

Moore's "Proof" should be seen as a comment on this program. I don't claim that his proof *succeeds* in refuting Descartes's skeptic in terms that even the skeptic would have to accept. I don't even claim that it *attempts* to do so. As I see it, Moore attacks the presuppositions of such attempts. His goal is, first, to understand what the skeptic is asking for and why, and second, to undermine the skeptic's position by questioning the implicit assumptions that lead him to doubt our knowledge in the first place, and to demand a kind of proof that can't be given. Moore's aim is not to provide the skeptic with anything the latter would recognize to be an *answer* to his challenge, but to question why, if at all, that challenge should be taken seriously.

He begins by asking what exactly philosophers have been trying to prove. The question at issue in the quote from Kant is the existence of *things outside of us*. However, Moore notes an ambiguity in this phrase. According to Kant, one of its meanings is *thing-in-itself, distinct from us*, which presumably involves independence from us. The second meaning he attaches to the phrase is expressed in various ways: *things belonging to external appearance, empirically external objects, things to be met with in space*, and *things presented in space*. The contrast between these two meanings may seem strange. We normally take many things that are met with in space to be things that exist in their own right, distinct from and independent of us. However, on Moore's interpretation, this was not the way Kant thought of them. There is a natural way of reading Kant according to which he does not regard the objects met with, or presented, in space to be wholly distinct from us; rather they are mind-dependent entities the organization and constitution of which are due in part to our cognitive categories of perception and understanding. Since space, for Kant, is one of these categories, it is natural for him to use the phrases "things to be met with in space" and "things presented in space" to indicate a class of mind-dependent entities he calls "external appearances."

Moore doesn't dwell on this, but he may think that Kant can be criticized for trading on the ambiguity in his use of the term "things outside us." On the interpretation in which things outside us are *not* dependent for their existence on our minds, one can understand why a philosopher might take it to be a scandal that no one has been able to prove their existence. Ordinarily we think of material objects like the earth, rocks, and trees as things which, if they exist, exist independently of us. So, one naturally interprets Kant's remark about the scandal to philosophy as the claim that it is a scandal that, prior to Kant, no one could prove to the Cartesian skeptic that things independent of our minds, like the earth, really exist. One then takes Kant's claim to have provided the required proof as the claim to have proved to the skeptic that mind-independent objects do exist. But it is not clear that he did try to prove this. Instead, Kant can be interpreted as attempting to demonstrate various things about the existence and constitution of a world of mind-dependent appearances. However, the existence of such appearances is *not* what philosophers since Descartes have tried to prove.

Although this is not the place to go into it, there is another, more charitable, interpretation in which what Kant tried to prove was neither about cognitively inaccessible things-in-themselves nor about mind-dependent appearances, but rather about tables and chairs in the sense in which we ordinarily think of them. On this interpretation, he didn't so much attempt to prove that they exist; rather he attempted to prove that the very ability to formulate and take seriously the skeptical question presupposes that one already is implicitly committed to the existence of such objects—i.e., objects that are external to, and independent of, oneself. Such a position is quite interesting. Unfortunately, Kant himself did not carefully distinguish it from other, more problematic, interpretations, with the result that his distinction between things-in-themselves and external appearances has been subject to serious confusion. This confusion illustrates why it is important to be clear about what one is asking when one asks for a proof of the existence of *things outside us*, *things external to our minds*, or *things to be met with in space*. Thus, a necessary preliminary for Moore's proof is that he clarify what *he* means.

3.1.2. EXTERNAL OBJECTS VS. OBJECTS INTERNAL TO, OR DEPENDENT ON, OUR MINDS

Moore approaches this task by distinguishing two classes of things: *things to be met with in space* and *things presented in space*. Examples of *things to be met with in space* are tables, chairs, bubbles, rocks, trees, and the earth. Examples of *things presented in space* are pains (such as the throbbing I sometimes feel just behind my eyes when I have a headache), afterimages (such as the bright gold circle that gradually changes to blue in the middle of my visual field that I seem to see when I close my eyes after staring at a bright light against a dark background), and double images (such as the images I see when I hold a pencil close to my face and press my finger against one of my eyes until I see double). Moore notes two general differences between these classes of things.

First, he takes afterimages, double images, and pains to be logically (conceptually) private, which may be defined as before:

> x is logically (conceptually) private to y iff it is conceptually possible for y to perceive or experience x, but conceptually impossible for someone other than y to perceive or experience x.

Consider pains. Moore would say that although the pain you feel may be very similar to the pain I feel, it cannot be the very same pain. So, if you have a pain in your leg and I have one in mine, then two pains exist, not one that is simultaneously in both of our legs. This is no accident of nature; it is supposed to be part of what we mean by *pain* that it is conceptually impossible for two people to experience the same one. Moore takes the same to be true of afterimages and double images. They are all logically (conceptually) private. This is not true of things met with in space—like tables, chairs, and bubbles. Some bubble may in fact be perceived by only y, but it isn't conceptually absurd or impossible for it to be perceived by someone other than y. So bubbles, along with other things met with in space, are *not* logically (conceptually) private.

The second difference between *things to be met with in space* and *things presented in space*, as Moore here uses these terms, is that for the latter, but not the former, *to exist is to be perceived*. Afterimages, double images, and pains can exist only when they are experienced. After my foot stops hurting, we don't suppose that the pain continues to exist unfelt (though the cause of the pain might). When my afterimage fades away we don't think it still exists somewhere unperceived. Again, this is no accident. According to Moore, these are things for which it is inconceivable that they could exist unexperienced. As we have seen, this is not true of tables, chairs, and bubbles. Indeed, we commonly suppose that many such things do in fact exist without anyone perceiving them. Thus, Moore will try to prove that there are things to be met with in space, where, by definition, if x is to be met with in space, then x is the sort of thing that could exist unperceived, and that could be perceived by more than one person (if it could be perceived at all). Surely, if rocks, trees, hands, or shadows exist, they are capable both of existing unperceived and of being perceived by more than one person. So, if there are rocks, trees, hands, or shadows, there are things to be met with in space.

Next, consider the phrase 'things external to our minds'. According to Moore, philosophers have used this expression in accordance with the following definitions:

> x is *in my mind* iff it is conceptually impossible for x to exist at a time when I am having no experiences—in particular, at a time in which I am not experiencing x.

> For x to be *external*, not only to my mind, but to all human minds, is for it to be conceptually possible for x to exist without anyone perceiving or experiencing x.

This last was also a criterion for something to be met with in space. So, Moore uses 'thing to be met with in space' and 'thing external to our minds' in such a way that it follows that anything falling under the former also falls under the latter.

3.2. The Proof

We have already seen that if there arc rocks, trees, hands, or shadows, then there are things to be met with in space. We now see that if there are tables, chairs, hands, or shadows, then there are things external to our minds. What then is Moore's proof that there are things external to our minds? It is very simple.

Premise 1.   Here (holding up one hand) is one hand.

Premise 2.   Here (holding up his other hand) is another hand.

Conclusion 1. Therefore, there are at least two hands.

Conclusion 2. Since there are two hands, there are at least two things to be met with in space.

Conclusion 3. Therefore, there are at least two things external to our minds.

This argument is so simple that one might wonder whether it really is a proof. Moore insists it is, citing three requirements an argument must satisfy if it is to count as a proof.

The first requirement is that the premises must be different from the conclusion. Since Moore's conclusion—that at least two things external to the mind exist—could be true even if the premises—that he has hands—were not, the conclusion differs from the premises, and Moore's first requirement is satisfied. The second requirement an argument must satisfy in order to be a proof is that the conclusion must follow from the premises—it must be *impossible* for the premises to be true while the conclusion is false. Moore's argument also satisfies this condition. He has explained that he is using the expressions 'hand', 'thing to be met with in space', and 'thing external to our minds' in such a way that it follows that *if* there are hands, then there are things to be met with in space, and hence things external to our minds. So, Moore's conclusion *does* follow from his premises.

His final stated requirement that an argument must satisfy in order to qualify as a proof is that its premises must be *known* to be true. Does he really know, when he holds them up, that he has hands? Recognizing that any philosopher who was initially skeptical about whether one can know that external objects exist will be skeptical of his claim to know his premises to be true, Moore nevertheless does claim to know them. In defending this claim, he starts out in a way that may superficially seem naïve—baldly asserting that, of course, he knows he has hands. It would, he thinks, be as absurd to suggest that he didn't as it would be to claim that you don't know you are reading these words. Nothing could be more obvious. Well, yes, one is inclined to think; I know I am reading these words, and Moore knew he had hands. But surely that can't be enough to prove what philosophers for centuries have despaired of proving, can it?

If it were enough, wouldn't it show that something at the heart of philoso-phy had been monumentally wrong for hundreds of years?

Indeed it would, which is precisely what Moore is suggesting. He is well aware that any philosopher who thinks that a proof of the external world is needed will reject his argument on the grounds that his premises require proof. He simply has no sympathy with this response. According to him, his premises don't need proof, and in any case no proof of them can be given that would satisfy the skeptic. Thus, he rejects the view that if you can't prove you have hands in a way that would satisfy the skeptic, then you don't know you have hands. But then, since he *does* know that he has hands, he concludes that the argument he has called "a proof of an external world" really is a proof of what philosophers have (wrongly) claimed needed proving.

In one revealing passage he uses a comparison to bring out the ordinary nature of his proof. He asks us to imagine someone claiming that there are three misprints on a certain page, and someone else disputing this. The first person then *proves* that there are three misprints on the page by read-ing the page and pointing them out. "Here is a misprint, here is another misprint, and here is a third; therefore there are at least three misprints on the page." As Moore insists, it would be absurd to suppose that no such proof could be legitimate. Any of us would accept such a proof from a copy editor; and if one can prove in this way that there are three misprints on a page, one can *know* the premises of the proof to be true. But if one can know that certain things are misprints, surely, one can know that other things are hands.

It is hard to dispute the compelling character of what Moore says. No one dealing with a copy editor would deny that we can prove that something is a misprint. Why should proofs in philosophy be held to a different, absurdly high standard that other proofs are not? The skeptic in philosophy asks for a proof of the external world. Very well, Moore implicitly replies, let's figure out what counts as a proof by finding out what everyone routinely takes to be a proof. The misprints example is a case in point. Since such proofs are genuine, Moore's proof of the external world should also be gen-uine. Of course, the skeptic may protest that he means something different by 'proof'—something special, stricter, and more demanding. But now the burden is on him. Perhaps he can show that philosophy will progress faster and achieve deeper results with his notion of proof. But no such argument has been given, and history since Descartes doesn't inspire optimism about such a conclusion. Perhaps the skeptic can convince us that there is some-thing wrong with what we all take to be genuine proofs outside of philos-ophy. Fair enough, but to do this, he will have to find among our firmest convictions some that are inconsistent with our normal epistemic practices, while still being sufficiently well-grounded to force a radical reassessment of them. Although Moore hasn't said much to illuminate why exactly this can't be done, it is hard not to agree with him that it can't.

3.3. Does Moore's Argument Satisfy the Requirements for Being a Proof?

Even if Moore's argument for the existence of an external world satisfies the three requirements he lists for being a proof, some philosophers have contended that there is a fourth requirement that his argument does not satisfy. In order for an argument to count as a proof, it must provide a rational route by which one could *come to know its conclusion*; and in order for this to be so, knowledge of the premises must not presuppose, or be based upon, prior knowledge of the conclusion. Although Moore would surely agree, this point is coupled, in Martin Davies (2000), with an idea that directly challenges Moore's "proof." The contention is that even if his premises, that he has hands, are knowable, knowing them depends on already knowing the conclusion he draws from them. Otherwise put, the perceptual experience that gives Moore, and us, knowledge that he is holding up his hands does so only because he, and we, already know that there is an external world about which our perceptions provide information. If for some reason we started out (wrongly) thinking that such experiences were only dreams, or visions of artificially created Matrix images, both Moore's experiences and ours would be taken to be just more entertaining dreams or images. Neither would convince us, or provide justification for the claim that we were seeing real, existing hands, or even that such things exist. According to this anti-Moorean critique, it may very well be that we know that there is an external world, but if we do, nothing like Moore's argument establishes that. Thus, Moore's argument isn't a proof.

To evaluate this case against Moore, we must make two distinctions: (i) between the role of perceptual evidence in justifying a belief and its role in leading one to adopt that belief, and (ii) between situations in which potential evidence fails to justify because one has reason to believe it is inaccurate and situations in which such evidence retains its justificatory force despite one's recognition of the possibility that it may be misleading. Regarding (i), a person who is suffering from a massively systematic delusion may have sufficient cognitive resources to incorporate any experience into his or her delusional scheme while retaining a set of fixed delusional beliefs. The fact that for some true propositions p such a person would not be moved by any experience to believe p doesn't show that none of those experiences provide justifying evidence for p. Of course, being in possession of evidence that would justify one's belief, if one were to come to believe p, is not sufficient for knowledge of p. For that, one must really believe p (which must also be true). However, if, due to some psychological cause, the delusion loses its hold on the sufferer, who then becomes willing to consider alternative beliefs, the justificatory force of available perceptual evidence stands ready to underwrite knowledge of p, once the agent comes to firmly believe p. This point applies also to Moore's argument. It is, admittedly, difficult to imagine anyone insane enough to be

under the delusion that his or her perceptual experiences are merely images and impressions, providing no information about an external world.
However, to the extent that we can imagine it, we may grant that seeing
Moore hold up his hands, and hearing him present his argument, could
not be expected to persuade the sufferer to replace his or her delusional
beliefs with beliefs in Moore, his hands, and the external world. However,
if the agent were to suddenly snap out of it and acquire those beliefs, he or
she would have perceptual justification for them.

Next consider (ii)—the distinction between cases in which potential evidence fails to justify because one has reason to believe it to be unreliable
and cases in which the experience in question retains its justificatory force
despite one's recognition of the possibility that it could be misleading. The
following scenarios illustrate the difference.

Scenario 1

Entering a room, you see a certain book B, which you perceive *as blue*. Normally when something appears blue, you judge, or take it for granted, that
it is blue—which you do here. Being aware of perceptual illusions, you
know you aren't infallible. But, although you realize that error is possible,
you don't take it to be the norm, and nothing supports suspicion in this
case. So you judge B to be blue, and conclude that B is the same color as
another book C you have at home. You thereby come to know *that B is the
same color as C* by deriving it from a premise you already knew—that C is
blue—plus a premise you know on the basis of your perceptual experience
in the room—that B is blue. In so doing you prove your conclusion by relying on your perceptual knowledge.

Scenario 2

The situation is the same as before, except that this time before entering the
room you are given somewhat credible (though not entirely conclusive)
evidence that the room is color-distorting, so that nothing in it has the
color it appears to have. In fact, the room is perfectly normal, and not
color-distorting. But you don't know this. On entering, you see the book
B, which appears (and really is) blue, just as before. Not sure whether to
trust the discounting evidence you received before entering the room, you
"go with your gut" and cautiously believe that it is blue, and hence that B
is the same color as C. In this way, you arrive at the some conclusion as in
scenario 1, on the basis of the same experience. In this case, however, you
don't *know*, and you don't take yourself to know, that conclusion. Having
been given positive reason not to trust your perceptual experience in the
room, the normal justificatory force of your visual experience of B will
be defeated, and will not justify a claim of knowledge, unless it is supplemented by further evidence defeating the defeater. Since you lack such
evidence, you don't know.

Scenario 3

> The situation is just like scenario 1, except that this time you are given the
> (false) defeating evidence of color-distortion after you have left the room.
> In this case you did have knowledge when you were in the room, but you
> lose it when provided later with the defeater that you are unable to rebut.

These scenarios illustrate the difference, for our assessment of knowledge
claims, between (a) cases in which empirical evidence (e.g., one's perceptual experience) justifies one's knowledge of p, even though (one realizes
that) it is possible for such experience to mislead, and (b) cases in which
some experience E, which would otherwise provide justifying evidence
for p, fails to provide knowledge of p, because one is in possession of
other evidence that E is unreliable. Roughly put, *unrebutted evidence of
unreliability or error is inconsistent with knowledge, but the mere possibility of
such is not.*

Applied to Moore's argument, this means that if he, or we, had *independent reason* to believe either (i) that, despite our perceptual experience,
there were no hands or other external objects we were then (or ever) perceiving, or (ii) that our perceptual evidence was systematically unreliable,
then his simple appeal to such evidence would not support knowledge
either of his premises or of his conclusion. In point of fact, however, it
would seem that all the skeptic has given us is the *mere possibility* that there
are no hands or other external objects presented to us in perception. *But
the mere possibility that something isn't so is not a reason to believe that it isn't so.*
Since the perceptual evidence that Moore implicitly appeals to has no independently justified burden of inaccuracy or unreliability to overcome, he
is in a position to argue that it can successfully play its intended role of justifying his claim to know both his premises and his conclusion to be true.
In this way, his claim to have presented a proof (of sorts) of an external
world can be given a plausible, though admittedly incomplete, defense.[25]

3.4. Moore versus the Skeptic: What Is the Point of Moore's Proof?

The discussion just concluded is a mere sample of the much larger issue
of how, in light of Moore's proof, we should view skepticism. Beyond providing what might be counted as a plausible, though contentious, proof
of a conclusion that is incompatible with skepticism, Moore showed remarkably little interest in diagnosing why many have found skepticism so
seductive, what subtle errors have contributed to its enduring power, what
positive lessons we can learn from it, and what enlightening distinctions
are required in order for us to avoid falling into confusion about it. These
issues, with which philosophers continue to struggle, are barely touched

---

[25] A strong defense of Moore along these lines is given in Pryor (2000). For further relevant discussion, see Pryor (2004), and Wright (1985, 2000, 2002, 2003, 2004).

in Moore's otherwise ground-breaking and highly influential writings on epistemology. What then was the point of his proof? He was as aware as anyone else that no one who thought a proof was needed in the first place would be convinced by the one he provided. Unlike far too many, he was also aware that failure to convince does not show that an argument isn't a proof. Still, the presentation of proof must have some point—some message that Moore deemed to be important for other philosophers. What was it?

In my opinion, the implicit message of "Proof of an External World" is briefly touched on in Moore (1909), and more explicitly stated in his 1910–11 lectures, later published as chapters 5 and 6 of *Some Main Problems of Philosophy*. His message is that prior to turning themselves into knots attempting to "answer the skeptic," philosophers should ask the skeptic to justify his claim that we can't know that there are things like hands, or misprints. As Moore saw it, skeptics have typically based their supposedly unanswerable question "How do you know?" on restrictive theories of what knowledge is, and what is required for achieving it. In section 1.3 of this chapter, I discussed his response to the skepticism inspired by Hume's theory of knowledge, which is, I believe, his model for responding to all versions of skepticism arising from claims of the following form:

P1.   All knowledge is thus-and-so. (E.g., to know p, one's evidence must strictly entail p—and so rule out the possibility that p is untrue. Also, nothing counts as evidence unless one couldn't be mistaken about it under any circumstances—even if one turned out to be dreaming, or to be deceived by an evil demon. Such evidence is restricted to statements about oneself, one's thoughts, and one's private sense experience.)

P2.   Alleged knowledge of hands, misprints, etc., is not thus-and-so.

C.   Thus, no one ever knows that there are hands, misprints, etc.

Moore's reply to all such arguments is "How do *you* know that the premises of *your* argument are true?"

Restrictive premises, like Humean versions of P1 and P2, are not without plausibility. If one builds the skeptical case carefully, one can give a chain of reasoning leading to something very much like, P1, P2, and C, each step of which appeals to what seem to be ordinary, commonsense views about knowledge and evidence. For example, we would normally be quite uncomfortable making any claim to the effect *I know that S, but it is possible, given my evidence, that not S*. Moreover, if asked to imagine the possibility that a brain in a vat could be artificially stimulated to have precisely the experiences we have had in the past, are having now, and will have in the future, many of us would be uncomfortable denying that such a scenario is possible. Finally, asked whether, since the brain in the vat has the same experiences we do, the brain's perceptual evidence for its view of the world must be the same as ours (despite the fact that it never really perceives any hands, or misprints), many would be tempted to admit that the brain's evidence *is* the same as ours. Taken singly, each step in the reasoning has intuitive appeal. Taken together, they seem to support a view much like that expressed by (Humean versions of) premises P1 and P2, according to which (i) it *is* possible, given our evidence, that we have never perceived hands or misprints, and even, that there are no such things, and (ii) it follows that our pre-theoretic claims to know otherwise are false. Since we surely want to preserve these claims, we would like an explanation of precisely which steps in this intuitive line of skeptical reasoning are incorrect and why. Unfortunately, Moore doesn't oblige us.

What he does seek to do is to assure us—even before we are able to identify the precise intuitive missteps leading to P1, P2, and, thereby, to C— that no such line of reasoning could ever be correct. Since C does follow from P1 and P2, what we learn is that one cannot simultaneously accept P1, P2, and (7).

7. I know that this is a hand/misprint (demonstrating a relevant hand/ misprint).

Moore reminds us that, although at least one of these statements must go, nothing in the argument dictates which. So one must decide which statement or statements one has least reason to accept, and which one has most reason to accept. His point seems to be that anyone who honestly asks this question will find (7) to be the most secure, and so will reject either P1 or P2. As Moore sees it, the problem with the skeptic is that he has adopted a philosophical theory about what knowledge consists in that is far too restrictive. *The skeptic assumes that we can be certain about what knowledge is before we decide whether what we all ordinarily take to be paradigmatic cases of knowledge are genuine.* But this is backwards. For Moore any philosophical theory about what knowledge is, including any theory of the necessary and sufficient conditions for knowledge, must be tested against what we all recognize to be the clearest and most fundamental examples of knowledge. Since these constitute *evidence* for, or against, the theory, any theory inconsistent with a substantial range of such examples is strongly disconfirmed. Once we see that the skeptic's assumptions about knowledge are themselves both typically unsupported by anything more than their initial intuitive appeal, and less plausible than the commonsense convictions they conflict with, we have little choice but to reject the way in which the skeptic poses the problem. The real problem, according to Moore, is not to prove that we know that there are hands, or to deny this, but to construct a theory of knowledge that is consistent with obvious instances of knowledge such as this, and that explains how such knowledge arises.

For Moore, both the skeptic and the philosopher who tries to provide the kind of proof demanded by the skeptic accept an unjustified theory of what knowledge consists in. This conviction drives the ironic nature of his presentation. No one who believed that a proof of the external world was needed would be satisfied by Moore's proof, because anyone who demanded such a proof would already have accepted the skeptic's restrictive conception of knowledge, and so would deny that Moore knew that he was holding up his hand. What then was Moore's purpose in presenting his proof? His purpose was to underline that there is no need for such a proof in the first place. What he wants us to see is that if our knowledge of the external world presents a problem to philosophy, the scandal does not lie in the inability of philosophers to show that this knowledge meets the conditions demanded by the skeptic. Rather, the scandal lies in philosophers' uncritical acceptance of the legitimacy and presuppositions of the skeptic's demands. It is hard to resist the idea that there is an important insight here. Would that it were accompanied by a positive theory of what knowledge is that made it clear at precisely which points the skeptic goes wrong, and explained how we know what we really do know.

4. PERCEPTION, SENSE DATA, AND ANALYSIS

Unfortunately, when Moore did turn to such an explanation, in "A Defense of Common Sense," the strategy he seemed to regard as the most promising one turned out to be unproductive. The key idea was to analyze precisely *what it is we know* when we know a claim about the external world to be true. In giving his proof of an external world, he concentrates on propositions, like those about his hands, that he knows by perception. However, by 1925, when writing "A Defense of Common Sense," he was most inclined to think of his perception of hands and other external objects as being mediated by the direct apprehension of private sense data, as explained in section 1 above. This created a tension in his epistemology. How could his direct apprehension of private, mind-dependent sense data provide knowledge of things that are both public and mind-independent? In section 4 of "A Defense of Common Sense" he struggles to formulate *an analysis of perceptual statements* that answers this question.

His basic idea is that in order to understand how perception can give us knowledge that there are material objects, we must *analyze* exactly what we mean by such elementary claims as:

8. I see this and this is a table.

At this point, his task is not to try to decide whether or not propositions such as this are ever true. Of course, they are. Accepting this, he believes that philosophers face the task of providing an analysis of these propositions that explains how we are able to know them to be true. How, then, are we to analyze propositions like (8)? Moore suggests three alternatives among which he cannot make up his mind.[26]

---

[26] I will omit here the distinction between talking about a table and talking about the surface of the table. Although Moore spends quite a bit of time on this, the distinction does not substantially affect the central philosophical questions at stake.

The first alternative is *Direct Realism*, which involves scrapping sense data for cases of normal perception (excluding after images, double images, and hallucinations). On this alternative, what I perceive is not an array of private sense data, but simply the table. In addition, there is no more basic proposition that gives the content of (8). Although Moore grants that this view might possibly be correct, he cites two objections to it that make him doubt that it is. First, this view requires giving up an analysis of normal perception that he favored, in part because he was inclined to accept the Appearance Principle.

The Appearance Principle

Whenever something looks, e.g., white, rectangular, and small to you, you are seeing something that is white, rectangular, small, etc.

This is the principle—from chapter 2 of his 1910–11 *Some Main Problems of Philosophy* lectures (discussed in section 1 above)—that underwrites his inference from (i) the fact that the envelope he holds up in front of his class looks different to the different students to (ii) the conclusion that they must be seeing different patches—i.e., sense data. Since Direct Realism denies this principle, which Moore is inclined to accept, he takes this denial to be an objection to Direct Realism (though not necessarily a fatal one, since he admits that he isn't completely sure of the principle). Of course, if one doesn't think that the principle is plausible in the first place, as many now do not, then one won't see this as a problem. However, Moore had another objection to Direct Realism as well. He thought that it was obvious that in cases involving hallucination, afterimages, and double images, we really do see sense data. Furthermore, he thought that what we see in these cases is so much like what we see in normal perception that the most plausible explanation for the similarity is that we *always* see sense data. If so, then Direct Realism is out.

Moore's second alternative is that in normal, veridical cases (in which, unlike cases of illusion or hallucination, things really are as they seem), what we directly perceive are mind-dependent sense data related to material objects in a certain way. On this alternative, (8) is analyzed as meaning the same as some version of (9).

9. There is exactly one thing of which it is true both that it is a table and that it bears relation R to this sense datum I am now seeing.

Different versions of this analysis come from different choices of R. On one version, R is the causal relation, and seeing a table is seeing a sense datum caused (in the right way) by a table. Moore himself didn't accept this version, but rather preferred a version according to which R is an *unanalyzable* relation that holds between x and y iff y is an appearance of

x. But no matter how R is characterized, being justified in believing that one sees a table depends on being justified in inferring something from one's perceptual knowledge of sense data. One must be able to justifiably infer from the fact that one is perceiving a certain sense datum that there is something that bears R to that sense datum. Although Moore thought that this analysis might be correct, he took the basis for the inference to be problematic. If all we ever directly perceive are sense data, how do we know that anything bears R to them, or, if some things do, how do we know what those things are like? Having posited intermediaries between us and material objects, this alternative has no obvious explanation of how we get beyond the intermediaries.

Although Moore takes this to be a powerful objection, he doesn't regard it as absolutely conclusive. As I discussed earlier, he notes at the end of chapter 2 of *Some Main Problems of Philosophy* that there are cases in which we know, on the basis of mental images that are presently before our minds, of the existence of other things that are not immediately before our minds. One example is memory. He says that he can remember today that he saw something red yesterday, even though the red sense datum the existence of which he remembers is not identical with any memory image that he now has. He takes this to show that sometimes our direct awareness of certain images or sense data makes it possible for us to know of the existence of other things to which those images or sense data are related. According to the second alternative view of perception, and analysis of perceptual statements, our knowledge of the existence of material objects on the basis of our perception of sense data is analogous to this. Moore acknowledges that this might be the correct account, but he admits to being uncertain about it.

So far we have considered two alternatives. The first scraps sense data for normal perception and claims that a statement like (8) doesn't have any more fundamental analysis. The second posits sense data as objects perceived in all cases of perceptual experience, and takes the meaning of (8) to be given by (9). As we have seen, Moore thinks that there are substantial, but not absolutely conclusive, objections to each. There is also a further consideration that may have made both alternatives unattractive to him, though he doesn't mention it himself. This consideration is based on the reason he is looking for what he calls an analysis of statements like (8) in the first place.

The main reason he wants such an analysis is to help explain how we can come to know these propositions to be true. However, the key problem in providing such an explanation will arise no matter whether one takes sense data to be objects of perception or not. Either way, one must admit that people sometimes have hallucinatory experiences that are indistinguishable to them from normal perceptions. If we can sometimes be fooled in this way, how do we know that we are not always fooled? How does anyone know that he or she is not a brain in a bottle, whose sensory pathways are electronically stimulated by a computer in just the ways they would be if he or she were living a normal life? Does it really matter for the answer to this question whether we describe the brain as seeing sense data to which no material objects correspond, or as not really seeing anything (including sense data), but only seeming to see? Either way, it is possible for me to have experiences indistinguishable from those I am now having without there being any table, computer, or window in front of me. How, then, does my actual experience succeed in ensuring that I do know what I really do know—namely, that these things are really there? Won't the chief difficulties involved in answering this question remain whether or not we take sense data to be objects of perception? If, according to Direct Realism, statements like (8) do not have any more fundamental analysis, then analyzing *what we know* when we know (8) to be true doesn't help answer this question about *how we know*. The same is true of the second alternative. If (8) is analyzed as (9), then the job of explaining how we can know it to be true doesn't get any easier. Since Moore hoped, rightly or wrongly, that the analysis of statements like (8) would help with such an explanation, he had reason to be dissatisfied with both alternatives.

This brings me to the final, very radical alternative, that Moore thought might provide a correct analysis. On this alternative, material objects are *not* fundamentally different from sense data, but rather are what John Stuart Mill called *permanent possibilities of sensation*. On this view, the meaning of a statement like (8) is given by a long list of categorical and hypothetical statements about sense data. Roughly speaking, (8) means something like (10).

10. I am seeing a certain table-like visual sense datum; and if I were to walk a little to the side, then I would have certain other slightly different table-like visual sense data; and if I were to put my hand down, then I would have certain tactile sense data of hardness and smoothness; and so on, and so on, and so on.

Although Moore doesn't say what the virtues of this analysis are supposed to be, it is pretty clear what he has in mind. According to the analysis, to say that I am seeing a table is just to say something about my own sense data—the ones I am having now, and the ones I would have if certain conditions were fulfilled. I know what sense data I am having now because I perceive them, and because they are the kinds of things I can't be mistaken about. Do I know what sense data I would perceive if certain conditions were fulfilled? Well, if in a particular case of "seeing a table" I gather enough visual and tactile sense data, then because I have experienced such combinations of sense data in the past, and seen what other sense data follow from them, it is plausible to suppose that I am justified in believing that all the conditions for "seeing a table" are fulfilled. If they are fulfilled, it is natural to suppose I know this. So, if *I am seeing a table* is really a statement about my own sense data, then it is understandable how I can come to know it to be true.

Still, Moore doubts that it is the correct analysis. For one thing, he doubts that the conditions specified in the analysis of material-object statements like (8) can be spelled out without again referring to material objects. In providing the schematic sample analysis (10), I included such things as *If I were to walk a little to the side . . .* , and *If I were to put my hand down . . . .* But *walking* implies I have a body, and *putting my hand down* implies I have a hand. If all material objects are supposed to be permanent possibilities of sensation, then these references to hands, bodies, and the rest would themselves have to be spelled out completely in terms of sense data. Moore doubts this could be done. Second, he rightly thinks that statements about *one's own sense data*—no matter how complex—can never be equivalent to statements about material objects. We might, of course, revise the analysis so as to make reference not only to one's own sense data, but also to the sense data of others. However, this would raise the question of how one individual can *know* of the existence and quality of sense data of other agents. If it is hard to explain how we come to have knowledge of material objects, like the bodies of other people, then surely it can't be easier to explain our knowledge of their sense data. Moore seems to think (for good reason) that there is an irreducible residue in our talk about material objects that cannot be captured by any talk that is solely about sense data.

Since he was unsatisfied with every analysis of statements like (8) he could think of, he was left without an answer to his central problem. *Granted that we do know about material objects, how is this knowledge to be explained?* He was, of course, not alone in this, and the fact that he left this question unanswered contributed to the urgency of the attempts by others to answer it. Three aspects of his position were particularly influential:

(i) his conviction that we do know that there are material objects and other people,
(ii) his insistence that the job of philosophy is not to dispute this but to explain how such knowledge is possible, and
(iii) his belief that a satisfactory explanation must rest on a philosophical analysis of the meanings of statements about material objects, other people, and so on.

This was an important legacy, as was Moore's other work in epistemology. However, it was rivaled, if not surpassed, by his extraordinary influence on moral philosophy in the first half of the twentieth century. Having dissected the arguments for his chief metaethical doctrines about goodness in the previous chapter, in the next chapter I will try to put Moore's moral epistemology in a broader context.

CHAPTER 6

The Mixed Legacy and Lost Opportunities of Moore's Ethics

1. Improving Moore's Failed Moral Epistemology
2. The Incompleteness of the Good: Attributive, Predicative, and More
3. Definability, Consequentialism, and the Primacy of Goodness
4. Moore's Argument against Subjectivism
5. Moore's Philosophical Credo

1. IMPROVING MOORE'S FAILED MORAL EPISTEMOLOGY

Moore's two most influential and long-remembered contributions to philosophy were (i) his proof of an external world (and the defense of Common Sense that accompanied it) and (ii) his metaethical doctrines that 'good' (and other ethical notions) are not definable in nonethical terms, and that, because of this, fundamental ethical conclusions are neither provable, nor capable of support, confirmation, or disconfirmation by evidence. Though Moore was, I think, comfortable holding these views together, they tended to push the philosophy of their day in opposite directions. Lecturing to the British Academy on November 22, 1939, the longtime defender of Common Sense and opponent of skepticism could assert the existence of his two hands, conclude that at least two external objects exist, and plausibly claim to *know* the latter (in part) because he *knew* the former. If challenged to defend his knowledge claims, his response would have been that his (justified) confidence that he knew these things exceeded his, or anyone's, (justified) confidence in any philosophical theory of knowledge that does not allow for knowledge of hands.

By contrast, he could not, on that day, have given a similar proof of the existence of at least two states of affairs that were good in themselves, or at least two acts that were wrong, by describing any two states of (parts of) the universe, no matter how widely they might be approved, or any two actions, no matter how widely condemned. He could not have done so because it would have been difficult for him to credibly maintain that he *knew* the needed premises—that certain specified states of affairs are good in themselves, and that the acts in question, being of a certain sort, were therefore wrong. It's not that he wouldn't have taken himself to know these things. He would have. Nor would he have been wrong. Surely there are some premises of the needed kind about which he would have been right to think that he knew them. However, by 1939 this was a position that had too little currency in philosophy to be assumed or asserted without a clear and cogent refutation of the "moral skeptics" of his day (the emotivists) that exposed precisely where and why they had gone wrong. What makes this contrast ironic is that Moore himself was in no small degree responsible for it.

The preface and first chapter of *Principia Ethica* had a profound impact on philosophical ethics throughout most of the twentieth century. The doctrine that conclusions about goodness and badness, as well as those about rightness and wrongness, can neither be proved by philosophical argument from nonevaluative premises, nor established by empirical evidence, was intended by Moore to carve out the domain of an autonomous "science" of ethics.[1] For him to take ethics to be "a science," which today sounds so quaintly anachronistic, was simply to take it to be a systematic body of knowledge, independent not only of psychology and other natural sciences, but also of metaphysics and other fields of philosophy. It was the *autonomy* of ethics he sought by freeing it from "naturalistic" analyses of ethical notions. However, it was *noncognitivism* to which his metaethical doctrines inadvertently contributed the most.

While Moore himself could live with goodness as an unanalyzable, nonnatural property that supervenes on, but is not identical with, the natural properties of a state of affairs that has it, others understandably found the doctrine mysterious.[2] Convinced by him that goodness was neither a simple nor a complex natural property, they were attracted to the idea that it didn't express a property at all—from which they jumped to the conclusion that 'good' is used, not describe anything, but to express the emotion, or the evaluative attitude, of an agent. From this perspective, Moore's open-question argument—which had always seemed more compelling than his explanation of it—became instantly comprehensible.[3] According to emotivism, which had succeeded Moore's difficult doctrine as the dominant metaethical view of analytic philosophers at the time of his 1939 lecture, the question ⌈Granted α is D, is α good?⌉ is always open because no matter what property you take the referent of α to have, it is always open to you to respond to it either negatively, or with no emotion at all. Since utterances of ⌈α is good⌉ were thought to make no statement

---

[1] Sections 2 and 3, *Principia Ethica*, revised edition (Moore 1993), p. 55.

[2] Moore discusses the relationship between the goodness of a state of affairs and the natural properties it supervenes on in Moore (1922b), "The Conception of Intrinsic Value."

[3] Thomson (2003) contains an illuminating discussion of how Moore's open-question argument, and his own inadequate explanation of it in terms of "nonnatural properties," fed versions of noncognitivism from emotivism to expressivism.

about the world, it was deemed to make no more sense to apply the categories of truth and falsehood to them, or to claim to know them to be true, than it would to apply the categories of truth and falsity to the imperative 'Close the door!' or to claim to know an utterance of it to be true. In this way, Moore's open-question argument, and the conclusions he drew from it, fed forms of skepticism and noncognitivism in ethics that he never endorsed, and of which he never approved.

Unfortunately, the shortcomings of his own metaethical view made it untenable. His central insight, which was both correct and important, was that *interesting* claims about goodness and other moral notions—of the sort about which we hope to receive guidance from ethical theory—are resistant to proof. However, his account of why they are so was woefully inadequate, in large part because of his insecure grasp of the fundamental methodological notions he employed—including *analysis, definability, entailment, logical consequence, analyticity, necessity, possibility, meaning,* and *proof.* At first glance, Moore's use of these notions to discuss the central issues in ethics appears to be a model of clarity and precision, and there is no doubt that he strove mightily to try to make it so. But the appearance of clarity and precision in his discussion is misleading. As I explained in chapter 4, the definability or indefinability of 'good' (in his sense) is irrelevant to any serious attempt to establish his central metaethical conclusions—as is the question of whether any statements in which it occurs are, or not, Frege-analytic (which, I argued, was roughly what he had in mind). At best, one can reconstruct a speculative argument—based on an expansive reading of the open-question argument—for the conjectures (i) and (ii).

(i) No statement predicating *goodness* of an individual or state of affairs contingent on its having any "natural" (non-evaluative) properties is *analytically obvious.*

(ii) Because of this, no statement characterizing an individual or state of affairs as good is provable from analytically obvious premises by analytically obvious steps.

Though the wording "analytically obvious" was chosen for its Moorean flavor, an analytically obvious premise is just one that is necessary, a priori, and so obvious as to be difficult to deny by anyone who understands or apprehends it; an analytically obvious step is truth preserving in the same sense. Putting aside worries mentioned in chapter 4 concerning the notion *analytic obviousness,* one can make a plausible argument that both (i) and (ii) are counter-exemplified by highly specific and seemingly uncontroversial claims—like (22a–g) at the end of chapter 4—about the goodness or badness of particular individuals or states of affairs, and the rightness or wrongness of certain acts.

Despite these negative results about Moore's main metaethical theses, one important sub-case of conjecture (ii) might be maintained:

(ii') No *interesting* ethical thesis—about which we may look to philosophy for guidance to resolve controversy or overcome uncertainty—is either itself analytically obvious, or provable from analytically obvious premises by analytically obvious steps.

Though less ambitious than his original metaethical claims, (ii') is both plausible and potentially important. Had Moore been able to make the case for it—instead of his more sweeping and exciting claims—his influence in ethics might have been different, and more to his liking. Unfortunately, his own moral epistemology prevented him from doing so.

Although it was central to his view that interesting ethical claims are resistant to proof, it was equally central that some, for example (1), are both true and knowable.

1. The appreciation of beautiful objects and the pleasures of human companionship are (intrinsically) good, and only these things are (intrinsically) good.

Since this was his most fundamental ethical principle, he thought that other ethical claims could be justified by appealing to it, but it could not be justified by appealing to anything. In this way, he was driven to the view that (1) is necessary, a priori, and *self-evidently obvious*, even though (a) it is not a counterexample to (ii'), and (b) the question expressed by (2) is genuinely open, in the sense that knowing the answer to it is not guaranteed by understanding the interrogative sentence and grasping the question it expresses.

2. Granted that x is the appreciation of beautiful objects or the enjoyment of each other's companionship by human agents, but is x good?

But how can Moore take (1) to be self-evidently obvious, while taking it not to counter-exemplify (ii'), and taking the question corresponding to (1) to be genuinely open?

He got himself into this predicament by maintaining three general principles:

P1.　　The most general ethical claims, ⌜Things that are D (and only those things) are good⌝, are neither analytic nor susceptible to philosophical proof, for any relevant D, and for any such D the question ⌜Granted that α is D, is α good?⌝ is genuinely open.

P2.　　Some ethical claims are both true and capable of being known to be true; hence either they are self-evident, or they can be justified.

P3.　　Justification of ethical claims flows from the general to the specific. Particular claims about this or that being good are justified by appeal to generalities under which they fall. Low-level generalities are justified by higher level generalities and equivalences, until we reach a fundamental claim ⌜Things that are D (and only those things) are good⌝.

P2 and P3 together tell us that some highly general, yet epistemically fundamental, claims must be self-evident, since they serve as the justification for lower-level claims which, being knowable, must be capable of justification. Since there is nothing else on which to base these most fundamental claims—⌜Things that are D (and only those things) are good⌝—we have no choice but to regard them as self-evident. But it is hard to square this with P1. It is not easy to see how such claims could be self-evident without being either analytically obvious or provable by analytically obvious means. Moore did nothing to resolve this tension.

This is a pity, since an alternative was available. As I pointed out at the end of chapter 4, he could have given up P3, while retaining P1, P2, and (ii'). Instead of thinking that particular, or highly restricted, claims about goodness, badness, rightness, and wrongness are justified by appealing to selfevident but highly abstract equivalences or generalities like (1), he could have held that the starting point in ethics consisted in our pre-theoretic moral certainties about particular cases and severely restricted generalities— such as (22a–g) of chapter 4. If any moral claims are self-evident, these are. Of course, these restricted generalities don't cover nearly all the cases for which evaluations are needed. Hence, the central problem in ethics is to systematize and extend these judgments by forming more encompassing generalizations that may be justified as *explaining* what we antecedently take to be self-evident cases, by having independent plausibility themselves, and by fitting in well with already accepted principles. On this conception, the most encompassing generalizations in ethics are not themselves self-evident; rather, they are justified by how well they explain and systematize an array of more limited claims, many of which are self-evident.

Had Moore adopted this picture, his conception of proper methodology in ethics would have been more in harmony with his well-known epistemological views. Unlike many philosophers (among them, Hume) who have thought that we can first establish a general theory about the necessary and sufficient conditions for knowledge, and then use it to assess the claim that one knows that one has hands, that there are other bodies, and the like, Moore insisted that our pre-philosophical certainties about individual instances of knowledge provide a foundation for evaluating any such general theory of knowledge. No idea is more associated with him than that of starting with pre-philosophical certainties about particular cases, and using them to confirm or disconfirm general philosophical principles, rather than going the other way around. None of Moore's contributions to philosophy match this for lasting importance. How ironic, and what a pity, that he didn't follow this method in ethics.

Had he done so, his metaethical legacy might have been rather different. On this alternative view, the resistance of interesting ethical claims to proof in the sense of (ii'), and the openness of the corresponding ethical questions, is not obviously different from the resistance to proof of other sweeping philosophical claims—about, e.g., the necessary and sufficient conditions for knowledge, rationality, or personal identity (though time)—or the openness of the corresponding philosophical questions about them. None of these interesting philosophical claims is uncontroversially provable in the sense in which (ii') denies that interesting ethical claims are. On the contrary, the resistance of ethical claims to proof noted by Moore, and the openness of certain corresponding questions, have their counterparts in all areas of philosophy. Since there is nothing in this to suggest noncognitivism in every philosophical domain, there is nothing in this way of construing Moore's central metaethical observations to create tension with his central contention that some important, interesting, and highly general ethical judgments are both true and knowable. This, then, is a way of modifying his metaethics to make it coherent, while giving up little that was truly important to him.

One might, of course, think that there really is something special about the resistance of interesting ethical claims to proof, and the corresponding openness of questions corresponding to them, that goes beyond the normal resistance of interesting philosophical claims to proof, and the openness of the related questions. Is there something to this alleged specialness that goes beyond the fact that the central issues of ethics have a strong practical interest to us that the central issues of many other areas of philosophy do not? If so, what is it? It seems to me that the jury is still out on these questions, more than a century after the publication of *Principia Ethica*.

We now turn, in the rest of this chapter, to a collection of important, related, and historically significant issues concerning Moore's ethics.

2. THE INCOMPLETENESS OF THE GOOD: ATTRIBUTIVE, PREDICATIVE, AND MORE

The epistemological issues under discussion have concerned how claims formulated using the word 'good' are established. The focus on 'good' derives from the fact that Moore takes it to be the most fundamental term in ethics—one that can be used to define other ethical terms, such as 'duty', 'obligation', and 'morally right action'. In section 3, I will address the alleged primacy of goodness among the moral notions. Here, I note that the issue of primacy does not (in my view) affect the epistemological conclusions we have reached so far, since those conclusions carry over to the other ethical notions as well. There is, however, a central aspect of Moore's treatment of 'good' that has been subjected to a historically influential, and potentially far-reaching, criticism of which everyone should be aware. This criticism, made in Peter Geach (1956), has had an important effect both on the prevailing view of Moore's ethical theory, and on more recent alternative theories.

Geach's criticism focuses on Moore's comparison of the word 'good' to the word 'yellow'. Since Moore takes both to pick out properties, he is committed to a certain parallel between the two. Since ⌜α is a yellow N⌝ is equivalent to the claim ⌜α is yellow and α is an N⌝—which says of the referent of α that it has both the property *being yellow* and the property expressed by N—the view that 'good' also expresses a property leads one to expect that ⌜α is a good N⌝ is equivalent to ⌜α is good and α is an N⌝— which says of the referent of α that it has both the property *being good* and the property expressed by N. However, this is typically not so, as shown by the following example:

P1. α is a good driver.

C1.   Therefore α is good and α is a driver.

C2.   Therefore α is good.

P2. α is a man.

C3.   Therefore α is good and α is a man.

C4.   Therefore α is a good man.

If ⌜α is a good N⌝ were always equivalent to ⌜α is good and α is an N⌝ then this would be a valid argument, and we could derive the conclusion that x is a good man from the premises that x is a good driver and x is a man. Since, in fact, this conclusion does not follow from the premises, ⌜α is a good N⌝ is not always equivalent to ⌜α is good and α is an N⌝. This in turn means that 'good', as used in the phrase ⌜a good N⌝, does not stand for a property common to all and only good things. There is no significant property common to all good men, good carpenters, good burglars, good cooks, good houses, good cheese, and so on.

When 'good' is used in these constructions it has an entirely different function from picking out a property. It is, in Geach's words, an *attributive* predicate modifier rather than predicative adjective, or separate predicate itself. When one says ⌜α is a good N⌝, one is saying, roughly, ⌜α is an N that satisfies certain contextually relevant interests taken in N's to a higher degree than most N's⌝.[4] Since it is often a straightforward matter to determine what the relevant interests are, one can often provide true, informative, and relatively uncontroversial statements of the conditions that are necessary and sufficient for the predicate ⌜is a good N⌝ to apply to something. For example, typically, someone is a good sprinter if and only if that person runs faster than most sprinters; something is a good watch if and only if it does a better job than most watches in keeping accurate time, while being durable, attractive, and comfortable to wear. Similar results are forthcoming whenever N is a noun (or noun phrase) that stands for things with a highly specific function, or for things for which it is otherwise obvious what the interests taken in them are.

---

[4] What these interests are, and who takes these interests in N's, are matters often left implicit; they may vary from one context of utterance to the next.

When N is a noun standing for things with which no specific function is associated, it is often difficult, if not impossible, to specify what it is for the predicate ⌈is a good N⌉ to apply. For example, when N stands for a class of things that no one has any interest in—particles of dust, for example—the claim expressed by ⌈α is a good N⌉ (the claim that something is a good particle of dust) will seem strange and hard to make sense of (except, perhaps, in specialized or artificial contexts). Another class of problematic cases are those in which N stands for a class of things that people do have interests in, but interests of many different and varied kinds. A case in point is the predicate 'is a car'. One reason why it sometimes may be hard to get a handle on what is being said when an automobile is called "a good car" is that it may be difficult to pin down precisely which of the interests standardly taken in cars are the most relevant in the context in which the remark occurs. A similar point holds when N is a highly general or abstract predicate like 'event', or 'state of affairs'. Since it is unclear and indefinite what, if any, the relevant interests taken in arbitrary events, or states of affairs, might be, it is understandably unclear and indefinite what sorts of events count as good events, and what sorts of states of affairs count as good states of affairs.

The predicate 'is a good state of affairs' was, of course, particularly significant for Moore, who regarded it as expressing the fundamental moral concept in terms of which the notions *duty, obligation,* and *morally right action* could be defined. One problem with relying so heavily on this abstract predicate is that it is very difficult to figure out what conditions are necessary and sufficient for a state of affairs to be properly called 'good'. Moore, and later the emotivists, had their own explanations of why this is so, the one emphasizing nonnaturalism and the other noncognitivism. We now see that there is yet another possible explanation of why it is so difficult to establish any such conditions as correct. If, as Geach maintains, 'good' *always* functions as an attributive predicate modifier, rather than as a predicate itself, then it may be fully descriptive without standing for any property—natural or nonnatural. If, in addition, ⌈a good N⌉ means something like ⌈an N that satisfies the contextually relevant interests taken in N's to a higher degree than most N's⌉, then the claim expressed by ⌈α is a good N⌉ will be unclear, open-ended, and hard to establish whenever it is unclear and indefinite what, if any, the relevant interests taken in things denoted by N are supposed to be. This is just what we seem to find when we let N be the abstract predicate 'state of affairs'. Since states of affairs have no function, and since there is no specific interest we standardly take in them, the claim that something is a good state of affairs is apt to seem vague and indefinite. Something can be a good state of affairs for me (to do x), while also being a bad state of affairs for you (to do y). Of course, Moore wants us to abstract away from the goodness or badness of a state of affairs *for someone,* or *for some purpose,* or *for doing some particular type of thing.* No, we are admonished, "I just want to know whether the state of affairs is good in and of itself—as opposed to good for some reason, for some purpose, or for some agent." Since it is not at all clear what we are being asked to look for, it is no surprise that we have a hard time demonstrating to others that we have found it. No wonder it is so difficult to prove that something is "intrinsically good."

This is the most important criticism of Moore's discussion of goodness that can be extracted from Geach's thesis that 'good' is an attributive predicate modifier. It is useful, in evaluating this thesis and assessing its import, to separate uncontroversial matters of more or less established fact from issues that remain contentious. It is obvious that 'good' does often function as an attributive predicate modifier in Geach's sense. It also seems clear that when it is used attributively it has an analysis of roughly the sort indicated above—one in which ⌜good N⌝ applies to things that satisfy certain interests taken in things denoted by N. However, the precise details of this analysis are debatable, and remain open to fine-tuning. Which interests in things designated by N are the ones relevant to determining which things are designated by ⌜good N⌝, and whose interests are they? Are they the interests of everyone, the interests of those who may be choosing among things denoted by N, the interests of the speaker, the interests of an ideally situated observer who shares the speaker's values and knows all the relevant facts, or are they the interests of some group that the speaker has in mind to which he implicitly refers? It seems likely that the answers to these questions may vary from one context of utterance to the next.

Another important question is whether 'good' is always used attributively, in the manner suggested by Geach. Certainly it is sometimes used on its own, without an accompanying noun or noun phrase. In many of these cases it is clear from the context of utterance that some implicit N is intended. Geach maintains that this is always so.

> Even when *good* or *bad* stands by itself as a predicate, and is thus grammatically predicative, some substantive has to be understood; there is no such thing as being just good or bad, there is only being a good or bad so-and-so. (If I say that something is a good or bad *thing*, either 'thing' is a mere proxy for a more descriptive noun to be supplied from the context; or else I am trying to use 'good' or 'bad' predicatively, and its being grammatically attributive is a mere disguise. The latter attempt is, on my thesis, illegitimate.)[5]

Although Geach's claim is a bold one, it is not obviously correct. If you say "Dick just got out of the hospital," and I say "That's good," my remark is, I think, perfectly ordinary, legitimate, and intelligible, even though it is not obvious what, if any, background noun or noun phrase 'good' is modifying—short, perhaps, of the highly abstract 'thing', 'event', or 'state of affairs' (which Geach takes to be "illegitimate" completers). Contrary to Geach, this seems to be a legitimate predicative use of 'good'. Whether it is a use to which Moore might appeal to elucidate his notion of a good or desirable state of affairs is another matter.

[5] Geach (1956), "Good and Evil," p. 65.

A little investigation quickly reveals many legitimate predicative uses of 'good' in which the adjective is completed by prepositional phrases that are either explicitly parts of the sentences uttered, or implicitly understood by speakers and hearers.

3a. Dick just got out of the hospital.
   That's good *for Dick/for his family/for us.*

b. What do you think of the current state of the economy?
   It is good *for commodities investors, but bad for everyone else.*

c. I like the way the new man is playing.
   Yes, he is good *for a rookie.*

d. Are you happy with your new motorbike?
   On the whole, yes. It is very good *for off-road driving,* though less good *for highway driving.*

e. Did you like the dessert?
   The chocolate was good *to eat.*

f. How is the new quarterback doing?
   He is good *at reading the defense,* but not very good *at finding his secondary receivers.*

g. What is your current view of gold?
   It isn't good *as an investment,* but it is fine *as insurance against inflation.*

h. How is your new employee working out?
   He is good *with customers,* but not *with his fellow employees.*

Perhaps all uses of 'good'—whether attributive or predicative—are legitimate, provided that 'good' is completed either by the content of an explicit phrase it combines with, or by a content of the appropriate type that is understood in the context of utterance. If something along these lines is correct, then the following updated version of Geach's incompleteness thesis might be defensible.

> The Incompleteness of the Good
>
> There is no such thing as just being good, or just being bad; there is only being *a good or bad so-and-so,* being *good or bad for a so-and-so,* being *good or bad for V-ing,* being *good or bad to V,* being good or bad *at V-ing,* being *good or bad as a so-and-so,* being good or bad *with so-and-so,* or in general, being good or bad in a certain way, for a certain activity, or in a certain respect.

This linguistically based thesis reinstates Geach's original challenge to Moore's claim that the meaning of 'good' (on one of its central uses) is a complete and morally fundamental property—*intrinsic goodness.*[6]

---

[6] See Thomson (1992) and (2003), which argue that all good is *good-in-a-way.* See also Thomson (2008).

Whether or not 'good' turns out to be analyzable, when properly understood as a term uses of which require implicit or explicit conceptual completion, is a further question. I have already indicated that typically ⌜good N⌝ can be understood as being roughly equivalent to ⌜N that satisfies the contextually relevant interests to a greater degree than most N's⌝. If a similar story can be told about the common content contributed by 'good' to the complete contents of the different predicate phrases in which it occurs—⌜good for T⌝, ⌜good for an N⌝, ⌜good as an N⌝, ⌜good with N's⌝, ⌜good for V-ing⌝, ⌜good to V⌝, ⌜good at V-ing⌝, etc.—(perhaps by reducing this variety to some one or more common forms), then 'good' may turn out to be (naturalistically) analyzable after all.[7] Whether or not one can find this sort of conceptual unity amidst the syntactic variety of constructions containing 'good' is an important topic of ongoing investigation.[8]

3. DEFINABILITY, CONSEQUENTIALISM, AND THE PRIMACY OF GOODNESS

In chapter 4, Moore's stringent conception of definition and his argument that 'good' is indefinable were discussed at length. For him, no expression D counts as definitionally equivalent to 'good' unless (i) it expresses the very same property as 'good', (ii) a competent speaker who understands both D and 'good' would recognize that they mean the same thing, and (iii) substitution of one for the other in an ordinary declarative or interrogative sentence S preserves the proposition, or question, that S expresses. Philosophers who did not recognize that 'good' is indefinable in this sense—including those who maintained either that goodness was a complex and hence an analyzable property, as well as those who identified it with a simple natural property (like pleasure)—were regarded by Moore as guilty of having committed what he called *the naturalistic fallacy*, which he described as follows:

> It may be true that all things which are good are also something else, just as it is true that all things which are yellow produce a certain kind of vibration of light. And it is a fact that Ethics aims at discovering what are those other properties belonging to all things which are good. But far too many philosophers have thought that when they named these other properties they were actually defining good; that these other properties, in fact, were simply not

---

[7] Here, T is a singular term (or definite description), N is a common noun phrase, and V is a verb phrase.

[8] One of the most interesting critiques of Geach, defenses of genuinely predicative uses of 'good', and proposals for capturing the unity of different uses of 'good' is Pigden (1990). For an illuminating and ambitious attempt to find a naturalistically analyzable account of the conceptual unity of uses of 'good' across a wide range of syntactic enviornments, see chapter 3 of Finlay (forthcoming).

"other," but absolutely and entirely the same with goodness. This view I propose to call the "naturalistic fallacy" and of it I shall endeavor to dispose.[9]

By contrast, Moore claims that the notions of an act being right, being our duty, and being one that we ought to perform *are definable*—in terms of goodness. Not only does he think that all and only right actions share the property of causing consequences the goodness of which is not exceeded by those that would be caused by any alternative action open to the agent, he also believes that rightness is entirely the same as this property.[10] He expresses this belief in sections 88 and 89 *of Principia Ethica*.

> To ask what kind of actions we ought to perform, or what kind of conduct is right, is to ask what kind of effects such action and conduct will produce. Not a single question in practical Ethics can be answered except by a causal generalization. All such questions do, indeed, also involve an ethical judgment proper—the judgment that certain effects are better, in themselves, than others. But they do assert that these better things are effects—are causally connected with the actions in question. Every judgment in practical Ethics may be reduced to the form: This is a cause of that good thing.[11]

> What I wish first to point out is that 'right' does and can mean nothing but 'cause of a good result', and is thus identical with 'useful'; whence it follows that the end always will justify the means, and that no action which is not justified by its results can be right.[12]

However, at this point an obvious question arises. Can it really be that the two expressions ⌈α is a right action⌉ and ⌈α is the cause of a good result⌉[13] satisfy Moore's stringent criteria for meaning the same thing? To suppose they do is to suppose that any (fully) competent speaker of English who understands both will recognize (i) that they mean the same thing, and (ii) that Q1 expresses the same trivial, self-answering question as Q2.

Q1.   Granted that α causes a good result, is α right?

Q2.   Granted that α causes a good result, does α cause a good result?

But this simply is not so. Someone might feel unsure whether, in a particular case, lying or breaking a promise to produce a certain good result is right. Such a person might have no doubt that a good result would be achieved, while wondering whether the wrong-making features of the act

---

[9] *Principia Ethica*, Moore (1903b), sec. 10, p. 62.

[10] In this discussion I bracket the critique in section 2 that there is no property goodness, expressed by 'good'.

[11] Ibid., section 88, p. 196.

[12] Ibid., sec. 89, p. 196.

[13] A result the goodness of which is not exceeded by the goodness of the result caused by any alternative action open to the agent.

itself, or its relation to past events, outweigh the goodness of the states of affairs that the action would cause to exist. Whatever the correct answer may be in a case like this, a person confronted with this dilemma may naturally use Q1 to express a genuine question that cannot be identified with the triviality expressed by Q2. Thus, it would seem that, by Moore's own standards, *a right act* is not definable as *a cause of a good result*.

In 1930, in his classic work *The Right and the Good*, Sir David Ross made precisely this argument.[14] He accused Moore of being guilty of a fallacy with regard to *right* of the same type as the (supposed) naturalistic fallacy with regard to *good*. Here is an illustrative passage.

> The most deliberate claim that 'right' is definable as 'productive of so-and-so' is made by Prof. G. E. Moore. . . . Now it has often been pointed out against hedonism . . . that the claim that 'good' just means 'pleasant' cannot seriously be maintained; that . . . the statement that the good is just the pleasant is a synthetic, not an analytic proposition; that the words 'good' and 'pleasant' stand for distinct qualities, even if the things that possess the one are precisely the things that possess the other. If this were not so, it would not be intelligible that the proposition 'the good is just the pleasant' should have been maintained on the one hand, and denied on the other, with so much fervor; for we do not fight for or against analytic propositions. . . . Must not the same claim be made about the statement 'being right means being an act productive of the greatest good producible in the circumstances'? Is it not plain on reflection that this is not what we *mean* by 'right', even if it be a true statement about what *is* right? . . . 'Ideal utilitarianism' is, it would appear, plausible only when it is understood not as an analysis or definition of the notion of 'right' but as a statement that all acts that are right, and only these, possess the further characteristic of being productive of the best possible consequences, and are right because they possess this other characteristic.[15]

---

[14] Ross was not the only one. Russell (1904b; p. 101 of Russell 1999) made essentially the same point almost immediately in his review of *Principia Ethica*.

Chapter V, on *Ethics in Relation to Conduct*, though it abounds in important distinctions, appears to me the least satisfactory in the book. The question discussed in this chapter is: "What ought we to do?" It is held that what we ought to do is that action, among all that are possible, which will produce the best results on the whole; and this is regarded as constituting a definition of *ought*. I hold that this is not a definition, but a significant proposition, and in fact a false one. It might be proved, in the course of moral exhortation, that such and such action would have the best results; and yet the person exhorted might inquire why he should perform the action. The exhorter would have to reply: "Because you ought to do what will have the best results." And this reply distinctly adds something. The same arguments by which good was shown to be indefinable can be repeated here, *mutatis mutandis*, to show the indefinability of ought.

[15] Ross (1930), pp. 8–9.

Given Moore's own standards of definition, one is hard pressed not to agree with Ross that the proposed definition of the rightness of an action in terms of the goodness of its consequences fails to satisfy them.

How could Moore have thought otherwise? He tells us most clearly in section 89 of *Principia Ethica*:

> [T]he assertion 'I am morally bound to perform this action' is identical with the assertion 'This action will produce the greatest possible amount of good in the Universe'.... *[W]hen we assert that a certain action is our absolute duty, we are asserting that the performance of that action at that time is unique in respect to value.* But no dutiful action can possibly have unique value ... [by being] the sole thing of value in the world. . . . [F]or the same reason its value cannot be unique ... [by having] more intrinsic value than anything else. . . . *It can, therefore, be unique only in the sense that the whole world will be better, if it be performed, than if any possible alternative were taken. . . . [W]hether this is so cannot possibly depend solely on the question of its own intrinsic value. For any action will also have effects different from those of any other. . . .* [H]owever valuable an action may be in itself, yet, owing to its existence, the sum of good in the Universe may conceivably be made less than if some other action, less valuable in itself, had been performed. But to say that this is the case is to say that it would have been better that the action should not have been done. . . .
>
> Our 'duty, therefore can only be defined as that action, which will cause more good to exist in the universe than any possible alternative. And what is 'right' . . . only differs from this, as what will *not* cause *less* good than any possible alternative.[16]

In this passage, we see a remarkable transformation. Consequentialism is often understood as the doctrine that the rightness of an act depends *not at all* on the intrinsic character of the act itself, the agent's motivation in performing it, or the relation between the act and past actions or states of affairs, but *only* on the value of the consequences that come after, and are caused by the act. Moore's own language throughout *Principia Ethica* suggests this—for example, his repeated instance that rightness is a matter of the goodness of that which an action *causes* (which must therefore come after the action). Certainly this is how Ross understood Moore's claim that 'right' simply means 'cause of a good result'. Although this *is* the natural way to understand Moore's language throughout the work, it is clear that, at least in the passage above, it is not what he really meant. There, in the process of defending the claim that consequentialism is true by definition, Moore transforms it from a highly interesting, but debatable, ethical thesis into something approaching an uninformative triviality.

The gist of his argument in the passage is this: To say that an action is our duty is to say that it is the action that it would be best for us to perform, which is to say that it would be better, all things considered, for us to

---

[16] Moore (1903b), sec. 89, pp. 197–98; the italicized sentences are my emphasis.

perform it than for us not to do so. Moreover, for it to be better, all things considered, for us to perform the action, rather than not, is for all the positive, morally relevant factors bearing on the action to outweigh the negative morally relevant factors associated with its performance. Here, by a *morally relevant factor* we mean anything that bears on the potential rightness or wrongness of the act—the value of the effects it causes, the intrinsic character of the act itself (e.g., whether or not it is a lie), the relation of the act to past actions and events (e.g., whether it involves doing what one has previously promised to do), the motivation it grows out of (e.g., gratitude for past service), or any number of other things. When, taking all these things into consideration, we judge it to be better to perform the act than not, we are saying that the universe would be better if the act were performed than if it weren't. Thus, when we say that an act is our duty we are saying that it maximizes value in the universe as a whole. In short, consequentialism is true by definition.

Like many sophistical arguments, this one confronts us with a choice. If one takes consequentialism to be the highly interesting, but debatable, thesis that the rightness of an action is determined solely by the goodness of the events or states of affairs that follow and are causally produced by it—and not at all by the intrinsic nature of the act itself, or its relations to past events—then the argument does *not* establish that consequentialism is true by definition; in fact it tacitly presupposes that consequentialism may well be false. By contrast, if one includes every state of affairs involving the action as among its consequences, while including every morally relevant feature of the action in the value of these "consequences," then one can understand how the conclusion that consequentialism is true by definition might seem tempting. However, the cost of adopting this strategy is to drain the doctrine of most of its philosophical significance. But whatever the merits of the strategy, the one thing that one must *not* do is combine the two options—treating consequentialism as a highly informative and substantial ethical doctrine, while regarding it as true by definition, in Moore's sense. It is a defect of *Principia Ethica* that the overall impression given by the work is of just such a combination—which is precisely how Ross interpreted the work.

In fairness, it should be pointed out that in time Moore himself seemed to recognize the validity of this criticism. In his little book *Ethics*, originally published in 1912, nine years after *Principia Ethica*, he vigorously defends consequentialism in its interesting and debatable form. As for the question of whether consequentialism about rightness or duty is true by definition, he says the following:

> [E]ven if we admit that to call an action expedient is the same thing as to say that it produces the best possible consequences, our principle still does not compel us to hold that to call an action expedient is *the same thing* as to call it a duty. All that it does compel us to hold is that whatever is expedient is always *also* a duty, and that whatever is a duty is always *also* expedient.

That is to say, it *does* maintain that duty and expediency *coincide*; but it does *not* maintain that the meaning of the two words is the same. It is, indeed, quite plain, I think, that the meaning of the two words is *not* the same; for, if it were, then it would be a mere tautology to say that it is always our duty to do what will have the best possible consequences. Our theory does not, therefore, do away with the distinction between the *meaning* of the words 'duty' and 'expediency'; it only maintains that both will always apply to the same actions.[17]

The import of this change for Moore's overall position is that now he has the task of defending his fundamental consequentialist claims about rightness and duty in the same way—either by appeal to self-evident moral facts revealed by moral intuition, or in some other way—that he defends his fundamental claims about goodness.[18]

4. MOORE'S ARGUMENT AGAINST SUBJECTIVISM

In addition to containing this significant change in view, Moore's *Ethics* contains an important chapter devoted to the objectivity of moral judgments. According to Moore, it is the essence of objectivity that if one person says of a given act "it is wrong" and another says of the same act "it is right" (or "not wrong"), then they cannot both be correct. Even if both are equally sincere and conscientious, x cannot be both wrong and right, and so, Moore thinks, one of them must be in error.

Recognizing that there are those who would dispute this, he points out that many who would do so believe that to assert of an act that it is right, or wrong, is to assert something about someone's feelings toward the act. A familiar version of this subjectivist view holds that

> whenever any man asserts an action to be right or wrong, what he is asserting is merely that he *himself* has some particular feeling towards the action in question. Each of us, according to this view, is merely making an assertion about *his own* feelings: when *I* assert that an action is right, the *whole* of what I mean is merely that *I* have some particular feeling towards the action; and when *you* make the same assertion, the *whole* of what you mean is merely that *you* have the feeling in question towards the action.[19]

Moore points out the following consequence of this view:

> If, whenever I judge an action to be right, I am merely judging that I myself have a particular feeling towards it, then it plainly follows that, provided I really have the feeling in question, my judgment is true, and therefore the

---

[17] Moore (1912), p. 73.
[18] Being the careful commentator that he was, Ross noted this change in Moore's position between *Principia Ethica* and *Ethics,* calling attention to the passage from *Ethics* cited above.
[19] Moore (1912), p. 37.

action in question really is right. And what is true of me, in this respect, will also be true of any other man. . . . It strictly follows, therefore, from this theory that whenever *any man whatever* really has a particular feeling towards an action, the action really is right; and whenever *any man whatever* really has another particular feeling towards an action, the action really is wrong. . . . And now . . . it seems plainly to follow that, if this be so, one and the same action must quite often be both right and wrong.[20]

Although Moore makes a significant mistake in this passage, it is correctable. The subjectivist he describes *is* committed to the view that two different men, one who says of a certain act x "it is right" and the other who says of x "it is wrong," may both be correctly describing their feelings, and hence be speaking truly. But the subjectivist is *not* thereby committed to saying of x "it is both right and wrong." A Moorean subjectivist who said this would be saying of x that he, the subjectivist, had both the requisite right-making feeling about x and the requisite wrong-making feeling about x—feelings he may well not have. Depending on what the requisite feelings are, the subjectivist might even tell us that it is impossible for anyone to simultaneously have both toward the same act. Such a subjectivist would vigorously, and correctly, dissent from the sentence 'one and the same action can be both right and wrong'.

Nevertheless, the subjectivist described by Moore does remain committed to the view that when one person says of x "it is right" and the other says "it is wrong," or even "it is not right," the two speakers do *not* contradict each other, and both may be speaking truly. Moore correctly thinks that this alone is a fatal objection to the subjectivist view. He asks whether one who judges an action to be right, or to be wrong, is merely asserting that one has a certain feeling of approval, or disapproval, toward it. Moore gives the following reason for thinking that such an analysis can't be correct:

If, when one man says, "This action is right," and another answers, "No, it is not right," each of them is always merely making an assertion about *his own* feelings, it plainly follows that . . . the one of them is never really contradicting what the other is asserting. They are no more contradicting one another than if, when one had said, "I like sugar," the other had answered, "I don't like sugar." In such a case . . . it may quite well be . . . that the one man really does like sugar, and the other really does *not* like it. The one, therefore, is *never* denying what the other is asserting. And what the view we are considering involves is that when one man holds an action to be right, and another holds it to be wrong or not right, here also the one is *never* denying what the other is asserting. It involves, therefore, the . . . consequence that no two men can ever differ in opinion as to whether an action is right or wrong. And surely the fact that it involves this consequence is sufficient to condemn it. It is surely a plain matter of fact that when I assert an action to be wrong, and

[20] Ibid., pp. 38–39.

another man asserts it to be right . . . he sometimes is denying the very thing which I am asserting. But, if this is so, then it cannot possibly be the case that each of us is merely making a judgment about his own feelings.[21]

This argument shows that a certain form of subjectivism cannot account for the reality of ethical disagreement, and therefore must be rejected. What the argument does *not* show is that no form of subjectivism can accommodate this reality, and hence that ethical judgments are "objective" in some robust sense. For example, a form of subjectivism which maintained that to say that an act is right is to say that everyone who both satisfies a certain condition and considers the act will have a certain attitude toward it might well accommodate the fact that a person who says of x "it is not right" does indeed contradict a person who says of x "it is right." There may, of course, be other objections to such a subjectivist view, but at least it is compatible with Moore's argument.

Later, when emotivism came along, the leading emotivist, Charles Stevenson, had to deal with this argument by finding a way in which conflicting noncognitivist utterances may contradict one another, even though no propositions are asserted or expressed, and hence neither truth nor falsity is at issue. He thought that conflicting utterances about, e.g., what we should or should not do could be likened to conflicting orders or recommendations—as in "Let's support the army against the terrorists!" vs. "No, let's not!"[22] Whatever the ultimate merits of this or other subjectivist views, the Moorean argument in *Ethics* presented a challenge which, though fatal to some forms of subjectivism, could be accommodated by others.

5. MOORE'S PHILOSOPHICAL CREDO

In these chapters I have concentrated on Moore's lasting, and historically influential, contributions to ethics and epistemology. However, there is one other way in which he contributed greatly to the developing tradition known as *analytic philosophy*. This contribution—which consisted in a certain way of doing philosophy and a corresponding attitude toward the subject—was not confined to any subarea of philosophy, and was independent of his substantive doctrines concerning particular philosophical questions. Since I have elsewhere said a few words about this, I will here simply let Moore speak for himself by citing what are to me are the most memorable words he ever wrote—the very first paragraph of *Principia Ethica*.[23]

It appears to me that in Ethics, as in all other philosophical studies, the difficulties and disagreements, of which its history is full, are mainly due to a very simple cause: namely to the attempt to answer questions, without first

---

[21] Ibid., p. 42.
[22] Stevenson (1937).
[23] See the "Introduction to the Two Volumes," pp. xi–xviii of Soames (2003c).

discovering precisely *what* question it is which you desire to answer. I do not know how far this source of error would be done away, if philosophers would *try* to discover what question they were asking, before they set about to answer it; for the work of analysis and distinction is often very difficult: we may often fail to make the necessary discovery, even though we make a definite attempt to do so. But I am inclined to think that in many cases a resolute attempt would be sufficient to ensure success; so that, if only this attempt were made, many of the most glaring difficulties and disagreements in philosophy would disappear. At all events, philosophers seem, in general, not to make the attempt, and, whether in consequence of this omission or not, they are constantly endeavoring to prove that 'Yes' or 'No' will answer questions, to which *neither* answer is correct, owing to the fact that what they have before their minds is not one question, but several, to some of which the true answer is 'No', to others 'Yes'.

The admirable philosophical credo expressed in these simple words is one to which Moore devoted his philosophical life, inspiring similar effort and commitment in those who followed. Though Frege was, of course, a very different philosopher with a very different career, much the same could be said about him; he also fit the mold. Here in two of the great founders of the analytic tradition we have men whose commitment to clarity, precision, intellectual honesty, and argumentative rigor continue to inspire the generations that have followed them.

Part 3

· RUSSELL ·

CHAPTER 7

⮜⮞

Early Russell:
Logic, Philosophy and
The Principles of Mathematics

1. Russell's Introduction to Philosophy
2. Russell, Cantor, and the Paradox in Frege's System
3. Frege's Problem and the Germ of a Russellian Strategy
4. Russell's 1903 Conception of Language, Meaning, and Propositions
    4.1. The Basic Properties of Russellian Propositions
    4.2. Propositional Structure: Terms and Concepts
    4.3. The Theory of Denoting
    4.4. Names, Negative Existentials, and Denoting
    4.5. The Problem of the Unity of the Proposition
5. The Road to "On Denoting"

1. RUSSELL'S INTRODUCTION TO PHILOSOPHY

Most of this chapter will be devoted to Russell's *Principles of Mathematics*. Like Moore's *Principia Ethica*, it was published in 1903. Also like *Principia Ethica,* it was both its author's most ambitious philosophical work to date, and on a subject—in Russell's case the philosophical foundations of mathematics—with which the author would forever be identified. However, unlike *Principia Ethica,* it did not become the author's canonical text on that subject, which for Russell would come in the years 1910–13 with the publication of his magisterial three-volume classic, *Principia Mathematica,* coauthored with Alfred North Whitehead. Also unlike *Principia Ethica,* it was not its author's first book. In 1896, Russell published *German Social Democracy*, a work in political theory and practice based on lectures he gave at the London School of Economics; in 1897 he published his Cambridge Fellowship dissertation, *An Essay on the Foundations of Geometry*; and in 1900 he published *A Critical Exposition of the Philosophy of Leibniz*—which (like his first book) was based on a series of lectures, this time at Cambridge in 1899, when he stepped in to replace the originally scheduled lecturer, J.M.E. McTaggart, who was unavailable due to a trip to New Zealand. While the first of these books presages Russell's lifelong

concern with social and political improvement, the second and third illustrated his abiding interest in logic, the foundations of mathematics, and
the importance of logic to philosophy generally. (In the book on Leibniz,
he argued that the former's astonishing metaphysics was, in effect, derived
from the fundamental principles of his logic.) In addition to these books,
prior to 1903 Russell published eight articles (exclusive of reviews), all
on topics concerning the foundations of geometry in particular or mathematics in general, including such notions as *space, time, motion, order,
continuity,* and (Cantorian) *infinity.*

In 1890, at age 18, Russell entered Cambridge to study mathematics,
where he met and formed a close relationship with Whitehead, who was
one of his entrance examiners. For three years he devoted himself to
mathematics, turning his attention to philosophy in his fourth year, when
he studied ethics with Henry Sidgwick, Kant with James Ward, and Idealist metaphysics with G. F. Stout and McTaggart. Ward and McTaggart
initially won him over to the Absolute Idealism first of McTaggart himself,
and then of F. H. Bradley. This was a striking collegiate introduction to
philosophy for the man who was to become both a leading opponent of
Idealism and a towering figure in philosophical logic and the philosophy of mathematics. As suggested in Stove (1991), Allard (2003), Griffin
(2003b), and Pigden (2007a), much of the attraction of Absolute Idealism
for Russell and other young Victorian intellectuals appears to have been
its prospects for satisfying the moral and religious impulses of former or
questioning Christians. The son of lapsed Christians who were earnest
social and political liberals as well as friends and followers of John Stuart
Mill, Russell was raised by his devoutly religious, rigidly moral, and po-
litically courageous Scotch Presbyterian grandmother. It was doubtless
due to her influence that he considered himself a Christian until shortly
before entering Cambridge, when his free-ranging intellect could no longer reconcile itself to her traditional faith. As he puts it in "My Mental
Development" in 1944:

> At fourteen or fifteen I became passionately interested in religion, and set to
> work to examine successively the arguments for free will, immortality, and
> God. For a few months I had an agnostic tutor with whom I could talk about
> these problems, but he was sent away, presumably because he was thought to
> be undermining my faith. Except during those months, I kept my thoughts
> to myself, writing them out in a journal in Greek letters to prevent others
> from reading them. I was suffering the unhappiness natural to lonely adoles-
> cence, and I attributed my unhappiness to loss of religious belief. For three
> years I thought about religion, with a determination not to let my thoughts
> be influenced by my desires. I discarded first free will, then immortality: I
> believed in God until I was just eighteen, when I found in Mill's *Autobiog-
> raphy* the sentence: "My father taught me that the question 'Who made me?'
> cannot be answered, since it immediately suggests the further question 'Who

made God?'" In that moment, I decided that the First-Cause argument was fallacious.[1]

This is the background against which Russell's introduction to philosophy at Cambridge should be understood. When, in the 1903–4 academic year, he took Sidgwick's course in ethics, he became concerned with a problem, called the *Dualism of Practical Reason* in Pigden (2007a), arising from one of Sidgwick's doctrines. Being an earnest utilitarian, Sidgwick believed it to be both rational and our moral duty to maximize the happiness, or pleasurable consciousness, of all sentient beings. However, he also believed it to be rational to promote one's own happiness, and that of the small circle of intimates one cares about. Moreover, he was vividly aware that these two courses of action may come into conflict—hence the duality of practical reason. The problem with which he was so concerned was that he could not discern any basis for maintaining that the morally required course of action would always be the more rational one.[2]

Sidgwick introduces the problem in the following passage:

> In chap. ii of the Book we have discussed the rational process (called by a stretch of language "proof") by which one who holds it is reasonable to aim at his own greatest happiness may be determined to take Universal Happiness instead, as his ultimate standard of right conduct. We have seen, however, that the application of this process requires that the Egoist should affirm . . . that his own greatest happiness is not merely the rational ultimate end for himself, but part of the Universal Good: and he may avoid the proof of Utilitarianism by declining to affirm this. It would be contrary to Common Sense to deny that the distinction between any one individual and any other is real and fundamental, and that consequently "I" am concerned with the quality of my existence as an individual in a sense, fundamentally important, in which I am not concerned with the quality of the existence of other individuals; and this being so, I do not see how it can be proved that this distinction is not to be taken as fundamental in determining the ultimate end of rational action for an individual.[3]

With the problem thus posed, Sidgwick first examines whether one's *enlightened self-interest* (taken to include interest in one's friends, family, and other intimates) can be shown inevitably to coincide with a concern for universal happiness. After taking into account the rewards and punishments associated with conforming to, or violating, social sanctions, as well as the benefits of cultivating genuine sympathy for at least some other people, he rightly concludes "that the inseparable connection between

---

[1] Russell (1944), pp. 7–8.
[2] Sidgwick discusses this problem at length in the last chapter of *The Methods of Ethics*. See chapter 4 of Shultz (2004) for discussion of the importance Sidgwick attached to it.
[3] Sidgwick (1874), at pp. 497–98 of Sidgwick (1907).

Utilitarian Duty and the greatest happiness of the individual who conforms to it cannot be satisfactorily demonstrated on empirical grounds."[4]

He then turns to his last hope for reconciling the prudential rationality
of enlightened self-interest with the rationality of doing one's moral duty—
namely, the rewards and punishments meted out by a just, good, and om-
nipotent God. The problem, of course, was that he could not demonstrate
the existence of such a being, and hence had to conclude that he had no
solution to the "contradiction" between the equally rational demands of
duty and self-interest.

> I cannot find inseparably connected with this conviction [that it is right and
> rational to promote universal happiness], and similarly attainable by mere
> reflective intuition, any cognition that there actually is a Supreme Being
> who will adequately reward me for obeying these rules of duty, or punish
> me for violating them. Or—omitting the strictly theological element of the
> proposition—I may say that I do not find in my moral consciousness any
> moral intuition, claiming to be clear and certain, that the performance of
> duty will be adequately rewarded and its violation punished.[5]

Having come to this end, he concludes *The Methods of Ethics* with what he
takes to be an unresolved threat to the rationality of ethics—its conflict
with rational self-interest.

According to Pigden (2007a), Russell became concerned about this
problem during his student days and initially attempted to solve it by appealing not to God, but to what the Absolute Idealists took to be Reality.[6]
This view is supported by a paper Russell wrote in 1893, which sketches
his own version of utilitarianism incorporating McTaggart's conception
of the Absolute, Eternal Reality as a community of immortal souls recip-
rocally aware of one another, united in love. Russell writes:

> This view would estimate the goodness of an act by its tendency to promote
> absolute harmony among spirits; since this harmony when established would
> involve the eternal happiness of all spirits, the passing pleasures and pains
> of our present existence in time would be of no account to it; and its pre-
> cepts would often lead to acts which might increase human misery for a time,
> though it would reckon on an ultimate recompense.[7]

The idea, roughly, is that (i) the passing world of pleasures and pains in
which self-sacrifice sometimes seems to be called for is merely insignificant

---

[4] Ibid., p. 503.

[5] Ibid., p. 507.

[6] Russell makes a general comment about this in Russell (1961, p. 35): "I found that all
I had thought about ethics and logic and metaphysics was considered to be refuted by an
abstruse technique that completely baffled me; and by this same technique it was proved
that I should live forever . . . for a time I more or less believed it."

[7] Russell (1893), originally published in Russell (1983) and reprinted with useful commentary in Russell (1999). The passage quoted is from p. 34 of Russell (1999).

Appearance, and (ii) in the Ultimate Harmony of Immortal Souls no conflict between the welfare of one soul and that of others is possible. Hence, the Duality of Practical Reason is dissolved. In support of (ii), Russell adds:

> the more perfection is approached, the less often will self-sacrifice be necessary. When sympathy is more developed no person will be able to feel happiness in the pursuit of his own selfish pleasures if he knows he might be improving the condition of another, and thus gradually selfishness and unselfishness will become indistinguishable, the end of each will be the end of all. . . . [I]n the perfect state we shall be neither virtuous nor vicious, any more than the soul is either round or square: the words will have lost their meaning.[8]

In a paper delivered to the Apostles Society in November of 1894, Russell reprised this solution of Sidgwick's dilemma, this time with growing doubt. In the paper, he takes the good to be, in one form or another, that which is desired, and the good life to be that in which one's desires are harmonious and without serious conflicts. However, Russell also takes the Ultimate Good, which one has a duty to promote, to involve not just one's own good, but the good of all. His problem, as before, is to reconcile this with self-interested desires.

> But how to prove, a priori, that the satisfaction of the individual is necessarily that of the Universe, I do not see, and this is to me *the* fundamental problem of Ethics. . . . If with McTaggart, we bring in personal immortality and progress toward perfection (waiving the difficulty about Time), this limitation to Self involves no great difficulties, for with higher sensibility comes acuter sympathy, and so personal satisfaction cannot be perfect until it is shared by all.[9]

Unfortunately, by this time Russell had stopped believing in personal immortality, and so was dissatisfied with his old solution. The natural progression was to move from McTaggart's version of the Absolute as a community of immortal souls to Bradley's Absolute Spirit, in which all distinctions between what in Appearance seem to be different individuals are obliterated in the all-encompassing One. For if you and I are at bottom one, then there can be no real conflict in our interests.

Russell flirts with this idea in the address to his fellow Apostles.

> But with a more Bradleian view of the Subject, this theory [the McTaggart version of the solution] becomes unsatisfactory. . . . I am vastly tempted to regard the Subject, as apparently Bradley does, as a mere fluid nucleus of Feeling, of uncertain and constantly changing boundaries, and so adopt an almost Spinozistic monism, in which our terms become merely Desire on the one hand and Satisfaction on the other. This would obviate all these ethical difficulties, and reduce Hatred and similar passions to my former case of a

---

[8] Ibid., p. 35.
[9] Russell (1894), at p. 66 in Russell (1999).

conflict, for reciprocal hatreds do not form a harmony like reciprocal loves, and cannot both be satisfied.[10]

However, he didn't truly accept the idea, and closes the talk on an uncertain note without real confidence in any solution to the problem.

By December of 1897, when he delivered another paper to the Apostles on metaphysics and morality, the Absolute—supposedly standing behind that everyday world of lived experience—had ceased to satisfy Russell's yearning for a moral universe. His point is that the only universe we know is the one we experience in time and space. This—not an imagined timeless realm reached only by abstract argument—is the true locus of our interests, our desires, and our concerns about good and evil. Even if there were a timeless reality beyond Appearance, it would be irrelevant to us. He says:

> As I do not wish to discuss the truth of philosophy, but only its emotional value, I shall assume a metaphysic which rests on the distinction between Appearance and Reality, and regards the latter as timeless and perfect. . . . The emotional value of a doctrine, as a comfort in adversity, appears to depend upon its prediction of the future . . . we are concerned always with appearances in time, and unless we are assured that the future is to be better than the present, it is hard to see where we are to find consolation. . . . All our experience is bound up with time, nor is it possible to imagine a timeless experience. But even if it were possible, we could not, without contradiction, suppose that we ever *shall* have such an experience. All experience, therefore, for aught that philosophy can show, is likely to resemble the experience we know—if this seems bad to us, no doctrine of a Reality distinguished from Appearances can give us hope of anything better. We fall indeed into a hopeless dualism. On the one side we have the world we know, with its events pleasant and unpleasant, its deaths and failure and disasters—on the other hand an imaginary world, which we christen the world of Reality, atoning, by the largeness of the R, for the absence of every other sign that there really is such a world.[11]

Two things seem clear: (i) The Absolute had ceased to satisfy the moral, emotional, and religious needs that initially attracted the young Russell; and (ii) realizing this, he no longer really believed any version of the metaphysical Idealism propounded by McTaggart, Bradley, and others, despite the fact that he had still produced no directly metaphysical arguments against them. Although he did, at about this time, develop such arguments, his maturing investigations of the foundations of logic, arithmetic, geometry, and mathematics provided him with other, more important, fish to fry. Thus, he didn't publish his refutations of what he called the

---

[10] Ibid., pp. 66–67.
[11] Russell (1897c) at pp. 81–82 of Russell (1999).

Idealist's "Monistic Theory of Truth and Reality" until several years later. Although these arguments are interesting in their own right, they are best discussed after some of the tools of Russellian logical analysis have been presented; I will, therefore, take them up in the first section of chapter 9. For the rest of this chapter I will examine Russell's early philosophical logic and the uses to which he hoped to put it in grounding mathematics.

2. RUSSELL, CANTOR, AND THE PARADOX IN FREGE'S SYSTEM

It is useful to begin by recalling Frege's criterion in *The Foundations of Arithmetic* for determining the truth or falsity of claims of the form *The number of F's = the number of G's*. Such statements are true iff the extension of the concept F can be put into one-to-one correspondence with the extension of the concept G—i.e., iff there is a one-to-one function mapping all the F's onto all the G's.[12] In chapters 1 and 2, I concentrated on cases in which these extensions are finite. However, the criterion can also be applied to concepts with infinite extensions. When we do this, we get the result that the number of positive integers = the number of even numbers = the number of prime numbers. Although this result may initially seem mildly surprising, its rationale can easily be grasped by noticing that 1 is the first (least) prime number, 2 is the second prime, 3 is the third, 5 is the fourth, 7 is the fifth, 11 is the sixth, and so on. In saying "and so on" we recognize that every prime number will eventually find a place in the list, and—since there is no largest prime—for any positive integer n, there will be a unique prime number occupying the nth place on the list. In other words, there is a one-to-one mapping from the positive integers to the primes that exhausts both sets. This is the natural sense in which the two sets are the same size, and so have the same number.

Having seen this, one might naïvely suppose that all infinite sets are the same size. That this is not so was shown by an elegant argument due to Georg Cantor in 1891. The general form of the result shows that the power set PA—i.e., the set of all subsets of A—cannot be put into one-to-one correspondence with any subset of A (including A itself), no matter what set A may be.[13] This result has come to be known as *Cantor's Theorem*. One instance of it is obtained when we let A be the infinite set N of natural numbers, in which case PN is the set of all sets—finite, infinite, and empty—of natural numbers. Since PN can't be put in one-to-one correspondence with N (or any subset of N), the number of natural numbers ≠ the number of sets of natural numbers. Since N can (trivially) be mapped 1-1 onto a subset of PN (namely itself), PN "is larger than" N. Of course,

---

[12] In this paragraph 'F' and 'G' are used as schematic letters.

[13] Here, and throughout, I use the terms 'class' and 'set' interchangeably.

PPN is also "larger than" PN, and so on without end. In this way, we get an unending order of greater and greater infinities. Any infinity of the first order—that has the same number as N—is called *countable*. The others are called *uncountable*.

The general form of Cantor's argument is *reductio ad absurdum*. Let A be any set and PA be its power set. We then assume (1):

1. There is a 1-1 function f mapping each member of PA onto some subset A′ of A.

Cantor's argument is a demonstration that (1) leads to contradiction—in which case it must be false, and its negation—that there is no such function—must be true. To derive the contradiction and establish this result, we note that if (1) is true, then since for each subset x of A, f(x) is a member of A′, we can always meaningfully ask whether f(x) is, or isn't, a member of x. With this in mind, we define a certain subset s_f of A′ (and hence of A). We let s_f be the set of those members y of A′ that are not members of the subset x of A such that f(x) = y. (Given that f is 1-1, we know that for each y there will always be exactly one such x.) Since s_f is a subset of A, f must map it onto some member s* of A′ (i.e., $f(s_f) = s^*$). Is s* a member of s_f or not? If it is, then it is not a member of s_f—since, by the definition of s_f, s* is *not* a member of the subset x of A—namely s_f—such that f(x) = s*. This means that *if* s* is a member of s_f, then s* is *not* a member of s_f, from which it follows that s* must *not* be a member of s_f. However, this won't do either, since, by definition, *the members of s_f are* all those members of A′ that are not members of the set that f maps onto them. In the case of s*, this set is s_f. So, if s* is *not* a member of s_f, then s* *is* a member of s_f, from which it follows that s* *is* a member of s_f. But now we have contradicted our earlier result that s* is *not* a member of s_f. Since this contradiction depends only on (1), there is no 1-1 function mapping PA onto any subset A′ of A (including, of course, A itself). This is Cantor's Theorem.

Though both Russell and Frege had read Cantor, Russell noticed something Frege didn't. Suppose there is a universal set U that contains all objects (both sets and nonsets alike). For Frege, U is the extension of the concept *is an object that is identical with itself*. Prior to reading Cantor, Russell also accepted the existence of U. On reading Cantor, however, he asked whether there is a 1-1 function f from the subsets of U onto some subset U′ of U. Well, he reasoned, since U contains every set—including, of course, every subset of U—there must be such a function. Just let f be the identity function that maps any set onto itself. Surely, there is no denying that if U exists, this is a 1-1 function that maps every subset of U onto a member of a certain subset U′ of U—namely the set of all sets. But, since Cantor proved that for *any set A* there is *no* 1-1 function from its subsets to any subset of A′ of A, this *must* mean that there is no universal set. We can see this by noting that when Cantor's reasoning is applied to U and f is the identity function just mentioned, s_f is *the set of those sets that are not members of themselves.* As Russell saw, there can't be any such set s_f, since if there were it would be a member of itself iff it is not a member of itself. Since this is contradictory, there is no universal set.

The universal set comes from a simple comprehension principle stating that for every meaningful formula ϕ, there is a set (perhaps empty) of all and only the objects of which ϕ is true. Without further restrictions, then, 'x = x' will give one the universal set. If, in addition, the language allows one to express the claim that any object is, or isn't, a member of any set, then one will get a formula analogous to '~x ε x' (*x isn't a member of x*), which yields the set of all non-self-membered things (including all non-self-membered sets). But then one is stuck with the paradox, which was initially as much a problem for Russell as for Frege.

However, Frege's commitment to problematic sets came about by a more circuitous route. As we saw in chapter 1, his semantic theory—according to which meaningful predicates/formulas denote concepts that determine which objects they are true of—takes the following comprehension principle for concepts for granted.

Concept Comprehension

For every stateable condition ϕ on things, there exists a concept C that is true of all and only those things that satisfy the condition. In symbols: $\exists C \, \forall y \, (Cy \longleftrightarrow \phi y)$

Since Fregean concepts are simply assignments of truth values to objects, concepts that assign the same values to the same arguments are identical, guaranteeing the truth of the following principle of extensionality for concepts.

Extensionality

Concepts P and Q are identical iff everything that falls under one falls under the other. In symbols: $\forall P \, \forall Q \, (P = Q$ iff $\forall x \, (Px \longleftrightarrow Qx))$

Still, there is, so far, no commitment to a set of non-self-membered sets and thus no set-theoretic paradox. Frege's system is also not subject to a concept-theoretic version of the paradox. To get that, his logical language would have to contain a predicate (formula) designating the concept *being a concept that is not true of itself.* For this, he would need to allow propositions in which n^{th}-level concepts take n^{th}-level concepts as arguments, and formulas in which n^{th}-level predicates occupy the argument positions of nth-level predicates. However, the former was ruled out by his metaphysical principle M, while the latter was ruled out by a syntactic principle mirroring M.

M. A first-level concept can combine only with an object, or with a second-level concept, to form a proposition; a higher level concept can combine only with a concept of the preceding level, or with a concept of the succeeding level.

As a result, Russell's paradox cannot be recreated for Fregean concepts.

However, for Frege, like Russell at the time, numbers aren't concepts; they are sets (which he takes to be the extensions of concepts). Thus, he needs a theory of what sets there are. As we saw in chapter 1, this was provided by his notorious Axiom V.

Axiom V: For all (first-level) concepts P and Q, the extension of P (the class of things falling under P) = the extension of Q (the class of things falling under Q) iff ∀x (Px ⟷ Qx).

Since his language contains '∃Y(x = Extension(Y) & ~Yx)', unrestricted comprehension plus Axiom V commits him to a concept the extension of which includes all and only those concept extensions of which their associated concepts are not true, which in his system amounts to the set of all and only those sets that are not members of themselves. Hence, he is trapped in Russell's paradox.[14]

But why does Frege take numbers to be sets—i.e., extensions of concepts—rather than concepts themselves? The official answer is given in his "Concept and Object," critically discussed in section 2 of chapter 2. As we saw, for Frege, *concepts* are the referents of predicates—a category that includes simple predicative expressions, formulas containing free occurrences of variables, and quantifiers. By contrast, *objects* are the referents of singular terms—a category that includes ordinary proper names, singular definite descriptions, and complete sentences (which refer to truth values). Just as predicates are parts of language that need to be completed by singular terms (or higher level predicates) in order to form sentences, so, for Frege, their senses and referents (i.e., concepts) are incomplete, and in need of supplementation by the senses and referents of singular terms (or higher level predicates) in order to arrive at thoughts, or truth values. By contrast, objects (including ordinary material objects, sets, thoughts, and truth values) are complete in themselves. According to Frege's combinatorial semantic and metaphysical principles, no expression that can be used predicatively has the same sense or referent as any non-predicative expression. Thus, no concept is identical with any object.[15]

[14] Unlike concepts, which Frege saw as coming in a hierarchy of levels, all objects—including sets—are present at the first level. Thus, whereas in his system quantification over concepts is always restricted to a given level, and conditions on concepts can only be stated piecemeal, level by level, quantification over sets (and other objects) is unrestricted, and set-defining conditions can be stated that encompass every set, including the set one is defining.

[15] For a critique of these doctrines, and the use to which Frege puts them in addressing the problem of the unity of the proposition, see section 2 of chapter 2.

This was sufficient to prevent Frege from taking numbers to be concepts. Consider sentence (2).

2. The number of fingers on my left hand = 5.

Since the number five is designated by the singular terms flanking the identity sign, it can't be a concept. Nevertheless, as we saw in chapter 1 (section 5.3.1), for Frege "the content of a statement of number is an assertion about a concept."[16] How, one might wonder, can this be? How can concepts be crucial to the account of number, and indeed be what a statement of number is about, if concepts are not themselves numbers? As we saw, the trick was to take numbers to be *sets of concepts* that bear a certain relation to one another in virtue of a relation holding among their extensions. Since sets are objects, they can be referents of singular terms, including numerals and definite descriptions. For any concept F, Frege identified the number belonging to F with the extension of the concept *equal to F*—where the extension of a concept is the set of things of which it is true, and for one concept to be equal to another is for their extensions to be equinumerous (i.e., capable of being mapped 1-1 onto one another).[17] So, the number belonging to F is the set of all and only those concepts the extensions of which are equinumerous with the set of things of which F is true. For example, the number of fingers on my left hand is the set of concepts the extensions of which can be put in one-to-one correspondence with the fingers on my left hand; it is the set of concepts with five-membered extensions. If we weren't distinguishing concepts from their extensions, we could say, with Russell, that the number of fingers on my left hand is the set of all five-membered sets. For the present point, this difference between Frege and Russell is no matter. Both initially needed principles generating a rich ontology of sets, which they got from comprehension principles that landed them in contradiction.

3. FREGE'S PROBLEM AND THE GERM OF A RUSSELLIAN STRATEGY

In 1903, when he published *The Principles of Mathematics,* Russell had not yet arrived at a workable strategy for simultaneously avoiding the paradox and carrying through his own Frege-like reduction of arithmetic to logic. That wouldn't come until 1908, when he published an article announcing the strategy that would be pursued in *Principia Mathematica.*[18] As we will see in chapter 10, the strategy included some broadly Fregean factors, plus some non-Fregean ones. Most notable of these was Russell's theory

---

[16] Section 46 of *The Foundations of Arithmetic*, Frege (1950), p. 59.
[17] Ibid., section 68.
[18] Russell (1908a).

of types, which bears some resemblance to Frege's hierarchy of concepts. One can get a glimmer of what Russell was looking for, and Frege failed to find, by noticing why Frege couldn't simply dispense with extensions of concepts for purposes of the reduction, and make do with concepts on their own.

Remember, apart from Frege's metaphorical talk about concepts being "incomplete" entities, and his counterintuitive, and even paradoxical, talk about the impossibility of using singular terms to refer to them, Fregean concepts are simply functions from arguments to truth values. Since they are the referents of meaningful formulas, we have comprehension for concepts. Since functions that assign the same arguments the same values are identical, we have extensionality for them. Given this, one might think that we can hardly go wrong—at least for technical or mathematical purposes—by letting the *concept* that assigns truth to x, y, and z, while assigning falsity to everything else, play the role of the set the only members of which are x, y, and z. In this way, we might dispense with extensions, i.e., sets, and make do entirely with concepts—while retaining the restrictions of Frege's hierarchy of concepts, and ascending orders of quantification over them, in order to avoid Russell's paradox.

Why, given all this, couldn't Frege identify numbers with *concepts* under which other concepts fall—rather than with *extensions of concepts* under which other concepts fall? On this alternative, the number that belongs to (a concept) F is the concept *equal to F*—rather than the extension of that concept. As before, concepts F and G are equal iff there is a function that maps each object falling under F onto a unique object falling under G (with different arguments always assigned different values), and every object falling under G is the value of the function for some object that falls under F. With this in mind, consider the first-level concept *is not identical with itself*, which assigns falsity to every object, and so is a concept under which no object falls. (As before, objects are assumed to be distinct from concepts, first-level concepts are distinct from second-level concepts, and so on). On this conception, 0 is the second-level concept under which all first-level concepts that are true of no objects fall. (Given our assumption that concepts that assign the same truth values to the same objects are identical, there is only one such first-level concept.) Successor is then defined for concepts. We say that n is the successor of m iff for some concept F, and object x falling under F, n is the number belonging to F and m is the number belonging to the concept *falling under F but not identical with x*. So, n is the successor of 0 iff for some concept F, and object x falling under F, n is the number belonging to F, and 0 is the number belonging to the concept *falling under F but not identical with x*. It follows that 1 (the successor of 0) is the second-level concept under which fall those first-level concepts that are true of some object x, and nothing else; 2 is the second-level concept under which fall those first-level concepts C that are true of some objects x, y, such that (i) x ≠ y, and

(ii) every object that falls under C is identical with x or y. The concept *natural number* is, on this account, the third-level concept *being an inductive concept*, where an inductive concept C is one under which the second-level concept zero falls, and under which the successor of a concept falls whenever the concept itself falls under C.

Since, on this conception, the arguments of first-level concepts are always objects, and the arguments of n-level concepts are always (n − 1)-level concepts, no concept can be an argument of itself, and no well-formed formula ...v... can contain a variable ranging over concepts of the level of the concept C designated by the formula itself. Thus, although for each level of concepts we get a universal concept applying to the entities of the preceding level, we get no universal concept that is true of all concepts. So, paradox is avoided.

There are, however, problems with this approach. One that would have worried Frege is that, for him, numbers would cease to be referents of singular terms, and be more naturally taken to be the denotations of quantifiers. As a result, what he expressed by examples like (2a) and (3a) would be more naturally expressed along the lines of (2b) and (3b).

2a. The number of fingers on my left hand = 5.
 b. There are five fingers on my left hand.
3a. The number of F's = n.
 b. There are n F's.

Although in these cases the change may be no loss, more is needed to extend the idea to the range of purely arithmetical sentences like '$(2 + 3) \times 7 = 35$'.[19]

A related problem involves generalizing examples like those in (2) to cover all instances of (3). On the picture just sketched, 5 is the second-level concept under which fall all and only those first-level concepts C for which there are objects x, y, z, w, u each distinct from the others which fall under C, and which are such that anything that falls under C is identical with one of them. One of these first-level concepts is, of course, the concept *being a finger on my left hand*. So, the translation of (2) into our logical language ends up being straightforwardly true. Suppose, however, that I had given exactly five examples of Fregean concepts—either from a single level (say level 1), or from different levels. In such a circumstance, one would quite naturally think that (4) or (5) should be true. (I revert to the Fregean, singular term formulations.)

4. The number of first-level concepts mentioned by Soames = 5.
5. The number of concepts of any level mentioned by Soames = 5.

---

[19] See Rayo (2002), which builds on a comment in Frege (1919b) about reconstructing arithmetic with numbers *as concepts rather than objects* and an earlier development in Hodes (1990). Rayo makes good on Frege's comment by deriving arithmetic from a system of second-order logic plus an extra logical assumption ensuring a large enough universe.

However, since the concepts *first-level concept* and *concept of any level* are not first-level concepts (indeed the latter can't be a Fregean concept at all), strictly speaking, 5 is *not* the number belonging to either of them, and the system just sketched doesn't straightforwardly account for these examples. Although one might find a way of living with this result, Frege himself would, I think, have been worried.

Lest one think this is a glitch, one should ask oneself, "How many second-level concepts are there anyway?" Since natural numbers are here identified with second-level concepts, the answer had better be "Infinitely many!"—if the reduction of arithmetic to logic is to go through. However, since second-level concepts are assignments of truth values to first-level concepts (where assignments of the same values to the same arguments are identical), there can be infinitely many such concepts only if there are infinitely many first-level concepts, which in turn requires infinitely many objects—i.e., non-concepts. But how can one prove by logic alone that there are infinitely many objects? When, in Frege's actual system, sets—i.e., the extensions of concepts at any level—are counted as objects, one can guarantee an infinity of them. However, if extensions (sets) are dropped entirely from the construction, because of Russell's paradox, there is a danger of running short of the objects needed for the construction of the natural numbers. Thus, even though the idea of using hierarchy to avoid paradox was promising, it did not provide a quick fix for Frege's—or the early Russell's—problem.

We will return to this in chapter 10 when we look at Russell's version of the logicist reduction in more detail. In the meantime more must be said about how the conceptual apparatus he brings to his philosophy of mathematics from his general account of language differs from that of Frege. The central notions of Frege's semantics were, of course, sense and reference, the latter being determined by the former. The most important of these semantic notions for his account of logic and mathematics was the notion of a concept, which is the referent of a predicate (where quantifiers are higher-order predicates expressing concepts of lower-order concepts). As we have seen, concepts are very closely related to sets: for any concept, the corresponding set is the set of those entities x to which the concept assigns the value the True, and for any set the corresponding concept is the function that assigns the True to all and only members of the set. Given sets as the extensions of concepts, Frege gets the extensionality of sets, used in the logicist reduction, from the extensionality of concepts.

Since Russell's semantic theory differs from Frege's, the key semantic notion he brings to his account of logic and mathematics is quite different from that of a Fregean concept. For Russell, it is the notion of a *propositional function* that is central. This notion, like much else in his semantics, was a work in progress, changing in various ways over the course of his career. At this early stage, however, propositional functions can, for our purposes, best be regarded as functions that assign propositions as values to objects as arguments.[20] Propositions are the Russellian counterparts of Fregean thoughts, except for the fact that propositions (like the proposition that I am hungry) can contain objects (me, rather than a sense that determines me as referent) of which properties can be directly predicated (in this case *being hungry*). Like Fregean thoughts, Russellian propositions are bearers of truth and falsity, they are objects of attitudes like knowledge, belief, and assertion, and they are also the meanings of sentences. A propositional function of n arguments is the meaning of a formula ...*x*...*y*...*z*... in which exactly n distinct variables have free occurrences. The proposition it assigns to an n-tuple of arguments is the proposition expressed by the formula relative to an assignment of those arguments to the free variables in the formula. By 1905, higher-order properties of propositional functions would be central to Russell's account of quantification (just as higher-order concepts of lower-order concepts were central to Frege's), and by 1910 "propositional functions" would be central to his project of reducing arithmetic to logic (just as concepts were to Frege's project).

Even by 1903 it was clear that propositional functions were importantly different than Fregean concepts. Whereas the latter are *referents* of predicates/formulas, the former are *meanings* of those linguistic items. This is reflected in the different values they assign to their arguments. Whereas (first-level) concepts assign *truth values* to objects, (first-level) propositional functions assign *propositions*. Whereas each proposition determines a unique truth value, there are many propositions with the same truth value. Propositions are called *extensionally equivalent* when they have the same truth value. First-level propositional functions are *extensionally equivalent* to one another iff for every object o, they map o onto propositions that are extensionally equivalent. Similarly for higher-level propositional functions (whose arguments are lower-level propositional functions). Given propositional functions as primitive, one can define classes in terms of them, as Russell does in *Principles of Mathematics*. When F(x) is a formula in which only the variable 'x' is free, and g is the propositional function expressed by F(x), he takes ⌜the class of x's such that F(x)⌝ to stand for

---

[20] This is a convenient reconstruction of Russell's actual view, according to which a propositional function is what you get from a proposition by replacing one of its constituents with "a variable," where the latter is taken to be the most general denoting concept (*Principles of Mathematics* [Russell 1903a], pp. 89, 94, 263). Like the denoting concept expressed by 'any man', which he spoke of as "ambiguously denoting" each individual man, Russell took a variable to be an even more general concept "ambiguously denoting" a wider class of things. See Klement (2004), pp. 14–16, for explanation. As we shall see in this chapter, the theory of denoting to which this view belonged faces many problems. Since it is helpful to have a notion free of these problems, I will take propositional functions to be genuine functions the values of which are propositions. For many issues, this simple reconstruction of Russell's more difficult view won't make a significant difference. Where it does, I will flag those cases with a qualifying note.

the class of things to which g assigns a true proposition.[21] Thus, extensionally equivalent propositional functions determine the same class. Given this way of generating classes, one can introduce predicates applying to them, and so develop a calculus of classes, including an account of natural numbers as classes of classes.

However, one can also proceed in a different way, talking exclusively of propositional functions rather than classes, and trading each predicate P of classes for a corresponding *extensional predicate* P* of propositional functions—where a predicate of propositional functions is extensional iff whenever it is true of a propositional function *pf*, it is true of all propositional functions extensionally equivalent to *pf*. Although such predicates are officially true of propositional functions, one can read them as if they were true of classes, or of class concepts (functions from arguments to truth values). It is plausible to suppose, as Russell did, that only extensional predicates of propositional functions (including quantifiers, which he came in 1905 to see as predicates of propositional functions) are relevant to mathematics. Thus, when he came, in *Principia Mathematica*, to develop his type-theoretical hierarchy, his resulting logicized versions of arithmetical statements were officially about the things he then called "propositional functions," rather than classes or concepts, while nevertheless being equivalent to, and in effect translatable into, corresponding statements about such. Some, including by that time Russell himself, have professed to see an important philosophical advantage in this—namely, the "ontological economy" allegedly achieved by "eliminating classes from one's ontology."[22] In chapter 10, I will argue that this is a mistake (which fortunately never really caught on).[23] However, in order to properly understand this and related issues, we must first trace the evolution of Russell's highly influential views about language and meaning, which are immensely important in their own right.

4. RUSSELL'S 1903 CONCEPTION OF LANGUAGE, MEANING, AND PROPOSITIONS

Russell's 1903 conception of language is found mostly in chapters 4 and 5 of *Principles of Mathematics*. The notions central to this conception are *propositions*, *propositional functions*, *terms*, *concepts*, and *denoting concepts*. Having already covered propositional functions, I turn to the remaining notions.

---

[21] Russell (1903a), p. 88. Russell uses the word 'class' rather than 'set', but given my usage, this makes no difference. He does, however, have nonstandard views of the null set, as well as sets with only a single member. See sections 69 and 73 of *Principles of Mathematics*.

[22] Kremer (2008).

[23] See Soames (2008b).

4.1. The Basic Properties of Russellian Propositions

During this period, Russell followed the early Moore in thinking of propositions as the objects of the attitudes, the primary bearers of truth value, and the meanings of sentences. In speaking of them as objects of attitudes such as judgment and belief, he implicitly distinguished *what is judged or believed* from particular cognitive events of judging, and mental states of believing. On this view, when speaking of John's judgment or belief that at least one sentient being exists as *being true*, but such that *it could have been false*, or as *following from* the judgments or beliefs that John exists and that John is a sentient being, we are referring to the propositions judged or believed, and attributing certain logical properties to them. By contrast, when speaking of a particular judgment or belief as *irrational*, *ill-conceived*, or *unshakable*, we are speaking of a particular cognitive act or state, and attributing psychological properties to it. Judgment and belief themselves are relations between an agent who judges or believes and the thing so judged or believed. In this respect, these attitudes are like seeing, which is a relation one bears to something seen. Just as when one sees a tree, there is something one sees, so when one judges or believes that the tree is green, there is something that one judges or believes.

During this period, Russell followed Moore in identifying much (though mercifully not all) of what we see, or otherwise perceive, with existential propositions—such as, as he might put it, *the existence of redness here now,* or *that redness exists here now.* Thus, writing in 1904, Russell says:

> I have spoken hitherto, being concerned with what is commonly called perception, only of the awareness of *propositions*; for all cases concerned are . . . cases where something is known to exist, and where, consequently, the object of perception is an existential proposition. But it seems undeniable that there is also a mere awareness, in which the object is not a proposition; for unless we were aware what redness is, we could not know that redness exists.[24]

This view is, as I indicated in section 4 of chapter 3, most implausible. However, it does contain a kernel of truth. Although we don't literally *see* propositions, and although seeing something needn't involve being aware of a proposition in the sense of making it the object of our attention, still, whenever we see something we are cognitively related to a proposition that represents the world as being the way we perceive it to be. When I see an object, I see it *as being a certain way* (and so as having a certain property). This doesn't mean that I always judge or believe the object to be that way (or to have that property); I may suspect that things are not as they visually appear. But it does mean that my visual experience represents (a part of) the world as being one way rather than another. Since my perception is *veridical* iff the world is as my perception represents it to be, one

---

[24] Russell (1904a); reprinted in Russell (1973), at p. 34. See also pp. 35, 37, 76.

may plausibly maintain (i) that it puts me in an important cognitive relation to a proposition that is the representational content of my perceptual state, and (ii) that my perception is veridical iff this proposition is true.

For Russell, propositions are the *primary* bearers of truth and falsity; other things—e.g., sentences, utterances, acts of judgment, and states of believing—are true or false only in virtue of expressing propositions that are true or false. If John's prepared statement, which lasted for over two minutes, is entirely true, it is so because his lengthy oration resulted in the assertion of one or more propositions, all of which are true. What is it for a proposition to be true? One might think it is for the proposition to correspond to reality, or to a fact. Although some philosophers have held this to be so, Russell did not. Instead, he followed Moore in adopting the view—discussed above in section 3 of chapter 3—that truth and falsity are simple, unanalyzable properties of propositions. To paraphrase Moore on goodness, "If I am asked 'What is true?', my answer is that true propositions are true, and that is all I have to say about it."[25] Russell would not have denied that the proposition that the earth is round is true iff the earth is round, and false iff the earth is not round—and so on for every proposition. However, he would not have seen this as providing any sort of analysis or philosophical illumination.

In this period he and Moore took propositions to have their truth values eternally, but not essentially. To say the former is to say that no proposition that was once true (or false) has now, or will ever, become false (or true). To say the latter is to say that some propositions—e.g., the proposition that I (SS) am sitting—are true, but they could have been false. The latter is surely right; the proposition that I am standing at this very moment could have been true, even though it isn't. But, one is inclined to object, shouldn't an analogous point be made about change of truth value over time? Although I am sitting now, soon I won't be, so the proposition that I am sitting is true now, even though it will soon be false. According to Moore and Russell, this is an illusion. The proposition that I am sitting (expressed by me now) is really the proposition that SS is sitting at 5:19 PM on December 15, 2010—which is true, and will forever remain so.

Just as propositions have their truth values eternally, so Russell (and Moore) thought, if there is such a thing as a certain true (or false) proposition p at one time, then there is such a thing as that proposition p at all times. In 1903 Russell would have expressed this by saying that propositions have their being eternally. Although it is tempting to put this by saying that for him propositions *exist* eternally, we will resist this, since during this period he distinguished *existence* from (mere) *being*. Thus, in Russell (1904a) he says that "except for space and time themselves [which exist], only those objects exist which have to particular parts of space and

---

[25] See chapter 4, section 2.1.

time the special relation of *occupying* them."[26] So, although he took there to be such things as numbers and sets—all of which "have being"—he denied that they exist.[27] In the case of propositions (at least some of which only have being), his recognition that they are objects of the attitudes was coupled with an insistence that whether or not there are propositions at a given time doesn't depend on their being objects of anyone's attitudes at that time (or ever). Propositions are the kinds of things that *can be* believed, doubted, disbelieved, and the like—irrespective of whether or not they are ever the objects of anyone's attitudes.

This last is, in one form or another, a plausible and perhaps unavoidable feature of any viable theory of propositions. However, it is also one which—when combined with other features of Russell's view—can all too easily lead to trouble. Recall the passage quoted above in which he speaks of our "awareness" of propositions in perception—where he (seemingly) confuses the relation of visual awareness that holds between an agent and an object o the agent sees with the special cognitive relation that an agent bears to the *proposition that o is so-and-so when the agent's perceptual experience represents o as being just that way.*[28] It is striking how much his discussion resembles Moore's discussion in "The Refutation of Idealism" of the relation between the blue one sees and the agent who sees it. As observed in chapter 3, Moore thought that seeing something is a relation between an agent and an independently existing thing seen, in which the agent's visual perception is a complex consisting of consciousness—which is notoriously "transparent"—plus the object of which the agent is conscious. The perceptual state itself is portrayed by Moore as passive—the mere apprehension of something the existence and observed characteristics of which have nothing to do with the agent's cognition. This is the troublesome picture Russell adopts, and applies to judgment, belief, and other attitudes.

It is illustrated by another passage from Russell (1904a).

> Suppose, for the sake of definiteness, that our judgment is 'A exists', where A is something that does as a matter of fact exist. Then A's existence, it seems plain, subsists independently of its being judged to subsist. . . . In this case the Objective [i.e., the proposition] of the judgment—at least in the view of common sense—is as truly independent of the judgment as is A itself. But the peculiarity of the cognitive relation, which is what we wish to consider, lies in this: that one term of the relation *is* nothing but an awareness of the

---

[26] Russell (1904a), p. 29 of Russell (1973). See also Russell (1903a), pp. 449–50.

[27] Since, on Russell's view, there is also someone who is the referent of my use of 'Socrates' (namely the teacher of Plato), Socrates still has being (even if we recognize that he no longer exists).

[28] Although Russell distinguishes such propositional awareness—e.g., of the proposition that redness exists here now—from the "mere awareness" of redness when one sees something red, his discussion (wrongly) suggests that the former amounts simply to the latter plus knowledge that its object exists.

other term. . . . This makes the relation more essential, more intimate, than any other; for the relatedness seems to form part of the very nature of one of the related terms, namely of the psychical term. . . . Here again, however, the very great difficulty of thinking of contents [by this Russell means the properties of the psychic side of cognitively relational states], as opposed to objects [i.e., the independent, external things to which these states are relations], has caused a confusion; there is no way of describing a particular judgment except as a judgment that so-and-so, i.e., by means of its object.[29]

The difficulty here, as I see it, is that this passive-object-of-attention conception of what it is to bear a cognitive attitude to a proposition encourages a conception of what propositions are that makes it very hard to believe that anything could fill the bill. The conception is one in which the key defining feature of propositions—the fact that they are *about* certain things, which they *represent* as being one way or another, and so are properly characterized as *true* (false) iff those things are (or are not) the way they are represented to be—is in no way derivative from, or attributable to, conceptually prior cognitive activities of agents who entertain them. On the contrary, since propositions are the *primary* bearers of intentionality, the secondary intentionality and truth conditions of cognitive acts or states must, for Russell, be explained in terms of substantially passive acts of perception-like awareness of propositions. But, one is inclined to ask, how can that be? Are there really eternal, abstract objects of this intrinsically representational sort, the essential nature of which is to be understood entirely independently of conscious agents, and the mere apprehension of which provides the basis of all cognition? It is hard for even a confirmed believer in propositions (like me) to think that there are—which makes one suspicious of the way in which Russell's quasi-perceptual epistemology of propositions feeds off his robustly Platonic metaphysics of them, and vice versa.[30] To his credit, he himself expressed what I take to be related doubts in his worries about "the unity of the proposition," which we will examine in section 4.5.

It should be added that, for Russell, there are also—how to put this?—a great many propositions. For every object o and property P of objects, there is a proposition in which P is predicated of o (and nothing else is predicated of anything). In addition, for every proposition there is a distinct proposition that is its negation. For every finite set of propositions there is at least one proposition that is their conjunction, and on and on and on. In fact, there are all the propositions there could possibly be. Just as there couldn't have been more, or fewer, numbers than there actually are, so, according to Russell, there couldn't have been more, or fewer, propositions than there actually are. For a proposition to "have being" its

[29] Russell (1904a); p. 60 of Russell (1973).
[30] See Soames (2010b) and the updates, Soames (2014c and forthcoming), for a Russell-inspired account of propositions that lacks these questionable features.

constituents must have being. However, as we shall see, during this period he also thought that "all possible objects of thought"—and so, I take it, all possible objects and all possible propositions—have being. This was bound to lead to trouble.

Finally, I mentioned above that propositions are the meanings of sentences. Since meaningful sentences are grammatically structured complexes composed of meaningful constituents, it was natural for Russell to take propositions to be similarly structured complexes the constituents of which are those elements of reality—objects and properties—that can be meanings of sub-sentential expressions. Russell gives expression to this idea in the first section of chapter 4 of *The Principles of Mathematics*.

> Although a grammatical distinction cannot be uncritically assumed to correspond to a genuine philosophical difference, yet the one is *prima facie* evidence of the other, and may often be most usefully employed as a source of discovery. Moreover, it must be admitted, I think, that every word occurring in a sentence must have *some* meaning: a perfectly meaningless sound could not be employed in the more or less fixed way in which language employs words. The correctness of our philosophical analysis of a proposition may therefore be usefully checked by the exercise of assigning the meaning of each word in the sentence expressing the proposition. On the whole, grammar seems to me to bring us much nearer to a correct logic than the current opinion of philosophers; and in what follows, grammar, though not our master, will yet be taken as our guide.[31]

For Russell, the proposition expressed by a sentence S is a nonlinguistic correlate of S in which the meanings of S's constituents bear relations to one another that correspond to the grammatical relations that S's constituents bear to one another. As he stresses, however, this picture is only a guide, not a governing principle. Moreover, although he shows remarkable interest—in a book focusing on logic and the philosophy of mathematics—in the general theory of meaning and of propositions expressed, he was not, after all, trying to construct a general semantic theory for natural language. Thus, there is no reason to think that he would have assigned the grammatically different sentences of ordinary language in (6), (7), and (8) different propositions.

6a. There is now likely to be a mouse in the bathtub.
 b. It is now likely that a mouse is in the bathtub.
 c. That a mouse is in the bathtub is now likely.
7a. John gave a book to Mary.
 b. John gave Mary a book.
8a. John expects himself to be elected.
 b. John expects to be elected.

---

[31] Russell (1903a), p. 42.

By contrast, his view of the propositions expressed by (9a) and (9b) was guided by his basic picture.

9a. Socrates is wise.
 b. Wisdom characterizes Socrates.

Although the propositions expressed by these sentences are said to be logically equivalent, Russell takes them to be nonidentical. The first is said to contain two constituents—the man Socrates and the property wisdom—the latter understood as predicated (or "asserted" as he puts it) of the former. (The copula, or 'is' of predication, merely serves to indicate what is predicated of what, and so does not introduce another constituent into the proposition expressed.) The proposition expressed by the second sentence, (9b), is said to contain three constituents—Socrates, wisdom, and the instantiation relation (which holds between an individual and a property when the individual has the property). According to Russell, these propositions also differ in what they are "about." Whereas the first is said to be about only Socrates (and not about wisdom), the second is said to be about both Socrates and wisdom (and not about instantiation). He puts this by saying that whereas (the man) Socrates occurs *as a term* and wisdom occurs *as a concept* in the proposition expressed (9a), both occur *as terms*, while instantiation occurs *as a concept*, in the proposition expressed by (9b).

4.2. Propositional Structure: Terms and Concepts

Russell's conception of terms is expressed by the following definitions.

Occurring as a Term in a Proposition

For anything x whatsoever, and proposition p, x occurs as a term of p iff x is a constituent of p and p is about x.

Termhood

For anything x whatsoever, x is a term iff there is some proposition p in which x occurs as a term.

Since for anything x, Russell took the proposition that x is a term (or that x isn't a term) to be a proposition about x, he concluded that everything is a term. In section 47, he tells us how much is included in "everything."

Whatever may be an object or thing, or may occur in any true or false proposition, or can be counted as *one*, I call a *term*. This, then, is the widest word in the philosophical vocabulary. I shall use as synonymous with it the words unit, individual, or entity. The first two emphasize the fact that every term is *one*, while the third is derived from the fact that every term has being, i.e. *is* in some sense. A man, a moment, a number, a class, a relation, a chimera, or anything else that can be mentioned, is sure to be a term; and to deny that such and such a thing is a term, must always be false.[32]

Here, what starts out sounding like a pedestrian discussion of terminology ends up in a surprising metaphysical claim. We are told that certain merely mythological creatures, chimeras, are terms, *and hence have being,* which means that *there are chimeras*! Russell repeats essentially the same thought later, in section 427 of *Principles of Mathematics.*

> *Being* is that which belongs to every conceivable term, to every possible object of thought—in short to everything that can possibly occur in any proposition, true or false, and to all such propositions themselves. Being belongs to whatever can be counted. If A be any term that can be counted as one, it is plain that A is something, and therefore that A is. "A is not" must always be either false or meaningless. For if A were nothing, it could not be said not to be; "A is not" implies that there is a term A whose being is denied, and hence that A is. Thus unless "A is not" be an empty sound, it must be false—whatever A may be it certainly is. Numbers, the Homeric gods, relations, chimeras and four-dimensional spaces all have being, for if they were not entities of a kind, we could make no propositions about them. Thus being is a general attribute of everything, and to mention anything is to show that it is.[33]

In these passages, Russell seems to be thinking along the following lines without clearly distinguishing among them.

A1. Since one can mention chimeras, Homeric gods, four dimensional-spaces, etc., they must be terms, and so have being.[34]

A2. Let A be any meaningful singular term (name or definite description) that can occur as indicated in ⌜A is not a term⌝, ⌜There is no such thing as A⌝, and ⌜A is not⌝. If these sentences are meaningful, then the propositions expressed by the following sentences are all true: ⌜The proposition that A is not a term denies the termhood of A, and so is *about* A⌝, ⌜The proposition that there is no such thing as A denies that there is such a thing as A, and so is *about* A⌝, and ⌜The proposition that A is not denies the being of A, and so is *about* A⌝. But if that is so, then the propositions expressed by ⌜A is a term⌝, ⌜There is such thing as A⌝, and ⌜A is⌝ are also true. So, if ⌜A is not a term⌝, ⌜There is no such thing as A⌝, and ⌜A is not⌝ are meaningful, they must be false.

A3. Let B be any meaningful plural or quantificational expression that can occur as indicated in ⌜B's are not terms⌝, ⌜There are no such things as

---

[32] Ibid., p. 43.

[33] Ibid., p. 449.

[34] Though Russell was often pretty liberal about chimeras, he was not entirely consistent in *Principles of Mathematics*, seeming to suggest on p. 74 that 'x is a chimera' is false for all values of 'x'. Perhaps he was of two minds about this, or perhaps he thought we sometimes use 'chimera' with the implicit restriction 'existing chimera'.

B's⌉, and ⌈B's are not⌉. If these sentences are meaningful, then the propositions expressed by the following sentences are all true: ⌈The proposition that B's are not terms denies the termhood of B's, and so is *about* B's⌉, ⌈The proposition that there are no such things as B's denies that there are such things as B's, and so is *about* B's⌉, and ⌈The proposition that B's are not denies the being of B's, and so is *about* B's⌉. But if that is so, then the propositions expressed by ⌈B's are terms⌉, ⌈There are such things as B's⌉, and ⌈B's are⌉ are also true. So, if ⌈B's are not terms⌉, ⌈There are no such things as B's⌉, and ⌈B's are not⌉ are meaningful, they must be false.

Far from being established by Russell's argument, his conclusion—which we may formulate as UB (Universal Being)—is self-refuting, and so demonstratively false. Here, it is convenient to divide this conclusion into two parts: UB singular, and UB plural.

UB$_{Sing}$ For any meaningful singular term (name or definite description) A that can occur as indicated in the meaningful sentences ⌈A is (or is not) a term⌉, ⌈A is (or has being)⌉, ⌈A is not (or does not have being)⌉, and ⌈There is (no) such thing as A⌉, the sentences ⌈A is not a term⌉, ⌈A is not (or does not have being)⌉, and ⌈There is no such thing as A⌉ all express false propositions, while their positive counterparts express true propositions.

UB$_{Plu}$ For any meaningful plural or quantificational expression B that can occur as indicated in the meaningful sentences ⌈B's are (or are not) terms⌉, ⌈B's are (or have being)⌉, ⌈B's are not (or do not have being)⌉, and ⌈There are (no) such things as B's⌉, the sentences ⌈B's are not terms⌉, ⌈B's are not (or do not have being)⌉, and ⌈There are no such things as B's⌉ all express false propositions, while their positive counterparts express true propositions.

Let UB be the conjunction of these two theses. The demonstration that UB is false is a *reductio ad absurdum* starting from UB.[35]

P1.   UB

P2   If ⌈There is no such thing as A⌉ expresses a false proposition, then ⌈There is such thing as A⌉ expresses a true proposition.

P3.   'The false proposition here expressed by the sentence labeled *UB$_{sing}$*' is a meaningful singular term that can occur in the indicated position in any of the relevant sentences mentioned in UB$_{Sing}$.

C1.   So (from P1, P2, and P3), the sentence 'There is such a thing as the false proposition here expressed by the sentence labeled *UB$_{sing}$*' expresses a true proposition.

C2.   So (from C1), there is such a thing as the false proposition here expressed by the sentence labeled 'UB$_{Sing}$'.

---

[35] See Richard Cartwright (1987b), p. 98.

C3.   So (from C2), UB_{Sing} is false, which means that its negation is true, which means that it is not the case that . . . (where the dots are filled in by repeating UB_{Sing}).

C4.   Since C3 contradicts UB_{Sing}, which follows from UB, C3 contradicts UB. Since P2 and P3 are clearly true, UB is false.

In section 4.4, it will be interesting to investigate which assumption or assumptions leading to UB Russell must give up.[36] However, this will require familiarity with more of the conceptual apparatus involved in his conception of the structure of propositions.

We already have the notion of an entity *occurring as a term* in a given proposition. Using this, we get Russell's notion of a "thing."

Thinghood

For anything x whatsoever, x is a thing iff for every proposition p of which x is a constituent, x occurs as a term in p.

Since, as we have seen, wisdom occurs in the proposition expressed by (9a) without occurring as a term in that proposition, it is not a thing. Instead, Russell calls it "a concept."

Being a Concept

For any x whatsoever, x is a concept iff for some proposition p, x is a constituent of p without occurring as a term in p.

From these definitions it is clear that, in Russell's terminology, properties and relations are concepts. Of course, concepts are also terms, since for any concept C, there are propositions about C which also contain C (as a constituent)—e.g., the proposition that C is a concept.[37] However, some entities—namely "things" like Socrates, Los Angeles, or the planet Earth—are not concepts, since every proposition in which they occur is a proposition about them. What this amounts to for Russell is, it seems, that in every proposition in which they are constituents they are among the subjects of predication in the proposition. By contrast, concepts—at any rate "non-denoting concepts" like wisdom or humanity—are capable

---

[36] The move from C2 to C3 might be questioned on the grounds that it assumes that UB_{Sing} expresses only one proposition. But if this is thought problematic the meaningful singular term mentioned in P3 could be changed to 'the proposition that is both false and the only one expressed by the sentence labeled UB_{Sing}'.

[37] Compare with Frege. Whereas for Russell the concept *horse* can be truly said to be a concept (by asserting the proposition about that concept that predicates *being a concept* of it), for Frege this is paradoxically not so.

of playing a different role in the propositions in which they occur, since they can be what is predicated of something else. *Denoting concepts* require special treatment.

4.3. The Theory of Denoting

Chapter 5 of *The Principles of Mathematics* is devoted to a crucial sub-class of concepts that Russell calls *denoting concepts*, which are defined in section 56.

> A concept *denotes* when, if it occurs in a proposition, the proposition is not *about* the concept, but about a term connected in a peculiar way with the concept.[38]

Among Russell's examples are the concepts *a man, any number,* and *man* as used in (10).

10a. I met *a man.*
   b. *Any number* is odd or even.
   c. *Man* is mortal.

About these, he says:

> If I say "I met a man," the proposition is not about *a man*: this is a concept which does not walk the streets, but lives in the shadowy limbo of the logic-books. What I met was a thing, not a concept, an actual man with a tailor and a bank-account or a public-house and a drunken wife. Again, the proposition "any finite number is odd or even" is plainly true; yet the *concept* "any finite number" is neither odd nor even. It is only particular numbers that are odd or even: there is not, in addition to these, another entity, *any number*, which is either odd or even. . . . People often assert that man is mortal: but what is mortal will die, and yet we should be surprised to find in the "Times" such a notice as the following: "Died at his residence of Camelot, Gladstone Road, Upper Tooting, on the 18th of June 19___, Man, eldest son of Death and Sin." *Man*, in fact, does not die; hence if "man is mortal" were, as it appears to be, a proposition about *man,* it would be simply false. The . . . proposition is about men: and here again, it is not about the concept *men*, but about what this concept denotes. The whole theory of definition, of identity, of classes, of symbolism, and of the variable is wrapped up in the theory of denoting. The notion is the fundamental notion of logic.[39]

Here, when Russell argues that a proposition containing denoting concept C is not *about* C, he does so by noting that C is not the subject of the predication in the proposition—it is not that of which the proposition predicates a concept. It is not what is said in (10a–c) to be *mortal, odd or*

---

[38] Russell (1903a), p. 53.
[39] Ibid., pp. 53–54.

even, or *one I met*. We know, however, from the definition of a denoting concept that the proposition is, in each case, *about* something—and indeed something connected "in a peculiar way" with the concept. What is it? Russell's reasoning here seems to provide a criterion for assessing answers to this question—for, if his reasoning is correct, it would seem that whatever is connected "in a peculiar way" with the denoting concept must be what is said to be mortal, odd or even, or one I met, in (10a–c). What objects, denoted by denoting concepts, satisfy this criterion?

Since the answer to this question turns out to be more difficult than one might first think, it will be helpful to begin by getting a clearer conception of the difference between denoting and non-denoting concepts. We begin by comparing (11a) and (11b).

11a. Socrates is mortal.
  b. Every man is mortal.

For Russell, the propositions expressed by these sentences have the same structure, while differing in that where the first has Socrates as a constituent the second has the concept *every man*. Since the proposition expressed by (11a) is about Socrates, whereas the proposition expressed by (11b) is not about its constituent *every man*, the latter occurs in (11b) as a concept—just as *mortality* occurs as a concept in both propositions. The difference in the way these two concepts function is connected to certain structural differences between the positions they occupy. Call the position occupied by a constituent of a proposition p a *term-accessible position* in p iff there is some proposition p* that differs from p at most (if at all) in having something that occurs as a term in p* occupying that position.[40] Then, Socrates occupies a term-accessible position in the proposition expressed by (11a) by virtue of the fact that Socrates is himself a term in that very proposition, while the concept *every man* occupies a term-accessible position in the proposition expressed by (11b) by virtue of the role of Socrates in the proposition expressed by (11a). By contrast, *mortality* does not occupy a term-accessible position in either proposition, since replacing *mortality* in those propositions with other items never results in propositions in which those items occur as terms. If *mortality* is replaced by another non-denoting concept—e.g., wisdom— the result will be a proposition, but not one in which wisdom is a term; if *mortality* is replaced by a thing—e.g., Aristotle—one fails to get a proposition at all.

In this connection, it is important to realize that for Russell (12a) and (12b) are not counterexamples to this claim.

12a. Socrates is Aristotle.
  b. Every man is Aristotle.

[40] See pp. 102–3 of Cartwright (1987b) for useful discussion.

Though he would not deny that these sentences are meaningful, and so express propositions, he would maintain that this is so only when they are understood as containing the 'is' of identity, rather than the 'is' of predication that occurs in (11). Thus, for Russell, the propositions expressed by the sentences in (12) contain three constituents (one of which is the concept *identity* expressed by 'is'), whereas those expressed by the sentences in (11) contain only two (with 'is' contributing no constituent).

With this in mind, we adopt the following definition.

Occurring in a Proposition as a Denoting Concept

For any concept C, C *occurs as a denoting concept* in a proposition p iff C occurs in a term-accessible position of p without itself being a term of p.

Further examples of constituents occurring as denoting concepts are given in (13).

13a. Martha can outsmart any man.
  b. Nora ate lunch with a man she met this morning.
  c. Some man shouted at Susan.
  d. Jill likes the man she met.

Remembering that everything whatsoever—including concepts of all sorts—can occur as terms in some propositions, we define what it is to be a denoting concept as follows:[41]

Denoting Concepts

A is a denoting concept iff A occurs as a denoting concept in at least one proposition.

With this way of thinking about denoting concepts, we return to the question of what they denote. For each denoting concept DC, and proposition ...DC... in which it occurs as a denoting concept, there will be a class of corresponding propositions, ...term$_1$... , ...term$_2$... , ...term$_3$... , etc., in which different terms occupy the position of DC in the original proposition. For different denoting concepts, what Russell would call "the logical relationships" between ...DC... and members of the class will be different. We can illustrate this by considering the simplest kinds of propositions containing DC—e.g., propositions like those expressed by the relevant examples in (10–13). One can think of these as "atomic propositions" each of which contains a single denoting concept. In these simple

---

[41] These definitions, plus discussion of some shortcomings, are found on p. 103 of Cartwright (1987b).

cases, when DC is the concept *every man*, the resulting class is gotten by forming a proposition for each man, and noting that the original proposition is true iff each of the propositions in the class is true. When DC is the concept *some man,* the original proposition is true iff at least one of the propositions in the resulting class is true. When DC is the concept *the man*, the original proposition is true iff there is exactly one proposition in the resulting class, and it's true. In principle, the idea could be extended to encompass *no men, many men, most men, few men, 17 men*, and so on— though Russell was concerned with only a small subset of the whole class of denoting concepts. The task for him in 1903 was to assign denotations to all denoting concepts in this subset from which he could extract results like these for all propositions in which these denoting concepts occur. This, it turns out, was easier said than done.

To see why, let's go back to his remarks about (10a–c) and about denoting itself: "A concept *denotes* when, if it occurs in a proposition, the proposition is not *about* the concept, but about a term connected in a peculiar way with the concept."

10a. I met *a man*.
  b. *Any number* is odd or even.
  c. *Man* is mortal.

If I say "I met a man," the proposition is not about *a man*: this is a concept which does not walk the streets, but lives in the shadowy limbo of the logic-books. What I met was a thing, not a concept. . . . Again, the proposition "any finite number is odd or even" is plainly true; yet the *concept* "any finite number" is neither odd nor even. . . . Of the *concept* "any number," almost all the propositions that contain the *phrase* "any number" are false. . . . People often assert that man is mortal: but what is mortal will die. . . . *Man*, in fact, does not die; hence if "man is mortal" were, as it appears to be, a proposition about *man,* it would be simply false. The fact is, the proposition is about men: and here again, it is not about the concept *men*, but about what this concept denotes. [42]

Here, the proposition expressed by (10c) is said to be (a) about men, and (b) about what the concept *men* denotes—apparently suggesting that these are one and the same. Thus, one might imagine that, for Russell, this proposition is about individual men, each of which is denoted by the concept. Given this, one might further suppose that a parallel result holds for the proposition expressed by (10b), and hence that the concept *any number* denotes each individual number. Although this is a natural thought, it was not Russell's view. First, it doesn't quite fit his informal definition of a denoting concept as something which, when it occurs in a proposition (as a denoting concept), makes it the case that the

[42] Russell (1903a), pp. 53–54.

proposition is about "a term [singular, not plural] connected in a peculiar way with the concept."[43] Second, if the natural thought were correct, and if, in addition, there are cases in which a meaningful class concept F isn't true of anything (which one would suppose there must surely be), then examples ⌜Any F is G⌝ and ⌜F is H⌝ (analogous to (10b) and (10c)) would be meaningful, and hence express propositions containing denoting concepts that are not about anything, and so, again, contradict Russell's definition.

One might respond that with his expansive ontology, in which everything that can be mentioned has being, and plenty of nonexistent things can be mentioned, there simply won't be any such cases. However, that goes a bit too far. Though Russell's ontology at the time was extravagantly expansive, he did reject some things outright—including the universal set, the set of all and only non-self-membered sets, and, somewhat idiosyncratically, the null set.[44] Surely there must have been many others from mathematics that he rejected, including the largest prime number. Thus, he cannot really be taken to have ruled out denoting concepts that don't denote anything, despite the many passages to the contrary in *The Principles of Mathematics*—which must be regarded as somewhat misleading, but mostly harmless, oversimplifications.[45]

This aside, the fundamental problem with the natural thought is that it doesn't generalize to (10a), as Russell, in effect, tells us in section 62.

---

[43] Ibid., p. 53.

[44] He denies what he calls "the null class," on ibid., p. 75, and calls concepts that denote nothing "null class-concepts," adding:

> But now a new difficulty has to be met. The equality of class concepts, like all relations which are reflexive, symmetrical, and transitive, indicates an underlying identity, *i.e.* it indicates that every class-concept has to some term a relation which all equal class-concepts have to that term, the term being different for different sets of equal class-concepts, but the same for the various members of a single set of equal class-concepts. Now for all class-concepts which are not null, this term is found in the corresponding class [it is the common extension of the given class of equal class-concepts]; but where are we to find it for null class-concepts [which have no extension]?

Russell's answer is that for logical and mathematical (as opposed to philosophical) purposes we let the nonempty class of null class-concepts play the role of the null class wherever necessary. This artificial substitute can't be counted as the denotation of a null denoting concept, as it would make nonsense of Russell's characterization of what propositions containing them are about. Rather such denoting concepts must, I think, be seen as denoting nothing, with the result that propositions containing no other terms or non-null denoting concepts are about nothing.

[45] On p. 75 Russell says, "*Nothing* is a denoting concept which denotes nothing," while on p. 74 he says, "The denoting concepts associated with *a* will not denote anything when and only when 'x is an *a*' is false for all values of *x*. This is a complete definition of a denoting concept which does not denote anything; and in this case we shall say that *a* is a null class-concept, and that 'all *a*'s' is a null concept of a class." The brevity of his treatment of this class of denoting concepts, and his struggles over the few explicit examples considered, indicate that he doesn't take the class of null denoting concepts to be large and important.

Consider again the proposition "I met a man." It is quite certain, and implied by this proposition, that what I met was a perfectly unambiguous and perfectly definite man: in the technical language which is here adopted, the proposition is expressed by "I met some man." But the actual man whom I met forms no part of the proposition in question, and is not specifically denoted by [the denoting concept] *some man*. Thus the concrete event which happened is not asserted in the proposition. What is asserted is merely that some one of a class of concrete events took place. The whole human race is involved in my assertion: if any man who ever existed or will exist had not existed or been going to exist, the purport of my proposition would have been different. Or, to put the same point in more intensional language, if I substitute for *man* any of the other class concepts applicable to the individual whom I had the honour to meet, my proposition is changed, although the individual in question is just as much denoted as before. What this proves is, that [the denoting concept] *some man* must not be regarded as actually denoting Smith and actually denoting Brown, and so on: the whole procession of human beings throughout the ages is always relevant to every proposition in which *some man* occurs, and what is denoted is essentially not each separate man, but a kind of combination of all men.[46]

Here, Russell takes the expression 'a man', as it occurs in (10a), to express the denoting concept *some man*. It is clear from the passage, plus what has gone before, that, according to Russell, (i) the denoting concept *some man* does not denote individual men, (ii) it does denote something, (iii) what it denotes is not part of the proposition in which the denoting concept occurs, (iv) what it denotes is what that proposition is about, and (v) this denotation is a kind of complex to which each individual man makes a contribution—in Russell's words, "a kind of combination of all men."

Point (v) can, I think, be clarified by focusing on two of the more puzzling sentences in the above passage.

The whole human race is involved in my assertion: if any man who ever existed or will exist had not existed or been going to exist, the purport of my proposition would have been different. Or, to put the same point in more intensional language, if I substitute for *man* any of the other class concepts applicable to the individual whom I had the honour to meet, my proposition is changed, although the individual in question is just as much denoted as before.

How would "the purport" of Russell's proposition have been different if any man who had ever existed, not existed? The proposition expressed in that counterfactual circumstance would have been no different, and it is likely that its truth value would not have been different either—since it is unlikely that Russell would have failed to meet a man (on the given occasion), had some hermit who actually lived centuries ago never existed.

[46] Russell (1903a), p. 62.

Russell's point, is, I think, that *what it is* for the proposition that he met a man *to be true* is for at least one member of a certain related set of propositions to be true—the set of propositions differing only from the original in having some man, past or present, in the position that the denoting concept *a man* occupies in the original proposition. As things stand, that set contains one proposition for each man m who ever existed—a proposition stating that Russell met m. However, had any one of those men never existed, *the set of propositions in terms of which the truth conditions of Russell's proposition (10a) are defined* would have been different (as would the denotation of the concept *some man*). Similarly, were we to substitute, for the concept *man*, some concept *so-and-so* that is true not only of the man Russell actually met, but also of some things that are not men, the resulting proposition—that Russell met a so-and-so—would be true, but the canonical set of propositions in terms of which its truth conditions are defined would be different yet again (as would the denotation of the denoting concept). For Russell, this change in truth conditions goes hand in hand with a change in denotation. In both cases—the counterfactual and the substitutional—the denotation of the relevant denoting concept differs from *the actual denotation* of the concept *some man* in the proposition expressed by (10a). Since the denotations change from case to case, though the man m whose meeting with Russell makes the proposition true in each case remains the same, Russell concludes that m contributes to, but isn't the denotation of, the denoting concept in any of the cases. Fair enough.

Looking at this example, it might seem that the denotation of the concept *some man*, should be the set of all men, past and present. Moreover, one might imagine we had a recipe for identifying the denotation of denoting concepts *every F, some F, the F, most F's*, etc., too: (i) Find the class of propositions needed to define the truth conditions of the proposition p containing the denoting concept, (ii) notice that this will be a class of propositions p* differing from the p only in containing a genuine term t in the term-accessible position in p* occupied by the denoting concept in p, (iii) define the denotation of the denoting concept to be the class of such terms t. However, this won't do, as is evident from the fact that applying this recipe to (10a′) and (10c) will yield the result that the denoting concepts *some man, every man*, and *man* (as it functions in (10c)) all denote the same thing.

10a′.   Russell met every man.

The same result could be extended to the concepts *many men, most men, few men, 17 men*, and so on. As natural as this may seem, it is, from Russell's point of view, absurd. It is absurd because it is their *denotations* that denoting concepts are supposed to contribute to the truth conditions of the propositions in which they occur. So, if all these denoting concepts denoted the same thing, then substitution of one for another in a Russellian proposition would never change truth conditions—which really is absurd.

Russell's problem is that although it is easy to associate each denoting concept DC with a set of terms that play a crucial role in determining the truth conditions of propositions in which DC occurs as a denoting concept, the role played by that set is incomplete and must be supplemented by a further condition, which differs from one denoting concept to another. To wax expansive, we note: whereas the relevant set for the denoting concepts *some man, every man, the man, many men, most men, few men, 17 men,* etc. is always the set of men, (i) the condition for *some man* is that at least one member of the set is such that substituting it for the denoting occurrence of the concept in the original proposition produces a true proposition, (ii) the condition for *every man* is that every member of the set have this property, (iii) the condition for *the man* is the same as that for every man, plus the condition that the set have only one member, (iv) the condition for *many men* is that many members of the set have it, (v) the condition for *most men* is that most members of the set have it, (vi) the condition for *few men* is that few members of the set have it, (vii) the condition for *17 men* is that seventeen members of the set have it, and so on. If, for each denoting concept, we could somehow combine the condition peculiar to it with the set it shares with many other denoting concepts to form a single complex object, we could use that complex as the denotation of the denoting concept. To think of things in this way is to imagine accounting for what are now recognized to be generalized quantifiers, not by invoking higher-order properties of lower-order properties (which, generalizing Frege's treatment of 'every' and 'some', is how they are now standardly treated), but by adding to one's ontology of ordinary objects further "logically complex" objects formed by applying "logical" operators not to expressions, or sentences, or propositions, but to ordinary objects themselves.

This is what Russell tried, quixotically, to do for the denoting concepts expressed by ⌜all F's⌝, ⌜every F⌝, ⌜any F⌝, ⌜an F⌝, ⌜some F⌝, and ⌜the F⌝. Although I will concentrate only on *every, some,* and *the,* I will try to say enough about the whole group to convey what he took himself to be up to. He gets down to business in section 58. After telling us that *all men, every man, any man, a man,* and *some man* are denoting concepts for each of which there is "an object denoted," he adds in a footnote that he is using 'object' "in a wider sense than *term* [which he had already called *the widest word in the philosophical vocabulary*], to cover both singular and plural."[47] Here, he employs 'singular' and 'plural' not as predicates of expressions (as they are normally understood), but as predicates of *objects,* without clearly indicating what it means to say that some (complex) objects are singular and some are plural. He continues:

> The combination of concepts as such to form new concepts, of greater complexity than their constituents, is a subject upon which writers on logic have

[47] Ibid., p. 55.

said many things. But the combination of terms as such, what by analogy may be called complex terms, is a subject which logicians, old and new, give us only the scantiest discussion. Nevertheless, the subject is of vital importance to the philosophy of mathematics, since the nature both of number and of the variable turns upon just this point. Six words, of constant occurrence in daily life, are also characteristic of mathematics: These are the words *all, every, any, a, some* and *the*. For correctness of reasoning, it is essential that these words should be sharply distinguished one from another: but the subject bristles with difficulties, and is almost wholly neglected by logicians. It is plain, to begin with, that a phrase containing one of the above six words always denotes.[48]

There are three points to note. First, the contrast in the first two sentences between complex concepts and complex terms is a contrast between certain constituents of propositions (including denoting concepts) and the elements in the world that such propositions are used to talk about (complex objects). Russell notes that logicians, old and new, say a great deal about the former, but next to nothing about the latter, which is surely right. His message is unusual: that to understand logic, and also reasoning, we need a kind of logical metaphysics to inform us about the "logically complex objects" in the world that are denoted by denoting concepts. The second point is the claim that the words 'all', 'every', 'any', 'a', 'some', and 'the'—which today we classify grammatically as determiners and semantically as quantifiers—are said by Russell to be vital to mathematics. This also sounds strange, and was nonstandard for most of the twentieth century, when it was usually thought that 'every' or 'some' would be sufficient for mathematics (even though there is much to be said about the differences between the six determiners that is important for the syntax and semantics of English). The third point to emphasize is Russell's categorical statement that "a phrase containing one of the above six words always denotes." Various formulations of the claim reoccur again and again in *The Principles of Mathematics*, giving the impression that for any meaningful class-concept F, the phrases ⌜all F's⌝, ⌜every F⌝, ⌜any F⌝, ⌜an F⌝, ⌜some F⌝, and ⌜the F⌝, and the denoting concepts they express, *always* denote something.[49] However, as already noted, this can't be quite right, but must be taken to be an oversimplification. Thus, at the end of section 58, Russell adds that whenever F is a null class-concept, the propositions expressed by ⌜All F's are G⌝, ⌜Every F is G⌝, ⌜Any F is G⌝, ⌜An F is G⌝, ⌜Some F is G⌝, and ⌜The F is G⌝ *are*

---

[48] Ibid., pp. 55–56.

[49] See, for example, ibid., p. 43, where Russell says: "In every proposition . . . we may make an analysis into something asserted [predicated] and something about which the assertion is made." To accept this claim as true, one must not accept denoting concepts that fail to denote anything. For, if there are such concepts, then some propositions containing them will be about nothing, and so be counterexamples to this thesis.

always false.[50] Together, the ontological expansiveness that led him to minimize the number of null class-concepts there are, plus what he took to be the dearth of *truths* involving the relatively few genuinely null denoting concepts he was willing to recognize, led him, at various points, to regard the exceptions to the claim that denoting concepts always denote to be few, and scarcely worth mentioning.

Returning to the genuinely denoting cases, he concludes, six pages later, that

> the objects denoted by *all men, every man,* etc. are certainly distinct. It seems therefore legitimate to say that the whole difference lies in the objects, and that denoting itself is the same in all cases.[51]

Here we are told that the six different denoting concepts denote correspondingly different objects. Although Russell treats ⌜the F⌝ as a special case, taking it to denote an ordinary individual (that uniquely satisfies F), the other five are said to denote complex objects.

> There is, then, a definite something, different in each of the five cases, which must, in a sense, be an object, but is characterized as a set of terms combined in a certain way, which something is denoted by *all men, every man, any man, a man,* or *some man;* and it is with this very paradoxical object that propositions are concerned in which the corresponding concept is used as denoting.[52]

In the previous sections (59–61), Russell attempts to explain what these "very paradoxical objects" are, which propositions are supposed to be about. The explanation begins with logical distinctions among propositions that are supposed to correspond to logically relevant distinctions among composite objects denoted by denoting concepts.

> Let us begin by considering . . . Brown and Jones. The objects denoted by *all, every, any, a* and *some* are respectively involved in the following five propositions. (1) Brown and Jones are two of Miss Smith's suitors; (2) Brown and Jones are paying court to Miss Smith; (3) if it was Brown or Jones you met, it was a very ardent lover; (4) if it was one of Miss Smith's suitors, it must have been Brown or Jones; (5) Miss Smith will marry Brown or Jones. . . . I maintain that five different combinations [of objects] are involved. . . . In the first proposition, it is Brown *and* Jones who are two, and this is not true of either separately; nevertheless it is not of the whole composed of Brown and Jones which is two, for this is only one. The two are a genuine combination of Brown with Jones [as opposed to a conjunction of words, or propositions]. . . . In the

---

[50] This claim, questionable with 'all' and 'every', is clearly false for 'any'. One who says "Any student found to have cheated on this examination will be expelled from school" is not committed to the claim that at least one student will be found to have cheated on this examination.

[51] Russell (1903a), pp. 61–62.

[52] Ibid., p. 62.

second proposition . . . what is asserted is true of Brown and Jones severally; the proposition is equivalent to, though not (I think) identical with, "Brown is paying court to Miss Smith and Jones is paying court to Miss Smith." Thus the combination [of objects] indicated by *and* is not the same here as in the first case: the first case concerned *all* of them collectively, while the second concerns *all* distributively. . . . (It should be observed that the conjunction of propositions in question is of a wholly different kind from any of the combinations we are considering. . . .)[53]

The contrast between 'all' and 'every' to which Russell calls attention is illustrated by the following examples.

14a. All of those here (Brown and Jones) are (make up) two.
  b. All my friends (Brown, Jones, and Smith) are scattered.
  c. All members of the family (Al, Betty, Dick, and Susan) criticize each other.

15a. *Every (each) person here (Brown and Jones) is two.
  b. *Every one (each) of my friends (Brown, Jones, and Smith) is scattered.
  c. *Every (each) member of the family (Al, Betty, Dick, and Susan) criticizes each other.

In (14) 'all' is used with a collective interpretation that isn't carried by 'every' or 'each'. Russell struggled to explain this difference by assigning one "logically" complex object (somehow constructed from ordinary individuals) as the denotation of the concept expressed by ⌜all F's⌝ and a different "logically" complex object (somehow constructed from the same ordinary individuals) as the denotation of the concept expressed by ⌜every F⌝ and ⌜each F⌝.

By contrast, many today would dispense with such logically complex objects and characterize the contrast as that between singular and plural predicates (i.e., those true of individuals vs. those true of pluralities of individuals) plus singular or plural *quantification* over ordinary individuals.[54] On this way of looking at things, 'singular' and 'plural' function as they always do—to mark a linguistic, not an ontological, distinction. The difference, expressed in familiar talk of quantifiers and variables, is that whereas in singular quantification (involving 'every' and 'each') a variable is assigned a single individual, in plural quantification (involving the collective 'all') a variable is assigned multiple individuals—not a set, or combination, or fusion, or plurality (thought of as a single thing) consisting of those individuals. Collective predicates, like 'two' and 'scattered', are then understood as being true of multiple individuals—rather than of sets or other "combinations" of individuals.

[53] Ibid., pp. 56–57.
[54] For more on plural quantification, see Rayo (2007), and Linnebo (2003, 2010).

For example, let 'X' be a second-order variable of plural quantification, assignments to which are always pluralities of two or more individuals, let ⌜All X ΦX⌝ be true iff ΦX is true for all plural assignments to 'X', and let ⌜[All X: FX] GX⌝ be true iff GX is true for all plural assignments to 'X' that satisfy FX. Then, the quantificational versions of (14) might be represented along the following lines.

14a'. [All X: ∀y Xy ⟷ here y] X are (make up) two.
  b'. [All X: ∀y Xy → my friend y] X are scattered.
  c'. [All X: ∀y Xy → y is a member of my family] X criticize each other.

By contrast, since 'every' and 'each' are singular, and so bind variables that are assigned individuals, while the predicates in these examples are plural, and so true only of pluralities, the formal counterparts of (15) turn out to be incoherent (as they should).

15a'. *[Every (each) y: here y] y is (make up) two.
  b'. *[Every (each) y: my friend y] y is scattered.
  c'. *[Every (each) y is a member of my family] y criticizes each other.

In this way, one avoids the incoherence inherent in Russell's repeated insistence that the concept expressed by ⌜all F's⌝ denotes *a single complex object* that a proposition containing it is about, even when the concept predicated by the proposition does *not* apply to single objects *of any sort*. It is just this incoherence he struggles with in the previous passage, when he says:

> In the first proposition [*that Brown and Jones* are two of Miss Smith's suitors, or in our example (14a)], it is Brown *and* Jones who are two, and this is not true of either separately; nevertheless it is not the whole composed of Brown and Jones [namely the complex object denoted that is "the conjunction" of the man Brown and the man Smith] which is two, for this is only one.

The resolution of this incoherence is that these examples do not support the postulation of any "conjunctive object" that is "the whole composed of Brown and Jones." Whatever may be the correct metaphysical view about complex objects composed of individual men, a proper understanding of Russell's examples of the collective 'all' doesn't involve them.

A less dramatic, though similarly important, point can be made about his discussion of the supposed denotation of the concept expressed by ⌜every F⌝. His task was to identify a kind of *ontological conjunction* associated with the concept *every* that produces a complex object from individuals of which F is true—different from the complex object he imagined to be produced from the same individuals by the special kind of ontological conjunction associated with the collective *all*. The simple, nonquantified proposition that he used to illustrate what he imagined to be *every*-conjunction was his proposition (2): that Brown and Jones are paying court to Miss Smith. Here, repeated from above, are his remarks.

In the second proposition, on the contrary, what is asserted is true of Brown and Jones severally; the proposition is equivalent to, though not (I think) identical with, "Brown is paying court to Miss Smith and Jones is paying court to Miss Smith." Thus the combination [of terms—i.e., objects] indicated by *and* is not the same here as in the first case: the first case concerned *all* of them collectively, while the second concerns *all* distributively, i.e. each or every one of them.

The problem here is a variant of the one found in the previous case. What the predicate applies to, if the proposition is true, are the *individuals* Brown and Jones themselves—*not* a complex object formed by a special (distributive) way of "conjoining" them. There is no one thing that is paying court to Miss Smith, whenever either Brown or Smith is courting her, and which, if successful, will marry her.

It is odd that although Russell seems to acknowledge this in the passage, he fails to see its implications.[55] Earlier, he had great and amusing fun in ridiculing the idea that the propositions (10a), that he met a man, and (10c), that man is mortal, are about the denoting concepts expressed by 'a man' and 'man'. As he rightly observed in the first case, this can't be so because *what he met* "was a thing, not a concept, an actual man with a tailor and a bank-account or a public-house and a drunken wife." But, as just indicated, the same point applies to the courtship of Miss Smith, whose suitors are each individuals with properties that only individuals, not combinations of individuals, can have. So, if Russell's observations about (10a) are sufficient to show that it isn't about the denoting concept expressed by 'a man', a corresponding observation about the propositions expressed by

16a. Brown and Jones are paying court to Miss Smith.
   b. Every member of the club who has met her is paying court to Miss Smith.

should suffice to show that they are not about the complex conjunction of objects that he imagines to be denoted by the relevant denoting concepts involving *every*. As for the proposition that man is mortal not being about the concept *man*—because what is mortal lives and dies, which the concept *man* does not—an analogous point can be made that the proposition expressed by (17)

17. Every man is mortal, and will live a span of less than 200 years.

---

[55] He also fails to see the implications of a corresponding case involving the collective 'all'. On pp. 76–77, in discussing the kind of conjunction involved in collective understandings, he says: "In such a proposition as 'A and B are two,' there is no logical subject: the assertion is not about A, or about B, nor about the whole composed of both, but strictly and only about A and B. Thus it would seem that assertions are not necessarily *about* single subjects, but may be about many subjects." Why then posit the "collective conjunction" of objects at all?

is not about a complex "conjunction" of all past, present, and future men—because, presumably, such a conjunction is not itself something that is born, lives, and dies (and even if it were, its "life span" would be too long to make (17) true).

What is true of Russell's "ontological conjunction" is equally true of his "ontological disjunction," needed for the denotation of the denoting concept expressed by ⌜some F⌝—supposedly illustrated by his example above, that Miss Smith will marry Brown or Jones. About this he says:

> This [complex object] is what I shall call the *constant* disjunction, since here either Brown is denoted, or Jones is denoted, but the alternative is undecided. This is to say, our proposition is now equivalent to a disjunction of propositions, namely "Miss Smith will marry Brown, or she will marry Jones." She will marry *some* one of the two, and the disjunction [i.e., "Brown or Jones"] denotes a particular one of them, though it may denote either particular one.[56]

This description is incoherent, and inconsistent with what I quoted above from section 62—namely, that the denoting concept *some man* (the complex denotation of which Russell is here, in section 59, explaining to be a "constant disjunction" of objects) does *not* denote any individual man, but rather denotes a complex object in which all men past and present are somehow combined. But surely Miss Smith is *not* about to marry this decrepit entity. Nor does it make sense to say, as Russell does in section 59, that either Brown is denoted or Jones is denoted, "but the alternative is undecided." Undecided by whom—Miss Smith, her father, Fate, Destiny? What he means, I suspect, is that although Brown isn't specifically denoted and Jones isn't either, one or the other of them is (nonspecifically) denoted. But this makes no sense. Here, as elsewhere, it is hard to resist the conclusion that Russell can't keep his story straight, and that his theory of denoting concepts is an inextricable tangle of insights, problems, and implausibilities.

So far I haven't said anything about what he takes to be the special case of the denoting concept expressed by ⌜the F⌝, to which he devotes section 63. It is with some relief that one finds him here dispensing with the mysteries of ontological conjunction/disjunction. This denoting concept, it seems, denotes an individual—the unique individual of which F is true.

> The word *the*, in the singular, is correctly employed only in relation to a class-concept of which there is only one instance. We speak of *the* King, *the* Prime Minister, and so on (understanding *at the present time*); and in such cases there is a method of denoting one single definite term by means of a concept, which is not given us by any of our other five words.[57]

[56] Russell (1903a), p. 58.
[57] Ibid., p. 62.

To this Russell adds an account of identity statements according to which (i) the singular referring expressions flanking the identity sign in (18) designate one and the same man, and (ii) what the identity relation is predicated of—i.e., *what is said to be identical* by true propositions expressed by sentences of this sort—is always an object and itself.

18a. Mark Twain = Mark Twain
   b. Mark Twain = Samuel Clemens
   c. The author of *Life on the Mississippi* = Mark Twain
   d. The author of *Life on the Mississippi* = the author of *The Adventures of Tom Sawyer*

About this, Russell says:

> The connection of denoting with the nature of identity is important, and helps, I think, to solve some rather serious problems. The question whether identity is or is not a relation, and even whether there is such a concept at all, is not easy to answer. For, it may be said, identity cannot be a relation, since, where it is truly asserted we have only one term, whereas two terms are required for a relation. . . . Nevertheless identity must be something. . . . Thus identity must be admitted, and the difficulty as to the two terms of a relation must be met by a sheer denial that two different terms are necessary. There must always be a referent and a relatum, but these need not be distinct; and where identity is affirmed, they are not so.[58]

At long last, Russell has found a denoting concept and denotatum that fits the general conception into which he tries so hard to force his other denoting concepts. The denoting concept *the so-and-so* denotes something x that is an argument of the property or relation occurring as a non-denoting concept in the proposition in which the concept *the so-and so* occurs as a denoting concept; hence x is among the subjects of the predication the proposition encodes. Though Russell's official doctrine maintains that this is true for all denoting concepts, the only denoting concepts for which he manages to provide a verifying analysis are those expressed using 'the'. A further virtue of this analysis of definite descriptions is that it explains the informativeness of the propositions expressed by (18c) and (18d), and their distinctness from the proposition commonly expressed by (18a) and (18b)—even though in all three propositions the identity relation is predicated of the same object and itself.[59] Russell does not address the puzzle of how sentences (18a) and (18b) can express the same proposition, if propositions are meanings.

Another question not addressed by his analysis is "What does the denoting concept expressed by ⌈the F⌉ denote when F is true either of nothing, or of more than one thing?" In such cases, he must say either (i) that it

[58] Ibid., pp., 63–64.
[59] See section 64.

fails to denote anything, or (ii) that it denotes something other than what it denotes when F is true of exactly one thing. Since Russell rejects the empty set, it is not a candidate—though, when F is true of several things, some ontologically complex entity composed of those things could be chosen. Whereas (i) would be a further counterexample to his rough and ready generalization that all denoting concepts denote something, (ii) further conflicts with his view that the denotation of such a concept is always what the proposition containing it is about (by being one of the subjects of predication). Though this worry about 'the' is not the most serious worry facing Russell's problematic 1903 theory of denotation, it conforms to what was, shortly after its completion, his own assessment of it as a work in progress, with much about which to remain concerned.

4.4. Names, Negative Existentials, and Denoting

Russell's 1903 theory of denotation was also one of two specifically logico-linguistic theses entangled with the ontological promiscuity of *The Principles of Mathematics*. The other was his doctrine that proper names— e.g., 'Socrates', 'Moore', 'London', 'Carthage', 'Zeus', and 'Lucifer'—refer to objects (their bearers), which are constituents of the propositions expressed by sentences containing the names. Unlike Frege, who took such names to express descriptive senses the contents of which varied from speaker to speaker, Russell took names to be mere tags for items with which one was cognitively acquainted. Although variants of this idea would remain an enduring feature of his thought throughout his career, his notion of acquaintance during this early period was very broad— covering the people and things with whom or which one is personally familiar, those of whom or which one has heard, or read, as well as beings like Romulus and Remus, who may once have been thought (by some) to genuinely exist, but who are now recognized to be mythical. As a consequence, whenever N could be recognized by ordinary criteria to be a name that could occur as a constituent of a meaningful sentence S, the proposition expressed by S must, Russell thought, contain the bearer of N as a constituent.

This doctrine about names may have been among the factors leading to his formulations of the passages in *The Principles of Mathematics* in which he gives the (slightly exaggerated) impression of accepting A2 and UB_{Sing}.

A2.   Let A be any meaningful singular term (name or definite description) that can occur as indicated in ⌜A is not a term⌝, ⌜There is no such thing as A⌝, and ⌜A is not⌝. If these sentences are meaningful, then the propositions expressed by the following sentences are all true: ⌜The proposition that A is not a term denies the termhood of A, and so is *about* A⌝, ⌜The proposition that there is no such thing as A denies that there is such a thing as A, and so is *about* A⌝, and ⌜The proposition that A is not denies the being of A, and so is *about* A⌝.

But if that is so, then the propositions expressed by ⌜A is a term⌝, ⌜There is such thing as A⌝, and ⌜A is⌝ are also true. So, if ⌜A is not a term⌝, ⌜There is no such thing as A⌝, and ⌜A is not⌝ are meaningful, they must be false.

UB$_{\text{Sing}}$ For any meaningful singular term (name or definite description) A that can occur as indicated in the meaningful sentences ⌜A is (or is not) a term⌝, ⌜A is (or has being)⌝, ⌜A is not (or does not have being)⌝, and ⌜There is (no) such thing as A⌝, the sentences ⌜A is not a term⌝, ⌜A is not (or does not have being)⌝, and ⌜There is no such thing as A⌝ all express false propositions, while their positive counterparts express true propositions.

However, the doctrine about names cannot have been the whole story, since (i) A2 and UB$_{\text{Sing}}$ also cover cases involving definite descriptions, and (ii) the passages in question give the further (somewhat exaggerated) impression that Russell subscribed to A1, A3, and UB$_{\text{Plu}}$ in the same breath in which he subscribed to A2 and UB$_{\text{Sing}}$.

A1. Since one can mention chimeras, Homeric gods, four-dimensional spaces, and the like, they must be terms, and so have being.

A3. Let B be any meaningful plural or quantificational expression that can occur as indicated in ⌜B's are not terms⌝, ⌜There are no such things as B's⌝, and ⌜B's are not⌝. If these sentences are meaningful, then the propositions expressed by the following sentences are all true: ⌜The proposition that B's are not terms denies the termhood of B's, and so is *about* B's⌝, ⌜The proposition that there are no such things as B's denies that there are such things as B's, and so is *about* B's⌝, and ⌜The proposition that B's are not denies the being of B's, and so is *about* B's⌝. But if that is so, then the propositions expressed by ⌜B's are terms⌝, ⌜There are such things as B's⌝, and ⌜B's are⌝ are also true. So, if ⌜B's are not terms⌝, ⌜There are no such things as B's⌝, and ⌜B's are not⌝ are meaningful, they must be false.

UB$_{\text{Plu}}$ For any meaningful plural or quantificational expression B which can occur as indicated in the meaningful sentences ⌜B's are (or are not) terms⌝, ⌜B's are (or have being)⌝, ⌜B's are not (or do not have being)⌝, and ⌜There are (no) such things as B's⌝, the sentences ⌜B's are not terms⌝, ⌜Bs are not (or do not have being)⌝, and ⌜There are no such things as B's⌝ all express false propositions, while their positive counterparts express true propositions.

It is time to sort this out.

First consider the restriction UB$_{\text{N}}$ of UB$_{\text{Sing}}$ in which A is required to be a proper name N.

UB$_{\text{N}}$. For any proper name N that can occur as indicated in the meaningful sentences ⌜N is (or is not) a term⌝, ⌜N is (or has being)⌝, ⌜N is not (or does not have being)⌝, and ⌜There is (no) such thing as N⌝, the sentences ⌜N is not a term⌝, ⌜N is not (or does not have being)⌝, and ⌜There is no such thing as N⌝ all express false propositions, while their positive counterparts express true propositions.

One can reach UB_N by appealing to A2 as stated, or by invoking the slightly different form of argument indicated in $A2_N$.

A2_N.   Let N be a proper name that can occupy the indicated position in ⌜N is not a term⌝, ⌜There is no such thing as N⌝, and ⌜N is not⌝. If these sentences are meaningful, they must express propositions p, q, and r, one of the constituents of each of which is the bearer of N. Since p, q, and r have being, this constituent must also have being. So, if ⌜N is not a term⌝, ⌜There is no such thing as N⌝, and ⌜N is not⌝ are meaningful, they must be false.

Since we have already refuted the unrestricted versions of A2 and the UB_{Sing} using an example involving a definite description, the restricted versions $A2_N$ and the UB_N have the advantage of being so far unrefuted. Since it is unclear that a meaningful proper name can be introduced using the description 'the false proposition here expressed by the sentence labeled 'UB_N,'' without first showing, independently, that the proposition in question is false, it does not appear that the restricted thesis can be refuted in the same way.

With this in mind, let us return to the unrestricted A1–A3, and UB_{Sing} and UB_{Plu}, which should be assessed together. I have already indicated that, though some of his formulations were incautious, Russell was not really committed to the full force of A2, A3, UB_{Sing}, or UB_{Plu}. However, he was committed to A1 plus a very expansive view of what is involved in mentioning something. Taking the truth of ⌜Any proposition that mentions A is about A, and vice versa⌝ for granted, we may formulate versions of A2 and A3 that he would have found acceptable as follows.

A2_A.   Let A be any meaningful singular term (name or definite description) that can occur as indicated in (i) ⌜A is not a term⌝, (ii) ⌜There is no such thing as A⌝, and (iii) ⌜A is not (does not have being)⌝. If ⌜The propositions expressed by (i), (ii), and (iii) are *about* A⌝ is true, then the propositions expressed by (i), (ii), and (iii) are false, and the propositions expressed by ⌜A is a term⌝, ⌜There is such thing as A⌝, and ⌜A is (has being)⌝ are true.

A3_A.   Let B be any meaningful plural or quantificational expression that can occur as indicated in (i) ⌜B's are not terms⌝, (ii) ⌜There are no such things as B's⌝, and (iii) ⌜B's are not (do not have being)⌝. If ⌜The propositions expressed by (i), (ii), and (iii) are *about* B's⌝ is true, then the propositions expressed by (i), (ii), and (iii) are false, and the propositions expressed by ⌜B's are terms⌝, ⌜There are such things as B's⌝, and ⌜B's are (have being)⌝ are true.

From these, plus expansive claims about what can be mentioned and/or what various propositions are about, we can draw expansive ontological conclusions.

We know, of course, that Russell was committed to Homeric gods. One way in which this commitment may have arisen is from acceptance of 'Zeus and Athena are among those spoken about in the stories told by Homer' and 'Zeus and Athena are gods'. However, Russell's ontological commitments were not, I think, exclusively tied to his acceptance of sentences containing proper names for fictional or mythical characters. Many such characters, though lacking proper names, are just as mentionable as Zeus and Athena—e.g., the three witches whose prophesies haunted Macbeth, the nine Nazgûl searching for the ring of power in *The Lord of the Rings*, the giant in "Jack and the Beanstalk," the ghosts of Christmas past, present, and future in "A Christmas Carol," and a great many more. If Homer's tales were enough to generate Russell's commitment to the gods of Mount Olympus, then the tales of Shakespeare, Tolkien, Tabart, and Dickens should be sufficient to guarantee the being of witches, Nazgûl, giants, and ghosts—to name just a few. Does it make a difference whether the tales were told as fiction, as opposed to being, at least initially, believed to be true? Nothing in *Principles of Mathematics* so indicates. Can't one mention the planet Vulcan and the substance phlogiston, postulated by false empirical theories, every bit as much as one can mention Zeus or Athena? If so, then Russell's early ontological commitments can be pushed a long way.

In traveling this road, I have placed heavy weight on fictional characters, dramatic roles, legendary figures, and similar "information-theoretic" things. This raises an important issue that must be addressed in understanding Russell. On the one hand, I, like nearly all commentators on *Principles of Mathematics*, have characterized its ontological claims as highly expansive. On the other hand, it ought to be uncontroversial, and not ontologically contentious, to recognize the existence of fictional characters, dramatic roles, and figures of legend. Does anyone without a special philosophical ax to grind doubt such things? If not, how can Russell's commitment to them be properly characterized as ontologically expansive?

The answer involves the contrast between the sense in which Russell is committed to these things and the sense in which commitment to them is, or ought to be, commonsensical. The commonsensical commitment, which involves no distinction between existence and mere being, puts the existence of these things on a par with the existence of the things of which they are parts—books and their chapters, plays and their acts, movies, poems, stories, legends, and theories. These wholes may be thought of as contents of "texts" in an extended sense. They are abstract representational objects that come into being when they are created by us. Particular concrete instances of these abstract contents are bound volumes on bookshelves, live performances, old cans of film, compact discs, sequences of spoken sounds, and inscriptions on paper. Characters—like Zeus, Athena, the three witches haunting Macbeth, the Nazgûl and their mounts, the giant slain by Jack, the ghosts of Christmas who frighten Scrooge—are entities of this sort; they are abstract representational things.[60] Although some are *portrayed* as gods, witches, undying horsemen on an evil mission, giants, or ghosts—and are *said* in the relevant "texts" to be such—none of them *is* any of these kinds of thing, and so none is in the extension of any of the relevant concepts. Consequently, admitting their existence doesn't mean admitting that gods, witches, undying horsemen, giants, or ghosts exist, or have being, *in any sense*.[61] Because they exist, we can agree with Russell that they can be and often are mentioned, and hence that there are propositions about them. Where he came to grief is in failing to distinguish the properties such characters are portrayed as having from the properties they really have.

When he (and Meinong) talked of these things, he (they) *did* think of them as members of the extensions of the relevant concepts—and hence as gods, ghosts, monsters, n-dimensional spaces, golden mountains, and the like. For every such Russellian commitment there will be a concept F which, even if it fails to be true of any existing thing, will, on his account, be true of one or more things that have being. Thus, in all such cases ⌜There is at least one F⌝ will be true. Similarly, the denoting concepts ⌜all F's⌝, ⌜every F⌝, ⌜any F⌝, ⌜an F⌝, ⌜some F⌝, ⌜at least one F⌝, as well as others, will, on Russell's theory, denote "conjunctive" or "disjunctive" ontological complexes which themselves have being. As a result, the propositions expressed by ⌜All F's are G⌝, ⌜Every F is G⌝, ⌜Any F is G⌝, ⌜An F is G⌝, ⌜Some F is G⌝, and ⌜At is least one F is G⌝ will always be true when the predicate G expresses the property *having being*, and will typically be true for some choices of G that express other properties that things that merely have being can have—such as being *mentioned* or *thought about*, or being *similar*, or *related in a certain way*, to something else (whether existent or nonexistent). The only case in which all such propositions are false for Russell is when F isn't true of anything at all (existent or nonexistent). So, whenever he was inclined to accept the truth of any such proposition, he had to admit the truth of ⌜There is at least one F⌝. This is how Russell's theory of denoting concepts became entangled with the independent factors pushing him to accept the highly expansive and problematic ontology of *Principles of Mathematics*.

---

[60] Characters are representational in the sense of being part of stories, plays, legends and the like, which represent *them* as having various properties. It is in virtue of this that the stories, etc., have truth conditions. Since often the characters themselves—which are mere creations—don't really have the properties they are represented to have, the truth conditions of the larger representational text are not satisfied. In fiction we don't expect them to be satisfied, but treat the text as a kind of pretense.

[61] See Nathan Salmon (1998) for a well-worked-out version of a view of this general sort.

The determiner 'the' was, of course, a bit of a special case for Russell, since when there is exactly one thing of which F is true, he took that thing to be the denotation of the concept expressed by ⌜the F⌝. As we have seen, he left it unclear what its denotation is when this is not so; when F is true of several things, there is room to treat the denotation as one of his complex objects, but when F is true of nothing, he had little choice but to take it to fail to denote. Let us, in light of this, generalize the latter case to cover the former as well.

With this in mind, consider (19).

19a. The author of *Principia Mathematica* was born in 1872.
  b. There is such a thing as the author of *Principia Mathematica* / The author of *Principia Mathematica* has being.

Since Russell and Whitehead wrote *Principia Mathematica* together, the extension of the class-concept expressed by 'author of *Principia Mathematica*' contains at least two individuals, and the proposition expressed by (19a) is, by Russell's lights, false. Of course, some might be unaware of the joint authorship, and others—even if they are aware—can surely imagine the book being written by a single author. In light of this, one may wonder whether one can mention, or think about, *the* (unique) author of *Principia Mathematica*. Presumably one could do so if an elaborate fiction had been written in which the central character was portrayed as being the unique author. If this were sufficient for one to mention or think about the character portrayed as "the unique author of *Principia Mathematica*," then A1 plus the failure to distinguish the properties the character really has from the properties it is portrayed as having would generate the absurd results that (19b) is true and that the denoting concept *the author of Principia Mathematica* denotes exactly one thing—which is impossible, since the concept expressed by 'author of *Principia Mathematica*' is, as we know, true of both Russell and Whitehead. This may be taken as a cautionary tale, if one is needed, about the wisdom of combining A1 with expansive claims about what one can mention that do not take the special nature of talk about the fictional into account.

The examples in (20) carry the same lesson.

20a. The author of *Principles of Mathematics* was born in 1872.
  b. There were two coauthors of *The Principles of Mathematics* / The two coauthors of *The Principles of Mathematics* have being.

The proposition expressed by (20a) is true, because Russell, who was born in 1872, wrote *The Principles of Mathematics* by himself. On his 1903 theory of denoting, this means that the denoting concept *the author of The Principles of Mathematics* denotes only him, which in turn requires him to be the only one in the extension of the class-concept 'author of *The Principles of Mathematics*'. However, if it is also possible to *mention* the two coauthors of that work—after reading a historical fiction in which two characters are so portrayed—Russellian principles will, as before, lead to absurdity.

The examples in (21) seem to be of a different sort.

21a. Plane figures that are round and square are round.
   b. The set of all and only non-self-membered sets has members.

Since the supposed figures and the supposed set are not part of any legend or fiction, it would be implausible to take uses of these sentences to *mention* real characters that are portrayed as having properties—*being round and square,* or *containing all and only non-self-membered sets*—that nothing could have. Best in these cases simply to deny that uses of (21a) or (21b) mention anything and to affirm the truth of (22a) and (22b).

22a. There are no such things as plane figures that are round and square.
   b. There is no set of non-self-membered sets.

Even in 1903, Russell would have agreed. What he didn't then see was how to relate his correct treatment of this case to his incorrect treatment of others.

4.5. The Problem of the Unity of the Proposition

At the end of section 4.1, I mentioned a pair of elements that Russell, Moore, and Frege all took to be essential to their conception of propositions. The first element is that propositions are *intentional*—by which I mean that they are *about* certain things, which they *represent* as being one way or another, and so are properly characterized as *true* (false) iff those things are (or are not) the way they are represented to be. The second element is that the intentionality of propositions is in no way derivative from, or attributable to, conceptually prior cognitive activities of agents who entertain them. On the contrary, since propositions are the *primary* bearers of intentionality, the secondary intentionality of cognitive acts or states results from the cognitive apprehension of propositions. In short, for Russell, Moore, and Frege, propositions are intrinsically representational abstract objects the essential nature of which is entirely independent of conscious agents, and the apprehension of which provides the basis of all cognition.

The problem of the unity of the proposition for Russell was to explain what propositions are in a way that makes clear how they can have the properties this conception requires of them. Since propositions are the meanings of sentences, which are themselves structured complexes of meaningful parts, he took them to be structured complexes of entities that are the meanings of those parts. In the simplest of sentences, like (23), the subject expression is used by the speaker to designate something that the other part of the sentence, the predicate, is used to say, or assert, something about.

23. Socrates is human.

Similarly, Russell thought, one part of the *proposition* expressed by the sentence—the concept/property humanity—is applied to, or asserted of, the other part of the proposition—(the man) Socrates. This was Russell's model for all propositions.

> In every proposition . . . we may make an analysis into something asserted and something about which the assertion is made.[62]

Although there are problems with this idea, there is also something correct and revealing about it. When *we* agents say of something—e.g., Socrates—that it is so-and-so—e.g., that he is human—we can be thought of as asserting the property being so-and-so—e.g., *being human* (a.k.a. *humanity*)—of that thing. In so doing *we agents represent* the subject of our assertion (Socrates) as being a certain way (*human*). It is because of this that the performance that is our assertion that Socrates is human has truth conditions; it is true iff that which it represents (Socrates) is as it/he is represented to be (*human*). All of this is plausible and commonsensical. However, for Russell, it was also something to be explained in terms of the conceptually prior properties of propositions. Since for him, propositions are both the things asserted and the primary bearers of intentionality, what he did, in effect, was to replace this commonsense talk about what *we do*—assert of things that they are so-and-so, and thereby represent them as being certain ways—with talk about what propositions "do," with the result that propositions are seen as the fundamental bearers of truth conditions.

The problem of the unity of the proposition is, at base, to spell out how it is that propositions can be properly thought to do these things—assert and represent—and thereby to have truth conditions. Regarding the proposition expressed by (23)—*that Socrates is human*—in which the concept *humanity* is "asserted" of the term Socrates, Russell says something puzzling in attempting to explain how this relation of "assertion" between humanity and Socrates is to be understood.

> Thus, we shall say that 'Socrates is human' is a proposition having only one term; of the remaining components of the proposition, one is the verb, the other is a *predicate*.[63]

The term is Socrates, and the predicate is humanity. What is the verb? Russell returns to this a few pages later with the following difficult remarks.

> It may be asked whether everything that, in the logical sense we are concerned with, is a verb, expresses a relation or not. It seems plain that, if we were right in holding that [23] is a proposition having only one term, *the 'is' in the proposition cannot express a relation in the ordinary sense [my emphasis]*. In fact, subject-predicate sentences are distinguished by just this non-relational character. Nevertheless, a relation between Socrates and humanity is certainly *implied*, and it is very difficult to conceive the proposition as expressing no relation at all. We may perhaps say that it is a relation, although it is

---

[62] Russell (1903a), p. 43.
[63] Ibid., 45.

distinguished from other relations in that *it does not permit itself to be regarded as an assertion concerning either of its terms indifferently, but only as an assertion concerning the referent [my emphasis]*.[64]

These remarks are confusing. Though Russell seems to be talking about expressions, he is really talking about what they stand for. His concern is that if Socrates and humanity are constituents of the proposition, then it would seem that 'is' must stand for a "verb"—i.e., a special kind of relation that "binds the two constituents together" in a propositional unity by relating them. However, Russell is concerned that the "verb" not be seen as relating two *terms* of the proposition—as the relation *instantiates* does in the proposition that Socrates instantiates wisdom. In my opinion, this complication is unnecessary. He would have done better to have said that the proposition expressed by (23) has two constituents, Socrates and humanity, but that the latter is related in a special way to the former, which allows it to be "asserted" of the former. In the *sentence*, the copula 'is' marks the fact that the predicate is "asserted" of the referent of the name 'Socrates'. In the *proposition* no extra relation, expressed by 'is', is needed as a constituent. However, *something* about the proposition indicates that, in it, humanity is "asserted" of Socrates. What is it? This is what Russell is struggling with.

The nature and identity of Russell's elusive propositional "verbs" come up in his tangled discussion of verbs vs. verbal nouns—e.g., 'die' vs. 'death'.

> It is plain that the concept that occurs in the verbal noun is the very same as that which occurs as verb. . . . But . . . there is a further point. By transforming the verb, as it occurs in a proposition [i.e., as concept, rather than as term], into a verbal noun, the whole proposition can be turned into a single logical subject, *no longer asserted and no longer containing in itself truth or falsehood.* But here too, there seems to be no possibility of maintaining that the logical subject which results is a different entity from the proposition. "Caesar died" and "the death of Caesar" will illustrate this point.[65]

Russell's idea is (i) that 'Caesar died' and 'the death of Caesar' stand for the same proposition, which (of course) contains a propositional "verb," (ii) that when this proposition occurs as a "logical subject" (predication target) in another proposition, the "verb" doesn't function as it does when the proposition occurs unembedded (and so "is asserted"), and (iii) that when occurring as a "logical subject" the verb somehow continues to "bind the constituents of the proposition together" *without* (incredibly) doing so in a way that renders the proposition intentional, and so the bearer of truth conditions—as evidenced by the absurdity of the claim that *the death of Caesar is true*, as well as the claim *that it is false*. Hence,

---

[64] Ibid., p. 49.
[65] Ibid., p. 48, my emphasis.

Russell seems to think, it is precisely the mysterious functioning of the propositional "verb"—which is lost when the proposition is made a logical subject—that is the source of intentionality.[66]

Russell's investigation of propositions as logical subjects is made more difficult by running it together with the vexed question of the relationship between 'the death of Caesar'—which can, at least sometimes, be used to designate an *event* in which Caesar dies rather than a proposition—with the nominal complement 'that Caesar died', which is the more natural linguistic means of making the proposition expressed by 'Caesar died' a Russellian "logical subject." This is seen by substituting 'that Caesar died' for 'the death of Caesar' in the following passage.

> If we ask: What is asserted in the proposition "Caesar died"? the answer must be "the death of Caesar is asserted." [Better: *that Caesar died* is asserted.] In that case, it would seem, it is the death of Caesar which is true or false [Better: *that Caesar died* is true or false]; *and yet neither truth nor falsehood belongs to a mere logical subject. . . . There appears to be an ultimate notion of assertion, given by the verb, which is lost as soon as we substitute a verbal noun, and is lost when the proposition in question is made the subject of some proposition.*[67]

When we now apply Russell's reasoning to the examples in (24) we get a result at variance from the one he arrives at.

24a. Caesar died.
   b. That Caesar died is widely believed.

Although this is not a case involving a verb and a verbal noun ('die' and 'death'), it is a case in which the proposition expressed by one sentence is what Russell calls "the logical subject" of the proposition expressed by another sentence. However, when applied to (24), his comment that "neither truth nor falsehood belongs to a mere logical subject" is problematic, since the logical subject of (24b) is the true proposition *that Caesar died*.[68]

---

[66] Since Russell regards it as "self-contradictory" to suppose that any entity cannot be the subject of predication, he is driven to claim that propositions can occur as "logical subjects"—even though he thinks that when they do, they lose something crucial to their normal functioning. See p. 48.

[67] Ibid., p. 48, my emphasis.

[68] Russell should have recognized this, since he was aware that his problem was not limited to the examples that don't involve verbal nouns. He says (p. 48):

> This does not depend upon grammatical form: for if I say "*Caesar died* is a proposition," I do not assert that Caesar did die, and an element which is present in [the proposition] "Caesar died" has disappeared. Thus the contradiction which was to have been avoided, of an entity [the proposition that Caesar died] which cannot be made a logical subject, appears to have here become inevitable. The difficulty, which seems to be inherent in the very nature of truth and falsehood, is one with which I do not know how to deal satisfactorily.

Russell was here in a tangle, and knew it.

It is, of course, correct that when one proposition is the logical subject of another, *asserting* the latter needn't involve *asserting* the former. But why is this worth noting? You would think it so if you thought that *assertion* (in some sense carried by a fully functioning propositional "verb") was what distinguishes a genuinely intentional proposition from a mere collection of its constituents. For under this conception, failing to *assert* a proposition—e.g., the proposition (24a)—that is the logical subject of another proposition—e.g., the proposition (24b)—would threaten the intentionality of the former.

What these observations show is that the relation ___*is asserted of*___, as illustrated by 'Humanity is asserted of Socrates' and 'Dying is asserted of Caesar', is not the relation that holds between *humanity* and Socrates in the proposition expressed by (23), and between *dying* and Caesar in the proposition expressed by (24a), in virtue of which those propositions are genuinely intentional entities. More cautiously, it is not that relation, when 'assertion' is understood in the ordinary way, as indicating something *agents* do. Though Russell was perplexed and confused by the problem of propositional unity, he did, of course, realize this much.

> The most obvious course would be to say that the difference between an asserted and an unasserted proposition is not logical, but psychological. In the sense in which false propositions may be asserted, this is doubtless true. *But there is another sense of assertion, very difficult to bring clearly before the mind, and yet quite undeniable, in which only true propositions are asserted.* True and false propositions alike are in some sense entities, and are in some sense capable of being logical subjects; but when a proposition happens to be true, it has a further quality, over and above that which it shares with false propositions, and it is this further quality which is what I mean by assertion in a logical as opposed to a psychological sense.[69]

Since there is no ordinary sense in which only true propositions can be asserted, it is quite mysterious what Russell's "assertion in the logical" sense was supposed to mean. Worse, no matter what it means, no notion of assertion can do the job that needs doing. We are looking for a relation holding between an n-place property occurring in a proposition as a concept and the constituents of the proposition that occur there as terms (or, alternatively, the denotations of constituents occurring there as denoting concepts). Crucially, the needed relation must hold in order for the proposition to be intentional, in the sense of representing its terms (or the denotations of its denoting concepts) as being a certain way. Since both true and false propositions are intentional in this sense, the relation Russell needs to explain the unity of the proposition can't be one that is found only in true propositions. Since both propositions that have been asserted by someone and those that haven't been asserted are genuinely

---

[69] Ibid., pp. 48–49.

intentional, no notion of assertion, whether "logical" or "psychological," will provide the needed explanation.

Fortunately, there is another relation at hand, though, as we shall see, it only postpones Russell's day of reckoning. To grasp what it is, we need to go back to the acts *agents* perform with sentences and sub-sentential expressions. Assertion is one such act. But so are referring and predicating. With this in mind, consider the sentences in (25).

> 25a. Socrates is human.
> b. If Socrates is human, then Socrates is mortal.
> c. That Socrates is human is widely believed.
> d. I wonder whether Socrates is human.
> e. Is it true that Socrates is human?
> f. Is Socrates human?

Whereas one who assertively utters (25a) asserts that Socrates is human, one who assertively utters (25b), (25c), or (25d) does not assert this, while one who uses (25e) or (25f) to ask a question doesn't assert anything. In each case, however, the speaker uses the name 'Socrates' to refer to Socrates, and the predicate 'is human' to represent him as being a certain way. In (25a) Socrates is asserted to be that way; in (25b) it is asserted that if he is that way, then he is mortal; in (25c) it is asserted that he is widely believed to be that way; in (25d) I indicate that I wonder whether he is that way, and in (25e) and (25f), I ask whether he is that way. In each case part of what a speaker does in performing his or her overall speech act (of asserting, questioning, etc.) is to represent Socrates as being human by *predicating* the property humanity of him. Since, for Russell, the intentional properties of the overall speech acts performed are derived from the propositions expressed, including in these cases the proposition that Socrates is human, the relation he needs to "unify" that proposition is predication. In the proposition that Socrates is human, *humanity* is predicated (not asserted) of Socrates.

The problem is that predication, as I have explained it, is something that agents do; so, what Russell needs is "a logical sense of predication." It is, admittedly, difficult to see what this could amount to. Indeed, it may have been this difficulty that led Russell to think of assertion, rather than predication, as the crucial "unifying" relation. Since, for him, propositions are objective entities, entirely independent of agents, the intentional properties of propositions are *sui generis*, and conceptually prior to the secondary intentionality of the cognitive activities of agents, linguistic or otherwise. It is, therefore, not surprising that when searching for his notion of "assertion in the logical sense," he was irresistibly drawn to the notion of truth.

One point on which he never wavered was that whether or not a potential truth bearer is, in fact, true is entirely independent of human or other cognizing agents. By contrast, it is not clear that a relation of predication holding between a property, occurring as a concept in a proposition, and other elements of the proposition (or their denotations) has the ontological independence from the cognitive activities of agents required by his robustly Platonic conception of propositions. Recognizing that "logical assertion"—*thought of as truth*—did have the desired independence, he may have looked to it to somehow provide propositional unity. The obvious problem, of course, is that no relation that fails to apply to false propositions can possibly do the job of "unifying" them. In addition, since, for Russell at this stage, there is no intentionality without propositions, and hence no truth to be appealed to prior to having been given propositions, the unifying notion he needs is one that is prior to the one he employed. At this stage of our investigation, we do better by shifting the burden of "unifying" propositions to predication, while deferring until later the discussion of whether propositions so conceived can have whatever ontological independence from agents turns out to be needed.

This brings us to Russell's most famous remark on propositional unity.

> Consider, for example, the proposition "A differs from B." The constituents of this proposition, if we analyze it, appear to be only A, difference, B. *Yet these constituents, thus placed side by side, do not reconstitute the proposition. The difference which occurs in the proposition actually relates A and B, whereas the difference after analysis is a notion which has no connection with A and B.* It may be said that we ought, in the analysis, to mention the relations which difference has to A and B, relations which are expressed by *is* and *from* when we say A is different from B. These relations consist in the fact that A is referent and B relatum with respect to difference. But A, referent, difference, relatum, B, is still merely a list of terms, not a proposition. *A proposition, in fact, is essentially a unity, and when analysis has destroyed the unity, no enumeration of constituents will restore the proposition. The verb, when used as a verb, embodies the unity of the proposition, and is thus distinguishable from the verb considered as a term, though I do not know how to give a clear account of the precise nature of the distinction.*[70]

Russell reiterates this point a few pages later, when he says:

> Owing to the way in which the verb actually relates the terms of a proposition, every proposition has a unity which renders it distinct from the sum of its constituents.[71]

A central point in these passages is that there is more to the proposition *that A differs from B* than the fact that its constituents are A, B, and difference. In addition, there is both the manner in which these constituents occur in the proposition, and how their occurring as they do *represents* the terms of the proposition as being a certain way. Following my earlier suggestion, we may express this by saying that, in the proposition, difference

[70] Ibid., 49–50, my emphasis.
[71] Ibid., 52.

is *predicated* of A and B, with the result that they are *represented as being different*. In a mere list, nothing is *predicated* of anything, and so the list doesn't *represent* the items listed as being one way rather than another. Consequently propositions are true or false, whereas lists are neither.

Though I have given examples above illustrating what predication is, I haven't offered an *analysis* of it, nor is it clear that there is an informative analysis to be given. Unfortunately, what Russell says in the passage—namely that "the difference [relation] which occurs in the proposition actually relates A and B"—is of no help, since for a relation R to "actually relate" x and y is, one would have thought, for x to actually bear R to y. Since this brings with it the absurd result that all propositions are true, it isn't what Russell needs. Thus, if we want to preserve any semblance of his view, we must think of the crucial relation—here dubbed "predication"—in another way. Perhaps we don't need *an analysis* of it. After all, some logical and semantic notions, like negation, are primitive. Since this elementary point typically isn't taken to be alarming, it is not obvious that the primitiveness of predication should be. However, whether we take predication to be primitive or not, we know that adding the relation to the proposition that A differs from B *as an extra constituent* would simply reintroduce the problem Russell struggled to solve. Rather, we must hold that the concept *difference* somehow stands in the predication relation to A and B *in the proposition that A differs from B*.

The question for the neo-Russellian is how one should understand this. What is it about a proposition that indicates which constituent is predicated of which things? There seems to be only one remotely plausible answer to this question from a neo-Russellian perspective. Just as it is the structural relations holding among the syntactic constituents of a sentence that *show* how they are to be understood, so, one might think, it must be the structural relations holding among the constituents of the proposition that *indicates* what it predicates of what. Very well, then. What structural features of a proposition *do* show what is predicated of what, and *how*, exactly, do they manage to do that? Consider the proposition expressed by (26), the constituents of which are the relation *identity*, occurring as a term, *difference*, occurring as a concept, and *difference*, occurring again as a term.

26. Identity is different from difference.

In this proposition, the *difference* relation is predicated of *identity* and *difference*. What feature of the proposition shows this?

Consider some candidates for being that proposition.

27a. <difference, <identity, difference>>
 b. {{difference}, {difference, {{identity}, {identity, difference}}}}
 c. <<identity, difference>, difference >
 d. {{{identity}, {identity, difference}}, {{{identity}, {identity, difference}}, difference}}

e. <difference, <difference, identity>>
f. {{difference}, {difference, {{difference}, {difference, identity}}}}
g. <<difference, identity>, difference>
h. {{{difference}, {difference, identity}}, {{{difference}, {difference, identity}}, difference}}

Any of these could be used as a formal model of the Russellian proposition expressed by (26), as could any number of tree structures, two of which are pictured in (28).

28a.

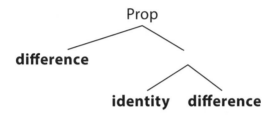

28b.

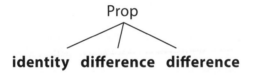

Which of the structures of the sort illustrated by (27) and (28) is the proposition expressed by sentence (26)? Expressed in this direct and uncompromising way, the question seems absurd. The problem is *not* that there is no determinate answer to it. The problem is that it is hard to see how *any formal structure of any of these, or any similar, sorts* could be the proposition we are looking for. The proposition expressed by (26) is something that *represents the relation of identity as being different from the relation of difference*—by virtue of the fact that *difference* is predicated of the two relations. But there is nothing in the sets or sequences of (27), in the tree structures of (28), or in any other formal structure we might construct to organize the constituents of the neo-Russellian proposition which, *by its very nature*, indicates that anything is predicated of anything. Hence, there is *nothing* intrinsic to such structures that makes them representational, and so capable of being true or false. Whatever else these may be, no structures of this sort are the primary bearers of intentionality.

We *could*, if we wished, adopt rules that would allow us to read off the needed information about predication from these structures, and so *interpret* them. To do this would be to *endow* the structures with representational meaning or content, thereby making them bearers of truth and falsity. However, it would *not* make them propositions in any sense that Russell would recognize. For him, propositions are *not* things that *have meanings*, or *get interpretations from us*. Rather, they *are* the meanings that sentences come to express when we initially endow linguistic expressions with meaning, or that we discover when we come to understand a sentence that already has meaning. The real problem posed by Russell's discussion of the unity of the proposition in *The Principles of Mathematics* is that his conception of what propositions are makes it difficult to answer a question he finds no way of avoiding: "*What makes propositions representational, and, thereby, bearers of truth and falsity, as well as things we know, believe, assert, and bear other representational attitudes to?*" This is a question he would struggle with until 1910–12, when, as we shall see in chapter 9, he came to the conclusion that there are no propositions in the sense he previously imagined. This led him to propose, in *The Problems of Philosophy,* an alternative theory of the bearers of truth and falsehood, plus a different analysis of knowing, believing, and asserting.

5. THE ROAD TO "ON DENOTING"

The theory of denoting and related issues involving ontological commitment were matters of concern to Russell in the two years between the publication of *The Principles of Mathematics* in 1903 and the appearance of "On Denoting" in 1905. These concerns, touched on already in Appendix A of *Principles*, were the subject of three unpublished manuscripts written between late 1903 and very early 1905: "On the Meaning and Denotation of Phrases" (1903b), "Points about Denoting" (1903c), and "On Meaning and Denotation" (1903d). These were followed by "The Existential Import of Propositions" (1905a), written late in 1904, and by "Review of Meinong et al., *Untersuchungen zur Gegenstandstheorie und Psychologie*" (1905b). Finally, there was the manuscript "On Fundamentals" (1905c), which Russell began in June of 1905, and on which he was working when he discovered the theory published as "On Denoting" (1905d).[72]

The import of the three unpublished manuscripts in 1903 is found in clarifications of the theory of denoting of *Principles*, a change in Russell's view of some names, and a clear retreat from his earlier expansive ontology. One of the early developments was his explicit recognition of nondenoting definite descriptions—which I indicated above to be implicitly required in *Principles*, in any case. In (1903b) we find

> It is impossible to deny *meaning* [i.e., the expression of a genuine denoting concept] to this phrase ['the present King of France']; it has just as distinct

[72] A good account of Russell's development in this period can be found in Cartwright (1987b).

a meaning as 'the present King of England'. But unlike this latter phrase it denotes nothing [because the denoting concept expressed denotes nothing].[73]

while in (1903d) we find

The same holds of 'the even prime other than 2', 'the rational square root of 2', 'the bed in which Charles I died', and 'the difference between Mr. Arthur Balfour and the present Prime Minister of England'. In all such cases, the meaning [denoting concept] expressed is perfectly intelligible, but nothing whatever is designated.[74]

Although this recognition may have relieved some of the ontological pressure Russell previously felt, its chief import is simply to remove what had been a source of confusion.

The change in his view of names was more substantial. Now, "names" of fictional or legendary characters are taken not to be genuine names at all, but rather "substitutes for descriptions."[75]

These appear to be proper names, but as a matter of fact they are not so. 'Odysseus' may be taken to *mean* 'the hero of the *Odyssey*,' where the meaning of this phrase [i.e., the denoting concept it expresses] is involved, and not the imagined object designated. If the *Odyssey* were history, and not fiction, it would be the designation that was in question: 'Odysseus' would then not express a meaning, but would designate a person, and 'the hero of the *Odyssey*' would not be identical in *meaning* with Odysseus [Russell means the name 'Odysseus'], but would be identical in designation.[76]

At this time, Russell takes genuine names to have reference (designation), but not what he calls "meaning." This doesn't mean they don't make contributions to the meanings of sentences, or other complex constituents, in which they occur. On the contrary, they contribute their bearers to such meanings, including the propositions expressed by sentences. That Russell still takes this to be true of ordinary (nonfictional) names, which he continues to contrast with descriptions, is indicated by the following passages.

'Arthur Balfour' and 'the present Prime Minister of England' differ profoundly. When we make a statement about Arthur Balfour, he himself forms part of the object before our minds, i.e. of the proposition stated. If we say . . . "Arthur Balfour advocates retaliation," that expresses a thought which has for its object a complex containing as a constituent the man himself; no one who does not know the designation of the name 'Arthur Balfour' can understand what we *mean*: the object of thought cannot, by our statement,

---

[73] Russell (1903b), pp. 285–86 of Russell (1994).
[74] Russell (1903d), p. 318 of Russell (1994).
[75] Russell (1903b), p. 285 of Russell (1994).
[76] Russell (1903d), p. 318 in Russell (1994).

be communicated to him. But when we say "the present Prime Minister of England believes in retaliation," it is possible for a person to understand completely what we mean without knowing that Mr. Arthur Balfour is Prime Minister, and without his even having heard of Mr. Arthur Balfour. . . . [I]f he does not know what England is, or what we mean by *present*, or what it is to be Prime Minister, he cannot understand what we mean. This shows that Mr. Arthur Balfour does not form part of our meaning, but that England and the present and being Prime Minister do form part of it.[77]

[Descriptive] phrases [like 'the Prime Minister of England'] may be regarded as names for that which they describe, but they differ from names in the narrow sense by the fact that they do *describe* that which they name. A name in the narrow sense is merely a symbol arbitrarily selected to designate some object.[78]

What Russell is saying in the passage about Odysseus is that fictional names are descriptive, and so aren't really names at all (in the sense in which 'Arthur Balfour' is). The paraphrase he provides for 'Odysseus' is, however, most implausible, because (i) a character in the story who says ⌜Odysseus is F⌝ is surely not to be understood as asserting the proposition expressed by ⌜The hero of the *Odyssey* is F⌝, and (ii) a misguided critic who wrongly claims "Odysseus is not really the hero of the *Odyssey* (a different character is)," may be foolish, but he hasn't contradicted himself. Thus, it is not clear that Russell's new view is really an advance.

Whether or not it frees him from the need to countenance an object to which he would previously have accorded a kind of *being* is also unclear. It does so only if he would be correct in saying that the *Odyssey* has no (main) hero. Since this claim would *not* be correct, Russell still has further to go before he can properly claim an ontological advance. To be sure, his new position no longer requires Odysseus to be a constituent of propositions expressed by sentences containing the name. But, as we saw in discussing the three witches in Macbeth, the source of the conviction that there are fictional characters, named and unnamed, goes deeper than that. The idea that thought and talk involving such characters is genuinely about something—which was central in motivating the ontology of *Principles*—can't be dispelled simply by adopting a descriptive theory of fictional names, while noting that definite descriptions can be meaningful even when they fail to denote anything.

Nevertheless, by early 1905, before he discovered the theory of "On Denoting," Russell believed he had worked his way clear of his earlier ontology. Responding to a paper by Hugh MacColl advocating the recognition of "*non-existences*, that is to say . . . *unrealities* such as *centaurs, nectar, ambrosia, fairies,* [along] with self-contradictions, such as *round squares,*

---

[77] Ibid., pp. 315–16.
[78] Ibid., p. 314.

square circles, flat spheres, etc.,"[79] Russell maintained that realities alone are enough. MacColl's "unrealities" are dismissed as follows.

> Concerning all these we shall simply have to say that they are classes which have no members, so that each of them is identical with the null class. There are no Centaurs: 'x is a Centaur' is false whatever value we give to x. . . . Similarly, there are no round squares. The case of nectar and ambrosia is more difficult, since these seem to be individuals, not classes. But here we must presuppose definitions of nectar and ambrosia; they are substances having such and such properties, which, as a matter of fact, no substances do have. We have thus merely a defining concept for each, without any entity to which the concept applies. In this case, the concept is an entity, but it does not denote anything. To take a simpler case: 'The present King of England' is a complex concept denoting an individual: 'the present King of France' is a similar complex concept denoting nothing. The phrase intends to point out an individual, but fails to do so; it does not point out an unreal individual, but no individual at all. The same explanation applies to mythical personages, Apollo, Priam, etc. These words have a *meaning*, which can be found by looking them up in a classical dictionary; but they have not a *denotation*: there is no entity, real or imaginary, which they point out.[80]

In assessing this passage, it is important to distinguish Russell's ontological progress from his questionable logico-linguistic explanation of it. There are indeed, as he here insists, no centaurs, Greek gods, or substances with the properties attributed to nectar or ambrosia. But just as something more, or other, than a descriptive theory of fictional names is needed to avoid his previous commitment to centaurs and Homeric gods, so something more, or other, than a descriptive theory of substance names is needed to avoid commitment to fictitious or nonexistent substances like nectar and ambrosia. In general, natural kind terms—like 'water', 'gold', 'tiger', 'heat', and 'light'—are not abbreviations for definite descriptions "defining" the various natural kinds—substances, species, etc.—they stand for.[81] Thus, Russell's suggestion that substance and species terms are really disguised descriptions does not suffice to defuse the problems illustrated by terms like 'nectar' and 'ambrosia'.

Aside from questions about the adequacy of Russell's explanations, it is significant that he moved so far from the extravagant ontological views of *The Principles of Mathematics* while, to this point, changing so little of the philosophical logic and philosophy of language of that work. By mid-1905, the theory of denoting had been clarified a bit, but not much more, while

[79] MacColl (1905), p. 308.

[80] Russell (1905a), at p. 100 of Russell (1973).

[81] See Kripke (1972) and Putnam (1970, 1973, 1975). For secondary commentary, see Salmon (1981), Part Two; and Soames (2002), chapter 10, (2005c), pp. 64–68, (2010a), pp. 88–91, and (2007a).

the theory of names had remained essentially intact, except for the special and problematic case of fictional names. This was to change in June of 1905, when Russell was working on his manuscript "On Fundamentals." Here, in the portion of the manuscript prior to his abrupt discovery of the theory of descriptions, he explores three main concerns. First, he narrows what he is willing to regard as acquaintance with an object, thereby limiting both the entities he takes agents to be capable of naming, and the propositions in which those entities occur that agents are capable of apprehending. Second, recognizing the extra epistemological weight this places on the theory of denoting, he explores denoting occurrences of denoting concepts in a manner slightly different from, and in a wider range of cases than, he did in *The Principles of Mathematics.* Finally, this investigation brings him to the concern that brought his theory of denoting concepts to an end, and prompted the new theory of "On Denoting." The concern is over propositions *about* denoting concepts—which, one would suppose from *Principles,* are those in which denoting concepts have *non-denoting occurrences.* It was when Russell discovered that there is a problem with the idea that such occurrences are even possible that he came to regard his earlier theory as hopeless, and straightway developed his new alternative.[82]

Regarding acquaintance—the relation one must have to each of the constituents of a proposition in order to entertain it, or to name any of its constituents—Russell says:

> Thus Jones = the person who inhabits Jones's body. We don't have *acquaintance* with Jones himself, but only with his sensible manifestations. Thus if we think we know propositions about Jones, this is not quite right; we only know propositional functions which he satisfies, unless we *are* Jones.[83]

Passing his otherworldly view of persons as non-perceivable without comment, we may focus on the drastic restriction imposed on the things that may occur as terms in propositions we can entertain. The only such propositions now available are those the terms of which include things we have perceived ourselves, in a sense of 'perceived' narrow enough to rule out perceiving persons, while allowing their bodies to be perceived. Since entertaining such propositions is one of only two ways Russell recognizes by which one can think *about* items in the world, propositions containing denoting concepts now carry most of the burden of our cognitive connection to tangible reality. In addition, many expressions that, by ordinary grammatical standards, count as names are now disqualified from counting as genuine "logically proper" names (as opposed to disguised definite descriptions, varying, one would suppose, from speaker to speaker).

In the passage, Russell says that "if we think we know propositions about Jones, this is not quite right; we only know propositional functions

[82] See Cartwright (1987b) for an excellent extensive discussion.
[83] Russell (1905c), p. 369.

which he satisfies." Read strictly, this would seem to rule out something on which he has previously been insistent—namely, that propositions containing denoting occurrences of the denoting concept expressed by ⌜the F⌝ are *about* the unique thing designated by the description. Since we may well be acquainted with propositions containing such concepts that denote Jones, Russell might here be seen as repudiating the idea that propositions containing denoting occurrences of denoting concepts are *about* the things they denote. Though this would be reading too much into a single comment, the remark does, I think, represent a subtle shift that was occurring in Russell's thinking. He was, by this time, coming to appreciate that the sense in which propositions containing denoting occurrences of the concepts expressed by definite descriptions are genuinely *about* the unique things satisfying the descriptions was rather slight. He was perfectly aware that one could believe such a proposition without *knowing of* anything x that the proposition was about x, and without having any idea what or whom the denoting concept denoted. He also realized that had circumstances been different, the same proposition could have been *about* something other than what it was actually about (without, in many cases, losing its actual truth value).

So in what sense are such propositions about the denotations of descriptions? One might, of course, simply stipulate that, by definition, any proposition containing a denoting occurrence of a denoting concept expressed by a definite description is *about* the unique satisfier of the description (if such there be). But nothing of epistemological or general philosophical importance will follow from such a stipulation, and it is hard to see how there could be much of significance in the offing. Think of it this way: according to Russell, (29a) is logically equivalent to (29b), (29c), and (29d).

29a. The F is G.
   b. Some F is G & at most one thing is F.
   c. Some F is G & some F is such that every F is identical with it.
   d. Something is both F and G, and identical with everything that is F.

Since the latter three don't contain definite descriptions, they don't fall under the imagined stipulation; nor does Russell give any reason to think he would count them as being *about* a unique individual. How, then, could the *aboutness* of (29a) cut any ice? The contents of our cognitive lives would be essentially unchanged if we scrapped definite descriptions altogether, in favor of some translation of the sort indicated here. At any rate, we wouldn't lose any truths or gain any falsehoods. We could, perhaps, extend our arbitrary stipulative definition to cover such cases. But what difference would it make?

Perhaps because of thoughts of this sort, Russell's extensive discussion in "On Fundamentals" of the ways in which items of different sorts can occur as constituents of propositions is formulated without reference to what those propositions are *about*. For example, he had previously defined a *term-accessible position* using the notion of an *occurrence as a term in a proposition*, which involved a claim concerning what the proposition was about. Now, he defines what had been the distinction between term-accessible and other positions as a distinction between *entity occurrences* and *meaning occurrences*. An entity x (of any sort) has an entity occurrence in p iff for any y, there is a proposition p* just like p except for having y where p has x; all other occurrences are meaning occurrences.[84] What had been term occurrences and denoting occurrences of denoting concepts are now *entity* occurrences. Next, he divides *entity* occurrences of what he here calls "denoting complexes" into two subtypes—*primary* and *secondary*.

> When a *denoting* complex A occurs in a complex B [e.g., a proposition], it may occur in such a way that the truth-value of B is unchanged by the substitution of A for anything having the same denotation (for the sake of brevity, it is convenient to regard anything which is not a denoting complex as denoting itself.) This is the case with "the author of *Waverly*" in "Scott was the author of *Waverly*." . . . We will call A a *primary constituent* of B when only the denotation of A is relevant to the truth-value of B, & we will call the occurrence of A a *primary occurrence* in this case; otherwise we will speak of [the occurrence of] A as a *secondary* occurrence.[85]

The distinction between primary and secondary occurrences of a denoting concept is illustrated by the propositions expressed by (30a) and (30b).

30a. Walter Scott was the author of *Waverley*.
  b. The proposition that Walter Scott was the author of *Waverley* is one the truth of which surprised many people.

The occurrence of the denoting concept DC expressed by 'the author of *Waverley*' in the proposition expressed by (30a) is a *primary occurrence*, because substituting the man Walter Scott (who is denoted by DC) for DC results in a true proposition, different from the original, as does substituting any other denoting concept that denotes the same individual that DC does. In contrast, the occurrence of DC in (30b) is a *secondary occurrence* because substituting Walter Scott for DC in this true proposition would result in the false proposition expressed by (30c).

30c. The proposition that Walter Scott was Walter Scott is one the truth of which surprised many people.

At this point Russell turns to what was to become the crucial topic in the manuscript—non-denoting occurrences of denoting concepts. What is such an occurrence? For this, we must return to the vexed notion of aboutness. A non-denoting occurrence of a denoting concept is (roughly put) an occurrence in a proposition that is *not about* what the concept denotes,

---

[84] Ibid., p. 374.
[85] Ibid., 374. Russell here treats 'Scott' as a genuine name.

but rather *is about* the concept itself. An example is the occurrence of the concept DC—*the philosopher who informed Frege of the contradiction in his system*—in the proposition *that DC is a concept*. According to the Russell of *Principles*, this proposition is a singular proposition, containing DC as a constituent, which says *of DC* that it is a concept—which, of course, it is. That this occurrence of DC must be a *non-denoting* occurrence is shown by the fact that if it were, on the contrary, a denoting occurrence, the proposition would tell us something quite different; it would tell us—absurdly— that the philosopher who informed Frege of the contradiction in his system is a concept. Since that philosopher was Bertrand Russell, who was no concept, the proposition would then be false. Hence, the need to distinguish between denoting and non-denoting occurrences of denoting concepts.

However, the need of a defender of the system of *Principles* to make a distinction is one thing; the ability to make it is another. The difficulty is easy to state. Where in propositions do non-denoting concepts occur? According to Russell, they occur in what were formerly called *term-accessible positions*, but are now called *entity positions*. But—and here is the problem— whenever they do so occur, it is the entity denoted, not the denoting concept itself, that is the argument of the predication in the proposition—in the sense of being that to which the predicate must truly apply in order for the proposition to be true. For example, since DC occurs in entity position in the proposition that DC is a concept, the proposition predicates *being a concept* not of DC, but of the philosopher who informed Frege of the contradiction in his system; hence, it is true only if Russell himself is a concept. According to the philosophical logic of *Principles*, whenever one tries to *say of* a denoting concept *the so-and-so* that it is such-and-such, one instead ends up *saying that* the so-and-so is such-and-such (the truth of which requires the denotation of the concept, rather than the concept itself, to be such-and-such).

When Russell discovered this problem, working on the manuscript "On Fundamentals," he immediately took it to be fatal to his previous theory of denoting. It was, there is no denying, a serious problem. But should he really have regarded it as fatal? One corollary of the problem is that, even though we are acquainted with denoting concepts, we cannot name them—since if I could (as I implicitly assumed above) use 'DC' as a name of the concept *the philosopher who informed Frege of the contradiction in his system*, then (according to *Principles*) I could use the sentence 'DC is a concept' to express a truth about that concept, which I can't. In fact, the idea (used by Russell throughout) that one can name a concept—whether it be a denoting concept or not—by italicizing and prefixing the words 'the concept' to a phrase expressing it, is now doubtful. These results are clearly troubling.

If they showed that there could be no propositions about denoting concepts—in the weak sense in which the proposition *that the center of mass of the solar system is a point* is about a certain point—then they would indeed show there to be no such things as the denoting concepts of *The Principles of Mathematics*. However, the results don't show this. Descriptions of denoting concepts expressing what might be called higher-level denoting concepts denoting lower-level concepts are still possible. For example, if I wish to assert a proposition that is true iff the entity expressed by 'the philosopher who informed Frege of the contradiction in his system' is a denoting concept, I need only say, "The meaning of the English description 'the philosopher who informed Frege of the contradiction in his system' is a denoting concept." Rather awkward, to be sure, but nothing so far said about the problem Russell discovered in June 1905 clearly demonstrates it to be untrue.

The puzzle, then, is why, upon discovering the problem, he took it to be fatal. His discussion of this point provides no clear and explicit answer, either in "On Fundamentals" or in "On Denoting" (where the problem becomes the central argument against competitors to the new theory of denoting developed there). There is, however, a powerful, and thoroughly Russellian, line of argument he may have had in mind. What, after all, are denoting concepts supposed to be? For Russell in *Principles*, they are the meanings of denoting phrases. But, he could now ask, "How could they be such meanings?" To understand a denoting phrase, one must be acquainted with its meaning, and *know of* that meaning *that it is the meaning of the phrase*; to understand ⌜the F⌝ one must *know of* a certain meaning M that it is the meaning of ⌜the F⌝. But this is precisely what Russell's discovery shows one cannot know. To *know of* any entity x that it is so-and-so, one must know the singular proposition in which x occurs in entity position as the subject of predication of the concept *so-and-so*. Since, when x is a denoting concept, there is no such proposition, it is impossible to *know of* such a concept that it is the meaning of anything. But surely whatever *is* the meaning of an expression can be known to be so; the idea that M is the meaning of E, even though it is impossible for anyone to ever *know of* M that it is the meaning of E, is, as Russell would surely have insisted, absurd. So, denoting concepts can't be the meanings of anything. Since that was their *raison d'être*, there are no denoting concepts.[86]

There are three crucial assumptions required by this argument. The first is the result that Russell labors to establish, and takes himself to have discovered, in "On Fundamentals"—namely, that denoting concepts that are constituents of a proposition cannot be among the subjects of predication of that proposition. Although I do not believe this assumption to be true, I will postpone further discussion of it until the next chapter, where I examine the central role it plays in "On Denoting."

---

[86] This account of Russell's view of the significance of his discovery in "On Fundamentals" is based in substantial part on the important and illuminating discussion in Salmon (2005) of the Gray's Elegy passage in "On Denoting."

The second assumption concerns the distinction between *knowledge of* and *knowledge that*. On this point, I believe Russell to have been on firmer ground. Although I *know that* the oldest person alive today is older than all other persons alive today, there is no person x *of whom I know* that x is older than all other persons alive today. To know of a particular person x, that x is older than all other persons alive today, I must know the proposition p expressed by 'x is older than all other persons alive today' relative to an assignment to 'x' of that person himself, or herself. Since the contribution to p of 'x', relative to this assignment, is that very person, p is the singular proposition in which that person occurs as subject of the predication *being older than all other persons alive today*. I don't *know of* anyone that he or she is older than everyone else alive today because I don't know any singular proposition of this sort. If, by extension, there are things that are such that I can't know any singular propositions in which they occur, then I can't have *knowledge of* these things—even though I may *know that* such things exist and have certain properties. If, as Russell believed, there are things I can't be acquainted with, they are of this sort.

The third assumption identifies meanings as things one must have *knowledge of*, in order to understand expressions—which has the consequence that nothing we can have no *knowledge of* can be the meaning of anything. The thought is very natural. How is it that I can *know that* the unique person with property P (e.g., the oldest person alive today) has property P, without *knowing of* a certain person A (who is in fact the oldest person alive today) that he/she has P? The answer, according to Russell, is that I can know (i) that some unique person has P, and (ii) that whoever is the unique person with property P has P, even though I have no idea who the unique person with P is, and can't truly *say of* any individual that I know that he or she has P. With this in mind, let E be an expression and M be its meaning. It is clear that one can know *that the thing that is the meaning of E is what E means,* without having the least understanding of E—even though the proposition one knows is (weakly) *about* M. The same is true for the proposition expressed by ⌜D is what 'E' means⌝, for any description D which, though it denotes M, one can understand without having any idea what potential meaning D denotes, and without being able to truly say of any such candidate, ⌜I know that it is D⌝. In all such cases, knowledge of the proposition expressed by ⌜'E' means D⌝ fails to bring with it an understanding of E. Since this will always be so whenever *knowledge of* M is not forthcoming, it is reasonable to suppose that *knowledge of* meaning is required for understanding. Since Russell's argument in "On Fundamentals" purports to show that we can't have such knowledge of denoting concepts, he quite naturally takes it to show that such concepts can't be meanings at all. This, I believe, is why he took his alleged discovery that the denoting concepts of *The Principles of Mathematics* can't have non-denoting occurrences in propositions to show not just that there are no such concepts, but that there couldn't possibly be any.

༄༅༅

CHAPTER 8

Russell's Theory of Descriptions:
"On Denoting"

1. The New Theory of "On Denoting"
   1.1. The Nature, Scope, and Importance of the Theory
   1.2. Initial Analyses of Denoting Phrases
   1.3. Logic, Language, and Logical Form
   1.4. Russell's Analysis of 'The'
2. Russell's Arguments against Other Theories
   2.1. Contra Meinong
   2.2. Contra Frege
   2.3. Contra Any Possible Theory of Definite Descriptions as Singular Terms
        2.3.1. The "Gray's Elegy" Argument from "On Fundamentals"
        2.3.2. Extending the Argument to a *Reductio Ad Absurdum*
        2.3.3. Locating the Offending Premise
        2.3.4. The Epistemology of Meaning, Understanding, and Acquaintance
        2.3.5. Remaining Questions about Propositions
        2.3.6. Application of Russell's Impossibility Argument to Frege's Theory
3. Solutions to Logical Puzzles as Arguments for Russell's Theory
   3.1. Excluded Middle and Logical Scope
   3.2. George IV and The Author of *Waverley*
   3.3. More on Scope: Russell and the Yacht Owner
   3.4. Negative Existentials
4. Problems, Challenges, and Refinements
   4.1. The Clash between Russell's Epistemology and His Theory of Descriptions
   4.2. No Meaning in Isolation?
   4.3. Names and Negative Existentials Revisited
   4.4. Incomplete Descriptions
   4.5. Foundational Issues: Logic, Language, Meaning, and Thought

1. THE NEW THEORY OF "ON DENOTING"

1.1. The Nature, Scope, and Importance of the Theory

Russell's first words in "On Denoting" sketch the scope of the new theory to be developed in what was to become one of the most celebrated and influential philosophical articles in the twentieth century.

By a "denoting phrase" I mean a phrase such as any one of the following: [here the reader should supply quotes around each phrase] a man, some man, any man, every man, all men, the present King of England, the present King of France, the centre of mass of the Solar System at the first instant of the twentieth century, the revolution of the earth round the sun, the revolution of the sun round the earth. Thus a phrase is denoting solely in virtue of its *form*. We may distinguish three cases: (1) A phrase may be denoting, and yet not denote anything; e.g., "the present King of France". (2) A phrase may denote one definite object; e.g., "the present King of England". (3) A phrase may denote ambiguously; e.g., 'a man' denotes not many men, but an ambiguous man.[1]

The examples of the denoting phrases given here nicely illustrate a large and interesting class of expressions. In addition to those Russell mentions, the class includes: 'at least one man', 'a least two men,' 'several men'. 'many men', 'more than 20 but fewer than 50 men', 'most men', and 'no men'. Today, members of this class are called *generalized quantifiers*, which are typically given a unified semantic analysis. Russell, of course, was not interested in all members of this class. However, it will be useful, as we proceed, to attend to the question of what might have to be added to, or subtracted from, his explicit analyses in order to produce a systematic treatment of the whole class. Even at this early stage, an important point can be discerned from his list. In including 'the man' along with 'every man', 'any man', 'all men', and 'some man', Russell is signaling that it functions quite differently from (logically) proper names, and so is not to be counted as a singular term. This point—which still remains somewhat controversial today—was among his most important insights.

Having indicated the scope of his theory of denoting, Russell uses the next paragraph to explain why the theory of denoting is important.

The subject of denoting is of very great importance not only in logic and mathematics, but also in the theory of knowledge. For example, we know that the centre of mass of the Solar System at a definite instant is some definite point, and we can affirm a number of propositions about it, but we have no immediate *acquaintance* with this point, which is only known to us by description. The distinction between *acquaintance* and *knowledge about* is a distinction between the things we have presentations of, and the things we reach by means of denoting phrases. It often happens that we know that a certain phrase denotes unambiguously, although we have no acquaintance with what it denotes; this occurs in the above case of the centre of mass. In perception we have acquaintance with the objects of perception, and in thought we have acquaintance with objects of a more abstract logical character [e.g., universals and propositional functions]; but we do not necessarily have acquaintance with the objects denoted by phrases composed of words with whose meanings we are acquainted. To take a very important instance: There seems no reason to believe that we are ever acquainted with other people's minds, seeing that these are not directly perceived; hence what we know about them is obtained through denoting. All thinking has to start from acquaintance: but it succeeds in thinking *about* many things with which we have no acquaintance.[2]

On Russell's view, the chief reason we need a theory of denoting phrases is to understand the key role of denoting in thought. Taking it to be axiomatic that all propositions we can entertain are composed entirely of things with which we are acquainted, he realized that we can think of, or about, many things with which we are not acquainted—including many things that can't be constituents of any entertainable proposition. This, he believes, is done by means of denoting.

Several aspects of this idea are worth noting. One is the implicit priority Russell gives to thought in his analysis of language. It is from its role in expressing thought that language derives its chief importance for him. Since he took thought to be private, and restricted by what one can "directly perceive" plus one's ability to cognitively apprehend abstract objects (universals and propositional functions), the primacy accorded to thought carried with it an implicit linguistic individualism. For Russell, language is *not* a social institution participation in which expands one's cognitive reach by enabling one to entertain propositions beyond one's solitary grasp. Rather, it is the expression of capacities the scope of which is fixed by that with which one can be nonlinguistically acquainted. This, as we shall see, limited the analyses he was capable of taking seriously.

The second thing to notice about the passage is the presence of his famous distinction between *knowledge by acquaintance* and *knowledge by description*. When we are acquainted with something, we can think about it directly. Having it before our minds, we predicate a property of it, thereby entertaining the singular proposition containing both the object and the property. When we are not acquainted with something, the best we can do is to entertain a proposition, which, though it doesn't contain the object as a constituent, is nevertheless, somehow, *about* the object. The implicit promise in the passage is that the new theory of denoting that Russell is about to propose will explain what denotation is, and how, precisely, it does this job.

Next, the passage inadvertently sounds a cautionary note about the explanation we can expect. In order for the promised explanation to work, it would seem that denoting must be a feature of *propositions*. Since propositions are, for Russell in 1905, the things we assert, believe, and know, they must also be the focus of any explanation of how we can speak, think, or know about things with which we are not acquainted. So we expect to be told how the propositions he identifies end up being *about* those things. Russell seems to indicate his adherence to this picture when he says (my emphasis added):

we know that the centre of mass of the Solar System at a definite instant is some definite point, and we can affirm a number of *propositions* about it, but

[2] Ibid., 479–80.

we have no immediate acquaintance with this point, which is only known to us by description.

> The distinction between acquaintance and knowledge about is a distinction between the things we have presentations of, and the things we reach by means of *denoting phrases*. It often happens that we know that *a certain phrase* denotes unambiguously, although we have no acquaintance with what it denotes; this occurs in the above case of the centre of mass.

Here, Russell seems to take it for granted that *denoting* is a relation that holds not between a proposition, or one of its constituents (which does the denoting), and an object (which is denoted); rather, we are told, it is a relation between a *phrase* and an object. He seems to be saying that the things that denote other things are certain *phrases*. This is puzzling. Since phrases aren't constituents of thoughts, any problem about how thoughts can have a crucial representational feature should—one would have supposed—focus on the representational features, not of phrases, but of the constituents of propositions corresponding to those phrases.

Were the above paragraph drawn from *The Principles of Mathematics*, there would be no cause for alarm. According to the denoting theory given there, meaningful *denoting phrases* always contribute constituents (*denoting concepts*, which are their meanings) to the propositions expressed by sentences containing them. Thus, one can easily move back and forth between representational talk of phrases and similar talk of their meanings. However, because we have not yet been told in "On Denoting" that the same will be true in the new theory, the reader must remain wary. Since, as we shall see, this is a point on which the new theory will, in fact, differ radically from the old, we will need to revisit the expansive epistemological message of Russell's second paragraph, once his new logical analysis is in place.

The final point about this paragraph is the hint in its penultimate sentence about how narrow Russell's conception of acquaintance and *knowledge by acquaintance* is becoming, and hence how far his conception of denoting and *knowledge by description* will be forced to expand in order to take up the slack. If, as he seems to suggest, one is never acquainted with another person, then the lion's share of the burden of connecting us cognitively to the world will have to be borne by denoting.

1.2. Initial Analyses of Denoting Phrases

Russell's initial statement of his theory is as follows:

> I use "C (x)" to mean a proposition (more exactly a propositional function) in which x is a constituent, where x, the variable, is essentially and wholly undetermined. Then we can consider the two notions "C (x) is always true" and

"C (x) is sometime true". (The second of these can be defined by means of the first, if we take it to mean, "It is not true that 'C (x) is false' is always true".) Then *everything* and *nothing* and *something* (which are the most primitive of denoting phrases) are to be interpreted as follows:

C (everything) means "C (x) is always true";
C (nothing) means "'C (x) is false' is always true";
C (something) means "It is false that 'C (x) is false' is always true".

Here the notion "C (x) is always true" is taken as ultimate and indefinable, and the others are defined by means of it. *Everything, nothing, and something*, are not assumed to have any meaning in isolation, but a meaning is assigned to *every* proposition in which they occur. This is the principle of the theory of denoting I wish to advocate: that denoting phrases never have any meaning in themselves, but that every proposition in whose verbal expressing they occur has a meaning.[3]

According to Russell, ⌜Everything is F⌝ expresses the proposition that predicates the property *being always true* of the propositional function for which the formula ⌜x is F⌝ stands. In the above passage, as well as in much of the rest of "On Denoting," he uses the word 'proposition' very loosely, sometimes when speaking of sentences, and sometimes when he has their meanings—propositions proper—in mind. A similar looseness accompanies his use of 'propositional function' for a formula, or for its meaning. Since, at this stage of his career, Russell was still a believer in fully fledged propositions, I will reconstruct his remarks in those terms. At this stage, he was still a realist of sorts about propositional functions as well—which I will continue to characterize as genuine functions taking entities as arguments and assigning propositions containing those entities as values.[4] So understood, ⌜Everything is F⌝ expresses the proposition that p_F is always true—e.g., when F = 'human', (i) p_F is the function that assigns to any object o the proposition *that o is human*, and (ii) p_F is always true iff it assigns a *true* proposition as value to every object o as argument (e.g., for every object o, the proposition *that o is human* is true). Similarly, ⌜Nothing is F⌝

---

[3] Ibid., p. 480.

[4] It should be noted that the logic of "On Denoting"—which requires eliminating all denoting concepts in the sense in which Russell accepted them in *The Principles of Mathematics*—requires eliminating what he there meant by a "variable" (the most general denoting concept). Since *Principles of Mathematics* took a propositional function to be a proposition in which an ordinary constituent is replaced by a "variable," the logic of "On Denoting" requires a new conception of propositional functions. Nevertheless, this subject is not treated in the article. In the following year it was. Since this reconstrual plays no role in "On Denoting," I will not go into it here, but rather will defer discussion of it until chapter 10, where I will explain how Russell's evolving views of propositional functions were connected with his views about paradox and his conception of the theory of types in *Principia Mathematica*.

and ⌜Something is F⌝ mean, (something equivalent to) respectively, that p_F is never true, and p_F is sometimes true.

At this point a serious foundational issue must be faced. Although it is, of course, taken for granted that a propositional function that is *always true* is one that assigns a true proposition to every object, Russell does *not* take this to be a definition of that notion. Rather, he takes *the property of being always true* to be primitive. From his perspective, it is the quantifier 'every' that is defined in terms of the unexplicated and antecedently understood notion of a propositional function *being always true*. In this way he avoids the problem we had (in section 1 of chapter 2) in making sense of Frege's analysis of quantification as the predication of a higher-order concept (expressed by the quantifier) of a lower-order concept (expressed by the grammatical predicate). Our problem came from using the very quantifier being analyzed to explain the higher-order concept it expressed—thereby generating the need for still further analysis in terms of a yet higher-order concept. In the end, we were left with an unending hierarchy of logically equivalent, but structurally different, propositions each with an equal claim on being "the proposition expressed by the original sentence." Being intolerable, the result is one Russell does well to avoid. Since his account of quantification involving quantifiers like 'everything' and 'something' is essentially the same as Frege's—differing primarily in taking propositional functions, rather than Fregean concepts, to be the arguments of the higher-order properties/concepts expressed by the quantifiers—Russell's options for avoiding the problem are essentially the same as Frege's. The cost of the option he selected is, of course, the difficulty one may naturally feel in acquiescing to the idea that *being always true* is an indefinable primitive.[5]

In addition to taking it to be primitive, Russell uses this notion to define each of the other quantifiers he considers. From the point of view of logic and mathematics, this is commendably elegant. However, as an analysis of what English speakers mean by the relevant sentences (and what propositions they entertain when they understand them), this analysis is rather doubtful, as is indicated by the psychological complexity that results from interspersing a few different quantifiers at the beginning of a sentence. Of course, this feature isn't essential to Russell's theory; he could, if he wished, take several different quantifiers to express different *primitive* properties of propositional functions.

This is connected to a further point in the initial statement of his view.

> *Everything, nothing,* and *something* are not assumed to have any meaning in isolation, but a meaning is assigned to *every* proposition in which they occur. This is the principle of the theory of denoting I wish to advocate: that

---

[5] There is, I think, a better way of avoiding the seeming hierarchical regress. See Soames (2014a), "A Puzzle about the Frege/Russell Analysis of Quantification."

denoting phrases never have any meaning in themselves, but that every proposition in whose verbal expression they occur has a meaning.

The idea that many denoting phrases don't have "meaning in isolation," even though they occur as meaningful grammatical constituents of larger, meaningful sentences, is central to Russell's new theory. For an expression to fail to have meaning in isolation is for its semantic role to be something other than that of contributing a constituent (its meaning) to the propositions expressed by sentences containing it. When E has no meaning in isolation, and S contains E, the structured proposition expressed by S does not contain any single constituent that is the meaning of E. Given Russell's definitions of 'nothing' and 'something' in terms of 'everything', one can see how they fit this profile. But what of 'everything'? Doesn't 'Everything is human' mean, and express the (false) proposition, *that p_F is always true*—with 'everything' contributing the property *being always true* that is predicated of p_F? If so, then 'everything' is a counterexample to Russell's general rule about denoting phrases not having meaning in isolation.

If it is a counterexample, then it is a lonely one, as is clear from Russell's next set of comments.

> Suppose now we wish to interpret the proposition, "I met a man". If this is true, I met some definite man; but that is not what I affirm. What I affirm is . . . "'I met x, and x is human' is not always false". Generally, defining the class of men as the class of objects having the predicate *human*, we say that: "C (a man)" means "'C (x) and x is human' is not always false". This leaves "a man," by itself, wholly destitute of meaning, but gives a meaning to every proposition in whose verbal expression "a man" occurs.
>
> Consider next . . . "all men are mortal". This proposition is really hypothetical and states that *if* anything is a man, it is mortal. . . . [I]t states that if x is a man, x is mortal, whatever x may be. Hence, substituting 'x is human' for 'x is a man,' we find "All men are mortal" means "'If x is human, x is mortal' is always true". . . . More generally, we say: "C (all men) means "'If x is human, then C (x) is true' is always true". Similarly,
>
> "C (no men)" means "'If x is human, then C (x) is false' is always true".
> "C (some men)" will mean the same as "C (a man)," and
> "C (a man)" means "It is false that 'C (x) and x is human' is always false".
> "C (every man)" will mean the same as "C (all men)".[6]

These remarks illustrate Russell's analysis of the denoting phrases ⌜every/all/some/an F⌝ as not having meaning in isolation. Although ⌜every F⌝ and ⌜all F's⌝ are grammatical constituents of the sentences ⌜Every F is G⌝ and ⌜All F's are G⌝, their contributions to the proposition p these sentences express are not found in any single constituent of p, but are distributed among p's constituents. On Russell's analysis, p predicates *being always*

---

[6] Russell (1905d), p. 481.

true (presumably contributed by 'every'/'all'), of the propositional function $p_{if,then}$ expressed by ⌜If x is F, then x is G⌝—which is not a grammatical constituent of the original sentences. What F contributes to $p_{if,then}$ is the property predicated of an object o supplied as argument in the antecedent of the conditional proposition that $p_{if,then}$ assigns to o as value. The case of ⌜no F⌝ is similar, while ⌜some F⌝ and ⌜an F⌝ are treated as variants of the same thing. The proposition expressed by ⌜Some F is G⌝ and ⌜An F is G⌝ is the negation of the proposition in which *being always true* is predicated of the propositional function $p\sim_{\&}$ expressed by ⌜$\sim$(x is F & x is G)⌝, with F contributing to $p\sim_{\&}$ the property predicated of an argument o in the first conjunct of the negated conjunctive proposition that $p\sim_{\&}$ assigns to o as value. Even before we get to the central case of ⌜the F⌝, the audacity of the analysis is already present in the gulf Russell posits between the grammatical forms of the sentences under analysis and what he takes to be their *logical forms*, which correspond to the forms of the propositions expressed by those sentences.

His remarks above about the denoting phrase 'a man', which he calls *an indefinite description,* warrant further attention. What does he mean when he says that if it is true that I met a man, then I met some definite man, "but that is not what I affirm"? Presumably, he means that if it is true that he met a man, then there is some man—call him "Sam"—whom he met; but when he asserts or believes that he met a man, what he asserts or believes is not that he met Sam. Rather, he asserts or believes the negation of the claim that a certain conjunctive propositional function is always false; in effect, he asserts or believes that it is "sometimes true." Although this sounds a little abstract, one gets the picture.

What about the analysis of 'I met a man' as 'For some x, I met x and x is *human*'? Why isn't it 'For some x, I met x and x is *a man*'? The answer, one imagines, is that if the latter were offered, it would be objected that the analysis had not succeeded in eliminating the phrase—'a man'—under analysis. In offering his own analysis, Russell avoids this potential objection by relying on the adjective 'human', which he takes to be synonymous with 'a man' when following the copula.[7] But this strategy doesn't generalize to all indefinite descriptions. For example, the most natural ways of expressing the Russellian analyses of '*I saw a tiger*' and '*I saw a large man*' are: '*For some x (I saw x & x is a tiger)*' and '*For some x (I saw x & x is a large man).*'[8] Is it a problem that the indefinite descriptions 'a tiger' and 'a large man' haven't been eliminated?

---

[7] Perhaps Russell was using 'man' with a meaning covering all male or female human beings of whatever age, though it doesn't sound very natural for 'I met a man'. Rather, one imagines Russell meant that he met an adult, male, human. Since 'adult' and 'male' are predicative adjectives, this doesn't substantially affect the point he is making.

[8] Since 'large' is an attributive, rather than a predicative, adjective, 'x is a large man' is not equivalent to 'x is large & x is male & x is adult & x is human'.

It might not be if an indefinite description ⌜a G⌝ is a predicate rather than a quantifier when it occurs after the copula, as suggested by the examples in (1).

　　1a. John is (isn't) *a philosopher.*
　　　b. *John is (isn't) some philosopher.
　　　c. *John is (isn't) at least one philosopher.

However, it can't be denied that some sentences containing indefinite descriptions do have quantificational readings, as indicated by the parallel between the sentences in (2) and those in (3) and (4).

　　2a. *A large man* will meet you.
　　　b. You will meet *a large man* on the bridge.
　　3a. Some large man will meet you.
　　　b. You will meet some large man on the bridge.
　　4a. At least one large man will meet you.
　　　b. You will meet at least one large man on the bridge.

Although the explanation of this data goes well beyond a discussion of Russell, it is not implausible to suppose that in (2) 'a large man' occurs as a predicate in the *restricted quantifier* '∃x: x is a large man'.[9] Since neo-Russellian readings as restricted quantifiers can be given for all complex denoting phrases discussed in "On Denoting," such a modification might not inhibit Russell's philosophical agenda, and so is not out of the question. I will return to this in section 4.2 below.

1.3. Logic, Language, and Logical Form

At this point in "On Denoting," Russell states his analysis of singular definite descriptions, which he characterizes as "by far the most interesting and difficult of denoting phrases."[10] Since the analysis is difficult, with details that are easy to lose track of when described informally, it will be useful to introduce a Russellian language of logical form. Although the language mostly parallels the one given in chapter 1 in the discussion of Frege, I will here use Russell's conceptual apparatus of propositions and propositional functions to state its semantics. The precise statement of the truth conditions for quantificational sentences given below, as well as the recursive assignment of propositions to sentences, and to formulas relative to assignments, are, though Russellian in spirit, traceable not to Russell himself, but to techniques introduced by Alfred Tarski, whose work on truth in the 1930s will be presented in volume 2.

　　In specifying the formal language, I first present its vocabulary, and then show how sentences are constructed from it. The notion of a formula is introduced to mediate between vocabulary and sentences. Whereas

---

　　[9] See Fara (2001) for illuminating discussion of data bearing on these issues.
　　[10] Russell (1905d), p. 481.

formulas express propositions relative to assignments of objects to variables, sentences need no such assistance.

The Formal Language
I. Vocabulary
  1. Predicates
     $=$, A, B, C, ... The predicates are sorted into 1-place, 2-place, . . . n-place predicates. 1-place predicates, like *is red*, express properties of individuals; 2-place predicates, like *is heavier than*, express relations holding between pairs of individuals; and so on. An n-place predicate grammatically combines with n terms to form a formula.
  2. Terms (These expressions designate or refer to single individuals.)
     a. Variables
        $x, y, z, x', y', z',$ . . .
     b. Names
        $\underline{x}, \underline{y}, \underline{z}, \underline{x}', \underline{y}', \underline{z}',$ . . . (Underlining a variable will involve treating it as a name.)
II. Formulas
  1. Atomic Formulas
     An n-place predicate followed by n terms is a formula (in the case of '=' we let the terms flank, rather than follow, the predicate).
  2. Others
     If Φ and Ψ are formulas, $\ulcorner \sim\Phi \urcorner$, $\ulcorner (\Phi \vee \Psi) \urcorner$, $\ulcorner (\Phi \,\&\, \Psi) \urcorner$, $\ulcorner (\Phi \rightarrow \Psi) \urcorner$, and $\ulcorner (\Phi \leftrightarrow \Psi) \urcorner$ are formulas. If v is a variable and $\Phi(v)$ is a formula containing an occurrence of v: $\ulcorner \forall v\, \Phi(v) \urcorner$ and $\ulcorner \exists v\, \Phi(v) \urcorner$ are also formulas. (Sometimes parentheses will be dropped when no ambiguity results.) $\ulcorner \sim\Phi \urcorner$, which is read $\ulcorner$not $\Phi \urcorner$, is the negation of Φ; $\ulcorner (\Phi \vee \Psi) \urcorner$, which is read $\ulcorner$Either Φ or $\Psi \urcorner$, is the disjunction of Φ and Ψ; $\ulcorner (\Phi \,\&\, \Psi) \urcorner$, which is read $\ulcorner \Phi$ and $\Psi \urcorner$, is the conjunction of Φ and Ψ; $\ulcorner (\Phi \rightarrow \Psi) \urcorner$, which is read $\ulcorner$if Φ, then $\Psi \urcorner$, is a conditional the antecedent of which is Φ and the consequent of which is Ψ; $\ulcorner (\Phi \leftrightarrow \Psi) \urcorner$, which is read $\ulcorner \Phi$ if and only if $\Psi \urcorner$, is a biconditional connecting Φ and Ψ; $\ulcorner \forall v\, \Phi(v) \urcorner$ which is read $\ulcorner$For all v $\Phi(v) \urcorner$, is a universal generalization of $\Phi(v)$; and $\ulcorner \exists v\, \Phi(v) \urcorner$, which is read $\ulcorner$There is at least one v such that $\Phi(v) \urcorner$, is an existential generalization of $\Phi(v)$. $\ulcorner \forall v \urcorner$ and $\ulcorner \exists v \urcorner$ are quantifiers.
III. Sentences
  1. A sentence is a formula that contains no free occurrences of variables.
  2. Free occurrences of a variable
     An occurrence of a variable in a formula Φ is free iff it is not bound.
  3. Binding occurrences of variables
     An occurrence of a variable in a formula Φ is bound iff it is within the scope of an occurrence of a quantifier in Φ using that variable.
  4. The scope of an occurrence of a quantifier $\ulcorner \forall v \urcorner$ and $\ulcorner \exists v \urcorner$ in a formula
     The scope of an occurrence of a quantifier in a formula Φ is the quantifier together with the (smallest complete) formula immediately following it in Φ.

IV. Examples

∀x (Fx → Gx) and ∃x (Fx & Hx) are each sentences, since in each, both occurrences of 'x' in the formula immediately following the quantifier are within the scope of the occurrence of the quantifier. Note, in these sentences (i) Fx does not immediately follow the quantifiers because '(' intervenes, and (ii) (Fx is not a complete formula because it contains '(' without an accompanying ')'. By contrast, (∀x Fx → Gx) and (∀x (Fx & Hx) → Gx) are not sentences because the occurrence of 'x' following 'G' is free in each case.

A Russellian Interpretation of the Language

I. Propositions and Propositional Functions

Sentences express propositions. Formulas that are not sentences ("open formulas") express propositional functions. A propositional function assigns propositions as values given objects as arguments. For example, if we use 'C' to mean 'is a cow', then the formula 'Cx' will express a function which, given o as argument, assigns as value the proposition that says of o that it is a cow. This proposition is true iff o is a cow, and is expressed by 'Cx̲' where 'x̲' names o.

II. Truth

1a. The proposition expressed by a sentence ⌜∀v Φ(v)⌝ is true iff the propositional function expressed by Φ(v) is true for all values of v—i.e., iff that function assigns to each object o as argument a true proposition about o as value. This is the case iff for every object o, the result Φ(v̲) of taking all free occurrences of v to name o expresses a true proposition.

b. The proposition expressed by a sentence ⌜∃v Φ(v)⌝ is true iff the propositional function expressed by Φ(v) is true for at least one value of v—i.e., iff that function assigns to at least one object o as argument a true proposition about o as value. This will be the case iff there is at least one object o such that the result Φ(v̲) of taking all free occurrences of v to name o expresses a true proposition.

2a. The proposition expressed by a sentence ⌜~Φ⌝ is true iff the proposition expressed by Φ is not true.

b. The proposition expressed by a sentence ⌜(Φ v Ψ)⌝ is true iff either the proposition expressed by Φ is true or the proposition expressed by Ψ is true.

c. The proposition expressed by a sentence ⌜(Φ & Ψ)⌝ is true iff the proposition expressed by Φ is true and the proposition expressed by Ψ is true.

d. The proposition expressed by a sentence ⌜(Φ → Ψ)⌝ is true iff it is not the case that: the proposition expressed by Φ is true and the proposition expressed by Ψ is false.

e. The proposition expressed by a sentence ⌜(Φ ⟷ Ψ)⌝ is true iff the proposition expressed by Φ and the proposition expressed by Ψ are either both true or both false.

3. Predicates stand for properties (or relations). Names stand for objects. An atomic sentence consists of names plus a single predicate. The proposition expressed by such a sentence is true iff the object (or objects) named have the property (or bear the relation) indicated by the predicate. For example, if 'C' stands for the property of being a cow, the proposition expressed by the atomic sentence 'C$\underline{x}$' is true iff the object named by '$\underline{x}$' is a cow. Every proposition that is not true is false.

The Structure of Propositions

I. The proposition expressed by a sentence in a logically perfect language is a complex entity the structure of which mirrors the structure of the sentence.

The proposition expressed by an atomic sentence $\ulcorner P\ t_1\ldots t_n\urcorner$ consisting of a predicate followed by n names is a complex $<P^*, O_1\ldots O_n>$ consisting of the property (or relation) expressed by the predicate, together with the referents of the names.[11]

An atomic formula $\ulcorner P\ t_1\ldots t_n\urcorner$ containing one or more free occurrences of a variable does not, in and of itself, express a proposition. However, such a formula does express a proposition relative to an assignment of objects as (temporary) referents of its free variables. Thus, the proposition expressed by $\ulcorner P\ t_1\ldots t_n\urcorner$ relative to an assignment A of objects to its free variables is a complex, $<P^*, O_1\ldots O_n>$, consisting of the property (or relation) expressed by the predicate, together with the referents of the terms with respect to A (A being relevant only in the case of variables with free occurrences in the formula). The proposition is true iff the object or objects have the property (or stand in the relation) P^*.

II. The proposition expressed by the formula $\ulcorner \sim\Phi\urcorner$ (relative to an assignment A) is the complex $<\text{Neg}, \text{Prop } \Phi>$, where Prop Φ is the proposition expressed by Φ (relative to A) and Neg is the property of being a proposition that is not true. $<\text{Neg}, \text{Prop } \Phi>$ is true iff Prop Φ is not true.

III. The proposition expressed by the formula $\ulcorner(\Phi\ \&\ \Psi)\urcorner$ (relative to an assignment A) is the complex $<\text{Conj}, \text{Prop } \Phi, \text{Prop } \Psi>$, where Prop Φ and Prop Ψ are the propositions expressed by Φ and Ψ, and Conj holds between a pair of propositions iff both are true. So $<\text{Conj}, \text{Prop } \Phi, \text{Prop } \Psi>$ is true iff Prop Φ and Prop Ψ are true. Similar rules specify the propositions expressed by $\ulcorner(\Phi\ v\ \Psi)\urcorner$, $\ulcorner(\Phi\ ^\circledast\Psi)\urcorner$, and $\ulcorner(\Phi \longleftrightarrow \Psi)\urcorner$.

IV. The proposition expressed by $\ulcorner \exists v\ \Phi(v)\urcorner$ (relative to an assignment A) is the complex $<\text{SOME}, g>$, where g is the propositional function that assigns to each object o the proposition expressed by $\Phi(v)$ relative to an assignment A′ that assigns o as the referent of v (and is otherwise

---

[11] Here and below, I use ordered n-tuples as formal models of structured Russellian propositions. In "On Denoting," Russell continued to think of propositions as being the same sorts of things he took them to be in *Principles of Mathematics*.

identical with A), and SOME is the property of being a propositional function that "is sometimes true" (and so assigns a true proposition to at least one object). Hence, <SOME, g> is true iff at least one object "is Φ."

The proposition expressed by ⌜∀v Φ(v)⌝ (relative to an assignment A) is a complex <ALL, g>, where g is the propositional function that assigns to each object o the proposition expressed by Φ(v) relative to an assignment A′ that assigns o as the referent of v (and is otherwise identical with A), and ALL is the property of being a propositional function that "is always true" (and so assigns a true proposition to every object). Hence, <ALL, g> is true iff all objects "are Φ."

With this machinery in place, I can now say more about the distinction between logical and grammatical form embedded in Russell's new theory of denoting phrases. So far, I have discussed his analysis of sentences containing 'everything', 'nothing', 'something', ⌜every F⌝, ⌜all F's⌝, ⌜no F⌝, ⌜some F⌝, and ⌜an F⌝. 'Everything' and 'something' correspond to ⌜∀v⌝ and ⌜∃v⌝ of the logical language, though for Russell, the latter is defined in terms of the former, as is ⌜no F⌝. Thus, for him the sentences in (5) express the same propositions as their logical counterparts in (6).

5a. Everything is F.
 b. Something is F.
 c. Nothing is F.
6a. ∀x Fx
 b. ~∀x ~ Fx
 c. ∀x ~ Fx

The Russellian proposition expressed by (5a) and (6a) is, therefore, a proposition in which *being always true* is predicated of the propositional function p_F that assigns to any object o the proposition in which the property expressed by F is predicated of o. The proposition expressed by (5c) and (6c) is similar, except in this case the propositional function is $p_{~F}$, which assigns to o the negation of the proposition that p_F assigns to o. The proposition expressed by (5b) and (6b) is the negation of the proposition expressed by (5c) and (6c).

We can already see, in the (b) and (c) cases, a difference between the grammatical form (structure) of these English sentences and their official Russellian logical forms. Since the proposition expressed by a sentence S of English directly encodes the grammatical structure of the sentence of the logical language that provides its logical form, it is the logical form of S, rather than its grammatical form, that reveals the true nature of the thought it expresses. The difference between grammatical form and logical form is brought out even more sharply by the contrast between the sentences in (7) and their (intermediate) Russellian analyses in (8).

7a. Every G is F.
 b. All G's are F's.
 c. Some G is F.

    d. A G is F.
    e. No G is F.
8a. $\forall$x (x is G → x is F)
  b. $\forall$x (x is G → x is F)
  c. $\exists$x (x is G & x is F)
  d. $\exists$x (x is G & x is F)
  e. ~$\exists$x (x is G & x is F)

Although (7a) and (7b) are both single-clause sentences in which G combines with 'every' and 'all' to form their grammatical subjects, their Russellian logical forms (8a) and (8b) are unrestricted universal quantifications of a conditional. The corresponding Russellian proposition encodes this logical structure; '$\forall$x' expresses the property of *being always true* that is predicated of the propositional function $p_{IfG,\ then\ F}$, which assigns to an object o the relevant conditional proposition involving predication of the property expressed by G in the antecedent, and predication of the property expressed by F in the consequent proposition. The intermediate analysis of the single-clause sentences (7c) and (7d) is similar, except that '$\exists$x' expresses the property *being sometimes true*, which is predicated of the propositional function $p_{G\&F}$, which in turn assigns to o the relevant *conjunctive* proposition involving predication of the properties expressed by G and F in the two conjuncts. I call this the "intermediate" analysis of (7c) and (7d) because, on Russell's official theory, the logical forms (8c) and (8d) should themselves really be understood as mere abbreviations for the more complicated (8f).

  8f. ~$\forall$x~(x is G & x is F)

Strictly speaking, the true language of logical forms corresponding to Russell's theory would not contain the existential quantifier ⌜$\exists$v⌝ at all. However, since allowing an independently defined existential quantifier reduces the psychological complexity of the formulas needed for Russell's analysis of ⌜the F⌝, without violating the spirit of his analysis, I will make use of both existential and universal quantifiers in discussing it.

1.4. Russell's Analysis of 'The'

Russell states his theory in two short paragraphs, the first of which illustrates it with a particular example.

> It remains to interpret phrases containing *the*. These are by far the most interesting and difficult of denoting phrases. Take as an instance 'the father of Charles II was executed'. This asserts that there was an x who was the father of Charles II and was executed. Now *the*, when it is strictly used, involves uniqueness. . . . Thus when we say 'x was *the* father of Charles II' we not only assert that x had a certain relation to Charles II, but also that nothing else had this relation. The relation in question, without the assumption of uniqueness, and without any denoting phrases, is expressed by 'x begat Charles II'.

> To get an equivalent of 'x was the father of Charles II', we must add, 'If y is other than x, y did not beget Charles II' or, what is equivalent, 'If y begat Charles II, y is identical with x'. Hence 'x is the father of Charles II' becomes 'x begat Charles II; and "if y begat Charles II, y is identical with x" is always true of y'. Thus 'the father of Charles II was executed' becomes: 'It is not always false of x that x begat Charles II and that x was executed and that "if y begat Charles II, y is identical with x" is always true of y'. This may seem a somewhat incredible interpretation; but I am not at present giving reasons, I am merely *stating* the theory.[12]

Russell's analysis of (9), which is not really "incredible," can be made somewhat less confusing by unpacking the putative logical forms (10), (11), and (12), which approximate, more and more closely, his remarks above. (Ignoring tense, we let 'E' stand for *being executed*, 'B' stand for *begetting*, and 'c' name Charles II.)

9. The father of Charles II was executed.
10. $\exists x \, [(Bxc \, \& \, \forall y \, (Byc \rightarrow y = x)) \, \& \, Ex]$
    Someone who both begat Charles II and was identical with anyone who did so was executed—i.e., someone who was unique in begetting Charles II was executed.
11. $\exists x \, [Bxc \, \& \, Ex \, \& \, \forall y \, (Byc \rightarrow y = x)]$
    Someone begat Charles II, was executed, and was identical with anyone who begat Charles II.
12. $\sim \forall x \sim [Bxc \, \& \, Ex \, \& \, \forall y \, (Byc \rightarrow y = x)]$
    It is not always false of x that [x begat Charles II & x was executed & x was identical with anyone who begat Charles II].

Working with (12), we see that it expresses the proposition that a certain propositional function—call it p_{12}—is *not always false*. This propositional function—p_{12}—assigns to any object o the conjunction of (i) the proposition that o begat Charles II, (ii) the proposition that o was executed, and (iii) the proposition expressed by '$\forall y \, (Byc \rightarrow y = x)$' relative to an assignment of o to the variable 'x'. Proposition (iii), the third conjunct of the proposition assigned by p_{12} to o, is the proposition that says of another propositional function, p_{iii}, that it is *always true*—where $p_{iii} \, (o^*)$ is the proposition that if o* begat Charles II, then o* is o itself. In short, proposition (iii) is the proposition that no one other than o begat Charles II. So, to say that p_{12} is not always false, and hence is sometimes true, is to say that for some object o, it is true that o begat Charles II, that no one else begat Charles II, and that o was executed. Since these are the truth conditions of (9), Russell's analysis is truth-conditionally correct.

But does the analysis correctly identify the proposition actually expressed by (9)? Since Russell's theory of propositions allows truth-conditionally equivalent propositions to differ from one another, nothing

[12] Russell (1905d), pp. 481–82.

we have said guarantees that it does. In fact, there is no evidence that Russell took this question seriously, or had anything credible to say about answering it. In addition to (10–12), the class of logically equivalent candidates for being the logical form of (9) includes (13–15).

13. $\exists x\ (Bxc)\ \&\ \exists x\ \forall y\ (Byc \rightarrow y = x)\ \&\ \forall x\ (Bxc \rightarrow Ex)$

Someone begat Charles II, at most one individual did so, and whoever did so was executed.

14. $\exists x\ [\forall y\ (x = y \rightarrow Byc)\ \&\ \forall y\ (Byc \rightarrow y = x)\ \&\ Ex]$

It is true of some individual that any individual he was identical with begat Charles II, that anyone who begat Charles II was identical with him, and that he was executed—in other words, since each thing is identical with itself (and only itself), some individual who was unique in begetting Charles II was executed.

15. $\exists x\ \forall y\ [(Byc \longleftrightarrow y = x)\ \&\ Ex]$

It is true of some individual both that he was identical with any individual whatsoever iff that individual begat Charles II, and that he was executed. In other words, some individual who was unique in begetting Charles II was executed.

Since there is no clear and principled way of making a definitive choice as *the* Russellian logical form of (9), I will select (15), purely because it is the most compact.

With this we return to Russell's most general statement of his theory of definite descriptions in "On Denoting."

> To interpret 'C (the father of Charles II)', where C stands for any statement about him, we have only to substitute C (x) for 'x was executed' in the above [i.e., in the analysis of (9)]. Observe that, according to the above interpretation, whatever statement C may be, 'C (the father of Charles II)' implies 'It is not always false of x that "if y begat Charles II, y is identical with x" is always true of y', which is what is expressed in common language by 'Charles II had one father and no more'. Consequently, if this condition fails, *every* proposition of the form 'C (the father of Charles II)' is false. Thus, e.g., every proposition of the form 'C (the present King of France)' is false.[13]

The passage is intended to generalize the discussion of (9) to all cases in which a singular definite description occurs in a sentence ⌐...the F...⌐. The idea is to use the previous remark,

> Thus 'the father of Charles II was executed' becomes: 'It is not always false of x that x begat Charles II and that x was executed and that "if y begat Charles II, y is identical with x" is always true of y'.

to illustrate a general rule R for translating an ordinary sentence containing a singular definite description into something more closely approximating its logical form.

---

[13] Ibid., p. 482.

R. C [the F] ⇒ ∃x ∀y [(Fy ⟷ y = x) & Cx]

R tells us that if a definite description occurs in a sentence along with additional material C, it can be eliminated (bringing us closer to the logical form of the sentence) by replacing the description with a variable, and introducing quantifiers plus the uniqueness clause as indicated. Russell's comment—that a sentence containing an occurrence of ⌜the F⌝ can be true only if F is true of one, and only one, thing—is vindicated by R, provided that the rule is understood in one particular, and restrictive, way.

The restriction concerns cases in which the description occurs in an embedded clause S′ of a larger complex sentence S. The application of R needed to vindicate Russell's remarks is one in which C is understood as encompassing all of S, as opposed to applying solely within S′. Sentence (16), containing 'the present king of France', illustrates the point.

16. If France presently has one and only one king, then the king of France is among a dwindling number of European monarchs.

To apply R in the manner indicated is to let (17a) play the role of C in the rule, yielding (17b) as logical form.

17a. If France presently has one and only one king, then _____ is among a dwindling number of European monarchs.
  b. ∃x ∀y [(y is presently a French king ⟷ y = x) & if France presently has one and only one king, then x is among a dwindling number of European monarchs]

Since the truth (17b) requires France to presently have a king, (17b) is false, and so conforms to Russell's remarks in the previous passage.

However, this is not the only, or most obvious, way of understanding (16)—as Russell himself would emphasize. To get the Russellian reading in which (16) is true, we apply R, not to the conditional sentence as a whole, but only to its consequent clause, with (18a) playing the role of C in the rule.

18a. _____ is among a dwindling number of European monarchs.

The result is (18b) as logical form of the consequent of (16), and (18c) as the resulting reading of (16) itself.

18b. ∃x ∀y [(y is presently a French king ⟷ y = x) & x is among a dwindling number of European monarchs]
  c. If France presently has one and only one king, then ∃x ∀y [(y is presently a French king ⟷ y = x) & x is among a dwindling number of European monarchs]

Clearly, Russell's rule for translating from grammatical to logical form must sometimes apply wholly within a sentential clause that does not encompass the entire containing sentence. As we will see when examining his notion of logical scope more carefully, applications encompassing the whole of complex sentences will also be required.

2. RUSSELL'S ARGUMENTS AGAINST OTHER THEORIES

Having at this point in "On Denoting" stated his analysis of ⌜the F⌝, Russell launches into a critique of alternative analyses, all of which lack what is for him the most crucial feature of the "incredible" analysis he has just offered. That feature is his treatment of singular definite descriptions as "incomplete symbols," which have "no meaning in isolation." By this he means that although ⌜the F⌝ is a perfectly meaningful phrase, there is no entity, its meaning, that it contributes as a constituent to the meanings of (i.e., propositions expressed by) sentences containing it. This was also a feature of his analyses of other denoting phrases, including ⌜every F⌝, ⌜all F's⌝, ⌜no F⌝, ⌜some F⌝, and ⌜an F⌝. However, the postulated gap between grammatical structure/constituency and propositional structure/constituency is far more dramatic for sentences containing ⌜the F⌝ than for sentences containing the others. Looking at the difference between (19a) and its Russellian logical form (19b), one can easily pinpoint the contributions of F and G to the proposition expressed.

19a. The F is G
  b. $\exists x \,\forall y\, [(Fy \longleftrightarrow y = x)\ \&\ Gx]$

Not so with 'the'. Somehow, everything else in the proposition expressed by (19a/b)—the pair of quantifiers (expressing properties of propositional functions), the conjunctive structure, the complex biconditional that is the first conjunct, and the identity predicate—is the responsibility of 'the'— even though no propositional constituent can be identified as its meaning. This is the heart of what Russell took to be his newly discovered truth.

It is also what, in his opinion, alternative analyses fatally miss. He begins with two focused criticisms of the theories of Meinong and Frege, both of which treat definite descriptions as contributing constituents— either objects denoted or meanings suited to denoting such objects—to the propositions expressed by sentences containing them. In each case, Russell isolates details of the view that he (rightly) takes to be problematic. However, these criticisms are only warm-ups for the devastating critique he offers against *every possible theory (of every possible language) that treats singular definite descriptions as genuine singular terms having meanings that (i) occur as constituents of propositions expressed by sentences containing them, and (ii) stand for individual objects they denote (which are referents of the descriptions themselves)*. The striking feature of Russell's argument, which is aimed at both Frege's theory and his own previous account in *The Principles of Mathematics*, is that it purports to uncover a conceptual incoherence in any theory of this sort. Since he (wrongly) seems to regard such a theory as the only possible serious competitor to the theory of "On Denoting," he takes the demonstration of such incoherence to be tantamount to establishing his new view. Thus, be prefaces his criticisms with the remark:

> The evidence for the above theory [of singular definite descriptions in "On Denoting"] is derived from the difficulties which seem unavoidable if we regard denoting phrases as standing for genuine constituents of the proposition in whose verbal expressions they occur.[14]

2.1. Contra Meinong

Russell continues the above remark:

> Of the possible theories which admit such constituents the simplest is that of Meinong. This theory regards any grammatically correct denoting phrase as standing for an *object*. Thus "The present King of France," "the round square," etc., are supposed to be genuine objects. It is admitted that such objects do not *subsist*, but nevertheless they are supposed to be objects. This is in itself a difficult view; but the chief objection is that such objects, admittedly, are apt to infringe the law of contradiction. It is contended, for example, that the existent present King of France exists, and also does not exist; that the round square is round, and also not round; etc. But this is intolerable; and if any theory can be found to avoid this result, it is surely to be preferred.[15]

Russell here calls attention to a difficulty in Meinong's postulation of somehow real objects corresponding to all meaningful denoting phrases. The problem was not quite as severe for Russell's own theory in *The Principles of Mathematics*—which did not countenance such objects *as constituents of propositions* expressed by sentences containing meaningful denoting phrases, and which denied the existence of at least some such objects. However, Russell's earlier theory did suffer from a version of the problem, even if (charitably interpreted) it may have managed to avoid some of its worst excesses. Here in "On Denoting," he draws the lesson that any theory according to which such objects, supposedly denoted by meaningful definite descriptions, figure as constituents of propositions expressed by sentences containing those descriptions, is to be avoided.

2.2. Contra Frege

Turning to Frege, Russell says:

> The above breach of the law of contradiction is avoided by Frege's theory. He distinguishes, in a denoting phrase, two elements, which we may call the *meaning* and the *denotation*. Thus, 'the centre of mass of the Solar System at the

---

[14] Ibid., p. 482.
[15] Ibid., pp. 482–83.

beginning of the twentieth century' is highly complex in *meaning*, but its *denotation* is a certain point, which is simple. . . . One of the first difficulties that confront us, when we adopt the view that denoting phrases *express* a meaning and *denote* a denotation, concerns the cases in which the denotation appears to be absent. If we say "the King of England is bald," that is, it would seem, not a statement about the complex *meaning* 'the King of England', but about the actual man denoted by the meaning. But now consider 'the King of France is bald'. By parity of form, this also ought to be about the denotation of the phrase 'the King of France'. But this phrase, though it has a *meaning* provided 'the King of England' has a meaning, has certainly no denotation, at least in any obvious sense. Hence one would suppose that 'the King of France is bald' ought to be nonsense; but it is not nonsense, since it is plainly false.[16]

This, of course, is no genuine critique of Frege, since on his view 'The King of France is bald' is not nonsense, but rather is perfectly meaningful, even though it is neither true nor false. Since sentences in this category express propositions/thoughts correctly characterized as untrue, Russell has so far failed to identify any problem for Frege. Nor do his remarks about what statements of this sort are "about" help his case. There is nothing evidently wrong with the Fregean reply to Russell that although the statement that the king of England is bald is *about* a certain man (supposing that England has a king at the time of utterance), the statement that the king of France is bald is not *about* anyone. Russell's seeming suggestion to the contrary is perhaps the remnant of the views expressed in the *Principles* that (i) denoting concepts, which are the meanings of denoting expressions, always denote, and (ii) propositions expressed by meaningful denoting phrases are always about the denotations of the denoting concepts they express—so that if nothing were denoted, there would be no meaning of the denoting phrase, and no proposition at all. Frege, of course, never held these views, and if Russell himself ever strictly adhered to them, one would have thought that time had passed.

Nevertheless, Russell does identify a genuine problem.

Or again consider such a proposition as the following: 'If u is a class which has only one member, then that one member is a member of u,' or, as we may state it, 'If u is a unit class, *the u* is a u'. This proposition ought to be *always* true, since the conclusion is true whenever the hypothesis is true. But 'the u' is a denoting phrase, and it is the denotation, not the meaning, that is said to be a u. Now if u is *not* a unit class, 'the u' seems to denote nothing; hence our proposition would seem to become nonsense [actually truth valueless] as soon as u is not a unit class. Now it is plain that such propositions do *not* become nonsense [truth valueless] merely because their hypotheses are false. The King in "The Tempest" might say, "If Ferdinand is not drowned, Ferdinand is my only son." Now 'my only son' is a denoting phrase, which, on the

16 Ibid., pp. 483–84.

face of it, has a denotation when, and only when, I have exactly one son. But the above statement would nevertheless have remained true, if Ferdinand had been in fact drowned.[17]

Minor points aside, Russell is clearly right. Frege's theory wrongly characterizes certain *true* sentences containing non-denoting definite descriptions as *not true*. One such sentence is our earlier example (16), the Russellian analysis of which was given above.

> 16. If France presently has one and only one king, then the king of France is among a dwindling number of European monarchs.

Here, we assume with Frege and Russell that the sentences in question are material conditionals. For Frege, this means that their truth values are the result of applying the two-place function f_{MC} that maps the pair consisting of truth (of the antecedent) followed by falsity (of the consequent) onto the value falsity, while mapping all the other pairs of truth and/or falsity onto truth. Frege's problem results from his compositional theory of reference according to which (i) the truth value of an atomic sentence consisting of an n-place predicate P and n singular terms is the value—truth or falsity—assigned by the n-place function designated by P to the n arguments that are referents of the terms, (ii) definite descriptions are singular terms, (iii) truth and falsity are the only truth values, and (iv) all truth-functional connectives designate functions from n-tuples of truth values to truth values. Given (i–iii), Frege must characterize the consequent of (16) as neither true nor false, and so as having no truth value. Given (iv), he must characterize (16) in the same way: since f_{MC} assigns truth values only to *pairs* of truth values, one of which is missing in this case, there is no such thing as the truth value assigned to (16).

Though this problem is genuine, it is not obvious that the culprit is the Fregean analysis of descriptions Russell criticizes. The problem could be avoided by modifying Frege's system in a variety of ways: e.g., (i) by assigning predicates sets of objects to which they apply, rather than functions from objects to truth values, and characterizing an atomic sentence as false whenever its n-tuple of terms fails to provide an n-tuple of referents that is a member of the set designated by its predicate, or (ii) by assigning non-denoting terms some entity to which the functions corresponding to predicates in the language always assign falsity (and over which the quantifiers do not range), or (iii) by expanding the number of truth values to include *neither-true-nor-false*, and adopting the truth function (20) for material conditionals, or (iv) by dispensing with functions as referents of truth-functional connectives, and characterizing the truth or falsity of truth functionally compound sentences using clauses like (21) in the theory of truth for the language.

---

[17] Ibid., p. 484.

20. *If A, then B.*

B	T	F	*
A			
T	T	F	*
F	T	T	T
*	*	*	*

'*' = *neither-true-nor-false*

21. A conditional sentence ⌜If A, then B⌝ is false iff A is true and B is not; otherwise it is true.

The point is not that these fixes are equivalent (they aren't), or even that there aren't further objections against some of them (there are). The point is that without a great deal of further argument, Russell's observation does not succeed in undermining Frege's analysis of definite descriptions.[18]

Although Russell does note the need for more argument to rule out solution (ii) above, he misses the other possibilities, and so comes to take the difficulty raised for Frege-style theories of descriptions to be more severe than it really is. Continuing the previous passage, he says:

> Thus we must either provide a denotation in cases in which it is at first sight absent, or we must abandon the view that the denotation is what is concerned in propositions which contain denoting phrases. The latter is the course that I advocate. The former course may be taken, as by Meinong, by admitting objects which do not subsist, and denying that they obey the law of contradiction; this, however, is to be avoided if possible. Another way of taking the same course, so far as our present alternative is concerned, is adopted by Frege, who provides by definition some purely conventional denotation for the cases in which otherwise there would be none. . . . But this procedure, though it may not lead to logical error, is plainly artificial, and does not give an exact analysis of the matter. Thus, if we allow that denoting phrases, in general, have the two sides of meaning and denotation, the cases where there seems to be no denotation cause difficulties both on the assumption that there really is a denotation and on the assumption that there really is none.[19]

Though Russell's conclusion clearly overstates the difficulties he has raised for Frege's theory of definite descriptions—which must so far be regarded has having remained more or less unscathed—his remarks in this passage about solution (ii) above—providing an artificial denotation for otherwise non-denoting definite descriptions—are correct and illuminating. Frege's primary concern in offering such a denotation was to

---

[18] For some further discussion of issues raised by some of the options above, see Soames (1979), Soames (1982), and Soames (1989a) at pp. 76–80, and 101–4 of the reprinted version in Soames (2009a).

[19] Russell (1905d), p. 484.

avoid wholesale failures of truth value that would otherwise result from occurrences of non-denoting singular terms in sentences of formal languages constructed for scientific and mathematical purposes. Thought of in this focused utilitarian light, the proposed solution is not unreasonable. If, however, more is desired—if one wants an accurate account of the thoughts expressed, and statements made, by uttering natural language sentences containing non-denoting definite descriptions—then such a "solution" is much less plausible. When advancing theses about logic and language, Frege and Russell had both narrowly scientific concerns, which could prompt technically fruitful departures from ordinary language, and broader concerns to lay bare the structure of thoughts and statements expressed by uses of natural language in less formal situations. Although the balance between these two concerns was not always clear, in "On Denoting" Russell displays a strong interest in the latter, as well as the former. Evaluated in this light, his dismissal of (ii) as a solution to the problem for Frege posed by examples like (16) is quite understandable. Nevertheless, his neglect of the other ways of solving the problem without giving up a Fregean account of definite descriptions defeats his claim to have shown that

> "if we allow that denoting phrases, in general, have the two sides of meaning and denotation, the cases where there seems to be no denotation cause difficulties both on the assumption that there really is a denotation and on the assumption that there really is none."

2.3. Contra Any Possible Theory of Definite Descriptions as Singular Terms

2.3.1. THE "GRAY'S ELEGY" ARGUMENT FROM "ON FUNDAMENTALS"

The following words introduce Russell's centerpiece argument against theories that treat definite descriptions as complex singular terms the meanings of which denote the objects designated by the terms:

> The relation of the meaning to the denotation involves certain rather curious difficulties, which seem in themselves sufficient to prove that the theory which leads to such difficulties must be wrong.
>
> When we wish to speak about the *meaning* of a denoting phrase, as opposed to its denotation, the natural mode of doing so is by inverted commas. Thus we say:

> The centre of mass of the Solar System is a point, not a denoting complex.
> "The centre of mass of the Solar System" is a denoting complex, not a point.

> Or again,

> The first line of Gray's Elegy states a proposition.
> "The first line of Gray's Elegy" does not state a proposition.

Thus taking any denoting phrase, say C, we wish to consider the relation between C and "C", where the difference of the two is the kind exemplified in the above two instances.

We say, to begin with, that when C occurs it is the *denotation* we are speaking about; but when "C" occurs it is the *meaning*. Now the relation of meaning and denotation is not merely linguistic through the phrase: there must be a logical relation involved, which we express by saying that the meaning denotes the denotation. But the difficulty which confronts us is that we cannot succeed in *both* preserving the connexion of meaning and denotation *and* preventing them from being one and the same; also that the meaning cannot be got at except by means of denoting phrases.[20]

Here, Russell uses double quotes, not to produce a name of the expression that occurs inside them, but to produce (what is intended to be) a logically proper name of the meaning of that expression. The theories he criticizes are those that take ⌜the F⌝ to express a complex meaning (of which the meanings of 'the' and F are presumably constituents) which, as a whole, denotes the unique thing of which F is true, if such there be. In saying "that when C occurs it is the *denotation* we are speaking about; but when "C" occurs it is the *meaning*," he is saying that when a definite description C occurs in a sentence S, the proposition S expresses is one we use to talk about the object that its meaning denotes; but when a name consisting of double quotes, followed by C, followed by double quotes, occurs in a sentence S′, the proposition S′ expresses is one we use to talk about the meaning of C. That is our intention. However, it is also what Russell believes he can show to be impossible.

His reason for taking the state of affairs imagined to be impossible is that it requires the meaning of C sometimes to occur in a proposition as a mere representative of its denotation—about which the proposition can be understood to say something—while occurring at other times not as a representative of its denotation, but simply as that of which the proposition predicates something. The problem, Russell thinks, is that meanings can't be ambiguous in this way. If definite descriptions have meanings that denote individuals, these meanings must either *always* represent their denotations, which the propositions in which they occur are ultimately about, or they must never do so, in which case the meanings can be subjects of predication in propositions containing them—but only at the cost of losing their *raison d'être* as constituents that denote other things. This is what Russell means by saying "that we cannot succeed in *both* preserving the connexion of meaning and denotation *and* preventing them from being one and the same." Finally, this point is connected to his final remark—"that the meaning cannot be got at *except by means of denoting phrases*"—which tells us that the meaning M of a denoting phrase could, in principle, be made the subject of predication only in propositions that do not contain M, but

[20] Ibid., pp. 485–86.

rather contain a higher-order meaning M* that denotes M. Russell, at this stage, doesn't specify what is problematic about this.

The next four paragraphs of "On Denoting," which spell out the argument, are among the most complex, confusing, and (somewhat) confused that Russell ever wrote. Referred to by scholars as "the Gray's Elegy passage," they were, for 100 years, mostly dismissed as a confused distraction from the main argument in "On Denoting." This situation persisted until October of 2005, exactly 100 years to the month from the original appearance of the article in 1905. It was then, in a special issue commemorating the centenary of Russell's original publication, that Nathan Salmon published "On Designating," which untangled the confusions, and clarified the master argument Russell intended. Fortunately, we need not follow all the twists and turns here, since the argument was previously introduced in the discussion of "On Fundamentals," in the previous chapter, at the end of section 5.[21]

Here, we let 'the first line of Gray's Elegy' be our example of a definite description expressing, according to the theories Russell wishes to refute, a complex meaning M that denotes 'the curfew tolls the knell of parting day' (which is the first line of the Elegy). Next we let 'Mthe-first-line-of-Gray's-ElegyM' be a proper name of M—not a description, but a name that contributes its bearer to propositions expressed by sentences containing it. With this in mind, consider (22) and (23).

22a. The first line of Gray's elegy is a sentence.
  b. Mthe-first-line-of-Gray's-ElegyM is a sentence.
23a. The first line of Gray's elegy denotes 'the curfew tolls the knell of parting day'.
  b. Mthe-first-line-of-Gray's-ElegyM denotes 'the curfew tolls the knell of parting day'.

If the theories being investigated were correct, and our convention about what is to count as a name of M were legitimate, then (22a) and (23b) would be true, while (22b) and (23a) should be false. But this can be so only if (a) and (b) express different propositions in (22) and (23). Russell's argument purports to show that these sentences can't do so.

What proposition is expressed by (22a)? It must be a proposition containing the property *being a sentence*, which is predicated of whatever is provided by its second constituent, M. Since M is, by hypothesis, a denoting concept, its role is to determine a denotation which, if it has the property predicated of it, will make the proposition true, and which, if it lacks the property, will make the proposition false. Knowing that the denotation of M is supposed to be a sentence, we judge proposition (22a) to be true. But now we are in for a surprise. What we didn't initially realize is that this line of reasoning would force us to take the proposition

---

[21] The argument in that section is what Russell reworks in the Gray's Elegy passage of "On Denoting."

expressed by (22b) to be true as well. *Since the first and second constituents of proposition (22b) are the same as those of proposition (22a), and since the positions occupied by these constituents are the same, both the structure and the constituents of the two propositions are identical. It follows that the propositions don't differ at all, and so aren't two propositions, but only one.* The same conclusion holds for (23).

Despite this, the result seems absurd. Surely, if there are meanings that denote, we should be able to name them, and truly say of them—just as we do of other meanings—*that they are meanings*. But, Russell is convinced, acquiescence in the result (I) just reached does not allow this.

> I. (a) If p and p* are propositions that consist of the same n-place property the predication targets of which are provided by the same n-tuple of further constituents, which together exhaust the propositions, then p = p*. So, (b) if definite descriptions express meanings that denote unique objects satisfying them (if such objects there be), then these meanings can occur in propositions *only* in the role of presenting their denotations as the subjects of predication in the propositions; thus, these meanings can never themselves be the direct subjects of predication in any proposition in which they occur.[22]

This, Russell thinks, prevents us from naming such meanings, and *saying of* them that they are meanings—or, indeed, from saying anything at all *of* them. The reason for this is given in (II), which he implicitly assumes.

> II. To *say of, believe of,* or *know of* an object o that it is so-and-so is to assert, believe, or know a singular proposition in which o occurs (in what Russell called in *The Principles of Mathematics* a "term accessible position" and what he called in "On Fundamentals" an "entity position") directly as subject of the predication *being so-and-so* in the proposition.[23]

Since (I) purportedly shows that there are no singular propositions of the sort mentioned in (II) in which a denoting concept occurs as direct subject of the proposition's predication, it follows that one cannot say, believe, or know, *of* any such concept, that it is the meaning of anything. But—and this brings his argument to a close—Russell also tacitly takes (III) to be an obvious truth about what is required in order for something to be the meaning of an expression.

> III. For any entity x whatsoever to be the meaning of an expression E for a group of speakers, it must be possible for those speakers to know *that E means x*, which is just to know the singular proposition in which the two-place relation *means* is directly predicated of the pair of E and x.

---

[22] We put aside, as irrelevant to our larger concerns, the bizarre but genuine technical possibility of a description the meaning of which denotes itself.

[23] Russell takes M to occupy the same term accessible/entity position propositions in (22) and (23).

Given (I–III), Russell concluded that there are not, and could not be, meanings expressed by definite descriptions that denote the unique objects satisfying the descriptions. Since he took theories of this sort to be the only credible alternative to his theory that definite descriptions are "incomplete symbols" with "no meaning in isolation," he concluded that his theory must be correct.

This argument has considerable force—particularly against Russell's own previous position in *The Principles of Mathematics*. Consider the first part of (III): for x to be the meaning of E, it must be possible to know *that E means x*. Surely that's right. What, then, is it for one to know *that E means x*? Russell would say, correctly, that it is for one to bear the relation of knowing to the proposition that 'E means x' expresses, when the variable 'x' is treated as a logically proper name of the entity M that E means. Since variables are devices of pure reference, free of any descriptive information, he would maintain that the contribution of 'x' to the proposition p expressed by 'E means x' is simply M itself. Thus, he would correctly conclude, p is the singular proposition in which the two-place relation *means* is directly predicated of the pair of E and M—which is precisely what (III) tells us. All this seems perfectly true.

In order to understand (II), one must understand the contrast between believing or knowing *of x* that it is so-and-so, and believing or knowing *that* D is so-and-so, when 'D' is replaced by an arbitrary description that happens to denote x.[24] To believe *of x* that it is so-and-so is to believe *that x is so-and-so*—which, as we have just seen, is to believe a singular proposition about x. This is different from believing *that D is so-and-so*, when 'D' is replaced by a description that denotes x. Obviously, for many such descriptions, believing the resulting proposition is not *necessary* for believing the singular proposition—since, for many descriptions that x happens to satisfy, one can believe *that x is so-and-so* without having any idea whether the corresponding proposition *that x is D* is true. Russell would further insist that for many x-denoting replacements of 'D', believing *that D is so-and-so* is *not sufficient* for believing *that x is so-and-so*. For example, suppose that M is the meaning of E. It seems evident that even one who has no idea what E means, and doesn't understand it, can know that it has a (single, unambiguous) meaning—and hence know *that the meaning of E is the meaning of E*—without knowing *that M is the meaning of E*. Again, all of this seems unassailable.[25]

---

[24] I here use 'D' as a schematic letter.

[25] Nothing in the argument requires the stronger conclusion that believing *that D is so-and-so* is *never sufficient* for believing *that x is so-and-so*. Russell needn't deny that there may be many cases in which one believes a singular proposition by virtue of believing a descriptive counterpart of it. What he does deny is that there are, or could be, any singular propositions in which meanings of definite descriptions are direct subjects of predication. If he is right about this, then given the rest of his argument, there can be no *knowledge of* them, in which case it is impossible for them to be meanings.

2.3.2. EXTENDING THE ARGUMENT TO A *REDUCTIO AD ABSURDUM*

With this in mind, we return to the linchpin of Russell's argument, which is (I). Here we face a dilemma. On one hand, it is hard to accept his conclusion, which seems too sweeping to carry conviction. On the other hand, given his conception of what propositions are, one is hard put to deny (I), which, when combined with his well-founded auxiliary assumptions, brings the far-reaching conclusion with it.

The first horn of the dilemma is illustrated by the examples in (24).

24a. 216 > 196
   b. $f_3(6) > f_2(14)$

Here, I will take the numerals '216', '196', '6', and '14' to be proper names of natural numbers, and I will let 'f_3' and 'f_2' stand for the functions that map a number onto the cube and the square, respectively, of that number. On this assumption, the propositions expressed by (24a) and (24b) are different. The former is one in which the two-place relation *greater than* is predicated of the pair of propositional constituents 216 and 196. The latter is one in which that relation is (in a sense) predicated of the same pair, *but only by virtue of the fact that the pair is the result of cubing 6 followed by the result of squaring 14* (which is what *being greater than* is really predicated of). This difference between the two propositions is due to their different constituents. Whereas the numbers 216 and 196 occur as constituents of the proposition expressed by (24a), they are not constituents of the proposition expressed by (24b)—which contains a pair of complex meanings, M_{3-6} and M_{2-14} expressed by the complex singular terms '$f_3(6)$' and '$f_2(14)$'. The former meaning, M_{3-6}, is a combination of the cubing function together with the number 6; the number it determines as referent of '$f_3(6)$' is the result of applying the function it contains to the argument it contains. The latter meaning, M_{2-14}, consists of the squaring function and the number 14, which determines the referent of '$f_2(14)$' in the same way. It is because of this difference in constituent structure of the propositions expressed by (24a) and (24b) that believing the former is not sufficient for believing the latter.[26]

What does this have to do with Russell's Gray's Elegy argument, which deals with definite descriptions, and doesn't say anything about function-argument terms? The answer is that Russell's argument *that it is impossible for a definite description to express a meaning the function of which in a proposition is to denote a unique satisfier* is correct iff an exactly corresponding argument *that it is impossible for a term* ⌜$f(\alpha)$⌝ *to express a meaning the function of which in a proposition is to denote a unique satisfier* is correct. Both arguments putatively rule out singular terms expressing denoting meanings. Since the arguments must either succeed together or fail together, Russell must

---

[26] Chapter 7 of Soames (2010b) explains why believing the latter isn't sufficient for believing the former.

either admit that the class of possible singular terms expressing denoting meanings contains both some that are definite descriptions and some that are function-argument expressions, or deny that it contains either.

To see this, compare (Ib) of his argument against the possibility of definite descriptions as singular terms with the corresponding principle (Ib′) dealing with function-argument expressions.

(Ib′) If a function-argument term $\ulcorner f(t_1 \ldots t_n) \urcorner$ expresses a complex meaning M that determines the object o that is the value of the function designated by f at the arguments designated by $t_1 \ldots t_n$ (provided that there is such an object), then M can occur in propositions only in the role of presenting this object as the subject of predication in those propositions; thus, M itself can never be the direct subject of predication in any proposition in which it occurs.[27]

Russell's case for (Ib), such as it is, applies with equal force to (Ib′). As with (Ib), if (Ib′) is correct, then the complexes M_{3-6} and M_{2-14} can't be direct subjects of predication in any propositions in which they occur, and so they can't occur as constituents of propositions in which they are said to be what '$f_3(6)$' and '$f_2(14)$' mean. (II) and (III) will then apply as before, with the result that neither M_{3-6} and M_{2-14}, nor any similar complex, can be meanings of '$f_3(6)$' and '$f_2(14)$'. So, we get the "result" that it is impossible for any singular term to be a function-argument expression.

I regard this as a *reductio ad absurdum* of Russell's conclusion. If his argument were sound, and his negative conclusions were correct, then $\ulcorner n + m \urcorner$, $\ulcorner n \times m \urcorner$, and $\ulcorner n' \urcorner$ could not be what they are standardly taken in mathematics to be—namely, singular terms designating numbers that are distinct from, but determined by, the function-argument combinations that are their meanings. There is a paragraph near the end of "On Denoting" that suggests that Russell himself may well have been willing to deny the possibility of such terms.[28] But if one isn't willing to grasp this nettle (as I am not), then one must reject the corresponding conclusion that complex denoting singular terms are impossible.

This point is strengthened by the observation that we know how, in formal work, to introduce definite descriptions as singular terms by treating them as special cases of function-argument expressions. Let 'ιx' stand for a function f_ι that takes a Russellian propositional function p_F as argument and assigns as value the unique object to which p_F assigns a *true* proposition, and otherwise is undefined. In introducing 'ιx' we stipulate that it combines with a formula $F(x)$, standing for p_F, to form a complex singular term $\ulcorner \iota x\ Fx \urcorner$ that designates the value of f_ι at p_F. The proposition

---

[27] As with (I), we put aside, as irrelevant to our larger concerns, the bizarre possibility of a function-argument expression the meaning of which is a function-argument complex, in which the value of function at the argument is the complex itself.

[28] Russell (1905d), p. 491–92.

expressed by $\ulcorner[\iota x\ Fx]$ is so-and-so$\urcorner$ consists of the property *being so-and-so*, plus the meaning of $\ulcorner \iota x\ Fx\urcorner$, which is a complex in which f_i is combined with its argument p_F. One who entertains this proposition is aware of both functions, and predicates *being so-and-so of* whatever results from applying the former to the latter. The proposition is true iff the function assigns the argument an object that is so-and-so.[29] So, if function-argument expressions can be genuine singular terms, then formal definite descriptions constructed with the 'ιx' operator can also be singular terms.

With this in mind, we can add (24c) and (24d) to our earlier examples (24a,b).

24a. 216 > 196
  b. $f_3(6) > f_2(14)$
  c. $\iota x\ [6 \times 6 \times 6 = x] > \iota x\ [14 \times 14 = x]$
  d. The result of multiplying 6 times 6 times 6 is greater than the result of multiplying 14 times 14.

My counterargument to Russell's conclusion in the Gray's Elegy passage can be summarized as follows: (i) if the function-argument expressions in (24b) can coherently be understood as genuine singular terms, then the formal definite descriptions in (24c) can also be understood in this way; (ii) the function-argument expressions in (24b) can be so understood; so (iii) the formal definite descriptions in (24c) can be coherently understood as singular terms, and (iv) Russell's Gray's Elegy argument does not rule out analyzing definite descriptions in English, like those in (24d), as genuine singular terms. This does not, of course, establish that English definite descriptions really are singular terms; nor does it show that there is anything wrong with Russell's positive analysis of them as "incomplete symbols." Which analysis of these expressions is correct is an empirical matter that depends on evidence concerning how they are used by English speakers across the whole range of environments in which they occur. The most that has been shown is that Russell's a priori argument in the Gray's Elegy passage does not establish that definite descriptions can't be singular terms.

2.3.3. LOCATING THE OFFENDING PREMISE

At this point, we must deal with an important unresolved issue. One who rejects Russell's impossibility argument for the reasons I have given may remain puzzled about how the meanings of complex singular terms can

---

[29] See Soames (2010b), pp. 110–19, and Soames (2014c and forthcoming) for more details, including an explanation of how it can be true that one predicates *being so-and-so* of the result of applying f_i to p_F, even in those cases in which f_i is undefined for p_F, and so there is no object x such that one predicates *being so-and-so* of x. The question of what it means for a proposition to predicate so-and-so of such-and-such will be revisited and discussed in greater detail in chapter 9, when Russell's robustly Platonic conception of propositions is revisited and compared with a more realistic alternative.

appear in some propositions as mere representatives of their denotations, while occurring in other propositions as direct subjects of predication. In addressing this puzzle, I will assume, simply for the sake of argument, that ⌜the F⌝ is a singular term that functions like ⌜ιx Fx⌝. I will also assume that enclosing a description in "meaning marks"—M . . . M—produces a logically proper name of the meaning of the description, just as enclosing the description in single quotes produces a logically proper name of the description itself. Just as a quote name—e.g., *'the curfew tolls the knell of parting day'*—can be replaced in any sentence S in which it occurs by a single symbol 'Q' conventionally selected to name the expression quoted, without changing the syntactic or semantic structure of S, or the proposition it expresses, so a meaning-mark name—e.g., *Mthe first line of Gray's ElegyM*—can be replaced in any sentence S in which it occurs by a single symbol 'M*' stipulated to name the meaning of the expression in question, without changing the syntactic or semantic structure of S, or the proposition it expresses.[30] With these assumptions in place, the puzzle is how the (a) and (b) sentences of (25) can express different propositions, as the sentences in (22) and (23) were intended to do.

25a. The F is G.
  b. Mthe FM is G.

Russell's reasoning was (i) that ⌜the F⌝ contributes its meaning M to the proposition expressed by (a) and ⌜Mthe FM⌝ contributes M to the proposition expressed by (b), and hence that the constituents of the propositions expressed by the two sentences are the same; (ii) that since (25a) and (25b) are both subject-predicate sentences, the propositions they express must have the same (subject-predicate) structure; (iii) that the constituents of a proposition, plus the structural relations they bear to one another, wholly determine all intentional properties of the proposition (including its truth conditions), which, in turn, determine the very identity of the proposition; and (iv) that, therefore, (25a) and (25b) must express the same proposition. This reasoning must be blocked if Russell's impossibility conclusion is to be avoided.

Consider the interaction of (i) and (ii) with (iii). Claim (i) maintains that because the subject expressions of the two sentences have the same meaning, they must contribute the same constituents to the propositions expressed. Claim (ii) maintains that because the sentences have the same subject-predicate structure, the propositions they express must have the same structure. Claim (iii) maintains that all there is to a proposition is given by its structure and constituents. I will argue that although there is a sense of 'constituent' in which (i) is true, there is no sense in which all three claims are true.

---

[30] Here, I use italics to produce quote names of (i) a quote name, and (ii) a meaning-mark name.

This can be made evident by looking more closely at the grammatical structures (25ag) and (25bg) of the two sentences.

25ag.   25bg.

If by 'constituent of a sentence' we mean *immediate constituent of the dominating 'S'* (the constituents NP and VP in these sentences), then the "constituents" of these sentences may be said to be the same. However, if we count constituents of a constituent as themselves (sub)constituents of the sentence—as, in any complete account, we must—then these *sentences* have different structures and different constituents. Whereas (25a) contains an occurrence of a determiner and a noun, (25b) does not, since its subject is a single constituent, with no grammatical subconstituents of its own.

The importance of the subconstituents of the main constituents of a sentence to its overall grammatical structure is shown by the fact that these subconstituents are visible to, and crucial for, many grammatical processes. The point is illustrated by comparing the behavior of (26a), (26b), and (26c), with respect to such grammatical processes as cleft formation (27), restrictive relative clause formation (28), quantificational binding (29), and dislocation (30).

26a. The author of *Waverley* is G.
  b. M* is G ('M*' is a single-symbol name of the meaning of 'the author of *Waverley*'.)
  c. Mthe author of *Waverley*M is G.
27a. It is *Waverley*, the author of which is G.
  b. *It is *Waverley*, M* is G.
  c. *It is *Waverley*, Mthe author of whichM is G.
28a. The book the author of which is G is popular.
  b. The book M* is G is popular.
  c. *The book Mthe author of whichM is G is popular.[31]

---

[31] Although (28b,c) might be understood as grammatical, though semantically deviant, sentences containing *nonrestrictive* relative clauses, they have no grammatical analysis as restrictive relatives.

29a. There is at least one book the author of which is G

   b. *There is at least one book M* is G.

   c. *There is at least one book Mthe author of whichM is G.[32]

30a. *Waverley*, the author of it is G.

   b. *Waverley,* M* is G.

   c. *Waverley,* Mthe author of itM is G.

In light of the grammatical differences between (26a) and (26b,c), it is reasonable to conclude that the grammatical structure and subconstituents of complex expressions like definite descriptions are, in some sense, parts of the total grammatical constituency and structure of sentences in which they occur, in a way in which that structure and those subconstituents are *not* parts of the constituency and structure of sentences in which special Russellian *names* of the meanings of those expressions are substituted for the expressions themselves. Given Russell's conception of *propositional* constituency and structure as encoding the *grammatical* constituency and structure of sentences, one has reason to suspect that this difference in grammar should be reflected in a difference between the proposition expressed by (26a) and the one expressed by (26b,c). *If this is right, then just as the grammatical constituents of the complex singular term in (26a) are significant grammatical (sub)constituents of the sentence as a whole, so the constituents of its meaning are—in some reasonable sense—significant (sub) constituents of the proposition expressed by (26a), without being constituents of the proposition expressed by (26b) and (26c).* With this, Russell's impossibility argument is threatened.[33]

The crucial point to notice here is the following: A complex meaning M with parts or constituents may be a constituent of a proposition p without M's constituents being (sub)constituents of p, even though M may occur in other propositions p* in which the constituents of M are (sub) constituents of p*. This may occur when N_E is a logically proper name for M and p is expressed by a sentence ...N_E... and C_E is a syntactically and semantically complex expression that expresses M and p* is expressed by the corresponding sentence ...C_E....

---

[32] Just as there is no quantificational binding from outside of quotation-mark names, so there is no such binding in the case of meaning-mark names.

[33] As indicated in Salmon (2005), the same point can be looked at in a slightly different way. Let 'B' be a Russellian proper name for a particular man's body. Then the proposition expressed by 'B is located in Santa Monica' is a singular proposition about a particular human body, of which that body is itself a constituent. Of course, the body has many parts—including, we may imagine, toes. However, the fact that it has ten toes plays no role in determining the identity of the proposition. Here, a "constituent" of something that is the subject of a singular proposition p is not itself a constituent of p. Something similar is true of a singular proposition about the meaning M of ⌜ɿx Fx⌝. As previously indicated, M is a complex the constituents of which include the propositional functions f and p_F. However, even though these are constituents of M, and also of the proposition expressed by ⌜ɿx Fx is so-and-so⌝, they are *not* constituents of the proposition expressed by ⌜Mɿx FxM is so-and-so⌝. It remains to be explained, how, exactly, this can be so.

The idea may be illustrated by letting 'logicism' name the proposition *that mathematics is reducible to logic*, expressed by (31).

31. Mathematics is reducible to logic.
32a. Russell attempted to establish that mathematics is reducible to logic.
  b. Russell attempted to establish logicism.
33a. Mary believes that Russell attempted to establish that mathematics is reducible to logic.
  b. Mary believes that Russell attempted to establish logicism.

On the supposition that 'logicism' and 'that mathematics is reducible to logic' name the same proposition, (31), which they contribute to the propositions expressed by the sentences in (32) and (33), it would appear that, on Russell's principles, the (a) and (b) sentences should mean the same thing, and so express the same propositions. But they don't, since it is possible to believe the proposition expressed (32b) without believing proposition (32a). Consider, for example, a student attending her first lecture in the philosophy of mathematics. She is told that logicism is a proposition defended by Russell about the relationship between logic and mathematics, formalism is a doctrine defended by Hilbert about the interpretation of mathematics, and so on. At this stage she is unable to distinguish logicism from other propositions about the relationship between logic and mathematics, or to describe its content in any more informative way. Being unfamiliar with the concept *theory reduction,* she may be unable even to *entertain* the proposition *that mathematics is reducible to logic,* in which case she surely can't *believe* that *Russell attempted to establish that mathematics is reducible to logic.* Nevertheless, she may acquire beliefs about logicism. She may be told "Russell attempted to establish logicism," and thereby come to believe *that Russell attempted to establish logicism.* Since she doesn't thereby come to believe *that Russell attempted to establish that mathematics is reducible to logic,* the (a) and (b) propositions in (32) and (33) must be different. This falsifies Russell's (Ia) and so leaves the crucial thesis (Ib) unsupported, thereby undermining his argument that definite descriptions (and other function-argument expressions) can't be singular terms.

2.3.4. THE EPISTEMOLOGY OF MEANING, UNDERSTANDING, AND ACQUAINTANCE

Though telling, this response to Russell's argument is incomplete for three reasons. First, while I have shown that the *necessarily equivalent* propositions (32a) and (32b) can differ despite the fact that they predicate the same property of *the same predication targets* (which are their major constituents), I have not yet explained how two propositions can be *non-equivalent* by virtue of having *different predication targets,* when their major constituents— which include the properties to be predicated and the constituents used to provide those targets—are identical. This is what must be explained, if we are to truly understand the difference between the crucial propositions (22a,b), and (23a,b) used in Russell's argument. Second, I have not explained what conception of propositions is needed in order to accommodate the difference between propositions (32a) and (32b). Explanations of both of these points will be sketched in the next section of this chapter, and finally put to rest in chapter 9, when I discuss Russell's 1910–12 critique of propositions as he had conceived of them up until then. There I will argue that his critique contains the germ of an idea—unfortunately undeveloped by him—for a new, more plausible conception of propositions that, among other things, allows us to properly characterize the genuine differences between propositions with the same major constituents.

In this section I will deal with aspects of Russell's 1905 view that would have prevented him from recognizing the significance of (32) and (33), even if they had been presented to him. In distinguishing between the propositions (32a) and (32b), I relied on what has become a commonplace in the philosophy of language of our time—namely, that one can acquire competence with an ordinary proper name (of a person, place, or thing) by picking it up in conversation with others who use it to refer to its bearer without oneself knowing very much about the bearer, or being able to give an accurate and uniquely identifying description of it.[34] For example, an agent A who has heard the name 'Peano' may be able to use it to express, and come to believe, singular propositions about Peano, even if A knows little more about him than that he was a mathematician, while failing to know, and even misdescribing, his major accomplishments, and being unable to uniquely, and noncircularly, identify the referent of the name. It was this feature of names that I drew on when I assumed that Mary's brief classroom introduction to the name 'logicism' was sufficient for her to be able to use sentences containing it to express, and come to believe, the singular proposition (32b), even though she had never entertained the proposition referred to by 'logicism' (and expressed by (31)), she couldn't describe it uniquely, and she knew little more about it than that it is a proposition about the relationship between logic and mathematics. By 1905 it was unlikely that Russell would have accepted this assumption about the use of names.

The reason for his reluctance would have been centered on his notion of acquaintance, which played two closely connected roles in his view of language and cognition. First, it imposed an epistemic constraint on the expressions that count as genuine names (as opposed to disguised descriptions). In order for an agent A to successfully use an expression n as a name for an object o, Russell required that A be acquainted with o. Second, in order for A to be able to entertain a proposition p, A must be acquainted with each of p's constituents. In 1903 and earlier, Russell seems to have had a relaxed view of acquaintance according to which I am genuinely acquainted with all the people and things I encounter in everyday life—including those like Pericles, Caesar, and Abraham Lincoln of whom I have heard only by name. However, his conception of acquaintance changed

---

[34] See Kripke (1972) and chapter 14 of Soames (2003d) for discussion.

between 1903 and 1905, when, in "On Fundamentals" and "On Denoting," he came to doubt that agents could be acquainted with anything they hadn't themselves perceived or cognitively encountered (in a narrow sense that allows perception of other bodies while denying perception of other people, on the grounds that they have, or are, unperceivable minds). By 1910, when he published "Knowledge by Acquaintance and Knowledge by Description," he had come to the unfortunate view that the only things one can name, and the only things that can be constituents of propositions one can entertain, are those to which we bear such a close epistemic relationship that we virtually cannot be mistaken about them—ourselves, our own private sense data, and the properties and relations in Plato's heaven.

The dynamic driving Russell down this road came from his conception of thought and meaning as transparent to the individual thinker and language user. It was axiomatic for him that whatever else an agent A might be mistaken about, A can be sure of what he means by an expression or a sentence, and of what he presently is, or is not, thinking. Since the meaning of a genuine name is its referent, if A thinks he means something by a name n, there must be something o that n really means and refers to; and if A thinks he means o by n, it can't turn out that n really refers to a different object o* that A has confused with o. As a consequence of these ideas, Russell thought that in order for n count as a genuine name, n must name an object the existence and identity of which it is all but impossible to be mistaken about. Moreover, the propositions one entertains must be made up exclusively of such constituents. By 1910, he would have taken these doctrines to rule out my use of 'logicism' as a genuine name to establish that propositions (32a) and (32b) differ despite predicating the same property of the same predication target. It is not unreasonable to think that he would have been of the same mind in 1905.

Since one should never confuse failure to convince a philosopher with failure to produce a good argument against him, this observation doesn't undermine the merit of the lessons drawn from (32) and (33). However, it does usefully connect what Russell took to be his master argument in "On Denoting"—against the possibility of definite descriptions being singular terms—with larger epistemological issues involving naming, meaning, and understanding. We know from the reconstruction of that argument in section 2.3.1 that according to Russell, in order for M to be the meaning of E for agent A, A must know of M that it is the meaning of E—where knowing this is knowing the singular proposition (34) in which *being the meaning of E* is predicated of M.

34. M is the meaning of E.

When $E = \ulcorner \iota x\ Fx \urcorner$, M is a complex the constituents of which include f_i and p_F—just as the meaning of the name 'logicism' is a complex the constituents of which are the (sub)constituents of the proposition *that mathematics is reducible to logic*. According to the critique given in section 2.3.3 above, f_i and

p_F are *not* themselves (sub)constituents of proposition (34)—in the sense of having to be identified by one who entertains the proposition—just as the constituents of proposition (31) are *not* themselves (sub)constituents of (35).

> 35. The proposition Russell defended, namely logicism, is the meaning of the name 'logicism'.

Russell would have denied this in both cases, while adding, in the case of the description, a further objection. Surely, he would have objected, one who knows that M is the meaning of ⌜ιx Fx⌝, thereby *understands* ⌜ιx Fx⌝—which requires one to know that 'ιx' means f, and that F(x) means p_F—and thereby *understands*, not just the description as a whole, but also its constituents. Since the critique of him doesn't account for this, Russell would have concluded that it is untenable.

However, he would have been wrong. One who knows no Spanish at all could be told by a reliable source, and so come to believe, that 'el profesor de filosofia' means *the professor of philosophy*, and so come to learn that the Spanish definite description means M, without either understanding its constituent expressions, or knowing which of them means what. (The point is even more obvious if one is told what proposition is expressed by a whole sentence none of the constituents of which one understands.) In fact, we might well say that such an agent doesn't really *understand* the description either, in the sense in which to understand an expression one must possess the knowledge and ability to use it in the expected way in communicating with genuinely competent speakers. But this only shows something we ought to have realized independently: *there is more to understanding most expressions than knowing, of that which they mean, that they do mean those things.*[35]

The critique of Russell in the previous section is consistent with this truth; the objection to that critique made here on his behalf is not. The objection implicitly assumes that knowing, of the meaning M of E, that it is the meaning of E, is all, or part, of the *explanation* of what understanding E amounts to. Not only is this contentious, it is, as I have argued elsewhere, false; often one knows semantic facts about an expression by virtue of understanding the expression, rather than the other way around.[36] Since the point applies to the expressions that are here in question, the critique of Russell is consistent with a proper understanding of the relationship between linguistic understanding and semantic knowledge.

2.3.5. REMAINING QUESTIONS ABOUT PROPOSITIONS

In my view, these considerations—the *reductio*, the critique of the Russellian premise (Ia), and the entanglement of his argument with questionable epistemological constraints on meaning, naming, and

---

[35] See Bowman (2012).
[36] Soames (1989b).

understanding—effectively dispose of the argument in the Gray's Elegy passage, *as an objection to Russell's earlier theory of denoting*. However, I am conscious of a pending explanatory debt that must be paid if we are to understand the perplexing issues raised by that argument. Without knowing more about what propositions are, beyond the fact that they are structured complexes in which one or more constituents are (somehow) predicated of others, it is hard to clearly understand how two propositions with the same major constituents—one of which is a property to be predicated and the others providing predication targets—can differ from one another, as they do in examples (22a,b), (23b,c), and (32a,b). Even if we are convinced that there is a crucial distinction between a complex constituent occurring in such a way that its constituents are also (sub)constituents of the proposition, versus occurring in a way in which they are not, the distinction will remain mysterious until we know what it is for something to *occur in a proposition* at all. What does this talk of the structure and constituents of a proposition amount to, anyway? How is it determined from the structure and constituents of a proposition what is required to entertain it, and what its intentional properties are—e.g., what is predicated of what, which things are represented in which ways, and what conditions must be satisfied in order for the proposition to be true? These are questions that Russell left largely unanswered, and that so far I haven't answered either.

The key to answering these questions is also the key to solving "the problem of the unity of the proposition" that puzzled Russell in *The Principles of Mathematics*. As I explained in the previous chapter, there the fundamental question was "How can propositions be bearers of intentionality —in ways in which sets, n-tuples, functions, and formal tree-structures specifying hierarchical dominance and linear precedence relations, are not?" I believe that the key to answering this question, as well as those raised here, is to replace the conception of propositions as Platonic entities in which objects, properties, and functions somehow stand in purely abstract relations to one another with a different conception that defines propositions in terms of the cognitive operations of agents who entertain them—relations of *focusing on, or thinking of, so-and-so*, of *applying a function to such-and-such*, of *predicating a property of an intended target*, and the like. When propositions are defined as complex acts in which agents perform these operations, it is natural (i) to take their constituents to be the objects, functions, and properties focused and operated on, or with, and (ii) to view their structure as given by the cognitive operations required to entertain the propositions.[37]

On this conception, the difference between propositions (32a) and (32b) is that whereas both require the agent to think of, and focus on, the man

---

[37] On this conception, a proposition isn't *composed* of its constituents, but defined in terms of them.

Russell and the proposition logicism, and to predicate *attempting to establish* of that ordered pair, only the former proposition imposes the further constraint that the agent think of, and focus on, its propositional argument *by entertaining it*—which includes performing the required cognitive operations on its constituents.

32a. Russell attempted to establish that mathematics is reducible to logic.
  b. Russell attempted to establish logicism.

In short, despite having identical truth conditions arising from predicating the same property of the same arguments, the two propositions differ by virtue of the fact that only one requires the constituents of its propositional argument to be cognitively accessed in the course of performing the operations in terms of which the larger proposition is defined. Whereas this constraint arises naturally on a conception of propositions as cognitive act types, the Platonic conception of propositions that Russell worked with has no plausible way of accommodating it.

In the case of (23a) and (23b)—on an analysis that treats the description 'the first line of Gray's Elegy' as a singular term—both propositions are cognitive acts in which an agent predicates *denoting 'the curfew tolls the knell of parting day'* of something provided by the complex meaning f_{the} *plus* g (where g assigns to an arbitrary object o the proposition that o is a line of Gray's Elegy that precedes all other lines).

23a. The first line of Gray's elegy denotes 'the curfew tolls the knell of parting day'.
  b. Mthe-first-line-of-Gray's-ElegyM denotes 'the curfew tolls the knell of parting day'.

The difference between the two propositions is the sense in which that complex meaning provides the predication target. This difference has nothing to do with passive gazing at abstract Platonic structure; instead it is a matter of *what the agent intends to be doing*. In the case of (23b) the agent intends to predicate *denoting 'the curfew tolls the knell of parting day'* of the complex meaning itself; in the case of (23a) the agent intends to predicate that content of *whatever is determined by that meaning*. One can think of this as involving two closely related senses of predication—one involving *direct predication* of the complex meaning (for which its constituents don't have to be cognitively accessed) and one involving *indirect predication* of *the result of applying one of its constituents to the other* (for which they do). On this conception, the two propositions differ in structure and truth value, because they involve different, though related, predication operations on different, though related, predication targets—even though those targets are provided by the same constituent.

Although this conception of propositions is not Russellian, it is one that can be reached by starting from a seminal idea in Russell's classic essay "On Truth and Falsehood," published in 1912 as chapter 12 of *The Problems of Philosophy*. Succumbing to his failure to solve the problem of propositional unity, he there abandons propositions entirely, proposing a *multiple relation theory of judgment* to do the work that propositions had previously been intended to do. The seminal idea is that although abstract Platonic propositions can never be unified, their constituents can be unified in judgment *by the mind of the agent doing the judging*. As we will see in the next chapter, which focuses on Russell's essay, there are serious problems with the new theory presented there. However, as we shall also see, the idea of appealing to the mind of the agent who entertains a proposition to define its constitutive features solves a number of important problems, including those with which we have struggled here.

2.3.6. APPLICATION OF RUSSELL'S IMPOSSIBILITY ARGUMENT TO FREGE'S THEORY

At this point, one final issue remains to be discussed before we can put the Gray's Elegy argument to bed. What is the force of that argument, not against Russell's earlier theory of *The Principles of Mathematics* and "On Fundamentals," but against Frege's theory of descriptions—which was, by this time, his main target? Here, the dialectic changes substantially. Since, for Frege, there are no singular propositions, the focus of concern shifts to requirements for naming, knowing-of, and quantifying-in. For Frege, whenever we think about anything in order to predicate some property of it, we think about it in some way or other. This "mode of presentation" of the object is one of the many Fregean senses capable of determining, or picking out, that object. For example, when Mary looks out the window and sees a tall man walking down the street, her visual acquaintance with the man provides her with a way of thinking about him—e.g., as the individual walking down the street who appears in such and such a way. On the basis of this acquaintance, she can, if she likes, introduce a name and use it in predicating properties of him. She can also be described as *believing of* the man that he has certain properties, and not others. In the same way, it would seem, she could introduce ⌜MtheFM⌝ as a name of the meaning M she is acquainted with through her understanding of ⌜The F⌝. So, it would seem, she should be able to say of M that it is a meaning, *knowing of* it that it is the meaning of ⌜The F⌝. How then does the Gray's Elegy passage present a problem for Frege?

The problem, if there is one, lies in an understandable worry that the Fregean explanation just given takes too much for granted. How, Russell would ask, can Mary's supposed acquaintance with M provide a *unique* higher-level sense that determines M? For anything x, whether it be a sense or not, Frege recognizes indefinitely many senses that denote x. So, Russell would insist, if a Fregean tells us that ⌜MtheFM⌝ is to be a name that denotes the sense of ⌜The F⌝, then the Fregean must also explain how we are supposed to figure out *which higher-level sense* in this vast array is to be the unique sense of the supposed new name. Russell doesn't think this challenge can be met. Presumably, when we learned the language we came to understand ⌜The F⌝ and so became acquainted with its sense. But, Russell would insist, there was never any instruction about what a name for its meaning would mean. So, he thinks, a true Fregean should be at a loss in trying to understand the new name; and if one can't understand such a name, it is hard to see how one could correctly be described as *knowing of* the meaning M that it is the meaning of ⌜The F⌝. After all, simply knowing that *the meaning of* ⌜*The F*⌝ is what ⌜The F⌝ means is not enough to *know of* M that it is what ⌜The F⌝ means. But then, Russell thinks, the Fregean has no way of explaining what the agent's knowledge of meaning could possibly consist in.

Although there are genuine difficulties here for Frege, nothing in the Gray's Elegy passage presents him with a new problem he didn't already have. The difficulties are variants of those presented by his hierarchy of indirect senses and referents, discussed in section 5 of chapter 2. In the case of (36), embedding S under 'believe' is supposed to result in the expression by S of a higher-level "indirect sense" that determines its ordinary sense, with further embeddings, as in (36b), yielding further movement up the hierarchy.

36a. A believes that S.
   b. B knows that A believes that S.

According to the orthodox Fregean story, one who understands unembedded occurrences of S is thereby *acquainted* with its ordinary sense, OS. Given (36a), the agent focuses on OS, knowing that the function designated by 'believe' must operate on it. Since thinking about anything requires *a way of apprehending it*, thinking about OS requires a Fregean mode of presentation. Frege maintains that this isn't a problem insofar as *acquaintance* with something *always* provides a way of thinking about it. This is the indirect sense, IS, of S, grasp of which allows the agent to understand (36a). The process is repeated for (36b). Since the agent has grasped the sense of (36a), he is already acquainted with IS (which is one of its constituents). This acquaintance provides him with the doubly indirect sense of S, required for understanding (36b). So, the Fregean contends, there is nothing problematic about the hierarchy. For the same reason, he would maintain, the very fact that we understand the denoting phrase ⌜the F⌝ means that we are acquainted with its sense M, which in turn provides us with a higher-level sense that may serve as the meaning of the name ⌜Mthe FM⌝ of M.

However, just as with the hierarchy, so with the Gray's Elegy problem, there must be more to the story. The meaning of (36a) doesn't change from agent to agent, depending on how they think of the meaning OS they all ascribe to S. Nor does it change from time to time in which they consider (36a), due to changes in the modes of presentation by which they apprehend OS. So, what Frege needs is not *an* acquaintance-based way of thinking of OS for each agent and time, but *the* acquaintance-based way of so doing, the same for every agent and time. Similarly in the Gray's Elegy case, the fact that understanding the description brings with it acquaintance with M, together with the fact that acquaintance always provides some mode of presentation or other of that with which one is acquainted, doesn't guarantee that different agents (at different times) converge on the same higher-level sense as the meaning of the name of M. Presumably, however, they must do so if each is able to report the beliefs and assertions of others concerning the properties of M—which each should, surely, be able to do. Unless the Fregean can explain such convergence, he will not have gotten to the bottom of Russell's concerns in the Gray's Elegy passage, any more than he will have answered corresponding concerns about the hierarchy.

In chapter 2, I pointed out a further worry: that in order for the Fregean story of the hierarchy of indirect senses to be adequate, it must guarantee that the indirect sense of S at a given level n *rigidly* picks out the same $n - 1^{st}$-level sense *at every counterfactual circumstance.* The point applies with equal force to the meaning of the name ⌜Mthe FM⌝. The problem for the Fregean is that nothing about acquaintance in and of itself ensures that the way of thinking about the object o of acquaintance that it provides will *rigidly* pick out o. After all, acquaintance with people, institutions, and physical objects doesn't guarantee any such unique and rigid sense by means of which agents think of them. All these things can appear to us in different ways, and—since they all have many properties—sometimes we think of them in terms of one set of salient properties, and sometimes we think of them in terms of another set. Since we don't think about them in the same way every time, the Fregean modes of presentation by which we apprehend them vary from agent to agent, and time to time. Moreover, these modes of presentation typically don't pick out their objects rigidly— since no matter how such an object may appear, it is usually possible for other objects to appear that way, and for that object not to so appear. Nor is the point limited to the objects mentioned so far. Books, poems, plays, musical pieces, and the like—thought of as abstract objects with which we are acquainted through their instances—can appear differently to us at different times, perhaps in ways in which it would be possible for different things of this kind to appear. If the same is true of Fregean senses, then the prospects of rendering his hierarchy harmless, and of giving an account of our ability to name Fregean senses, are not good.

As I mentioned in chapter 2, the only way out for Frege that I can discern requires embracing an ambitious Platonist epistemology about meanings/ thoughts/propositions. What he needs is a convincing argument that, unlike the objects we encounter in everyday life, abstract Fregean senses of his postulated "third realm of being" are cognitively transparent and inherently beyond appearance—with essential natures fully, rigidly, and immediately graspable in the same way by every mind acquainted with them. If this could be shown, then we would know that to be acquainted

with a sense s is to have access to a unique higher-level sense s* that reveals the complete and true nature of s, and so puts us *en rapport* with s.
With such special essence-revealing higher senses in place, Frege could
use such a sense M* for M in making the latter the predication target of
being the meaning of ⌜the F⌝, thus answering Russell's objection. If such
thoughts are available, then the Fregean analysis can withstand Russell's
attempted refutation in the Gray's Elegy passage.

Because I don't accept the robust Platonic epistemology required by
this response, I don't find the Fregean story plausible. However, since
Russell's own epistemology of acquaintance with properties, propositions, and propositional functions shared so much with Frege's Platonic
epistemology, he was not in the best position to resist this Fregean defense. Thus we must assess the argument of the Gray's Elegy passage, on
which Russell seemed to have placed such great store, as falling short.
Substantively, it does not establish that definite descriptions are "incomplete symbols" with "no meaning in isolation"; nor does it prove that they
can't be analyzed as singular terms. Historically, it refutes neither Frege's
theory of descriptions, nor the type of theory that Russell himself had
been working on between the publication of *The Principles of Mathematics*
and the publication of "On Denoting." What it does do is introduce an
intriguing problem about Russellian propositions that defenders of such
would do well to address.

3. SOLUTIONS TO LOGICAL PUZZLES AS ARGUMENTS FOR RUSSELL'S THEORY

To this point in "On Denoting," Russell has stated an intriguing analysis
of denoting phrases with special emphasis on singular definite descriptions, and has offered some mostly inconclusive arguments against alternative analyses of these phrases. Next, he turns to three logical puzzles,
his solutions to which provide important evidence in support of this theory. Whether or not this, and related, evidence is sufficient to establish his
theory as broadly correct is not a matter capable of proof from first principles. It is a question of whether his *explanations* of the relevant logico-
linguistic facts are the best and most fruitfully generalizable.

3.1. Excluded Middle and Logical Scope

One of Russell's puzzles involves the law of classical logic called *the law
of the excluded middle*. Here is his statement of the puzzle, which involves
sentences (37a–c).

> By the law of excluded middle, either 'A is B' or 'A is not B' must be true.
> Hence either 'The present King of France is bald' or 'The present King of
> France is not bald' must be true. Yet if we enumerated the things that are

bald and the things that are not bald, we should not find the present King of France in either list. Hegelians, who love a synthesis, will probably conclude that he wears a wig.[38]

37a. The present king of France is bald.
   b. The present king of France is not bald.
   c. Either the present king of France is bald or the present king of France is not bald.

In the passage, Russell gives a reason for supposing that neither (37a) nor (37b) is true, which in turn seems to suggest that (37c) is not true. But that violates a law of classical logic that tells us that for every sentence S, ⌜Either S or ~S⌝ is true. Since Russell regarded the law as correct, he needed a way of defusing this apparent counterexample.

The key to doing this lies in his general rule R for determining the logical form of sentences containing definite descriptions.

R. C [the F] ⇒ ∃x ∀y [(Fy ⟷ y = x) & Cx]

This rule for translating a sentence into its logical form says that if a definite description occurs in some sentence along with additional material C, then it can be eliminated (bringing us closer to the logical form of the sentence) by replacing the description with a variable, and introducing quantifiers plus the uniqueness clause as indicated. When we apply this rule to (37a), C corresponds to the phrase 'is bald' and the description is 'the present king of France'. Putting this in the form of the left-hand side of R, we have (37a').

37a'. B [the present king of France]

Applying R to this gives the logical form (lfa), in which 'B' abbreviates 'is bald', 'K' abbreviates 'is king of', and 'f' names France.

lfa. ∃x ∀y [(Kyf ⟷ y = x) & Bx]

In giving R, Russell takes himself to be explaining the contribution that a definite description makes to any sentence that contains it, which means that R is intended to apply to all sentences, no matter how complex.[39] With this in mind, we apply it to the slightly more complex example, (37b), which he would first express in the more convenient form (37b').

37b'. ~B [the present king of France]

There are now two ways of applying R, depending on what part of (37b') we choose to play the role of C. If we take C in (37b') to be just what it was in (37a'), namely 'B', then we are viewing (37b') as (37b'1) and applying R inside the parentheses.

[38] "On Denoting," p. 485.
[39] Russell's discussion on pp. 482 and 488–90 makes this clear.

37b′1. (B [the present king of France])

This gives us

lfb1. ~ ∃x ∀y [(Kyf ⟷ y = x) & Bx]

If, on the other hand, we take '~ B' in (37b′) to play the role of C, then we treat (37b′) as (37b′2); applying R will then give us (lfb2).

37b′2. (~ B [the present king of France])
lfb2. ∃x ∀y [(Kyf ⟷ y = x) & ~Bx]

Thus, Russell's rule R for relating English sentences to their logical forms yields the conclusion that negative sentences containing descriptions are ambiguous, which, in fact, they are.

What is the difference between these two interpretations of (37b)—i.e., between (lfb1) and (lfb2)? The former may be paraphrased: *It is not the case that there is someone who is both bald and unique in being king of France*; the latter: *There is someone who is not bald, who is unique in being king of France*. The latter logically entails that there is a king of France, whereas the former does not. Notice also that (lfa) is incompatible with both of the logical forms of (37b)—i.e., (lfa) and (lfb1) cannot be jointly true, and (lfa) and (lfb2) cannot be jointly true. However, (lfa) and (lfb2) can be jointly untrue; both are untrue when there is no unique king of France. This does not violate the law of the excluded middle, however, because (lfb2) is not the logical negation of (lfa). Rather, (lfb1) is the logical negation of (lfa); these two cannot both fail to be true. If one is untrue, then the other must be true; thus their disjunction must be true, exactly as the law maintains.

We can now see how the theory of descriptions solves Russell's puzzle about the law of the excluded middle. Like all laws of logic, it applies to logical forms. When we look at the logical forms of (37a) and (37b), they provide no counterexample to it. This is compatible with the observation that there is a way of understanding (37a) and (37b) in which their disjunction is untrue, because (37b) is ambiguous. On the interpretation of (37b) in which it is logically the negation of (37a), it is always true when (37a) isn't, and the law is upheld. On the interpretation of (37b) in which both (37a) and (37b) can be jointly untrue, (37b) isn't logically the negation of (37a), and we don't have an instance of the law. Hence the puzzle is solved.

This example of the interaction of negation and descriptions provides a convenient way of explaining some of Russell's terminology. When sentence (37b) is analyzed as (37b′1) and ultimately as having the logical form (lfb1), the description *the present king of France* is said to take *narrow scope* (relative to the negation operator), and to have *secondary occurrence*, in the sentence or proposition as a whole. When (37b) is analyzed as (37b′2), and ultimately as having the logical form (lfb2), the description is said to take *wide scope* over the negation operator, and to have *primary occurrence* in the sentence or proposition.

Another example of the same sort is provided by (38), which may conveniently be represented as (38′), where 'F' is taken to express the property of being famous.

38. John believes that the person sitting over there is famous.
38′. John believes that F [the person sitting over there].

As in the case of a negative sentence, Russell's theory predicts that there are two interpretations of (38), and hence that it is ambiguous. On one interpretation, the description 'the person sitting over there' has narrow scope (relative to 'believe'), and secondary occurrence in the sentence or proposition. On this interpretation, R is applied within the subordinate clause by itself to give the logical form

lf1. John believes that $(\exists x \forall y [(\text{sitting over there } (y) \longleftrightarrow y = x) \& Fx])$

When interpreted in this way, (38) tells us that John believes that there is just one person sitting over there and whoever that person may be, that person is famous. On this reading, (38) may be true, even if no one is sitting over there; it may also be true if Mary is sitting there, but John doesn't know that she is, or think that she is famous—all that is required is that he believe that some famous person or other is sitting alone over there.

On the other interpretation of (38), the description 'the person sitting over there' has wide scope over the belief predicate, and primary occurrence in the sentence or proposition as a whole. On this reading, R is applied to (38″), with the italicized expressions playing the role of C in the rule.

38″. *John believes F* [the person sitting over there]

This results in the logical form

lf2. $\exists x \forall y [(\text{sitting over there } (y) \longleftrightarrow y = x) \& \text{John believes that } Fx]$

When (38) is interpreted in this way, it tells us that there is one and only one person sitting over there and John believes that person to be famous. In order for this to be true, there really must be just one person sitting over there and John must believe that person to be famous; however it is not necessary that John have any idea where that person is, or believe that anyone is sitting over there.

3.2. George IV and the Author of *Waverley*

Another logical puzzle to which Russell took his theory of descriptions to provide a solution involves the interaction of a law of logic known as *the substitutivity of identity* with propositional attitude ascriptions (sentences with verbs like 'believe', 'know', 'assert', 'doubt', and 'wonder'), which report a relation between an agent and a proposition. Here is Russell's statement of the puzzle.

If *a* is identical with *b*, whatever is true of the one is true of the other, and either may be substituted for the other in any proposition without altering the truth or falsehood of that proposition. Now George IV wished to know whether Scott was the author of *Waverley*; and in fact Scott *was* the author of *Waverley*. Hence we may substitute *Scott* for *the author of "Waverley"*, and thereby prove that George IV wished to know whether Scott was Scott. Yet an interest in the law of identity can hardly be attributed to the first gentleman of Europe.[40]

Far from a model of clarity, the passage swings inconsistently back and forth between talking about expressions and talking about the individuals that the expressions designate, as well as between talking about sentences and talking about the propositions those sentences express. Nevertheless, the problem it poses is clear enough. Sentences P1 and P2 of the following argument appear to be true, even though the conclusion, C, appears to be false.

P1.   George IV wondered whether Scott was the author of *Waverley*.

P2.   Scott was the author of *Waverley*—i.e., Scott = the author of *Waverley*

C.   George IV wondered whether Scott was Scott

What makes this observation troubling is the apparent conflict created by the law of the substitutivity of identity, which may be stated as follows:

SI.   When α and β are singular referring expressions, and the sentence $\ulcorner \alpha = \beta \urcorner$ is true, α and β refer to the same thing, and so substitution of one for the other in any true sentence will always yield a true sentence.

If P1 and P2 are true, SI is truth preserving, and C follows from P1 and P2 by SI, then C must also be true. The problem is that it seems not to be. Russell claims that his theory of descriptions solves the problem.

The puzzle about George IV's curiosity is now seen to have a very simple solution. The proposition 'Scott was the author of *Waverley*,' which . . . [when written out in unabbreviated form], does not contain any constituent 'the author of *Waverley*' for which we could substitute 'Scott'. This does not interfere with the truth of inferences resulting from making what is *verbally* the substitution of 'Scott' for 'the author of *Waverley*,' so long as 'the author of *Waverley*' has what I call a *primary* occurrence in the proposition considered.[41]

The second sentence of the passage contains the key idea. Since 'the author of *Waverley*' is a singular definite description, it is not, logically, a singular referring expression, and so it does not figure in applications of

[40] Ibid., p. 485.
[41] Ibid., pp. 488–89.

SI. (In discussing this example, Russell treats 'Scott' as a logically proper name.) This rule, like every logical rule, applies only to logical forms of sentences. So, to evaluate the argument, P1 and P2 have to be replaced with their logical forms.

Since P1 is a compound sentence containing a definite description, it is ambiguous—having one reading in which the description has primary occurrence, and one reading in which the description has secondary occurrence. Thus, there are two reconstructions of the argument—one corresponding to each of these readings of P1.[42]

<u>Argument 1: Primary Occurrence of the Description in P1</u>

P1$_p$. $\exists x \forall y [(y \text{ Wrote } \textit{Waverley} \longleftrightarrow y = x) \text{ \& George IV wondered whether } x = \text{Scott}]$
>
> There was one and only one person who wrote *Waverley* and George IV wondered whether he was Scott.

P2. $\exists x \forall y [(y \text{ Wrote } \textit{Waverley} \longleftrightarrow y = x) \text{ \& } x = \text{Scott}]$
>
> There was one and only one person who wrote *Waverley* and he was Scott.

C. George IV wondered whether Scott = Scott.

<u>Argument 2: Secondary Occurrence of the Description in P1</u>

P1$_s$. George IV wondered whether $\exists x \forall y [(y \text{ Wrote } \textit{Waverley} \longleftrightarrow y = x) \text{ \& } x = \text{Scott}]$
>
> George IV wondered whether (there was one and only one person who wrote *Waverley* and he was Scott).

P2. $\exists x \forall y [(y \text{ Wrote } \textit{Waverley} \longleftrightarrow y = x) \text{ \& } x = \text{Scott}]$
>
> There was one and only one person who wrote *Waverley* and he was Scott.

C. George IV wondered whether Scott = Scott.

Russell takes the reading on which the description has secondary occurrence as the most natural one. With this in mind, we evaluate Argument 2. Suppose that P1$_S$ and P2 are true. Then George IV wondered whether a certain proposition—the one expressed by P2—was true. And in fact, it was true. However, since P2 is not a simple identity statement $\ulcorner \alpha = \beta \urcorner$, and there is no singular referring expression in P1$_S$ to be substituted for 'Scott', we cannot use the rule SI to derive C from P1$_S$ and P2. So far so good.

But this is not the whole story. In the last sentence of the passage Russell says: "This does not interfere with the truth of inferences resulting from making what is *verbally* the substitution of 'Scott' for 'the author of *Waverley*', so long as 'the author of *Waverley*' has what I call a *primary* occurrence in the proposition considered." His point is that when the description is

---

[42] In discussing these arguments, I ignore tense.

interpreted as having primary occurrence in P1$_p$, the truth of the premises P1$_p$ and P2 *does* guarantee the truth of the conclusion C. But, according to the theory of descriptions, SI no more applies in Argument 1 than it did in Argument 2. Hence one cannot explain the difference between the two arguments, and the invalidity of Argument 2, by noting that the theory of descriptions does not allow one to apply SI by substituting 'Scott' for 'the author of *Waverley*'.

To understand what is responsible for the difference in these arguments, it is best to begin by verifying that the step from premises to conclusion in Argument 1 is truth preserving. If P1$_p$ is true, then there is one and only one individual who wrote *Waverley*, and the sentence—(i) 'George IV wondered whether $\underline{x}$ = Scott'—is true when '$\underline{x}$' is taken as a logically proper name of that individual. This in turn will be true just in case George IV wondered whether a certain proposition p—namely, the one expressed by the sentence (ii) '$\underline{x}$ = Scott'—was true, again taking '$\underline{x}$' to be a logically proper name of the unique individual who wrote *Waverley*. If P2 is true, then this individual is Scott, in which case '$\underline{x}$' and 'Scott' are logically proper names of the same person. Because of this, their having the same reference guarantees that they mean the same thing, and hence that substitution of one for the other in any sentence doesn't change the proposition expressed. From this we conclude that 'Scott = Scott' expresses the same proposition p as (ii) '$\underline{x}$ = Scott'. Since we have already established that George IV wondered whether p was true, it follows that C is also true. Thus the inference from P1$_p$ and P2 to C *is guaranteed to be truth preserving*, in Argument 1.

Next consider Argument 2. If P1$_s$ is true, then George IV wondered whether a certain proposition q was true—where q is the proposition that a single person wrote *Waverley* and that person was Scott. If P2 is true, then q is, in fact, true. However, this tells us nothing about whether George IV wondered whether the proposition p, that Scott is Scott, was true. Since it is clearly possible to wonder whether q is true without wondering whether p is true, it is possible for the premises of Argument 2 to be true, while the conclusion is false. Hence the argument is invalid.

Does this solution of the puzzle about George IV support Russell's theory of descriptions? Yes, provided that there really are two ways of taking P1, both of which are capable of being true, and both of which figure in arguments, along with P2, to conclusion C, one of which is a valid argument and one of which isn't. If this is a correct description of how we understand the English sentences P1, P2, and C, then Russell's theory provides an elegant explanation of that fact. Does P1 really have a sense in which it could both be true and figure in such a valid argument? I believe it does, and also that Russell recognized the kind of situation in which P1 might be used with this reading.

> when we say 'George IV wished to know whether Scott was the author of *Waverley*', we normally mean 'George IV wished to know whether one and only one man wrote *Waverley* and Scott was that man', but we *may* also mean: 'One

and only one man wrote *Waverley*, and George IV wished to know whether Scott was that man'. In the latter, 'the author of *Waverley*' has a *primary* occurrence; in the former, a *secondary*. The latter might be expressed by 'George IV wished to know, concerning the man who in fact wrote *Waverley,* whether he was Scott'. *This would be true, for example, if George IV had seen Scott at a distance, and had asked 'Is that Scott?'*[43]

A similar example, not employing a proper name for Scott, is provided by (39).

39. Mary wondered whether the author of *Waverley* wrote *Waverley*.

The most natural interpretation of (39) is one in which the description has primary occurrence—one and only one person x wrote *Waverley* and Mary wondered, about that person x, whether x wrote *Waverley*. A speaker who assertively uttered (39), intending this interpretation, might know precisely who the author of *Waverley* was, and have overhead Mary say "Did he write *Waverley*?" asking about the man in question. It seems clear that if (39) were used in this way, it would express a truth. It is a virtue of Russell's theory that it explains this.

There is however, a discordant note in this otherwise pleasing melody. It occurs in the words Russell used when setting up the puzzle to emphasize the falsity of the conclusion C that might—but for his theory of descriptions—wrongly be derived from P1 and P2. There, Russell dismisses C with the humorous remark, "Yet an interest in the law of identity can hardly be attributed to the first gentleman of Europe"—which seems to suggest that it would be absurd to suppose that anyone might doubt whether the proposition that Scott was Scott was true.[44] What we have just seen is that his own discussion in "On Denoting" just a few pages later takes such doubt to be quite possible, and that without it his chosen example would fail to provide the support for his theory of descriptions that he (rightly) takes it to provide.

For Russell in 1905, propositions are the meanings of sentences, and the contributions made by logically proper names to propositions expressed by sentences containing them are the entities they name. On this view, if α and β are different logically proper names of the same object, then $\ulcorner \alpha = \alpha \urcorner$ and $\ulcorner \alpha = \beta \urcorner$ express the same proposition. Can someone understand both sentences without knowing this, and even while accepting the former sentence and rejecting the latter? One of the passages from "On Denoting" we have already examined implicitly answers the question.

The latter [interpretation of P1, in which the description has primary occurrence] might be expressed by 'George IV wished to know, concerning the

---

[43] Ibid., p. 489. The emphasis on the last sentence is mine.
[44] This supposed triviality of any proposition to the effect *that o = o* is reiterated in the antepenultimate paragraph of "On Denoting."

man who in fact wrote *Waverley,* whether he was Scott'. *This would be true, for example, if George IV had seen Scott at a distance, and had asked 'Is that Scott?'*

Here, Russell imagines the demonstrative 'that' being used as a logically proper name for Scott. Since he uses 'Scott' as such a name throughout the discussion, the question he imagines George IV asking must be one about the proposition expressed by 'That is Scott', in which both singular terms are logically proper names of the same individual, and 'is' stands for identity. In short, Russell seems to be presupposing that when α and β are used as different logically proper names of the same individual, it is possible for one to understand $\ulcorner\alpha = \alpha\urcorner$ and $\ulcorner\alpha = \beta\urcorner$ *without knowing that they express the same proposition p.* In such a case, one may accept the former sentence while wondering about the truth of the latter. It is a short step from here to the view that such an agent simultaneously believes p to be true while also wondering whether p is true, because the agent doesn't know that the proposition he or she wonders about is one that he or she already believes—and even knows.

Although such a position is coherent and defensible, there is reason—beyond the mocking reference to the lack of interest in the law of identity by the first gentleman of Europe (and its echo in the antepenultimate paragraph of "On Denoting")—to believe that it wasn't Russell's view.[45] For one thing, we know from both "On Fundamentals" and the penultimate paragraph of "On Denoting" that he had already decided that we are not acquainted with other minds (people), from which it followed that they could not be referents of logically proper names, or constituents of propositions we are capable of entertaining. Thus, the use of 'Scott' as a logical proper name in "On Denoting" must be regarded as a useful fiction to avoid epistemological complications that might otherwise distract from the logic-linguistic theory presented there.

Moreover, even though Russell seemed to retain the idea in "On Fundamentals" that we are acquainted with the bodies of other people, and so with many physical objects, at the end of "On Denoting" he indicates that matter "in the sense in which matter occurs in physics" is *not* among the objects of our acquaintance. By then he was on a fast track to eliminating everything physical, as well as everything mental outside oneself, from the charmed circle of possible objects of acquaintance. As I have mentioned, by 1910 he held that the only objects that can be referents of logically proper names are those the existence and identity of which one can't be mistaken about. Since material objects and other human beings don't satisfy this condition, he held that they couldn't be the referents of logically proper names, or occur as constituents of propositions we can entertain.

---

[45] For contemporary defenses of such a position, see Salmon (1984, 1989), Soames (1986b), especially sections III, IV, and IX, Soames (2002), and the introduction to Salmon and Soames (1988).

To sum up our whole discussion: We began by distinguishing two sorts of knowledge of objects, namely, knowledge by *acquaintance* and knowledge by *description*. Of these it is only the former that brings the object itself before the mind. We have acquaintance with sense-data, with many universals, and possibly with ourselves, but not with physical objects or other minds. We have *descriptive* knowledge of an object when we know that it is *the* object having some property or properties with which we are acquainted; that is to say, when we know that the property or properties in question belong to one object, and no more, we are said to have knowledge of that one object by description, whether or not we are acquainted with the object. Our knowledge of physical objects and of other minds is only knowledge by description, the descriptions involved being usually such as involve sense-data. All propositions intelligible to us, whether or not they primarily concern things only known to us by description, are composed wholly of constituents with which we are acquainted, for a constituent with which we are not acquainted is unintelligible to us.[46]

In section 4 of this chapter, I will return to the problems posed by this radical epistemological position. Here, it is enough to note that the pleasing example of George IV, and the support it provides for his theory of descriptions, rests on philosophical presuppositions that Russell was not really prepared to accept.

3.3. More on Scope: Russell and the Yacht Owner

In the midst of his discussion of George IV and the author of *Waverley*, Russell remarks about the (scope) ambiguity of logically compound sentences containing descriptions that is correctly predicted by his theory of descriptions, illustrating his point with a joke about a touchy yacht owner.

> When we say: "George IV wished to know whether so-and-so," or when we say "So-and-so is surprising" or "So-and-so is true," etc., the "so-and-so" must be a proposition. Suppose now that "so-and-so" contains a denoting phrase. We may either eliminate this denoting phrase from the subordinate proposition "so-and-so," or from the whole proposition in which "so-and-so" is a mere constituent. Different propositions result according to which we do. I have heard of a touchy owner of a yacht to whom a guest, on first seeing it, remarked, "I thought your yacht was larger than it is"; and the owner replied, "No, my yacht is not larger than it is." What the guest meant was, "The size that I thought your yacht was is greater than the size your yacht is"; the meaning attributed to him is, "I thought the size of your yacht was greater than the size of your yacht."[47]

[46] Russell (1910–11), pp. 127–28.
[47] Russell (1905d), p. 489.

Although this is one of the most widely known philosophical jokes, Russell's delivery of it was flawed. In order for the example to illustrate his theory of descriptions, we must understand the sentence uttered

40. I thought your yacht was larger than it is.

as equivalent to a sentence containing occurrences of a description 'the size of your yacht', one of which must have primary occurrence in the sentence/proposition, and so take scope over the propositional attitude verb.

41a. I thought the size of your yacht was greater than *the size of your yacht*.

Once this is seen, it is clear (i) that what the guest meant is the proposition expressed by (41b), in which the second occurrence of the description in (41a) has primary occurrence, and the first occurrence has secondary occurrence, and (ii) that what the yacht owner pretended to take him to mean is the proposition expressed by (41c), in which both occurrences of the description have secondary occurrence.

41b. $\exists x \, \forall y \, [(y$ is a size of your yacht $\longleftrightarrow y = x) \,\&\,$ I thought that $\exists z \, \forall w \, [(w$ is a size of your yacht $\longleftrightarrow w = z) \,\&\, z$ is greater than $x]]$

 c. I thought that $\exists z \, \forall w \, [(w$ is a size of your yacht $\longleftrightarrow w = z) \,\&\, \exists x \, \forall y \, [(y$ is a size of your yacht $\longleftrightarrow y = x) \,\&\, z$ is greater than $x]]$

Though Russell was correct in noting that the meaning attributed to the guest by the yacht owner is (equivalent to) (41c), he was incorrect in maintaining that the real meaning of the guest's remark is (equivalent to) (42).

42. *The size I thought your yacht was* is greater than the size your yacht is.

There are two things wrong with his characterization. First, the truth of (42) requires an agent A who utters it to have had *one and only one size previously in mind that A thought was the size of the yacht in question.* By contrast, what the truth of the guest's utterance of (40) really requires is simply that the guest previously thought that whatever (unique) size the yacht might turn out to have would exceed *the one and only one size that is the actual size of the yacht*—which is precisely what (41b) tells us. Second, Russell's contrast between (41c) and (42) is *not* a contrast between two examples that differ only in the relative scopes of the same description. Instead, he *changes* one of the descriptions, thereby making the yacht example wrongly appear as if it were *not* an instance of the general point enunciated in the sentences of the passage preceding it. Fortunately, these errors are correctable as indicated here—preserving the relevance of the example, and the support it provides for Russell's theory of descriptions.[48]

---

[48] Kripke (2005) offers a different analysis, plus a report on Nathan Salmon's contrasting view. My analysis of the example sides with Salmon over Kripke. Nevertheless, the Kripke paper contains an important larger point about examples like (41a) that contain multiple

3.4. Negative Existentials

The final logical puzzle mentioned by Russell in "On Denoting" to which his theory offers a solution is the problem of negative existentials, which he states as follows.

> Consider the proposition 'A differs from B'. If this is true, there is a difference between A and B, which fact may be expressed in the form 'the difference between A and B subsists'. But if it is false that A differs from B, then there is no difference between A and B, which fact may be expressed in the form 'the difference between A and B does not subsist'. *But how can a non-entity be the subject of a proposition? 'I think, therefore I am' is no more evident than 'I am the subject of a proposition, therefore I am,' provided 'I am' is taken to assert subsistence or being, not existence.* Hence, it would appear, it must always be self-contradictory to deny the being of anything; but we have seen, in connexion with Meinong, that to admit being also sometimes leads to contradictions. Thus if A and B do not differ, to suppose either that there is, or that there is not, such an object as 'the difference between A and B' seems equally impossible.[49]

Certain features of this example, involving 'differs' and 'difference', raise complications that I will temporarily put aside, before returning to them later. The fundamental point to notice at the outset is Russell's use of the notion "the subject of a proposition." Let A be a singular term—name, function-argument expression, or singular definite description. Next we consider the sentences in (43).

43a. A *does not exist.*
  b. A *does not subsist (have being).*
  c. A *is not among the things there are.*

Since each is a subject-predicate sentence, it is natural to think that the sentence is true iff the subject expression refers to something that has the property expressed by the predicate. Moreover, there is nothing special about singular subjects; we might make the same observation about the sentences in (44).

44a. B's *don't exist.*
  b. B's *don't subsist (have being).*
  c. B's *are not among the things there are.*

---

occurrences of descriptions. In certain complex cases (as when descriptions occur as constituents of other descriptions) Russell's rule R for eliminating them, plus other aspects of his philosophical logic, sometimes increase, rather than decrease, the number of occurrences of descriptions to be eliminated. Depending on what other logical symbols are taken to be primitive, the analysis may or may not eventually terminate—which is, of course, a serious defect.

[49] Russell (1905d), p. 485, my emphasis.

As with (43), it is natural to think that these sentences are true iff their subject expressions refer to things that have the properties expressed by their predicates. In both cases, we take it for granted that in order for a subject expression to refer to some thing, or some things, there must be some thing, or things, to which the expression refers. Thus, it would seem that the truth of (43a) and (44a) requires *there to be* some things that don't exist. That may seem puzzling in itself, but the truth of the (b) and (c) sentences is even more problematic. If what we have said is correct, they can be true only if *there are some things* that don't have being at all, and are not among the things there are. Since that is absurd, something has gone wrong. The puzzle is to identify the offending assumption, and to replace it with something better.

As we saw in the previous chapter, insofar as Russell had a solution to this problem two years earlier in *The Principles of Mathematics,* it was to distinguish sharply between *being* and *existence,* allowing being to all "objects of thought," while denying existence to many.[50] This latitude about the objects there are—i.e., that have being—was exhibited in the following passages.

> Whatever may be an object of thought, or may occur in any true or false proposition, or can be counted as *one,* I call a *term.* . . . A man, a moment, a number, a class, a relation, a chimera, or anything else that can be mentioned, is sure to be a term; and to deny that such and such a thing is a term must always be false.[51]

> *Being* is that which belongs to every conceivable term, to every possible object of thought. . . . If A be any term that can be counted as one, it is plain that A is something, and therefore that A is. 'A is not' must always be either false or meaningless. For if A were nothing, it could not be said not to be; 'A is not' implies that there is a term A whose being is denied, and hence that A is. Thus unless 'A is not' be an empty sound, it must be false—whatever A may be it certainly is. Numbers, the Homeric gods, relations, chimeras and four-dimensional spaces all have being, *for if they were not entities of a kind, we could make no propositions about them. Thus being is a general attribute of everything, and to mention anything is to show that it is.*[52]

The idea in these passages is much the same as before—that to deny the being of some thing, or things, is self-defeating, since, in order for one's remark to be meaningful, there must be some thing, or things, that one is talking about (referring to) and denying the being of (predicating *not being* of). Hence, meaningful denials that there is a so-and-so, or that there are so-and-so's, are always false. The difference between *The Principles of*

---

[50] As we also saw, Russell wasn't entirely consistent in adhering to this "solution," since even then he seemed to deny some objects altogether.

[51] Russell (1903a), p. 43.

[52] Ibid., p. 449, my emphasis.

Mathematics and 'On Denoting' is that in the former Russell was willing to assert this conclusion, while in the latter he sought to avoid it.

I will state the argument to be blocked with an even stronger conclusion (involving existence rather than being) than the one Russell embraced in *The Principles of Mathematics*. As we will see, it is a feature of the solution offered in "On Denoting" that it blocks not only the claim that meaningful denials of existence can't be true, but also the claim that meaningful denials of being can't be true. We start by characterizing *negative existentials* as sentences of the form (45a) or (45b)—where 'A' is to be replaced with a singular term , and 'B's' is to be replaced with a plural.

45a. A doesn't exist.
  b. B's don't exist.

Examples of negative existentials are (46–48).

46. Carnivorous cows don't exist.
47. The creature from the black lagoon doesn't exist.
48. Santa Claus doesn't exist.

The problematic argument to be blocked goes as follows:

P1.   Meaningful negative existentials, such as (46–48), are subject-predicate sentences. For example, the subject of (46) is *carnivorous cows* and the predicate is *don't exist*.

P2.   A meaningful subject-predicate sentence is true iff there is an object (or there are objects) to which the subject expression refers, and this object (or these objects) has (have) the property expressed by the predicate.

C1.   Sentence (46) can be true only if there are objects—carnivorous cows—to which its subject expression, 'carnivorous cows', refers, and these objects have the property of not existing. Ditto for (47), (48), and all other meaningful negative existentials.

P3.   No objects have the property of not existing. If there are objects to which the subjects of meaningful negative existentials refer, then they exist.

C2.   Meaningful negative existentials cannot be true.

C3.   So, there are no true, meaningful, negative existentials.

C4.   In other words, true, meaningful, negative existentials don't exist.

C4 is itself both a meaningful negative existential and a consequence of P1–P3. Since these premises entail a general claim that is a counterexample to itself, at least one of them must be false. The question is which. Russell's 1903 "solution" located the difficulty in P3. According to the view he held then, being comes in degrees, including a category of nonexistent things that *have being* even though they *don't exist*. On this view there really are such things as carnivorous cows, the 'f' in 'philosophy', and the present king of France. There are such things, even though they don't exist. These are to be contrasted with things that really do exist, such as the queen of England, the only even prime number, and Mount Vesuvius.

By the time of "On Denoting," Russell was no longer satisfied with this view, and was able to use the distinction between *logical form* and *grammatical form* ushered in by his new theory to avoid it. According to the new view, just as a sentence has a *grammatical form*, so the proposition expressed by the sentence has a *logical form*. Sometimes the logical form of the proposition expressed by S matches the grammatical form of S, and sometimes it doesn't. When it does, and S is grammatically of subject-predicate form, S is said to be *logically* of subject-predicate form. This is so when the proposition P expressed by S can be exhaustively divided into the property expressed by the predicate, and a constituent expressed by the grammatical subject of S. The logical form of S (and of the proposition expressed by S) is crucial for determining the conditions under which S is true.

With this in mind, we restate the paradoxical argument about negative existentials.

P1a.   Meaningful negative existentials like (46–48) are logically of subject-predicate form.

P2a.   A sentence that is logically of subject-predicate form is true iff there is an object (or there are objects) to which the subject expression refers, and this object (or these objects) has (have) the property expressed by the predicate.

C1.   Sentence (46) can be true only if there are objects—carnivorous cows—to which its subject expression, *carnivorous cows*, refers, and these objects have the property of not existing. Ditto for (47), (48), and all other meaningful negative existentials.

P3.   No objects have the property of not existing. If there are objects to which the subjects of meaningful negative existentials refer, then they exist.

C2.   Meaningful negative existentials cannot be true.

C3.   So, there are no true, meaningful, negative existentials.

C4.   In other words, true, meaningful, negative existentials don't exist.

Russell's 1905 solution to this version of the paradox is to deny P1a. Although negative existentials such as (46–48) are grammatically of subject-predicate form, the propositions they express aren't. His strategy is to produce, for each problematic negative existential S, a logically equivalent sentence S_1 that is not of subject-predicate form—where the grammatical structure of S_1 mirrors the logical structure of the proposition that both S and S_1 express.

In the case of C4, the relevant paraphrase might be C3 or C2. In the case of (46), it would be something along the lines of (49a) or (49b).

49a. Everything is such that either it isn't a cow or it isn't carnivorous.

   b. $\forall x$ (~ x is carnivorous $\vee$ ~ x is a cow)

When we look at (49a) or (49b), we see that no part of the sentence has the job of referring to something which is then said not to exist. On Russell's analysis, these sentences express a proposition that predicates *being always true* of the propositional function that assigns to any object o the proposition that either o isn't carnivorous or o isn't a cow. There is nothing paradoxical about declaring this to be true. So if (46) expresses the same proposition as (49a,b), its truth isn't paradoxical either.

Next we extend the analysis to (47), which Russell treats as the negation of (50).

47. The creature from the black lagoon doesn't exist.

50. The creature from the black lagoon exists.

In analyzing these sentences we let 'C' stand for *is a creature*, and 'B' stand for *is from the black lagoon*. Next consider (51), which is true iff the propositional function expressed by 'Cx & Bx' is true for at least one thing—i.e., iff at least one thing is a creature from the black lagoon.

51. $\exists x$ (Cx & Bx)

This is not quite what (50) tells us. Whereas (51) leaves it open that there might be several creatures from the black lagoon, the use of 'the' in (50) seems to indicate that there is supposed to be just one.[53] We have seen how this can be expressed in Russell's logical language. On his theory of descriptions, the logical form of (50) is (52), which is true iff there is one and only one creature from the black lagoon.

52. $\exists x \forall y$ ((Cy & By) $\longleftrightarrow$ y = x)

   There is an object x which is such that for any object y, x is identical with y if and only if y is a creature from the black lagoon.

Now that we have the analysis of (50), the analysis, (53), of its negation, (47), is automatic.

53. ~ $\exists x \forall y$ ((Cy & By) $\longleftrightarrow$ y = x)

This says that *it is not the case that there is exactly one creature from the black lagoon*, or, what comes to the same thing, *everything is either not a creature from the black lagoon or one of several such creatures*. The relation between (47) and its logical form (53) is like the relation between (46) and its logical form (49). Just as (46) initially seems to make reference to several things and say of them that they don't exist, so (47) initially seems to

---

[53] If I tell my class, "The student who got an A on the homework assignment won't have to take the exam," they will naturally assume that just one student got an A on the assignment.

refer to a single thing and say that it doesn't exist. In both cases, Russell resolves the paradox by analyzing the logical form of the proposition expressed in such a way that no such reference, and no such predication of nonexistence, is involved.

The next class of negative existentials are those like (48), the grammatical subjects of which are ordinary proper names.

48. Santa Claus doesn't exist.

By 1905, Russell had come to regard names that occur in myth and legend—as well as names of things with which we are not acquainted in any ordinary sense, plus names of "other minds" (other people)—as abbreviating definite descriptions. The idea is that when we use such a name we always have some description in mind we would be willing to substitute for it, indicating how we are using it. Which description gives the content of the name will vary somewhat from speaker to speaker and time to time. However, whenever (48) is used there is always some sentence containing a description that may replace it. So, when we use (48), we always mean something like (48a), the analysis of which is (48b).

48a. The so-and-so doesn't exist.
  b. $\sim \exists x \, \forall y \, (y \text{ is so-and-so} \longleftrightarrow y = x)$

Hence the truth of (48) doesn't require any object to have the property of not existing.

The key to this analysis is the first step—the claim that 'Santa Claus' is short for a descriptive phrase, which in turn is subjected to the usual Russellian analysis. On this view, many ordinary proper names don't function logically as names. Although they are called "names" in daily life, they are really used to describe rather than name. Are there words in English the logical function of which is *not* to take the place of a description, but simply to name? By 1910, when he published "Knowledge by Acquaintance and Knowledge by Description," Russell had eliminated nearly every candidate for such an analysis. Even then, however, there remained at least one word he took to function logically as a name—'this'. Suppose I hold up my wallet and say "This is empty." Here, 'this' simply indicates what I am talking about. If my wallet weren't present, I wouldn't say "This is empty," because my hearers wouldn't know what I was telling them to be empty. Instead, I would use a description like 'the wallet I normally carry'. When I have my wallet with me that isn't necessary, since I can show them what I am talking about. In this sort of case, 'this' doesn't function as a description; it is a bare label.

A point in support of this view is the seeming absurdity of utterances of (54).

54. This doesn't exist.

If I were to utter (54), directing my attention to something, or perhaps gesturing toward it, my remark would be hard to make out. My use of the demonstrative, plus my gesture, would indicate that I took myself to be referring to something. But then I would be in the odd position of purporting to refer to something I claimed not to exist. Hence, (54) is a rare case of a negative existential that really is bizarre: to use it sincerely is to presume that it isn't true. This indicates that the analysis of (54) is *not* like that of our earlier examples. In (54) the grammatical subject is a tag, not a description. Russell would put this by saying that 'this' is a logically proper name.

Well, almost. There is a complicating factor involving the objects that can be referents of logically proper names. So far, I have been speaking as if material objects, like my wallet, can be referents of such names. Russell casts doubt on this in the penultimate paragraph of "On Denoting," and by 1910 he was denying it, maintaining that the only things one can use a logically proper name to designate are oneself, one's own sense impressions, and one's thoughts, plus Platonic properties and relations (seen in the mind's eye). At this point he maintained that when 'this' is used as a logically proper name, it always names one of these objects; any other use must be regarded as one in which it functions as a disguised description.

Russell's reasoning can be partially reconstructed as follows: First, we define a logically proper name as a term the meaning of which is its referent. Next, we assume (for the sake of argument) that one can't be mistaken about whether or not one means something by one's words. Often when I use an expression it *seems* I can be certain that *I mean something* by it, even if I am not certain that what I mean is the same as what others mean by it, and even if I am not certain that the expression really refers to anything, when it is used with the meaning I attach to it. In these cases, I can be certain that *I mean something* by a term, even if I am not certain that the term succeeds in designating anything in the world. For example, I can be sure that I mean something when I use the words 'the house I once owned in Princeton' even though I am not sure that this expression refers to anything, since my former house may have burned down since I left. Similarly, Russell would say, just as I mean something when I use 'Santa Claus', even though it doesn't refer to anything, so I can be sure that I mean something when I use 'Thales', even if I am not completely sure that there really was such a man. Russell would express this by saying (i) that the term 'Santa Claus', as used by me, has a meaning, even though it lacks a referent, and (ii) that I can know that the term 'Thales', as used by me, has a meaning, even if I don't know that it has a referent.

Suppose that I do use N as a logically proper name—i.e., as a term the meaning of which is its referent. Then, one might argue, whenever I sincerely use N to mean something, it is guaranteed to do so. Moreover, the thing it both means and refers to is what I take it to mean and refer to. So, the only objects that can be referents of logically proper names are objects the existence of which I couldn't be mistaken about in any situation in which I can reasonably take myself to name them. Since material objects

and other human beings don't satisfy this condition, they can't be referents of logically proper names. The only concrete objects that do satisfy
the condition, and so can be referents of logically proper names, are oneself, one's own thoughts, and one's momentary sense data. By reasoning
in this way, Russell came to believe that whenever we think or talk about
material objects or other people, the words we use *describe* them, rather
than *naming* them directly. In addition, the propositions we believe never
contain material objects or other people as constituents, but rather are always made up of descriptive properties and relations, plus abstract logical
concepts, plus, perhaps, one or more of the few concrete particulars with
which we are acquainted. This was the view hinted at in the penultimate
paragraph of "On Denoting," and developed in "Knowledge by Acquaintance and Knowledge by Description."

Having come this far, I now return to Russell's remarks about "the difference between A and B" that Russell used to set up the puzzle about
negative existentials. After setting the stage earlier in the article, he offers
what he takes to be a resolution of the puzzle in the following passage.

> We can now see also how to deny that there is such an object as the difference
> between A and B in the case when A and B do not differ. If A and B do differ,
> there is one and only one entity x such that 'x is the difference between A
> and B' is a true proposition; if A and B do not differ, there is no such entity
> x. Thus . . . 'the difference between A and B' has a denotation when A and B
> differ but not otherwise.[54]

The problem we have making sense of this passage is figuring out how
to understand the seemingly straightforward result (56) of applying Russell's theory of definite descriptions to (55).

55. The difference between a and b is F.
56. $\exists x \forall y [(Dyab \longleftrightarrow y = x) \& Fx]$

There is much to wonder about. What are the entities in the world that are
supposed to count as *differences* between two things that are not identical?
Is it true that whenever two things are different, i.e., nonidentical, there is
exactly one thing that is *a difference between them* in the relevant sense—as
(56) seems to require? Often we think that different things can differ in
many respects. If so, *none* of the respects in which the things differ can be
the difference we are looking for.

I suspect that what Russell has in mind by "the difference between A
and B" is *that fact that A and B differ*. On this view, what (56) says is that
there is one and only one thing x of which (i) and (ii) both hold—(i) the
constituents of x are simply A, B, and the difference relation, and (ii) in x
A and B are (really) related by difference—and, in addition, x is F. Since I
am not fond of facts, I am not fond of this ontologically inflationary way

of construing (55), but Russell seems to have been, as suggested by the way in which he completes the above passage.

> This difference applies to true and false propositions generally. If 'a R b' stands for 'a has the relation R to b,' then when a R b is true, there is such an entity as the relation R between a and b; when a R b is false, there is no such entity. Thus out of any proposition we can make a denoting phrase, which denotes an entity if the proposition is true, but does not denote an entity if the proposition is false. E.g., it is true (at least we will suppose so) that the earth revolves round the sun, and false that the sun revolves round the earth; hence 'the revolution of the earth round the sun' denotes an entity, while 'the revolution of the sun round the earth' does not denote an entity.[55]

Though one might wish for a bit more clarity, I think that what Russell has in mind is a unique fact corresponding to each true sentence. On this view, when A differs from B, there will be a fact, denoted by "the difference between A and B," of which the formula '$\forall y \, (Dyab \longleftrightarrow y = x)$' is uniquely true, thereby guaranteeing the truth of (57).

57. There is such a thing as the difference between a and b.
$\exists x \, \forall y \, (Dyab \longleftrightarrow y = x)$

When A does not differ from B—i.e., when they are identical—(57) will be false, and so the negative existential, (58), will be true.

58. There is no such a thing as the difference between a and b.
$\sim \exists x \, \forall y \, (Dyab \longleftrightarrow y = x)$

Whatever one thinks of Russell's free and easy way with differences and facts, the theory of descriptions is not to blame. It functions here to avoid the usual problems about negative existentials, just as it does in other cases.

4. PROBLEMS, CHALLENGES, AND REFINEMENTS

4.1. The Clash between Russell's Epistemology and His Theory of Descriptions

In discussing Russell's solution of the puzzle about George IV, and his view of ordinary proper names (and demonstratives) vs. logically proper names, I noted the pressures leading him to restrict his circle of acquaintance, culminating in the extreme position enunciated in "Knowledge by Acquaintance and Knowledge by Description" (Russell 1910–11). According to the view developed there (Russell 1910–11, pp. 127–28, quoted in section 3.2), whenever we think or talk about material objects or other people, our words describe, rather than name, them. In addition, the propositions

[55] Ibid., 490–91.

we entertain never contain material objects or other people as constituents, but are always entirely made up of descriptive properties and relations, plus abstract logical concepts and momentary aspects of ourselves with which we are cognitively acquainted. It immediately follows that the only singular propositions we can believe are about these things.

Whatever else may be true of this thoroughly internalist conception of the objects of thought, it has disastrous consequences for the application of his theory of descriptions to propositional attitude ascriptions. The relevant cases are examples of the type (59a) and (59b), in which v is a verb (like *believe, doubt, assert,* or *wonder*) that relates an agent to a proposition, and the complement sentence S contains a description ⌜the D⌝ that can be interpreted as having a primary occurrence in the sentence as a whole.

59a. A v's that S(the D).
  b. A v's whether S(the D).

So interpreted, Russell's theory of descriptions tells us that (59a) is true iff (59a$_p$) is true, and (59b) is true iff (59b$_p$) is true.

59a$_p$. ∃x ∀y [(Dy ⟷ y = x) & A v's that S(x)]
59b$_p$. ∃x ∀y [(Dy ⟷ y = x) & A v's whether S(x)]

These in turn can be true only if the agent bears the cognitive relation (belief, assertion, wondering-about-the-truth-of) expressed by the verb v to the proposition expressed by S($\underline{x}$), when '$\underline{x}$' is a logically proper name of the unique object satisfying D. The central epistemological doctrine of "Knowledge by Acquaintance and Knowledge by Description" is that agents *cannot* bear any such cognitive relation to that proposition when the referent of '$\underline{x}$' is a physical object or another person. This doctrine has the consequence that all examples of the form (59a$_p$) and (59b$_p$) involving such objects are false. In this way, Russell's radical epistemological doctrine undermines one of the most impressive applications of his theory of descriptions.

4.2. No Meaning in Isolation?

Recall the first two sentences of "On Denoting."

> By a 'denoting phrase' I mean a phrase such as any one of the following: [here the reader should supply quotes around each phrase] a man, some man, any man, every man, all men, the present King of England, the present King of France, the centre of mass of the Solar System at the first instant of the twentieth century, the revolution of the earth round the sun, the revolution of the sun round the earth. Thus a phrase is denoting solely in virtue of its *form*.

What form are we being asked to attend to? At first blush it might appear to be the form *an/some/any/every/all/the F*. But surely, 'a', 'some', 'any', 'every', 'all', and 'the' are merely examples of expressions that can be combined with a simple common noun, or a complex phrase functioning as such. Alongside ⌜an F⌝, ⌜some F⌝, ⌜any F⌝, ⌜every F⌝, ⌜all F's⌝, and ⌜the F⌝, we have ⌜each F⌝, ⌜exactly n F's⌝, ⌜at least n F's⌝, ⌜at most n F's⌝, ⌜several F's⌝, ⌜many F's⌝, ⌜more than 20 but fewer than 50 F's⌝, ⌜most F's⌝, ⌜few F's⌝, ⌜no F's⌝, and many more. These do form a natural syntactic and semantic class. All are quantifiers consisting of a simple or complex common noun determining the range of quantification, together with a word or phrase (called a determiner by linguists) determining the extent of the quantification over that range. Being quantifiers, they are complex members of the same class as the simple quantifiers 'everything' and 'something', which Russell analyzes as expressing properties of propositional functions. One of the great insights of "On Denoting" is the recognition that definite descriptions ⌜the F⌝ can be given a natural analysis as members of this class, instead of being classified, along with proper names and demonstratives, as singular referring expressions.

Unfortunately, Russell combines this insight with the more questionable idea that quantifiers ⌜Det F⌝, consisting of a determiner and a common noun, are "incomplete symbols" that "have no meaning in isolation." Although definite descriptions were his favorite examples, every complex quantifier he discusses is treated as an "incomplete symbol." Whenever such a quantifier Q is a grammatical constituent of a sentence S, the proposition Russell takes S to express does *not* contain a single constituent that corresponds to, or is the meaning of, Q. It is striking that he gives this ubiquity of "incomplete symbols" in his analysis almost no defense. The inconclusive Gray's Elegy argument does try to refute analyses of definite descriptions as *singular referring expressions* the meanings of which occur as constituents of propositions. But even if this argument were successful, it would *not* rule out the possibility that definite descriptions are *complete symbols* by virtue of being *complex quantifiers*. Russell shows no awareness that such quantifiers can be analyzed as contributing their meanings, as constituents, to the propositions expressed by sentences containing them.

In fact the analysis is transparent, as indicated by (60) and (61).

60a. Every F is G.

$[\forall x: Fx]\ Gx$

The propositional function p_G that assigns to any object o the proposition expressed by 'Gx' relative to an assignment of o to 'x' is *true whenever o is F*—(i.e., p_G always assigns o a *true* proposition when o is an object to which p_F assigns a true proposition).

b. Some F is G.

$[\exists x: Fx]\ Gx$

P_G is *sometimes true when o is F* (p_G sometimes assigns o a true proposition when o is an object to which p_F assigns a true proposition).

c. The F is G.

$[\text{The } x: Fx]\ Gx$

P_G is *true of o when o is unique in being F* (p_G assigns o a true proposition to an object that is unique in being one to which p_F assigns a true proposition).

d. Exactly n F's are G.

[Exactly n x: Fx] Gx

P_G is *true in exactly n cases in which o is F* (p_G assigns o a true proposition to o for exactly n distinct objects o to which p_F assigns a true proposition).

e. At least n F's are G.

[At least n x: Fx] Gx

P_G is *true in n or more cases in which o is F* (p_G assigns a truth to at least n objects to which p_F assigns a truth).

61a. Most F's are G.

[Most x: Fx] Gx

P_G is *true of most of the objects o of which F is true* (p_G assigns a truth to most of the objects that p_F assigns a truth).

b. Many F's are G.

[Many x: Fx] Gx

P_G is *true for many of the objects o of which F is true* (p_G assigns a truth to many of the objects to which p_F assigns a truth).

c. Few F's are G.

[Few x: Fx] Gx

P_G is *true for some, but not many, of the objects o of which F is true* (p_G assigns a truth to some, but not many, of the objects to which p_F assigns a truth).

It is clear from these examples that our understanding of these denoting phrases conforms to a common pattern. So, if one is *describing* English, rather than *regimenting* its sentences in a system designed for other purposes, one should treat ⌜Det F⌝ as a semantic, as well as a syntactic, unit.

On this analysis, the denoting phrases in (62) are generalized quantifiers, and the sentences in which they occur have logical forms along the lines indicated.

62a. Every politician is slippery.

[∀x: Politician x] (Slippery x)

b. Some logician is brilliant.

[∃x: Logician x] (Brilliant x)

c. The man in an iron mask is innocent.

[The x: Man in an iron mask x] (Innocent x)

d. Several students are curious.

[Several x: Students x] (Curious x)

e. Most/many/few students are curious.

[Most/many/few x: Student x] (Curious x)

In each case, the logical form ⌜[Det x: Fx] (Gx)⌝ indicates that the sentence is true iff p_G has the property expressed by the quantifier. So, (62a) is true iff the propositional function that assigns to o the proposition that o is slippery *is true whenever o is a politician*; (62b) is true iff the propositional function that assigns to o the proposition that o is brilliant *is true in some case in which o is a logician*; (62c) is true iff the propositional function that assigns to o the proposition that o is innocent *is true of an object that is unique in being a man in an iron mask*; (62d) is true iff the propositional function that assigns to o the proposition that o is curious *is true of several students*; and (62e) is true iff that propositional function *is true of most, many, or some but not many, of those students.*

This analysis of the truth conditions of (62e) is not just natural, but required—since one can't get the correct truth conditions by treating 'most', 'many', or 'few' as simple unrestricted quantifiers (expressing the property of being true of most, many, or few things in general), and prefixing them to '(Student x → Curious x)', to '(Student x & Curious x)', *or to any other formula of Russell's language of logical form.* Given that we should provide a *unified* analysis of *all* expressions ⌜Det F⌝, the fact that we *must* treat ⌜Most/many/few F⌝ as generalized quantifiers (and hence as semantic units) requires anyone constructing a semantic theory of English to do the same for the other quantifier phrases as well. This is a significant modification of Russell's theory.[56]

Nevertheless, Russell shouldn't be judged too harshly for missing it. He wasn't concerned with constructing a systematic semantic theory for a natural language containing infinitely many generalized quantifiers understood by speakers in a uniform way. His primary concern in 1905 was with logic, mathematics, and the philosophical issues they raise. For this, either 'all' or 'some' would have been enough. Since 'the' is convenient, it was useful to define it from 'all' or 'some' (or both), plus identity. Numerical quantifiers in general, of the sort illustrated by ⌜exactly, at least, at most, n F's⌝, are similarly definable. Being a philosopher-mathematician, Russell had the familiar interest in specifying a minimal conceptual base for doing a maximum amount of intellectual work. Looming above all else was his grand project of reducing mathematics to logic. The denoting phrases relevant to this were few, and it was natural for one with his agenda to define them in terms of a single quantifier '∀x', plus identity.

One virtue of this was the assurance it provided that no numerical notions were being smuggled in, which is just what one wants if one's aim is to show how we *could* make sense of all of mathematics on a very slender base of logical primitives. Thus, for someone on Russell's quest, the following question was not a pressing concern.

Q. Are the propositions yielded by the logicist project merely *equivalent* (in some favored sense) to those grasped by ordinary English speakers when they do mathematics (or when they use one of the favored denoting

[56] Stephen Neale takes this position in his book *Descriptions* (Neale 1990).

phrases), or are the propositions yielded *identical* with those grasped by ordinary speakers?

It is not surprising that Russell wasn't very sensitive to Q or related questions. Although today we recognize such questions as being important for constructing empirical theories of meaning for natural languages, theories of this sort were not a top priority for either Russell or Frege. Despite the fact that their primary logico-mathematical projects laid important parts of the foundation of the scientific study of natural languages, the latter is a recent innovation that did not exist then in the form we know it now.

Before leaving the question of "incomplete symbols" and "meaning in isolation," there is a related point to be made. In section 1.2 of this chapter I noted the significance of the fact that Russell provides an analysis of 'everything' as expressing the supposedly primitive, and antecedently understood, property of being a propositional function that is *always true*. His intention in giving this *analysis* was to specify the structured propositions expressed by sentences containing 'every' and 'everything'. The idea, simply put, was to identify the proposition expressed by 'Everything is so-and-so' as predicating of a certain propositional function that it *is always true*.

Presented with this analysis, one is tempted first to ask, "What is it for a propositional function to be always true?" and then to answer, "It is for the function to assign a true proposition to every object—i.e., to everything." However, if one were to take this answer to be *an analysis* of *what it means* for a propositional function to be always true, it could be objected that one would be going around in circle; 'every' would be analyzed in terms of 'being always true', which in turn would be analyzed in terms of 'every'. Moreover, as we saw in section 1 of chapter 2, the identification of the propositional contribution of a quantifier occurring in an arbitrary sentence S containing it with a property that is itself *defined* in terms of the quantifier invites an unending hierarchy of equivalent, but structurally different, propositions each with an equal claim on being *the* proposition expressed by S. Russell avoids these absurdities by declaring *being always true* to be primitive.

Realizing that this primitive won't provide a basis for analyzing all generalized quantifiers, we are now faced with a similar problem for, e.g., ⌜Most/Many F⌝. There is, of course, no problem stating truth conditions of sentences containing these quantifiers, as I did in (61), provided that in doing so one can use 'most', 'many', and/or closely related notions. Suppose, however, that we are after a genuine Russellian *analysis* of

63. [Most x: Fx] Gx

and we say:

(i) The proposition expressed by (63) is the proposition that the propositional function p_G (which assigns to an object o the proposition that o is G) is true of *most* of the objects o to which the propositional function p_F (which assigns to an object o the proposition that o is F) assigns a truth.

If we do say this, it would seem that (63) will express the same proposition as sentence (ii), which in turn expresses the same proposition as sentence (iii).

(ii) The propositional function p_G (which assigns to an object o the proposition that o is G) is true of *most* of the objects o to which the propositional function p_F (which assigns to an object o the proposition that o is F) assigns a truth.

(iii) [Most x: p_F (x) is true] p_G(x) is true.

However, since (ii) and (iii) contain another 'most' quantifier, we are invited to apply the analysis again, with the result that, in addition to expressing the same proposition as (ii) and (iii), (63) also expresses the same proposition as sentence (iv).

(iv) The propositional function $p_{G\text{-}True}$ that assigns to an object o the proposition that the result of applying p_G to o is true (i.e., the proposition *that the proposition that o is G is true*) is true of most of the objects o to which the propositional function $p_{F\text{-}True}$ that assigns to o the proposition that the result of applying p_F to o is true (i.e., the proposition *that the proposition that o is F is true*) assigns a truth.

But now we have reached an absurdity. Since, for Russell, the constituents of the proposition expressed by (iv) are different from those of the proposition expressed by (ii) and (iii), the propositions are different. Since both can't be *the* proposition expressed by (63), the analysis fails.

To preserve a Russellian style analysis of examples like these, some step in the above *reductio* must be blocked. With 'everything' Russell did this by taking *being always true* to be an antecedently understood primitive—which prevented the analysis from reapplying to the sentence used to specify the proposition expressed by the original sentence being analyzed. For the same move to work here, we would have to take the property expressed by the most-quantifier in (63)—*being true of most objects that are F*—to be similarly primitive, with the result that the analysis would not reapply to sentences like (ii). Whether or not this move can be justified requires further investigation, which is provided in Soames (2014a), where I propose a way of looking at the Frege-Russell analysis of quantification that suggests a way out. Here, I will simply note that what was already a worry for the Russellian analysis of 'everything' has been compounded now that we have a broader range of examples to be considered.

4.3. Names and Negative Existentials Revisited

As the years went by, Russell's accelerating epistemic restrictions on acquaintance led him to adopt a view of all ordinary proper names (for people, places, and things) as disguised definite descriptions. On this view, the meaning of an ordinary name, for a speaker s at a time t, is identified with a description s is willing to substitute for it at t. In addition to fitting his doctrines of meaning and acquaintance, this allowed him to adopt a roughly Fregean solution to Frege's puzzle. Someone who doesn't know that (64b) and (65b) express truths simply associates different descriptions with the two names, and so means different things by them, while using the (a) and (b) sentences to express different propositions.[57]

64a. Hesperus is Hesperus.
  b. Hesperus is Phosphorus.
65a. Samuel Clemens is Samuel Clemens.
  b. Samuel Clemens is Mark Twain.

This semantic analysis of ordinary names is also supported by Russell's solution to the problems posed by negative existentials like (66).

66. Socrates doesn't exist.

Since (66) is true, he reasoned, 'Socrates' doesn't refer to anything. So, if 'Socrates' were a logically proper name, it wouldn't mean anything. But if it didn't mean anything, then (66) would be neither true nor meaningful. Since it is both, 'Socrates' isn't a name, but is short for a definite description.

However, examples like these are not so simple. Suppose 'Socrates' is short for 'the teacher of Plato'. Then, (66) means the same as (67a), which Russell would analyze as (67b).

67a. The teacher of Plato doesn't exist.
  b. $\sim \exists x \, \forall y \, (y \text{ taught Plato} \longleftrightarrow y = x)$

What, you may ask, happened to the predicate 'exist' in going from (67a) to (67b)? Since the existence claim is already made by the clause expanding the description, there is no need to add '& x exists' to the formula to which the quantifiers are attached. Moreover, Russell thought he had discovered that existence and nonexistence claims always involve a quantifier, and

---

[57] Russell addresses Frege's puzzle somewhat obliquely on the next to last page, 492, of "On Denoting."

The usefulness of *identity* is explained by the above theory. No one outside a logic-book ever wishes to say 'x is x', and yet assertions of identity are often made in such forms as 'Scott was the author of *Waverley*.' . . . The meaning of such propositions cannot be stated without the notion of identity, although they are not simply statements that Scott is identical with another term. . . . The shortest statement of 'Scott is the author of *Waverley*' seems to be: 'Scott wrote *Waverley*; and it is always true of y that if y wrote *Waverley*, y is identical with Scott'. It is in this way that identity enters into 'Scott is the author of *Waverley*'; and it is owing to such uses that identity is worth affirming.

Although Russell here uses 'Scott' as a proper name to illustrate his point, the logic of his position is that since it may occur with another name in an informative identity statement—one "worth affirming"—it can't really be a logically proper name. In short ordinary names, which can occur in nontrivial identity sentences, must be disguised descriptions.

that the grammatical predicate 'exist' never functions logically as a predicate. However, he was wrong about this. In fact, he makes the same three mistakes that Frege was shown to have made in the opening pages of chapter 2. The first mistake was holding that existence is the property of propositional functions expressed by the quantifier '∃x'. The second was thinking that it is in the nature of that quantifier, and its natural language counterparts, to range only over existing things. The third and most infamous mistake was in subscribing to the venerable canard "Existence is not a predicate." There is no logical or philosophical problem in recognizing that 'exist' functions semantically as a predicate.[58]

In fact, we need such a predicate in (67c), the logical form of (67a), which results from our revised analysis of definite descriptions as generalized quantifiers.

67c. ~[the x: x taught Plato] x exists.

This statement is true iff it is not the case that the propositional function p_{Exist}—which assigns to an object o the proposition that o exists—*is true of an object that is unique in having taught Plato* (i.e., that *is unique in being an object assigned a true proposition by the propositional function* $p_{taught\ Plato}$ *that assigns to an object o the proposition that o taught Plato*). More simply, (67c) is true iff it is not the case that an individual who uniquely satisfies 'x taught Plato' makes 'x exists' true.

Next, compare (67) with (68).

68a. The teacher of Plato is dead and so doesn't exist.
  b. ~([the x: x taught Plato] (x is dead and x exists))
  c. [the x: x taught Plato] (x is dead, and so ~ x exists)

The logical form of (68a) is clearly not (68b), but (68c)—which is true iff an individual who uniquely satisfies 'x taught Plato' makes 'x is dead and so ~ x exists' true, when assigned as value of 'x'. For this to be so, the range of the quantifier '[the x: x taught Plato]'—i.e., the range of objects to which the propositional function $p_{taught\ Plato}$ is applied—must include those who once existed, but no longer do. On this assumption, (68a) and (68c) correctly come out true—since 'x exists' is false, and 'x is dead and so ~ x exists' is true, when the nonexistent Socrates is assigned as value of 'x'. This is significant because the meanings of variables, relative to assignments, are, in the Russellian scheme, simply the objects assigned to them. But if formulas containing variables can be meaningful and true when assigned referents that no longer exist, then the fact that Socrates no longer exists doesn't show that 'Socrates' doesn't refer to him, that the referent of 'Socrates' isn't its meaning, or that (66) can't be both true and meaningful, even if 'Socrates' genuinely names Socrates. In short, Russell's historically influential argument to the contrary is inconclusive.

---

[58] Further explanation of Russell's errors about these matters is given in chapter 12.

What about true, meaningful negative existentials like (48)?

48. Santa Claus doesn't exist.

Is the Russellian argument that names of fictional characters like 'Santa Claus' must be short for (non-denoting) descriptions also inconclusive? Yes, I believe it is. For if 'Santa Claus' were simply short for some such description, then (69a) and (69b) would be obviously and straightforwardly false.

69a. Santa Claus lives at the North Pole and delivers presents on Christmas Eve.
  b. Santa Claus is a fictional character.

But they aren't false; both are naturally understood as saying something true. Standardly, someone who uses (69a) does so in order to assert the truth that *according to the traditional Christmas story, Santa Claus lives at the North Pole and delivers presents on Christmas Eve.* By contrast, (69b) is not used to report what is true according to the fiction; rather it is used to state a truth about the fiction as a cultural object. The claim made by (69b) is true because there really is a Christmas story, the main character of which is named 'Santa Claus'. Just as books, plays, and stories are real existing things that can be named, so parts of them—acts, scenes, and characters—are such things. 'Santa Claus' is the name of one of these things—a character in a story. (69b) is true because the story of which it is a part is a fiction; (69a) is true because it is used to truly report what is true in, or according to, the fiction. In what sense, then, is (48) true? It is true when used to assert that the fictional character Santa Claus does not exist *as a real person, with the properties the character is portrayed as having in the story.* All of this can, I think, be better explained by treating 'Santa Claus' as a logically proper name of a real part of an existing story, than by treating it as a disguised description. [59]

This failure of one of the chief negative arguments against treating *ordinary* proper names as *logically* proper names is significant. Russell always had a lively sense of the role of names in language as tags that merely label without describing, and he never gave up the category entirely. He did, however, end up drastically limiting the scope of naming, being pushed to this position by three main factors—the negative existentials argument, the need for a solution to Frege's puzzle when ordinary names are involved, and his general internalist epistemology. Now that the first leg of this trinity of descriptivism has been found wanting, it is worth noting that the combination of the second and third is also shaky.

Russell's treatment of his puzzle about George IV has much in common with Frege's solution to his puzzle, with the added benefit that Russell

---

[59] A well-worked-out version of this view is found in Salmon (1998).

recognized that attitude ascriptions have readings in which descriptions in content clauses take primary occurrence. One would expect the same to be true *if one took ordinary proper names to be disguised descriptions*, and indeed it is undeniable that ⌜A believes that n is F⌝ has a familiar use in which it is true iff ⌜[Some x: x = n] A believes that x is F⌝ is true. Putting aside Russell's problematic Cartesian epistemology of acquaintance, this can be captured either by treating n as a logically proper name, or by analyzing it as a description ⌜the x: Dx⌝ and giving it primary occurrence, ⌜[the x: Dx] A believes that x is F⌝. Bringing the problematic epistemology back into play ruins both, with the consequence that Russell's treatment of the attitude ascriptions relevant to Frege's puzzle is crippled.

There are, of course, common ways of construing attitude ascriptions in which more is asserted, and/or conveyed, by an ascription ⌜A believes that n is F⌝ than the proposition expressed by ⌜A believes that x is F⌝ relative to an assignment of the referent of n to 'x'. Russell was right to be concerned about such cases. Fortunately, conceptual apparatus is now available for accommodating this fact, thereby providing non-Fregean solutions to Frege's puzzle that do not follow Russell down the path of radically restricting the class of genuine names, the entities that can be named, or the singular propositions that can be entertained.[60]

With alternatives to descriptivism back on the table, it is worth listing a few of the difficulties faced by Russell's descriptivist treatment of ordinary proper names:

(i) In addition to being descriptivist, his account is individualist. Since I may associate N with a description without knowing which description another agent A uses N to abbreviate, it is a mystery how, after hearing A say ⌜N is F⌝, I can confidently report ⌜A said/believed that N is F⌝. Since, for Russell, the content of my use of N is presumably given by the description I associate with it, the proposition I end up characterizing A as asserting or believing should be the one I associate with ⌜N is F⌝. But then Russell has no account of why I am correct in routinely feeling justified in the truth of my assertion.[61] He also has no account of why, after hearing A's remark, I, knowing the person to whom N refers, can typically report ⌜There is an individual x such that A said/believed that x is F⌝. Although there are some descriptions D such that ⌜A said/believed that D is F⌝ will support the inference to ⌜There is an individual x such that A said/believed that x is F⌝, many will not. How, in light of this, can my report be routinely justified, even though in many cases I don't know what description A associates with N? By contrast, if the meaning of 'N' were that to which we all use it to refer (the least common denominator,

---

[60] Relevant literature includes Kripke (1972, 1979), Salmon (1984, 1989), Fine (2007), Soames (2002: chapters 3, 6, 8), and Soames (2005a and forthcoming).
[61] See Kripke (1979).

so to speak, of our different uses of the name), the answers to both these questions would be immediate.[62]

(ii) Since Russell so radically restricts the things that can be named, he is committed to the view that virtually all ordinary names are abbreviations of descriptions *which don't themselves contain any names at all, or if they do, contain only names of the speaker's private thoughts or experiences.* This is most implausible. Even when speakers can provide descriptions accurately describing the referents of ordinary names they use, in most cases those descriptions themselves contain names. (Try this with 'Winston Churchill', 'Aristotle', 'Cicero', 'Carthage', 'Honduras', and 'Gandhi'.) What Russell's view demands is that every speaker can uniquely and correctly describe the referent of every ordinary name that he or she uses in terms of purely qualitative properties and relations with which he or she is acquainted by unaided inspection of Plato's heaven. There is no evidence to support this radically Cartesian view of linguistic competence and language use.[63]

(iii) As we now know, names are rigid designators, whereas most ordinary descriptions speakers associate with them are not. Thus names are not abbreviations of such descriptions. Although there are ways of rigidifying descriptions, they create their own problems when taken to give meanings of names. Russell himself had a dim view of necessity and possibility, in terms of which rigidity is defined, and so it is natural that he didn't notice rigidity. But some way of accommodating the point is required for any adequate account of names.[64]

As important as these matters are to us, none needs to be of serious concern for one who is constructing a precise semantic model for understanding the relationship between logic and mathematics. Since that was Russell's main project, the warts we find when trying to absorb his pioneering work into our contemporary projects—like developing empirical theories of natural languages—should remind us again that despite all that Frege and Russell contributed to us, their projects and perspectives were not the same as ours.

4.4. Incomplete Descriptions

I have said that one of Russell's most important insights is that singular definite descriptions are naturally analyzed as quantifiers rather than singular terms. However, there have been important challenges to this insight stretching back to Peter Strawson's "On Referring," in 1950.[65] One

[62] See chapter 3 of Soames (2002).

[63] See Kripke (1972), chapter 1 of Salmon (1981), chapter 14 of Soames (2003d), and chapter 4 of Soames (2010a).

[64] For discussion of rigidity, rigidification, and the role they play in accounts of names see Kripke (1972), chapter 2 of Soames (2002), and chapter 14 of Soames (2003d).

[65] Strawson (1950).

of the features motivating Strawson's challenge, and those of similarly minded philosophers, focuses on *incomplete definite descriptions* ⌜the F⌝ in which F is true of many things, rather than only one. These terms occur in sentences ⌜The F is G⌝ that are routinely used by speakers to assert something true, and nothing false—even though their Russellian truth conditions seem not to be satisfied. This has led a line of theorists to insist that Russell's theory of descriptions is either false, or at best incomplete by virtue of missing one important use of definite descriptions.

Here is a passage from Strawson leading off the challenge.

> Consider the sentence, 'the table is covered with books'. It is quite certain that in any normal use of this sentence, the expression 'the table' would be used to make a unique reference, *i.e.* to refer to some one table. It is a quite strict use of the definite article, in the sense in which Russell talks on p. 30 of *Principia Mathematica,* of using the article "*strictly,* so as to imply uniqueness". On the same page Russell says that a phrase of the form 'the so-and-so', used strictly, "will have an application in the event of there being one so-and-so and no more." Now it is obviously quite false that the phrase 'the table' in the sentence 'the table is covered with books', used normally, will "only have application in the event of there being one table and no more." It is indeed tautologically true that, in such a use, the phrase will have an application only in the event of there being one table and no more *which is being referred to*. . . . To use the sentence is not to assert, but it is . . . to imply, that there is only one thing which is *both* of the kind specified (*i.e.* a table) *and is being referred to* by the speaker. It is obviously not to assert this. To refer is not to say you are referring.[66]

In this passage, Strawson both offers a criticism of Russell and indicates the nature of his alternative analysis. The criticism, which focuses on

70. The table is covered with books.

is (i) that a normal assertive utterance of (70) will succeed in saying something true, and nothing false, provided that one particular thing, correctly characterized by the speaker as a table, is covered with books (even though there are many tables in the world, and even if there are several in the context to which the speaker is not referring), and (ii) that if Russell's theory of descriptions were correct, this would not be so. Strawson's positive alternative analysis is, roughly, that ⌜the F⌝ is a singular term a use of which will designate an object o iff F is true of o, and o is unique in being what the speaker is using the term to refer to. Reconstructing this idea in terms of propositions (which Strawson himself would not do), one may say that the meaning of (70) is a set of instructions for using it to assert a singular proposition in which *being covered with books* is predicated of a contextually salient table to which the speaker is referring.

[66] Ibid., 332–33.

Sixteen years after Strawson's article appeared, Keith Donnellan drew on Strawsonian ideas in articulating his now well-known distinction between attributive and referential uses of descriptions.[67] Roughly put, an attributive use of ⌜the F⌝ in uttering ⌜The F is G⌝ is a use in which the speaker intends to assert the proposition expressed by the Russellian analysis of the sentence—that there is one and only one thing that is F, and that thing, whatever it may be, is G—with no idea of further asserting, of the individual o who is (or is taken to be) uniquely F, that it is G.[68] By contrast, a referential use of ⌜the F⌝ in uttering ⌜the F is G⌝ is one in which the speaker has an individual o in mind about whom he wishes to make an assertion; the speaker uses the description to identify o, and intends his remark to be taken as asserting, of o, that o is G. One of the interesting points noted by Donnellan was that since the speaker's primary purpose is to say this of o, his purpose is not automatically defeated if it turns out that o isn't F. Since the speaker's use of the description may still be successful in identifying for his audience the person about whom he wishes to make a statement, he may succeed in asserting the singular proposition *that o is G*, even if o is not F.

> When a speaker says, "The ϕ is ψ," where 'the ϕ' is used attributively, if there is no ϕ, we cannot correctly report the speaker as having said *of* this or that person or thing that it is ψ. But if the definite description is used referentially, we can report the speaker as having attributed ψ to something. And *we* may refer to what the speaker referred to, using whatever description or name suits our purpose. Thus, if a speaker says, "Her husband is kind to her," referring to the man he was just talking to, and if that man is Jones, we may report him as having said *of Jones* that he is kind to her. If Jones is also the president of the college, we may report the speaker as having said *of the president of the college* that he is kind to her. And finally, if we are talking to Jones, we may say, referring to the original speaker, "He said of you that *you* are kind to her." It does not matter here whether or not the woman has a husband, or whether, if she does, Jones is her husband. If the original speaker referred to Jones, he said of him that he is kind of her. Thus, where the definite description is used referentially, but does not fit what was referred to, we can report what a speaker said and agree with him by using a description or name that does fit.[69]

In the two decades following Donnellan's article a line of theorizing coalesced around the idea that singular definite descriptions are semantically ambiguous, having an attributive reading understood more or

---

[67] Donnellan (1966).

[68] Here, and later, I use 'F' and 'G' as schematic letters to be replaced with F and G, respectively.

[69] Donnellan (1966), p. 301. The connection between Donnellan's notion *saying of o that it is G* and *saying that o is G* (where o is the singular proposition predicating *being G* of o) is made on pp. 150–52 of Soames (1994).

less along Russellian lines, and a referential reading, in which they are context-sensitive singular terms used by speakers to refer to individuals about whom or which they wish to assert singular propositions.[70] Countering this, a powerful Russellian response effectively made three main points:

(i) Some propositions asserted by an utterance of a sentence S are not semantically expressed by S (on any meaning) or entailed by any proposition so expressed.

(ii) The singular propositions asserted by a referential use of ⌜the F⌝ (both when F is true of the referent and when it isn't) fall under (i) because in such cases the speaker (a) recognizes that his hearers take F to be true of a certain contextually salient individual o, (b) intends to make a remark about o, and (c) realizes that acceptance of the proposition expressed by ⌜The F is G⌝ on the standard Russellian interpretation will lead his hearers to accept the singular proposition that o is G, and (d) knows that his hearers are in a position to recognize all this.

(iii) "Referential" uses of both ordinary quantifiers and genuine proper names, which are clearly *not* semantically ambiguous, display the same contrasts with other "attributive" uses that Donnellan noted with definite descriptions, and are explainable nonsemantically by versions of the reasoning in (ii).

The upshot is a rebuttal of the claim that the distinction between referential and attributive uses of definite descriptions shows that they have non-Russellian readings.[71]

Despite this recent vindication of Russell's theory of descriptions, the more general problem posed by *incomplete* definite descriptions has remained a challenge. The seriousness of this challenge can be measured by the reaction to it of one of the theory's most prominent defenders. Writing in defense of Russell's theory against objections originating in Donnellan's distinction between attributive and referential uses of descriptions, Saul Kripke says the following:

> If I were to be asked for a tentative stab about Russell, I would say that although his theory does a far better job of handling ordinary discourse than many have thought, and although many popular arguments against it are inconclusive, probably it ultimately fails. The considerations I have in mind have to do with the existence of "improper" definite descriptions, such as 'the

---

[70] Different versions of this position were defended in many places, including Donnellan (1966, 1978), Stalnaker (1972), Partee (1972), Kaplan (1978), Devitt (1981), Wettstein (1981), and Barwise and Perry (1983).

[71] The line of argument featuring (i–iii) and leading to this conclusion was led by Kripke (1977), advanced in Salmon (1982), and Soames (1986a), and masterfully summarized and further advanced in chapter 3 of Neale (1990). Its connection with incomplete definite descriptions is discussed in Soames (2005b, 2009d).

table', where uniquely specifying conditions are not contained in the description itself. Contrary to the Russellian picture, I doubt that such descriptions can always be regarded as elliptical with some uniquely specifying conditions added.[72]

The chief difference between textbook examples of Donnellan-type cases of a referential use of a complete description D in uttering a sentence S and standard uses of an incomplete description D* in uttering S* is that in the former case *both* the proposition semantically expressed by S (on the Russellian analysis) and the derivative singular proposition about the presumed denotation of D are asserted by the speaker, while in the latter case the proposition semantically expressed by S (on the Russellian analysis) is often not asserted.

This difference is reflected in our reactions to cases in which the Russellian proposition expressed by the sentence containing the description is false. For example, a speaker under a widely shared misapprehension— that the man Bill, who arrived at the party with Susan, is engaged to be married to her—might comment on Bill's inappropriately flirtatious behavior with Mary by assertively uttering (71) to a group of guests who have noticed the same thing.

71. The man who is engaged to Susan has been coming on awfully strong to Mary, and he seems not to care who knows it.

On learning that Bill is not really engaged to Susan, the speaker (and hearers) will recognize the mistake in asserting that someone engaged to Susan has been flirting with someone else, while standing by the assertion that Bill was coming on to Mary without concern for who noticed. In such a case the speaker asserts something true and something false (the relative importance of which may vary depending on the context).

By contrast, one may truly utter

70. The table is covered with books.

speaking about a particular table, without falsely asserting that one and only one thing (in the world) is a table. Nor, as is shown by (72), can this problem be avoided simply by contextually setting the range of the neo-Russellian generalized quantifier (and all other quantifiers used in the conversational context) to include only things in the immediate vicinity.

72a. I parked the car just behind some cars across the street.
  b. [the x: x is a car] I parked x just behind some cars across the street

The problem is obvious. The apparent Russellian reading, (72b), of (72a) couldn't possibly be true, since it requires both that there be one and only one car x (in the range of things talked about) and also that I parked x behind some other cars. Nevertheless, my utterance of (72a) might well

---

[72] Kripke (1977), p. 6 of the reprinted version in French, Uehling, and Wettstein (1979).

result in the assertion of something true, and nothing false. Examples like this are common. If they cannot be accommodated, then Russell's theory of descriptions must be regarded as incapable of providing adequate semantic analyses of many sentences of ordinary English, and other natural languages.

In my view, the needed modification applies across the board, and has nothing special to do with descriptions. What must be revised is the traditional conception of meaning and assertion according to which a speaker who assertively utters S (speaking literally, non-metaphorically, and without conversational implicatures canceling the normal force of the remark) always asserts, perhaps among other things, the proposition semantically expressed by S (in the context). This inflexible tie between meaning and assertion leads to trouble, not only with incomplete descriptions, but also with other constructions.[73] A looser, more indirect relation between the two is needed in which the meaning of a sentence *constrains* what it is used to assert, without always *determining* it. On this view, meaning of a sentence S is a set of defeasible constraints which, together with conversational maxims and facts about the context of utterance, guide speaker-hearers in converging on one proposition as the most highly valued assertion candidate.[74] Although the meaning of S may, by itself, sometimes determine a complete proposition, and, hence, a possible assertion candidate, it may also provide only a partial specification of such a proposition. Often, the semantic content of S—whether it is a complete proposition or not—is enriched in contextually allowable ways resulting in an enriched proposition that it is the speaker's primary intention to assert. Other propositions count as asserted only when they are relevant, unmistakable consequences of the speaker's primary assertions, together with salient presuppositions of the conversational background.

In this framework, many facts about incomplete descriptions fall into place. Consider, for example, an utterance of (73a) said in the context of a particularly horrible murder.

73a. The murderer must be insane.

Although the proposition determined solely by the neo-Russellian semantics of this sentence is expressed by the quantification

73b. [the x: x is a murderer] x must be insane

---

[73] See Soames (2009d) and chapter 7 of Soames (2010a).

[74] There is a technical dispute in natural language semantics involving whether the problems I here focus on should be dealt with in the way I suggest, or by positing indexical elements that appear only in the logical forms of sentences and are provided "semantic contents relative to contexts." The latter approach is defended in Stanley (2000, 2002) and in Stanley and Szabo (2000). My response can be found in chapter 7 of Soames (2010a). Though the theoretical perspectives of the two approaches are quite different, they share important commonalities for accommodating incomplete descriptions into an essentially Russellian account of definite descriptions.

the utterance may result in a more specific assertion. In a context in which one comes across a mutilated body, with no idea who committed the crime, the contextually enriched proposition that (73a) is used to assert may be (73c).

> 73c. [the x: x is a murderer of v] x must be insane (where 'v' designates the victim)

Since the semantically determined proposition (73b) *does not follow* from the enriched proposition asserted, *it is not asserted*. So, if the murderer of v really is insane, we get the correct result that the speaker has said something true, and nothing false.[75]

Of course, (73a) can also be used referentially to say, of the murderer of v, that he must be insane. Thus, if it is assertively uttered in a context in which m has been correctly identified as the murderer of v, and the speaker intends to make a statement about m, then the contextually enriched proposition asserted is either (73d) or (73e), depending on whether the victim also has been identified.

> 73d. [the x: x is a murderer & x = m] x must be insane (where 'm' designates the man identified as the murderer)
>
> e. [the x: x is a murderer of v & x = m] x must be insane (where 'm' and 'v' are as before)

Since the semantically determined proposition (73b) associated with sentence (73a) is *not* a consequence of these assertions (plus relevant background presuppositions), it does not count as having been asserted—just as before. By contrast, the simple singular proposition expressed by (73f) *does* count as so asserted in both cases, since it is an obvious consequence of the primary, contextually enriched, proposition that is asserted.

> 73f. m must be insane. (where 'm' is as before)

So, when the murderer m is really insane, the speaker is characterized as asserting truths, while saying nothing false—exactly as it should be.

The same points are illustrated by the earlier example (72a) and the semantically determined proposition associated with it, (72b).

> 72a. I parked the car just behind some cars across the street.
>
> b. [the x: x is a car] I parked x just behind some cars across the street

---

[75] In this case, the speaker uses 'the murderer' to predicate the property *assigns a true proposition to one who uniquely murdered v* of the propositional function expressed by *must be insane*. This is the proposition entertained and asserted by the speaker, not the proposition semantically expressed by the sentence. To say that the proposition *that the unique murderer is insane* is semantically expressed by the sentence is to say it satisfies the purely semantic constraints placed on the proposition(s) asserted by an utterance of this sentence in contexts generally (including the context in question). However, since it does not satisfy the full set of constraints determining assertion in this context, it is not here asserted. Similar remarks apply to the other cases discussed here.

Since the truth of (72b) requires that there be exactly one car (in the domain of quantification), which must be parked behind other cars (also in the domain), (72b) must be false. However, this is of no concern to the speaker. Since (72b) is *not* a consequence of the contextually enriched proposition (72c) that is asserted, the false semantically determined proposition is not something the speaker asserts.

72c. [the x: x is a car & x = m] I parked x just behind some cars across the street (where 'm' designates the car under discussion)

Finally, this augmented Russellian approach unifies the treatment of standard Donnellan-type cases with that of incomplete definite descriptions. Donnellan's classic example is one in which a speaker assertively uttering (74a) uses the description it contains to pick out, and focus attention on, a certain man m, of whom the speaker predicates the property of being a famous philosopher.

74a. The man in the corner drinking champagne is a famous philosopher.

Although the proposition semantically determined by the Russellian semantics of the sentence uttered is given by (74b), the speaker asserts something else—namely, the singular proposition expressed by (74c).

74b. [the x: x is a man & x is in the corner & x is drinking champagne] x is a famous philosopher
　　c. m is a famous philosopher.

With the new conception of the relationship between meaning and assertion, this is no threat to a Russellian analysis of definite descriptions. In this context, the fact that it is evident to all that m is the intended denotation of the description results in the contextual enrichment of the speaker's utterance represented by (74d).

74d. [the x: x is a man & x is in the corner & x is drinking champagne & x = m] x is a famous philosopher

This is the primary proposition asserted by the speaker. Since propositions (74c) and (74e) are obvious consequences of it, they, too, count as asserted.

74e. m is a man & m is in the corner & m is drinking champagne

What about (74b), the proposition semantically associated with the sentence uttered? Although it is *not* a consequence of the enriched proposition (74d), it *is* an obvious consequence of (74d), plus proposition (Pre74).

Pre74. [the x: x is a man & x is in the corner & x is drinking champagne] x = m

Since in many Donnellan-type cases this proposition will be a background presupposition of the conversation, the proposition determined by the semantics of the sentence uttered will often count as having been asserted by the speaker's utterance, just as we expect.

In these cases, the speaker's referential use of the description in assertively uttering (74a) results in the assertion of propositions (74d), (74c), (74e), and (74b), all of which will be true provided that m is both the man in the corner drinking champagne and a famous philosopher. When there are *two* men in the corner drinking champagne, but it is, nevertheless, contextually obvious that the speaker is talking only about m (because the other man there is already known and m is the only new guy), the propositions—(74d), (74c), and (74e)—arising from contextual enrichment will all be true, but the semantically determined proposition (74b) will not be. However, this need not count as a black mark against the speaker, since in cases like this (Pre74) will standardly *not* be a background presupposition, and so (74b) will *not* count as asserted.

The speaker is, however, open to the charge of error in cases of misdescription—in which m is *not* a man in the corner drinking champagne. In these cases (74d) and (74e), and sometimes (74b), will be false. However, these culpable errors are mitigated by the fact that the asserted proposition (74c) remains true. Since in many cases this proposition will be more important to the conversation than whether m is in fact drinking champagne, or is really in the corner, the fact that the speaker has, strictly speaking, asserted one or more falsehoods will matter less than his having asserted an important truth. These results seem to match our intuitive reactions to the cases pretty well.

In sum, many of the problems dividing Russell from Strawson, Donnellan, and other challengers have less to do with the analysis of definite descriptions than with assumptions about the relation between meaning and assertion, or meaning and use more generally. The needed conception is one in which sentence meaning strongly contributes to what utterances assert without, in many cases, fully determining any of the several propositions asserted by an utterance. With this conception in place, Russell, Strawson, and Donnellan can each be seen as having had important central insights compatible with those of the others. Broadly speaking, Strawson was right in maintaining that the meaning of a sentence should be viewed as a set of rules conventionally followed in identifying the propositions asserted by utterances of sentences; Russell was right to insist that when descriptions are involved, the propositions asserted will standardly include those to which the descriptions contribute as quantifiers rather than as singular terms (plus other asserted propositions that follow from those); and Donnellan was right to observe that sometimes the propositions asserted are entirely Russellian, while at other times they include singular propositions free of any content associated with descriptions that occur in the sentences used to assert them.

The key element in this reconciliation of Russell and his critics is the conception of the meaning of a sentence in a language as constraining, rather than always fully determining, what it is used to assert (or otherwise

express). When meaning is understood in this way, a gap is created between *what a sentence means* and *what it is used to assert* that allows salient
features of contexts of utterance to interact with semantic features of sentences in systematic ways to determine what is, and what isn't, asserted.
Because incomplete descriptions are subject to routine contextual enrichment without affecting their austere neo-Russellian meanings, the problems they have traditionally been thought to pose for Russell can, I think,
be solved.

Nevertheless, my defense of Russell's semantic analysis is not thoroughly
Russellian. The conception of the meaning of S as merely constraining the
propositions asserted by uses of S cannot be found in Russell. Worse, it
stems from a perspective quite different from his. The project of giving
a theory of the meaning of a sentence in the common language of a linguistic community, along the lines that I have suggested, was *not* one of
his primary concerns. When he talked of meaning, he mostly had in mind
what an individual means by his or her use of a sentence at a given time.
From this perspective, the problems posed by incomplete descriptions are
not very serious. Since it is routine for speakers to contextually enrich
their utterances, what *they* mean by ⌜the F⌝ in one or another context is
typically *not* incomplete.

There is a lesson here. Incomplete definite descriptions are a serious
problem for broadly Russellian analyses of definite descriptions only if
one runs together two different objects of analysis—roughly, *what individual speakers mean (intend to assert)* by uses of sentences containing such descriptions, and *what those sentences mean* in the common language. Given
either choice, Russell's theory works pretty well. But, whichever choice
one makes, one must carry it through consistently. If one is analyzing
what speakers mean and assert, one must recognize that the *assertive contents* of uses of ⌜The F is G⌝—though broadly Russellian—differ widely
from one context to the next, and often are considerably richer than the
purely *semantic content* of the sentence in the common language. Something like this was Russell's preferred perspective. However, one can also
take the perspective of a semantic theory for the common language. I
have argued that Russell's theory of descriptions works well from this perspective, too—provided one does *not* assume that when speakers assertively utter S, what *they* mean, and assert, is what S means in the common
language—i.e., the proposition *semantically* determined by the meaning of
S. If I am right, then the problem for Russell posed by incomplete descriptions is essentially a pseudo-problem that arises from failing to properly
distinguish these two perspectives.

4.5. Foundational Issues: Logic, Language, Meaning, and Thought

"On Denoting" was a milestone in the history of philosophical logic.
The analysis of quantification in terms of propositional functions parallels Frege's seminal analysis in terms of concepts, with essentially the

same semantic utility in explicating the revolutionary symbolic logic of quantification of the day. The analysis of singular definite descriptions as quantificational, and subject to scope ambiguities leading to substantial differences between logical and grammatical form, was one of the most important contributions of all time to the semantics of natural language. The foundations for the later development of generalized quantifier theory, crucial to understanding natural language, are also lurking in "On Denoting." Finally, the general project of conceiving of natural language as a logico-linguistic system to be studied using the semantic notions underlying the new logic proved to be one of the most fruitful ideas of the twentieth century.

Though the accomplishments were monumental, they occurred within an extremely confining framework consisting of a general epistemology, philosophy of mind, and philosophy of language. The epistemology and philosophy of mind are essentially internalist and Cartesian, while the philosophy of language is both individualistic and subordinated to Russell's epistemology and philosophy of mind. It is this framework that he summarizes in the penultimate paragraph of "On Denoting."

[W]hen there is anything with which we do not have immediate acquaintance, but only definition by denoting phrases, then the propositions in which this thing is introduced by means of a denoting phrase do not really contain this thing as a constituent, but contain instead the constituents expressed by the several words of the denoting phrase. Thus in every proposition that we can apprehend . . . all the constituents are really entities with which we have immediate acquaintance. Now such things as matter (in the sense in which matter occurs in physics) and the minds of other people are known to us only by means of denoting phrases, i.e., we are not *acquainted* with them, but we know them as what has such and such properties. Hence although we can form propositional functions C (x) which must hold of such and such a material particle, or So-and-so's mind, yet we are not acquainted with the propositions which affirm these things that we know must be true, because we cannot apprehend the actual entities concerned. What we know is "So-and-so has a mind which has such-and-such properties," but we do not know "A has such and such properties," where A *is* the mind in question. In such a case, we know the properties of a thing without having acquaintance with the thing itself, and without, consequently, knowing any single proposition of which the thing itself is a constituent.[76]

On this view, perception acquaints us not with (ultimate) matter and other minds, but only with our own sense data. (By 1910 any ambiguity about whether or not Russell meant to exclude ordinary middle-sized material objects, along with the fundamental particles of physics, was decided by excluding them all from the charmed circle of acquaintance.)

---

[76] Russell (1905d), pp. 492–93.

On this Russellian picture, the constituents of one's thought, which fully determine the propositions one can entertain, are limited to oneself, one's fleeting ideas, feelings, and sense data, and the universals in Plato's heaven (which one can apparently grasp entirely on one's own). Though Russell speaks of having thoughts *about* things in the wider world that are denoted by denoting phrases, this ends up being a very weak reed. Despite his repeated insistence that it is this epistemological function that makes denoting philosophically important, he never articulates any interesting sense in which an agent's thoughts can be *about* any external object.

For one thing, one can never know, or even believe, *of any such object o* that it is the unique thing of which F is true, and hence that it is the denotation of the definite description ⌜the F⌝. For another, the description plays no role in one's thought, since, according to Russell, (i) propositions are that to which we bear cognitive relations, and (ii) the proposition expressed by ⌜The F is G⌝ doesn't contain any constituent corresponding to ⌜the F⌝. Instead that proposition is, or is equivalent to, a trio of propositions no one of which is, on Russell's account, *about* o or any other object—i.e., ⌜$\sim \forall x \sim (Fx)$⌝, ⌜$\forall x \forall y ((Fx \ \& \ Fy) \to x = y)$⌝, and ⌜$\forall x (Fx \to Gx)$⌝. Surely, there is no interesting sense of 'thinking about' in which one who thinks to himself *not everything isn't F and every pair of things both of which are F is a pair of an object and itself and everything is such that if it is F, then it is G* is thereby thinking about any specific object, including the object o that is uniquely F, if there is one. What one is really thinking about in these cases are properties, or, on Russell's account, propositional functions.

Russell's highly internalist and individualist philosophy of mind carries over into a similarly internalist and individualist philosophy of language. For him, language is first and foremost a vehicle of thought; each meaningful sentence is paired with a single unique proposition that is its meaning for a particular user at a particular time. There is no passing, in Kripke's sense, of a name or natural kind term with its externally derived content, from one user to the next, resulting in the acquisition by agents later in the chain of communication of a newly available propositional constituent occurring in newly entertainable propositions. There is no *linguistic division of labor* in Putnam's sense, in which language is recognized to be a social institution that provides a way of pooling the cognitive resources of a community and making new thought contents available to individual agents that otherwise would not be.[77] Finally, there is no awareness of the dynamics of assertion, or of language use more generally, in which acceptance of a sentence S (in a context) typically adds, not one favored proposition designated as *the meaning of S* to one's store of beliefs and assumptions, but a group of related propositions arising from the interaction of the context with the meaning of S—which, in turn, is thought

---

[77] Putnam (1975).

of as a set of conventional rules for associating possible propositional contents with uses of S.

From my point of view, 108 years after "On Denoting," these features of Russell's general epistemology, philosophy of mind, and philosophy of language are distortions of the nature of our thought, our language, and the relationship between the two. However, far from taking Russell to task, I see the deficiencies of his general view as a measure of how far we have advanced the project of understanding language and thought that he helped to initiate. It would be surprising and deeply disappointing if, in the century separating us from "On Denoting," we hadn't taken strides great enough to make some important aspects of his view look limited and parochial in retrospect. For Russell himself, the things I see as internalist and individualist deficiencies did not seriously inhibit, or detract from, the important progress he was making on his grand project of articulating a precise conceptual framework for understanding the relationship between logic and mathematics. In this way, my general anti-internalist and anti-individualist critique fits one of my recurring themes. Looking back on Russell today, we must *not* mistake his general perspective, his purposes, and his particular projects for ours—despite the fact that were it not for him, and a few others, we would never have gotten this far with ours.

CHAPTER 9

ᰄᱬᰂ

Truth, Falsity, and Judgment

1. Comrades in Arms: Russell's and Moore's Critiques of Pragmatic and Idealist Conceptions of Truth and Reality
    1.1. Russell and Moore vs. the British Idealists
    1.2. Russell (and Moore) vs. William James on Truth
2. The Bearers of Truth and the Problem of Propositions
3. Facts and Attitudes: The Multiple Relation Theory of Judgment
4. Problems
5. Propositions Regained: Salvaging Russell's (Nearly) Lost Insight
    5.1. Reversing Traditional Explanatory Priorities
    5.2. Complex Propositions and Attitudes
    5.3. Existence and Truth
    5.4. The Place of Propositions in Our Cognitive Architecture
    5.5. Further Light on the Central Argument of "On Denoting"
6. Russell's Struggle with a Dying Theory

1. COMRADES IN ARMS: RUSSELL'S AND MOORE'S CRITIQUES OF PRAGMATIC AND IDEALIST CONCEPTIONS OF TRUTH AND REALITY

The story of Russell's break with the British versions of Hegelianism he encountered at Cambridge was partially told in section 1 of chapter 7. That part of the saga focused on his early attraction to, but subsequent rejection of, Idealism as a substitute for religion and a way of securing a moral universe. But Russell's rebellion was not restricted to his discovery that Idealism could not fulfill his moral and religious impulses; it also stemmed from metaphysical disagreements with the Idealists about truth and reality. Together, these two aspects of his break with Idealism were crucial to his "becoming Bertrand Russell." I have waited until now to sketch the second half of this fateful transition both because his transformation wasn't truly complete without the lessons of "On Denoting," and because those tools will be useful to us in outlining some of the main points.

1.1. Russell and Moore vs. the British Idealists

In 1906–7, Russell published "On the Nature of Truth," the first two sections of which were reprinted in 1910 as "The Monistic Theory of Truth." There, Russell criticizes Harold H. Joachim's book *The Nature of Truth,* which articulates an Idealist conception of truth and reality similar to that of the leading British Idealist, F. H. Bradley. Russell begins the essay:

> In any inquiry into the nature of truth, two questions meet us on the threshold: (1) In what sense, if any, is truth dependent on the mind? (2) Are there many different truths, or is there only *the* Truth? . . . The view that truth is one may be called 'logical monism'; it is, of course, closely connected with ontological monism, i.e. the doctrine that Reality is one.[1]

His first target is Joachim's monistic theory of truth, which holds that "the truth itself is one and whole and complete."[2] Russell characterizes the view thusly:

> This doctrine, which is one of the foundation-stones of monistic idealism, . . . means that nothing is wholly true except the whole truth, and that what seem to be isolated truths, such as $2 + 2 = 4$, are really only true in the sense that they form part of the system which is the whole truth. And even in this sense isolated truths are only more or less true; for when artificially isolated they are bereft of aspects and relations which make them parts of the whole truth, and are thus altered from what they are in the system. . . . The truth that a certain partial truth is part of the whole is [itself] a partial truth, and thus only partially true; hence we can never say with perfect truth "this is part of the Truth."[3]

Russell's first criticism is the predictable, and perfectly correct, observation that from this Idealist doctrine it follows that the doctrine itself, and in fact all individual statements made by the Idealists, as well as the sum total of all their statements, are only partially true. But if that is so, then they must all be partially untrue as well, and hence incapable of being known, even by the Idealists who propound them. Russell goes on for awhile, ringing out particular instances of this self-defeating absurdity, exploiting the obvious but sometimes neglected principle that the propositions expressed by S and ⌈it is true that S⌉ are necessarily and a priori equivalent. Indeed any warrant for asserting, denying, believing, disbelieving, or doubting one is warrant for taking the same attitude toward the other. Thus, by disparaging individual "partial" truths, the Idealists implicitly disparage their own doctrines.

---

[1] Page 131 in Russell (1910c).
[2] Joachim (1906), p. 178.
[3] Russell (1910c), p. 132. In support, Russell cites a passage from p. 66 of Joachim (1906).

Russell's next significant criticism is that *The Truth*—the Idealist's imagined one coherent system incorporating all "partial truths"—can't itself be used to specify what truth is, because it presupposes an antecedent, ordinary notion of something being true *simpliciter,* for which the distinction between *partial* and *complete* is irrelevant.

> [T]here is a sense in which such a proposition as 'A murdered B' is true or false; and . . . in this sense the proposition . . . does not depend, for its truth or falsehood, upon whether it is regarded as a partial truth or not. . . . [T]his sense . . . is presupposed in constructing the whole of truth; for the whole of truth is composed of propositions which are true in this sense. . . . [T]he objection to the coherence theory lies in this, that it presupposes a more usual meaning of truth and falsehood in constructing its coherent whole, and that this more usual meaning . . . cannot be explained by means of the theory. The proposition 'Bishop Stubbs was hanged for murder' [a falsehood] is, we are told, not coherent with the whole of truth or with experience. But that means . . . that something is *known* which is inconsistent with this proposition. Thus, what is inconsistent with the proposition must be something *true*: it may be perfectly possible to construct a coherent whole of *false* propositions in which 'Bishop Stubbs was hanged for murder' would find a place. . . . [T]he partial truths of which the whole of truth is composed must be such propositions as would commonly be called true, not such as would commonly be called false; there is no explanation, on the coherence-theory, of the distinction commonly expressed by the words 'true' and 'false', and no evidence that a system of false propositions might not, as in a good novel, be just as coherent as the system which is the whole of truth.[4]

The whole truth—which for the Idealists is the one true description of Reality—can't be *the one coherent system of propositions,* when coherence is taken to be consistency, for there are many different but equally consistent and encompassing systems. Hence, on this understanding of *coherence,* ordinary "partial" truth cannot be defined as that which contributes to The One Coherent Whole. On the contrary, if one wishes to claim that *the whole truth* is the one coherent system of propositions, one must define *coherence* by appeal to our antecedently understood, ordinary, and unqualified notion of *truth*—in violation of central Idealist doctrine.

Having made these and related criticisms, Russell turns to what he regards as "the fundamental assumption of the whole monistic theory, namely its doctrine as to relations."[5] This doctrine, dubbed the *axiom of internal relations,* is stated by Russell as follows, "Every relation is grounded in the relation of the related terms."[6] About this, he says:

[4] Russell (1910c), pp 135–36.
[5] Ibid., p. 139.
[6] Ibid., p. 139.

If this axiom holds, the fact that two objects have a certain relation implies . . . something in the 'natures' of the two objects, in virtue of which they
have the relation in question. According to the opposite view, which is the
one that I advocate, . . . [relational facts] cannot in general be reduced to, or
inferred from, a fact about the one object only together with a fact about the
other object only; they [i.e., relational facts] do not imply that the two objects
have . . . any *intrinsic* property distinguishing them from two objects which
do not have the relation in question.[7] (139–140).

Although the content of this "axiom" is far from clear, Russell takes it
to entail (i) that, as Bradley maintains, there really are no relations, (ii)
that knowing everything about any single thing is, as the Idealists argue,
equivalent to knowing everything about everything, (iii) that, as they further maintain, every property that something A actually has—including
being related to B as it actually is—is an essential property of A, which A
couldn't have existed without having, (iv) that, because of this, Reality as
a whole is a single interconnected system every part of which is equally
essential to every other part, and (v) that, as Bradley maintains, there is,
in fact, no diversity at all, since only one thing, Reality itself, truly exists.

Presumably, (i) is entailed because, according to the *axiom of internal
relations*, relations are reducible to, and hence eliminable in terms of, intrinsic non-relational properties. Though I agree with Russell that this is
obviously false, there is no harm in assuming it for the sake of argument.
As for (ii), suppose that A stands in relation R to B, which in turn has
properties P_1 to P_n. Then A has the relational property *bearing R to something B with properties P_1 to P_n*, where this relational property is, by hypothesis, reducible to intrinsic non-relational properties of A. Hence knowing
that A has this property or properties will be sufficient for knowing that
B has P_1 to P_n. Since we can do the same for any object A that bears the
relation *coexists with* to any other objects, no matter what their properties,
it will follow that knowing all there is to know about A is necessary and
sufficient for knowing everything about every coexisting thing. Although
this sounds absurd, it is the result of a simple latitudinarian conception of
relations and relational properties that, for most purposes (apart from certain logical puzzles with which we need not be concerned here), is harmless enough. Roughly put, the conception holds that for any sentence S
containing two or more occurrences of singular terms, the result S(x,y) of
replacing at least two such occurrences with distinct variables expresses
a relation (possibly empty) between objects, while the result of adding
a quantifier to get ⌜∃y Sxy⌝ expresses a relational property of individuals (possibly empty).[8] Using this technique, one can encode any fact one

---

[7] Ibid., pp. 139–40.
[8] Although the conception is more general, this simple statement is enough to convey
the idea.

wants into a relational property of any object. On this highly expansive conception of properties, it is not surprising that knowing all of an object's properties, including all its relational properties, is tantamount to knowing everything. This result is trivial, not deep.

The real problem comes with (iii), which Russell states as follows: "*If A and B are related in a certain way . . . [then] if they were not so related they would be other than they are, and . . . consequently there must be something in them which is essential to their being related as they are.*"[9] Suppose this were so—i.e., that every relational property of an object were an essential property of it (or were reducible to its essential intrinsic properties). This would give us the initial statement of (iii)—that every property is essential. To show this, we let o be any object and P any relational or non-relational property of o. Let R1 be the relation *x is like y in possessing P* and RP1 be the relational property *being like o in possessing P*; let R2 be the relation *x differs from y in not possessing P* and RP2 be the relational property *differing from o in not possessing P*. Since o has P, it and everything else that has P has RP1; similarly, everything that lacks P has RP2. Given that relational properties are essential, we get the result that P is essential to everything that has it and that the negation (complement) of P is essential to everything that has it. More generally, for absolutely anything whatsoever, including the whole of Reality itself, every property of that thing is essential to it (and so could not have been a property that it lacked), and so is every relation in which it stands to other things. This is the Idealist's thesis (iv).

Although Russell correctly saw that (iii), and hence (iv), were the products of confusion, he didn't do a very good job, in "The Monistic Theory of Truth," of explaining what that confusion was. Fortunately, G. E. Moore did so in exquisite, if excruciating, detail in "External and Internal Relations," published in 1919–20. Although we need not follow the twists and turns of his painstaking discussion, we can illustrate the basic point using Russell's distinction between logical form and grammatical form. To this end, consider the following argument.

S1.   Necessarily, if a = b, then every property of a is a property of b.

S2.   Hence, if a has property P, then, necessarily, if b does not have P, then b ≠ a.

S3.   More generally, if a has P, then, necessarily, anything that doesn't have P isn't a.

S4.   So, if a has P, then it is a necessary truth that anything that doesn't have P isn't a.

S5.   If it is a necessary truth that anything that doesn't have P isn't a, then for every possible state of the world w (i.e., for every way w

[9] Ibid., p. 143.

that the world could have been) and for any object o whatsoever, if o were to lack P, were the world in state w, then o wouldn't be a.

S6.   Since a would always be a, no matter what possible state the world might be in (provided that a would exist were the world in that state), there is no possible state w such that, were the world in w, a would exist without having P.

S7.   Since there is no way that the world could be such that if it were that way, a would exist without having P, a could not exist without having P.

S8.   Since the same argument can be given for any property of any object, every property of an object is an essential property of that object—in the sense that the object could not exist without having that property.

The first premise of this argument is obviously true, each step has an air of plausibility; yet the conclusion is incredible. Why? Is our common sense conviction that we ourselves, as well as the things around us, could have had at least slightly different histories so befuddled and insecure as to be refuted by this little argument? No. The confusion is in the argument itself.

As indicated, S1 is fine, as is the progression from S4 to S8. The problem lies in an ambiguity in some sentences containing the word *necessarily* that affects the inferences to steps 2, 3, and 4. The argument can be understood in such a way that all occurrences of this word express the property of being a necessary truth. Thus, S1 can be understood as having the logical form LS1:

LS1. It is a necessary truth that [if a = b, then every property of a is a property of b]

Here, the property *being a necessary truth* is predicated of the proposition expressed by the sentence in brackets—i.e., the proposition that if a is the very same thing as b, then every property of a is a property of b. By contrast, S2 is ambiguous, due to different possible scopes of the necessity operator. Here we have an example of the pervasiveness of Russellian scope ambiguities in English; just as some sentences containing descriptions are ambiguous due to different possible scopes of the descriptions, so some are ambiguous due to different possible scopes of occurrences of the necessity operator.

On one interpretation the logical form of S2 is LS2a, and on another it is LS2b.

LS2a. It is a necessary truth that [if a has property P, then (if b doesn't have P, then b ≠ a)]
LS2b. If a has property P, then it is a necessary truth that [if b doesn't have P, then b ≠ a]

LS2a follows from LS1. Since the bracketed sentence of LS2a is a logical consequence of the bracketed sentence in LS1, if the one expresses a necessary truth, the other must do so as well. However, LS2b does *not* follow logically from LS1. LS1 tells us that there is no possible state w such that if the world were in w, a would be the very same object as b, while nevertheless not having the same properties as b. LS2 tells us something quite different: namely that if the world is *actually* in a state in which a has a certain property P, then there is *no possible* state w such that if the world were in state w, an object b that didn't have P would be the very same object as a. In order to draw this conclusion on the basis of LS1, one would have to add a further premise: namely, that if the world is actually in a state in which a has P, then there is no possible state w such that if the world were in w, a would lack P. But since this is what the argument is designed to *prove*, to introduce it as a premise would be to render the argument circular. So, if the argument is to have any chance of serving its purpose, S2 must be interpreted as having the logical form LS2a.

Similar reasoning establishes that if S3 is to follow from LS2a, it must have the logical form LS3a.

> LS3a. It is a necessary truth that [for any object o, if a has property P, then (if o does not have P, then o ≠ a)]

But now there is no way to get to S4, the logical form of which is, unambiguously, LS4.

> LS4. If a has P, then it is a necessary truth that [for any object o, if o does not have P, then o ≠ a]

Just as before, there is no way of validly inferring LS4 from LS3a, short of assuming what is supposed to be proved. Of course, since S3 is ambiguous, it has another interpretation in which S4 does follow from it, namely an interpretation in which S3 has the same logical form as S4. However, on that interpretation S3 doesn't follow from LS2a.

To sum up, the argument for corollary (iii) of the *axiom of internal relations* rests on a hidden ambiguity. Certain key sentences in it have more than one Russellian logical form. The fact that each step has an interpretation on which it follows logically and noncircularly from previous steps gives the argument its air of plausibility. However, there is no uniform way of interpreting the ambiguous sentences so that every step follows validly and noncircularly from the others. Because of this, the argument does nothing to rebut the commonsense conviction that we ourselves, and the objects around us, could have had slightly different histories. In short, the Idealists have done nothing to rebut the rational presumption in favor of this conviction, and nothing to establish their grand metaphysical theses. This was, essentially, Moore's conclusion, and Russell's too.

Having removed any plausible rationale for corollaries (iii) and (iv) of the *axiom of internal relations*, one may be pretty confident that corollary (v)—Bradley's incredible doctrine that exactly one thing exists, Reality as a Whole—will remain similarly unsupported. However, it may be of interest to recount Russell's argument that it too should be regarded as a corollary of the so-called *axiom*.

> This conclusion [corollary (v)] is reached by considering the relation of diversity [nonidentity]. For if there really are two things, A and B, which are diverse [nonidentical], it is impossible to reduce this diversity wholly to adjectives [intrinsic non-relational properties] of A and B. It will be necessary that A and B should have *different* adjectives [properties], and the diversity [nonidentity] of these adjectives [properties] cannot, on pain of an endless regress, be interpreted as *meaning* [being reducible to the claim] that they in turn have different adjectives [properties]. For if we say that A and B differ when A has the adjective [property] 'different from B' and B has the adjective [property] 'different from A', we must suppose that those two adjectives [properties] differ . . . and so on *ad infinitum*. We cannot take 'different from B' as an adjective [property] requiring no further reduction. . . . Thus, if there is to be any diversity [difference/nonidentity], there must [in order to avoid endless regress] be a diversity not reducible to a difference [nonidentity] of adjectives [properties]—i.e. not grounded in the 'natures' of the diverse [nonidentical] terms [thus falsifying the doctrine of internal relations]. Consequently, if the axiom of internal relations is true, it follows that there is no diversity [i.e., no nonidentity], and [hence] that there is only one thing. Thus the axiom of internal relations is equivalent to the assumption of ontological monism and to the denial that there are any relations [between different things?].[10]

Having gotten this far, Russell had no trouble finishing up the article by producing examples of central Idealist doctrines—e.g., that the several parts of a whole are different both from each other and from the whole they jointly make up—that cannot be intelligibly formulated without assuming the existence of nonidentical things. With this, we close the books on Russell's rejection of Absolute Idealism.[11] Having first concluded that the moral and religious appeal of this substitute for Christianity was an illusion, he later came to see that the logic, metaphysics, and epistemology of the system were hopeless.

1.2. Russell (and Moore) vs. William James on Truth

As I indicated earlier, the material later published under the title "The Monistic Theory of Truth" appeared as the first two sections of Russell (1906–7). In it, as we have seen, Russell makes the intellectual case against Idealist views of truth and reality—as opposed to the moral, religious, emotional, or practical case against it that he made in his (at this

---

[10] Ibid., pp. 141–42.
[11] For further discussion of Russell's critique of Idealism, see Coffa (1991), pp. 94–98.

point still unpublished) papers in the 1890s. At the same time, across the Atlantic in America, a different revolt was brewing against what its proponents, with reason, took to be the retreat from lived experience in favor of a bloodless, unworldly metaphysics exhibited by Anglo-Hegelians such as McTaggart, Bradley, and T. H. Green in Britain and Josiah Royce in the United States. This new movement in philosophy was the American Pragmatism of Charles Sanders Peirce, William James, John Dewey, and F.C.S. Schiller. Roughly put, its leading idea was that the meaning/significance/ importance/truth of a thought (precisely which of these alternatives was not always clear) is to be assessed in terms of its practical consequences— the empirical predications to which it leads, the beliefs and actions that flow from it, and even, for some leading pragmatists, the new experiences, emotions, and relationships that follow in its wake. Insofar as this pragmatic frame of mind represented experimental open-mindedness—as opposed to a priori metaphysical speculation in theoretical matters and the dead hand of tradition in moral and political matters—Russell welcomed it. Insofar as this openness was premised on a radically revisionary view of truth and reality, he judged it pernicious.

Russell articulated these views in two articles—one originally published in 1908 under the title "Transatlantic 'Truth'" (later renamed "William James's Conception of Truth" and reprinted in Russell 1910c) and the other published in 1909, called "Pragmatism."[12] Both distinguish what Russell calls the pragmatic method from the pragmatic theory of truth.

> Pragmatism represents, on the one hand, a method and habit of mind, on the other, a certain theory as to what constitutes truth. . . . The former, up to a point, is involved in all induction, and is certainly largely commendable. The latter is the essential novelty and the point of real importance.[13]

Unfortunately, this central point of importance, the new theory of truth, isn't easy to pin down. The most ambitious formulation of it is: *'True' means 'something useful to believe'*, which seems to be suggested by the following passages from James's *Pragmatism*.[14]

> I am well aware of how odd it must seem to some of you to hear me say that an idea is 'true' so long as to believe it is profitable to our lives. That it is good, for as much as it profits, you will gladly admit. . . . But is it not a strange misuse of the word 'truth' you will say, to call ideas also 'true' for this reason? . . . Let me now say only this, that truth is one species of good, and not, as is

---

[12] Russell was joined in his critique of James on truth by the like-minded, but more narrowly focused, critique in Moore (1907–8). Though the two agreed on a number of important points, they focused on somewhat different things. Here, the text of my discussion will follow Russell, with notes to Moore where appropriate.

[13] Russell (1908b), p. 114.

[14] See also section 1 of Moore (1907–8) for clear argument and documentation that James does intend to assert that 'true' means 'useful to believe'.

usually supposed, a category distinct from good, and co-ordinate with it. The true is the name of whatever proves itself to be good in the way of belief, and good, too, for definite assignable reasons.[15]

'What would be better for us to believe'! This sounds like the very definition of truth. It comes very near to say 'what we *ought* to believe': and in *that* definition none of you would find any oddity.[16]

Our account of truth is an account . . . of processes of leading, realized *in rebus*, and having only this quality in common, that they *pay*.[17]

'The true,' to put it very briefly, is only the expedient in the way of our thinking, just as 'the right' is only the expedient in the way of behaving. Expedient in almost any fashion; and expedient in the long run on the whole of course.[18]

One of Russell's main points is that the view that 'true' means 'what is useful to believe' is false; *being true* is not identical with *being something useful to believe,* or with *being what one ought to believe.* This can be seen by noting that any warrant for believing, doubting, or denying p is simultaneously warrant for believing, doubting, or denying *that p is true,* and conversely. Thus, if (i) were correct, any warrant for taking one of these attitudes toward p would be warrant for taking the same attitude toward the proposition *that p would be useful to believe,* and conversely. Since this is transparently not so, 'true' is not synonymous with 'something that is useful to believe'.

Russell implicitly makes this point time and time again. For example, on page 122 of "Transatlantic 'Truth'" (1908b) he considers the proposition *that other people exist,* while on page 124 he considers the propositions *that God exists* and *that there is life after death.* Where p is any of these propositions, we may desire that p be true while remaining uncertain whether it is and worried that it isn't. If we find ourselves in this state, it is no comfort to be told that we would be happier if we believed p to be true. W already knew that. We also *know* that the fact that p would be useful to believe *provides us with no grounds to believe either p or that p is true.* Since we clearly recognize our warrant for thinking that it would be useful to believe p while clearly recognizing that we are without warrant for thinking *that p is true,* 'true' doesn't mean 'something that is useful to believe'.

Russell makes a closely related point when he applies the Moorean open-question test for definability to (i).

Suppose I accept the pragmatic criterion, and suppose you persuade me that a certain belief is useful. Suppose I thereupon conclude that belief is true. Is

---

[15] James (1907), pp. 58–59. (*Pragmatism* was first published in 1907, but it was reprinted with different page numbering in 1965, and these are the page numbers I will use).

[16] Ibid., pp. 59–60.

[17] Ibid., pp. 142–43.

[18] Ibid., p. 145. See pp. 118–24 of the reprinting of Moore (1907–8) in Moore (1922a) for illuminating discussion of this and the immediately preceding passage from James.

it not obvious that there is a transition in my mind from seeing that the belief is useful to actually holding that the belief is true? Yet this could not be so if the pragmatic account of truth were valid. Take, say, the belief that other people exist. According to the pragmatists, to say 'it is true that other people exist' *means* 'it is useful to believe that other people exist'. But if so, then these two phrases are merely different words for the same proposition: therefore when I believe the one I believe the other. If this were so, there could be no transition from the one to the other, as plainly there is. This shows that the word 'true' represents for us a different idea from that represented by the phrase 'useful to believe'.[19]

Russell nicely supplements this point by noting that although, according to James, a hypothesis H is true if consequences useful to life flow from it, the useful consequences are those that flow *from H*, not from the claim *that H is useful to believe* (the consequences of which are quite different and do not include H among them).[20] Since H is a trivial and universally recognized consequence of the claim *that H is true*, it follows that the claim *that H is true* is different from, and not entailed by, that claim *that H is useful to believe*. So the properties *being true* and *being useful to believe* are not only different properties, they are also not necessarily coextensive. They could hardly even be actually coextensive (i.e., actually true of precisely the same things). Even if one denies what in fact seems very likely—namely that some falsehoods *are* on the whole useful to believe—surely many of the uncountable truths about any and all objects, concrete and abstract, are too irrelevant to our concerns and too complex for our limited minds to worry over.[21] Hence, like (i), (ii) and (iii) are false.[22]

(ii) Necessarily, a proposition is true iff it is one we ought to believe iff it is, all things considered, useful for us to believe.

(iii) A proposition is true iff it is one we ought to believe iff it is, all things considered, useful for us to believe.

What then, if anything, does pragmatism have to say about truth or belief that is itself a reasonable candidate for being both true and distinctive? To answer this question, one must understand, as Russell did, that what united pragmatists like James, Schiller, and Dewey was an interest, not in truth, but in the principles governing belief revision. James addresses

[19] Russell (1910c), pp. 119–20.

[20] Ibid., p. 124.

[21] Moore gives several commonsense examples both of truths that are not useful to believe (including many that are too irrelevant to be useful) and falsehoods that are useful to believe on pp. 107–15 and 118–23 of Moore (1922) (the reprinting of Moore 1907–8).

[22] Moore nicely distinguishes (ii) and (iii), arguing for the falsity of (ii) on pp. 127–28 of Moore (1922a), independently of his previous argument for the falsity of (iii) (which of course entails the falsity of (ii)). Here Moore emphases a certain type of possibility—in which it is useful to believe that someone exists, even though that person doesn't exist—as falsifying (ii), which Russell later uses in Russell (1908b).

this point in the following passages from chapter 2—"What Pragmatism Means"—of *Pragmatism*.

> The observable process which Schiller and Dewey particularly singled out for generalization is the familiar one by which any individual settles into *new opinions*. . . . The individual has a stock of old opinions already, but he meets a new experience that puts them to a strain. Somebody contradicts them; or . . . he discovers that they contradict each other; or he hears facts with which they are incompatible; or desires arise in him that they cease to satisfy. The result is an inward trouble . . . from which he seeks to escape by modifying his previous mass of opinions. He saves as much of it as he can . . . until at last some new idea comes up which he can graft upon the ancient stock with a minimum of disturbance. . . . The new idea is then adopted as the true one. It preserves the older stock of truths with a minimum of modification. . . . New truth . . . marries old opinion to new fact. . . . We hold a theory true just in proportion to its success in solving this 'problem of maxima and minima'. . . . The point I now urge . . . is the part played by the older truths. Failure to take account of it is the source of much of the unjust criticism leveled against pragmatism. Their influence is absolutely controlling. . . . The simplest case of a new truth is of course the mere numerical addition of new kinds of facts, or of new single facts of old kinds, to our experience—an addition that involves no alteration of old beliefs. . . . The new contents themselves are not true, they simply *come* and *are*.[23]

In this passage the concern is not with what it is for something to be true, but with how new beliefs are formed and old beliefs modified in light of the *facts* provided by experience and the need to ensure that one's beliefs are *consistent* both with those facts and with one another. Together, this emphasis on both facts and consistency indicates the pragmatists' implicit reliance on obvious, uncontroversial *truths*—in the ordinary sense of 'truth'—including both a priori truths of logic (and mathematics) and observational truths. These truths are simply taken for granted. The pragmatists' real concern is with what, given our unproblematic true beliefs, should determine our new beliefs.

Russell sees this point quite clearly.

> In order to understand the pragmatic notion of truth, we have to be clear as to the basis of *fact* upon which truths are supposed to rest. Immediate sensible experience, for example, does not come under the alternative of *true* and *false*. . . . Thus when we are merely aware of sensible objects, we are not to be regarded as knowing any truth, although we have a certain kind of contact with reality. It is important to realize that the *facts* which thus lie outside the scope of truth and falsehood supply the material which is presupposed by the pragmatic theory. Our beliefs have to agree with matters of fact: it is

---

[23] James (1907), pp. 50–51.

an essential part of their 'satisfactoriness' that they should do so. James also mentions what he calls 'relations among purely mental ideas' as part of our stock-in-trade with which pragmatism starts. He mentions instances '1 and 1 make 2', 'white differs less from grey than it does from black,' and so on. All such propositions as these, then, we are supposed to know for certain before we can get under way. . . . Thus it is only when we pass beyond plain matters of fact and *a priori* truisms that the pragmatic notion of truth comes in. It is, in short, the notion to be applied to doubtful cases.[24]

The genuine question that most exercised the pragmatists was what to do, and what, if anything, to believe, when confronted with a proposition p about which one needs to make a decision, even though (i) both p and its negation are consistent with all uncontroversial facts and (ii) the available empirical evidence doesn't clearly favor either over the other. James's answer is that one ought to believe the proposition the acceptance of which leads to the best consequences.

Pragmatists who gave this answer were wont to claim that *at least in cases such as this*, being true and being good to believe were one and the same. But there is no reason to follow them in this. Absent cogent argument to the contrary, for which none was given, there is no reason to think that the property predicated of p by saying "it's true" differs depending on the subject matter of p or the role it plays in our inquiry. The real issue raised by the pragmatists concerns the conduct of inquiry. What should we do when deciding whether to accept or reject p in the course of a theoretical or practical investigation? James's answer was that what we are naturally inclined to do, and in fact should do, is to believe the proposition that will lead us to the best consequences. But what are *consequences* and when do they count as *good*? James seems to have thought that it depends on the type of case we are considering.

In writing of scientific and other theoretical matters, James often seems to have in mind the observational consequences derived from a hypothesis by logical or a priori reasoning. In these cases, good consequences are those that verify the hypothesis.[25] So understood, an injunction to *accept* the hypothesis that is best verified by one's evidence is thoroughly sensible. However, to *accept* a hypothesis as being more highly confirmed by available evidence than any alternative hypothesis is not, necessarily, to *believe* it. One of Russell's most telling criticisms of James is that James runs the two together. Russell notes:

[Pragmatist] theories start very often from such things as the general hypotheses of science—ether, atoms, and the like. In such cases we take little interest in the hypotheses themselves, which, as we well know, are liable to

---

[24] Russell (1908b), pp. 117–18.

[25] Pages 98–107 of Moore (1922a) examines and persuasively critiques the thesis, sometimes urged by James, that all truths are verifiable.

rapid change. What we care about are the inferences as to sensible phenomena which the hypotheses enable us to make. All we ask of the hypotheses is
that they should 'work'—though it should be observed that what constitutes
'working' is not the general agreeableness of their results, but the conformity
of these results with observed facts. But in the case of these general scientific
hypotheses, no sensible man believes that they are true as they stand.[26]

Russell here vacillates between a commonsensical point about the relationship between acceptance of a scientific hypothesis and belief in it, on
the one hand, and a stronger, more philosophically contentious claim that
might itself be seen as a version of pragmatism.

The commonsensical point is that the verification of a non-observational
hypothesis by empirical evidence is seldom conclusive, and so may not be
belief-compelling. Derivations of observational claims from a theoretical
hypothesis often require subsidiary hypotheses to reach observational
conclusions. Because of this, a false prediction need not refute the hypothesis, since one might locate the fault in one of the subsidiary claims.
Even the derivation of true observation statements, while adding to the
credibility of the hypothesis, won't rule out alternative ways of making the
same predictions. For this reason, the proper attitude to take to many empirical hypotheses that are so far confirmed by the evidence is, as Russell
seems to suggest, not fully fledged *belief,* but *elevated credence* and *provisional acceptance.* In these cases, the Jamesian calculation of the utility of
believing the hypothesis is wrong both because *belief* is not the relevant
epistemic attitude and because utility plays no direct role in determining
the level of credence to assign a hypothesis and at best only a highly limited role in deciding whether or not to accept the hypothesis as part of
one's theoretical framework for further inquiry.[27]

To the extent that this was the essence of Russell's criticism of James in
the above passage (as well as other related passages in the two articles), he
was on firm ground. However, if that was his point, he slightly overstated
it in saying:

> we take little interest in the [general] hypotheses themselves. . . . What we
> care about are the inferences as to sensible phenomena which the hypotheses
> enable us to make. All we ask of the hypotheses is that they should 'work' . . .
> [in the sense of conforming] with observed facts. . . . [I]n the case of these
> general scientific hypotheses, no sensible man believes that they are true as
> they stand.[28]

Actually, many sensible men do believe that *some general scientific hypotheses* are true as they stand—not, perhaps that these hypotheses are the

[26] Ibid., pp. 121–22.

[27] The utility involved in accepting one of two theories that are compatible with the same
possible observations involves the ease of working with the theory and of modifying it
when required by unexpected evidence.

[28] Moore (1922a), p. 120.

whole truth about the theoretical items of which they speak, but that what they say about these items is, in fact, entirely true. I would venture that we *know* some scientific hypotheses to be true. What is more, many investigators do care about the picture of the universe given to us by the so far well-confirmed hypotheses of our best theories. Because they do care about what unobserved entities must exist if our theories are true, they *do not* agree with the anti-realist sentiment that all we ask of empirical theories is that their observational consequences be true. Putting these points together, a realist about science would claim to know some theoretical truths about some unobserved entities, despite the fact that those truths are underdetermined by the observational evidence for them.

It is clear that by 1914, when he published *Our Knowledge of the External World* (to be discussed in chapter 11), Russell rejected this realist contention about knowledge of the unobservable. He may have rejected it even in 1908, in which case he would have been in partial agreement with a much later version of pragmatism developed by Bas Van Fraassen in *The Scientific Image*.[29] Roughly put, this view holds (i) that for any consistent scientific theory T and observational conditionals entailed by T, there are multiple theories distinct from (and some inconsistent with) T that entail precisely the same observational conditionals as T, (ii) that although these observationally equivalent theories make different non-observational claims about the universe, we cannot know which such claims are true, (iii) that all we can justifiably ask of a scientific theory is that it be observationally adequate, (iv) that faced with the choice of which theory to accept—among observationally equivalent theories, each compatible with all currently available evidence—we may take various kinds of utility into account, and (v) that belief in an empirically adequate theory is never rationally *required* by the facts, but is always rationally *permissible*, making the option of believing a theory properly subject to evaluative concerns. Though admittedly a far cry from Jamesian pragmatism, Van Fraassen's version of pragmatism incorporates the Jamesian idea that non-epistemic utility in some quite broad sense may play a systematic and rationally defensible role in determining what one believes.

This brings us to Russell's last major objection to pragmatism. Whatever his skepticism may have been about attaining scientific knowledge of unobservable entities, he deeply opposed the idea that the utility of believing p might provide acceptable grounds for believing p—no matter what the subject matter of p (scientific, religious, etc.). The thought here is a variant of a point made early on. Recall his discussion of the propositions *that other people exist, that God exists,* and *that there is life after death.* Where p is any of these propositions, he pointed out that we might desire p be true and know that believing p would make us happy while remaining uncertain whether p is true and worried that it isn't. The point can be generalized to virtually any proposition q. Even if we don't already know

---

[29] Van Fraassen (1980). See Rosen (1994) for thoughtful discussion and critique.

that believing q would be useful or make us happy, coming to believe that it would do so will typically be of little help. Since we *know* that the utility of believing q provides no grounds for believing q, we typically *cannot* come to believe q on this basis. The reason we can't is that we implicitly recognize that to do so would be to violate the norms governing belief. Mightn't there be cases in which the greater good requires violating epistemic norms—e.g., by arranging to have oneself tricked into believing q—in something like the way that the greater good sometimes requires us to violate the norms against lying? Of course there might be such cases. But they provide no vindication of pragmatism. After one eliminates the pragmatists' confusion about truth, and reformulates their views as a theory of rational belief revision, the central doctrines of pragmatism are at bottom those that reduce epistemic norms to general practical norms. The fact that in certain special circumstances the latter can override the former does nothing to show that such a reduction is possible. Thus, there is reason to believe that Russell would have been right in rejecting even this sanitized version of pragmatism.

These, then, were Russell's chief criticisms of pragmatism as a serious philosophy.[30] However, they do not exhaust his critique of what might be called the spirit of pragmatism, or pragmatism as a way of life. Just as he took Absolute Idealism to task in the 1890s for failing to live up to its moral and religious pretentions, so he took on the pragmatist intellectual movement's offer of a general outlook on life to its adherents. Worse, he saw a connection between the failed serious philosophy of pragmatism and its flawed "philosophy of life." Bluntly put, the serious philosophy was, to far too great an extent, put in the service of the advocated life plan. It is notable that Russell does not speak at all of Peirce in this connection. The first, and by far greatest, of all the pragmatists, Peirce was the least associated with personal or societal uplift. He was also the least well known outside the tiny circle of professional philosophers in America plus the few Europeans interested in the foundations of logic. By contrast, James, Dewey, and Schiller, who wrote for more general audiences, made no clear distinction between their epistemology, metaphysics, and logic, on the one hand, and their prescriptions about life and society, on the other. This, Russell seems to suggest, was a serious, even a deplorable, mistake.

Although Russell himself had a great deal to say about personal happiness, individual morality, and social improvement, the tradition in philosophy that he, Moore, and Frege were building was then, and remains largely today, insistent that the core issues in epistemology, metaphysics, and logic must be rigorously investigated on their own, independently of moral, political, or religious concerns. This was not true of the alternate tradition

---

[30] James replies to Russell (and Moore) in "Two English Critics," which is chapter 14 of James (1909); see also his remarks in "Annotations on Bertrand Russell's "Transatlantic 'Truth,'" printed as Appendix 4 of that volume.

that was American Pragmatism. For Russell, this was an error—which he implicitly seems to suggest raised the issue of (presumably unconscious) bad faith in the case of some of the pragmatists—and so, for that reason, may have been as serious as all the other errors of pragmatism combined.[31]

This, I believe, is what lies in the background of the final seven pages of Russell (1910c). Having praised the empirical openness of "the pragmatic method" in the opening pages of Russell (1908b), and having critiqued the core logical and epistemological doctrines concerning truth and belief revision in the remainder of Russell (1908b) and the bulk of Russell (1910c) he closes the latter with what is mostly a diatribe against the larger "popular" pragmatic philosophy, chiefly inspired by Schiller and James. He says:

> Although . . . we do not ourselves accept the pragmatist philosophy, we nevertheless believe that it is likely to achieve widespread popularity, because it embraces some of the main intellectual and political tendencies of the time. This aspect of pragmatism deserves consideration, since the influence of a doctrine . . . is by no means proportional to its intellectual merit. On the intellectual side, pragmatism embodies scepticism, evolution, and the new insight into . . . scientific induction. On the political side, it embodies democracy, the increased belief in human power . . . and the Bismarckian belief in force.[32]

After articulating this largely critical general assessment of what he took to be the animating spirit and popular appeal of pragmaticism, Russell followed up with a more pointed list of particulars that included the following samples.

PRAGMATISM AND SKEPTICISM

The scepticism embodied in pragmatism is that which says, 'Since all beliefs are absurd, we may as well believe what is most convenient'. . . . Scepticism is of the very essence of the pragmatic philosophy: nothing is certain, everything is liable to revision, and the attainment of any truth in which we can

---

[31] If the attribution of bad faith to James seems questionable, I suggest close reading of Moore (1907–8), which, on issue after issue, patiently contrasts the extreme theses that James's words evidently express, and that he evidently intends, with the commonplace trivialities he offers in their defense. One persuasive example involves James's claim, examined in section 3 of Moore's article, that "to an unascertainable extent our truths are man-made products" (James quoted on pp. 138–39 of Moore 1922a). About this Moore (p. 139) says, "It is noticeable that all the instances which Professor James gives of the ways in which, according to him, 'our truths' are 'made' are instances of ways in which our *beliefs* come into existence." Although James's thesis is *that the truth of our beliefs is a human product,* the only support he offers is the triviality that *our beliefs are human products.* But surely the fact that we have a hand in bringing our beliefs into existence doesn't support what is evidently intended, namely that the various truths we believe—e.g., that the planets revolve around the sun, that the Alps arose in the distant past, or that the floor of the Pacific Ocean sank—were made true, at least in part, by us. See pp. 139–43 of Moore (1922a).

[32] Russell (1909), pp. 104–5 in Russell (1910c).

rest securely is impossible. It is, therefore, not worth while to trouble our heads about what really is true. . . . Instead of the old distinction between 'true' and 'false', we adopt the more useful distinction between what we persist in thinking true, and what merely seems true at first sight. Later on, the old meanings of 'true' and 'false' may slip back unnoticed, and we may come to think that what is true in the pragmatic sense is true in the old sense also; this happens especially in regard to religion. But on pragmatist principles, there is no reason to regret this; for the 'true' is what it is useful to believe. . . . Scepticism, therefore, though necessary at the start, must be banished later on. . . . In this there is no great psychological difficulty, since, as Hume confessed, the empirical attitude is one not easily maintained in practice.[33]

Pragmatism, Evolution, and Truth/Falsity

The philosophy of evolution has also had its share in generating the pragmatic tone of mind. It has led people to regard everything as fluid and . . . as passing by imperceptible gradations into everything else. . . . Hence it has come to be felt that all sharp antitheses, such as that of *true* and *false,* must be blurred, and all finality must be avoided. . . . Instead of 'the true' we shall have 'the more true'. . . . And between different claimants for truth, we must provide a struggle for existence, leading to the survival of the strongest.[34]

Pragmatism and Induction (Empirical Confirmation/ Disconfirmation)

Such general assumptions as causality, the existence of an external world, etc., cannot be supported by Mill's canons of induction, but require a far more comprehensive treatment of the whole organized body of accepted scientific doctrine. It is in such treatment that the pragmatic method is seen at its best; and among men of science its apparent success in this direction has doubtless contributed greatly to its acceptance.[35]

Pragmatism and Democracy

The influence of democracy in promoting pragmatism is visible in almost every page of William James's writing. There is an impatience of authority . . . a tendency to decide philosophical questions by putting them to a vote. . . . James claims for the pragmatist temper 'the open air and possibilities of nature as against dogma, artificiality, and the pretence of finality in truth'. A thing which simply *is* true, whether you like it or not, is to him as hateful as a Russian autocracy; he feels that he is escaping from a prison, made not by stone walls but by 'hard facts', when he has humanized truth, and made it, like the police force in a democracy, the servant of the people instead of their master.[36]

---

[33] Ibid., p. 105. Russell here alludes to Hume's confession that the skepticism about enduring external objects to which he is led when doing philosophy disappears when he leaves his study.

[34] Ibid., pp. 105–6.

[35] Ibid., p. 106.

[36] Ibid., p. 107.

PRAGMATISM AND HUMAN POWER

By the progress of mechanical invention, the possibilities of our command over nature have been shown to be much greater than they were formerly thought to be. Hence has arisen—especially in America . . .—a general feeling that by energy and hope all obstacles can be overcome. . . . Hence have arisen a self-confidence and a pride of life, which in many ways remind one of the Renaissance. . . . The . . . successful men of action generally . . . can find in pragmatism an expression of their instinctive view of the world. Such men . . . expect the world to be malleable to their wishes, and in a greater or less degree find their expectation justified by success. Hence arises a disbelief in those 'hard facts' which pragmatists tend to deny, and a confidence of victory in contests with the outer world, whether these contests be cognitive or more directly practical.[37]

PRAGMATISM AND THE RESORT TO FORCE

From the confidence of victory in contests it is an easy passage to the love of contest. For this pragmatism provides full scope. The many different 'truths as claim' must fight it out among themselves, and the victor will become 'truth validated'. . . . If [contrary to pragmatism] there is a non-human truth, which one man may know, while another does not, there is a standard outside the disputants, to which, we may urge, the dispute ought to be submitted; hence a pacific and judicial settlement of disputes is at least theoretically possible. If, on the contrary, the only way of discovering which of the disputants is in the right is to wait and see which of them is successful, there is no longer any principle except force by which the issue can be decided. . . . This philosophy, therefore, although it begins in liberty and toleration, develops, by inherent necessity, into the appeal to force and the arbitrament of the big battalions.[38]

There is far too much in this astonishing bill of particulars to discuss here. My own take is that although some of Russell's sweeping claims are exaggerated, and nearly all are debatable, a number are founded on nuggets of brilliant insight. Fortunately, sorting through which is which is not required here. For me, what is most striking is not that pragmatism is a flawed public philosophy, but that it is a public philosophy at all. For this reason alone, it stands, by my reckoning, largely outside the analytic tradition in philosophy. It is not that analytic philosophers, including Russell himself, haven't had a great deal to say about happiness, the art of living, morality, public policy, or the nature of a just society. Some have. What they have not done, or for the most part even tried to do, is to produce an integrated philosophical system—aimed at an intellectually sophisticated, but unspecialized general audience—in which the moral, social, and political are linked to, and influenced by, central metaphysical and epistemic doctrines, and from which important life lessons

[37] Ibid., pp. 107–8.
[38] Ibid., pp. 108–10.

and political programs can be extracted.[39] Whether or not this absence is progress is debatable.

That said, there is no denying that Russell too yearned for an integrated and comprehensive life picture which, it seems clear from his final summing up, he was trying to fashion, if only for himself.

> To sum up: Pragmatism appeals to the temper of mind which finds on the surface of this planet the whole of its imaginative material; which feels confident of progress, and unaware of non-human limitations to human power; which loves battle, with all its attendant risks, because it has no real doubt that it will achieve victory; which desires religion, as it desires railways and electric light, as a comfort and a help in the affairs of this world, not as providing non-human objects to satisfy the hunger for perfection, and for something to be worshipped without reserve. *But for those who feel that life on this planet would be a life in prison if it were not for the windows into a greater world beyond; for those to whom a belief in man's omnipotence seems arrogant, who desire rather the Stoic freedom that comes of mastery over the passions than the Napoleonic domination that sees the kingdoms of this world at its feet—in a word, to men who do not find Man an adequate object of their worship, the pragmatist's world will seem narrow and petty, robbing life of all that gives it value, and making Man himself smaller by depriving the universe which he contemplates of all its splendor.*[40]

It is hard not to be moved by these last lines. With that in mind, I invite the reader who feels so moved to revisit them, after digesting the diminishments of the universe resulting from Russell's proposed eliminations of propositions, numbers, classes, material objects, and even perceiving agents discussed in the remainder of this chapter and the following three.

2. THE BEARERS OF TRUTH AND THE PROBLEM OF PROPOSITIONS

Propositions, as conceived by Frege, the early Moore, and the early Russell, were the objects of assertion, belief, and knowledge, as well as being the (primary) bearers of truth and falsity. Since they were also taken to be the meanings of sentences, they were seen as structurally complex entities the constituents of which are the meanings of the grammatically significant constituents of sentences that express them. However, this raised a

---

[39] Analytic philosophers have developed broad, but quite specialized and focused, political and moral philosophies—e.g., Rawls (1971), Nozick (1974), and Scanlon (1998). But these are not, like those attacked by Moore and Russell, systems in which the metaphysical, epistemological, moral, and political are combined to yield life lessons and political programs.

[40] Russell (1909), pp. 110–11.

problem. Just as sentences aren't collections of unrelated expressions, but have a structural unity that distinguishes them from mere lists and allows us to use them to represent the world truly or falsely, so propositions aren't collections of unrelated meanings, but have a unity that endows them with truth conditions that mere aggregations of their parts do not have. The problem of "the unity of the proposition" was to explicate what this "unity" amounted to.

In chapters 2, 3, and 7, I emphasized that the problem is *not* to find some relation born by the constituents of a proposition to one another that "holds them together" as parts of a single complex entity; the problem is to explain the intentionality of propositions. The former, misconceived, problem stems from the idea that for any complex entity there must be some relation in which its parts stand by virtue of which they are all parts of a single thing. If this idea is correct, then there is such a relation involving being members of a set the only members of which are a, b, and c that "unites" the set {a,b,c}; there is another relation involving membership and order that "unites" the ordered triple <a,b,c>, and there is still another "uniting" relation involving hierarchical domination and linear order that "unites" the tree structure:

One might, of course, wonder what these relations amount to, and try to determine whether they have informative analyses. But since the same questions arise for all complex entities, there is no special "uniting" problem for propositions. What is special is that propositions must be—intrinsically and without further "interpretation" by us—capable of being true or false. Since it would seem absurd to characterize any set, sequence, or abstract tree as intrinsically representing things as being certain ways—and so as being true or false (depending on whether the things so represented are as they are represented to be)—the idea that propositions are any of these structures is a nonstarter. Of course, propositions can't be sentences either, since it is only by virtue of expressing propositions that sentences are supposed to be bearers of truth conditions themselves. So the problem remains. What is it about propositions that distinguishes them as being bearers of truth value from which all other bearers of truth value inherit that status?

In section 2 of chapter 2, I explained Frege's attempted solution to the problem—according to which the predicative elements of propositions, and the concepts they designate, are members of a special ontological category that both allows them to interact with their arguments in a special intentionality-creating way and prevents them from being predication targets of concepts applying to the referents of singular terms. But this was no solution at all. At best the imagined "intentionality-creating" interaction is mysterious and metaphorical. Worse, the supposed impossibility of making predicative elements the predication targets of concepts that apply to referents of singular terms was paradoxical in itself, while contradicting central elements of Frege's own presentation.

In section 3 of chapters 3 and 7, I discussed the early responses of Moore and Russell to the problem of "propositional unity." The central features of their shared early view were (i) that propositions are abstract, unchanging, and timeless constituents of reality, the identity and nature of which are entirely independent of the cognitive activity of agents, (ii) that assertion and belief (plus all other "world-representing" attitudes) are relations to propositions, (iii) that talk of the truth or falsity of any sentence is parasitic on talk of the truth or falsity of the assertion that the sentence is used to make or the belief it is used to express, (iv) that the truth or falsity of any assertion or belief is the truth or falsity of the proposition asserted or believed, and (v) that truth is a simple, unanalyzable property of propositions that is eternally (but not essentially) possessed by any proposition that has it.

This last view about truth played an important role in leading Moore, and Russell following Moore, to view the problem of the unity of the proposition through the prism of the relationship between propositions and facts. For this, we go back to Moore's very early work. In Moore (1899) we are told:

> A proposition is constituted by any number of concepts, together with a specific relation between them; and according to the nature of this relation the proposition may be either true or false. What kind of relation makes a proposition true, what false, cannot be further defined, but must be immediately recognized.[41]

Moore's primary concern here was to reject the view that truth is to be defined as correspondence with reality. As we saw in chapter 3, his argument against the correspondence theory was problematic. By 1902 he was able to offer an improvement.

> It is commonly supposed that the truth of a proposition consists in some relation which it bears to reality; and falsehood in the absence of this relation. The relation in question is generally called "correspondence" or "agreement"; and it seems to be generally conceived as one of partial similarity to something else, and hence it is essential to the theory that a truth should

[41] Moore (1899), p. 180.

differ in some specific way from the reality, in relation to which its truth is to consist. . . . It is the impossibility of finding any such difference between a truth and the reality to which it is supposed to correspond which refutes the theory.[42]

This argument, which also impressed Russell, is that for truth to be correspondence with reality is for the truth of an arbitrary proposition *that A is F* to consist in its correspondence to *the fact that A is F.* However, Moore thought, once we distinguish propositions both from the words used to express them, and from the ideas, attitudes, and mental states of agents, we see that there is no difference between a true proposition and the fact to which it is supposed to correspond. The idea is that the proposition and the fact share the same constituents—which we may take to be the individual A and the property *being F*—which, since the proposition is *true*, stand in the same relation of instantiation in the proposition and the fact. Hence, the proposition and the fact must be identical. On this view, truth is a simple, unanalyzable property of propositions. Although there are both true and false propositions, only the true ones are facts.[43]

But what seemed true in 1902 didn't seem so in 1911—when Moore, lecturing in London, criticizes his (and Russell's) earlier view as follows:

[A fact] does not, if you think about it, seem to consist merely in the possession of some simple property by a proposition—that is to say, by something which has being equally whether the belief is true or false. For instance, the fact that lions really do exist does not seem to consist in the possession of some simple property by the proposition which we believe, when we believe that they exist, even if we grant that there is such a thing as this proposition. *The relation of the proposition to the fact doesn't seem to consist simply in the fact that the proposition is a constituent of the fact—one of the elements of which it is composed.*[44]

As pointed out in chapter 3, this criticism confuses two theses: (i) that a fact is a true proposition, and (ii) that a fact is a complex entity consisting of a proposition's standing in the instantiation relation to the property *being true.* It was (i) rather than (ii) that was his (and Russell's) former view.

The implicit argument against (i), which probably did influence Moore and Russell, is based on the conception of facts that they then shared. Consider the facts that Jupiter is round and that Jupiter is larger than Venus. Moore and Russell would have conceptualized these as *Jupiter's being round* and *Jupiter's being larger than Venus,* which they would have taken to be complexes consisting, in the first case, of Jupiter and the property *being round,* and in the second case, of Jupiter, Venus, and *being*

---

[42] Moore (1902a), p. 717.

[43] Russell explicitly rejects the correspondence theory, and characterizes truth as simple and unanalyzable in Russell (1904a), p. 523.

[44] Moore (1953), p. 286, my emphasis.

larger than. In both cases, the constituents of the facts are genuinely re-lated to each other by *instantiation*. The fact that Jupiter is larger than Venus just is Jupiter's and Venus's instantiating *larger than*, while the fact that Jupiter is round is Jupiter's instantiating *roundness*. Given this, one may naturally take *being a fact* to be an essential property of anything that has it. For surely, if there exists such an object as *Jupiter's (really) being larger than Venus* (i.e., *Jupiter's and Venus's instantiating larger than*), then it could not have been a constituent of the universe if Jupiter hadn't been larger than Venus. By contrast, the proposition that Jupiter is larger than Venus doesn't have this property—which means that it is as much a constituent of reality in a possible scenario in which it is false as it is in a scenario in which it is true. Hence, the proposition can't be identical with the fact.

Russell and Moore regarded facts and propositions as complexes made up of constituents having essentially the same structure. Had they taken themselves to have an independently satisfying conception of what prop-ositions are, while taking the nature of facts to be an open question, they might have continued to identify facts with true propositions—while rec-ognizing that had Jupiter not been larger than Venus, there would have been no fact that Jupiter was larger than Venus, even though the proposi-tion that Jupiter is larger than Venus would have remained a constituent of reality. The conclusion drawn from this recognition would have been that propositions that are contingently true are also contingently facts; in other words, something that is a true proposition, and hence a fact, could have existed (as a false proposition) without being a fact. This is not so strange. After all, we speak both of *believing* what we know and also of *knowing* facts—as in "Because he knew all the facts, he was able to devise an effec-tive course of action." Taken together, these observations support the idea that facts are nothing more than propositions that happen to be true.

But this position wasn't open to Moore and Russell in 1911. By then, they thought they did know what facts were—and what they thought they knew carried with it the conviction that something that is a fact couldn't be a constituent of reality without being a fact. By contrast, they didn't take themselves to have an independently satisfying conception of prop-ositions. Hence, they felt compelled to allow the fate of propositions to depend on wherever their arguments might lead. The reason they didn't take themselves to have a satisfying conception of propositions was that they still couldn't answer the question "What distinguishes a mere list (1a) from the propositions (1b) and (1c)?"

    1a. *difference, identity, difference*
      b. *that difference is different from identity*
      c. *that difference is identical with difference*

According to the early Russell (and Moore), the constituents of these three are the same—the relation of identity plus the relation of difference, the latter occurring twice. How, then, do (1a), (1b), and (1c) differ from one another? Intuitively, they differ in that proposition (1c) predicates the identity relation of the pair of arguments *difference* followed by *difference*, whereas proposition (1b) predicates the difference relation of the pair of arguments *difference* followed by *identity*, while in (1a), nothing is predicated of anything. Because of this, (1c) represents difference as being identical with difference (and so is true), (1b) represents difference as being different from identity (and so is also true), and (1a) doesn't represent anything as being one way or another, and so doesn't have truth conditions.

Although this explanation of the differences between (1a), (1b), and (1c) is commonsensical, neither Moore nor Russell had any good way of making sense of it. The key to it, predication, is something that agents do. Properties don't predicate themselves of anything, nor, unless we have it explained to us, do we understand what it is for a complex of which various properties are constituents to predicate one of them of the others. This is what Moore and Russell were up against. They needed predication to make sense of propositions, but their conception of propositions made it impossible for them to find appropriate agents for that predication. It was fundamental to their view that propositions are (i) abstract, unchanging constituents of reality, the identity and nature of which are independent of the cognitive activity of agents, while also being (ii) the source of all intentionality, and hence that from which all other representational objects, events, or mental states inherit their representational properties, and so their truth conditions. This was the deadly combination that fueled Russell's and Moore's dissatisfaction with propositions, and rendered them ripe for elimination.

The fact that propositions were supposed to be composite and abstract wasn't the problem. So are sentence types, thought of as abstract complexes of equally abstract constituents that have instances (tokens) which are either (i) concrete events (utterances or inscribings) involving physical particulars (sounds or visually discernible portions of a relevant medium), or (ii) those physical products themselves. Yet we have no problem understanding what it is for one constituent of a sentence to be a predicate applied to the referents of the expressions that are its arguments. The reason this isn't taken to be a puzzling philosophical conundrum is that no one takes sentences to have their intentional properties intrinsically. They mean what they do because communities of speakers interpret them as they do. And what is interpretation? For the early Moore and Russell, it was for speakers to use sentences in conventional ways to make certain conventionally recognized assertions and to express certain similarly recognized beliefs, where it is the objects of these attitudes—propositions—that are the ultimate bearers of intentionality. This is what is rightly found mysterious and unexplainable when propositions are understood to be the type of entities that the early Russell and Moore conceived them to be.

3. FACTS AND ATTITUDES: THE MULTIPLE
RELATION THEORY OF JUDGMENT

By 1912, Russell had had his fill of propositions.[45] However, being troubled by them wasn't enough. In order to dispense with propositions, he
needed to find analyses of the attitudes, and bearers of truth and falsity,
to replace them. Since he took the latter to require explaining what truth
and falsity are, that too was central to his agenda. These were the tasks
he set himself in chapter 12 of *The Problems of Philosophy*.[46] His aim was
to accomplish them within the parameters set by three self-imposed constraints: (i) truth bearers must be the sorts of things that can also be false,
(ii) there would be no truth bearers, and no truth or falsity either, if there
were no beliefs, and (iii) whether on not a belief is true must be an objective matter of fact, independent of us. As he puts it:

> (1) Our theory of truth must be such as to admit of its opposite, falsehood.
> A good many philosophers . . . have constructed theories according to which
> all our thinking ought to have been true, and have then had the greatest dif-
> ficulty in finding a place for falsehood. . . .

> (2) [I]f there were no beliefs there could be no falsehood, and no truth
> either. . . . If we imagine a world of mere matter [without minds], there would
> be no room for falsehood in such a world, and although it would contain what
> may be called 'facts', it would not contain any truths. . . . In fact, truths and
> falsehoods are properties of beliefs and statements: hence a world of mere
> matter, since it contains no beliefs or statements, would also contain no truth
> or falsehood.

> (3) But . . . the truth or falsehood of a belief always lies outside the belief it-
> self. If I believe Charles I died upon the scaffold, I believe truly, not because
> of any intrinsic quality of the belief, which could be discovered by merely
> examining the belief, but because of an historical event which happened two
> and a half centuries ago. . . . Hence, although truth and falsehood are prop-
> erties of beliefs, they are properties dependent upon the relations of the be-
> liefs to other things, not upon any internal quality of the beliefs.

> The third of the above requisites leads us to adopt the view . . . that truth
> consists in some form of correspondence between belief and fact.[47]

---

[45] He had already officially and unequivocally renounced them in Russell (1910), "On the
Nature of Truth and Falsehood," where he first advocated the multiple relation theory of
judgment examined here. That article, in turn, was preceded by Russell (1906–7), "On the
Nature of Truth," in which he explored, without advocating, the multiple relation theory as
a theory of *false*, but not true, beliefs.

[46] Russell (1912). Finding some other entities to play the role of sentence meanings was
not on his agenda.

[47] Russell (1912), 120–21.

Russell takes the first constraint to eliminate propositions as truth bearers, since, he thinks, any reasonable conception of their "unity" will make it impossible for them to be false. He illustrates this with an example.

> The necessity of allowing for falsehood makes it impossible to regard belief as a relation of the mind to a single object, which could be said to be what is believed. If belief were so regarded, we should find that, like acquaintance, it would not admit of the opposition of truth and falsehood, but would have to be always true. This may be made clear by examples. Othello believes falsely that Desdemona loves Cassio. We cannot say that this belief consists in a relation to a single object, [denoted by] *'Desdemona's love for Cassio'*, for if there were such an object, the belief would be true. There is in fact no such object, and therefore Othello can't have any relation to such an object. Hence his belief cannot possibly consist in a relation to this object.[48]

As we have seen, for Russell, propositions are complexes the constituents of which are objects, properties, and relations, united somehow into a coherent whole. Thus, in order for there to be a proposition the constituents of which are Desdemona, loving, and Cassio (in that order), some relation must unite them into a single complex entity. Russell here assumes without argument that the only reasonable candidate for doing so is the loving relation. But for loving to unite Desdemona and Cassio is for Desdemona to stand in the loving relation to Cassio (and so to love Cassio)—in which case the complex *Desdemona's love for Cassio*, will, Russell thinks, be a fact. In short, the unity required by the existence of the proposition that Desdemona loves Cassio requires it to be true. But that can't be right, for then there would be no false propositions.

In framing the example this way—using a nominalized version of the sentence 'Desdemona loves Cassio' to designate the candidate object of belief, rather than the complement clause 'that Desdemona loves Cassio', Russell was stacking the deck—as he did in chapter 4 of *The Principles of Mathematics*, when he substituted 'Caesar's death' for 'that Caesar died' in discussing the unity of the proposition. This is tendentious. Even when the belief Mary expresses using the sentence 'Seattle is rainy' is true, we don't report Mary's attitude by saying *'Mary believes Seattle's being rainy'. So, there are grounds for the defender of propositions to argue that Russell's complex, nominalized phrases don't designate the same things (propositions) that the complement clauses normally used in belief ascriptions do.

What these nominalized phrases designate is a mixed bag. Although there is support for the idea that they sometimes designate facts—'Mary regrets (her) forgetting our appointment' seems pretty much on a par with 'Mary regrets the fact that she forgot our appointment'—often complex nominals stand for things other than either propositions or facts. If I say that Caesar's death was slow and painful, I am not saying that a fact was

---

[48] Ibid., 124, my emphasis.

painful, but that a certain event experienced by Caesar was. Similarly, if I say that Susan's love for her husband was both less intense and less constant than her strong and constant love for her children, I am comparing the intensity and changeable nature not of two facts, but of two emotional states. It is best then to put aside Russell's use of complex nominals, and simply grant him that propositions can't be facts, as he conceived them.

As for propositions being distinct from facts, while also being the objects of both true and false beliefs, Russell realizes that this is an option, but dismisses it.

> It might be said that this belief is a relation to a different object, namely [the object denoted by] 'that Desdemona loves Cassio'; but it is almost as difficult to suppose that there is such an object as this, when Desdemona does not love Cassio, as it was to suppose that there is [something denoted by] 'Desdemona's love for Cassio'. Hence it is better to seek for a theory of belief which does not make it consist in a relation of the mind to a single object.[49]

Although he here offers no argument, his reason is, I think, the one discussed at the end of section 2. Given his antecedent conception of what propositions would have to be (if there were any), he quite rightly saw there to be no way of explaining how such things could be bearers of truth and falsity.

His new alternative has two main parts. First, he takes the bearers of truth and falsity to be entities he calls "beliefs"—meaning by this something other than *what one believes*. Second, he takes believing, asserting, and other attitudes to be relations, not to single, objectively unified propositions, but to the very propositional constituents that he had come to realize can't be unified—covering true and false cases alike—in any objective, mind-independent way.

> The relation involved in *judging* or *believing* must, if falsehood is to be duly allowed for, be taken to be a relation between several terms, not between two. When Othello believes that Desdemona loves Cassio, he must not have before his mind a single object, [denoted by] 'Desdemona's love for Cassio', or 'that Desdemona loves Cassio', for that would require that there should be objective falsehoods, which subsist independently of any minds; and this, though not logically refutable, is a theory to be avoided, if possible. Thus it is easier to account for falsehood if we take judgment to be a relation in which the mind and the various objects concerned all occur severally; that is to say, *Desdemona and loving and Cassio must all be terms in the relation which subsists when Othello believes that Desdemona loves Cassio*. This relation, therefore, is a relation of four terms, since Othello also is one of the terms of the relation. . . . Thus *the actual occurrence, at the moment when Othello is entertaining his belief, is that the relation called 'believing' is knitting together into one complex whole* the four

[49] *The Problems of Philosophy*, 124.

terms Othello, Desdemona, loving, and Cassio. What is called belief or judgment is nothing but this relation of believing or judging, which relates a mind to several things other than itself.[50]

Under the old analysis of propositional attitudes, 'Othello believes that Desdemona loves Cassio' reports a relation that holds between the believer, Othello, and that which he believes, namely, *that Desdemona loves Cassio.* However, since Desdemona doesn't, in fact, love Cassio, this requires the existence of a false proposition, which Russell rejects. Under his new analysis, the sentence reports a four-place relation that unites Othello, the believer, with the several objects of his belief—Desdemona, the loving relation, and Cassio (in that order). Since Othello really does believe that Desdemona loves Cassio, the belief relation *really does relate* these objects—knitting them together into a complex entity, *Othello's belief that Desdemona loves Cassio,* which Russell takes to be a fact. (Note the familiar use of the nominalized phrase.) If this belief were true, then one of its objects—the loving relation—would *really relate* the other two—Desdemona and Cassio (in that order)—knitting *them* together into a different complex entity, *Desdemona's love for Cassio,* which would itself be a fact. But since Desdemona doesn't love Cassio, there is no such further fact, and the belief is false.

The reason this isn't taken to be problematic is that according to the new view, in saying that *the belief is false* we are *not* saying that *what Othello believes* is false. There is no one single thing that he believes. Rather, we are saying that the fact that consists of *Othello's believing that Desdemona loves Cassio* is false. Since this complex entity, which Russell calls the "belief," really does exist, he takes his theory to have successfully identified bearers of truth conditions that can, in fact, be false.

Whenever there is a relation which relates certain terms, there is a complex object formed of the union of those terms; and conversely, whenever there is a complex object, there is a relation which relates its constituents. When an act of believing occurs, there is a complex, in which 'believing' is the uniting relation, and subject and objects are arranged . . .by the 'sense' of the relation of believing. Among the objects, as we saw in considering 'Othello believes that Desdemona loves Cassio', one must be a relation—in this instance the relation 'loving'. But this relation, as it occurs in the act of believing, is not the relation which creates the unity of the complex whole consisting of the subject and the objects. The relation 'loving', as it occurs in the act of believing, is one of the objects—it is a brick in the structure, not the cement. The cement is the relation 'believing'. When the belief is true, there is another complex unity, in which the relation which was one of the objects of the belief relates the other objects. Thus, e.g., if Othello believes truly that Desdemona loves Cassio, there is a complex unity, 'Desdemona's love for Cassio', which is

[50] Ibid., 125–26, my emphasis.

composed exclusively of the objects of the belief . . . with the relation which was one of the objects occurring now as the cement that binds together the other objects of belief. . . . [W]hen a belief is false, there is no such complex unity composed only of the objects of belief.[51]

This, in a nutshell, is Russell's multiple relation theory of belief and other attitudes.

The new theory satisfies the first of Russell's three requirements: the bearers of truth are the sorts of things that can be bearers of falsity. For example, my belief that Seattle is larger than Portland is identical with *the fact that I believe that Seattle is larger than Portland.* It is true because this fact corresponds to another fact—*that Seattle is larger than Portland*—which consists of two of the constituents of "my belief" really standing in the relation *larger than,* which is (apart from me in my role as believer) the other constituent of "my belief." There are two reasons to suppose that this *is* the sort of thing that can be false. First, "my belief" is very similar to other "beliefs" that are false—for example, it is similar to Mary's belief that Portland is larger than Seattle. Second, my own belief—i.e., the fact that I believe that Seattle is larger than Portland—could have been false (even though if that belief were false, it would still be a fact).

The new theory also satisfies Russell's second requirement: if there were no beliefs (or other cognitive attitudes), there would be no bearers of truth or falsity. Why, one might wonder, is this a virtue? Russell's responds with a question of his own: "What sorts or things are true, or false, anyway?" That natural answer is: statements, hypotheses, assumptions, beliefs, predictions, and conjectures, plus perhaps utterances and sentences. Surely if there were no agents, there wouldn't be any of these things either. More pointedly, if there were no minds, there would be no *mistaken* statements, beliefs, predictions, and the like; and how, if there were no *mistakes*, could there be *falsehoods* either? As he puts it, "we feel that there could be no falsehood, if there were no minds to make mistakes."[52] This is, I think, reasonable as a default view; without the cognitive activity of agents there would exist no entities that were true or false.

Still, there are worries to which the default view gives rise. Chief among them is our free and easy talk of truth even when describing agentless scenarios. Consider, for example, a statement one might make in defending an anti-anthropogenic-global-warming view. First one asserts (let us suppose truly) that the small rise in global temperature over the past century is nothing more than the continuation of the gradual rise since the Little Ice Age ended around three hundred years ago. Next, one makes a counterfactual statement about that claim. One says, "That claim would have been true even if no human beings, or other sentient creatures, had

---

[51] Ibid., 127–28.
[52] Russell (1910), p. 152.

existed." On the face of it this remark seems to maintain that a certain previously asserted claim *would have been true even if there had been no cognitive agents*. How could that be? The defender of classical Moorean-Russellian propositions has an answer: since the asserted claim is an abstract bearer of intrinsic intentionality that doesn't depend on the existence of cognitive agents, it would have been present in the counterfactual scenario imagined, where it would have been true by virtue of representing the world as it, in fact, would have been. Since Russell rightly rejects classical propositions, he owes us an alternative answer to our question—which he never gives. We will return to this issue in section 5.

Paraphrasing Russell's third and final requirement, we may say that the truth or falsity of a belief is not intrinsic to it, but always depends on whether the constituents of the belief (apart from the agent) are, in reality, the way the belief represents them to be. As I would put it on Russell's behalf, *Othello's standing in the belief relation to Desdemona, loving, and Cassio involves Othello's predicating the loving relation of Desdemona and Cassio, and thereby representing her as loving him.* Whether or not Othello's belief is true depends on whether or not Desdemona and Cassio are as so represented, namely as standing in the loving relation. Since this is not a matter of any cognitive activity on the part of Othello, Russell's third requirement is met.

Russell's attempt to use the multiple relation theory to satisfy these requirements began in section 3 of Russell (1906–7), where the theory was explored as one possible analysis of *false beliefs*, while true beliefs were taken to be two-place relations between agents and facts. The other possible analysis of false beliefs held that they are also two-place relations, the second term being a Meinongian "objective non-fact" (i.e., a false proposition, quite different from the facts that are the objects of true beliefs).[53] Neither analysis combines well with the conception of true beliefs as relations to facts, since both lead to a disjunctive theory that failed Russell's first requirement—that bearers of truth and falsehood should be entities of the same kind. In addition, one theory posited "objective falsehoods," which he rightly found mysterious, and which failed to meet his second requirement. The other theory was, by his lights, not much better, since in positing two different belief relations, it failed his third requirement that truth and falsity not be *intrinsic* properties of beliefs—a point made in Russell (1910b) by noting that the disjunctive 1906–7 version of the multiple relation theory "would make an intrinsic difference between true and false judgments, and enable us (what is obviously impossible) to discover the truth or falsehood of a judgment merely by examining the intrinsic

---

[53] As Russell there puts it (1906–7, p. 48), "If we accept the view that there are objective falsehoods, we shall oppose them to facts, and make *truth* the quality of facts, *falsehoods* the quality of their opposites, which we may call *fictions*. Then facts and fictions together may be called *propositions*."

nature of the judgment [to see if it relates us to a single entity or to multiple entities]."[54] The solution reached in Russell (1910b, 1912) was to extend the multiple relation theory to all beliefs in the manner we have seen.

4. PROBLEMS

Given Russell's long-standing frustration with not being able to solve the problem of the unity of the proposition, one can well understand why the multiple relation theory appealed to him. One can also see that the version advocated in 1910 and 1912 was an advance over his hybrid theory of 1906–7. In section 5, I will argue that it also contained a genuine insight capable of supporting a more promising theory of propositions, an insight which, unfortunately, Russell didn't grasp. In this section, I will sketch some of the problems that undermine the multiple relation theory, and contributed to its abandonment in Russell (1919a), where he opted for an essentially Tractarian theory (to be examined in the next volume) quite different from any he had previously espoused.

One set of difficulties stems from Russell's permissive and, I believe, overly optimistic attitude toward facts. Taking them to be really existing truth makers is bad enough.[55] Taking them also to be the bearers of truth and falsity is a further affront. Surely there are many truths, and also, one would hope, many falsehoods, that no one has ever believed. Russell's theory can't account for this, since in such cases, there will be no *facts that an agent believes so-and-so* with which to identify them. Even when agents do have the relevant beliefs, the identification of facts as bearers of truth value is problematic. On our ordinary conception of facts, talk of "true facts" is redundant at best, while talk of "false facts" is either nonsensical or something that requires interpretation. Yet for Russell, facts are precisely the things that are, literally, true or false.

The second set of problems concerns the ways in which the multiple relation theory fails to capture the richness, variety, and utility of our ordinary talk of propositions and attitudes. At most, it offers an analysis of attitude ascriptions of the form *x knows/believes/asserts (the proposition) that S*. However, the theory is silent about, and makes no provision for, talk of propositions outside of attitude ascriptions, or for attitude ascriptions in which the complement of the attitude verb is a name, a singular definite description, or some other phrase or variable indicating quantification over propositions. Thus, the theory provides no analysis of examples like (2).

2a. Logicism is a thesis about the relationship between logic and mathematics.
  b. For every true proposition in the report, there are two other propositions in the report that are false.

---

[54] Russell (1910b), 152–53.
[55] For critical discussion, see Merricks (2007) and Soames (2008a).

   c. Bill asserted/denied Church's Thesis/Goldbach's Conjecture.

   d. Susan proved the proposition/several propositions that John denied.

   e. There are many propositions that no one has entertained, let alone proved or disproved.

But the main problem with the theory is that it plays fast and loose with the way in which truth and falsity are connected to the attitudes. Central to our conception of this connection is the notion *what is believed, assumed, doubted, predicted, denied, imagined, said, stated, whispered,* and the like. In every one of these cases, if John said/whispered/ believed/imagined/doubted/denied/assumed/predicted that the earth is round, then *what John said/whispered/believed/imagined/doubted/denied/ assumed/predicted* was true. How is Russell to account for this? Although one would think that the observation was too obvious to deny, that is just what his theory seems designed to do. According to it, these verbs don't take single objects; the multiple objects they do take are not bearers of truth and falsity; and their complement clauses ⌜that S⌝ are non-designating "incomplete symbols."[56] This is problematic. Either Russell must acquiesce in the incredible claim that our thought and talk about the truth or falsity of *what is believed, imagined, assumed,* and the like is grotesquely incorrect, or he must find a way of accommodating it within the confines of his theory (which he never succeeds in doing).

This is somewhat obscured by a fortuitous linguistic fact he takes advantage of. Some of the relevant verbs—'believe', 'assume', 'predict', and 'state'— have corresponding nominal forms—'belief', 'assumption', 'prediction', and 'statement'—that naturally occur as arguments of 'is true' or 'is false'. For example, we are perfectly comfortable with claims like those in (3).

   3a. John's belief (that so-and-so) is true (false).

   b. John's assumption (that so-and-so) is true (false).

   c. John's prediction (that so-and-so) came true (turned out to be false).

   d. John's statement (that so-and-so) is true (false).

The reason we are comfortable is that these nouns can be used in either of two related ways. On the one hand, they can be used to stand for *what one believes/assumes/predicts/states*; this is the sense in which "beliefs," "assumptions," "predictions," and "statements" can naturally be described as true or false, or as consistent or inconsistent with what others believe/assume/predict/state. On the other hand, the nouns can be used to stand for (i) one's cognitive state of believing or assuming that which one believes or assumes, or (ii) one's linguistic performance of predicting or stating that which one predicts of states. This is the sense in which one's "belief" may be irrational, one's "assumption" unproductive, one's "prediction" confident, and one's "statement" halting. However, Russell's story

---

[56] For the point about incomplete symbols, see Russell (1910), p. 151, and Russell (1913), p. 108.

is different. Dispensing with any literal notion of *what is believed/assumed/ predicted/stated,* he identifies *John's belief/assumption/prediction/ statement (that so-and-so)* with *the fact that John believes/assumes/ predicts/states that so-and-so.* There are several things wrong with this.

First, the strategy doesn't generalize. Suppose that John doubted/denied/imagined/ whispered that so-and-so. Although we are comfortable with the claim that *what John doubted/denied/imagined/whispered* turned out to be true (or false), we would never express this as in (4).

4a. *John's doubt (that so-and-so) is true (false).
  b. *John's denial (that so-and-so) is true (false).
  c. *John's imagining (that so-and-so) is true (false).
  d. *John's whisper (that so-and-so) is true (false).

Nor would it do to provide the Russellian substitutes in (5) for these deviant examples, since they also can't play the role of the unexceptionable claims in (6).

5a. *The fact that John doubted that so-and-so is true (false).
  b. *The fact that John denied that so-and-so is true (false).
  c. *The fact that John imagined that so-and-so is true (false).
  d. *The fact that John whispered that so-and-so is true (false).
6a. What John doubted is (in fact) true (false).
  b. What John denied is (in fact) true (false).
  c. What John imagined is (in reality) true (false).
  d. What John whispered is true (false).

Thus, Russell has no systematic way of accommodating our ordinary conception of *what a person believes/assumes/doubts/predicts/denies/imagines/ says/states/whispers,* etc.

Second, his identification of one's belief or statement that so-and-so with *the fact that one believes/states that so-and-so* is inaccurate. One's belief can be either *that which one believes,* which is off limits for Russell, or one's cognitive state of so believing. In this latter sense of 'belief' one's belief can be either strong or weak, rational and supported by evidence or irrational and impervious to evidence, recently formed or long enduring. None of these are properties of facts. Similarly, one's statement can be either *that which one states,* which is also off limits for Russell, or one's act of stating something. In this latter sense, one's statement can be confident or halting, lengthy or short, hurried or leisurely—none of which are properties of facts. So, Russell has no real account of (3).

Finally, his strategy of using

  (i) *the fact that one believes/assumes/predicts/states that so-and-so*

to play the role of

  (ii) *what is believed/assumed/predicted/stated* by one who *believes/assumes/ predicts/states that so-and-so* leads not simply to infelicities and subtle inaccuracies, but to absurdities. Suppose that each of the claims in (7) is true.

7a. John believes/assumes/predicts/states that so-and-so.
　b. Mary believes/assumes/predicts/states that so-and-so.

Then each of the following claims should also be true.

8a. What John believes/assumes/predicts/states is (=) that so-and-so.
　b. What Mary believes/assumes/predicts/states is (=) that so-and-so.

Now suppose, in accord with Russell's implicit strategy, that each of the claims in (9) is true.

9a. What John believes/assumes/predicts/states is (=) the fact that John believes/assumes/predicts/states that so-and-so.
　b. What Mary believes/assumes/predicts/states is (=) the fact that Mary believes/assumes/predicts/states that so-and-so.

From (7–9) we derive such absurdities as (10).

10a. The fact that John believes that so-and-so = the fact that John assumes/predicts/states that so-and-so.
　b. The fact that Mary believes that so-and-so = the fact that John assumes/predicts/states that so-and-so.

To block this *reductio ad absurdum*, Russell must either deny the seemingly undeniable observation that the move from (7) to (8) is truth preserving, deny (9), or deny that (8) and (9) jointly entail (10). Given his view of *that*-clauses as non-designating incomplete symbols, one might suppose that he could deny (8). However, this is too quick. Surely, there must be a way of understanding (8a) and (8b) on which they are true. If there is, then Russell needs an analysis of these so-called "incomplete symbols" that makes (8a) and (8b) true—presumably one that doesn't treat them as identities, and doesn't support the inference from (8a,b) and (9a,b) to (10a,b). For this, sloganeering about incomplete symbols not requiring designata is not enough; we need a precise analysis that Russell never gives. Short of giving such an analysis, he could deny (9). But then he faces the burden of defending his strategy of using *the fact that one believes/assumes/predicts/states that so-and-so* to play the role, as bearer of truth or falsity, that is intuitively played by *what one believes/assumes/predicts/states*. The prospect of succeeding with any of these moves is not good.

This point is related to another devastating problem. Suppose, for the sake of argument, that Russell is right in thinking that when Othello believes that Desdemona loves Cassio, he does something that creates a unified whole the constituents of which include Othello, as believer, plus the terms of his belief. What does he do? The answer, surely, is that he *predicates* the relation *loving* of Desdemona and Cassio (in that order).[57] Why doesn't he predicate Desdemona of *loving* and Cassio? Because that's impossible, of course. One can't predicate a person of anything. So if there is any "unifying" to be done, and any belief to be formed, the property must be predicated of the people. This sounds promising, and it leads Russell to think that he can give analyses of all beliefs without mentioning or presupposing propositions. He can't.

11a. Othello believes that some people are trustworthy.
  b. Othello believes that not many people are trustworthy.
  c. Othello believes that Iago is trustworthy and Desdemona is unfaithful.
  d. Othello believes that either Iago isn't trustworthy or Desdemona loves Cassio.
  e. Othello believes that if Iago is trustworthy, then Desdemona is unfaithful.
  f. Othello believes that it is a necessary truth that if Desdemona loves Cassio, then Desdemona loves Cassio.

First consider (11a). According to Russell's normal analysis of quantification, the constituents of the belief reported by (11a) are the property *being a function that assigns a true proposition to some object* and the *propositional function that assigns to any object o the proposition that o is trustworthy* (of which the property is predicated). But this presupposes that *there are propositions* that are the values of propositional functions. So, if the aim of the multiple relation theory is to allow us to dispense with propositions, either it fails to do so, or it must be supplemented by a reanalysis of quantification or propositional functions. As I will explain in chapter 10, Russell's views about propositional functions evolved very substantially between 1903 and 1910. For that reason, I won't dwell further on the problem here. Suffice it to say that it is serious. In order not to play on this problem in what follows, I won't presuppose any particular analysis of quantification in discussing the other examples in (11).

Consider the role of negation in (11b)—where by 'negation' I don't mean a particular word or symbol (no one of which would be familiar to all believers), but the content shared by the various words and symbols properly translated by the logician's '~'. With this understanding, the constituents of the belief reported by (11b) are *negation*, something corresponding to the quantifier 'many people', and something corresponding to the predicate 'trustworthy'. What does Othello do to "unify" these elements, along with himself as agent, in forming his belief? The most plausible answer is that he first does whatever is required to unify the contribution of 'many people' with the contribution of the predicate

[57] What is it to predicate a relation of a pair, *in a certain order*? Although the details won't matter for our purposes, one natural way of thinking about the example is that Othello operates on the two-place property *loving* and the individual Cassio to generate the one-place property *loving Cassio*, which he then predicates of Desdemona. For further discussion, see chapter 6 of Soames (2014c).

'trustworthy'.[58] Then, he negates that which he has unified. What does he negate? Since for Russell negation had always been conceived as an operator on a proposition, one would think that he was committed to saying that in forming the belief reported by (11b), Othello negates *the proposition* that many people are trustworthy. However, this can't be the analysis, since it presupposes propositions, which the multiple relation theory purports to eliminate. Thus, Russell needs a new analysis of negation.[59]

As the remaining examples in (11) illustrate, this argument can be repeated for all propositional operators, including conjunction, disjunction, and the content of the material conditional—all of which are used in forming complex propositions from pairs of simpler ones. With (11f) we add the necessity operator, which is there predicated of a complex proposition of the form *if p, then p*. Clearly examples of this sort could be multiplied far and wide. Short of a complete and radical reanalysis of Russell's previous philosophical logic, what these examples show is that the multiple relation theory is up to its neck in propositions. Without such a reanalysis, there is no understanding how it applies to any but the simplest examples.

The final problem with the multiple relation theory brings together all the previous difficulties, while pointing to a way of transforming the theory into a new and improved theory of propositions. It is a truism that a belief, assertion, hypothesis, or conjecture *represents* the world as being a certain way, and so is capable of being true or false. Ordinarily, what we mean by this is that *what is believed, asserted, hypothesized,* or *conjectured* represents the world, and so is true or false. Using the familiar name 'proposition' for these things, we may ask, *"In virtue of what are propositions representational, and hence bearers of truth conditions?"* This is the problem of *the unity of the proposition* that Frege, Moore, and Russell were unable to solve. One might think, as Russell apparently did, that in disposing of propositions he was disposing of the problem. He wasn't. Surely, beliefs, assertions, hypotheses, and conjectures *are* representational. Since Russell doesn't deny that these things exist (even if he does misidentify them), he needs to answer the question of what makes *them* representational, and so the bearers of truth conditions. This is the problem of *the unity of truth bearers*, no matter what one calls them.

---

[58] Assuming propositional functions, we would say that he predicates the higher-order property *being true of many people* of the propositional function that assigns to an object o the proposition that o is trustworthy.

[59] Russell realized that there was a difficulty here, which he planned to deal with in *Theory of Knowledge* (an aborted book manuscript on which he worked in 1913). Recognizing that in giving up propositions he must *reject* the standard assumption that "when a molecular proposition which is true appears to contain atomic constituents which are false, the apparent atomic constituents must really be constituents," he wrote, "We cannot enter into this question until we come to Part III; for the present, I shall assume by anticipation that a different analysis of such molecular propositions is possible" (Russell 1913, pp. 152–53). Russell never wrote Part III. Thanks to an anonymous referee for finding this passage.

Addressing this problem from the perspective of the multiple relation theory of judgment, we start with its central thesis: beliefs, assertions, hypotheses, conjectures, and the like are *facts* in which an agent is related by the relevant attitude (belief, assertion, etc.) to various objects, properties, and relations. If these facts are representational, what makes them so? The form of the answer dictated by the theory is obvious: what makes these facts representational is something that the agent's cognitive attitude adds to the objects toward which the attitude is directed to bring it about that the world is represented as being one way rather than another. When Othello believes that Desdemona loves Cassio, his cognitive attitude adds something to the raw material of the belief—Desdemona, loving, and Cassio—that brings it about that the resulting belief represents Desdemona as loving Cassio. What does it add?

In asking this question, it is important to bear two points in mind. First, what one agent adds to these constituents to bring it about that one's belief represents the world in this way is *the same* as what any other agent adds to bring it about that this other agent's belief represents the world in the same way. Second, there is reason to suppose that the same can be said about what is added when agents bear different attitudes to the same content. When agents believe, assert, deny, doubt, hypothesize, imagine, or conjecture that Desdemona loves Cassio, they take different cognitive stances toward representing Desdemona as loving Cassio. What is common to the different attitudes is that way of representing the world. What differentiates them from one another is the cognitive stance taken toward that representation. When these two points are kept in mind, the answer to our question is clear. *What the agent does* to bring it about that his or her belief, assertion, hypothesis, or conjecture involves *representing* Desdemona as loving Cassio is to *predicate* one constituent of the judgment—the loving relation—of the other two—Desdemona and Cassio, in that order.

This is the kernel of truth in the multiple relation theory. What unites the elements of a belief, assertion, hypothesis, or conjecture, and gives it representational import, is a cognitive operation agents perform on the constituents of the belief, assertion, hypothesis, or conjecture. In the case at hand, in which the agent believes, asserts, hypothesizes, or conjectures that Desdemona loves Cassio, he or she *predicates* the loving relation of Desdemona and Cassio. Since this is so no matter whether the representational content is believed, asserted, hypothesized, doubted, conjectured, or denied, we can transform the multiple relation theory back into a propositional theory by collecting the multiple constituents of representationally equivalent instances of believing, asserting, and the like, into a single formal structure the defining feature of which is that for an agent to entertain it is for the agent to predicate *loving* of Desdemona and Cassio.

5. PROPOSITIONS REGAINED: SALVAGING RUSSELL'S (NEARLY) LOST INSIGHT

In this section, I will use the powerful insight driving Russell's multiple relation theory to outline a new theory of propositions that solves the problem of their unity while both satisfying his three requirements on a theory of the bearers of truth value and avoiding the problems that undermined the multiple relation view.

5.1. Reversing Traditional Explanatory Priorities

The Russellian insight is that the intentionality of all truth bearers—the fact that they represent things as they do and so have truth conditions—is explained in terms of the intentionality of the cognitive activities of agents, rather than the other way around. Like the old conception, the new conception of propositions embraces the idea that both propositions and agents represent.

(i) Propositions are pieces of information that represent things as being certain ways, and so have truth conditions.

(ii) One who *entertains* a proposition *oneself* represents things as being certain ways.

According to the old conception, propositional intentionality was primary, and agents' intentionality was derivative. According to the new conception, the intentionality of propositions is derived from that of agents. How?

The simplest cognitive events are those in which one predicates a property of an object. This suggests that the proposition *that o is red* is the cognitive act (type) of predicating *being red* of o, the performance of which involves thinking of, perceiving, or imagining o as red. This act is representational because for an agent to perform the act is for *the agent* to represent o as red. Of course, the properties of agents—of doing this or that—are not literally *transferred* to the acts they perform. For agents to predicate redness of o and thereby to represent o as red is for them *to do* something. Since acts don't *do* anything, but rather are the things done, this is *not* precisely the sense in which the act *predicating redness of o* represents o as red. Rather, there is an extended sense of *representing o as red* that is attributable to acts, the function of which is to allow us to use the intimate relation these entities bear to the cognitive lives of agents to track their mental states and to assess their veridicality.

The extended sense in which acts are said to represent is related to the more the basic sense in which agents represent in a manner analogous to the way in which the extended sense in which acts can be said to be intelligent, stupid, thoughtless, vicious, irrational, or irresponsible is related to the more fundamental sense in which it is agents who are intelligent, stupid, thoughtless, vicious, irrational, or irresponsible. Very roughly, (i) for an act to be intelligent or thoughtful is for it to be one the performance of which marks one as behaving intelligently or thoughtfully, and (ii) for a cognitive act to represent o as red is for it to be one the performance of which marks one as representing o as red. We introduce this extended sense of representation in part because we wish to isolate individual aspects of agents' thought and perception in order to assess them for accuracy. When o is such that to perceive or think of o as red is to represent it accurately, it is handy to have an entity—a particular sort of perceiving or thinking—plus a property that entity has when this sort of perceiving or thinking is accurate. The entity is a proposition that is the cognitive act of representing o as red. The property is truth, which the act has iff to perform it is for an agent to represent o as o really is.

To *entertain* this proposition is to predicate redness of o, which is to perform the cognitive act that the proposition is. Using this notion, we say that the proposition that o is red is true (at a world-state w) iff (at w) o is as the proposition represents it to be—i.e., iff o is as it is represented to be by one who entertains the proposition (at any world-state). The representationality, and hence truth conditions, of the proposition are due to the representational features of agents who entertain it. Since it is necessary and sufficient for one to entertain the proposition that one represent o as being red, the proposition itself represents o as being red (without representing anything else), and so is true iff o is red. On this account, the truth conditions of the proposition are *inherent* to it in the sense that it couldn't be what it is without them, even though it bears its truth conditions by virtue of the intentionality of agents who entertain it. Being inherently intentional, it can be the interpretation of sentences and utterances, without itself being the sort of thing for which an interpretation is needed.

With this basic picture in place, I will say a word about the construction of complex propositions and some of the complex attitudes we bear to them.

5.2. Complex Propositions and Attitudes

Entertaining a proposition is the most basic attitude we bear to it, the one on which all others are based. For example, to *judge* that o is red is to predicate redness of o while affirming or endorsing that predication. To *believe that o is red* is to judge, or be disposed to judge, that it is. To *know* that o is red is, roughly, for o to be red, to believe that o is red, and to be justified in so believing. To *assert* that o is red is to commit oneself, by uttering something, to treating the proposition that o is red as something one knows. This is, of course, just a sample of the relevant attitudes. Rather than discussing others, I will turn to what is involved in entertaining more complex propositions.

To entertain the proposition *that it is not the case that o is red* is (i) to predicate redness of o, and thereby to entertain the proposition that o is red, (ii) to negate the property *being true,* and (iii) to predicate the resulting property *not being true* of that proposition. This can be done by thinking "That's not true," referring to the result of the initial predication—provided that one can so refer. Many, but not all, agents capable of entertaining the original proposition can do this. There is nothing inherent in the ability to entertain p that guarantees that one can think thoughts *about* p. The minimal form of acquaintance with propositions is the ability to cognitively represent the world by predicating properties of objects, thereby entertaining the relevant propositions. To gain a more robust form of acquaintance, one must be able to make propositions the targets of predication. This requires the ability to focus on one's own cognitive acts and distinguish them from one another. This, in turn, presupposes the ability to recognize differences and similarities in the events that make up one's perceptual and cognitive experience. One who can focus on such similarities and group together those in which *being red* is predicated of o is in position to make the cognitive act—*predicating redness of o*—an object of thought and subject of further predication. Given the means both of *thinking of o as red*, and of becoming aware of so doing, one can then make further predications about the proposition that o is red, which was the content of one's initial thought. For example, one may think, "That's not true," thereby predicating untruth of the proposition one has just entertained.

So far, I have mentioned two operations involved in proposition formation, negating properties and predicating them of objects. In addition to negating properties, agents also conjoin them. We entertain the proposition *that o is red and round* by conjoining *being red* and *being round*, and predicating the result of o. In addition to applying functions to properties, agents also apply them to objects, and to other functions. Thus, cognitively unself-conscious agents don't need to predicate properties of propositions to believe *that o isn't green* or *that o is red and round*. Think of the function *Neg* as a two-place relation in which the identity of its first argument determines the second. When P is a property, *NegP* is a property uniquely true of the property that is P's negation. An agent acquainted with *NegP* can predicate the property it determines of an object. Property conjunction is similar.

What about conjunctive and disjunctive *propositions*? One way of simulating such is to start with relations R& and RV. Predicating these of *a, redness, b,* and *roundness* represents *a as red and b as round* (and only this), and *a as red or b as round*, respectively. Performing this predication approximates entertaining the conjunctive and disjunctive propositions *that a is red and b is round,* and *that a is red or b is round.* To believe these new propositions is to be disposed to endorse such a predication, while to believe their negations is, in effect, to believe propositions in which one negates

R& and RV to get the relations ~R& and ~RV, which are then predicated of the relevant arguments, just as R& and RV were. None of these beliefs requires making propositions predication targets. By taking R& and RV to be two-place relations each argument of which is an n-place property followed by an ordered n-tuple, one can embed propositions formed using them under R& and RV themselves, thereby making the functional equivalent of full truth-functional cognition possible for agents that can't, for whatever reason, reflect on their own cognitive acts or experiences.

There is also a different and more direct way to get the result we are after. R& and RV are complex relations predicated of pairs of n-tuples of the constituents of arbitrary pairs of propositions, where each such proposition is itself the predication of a property or relation of its other constituents. Using this model, one can, for each truth-functionally compound proposition, generate an equivalent proposition that is itself a predication of such a pair of n-tuples. But we can also generate propositions that are genuine truth-functional compounds of other propositions. Let p be a proposition that represents things as *being so-and-so* (and nothing more) and q be a proposition that represents things as *being such-and-such* (and nothing more). Next consider a certain *disjunctive operation* the application of which to p and q represents *things as being so-and-so or things as being such-and-such* (and nothing more). To entertain this proposition is to entertain p, to entertain q, and to operate on them in this way—where operating on them *isn't predicating* anything of them. The result is a disjunctive proposition. Conjunctive propositions can be understood in the same way. So can negations of propositions; when p represents *things as being so-and-so*, to negate p is to represent *things as not being so-and-so*.[60] On this model, all propositions involve predications at some level, but some propositions are properly characterized as *operations* on constituents that themselves are, or depend on, predications. In what follows, I will sometimes ignore this complication, e.g., when speaking of entertaining an arbitrary proposition as predicating a property of certain things. In all such cases, a more complicated statement involving predicating a property of those things or operating on them could be supplied, without affecting the larger point at issue.

Next, I offer a more general sketch. The simplest propositions are those in which properties are predicated of objects. Complex propositions involve other operations such as conjoining, disjoining, and negating properties, or operating on, for example, a two-place relation R to form the reflexive, one-place property *self-Ring*. They may also involve applications of functions to objects, or to properties (or propositional functions). In addition, some complex propositions involve the ascription of higher-order properties to lower-order properties (or propositional functions), as in quantification. Propositions of any sort may also be arguments of

---

[60] For further discussion, see Soames (forthcoming).

further predications, which we find in modal propositions and attitude ascriptions. For example, the proposition *that it is a necessary truth that Frege isn't Russell* is the complex cognitive act of (i) negating the identity relation, (ii) predicating the result—nonidentity—of the pair consisting of Frege and Russell, and (iii) predicating *being necessarily true* of the act performed in (ii).[61] The proposition that John believes that Frege is Russell is the act of (i) predicating identity of the pair consisting of Frege and Russell, and (ii) predicating the belief relation of the pair consisting of John and the act (i).

The following examples illustrate these points. The proposition that Moore is wise is the act of predicating *being wise* of Moore; the proposition that he is eloquent and wise is the act of first conjoining *being eloquent* and *being wise*, and then predicating the result of Moore; the proposition that he shaves himself is the act of operating on the shaving relation to get the property *being one who shaves oneself*, and then predicating it of Moore. The proposition *that 6 cubed is greater than 14 squared* is the act of applying the cubing function to the number 6, applying the squaring function to 14, and predicating *being greater than* of the results (in that order). Functional application is also at work with Fregean definite descriptions, which are singular terms formed from attaching 'the' to a formula G. On a hybrid Russellian-Fregean analysis, 'the' denotes a function f_{the} that maps a propositional function g (which corresponds to G) onto the unique object to which g assigns a true proposition, if there is such an object; otherwise f_{the} is undefined. The proposition *that the G is H* is the act of applying f_{the} to g and predicating *being H* of the result. The proposition *that all G's are H* is the act of (i) applying the function f_{all} to g, yielding the property *being true of all objects to which g assigns a truth,* and (ii) predicating this property of *being H*.[62]

At this point, a word must be said about the verb 'predicate'. As a first approximation (to be modified shortly when we review Russell's Gray's Elegy example) one may think of it as analogous to the *intensional transitive* 'look for'. If Bill is looking for Maria, and Maria is Mary, who, in turn, is the chief of police, then Bill is looking for Mary, but it doesn't follow (on one reading) that he is looking for the chief of police. It also doesn't follow from that fact that he is looking for the fountain of youth that there is such a thing. Analogously, if Bill *predicates P of x,* and x is identical to y, which, in turn, is the unique so-and-so, then Bill predicates P of y, but it doesn't

---

[61] This is a bit of a simplification. In point of fact, there are two slightly different propositions that might correspond to the sentence 'Frege isn't Russell'. The first, indicated by (i) and (ii) above, is the proposition that Frege is nonidentical with Russell. The second corresponds to "~ Frege is identical with Russell," which comes by replacing (i) and (ii) with (i′) predicating identity of Frege and Russell, and (ii′) performing the negation operation on the proposition corresponding to (i′).

[62] Since I am here constructing an alternative to Russell's view, I make free and easy appeal to propositional functions.

follow that he predicates P of the so-and-so. It also doesn't follow from the fact that he predicates P of the so-and-so that there is a so-and-so. Like an intensional transitive (which expresses a cognitive relation between an agent and a content) the verb 'predicate' expresses a cognitive relation between an agent, a property, and a content. So, if we treat definite descriptions as singular terms, the proposition that the king of France is wise will be the act *predicating being wise* of the king of France, even though there is no such king. *The truth of the proposition depends on there being something of which being wise is predicated, but its existence doesn't.*

5.3. Existence and Truth

Cognitive acts, like acts of all kinds, are things that can be done—typically by different agents at different times who *do the same thing.* Thus, acts cannot be identified with particular concrete events in which agents perform them. They do, however, bear a close relation to event types in which some agent or other performs the act. I take no stand here on whether they are, or are not, identical with such types. However, I will explore existence conditions for acts that parallel those for the corresponding event types. On this way of looking at things, the conditions under which an act A exists are the same as those under which the event type of an agent's performing A exists. Thus, whether or not cognitive acts are themselves event types, their existence may be governed by the principles that determine the existence of types from the existence of instances of types. The point of exploring these existence conditions is in part to sketch a view that captures something close to one of Russell's three desiderata for any theory of truth and falsity—namely that if there were no minds, and hence no cognition, no truths or falsehoods would exist. Since this view has its own attractions, it is worth spelling out.

The simplest such principle is this: *If an event type E has instances that exist, then E exists.* For example, one can refer to Socrates even though he no longer exists. If I do so, then a concrete event e exists that is an instance of the minimal *event type* in which one refers to Socrates; thus the event type, and associated act, must also exist. Ditto for the (minimal) event type, and act, in which one thinks of (and perhaps refers to) Socrates and predicates *no longer existing* of him. Thus, the proposition that Socrates no longer exists *itself exists.* Since, in certain cases, one can also think of, and refer to, merely possible individuals, there exist propositions the "constituents" of which have never existed and never will.[63] To understand this,

---

[63] For more on referring to, or quantifying over, the nonexistent, see Nathan Salmon (1987); Soames (2007b); and pp. 128–29 of Soames (2010). In addition to the substantive issue, there is also a terminological one. I here use 'constituent' to stand for the entities in terms of which the crucial acts that make up the proposition are defined. There is, of course, a different sense of 'constituent' in which the acts that make up the proposition are

one must not confuse failing to refer with referring to a nonexistent. 'The present king of France' fails to refer, and so has no referent; 'Socrates' has a referent, just one that doesn't exist.

The view is *not* Meinongian—there is no such thing as the golden mountain, whether existent or not. It also eliminates what might otherwise seem to be a problem, namely, that if one of the so-called "constituents" of a singular proposition fails to exist, then the proposition also fails to exist. This false claim relating the existence of a proposition to the existence of its constituents comes from thinking of propositions in the wrong way. When a proposition is the act of predicating a property of a certain object, that object may legitimately be regarded as a constituent of the proposition—in the sense that the proposition is defined in terms of it—without the existence of the object being necessary for the existence of the proposition.

Here is another plausible principle about existence: if (i) P and R are each n-place properties for which there have been events in which an agent predicates them of things, (ii) $o_1 \ldots o_n$ are objects for each of which there have been events in which an agent thinks of the object, (iii) f is a function that maps n or fewer objects onto an object for which there have been events in which an agent applies f to objects, (iv) F is an operation on a property, or on a pair of properties, for which there have been events in which an agent applies it to a property, or to a pair of properties, and (v) Prop is an operation on a proposition, or on a pair of propositions, for which there have been events in which an agent applies the operation to a proposition, or to a pair of propositions; then (vi) there exist propositions p_R and p_P that are the (minimal) acts of thinking of $o_1 \ldots o_n$ and predicating R and P of them (respectively), (vii) there exist propositions just like p_R and p_P except for the fact that the predication targets for R and P include the results obtained by starting with $o_1 \ldots o_n$ and applying f any number of times (including to its own output), (viii) there exists a proposition p_F that is the (minimal) act of applying F to R, or applying F to P and R, and predicating the resulting property of $o_1 \ldots o_n$, and (ix) there exists a proposition p_{Prop} that is the (minimal) act of applying Prop to p_R and p_P—*even if no one has ever performed those predications or operations on those targets and hence there exist no concrete events in which agents entertain these propositions.*[64]

---

themselves its constituents. Both senses are legitimate, so long as they aren't confused. My use of the former is intended to preserve—within my cognitive theory of propositions—the identification of propositional constituents standardly used by defenders of more traditional accounts of structured propositions.

[64] The principles indicated here for ensuring the existence of propositions that have not been entertained are merely illustrative samples that can be expanded and made more complete in various ways. (For example, nothing here is said about propositional functions and quantification.) The idea is that complex propositions will exist when their most basic constituents have been cognized and the operations in terms of which the propositions are defined have been employed by some agents at some time. See chapter 12 of Soames (2014c) for some further discussion.

Consider an analog with sentences. If R is an n-place predicate that has been used by an agent, and $t_1 \ldots t_n$ are names, each of which has been used, and O is a sentential operator that has been used, then the sentence type $\ulcorner O(R\ t_1 \ldots t_n)\urcorner$ exists—*even if it has never been uttered or inscribed.* The reason we take ourselves to speak a language with indefinitely many sentences none of us has ever encountered is that each such sentence is built using combinatorial processes known by many of us from vocabulary items each of which is known by some of us. When propositions are taken to be cognitive acts, an analogous idea may apply to them. Acts the constituents of which are previously cognized objects, properties, functions, and operations, applied to one another in ways with which we are cognitively familiar, exist. If we were to take the further step of treating sentences themselves as complex acts, or event types instances of which are concrete events of uttering or inscribing in which agents produce auditory, visual, or tactile tokens, then the principle needed to guarantee the existence of the usual infinity of sentences would be an even closer analog of the one suggested for propositions as acts.[65]

In this way, we might come to recognize the existence of many propositions that have never been entertained. Still, one might worry, if propositions are acts, some propositions won't exist that should. One might have supposed that for each molecule in the universe, the proposition that it is a molecule exists and is true. Since many molecules have never been cognized by any agent, nothing guarantees the existence of these propositions. This would be a problem if propositions had to exist to be true. But they don't. Although many properties require things that have them to exist, some don't. An individual can have the properties *being dead, being referred to by me,* and *being admired by someone* despite not existing. Similarly, a pair of individuals—e.g., Frege and Moore—can instantiate the relation of non-identity without existing. By the same token, a proposition can be *true* whether or not it exists. Thus, there is nothing to prevent the nonexistent proposition that m is a molecule from *being true.* Since we can quantify over the merely possible, we can quantify over possible propositions, and say that if p predicates *being so-and-so* of o, then p is true (at world-state w) iff (at w) o is so-and-so, whether or not p exists (at w).

Although, on this account, a proposition p can be *true* at a world-state w without existing at w, p can't be *entertained* at w, *accepted* at w, *asserted* at w, *denied* at w, or *judged* at w to be true without existing at w. The reason

---

[65] This way of thinking of sentences requires distinguishing three things: (i) utterance or inscribing event types, (ii) concrete events of uttering or inscribing, and (iii) the objects, if any, produced by (ii). In the case of inscriptions, the objects will be visible or tactile shapes of some sort in one or another medium. In the case of utterances, it is not clear to me that there are separate products. If there are, they are sounds. But aren't those concrete events? Are those events different from utterance events? Supposing there are three things (at least in some cases), one may distinguish between sentences (event types), sentence instances (event instances), and the products traditionally called "sentence tokens."

is simple: to bear any of these attitudes to p at w, an agent must entertain p at w. Since in each case this involves producing an instance of the event type that corresponds to p, bearing any of these attitudes to p guarantees the existence of p. So, when we really need the existence of propositions as objects of attitudes, they are guaranteed to exist.[66] In this way, we satisfy a plausible version of Russell's second requirement of a proper theory of truth bearers: if no agents bore any cognitive attitudes to propositions, there would be no existing bearers of truth or falsity. Even better, we satisfy the requirement in a way that allows us to explain what Russell could not—namely, how certain propositions could have been true, even if there had been no minds to cognize them. In fact, our theory satisfies all of his requirements, since it also satisfies both his first requirement—that truths and falsehoods are things of the same sort—and his third requirement—that truth and falsity are not intrinsic properties of their bearers, but depend on the state of the world beyond themselves.

5.4. The Place of Propositions in Our Cognitive Architecture

In addition to satisfying Russell's requirements while avoiding the many problems of the multiple relation theory, the new theory provides a satisfying foundational account of what propositions are and how we are related to them. The account starts with the idea that we predicate properties of objects in cognition, thereby entertaining propositions. This is done before we have the concept *proposition*. Focusing on similarities and differences in our experience, we eventually acquire the concept, making propositions themselves objects of thought and subjects of predication. This allows us to acquire the notion of truth, in part by being given numerous examples— 'it is true that o is red if o is red', 'it isn't true that o is red if o isn't red', etc.—and in part by recognizing the general point that a proposition is true iff things are as it represents them to be. Given truth, properties can be conceptualized as *things true of other things*. With the concepts *truth, property, proposition*, and *modality* (what could be but isn't), we can characterize world-states as ways the world could be—maximally informative properties that the world could have had. Such a world-state w can be defined as the property of making true a set w* of basic propositions that tell a complete world-story. Roughly put, a proposition p is true *at w* iff p is an a priori consequence of w*. So, we can come to know that p is true at w by deriving p from w*. As for the actual world-state @, we can come to know p to be *true at @*, given knowledge of p, by noting that since p is true, it must be true *at this very world-state*—the one that is instantiated.[67]

---

[66] See Speaks (2014) for an objection to this claim, and chapter 12 of Soames (2014c) for a reply.

[67] See Soames (2007b), chapters 5 and 6 of (2010a), and chapters 3 and 6 of (2014c) for explanations.

5.5. Further Light on the Central Argument of "On Denoting"

Finally, the above theory of propositions sheds further light on the Gray's Elegy argument, which Russell took to be the centerpiece of "On Denoting." One of the crucial issues that arose from the discussion of that argument in section 2.3.3 of Chapter 8 concerned the examples in (12) and (13), in which 'logicism' is understood as a Russellian logically proper name of the very proposition *that mathematics is reducible to logic* that is designated by the directly referential *that*-clause.[68]

12a. Russell attempted to establish that mathematics is reducible to logic.
  b. Russell attempted to establish logicism.
13a. Mary believes that Russell attempted to establish that mathematics is reducible to logic.
  b. Mary believes that Russell attempted to establish logicism.

In my earlier discussion of this example, I observed that the propositions expressed by (12a) and (12b) are different—and that the truth of (13a) guarantees the truth of (13b), but not vice versa—*despite the fact that the propositions expressed by (12a) and (12b) predicate the same relation of the same predication targets (which exhaust their major constituents)*. However, I didn't explain how this is possible, except to suggest that the constituents of the proposition L—*that mathematics is reducible to logic* (which is a constituent of both the proposition expressed by (12a) and the proposition expressed by (12b))—must somehow occur as *sub-constituents* of the proposition expressed by (12a) without so occurring in the proposition expressed by (12b). The unsolved mystery left hanging at the time was "What must propositions be like in order for this to be so?"

If one tries to visualize propositions—e.g., by drawing them on a page or representing them on a graph—it is hard to make sense of this. In representing the propositional constituents pictorially on the page, one would use aspects of the spatial relationships their representations bear to one another to indicate the structure of the proposition, and so to represent what is predicated of what. But since pictorially representing proposition L on the page would require representing its constituents, the representations of the propositions expressed by (12a) and (12b) would be the same. Representing a proposition as visible in this way requires representing its constituents, and the constituents of its constituents, as similarly visible. So if one thought that entertaining a proposition was something like perceiving it with the mind's eye, one would think that to mentally "see" the proposition *that mathematics is reducible to logic* as a constituent of a larger proposition would require seeing its constituents too—as *sub-constituents* of the larger proposition. This, I suspect, is how Russell thought of propositions; if you do think of them in this way, you too will think that the

---

[68] For more detail, see Richard (1993) and Soames (2007a).

propositions expressed by (12a) and (12b) must be absolutely one and the same (on the assumption that 'logicism' and 'that mathematics is reducible to logic' are logically proper names of L).

But this is the wrong way to think about propositions; the propositions expressed by (12a) and (12b) are not the same. What is more, propositions, being cognitive act types, can't be visualized in the imagined way. According to this act-conception of propositions, understanding (12b) and entertaining the proposition it expresses require one to think of L, and to predicate *attempting to establish* of the pair consisting of Russell and L. Since one can think of L simply by possessing the name 'logicism', without knowing much about its referent, one who is competent with the name and accepts (12b) can, as I argued in chapter 8, entertain, and believe, the proposition it expresses without being able to state, or informatively identify, L. By contrast, in order to understand (12a) and entertain the proposition it expresses, one must first predicate *being reducible* of the pair consisting of mathematics and logic (in that order)—thereby entertaining L, which is expressed by the *that*-clause. Next, one predicates *attempting to establish* of Russell and L. This difference carries over to (13a) and (13b), with the result that the truth of the former requires the truth of the latter, but not vice versa. *Because propositions are cognitive acts that involve thinking of things and predicating properties of them, two propositions can place different constraints on how an agent thinks about their common predication targets, even if the truth conditions of the two propositions result from predicating the very same properties of the very same predication targets.* Although the propositions expressed by (12a) and (12b) predicate the same thing of the same targets, the former is a cognitive act in which the propositional predication target must be cognized by entertaining it (thereby making the constituents of that target sub-constituents of the proposition as a whole), while the latter is an act that doesn't require this. The difference in truth value between (13a) and (13b) is sensitive to this.

This is an important part, but not the whole, of the story needed to get to the bottom of the Gray's Elegy argument. The conclusion of Russell's argument is that complex singular terms are impossible, so no language, natural or artificial, can contain definite descriptions as singular terms. One of his key examples is (14), with 'M' as a genuine name for the meaning of 'the first line of Gray's Elegy' (taken to be a singular term).

14a. The first line of Gray's Elegy is 'the curfew tolls the knell of parting day'.
  b. 'The first line of Gray's Elegy' means M.
  c. 'The first line of Gray's Elegy' means the first line of Gray's Elegy.

As we saw in chapter 8, a key step in Russell's argument is (Ib).

(Ib) If definite descriptions express meanings that denote unique objects satisfying them (if such objects there be), then these meanings can occur in propositions *only* in the role of presenting their denotations as the subjects of predication in the propositions; thus, these meanings can never themselves be the direct subjects of predication in any proposition in which they occur.

Although (Ib) doesn't cause problems for the proposition expressed by (14a), it leads Russell to think that since the propositions expressed by (14b) and (14c) have the same structure and constituents, they must be identical. This is trouble, since if the description has a meaning, the proposition expressed by (14b) must be true, while that expressed by (14c)—which says that its meaning is the thing it denotes—must be false. Taking (Ib) to be true, Russell concludes that it is impossible for meaningful definite descriptions (of any language) to be singular terms.

In section 2.3.2 of chapter 8, I argued that Russell's conclusion is false, which means that (Ib) must also be false. It remains to show that the conception of propositions as cognitive acts provides a natural way of rejecting (Ib). We start by noting that the proposition expressed by (14a) is the act of (i) thinking of the function f_{the} and the function g (that assigns an object a truth iff it is a line in Gray's Elegy preceding all others), (ii) combining f_{the} and g into a single constituent in which g is understood to play the role argument-of-f_{the}, and (iii) predicating the identity relation of the pair consisting of 'the curfew tolls the knell of parting day' plus the result of applying f_{the} to g. Let it be part of the theory that the complex f_{the}-*plus*-g is the meaning of the definite description—which we take to be a constituent of the proposition. Since 'the curfew tolls the knell of parting day' is uniquely determined by this denoting complex, the proposition expressed by (14a) comes out true. Similar reasoning gives us the falsity of the proposition expressed by (14c).

What about the proposition expressed by (14b)? It seems that it should be the cognitive act type of predicating *means* of the pair 'the first line of Gray's Elegy' and f_{the}-*plus*-g. Since these are also the constituents of the proposition expressed by (14c), the assumption that in both cases the same relation is predicated of the same arguments requires the two propositions to have the same truth value. This is what generates the problem and leads to Russell's false conclusion. The conception of propositions as cognitive acts blocks the incorrect conclusion that the propositions expressed by (14b) and (14c) are identical by requiring one who entertains the latter (but not one who entertains the former) to cognize the individual sub-constituents f_{the} and g, and unite them in applying the former to the latter. However, nothing I have said up to now explains how the former can be true (which it must be), while the latter is false.

Since the two propositions have the same major constituents, and since the difference in the way that one of them is cognized in the two propositions doesn't, by itself, affect their truth values, they must also differ in their structure—which, on this view of propositions, means that they must differ in the predication relations involved in the two cases. Specifically, the manner in which the argument-providing constituents function in these predications can't be the same. In the proposition expressed by (14b), *being what 'the first line of Gray's Elegy' means* is *directly predicated* of the complex f_{the}-*plus-g* that is the meaning of the description; in the proposition expressed by (14c) it is *indirectly predicated* of whatever is determined by that complex—i.e., the value of f_{the} at g. In the former case, we predicate a property of something we have directly in mind as our intended target; in the latter case our intended predication target is whatever, if anything, is determined by the complex we are using to represent it. *The crucial difference between the propositions expressed by (14b) and (14c)—the one that gives rise to their different truth conditions—is a difference in cognitive operations performed on the same materials.*

More generally put, the relation *direct predication* holds of an agent A (who entertains a proposition p), a property F (to be predicated of something), and an item x (of which F is predicated), only if A has x in mind as the thing to be represented as having F. The *indirect predication* relation holds between A, F, and an item x that is the kind of thing (e.g., a function-argument complex) that determines something else (e.g., a value). In order for this relation to hold, A must have x in mind and intend to represent whatever, if anything, is determined by x as having F. The *direct predication* is veridical iff x has F; the *indirect predication* is veridical iff there is something uniquely determined by x and that thing has F.[69]

Thus, the crucial factors in determining the predicate-argument structure of the propositions expressed by (14b) and (14c) are the *intentions* of the agents concerning the role of the complex constituent in providing the arguments in the two cases. Since propositions are cognitive acts, it is perfectly possible for them to differ in this way. As noted above, this difference in the two propositions can't be drawn or visually represented. In both cases, any such representation would indicate *means* as combining with 'the first line of Gray's Elegy' to form the property to be predicated, plus the same argument-providing constituent. The different ways in which the agent *intends* that constituent to function in the two cases would be invisible. So, visualized in this way, the two propositions would "look"

---

[69] Let 'Pred$_D$' and 'Pred$_I$' express the relations *direct predication* and *indirect predication*, respectively, and let 'T' be a schematic letter to be replaced by a singular term. The proposition expressed by a sentence of the form (i) directly predicates Pred$_D$ of the triple consisting of A (or p), the property so-and-so, and *the referent*, if any, of T.

i. Agent A (or proposition p) *directly predicates* property so-and-so of T.

The proposition expressed by a sentence of the form (ii) directly predicates Pred$_I$ of the triple consisting of A (or p), the property so-and-so, and *the content* (meaning) of T.

ii. Agent A (or proposition p) *indirectly predicates* the property so-and-so of T.

The distinction is explained in greater detail in chapter 6 of Soames (2014c).

the same, as they did to Russell. That they are not the same indicates that he was operating with the wrong conception of propositions. Fortunately for us, his guiding insight in abandoning propositions in favor of his ill-fated multiple relation theory of judgment can be put to use in developing a more promising conception.

6. RUSSELL'S STRUGGLE WITH A DYING THEORY

The Russell-inspired theory outlined in the previous section was, of course, never contemplated by him, but remained undeveloped for nearly a century. The next step for Russell himself was to develop his earlier sketches of the multiple relation theory in more detail, and to place it at the center of his epistemology. This was the project undertaken in May of 1913 when he began work on a long manuscript entitled *Theory of Knowledge*.[70] The first part was largely devoted to elaborating the conceptual foundations of the multi-relation theory, while the third part was intended to extend it from simple "atomic" judgments to complex judgments involving negation, truth functions, and other logical operators. However, Russell encountered major difficulty right away, with the result that the work was never completed, and the third part on complex judgments was never written. By 1919, he had given up all hope of making any version of his ill-fated theory work. Although I will present a few aspects of this aborted work, I will spare the reader the epicyclical twists and turns of Russell's increasingly convoluted attempts to deal with the problems he faced. Instead, the focus will be on his interaction with Wittgenstein over these problems, with the aim of illuminating aspects of their thought that would show up later in Russell's 1918 lectures on logical atomism and in Wittgenstein's *Tractatus Logico-Philosophicus*.

One of the additions introduced in the 1913 version of the theory involved a new belief constituent that Russell called "a logical form." Suppose we are given a belief ascription formalized in accord with the multiple relation theory as (15a).

15a. Believes (Mary, identity, difference, difference)

Does this reflect Mary's belief *that identity is different from difference*, or does it reflect her belief *that difference is identical with difference*? Since both are possible, Russell must distinguish them. His solution was to introduce "logical forms." Mary's belief *that difference is identical with difference* is then represented as (15b), while her belief *that difference is different from identity* can be represented as (15c).

15b. Believes (Mary, identity, difference, difference, Rxy)
   c. Believes (Mary, difference, difference, identity, Rxy)

---

[70] The unpublished manuscript was posthumously published in 1984 (Russell 1913).

Very roughly, the idea was that in (15b) the agent, Mary, associates identity with 'R', and difference with both 'x' and 'y', while in (15c) difference is associated with 'R', while difference and identity are associated with 'x' and 'y' respectively.

The reality Russell was trying to get at is that what is predicated of what is different in the two cases, which must be reflected in the constituent structure of the two facts (wrongly characterized by Russell as the two "beliefs"). However, the idea of introducing these "logical forms" was deeply problematic. For one thing, we need to know what these new entities are. Since logical forms were not supposed to be expressions, one might suspect them to be proposition-like entities introduced in a theory meant to eliminate propositions. That, of course, was not Russell's intention. Trying on various explanations for size, he ended up claiming that logical forms were "general facts" of a certain quite special sort. Putting aside the problems posed by this answer, the question to ask is how adding *any entity* as an extra belief constituent could address any serious problem with the theory.

What distinguishes the two beliefs at issue in (15), or the two beliefs— *that John loves Joan* and *that Joan loves John*—in (16)?

16a. Believes (Mary, loving, John, Joan, Rxy)
   b. Believes (Mary, loving, Joan, John, Rxy)

In (15) it is the distinction between predicating identity of difference and difference versus predicating difference of difference and identity; in (16) it is the distinction between predicating the relation *loving* of the ordered pair <John, Joan> versus predicating it of <Joan, John>—where to predicate R of $<o_1, o_2>$ is to represent o_1 as loving o_2 (and o_2 as being loved by o_1). If belief constituents in (15) and (16) are already understood as ordered (and hence as already indicating what is predicated of what), then the addition of "logical forms" is superfluous, while if they are not, the addition doesn't rectify the problem. Although Russell tried to accommodate this point by complicating the account accordingly, it is not clear that anything worked.[71]

The fundamental problem he was struggling with was that of explaining how the cognitive activity of an agent combines the constituents of beliefs (and other attitudes) into something that represents the world, and so has truth conditions. That activity involves identifying properties and relations to be predicated of other constituents as well as identifying functions and other operations and applying them as the agent intends. Since ordering the arguments is sometimes necessary, as in (16), the predication target is naturally regarded as an ordered n-tuple. That Russell himself did not conceptualize things in this way may have reflected his

---

[71] For more on "logical forms," including their role in specifying the range of logically possible facts (complexes) in Russell (1913), see sections 2 and 3 of Pincock (2008). See also Landini (1991).

recognition of the threat this natural way of thinking poses to his theory. For consider a case like (17).

> 17. Mary believes that it is not the case that if John loves Joan, then Joan loves John.

Here, the unordered arguments to the belief relation are Mary, negation, the operation of forming a material conditional, loving, John, Joan, loving, Joan, John. What is needed seems clear: the negation operator must be provided a propositional target, which must be the conditional formed from the application of the conditional operation to a pair of propositions, which in turn are gotten from first predicating loving of <John, Joan> and then predicating it of <Joan, John>. Since this is a story that no multiple relation theorist can tell, the challenge was to stop it in its tracks—which left Russell with an unresolved (and ultimately irresolvable) difficulty even with simple examples like (16).

With this in the background, we are ready to explore Russell's interaction with Wittgenstein over the former's unfinished manuscript. Wittgenstein visited Russell on May 27, 1913, by which time Russell had drafted 240 pages of his new manuscript. Recounting the visit in a letter, Russell says:

> Wittgenstein came to see me—we were both cross from the heat—I showed him a crucial part of what I had been writing. He said it was all wrong, not realizing the difficulties—that he had tried my view and knew it wouldn't work. I couldn't understand the objection—in fact he was very inarticulate—but I feel in my bones that he must be right, and that he has seen something I have missed. If I could see it too I shouldn't mind, but as it is, it is worrying, and has rather destroyed the pleasure of my writing.[72]

Despite being troubled, and unsure of the content of the objection, Russell continued to work on the manuscript, finishing another 110 pages by June 6, at which time he ceased working on it in the midst of encountering difficulties with molecular judgment (involving complex propositions). Throughout this time Wittgenstein's criticism had been bothering him, as reported in another letter.

> All that has gone wrong with me lately comes from Wittgenstein's attack on my work—I have only just realized this. It was very difficult to be honest about it, as it makes a large part of the book I meant to write impossible for years to come probably. . . . I must be sunk—it is the first time in my life that I have failed in honesty over my work.[73]

Within a matter of days Wittgenstein wrote to Russell clarifying his objection.

---

[72] The letter is published in Russell (2002); the quotation is from p. 446.
[73] Russell (2002), p. 448.

I can now express my objection to your theory of judgment exactly: I believe it is obvious that, from the proposition 'A judges that (say) a is in a relation R to b', if correctly analysed, the proposition 'aRb ∨ ~aRb' must follow directly *without the use of any other premiss.* This condition is not fulfilled by your theory.[74]

A related point appears in Wittgenstein's "Notes on Logic," written in September of 1913.

> Every right theory of judgment must make it impossible for me to judge that "this table penholders the book." (Russell's theory does not satisfy this requirement.)[75]

It is widely agreed that these two formulations of Wittgenstein's worry come to essentially the same thing, which is later expressed in *Tractatus* 5.5422.

> The correct explanation of the form of the proposition 'A makes the judgment p', must show that it is impossible for a judgment to be a piece of nonsense. (Russell's theory does not satisfy this requirement.)[76]

The idea is that it should follow immediately from (18a) that (18b) is meaningful and so is true or false, which is just to say that in any correct account (18c) must immediately follow from (18a).

18a. A judges that n bears R to m.
  b. nRm
  c. nRm ∨ ~nRm

But why should this be seen as a devastating objection to Russell's multiple relation theory? For years the standard answer was that the constituents that can be combined by an agent into a judgment must obey Russellian (logical) type restrictions, which (supposedly) explain why some things can be meaningfully predicated only of a restricted range of arguments, and other things can't be predicated of anything—ruling out, for example, the possibility of judging *that the table penholders the book* or *that Desdemona Cassio's loving.*[77] So, some interpreters have thought, if Russell's theory of judgment is to conform to Wittgenstein's demand, it must presuppose his theory of logical types. However, the standard interpretation continues, this is impossible, since the theory of types itself depends on the theory of judgment to antecedently determine which predications are meaningful and which are not. Hence the impasse.

---

[74] Wittgenstein (1995), p. 29.
[75] Wittgenstein (1914–16), p. 96.
[76] Wittgenstein (1961), p. 65.
[77] See Black (1964), Griffin (1985, 1985/6, 1991), Hylton (1984, 1990), Landini (1991), Pears (1977, 1978, 1989), Somerville (1980), Stevens (2003), Weiss (1995).

Recently, however, the standard interpretation has come under sustained and persuasive attack in Stevens (2005), Hanks (2007), and Pincock (2008). Though the critical discussions are complex, two points stand out.[78] First, as Stevens and Pincock argue, all one needs (for the examples we are considering) is a distinction between different kinds of entities— individuals on the one hand, and properties and relations, on the other. If this is right, and if, as they contend, Russell's theory of types can be understood as leaving individuals, properties, and relations alone, while restricting the ascending orders of the type hierarchy to propositions and propositional functions, then we don't need to invoke type theory to deal with Wittgenstein's problem for the multiple relation theory. Second, as Hanks points out, there would no objectionable circularity even if type theory were involved in the response to Wittgenstein. Whereas the type hierarchy is *epistemologically* based on our ability to recognize certain judgments as conceptually coherent and others as incoherent, this doesn't prevent it from providing a *metaphysical* explanation of what makes a judgment fall into one, but not the other, of these categories.

What, then, is the core of Wittgenstein's objection? Hanks sees it as a version of the very problem of the unity of the proposition that the multiple relation theory was supposed to circumvent. Two key passages used to support this interpretation occur in "Notes on Logic," composed in September of 1913, which appears as an appendix on Wittgenstein (1914–16).[79]

When we say that A judges that, etc., then we have to mention a whole proposition which A judges. It will not do to mention only its constituents, or its constituents and form but not in the proper order. This shows that a proposition itself must occur in the statement to the effect that it is judged. For instance, however "not-p" may be explained, the question "What is negated?" must have a meaning.

Every right theory of judgment must make it impossible for me to judge that "this table penholders the book". (Russell's theory does not satisfy this requirement.)

The lesson Hanks draws from the first of these passages is similar to one mentioned in section 3 above in my critique of Russell's 1912 theory. There, my point was that Russell's insight—that it is the cognitive activity of the agent that unites the constituents of a belief into an intentional unit

---

[78] See section 3 of Hanks (2007) and section 4.1 of Pincock (2008).

[79] These passages occur one after the other in the Costello version of "Notes on Logic," which is reprinted on pp. 90–106 of Wittgenstein (1914–16). Scholars have found that this placing of the two next to each other is Russell's corrected and rearranged version of the original. In the original (found in the second edition of *Notebooks 1914–1916*) the passages do not appear next to each other. So it seems that Russell's putting the negation passage before the explicit objection to the multiple relation theory reflects his understanding of Wittgenstein's objection. Thanks to one of the excellent referees of the manuscript for pointing this out.

capable of bearing truth conditions—requires us to recognize one who believes *that not many people are trustworthy* as negating *the proposition* that many people are trustworthy. If this is right, then the very activity of belief formation required by the multiple relation theory presupposes propositions, in which case, Russell's theory can't succeed in eliminating them.

Hanks's point is related.

> The last sentence [of the first of the two passages from Wittgenstein quoted above] is helpful. Suppose we gave a multiple relation theory of negation, i.e., a theory in which we analyze 'a does not bear R to b' as 'Not(a,b,R)'. This treats negation as a three-place relation holding between a, b, and R. Following Wittgenstein's suggestion, let's now ask: in 'a does not bear R to b', what is negated? Given our multiple relation theory of negation, the answer is that a, b and R are negated—*but this makes no sense*. It makes no sense to negate two objects and a relation. Only propositions can be negated. This shows that a whole proposition has to be mentioned in the analysis of 'a does not bear R to b'.[80]

Here, he rejects what he calls a "multiple relation theory of negation" on the grounds that it can't answer the question "What is negated?" To answer this question properly (in the general case in which every proposition can be negated), we need a single thing—a proposition. Since this will be needed as a constituent of negative judgments as well, Hanks's point bleeds into mine. All of this seems to be essentially correct, both as an account of Wittgenstein's thinking, and as a telling objection to any attempt to extend the multiple relation theory to cover all negative judgments.

What about the impossibility of judging that the table penholders the book? Just as in the previous case we need a target for negation, so in this case we need a pair of arguments of which the agent can predicate *penholder*. But this is absurd, a penholder is not the sort of thing that can be predicated of other things. Hence it is impossible to judge that the table penholders the book. That is clear enough. What is less clear is the basis for Wittgenstein's conviction that Russell's theory can't accommodate this point. Here we return to Hanks's use of Wittgenstein's question "What is negated?" to rule out a "multiple relation theory of negation." As he sees it, Wittgenstein has a similar question in mind for any theory of judgment—namely "What is judged?" This is what Russell is alleged not to be able to answer. Here is Hanks again responding to the two passages from Wittgenstein (1914–16) cited above.

> I think Wittgenstein's point is that judging that p is always judging that p is true. This means that we can rephrase the question 'What does A judge?' as 'What does A judge to be true?' . . . [T]he answer that A judges that *a, b, and R are true* obviously makes no sense. . . . Only a proposition can be judged to be true—a collection of items, *even if they are of right number and variety of*

[80] Hanks (2007), p. 137.

types, is not the sort of thing that can be true or false. . . . When Wittgenstein says that any correct theory of judgment must show that it is impossible to judge nonsense, by "nonsense" he does not mean something that violates type restrictions. Rather, he means something that is not capable of being true or false.[81]

This strikes me as an insightful reading of the passage, with which, I think, Wittgenstein would probably have agreed. However, I am not sure that it addresses Russell's 1913 theory in a way that could reasonably be expected to move a proponent of that theory. Suppose the argument attributed to Wittgenstein is this: (i) to judge that so-and-so is to judge that it is true that so-and-so, (ii) which is to predicate truth of *that to which one bears the judgment relation*. Since (iii) according to the multiple relation theory *one bears the judgment relation* to a collection of unrelated things, and (iv) it makes no sense to predicate truth of such a collection, (v) Russell's theory of judgment is false. Although the argument has force, a proponent of the multiple relation theory of judgment might, I think, question the conjunction of (i) and (ii).

This may be brought out more clearly by considering a related version of the argument that identifies Russell's putative truth bearer with "one's judgment" (on a par with his 1912 discussion of "one's belief"). (i) To judge that so-and-so is to judge that it is true that so-and-so, (ii) which is to predicate truth of *one's judgment*. Since (iii) according to the multiple relation theory *one's judgment* is the fact that one judges that so-and-so, and (iv) the fact that one judges that so-and-so is clearly not something one predicates truth of when one judges that so-and-so, (v) *one's judgment* is not what Russell's theory says it is; so the theory is false. Although the multiple relation theorist can presumably accept (iii) and (iv), there is no evident reason for said theorist to accept the conjunction of (i) and (ii). In addition to the fact that (i) is implausible in its own right—since, e.g., nonlinguistic agents might judge/believe that so-and-so, without having, let alone applying, the concept of truth at all—(ii)'s implicit identification of *that so-and-so* with *one's judgment*, in the sense understood by Russell, is not something he was in a position to accept.

This doesn't mean that a good response to Wittgenstein's objection about meaningless judgments, understood along the lines suggested by Hanks, was available to Russell. It wasn't. It does suggest, however,

---

[81] Ibid., pp. 137–38. Graham Stevens's interpretation of Wittgenstein's penholder objection has points in common with those expressed in the final paragraph of this passage from Hanks. Like Hanks, he sees the objection as driven by the idea that breaking up what should be a single belief object into the plurality of its constituents requires treating those constituents as separate, unrelated things, none of which is capable of playing the crucial role of uniting them into something capable of being true or false. Because of this, there is no basis for treating the meaningless judgment to the effect that the table penholders the book any differently than any other judgment. See in particular Stevens (2005), 102–105.

that the objection, so conceptualized, could not reasonably have been expected to move him. One of the virtues of Pincock (2008) is that the author clearly sees this, and steers us toward Russell's take on the matter.[82] There is, to be sure, a kind of unity problem, which consists in specifying *that in virtue of which* the entities designated as truth bearers can properly be so regarded. In the context of Russell's multiple relation theory, this amounted to the attempt to show how certain facts—to the effect that the agent unites various terms into "a judgment," "a belief," or "an understanding"—intrinsically determine the possible facts correspondence with which would make them true. This problem—which Pincock calls "the correspondence problem"—is the one that Russell came to recognize as the Achilles' heel of his theory.[83] Otherwise put, Russell might be able to identify complex agent-involving facts corresponding to various attitude ascriptions, but he wasn't able to extract their truth conditions from their intrinsic nature—which meant that they couldn't really be the fundamental bearers of truth value that he needed.

How and why Russell reached this result is a complex and convoluted matter. Byzantine details aside, he concluded that where molecular judgments are concerned—those involving negation, conjunction, disjunction, and the like—properly specifying the facts in the world to which the attitude would have to correspond if it were to be true would require taking the attitude-fact (e.g., the judgment, belief, understanding) to contain atomic sub-complexes (sub-facts) as constituents (corresponding to what is negated, conjoined, etc.), even in cases when they were false. Since he saw these sub-complexes as being tantamount to false propositions, the existence of which was still an anathema to him, he gave up work on the theory.

My own take on the matter is that this was a pity, since on reaching this point Russell was not too far from the viable theory of propositions as cognitive acts sketched in section 4 above. To construct a theory roughly parallel to that one, using entities he was comfortable with, one may substitute, for example, *the fact that Othello predicates loving of the ordered pair of Desdemona and Cassio* for the event type consisting of Othello's performing that act of predication. The proposition that Desdemona loves Cassio may then be identified with the general fact of which that particular fact about Othello is an instance.[84] On this view, the proposition that Desdemona loves Cassio is *the fact that someone predicates loving of the ordered pair of Desdemona and Cassio*, on analogy with the earlier view that the proposition is the act of performing that predication (which is closely related to the event type in which some agent or other does). Entertaining the proposition could then be defined as performing the cognitive act that

---

[82] Pincock (2008), 122–23.

[83] Ibid., 124–30.

[84] Russell himself suggests something somewhat along these lines on p. 115 of Russell (1913).

results in the specific fact about oneself that is an instance of that proposition (i.e., the general fact). It might then be argued that what makes this fact/proposition a bearer of truth value is that any agent who entertains it thereby represents Desdemona as loving Cassio, and so represents her truly just in case she does love Cassio. From here, the overall structure of the new theory can, for the most part, be constructed in parallel with the earlier theory of propositions as cognitive acts. There are, to be sure, some important differences—which I believe favor the earlier view. But compared to the manifold inadequacies of the multiple relation theory, the differences and difficulties of this theory of propositions as facts of a special sort are relatively minor. For me, seeing how close Russell was to reconstituting a reasonable theory of propositions from the ashes of his multiple relation theory sheds light on the latter, illuminating both what was good and what was bad about it.

Still, this is not quite the end of the matter. There is more to be said about why he didn't explore either of these two ways of reconstituting a theory of propositions based on his idea that the judging agent is somehow responsible for unifying the elements of the judgment. For me, the way to develop his idea is transparent. What unifies the judgment that Desdemona loves Cassio is something the agent does: predicate a relation of an ordered pair. Somehow Russell failed to see this, or perhaps to appreciate its significance. Instead, he continued to think that the entity designated by the verb in the subordinate clause must somehow *itself* do the relating. But how could it, since (i) Desdemona didn't really love Cassio, and (ii) the way for a relation to relate two things is for them to really stand in that relation?

From my point of view, looking for a way for verbs to "really relate" is a dead end. For some interpreters, most notably Graham Stevens, the fact that they can't do this if they are merely terms in a multiple relation was the rock on which the multiple relation theory foundered. The version of the multiple relation theory on which Russell had been working required the loving relation to be simply one of several constituents of the judgment, in which case, some are inclined to think, "it can't relate" (whatever that may mean). As we will see in chapter 12, there is evidence in Russell's 1918 lectures on logical atomism that he himself came to see something like this as the chief import of Wittgenstein's objection. Even though he had ceased working on the *Theory of Knowledge* manuscript in 1913, he was, at the time of those lectures, hoping to somehow revive a "two-verbs" version of the multiple relation theory in which the loving relation somehow functions (along with relations designated by attitude verbs such as 'judge' or 'believe') "as a verb that really relates," while still being a constituent of the judgment. This, I believe, was backsliding. I will revisit Russell's thoughts on this when I discuss those lectures.

CHAPTER 10

⤳⊖⤳

Russell's Logicism

1. Russell, Frege, and the Strategy for Reducing Arithmetic to Logic
2. Reduction, Arithmetic, and the Scope of Philosophical Analysis
3. Russell's Logic and Reduction: First Pass
   3.1. The First-Order Set-Theoretic System
   3.2. The Reduction of Arithmetic to This System
   3.3. Types, the Axiom of Infinity, and the Need to Avoid Paradox
   3.4. The Philosophical Significance of This Reduction
   3.5. Logicism as Precursor
4. Russell's Higher-Order Logic and Reduction: Second Pass
5. Propositional Functions, Substitutional Quantification, and the No-Class Theory
6. Paradoxes, Types, and Vicious Circles

1. RUSSELL, FREGE, AND THE STRATEGY FOR REDUCING ARITHMETIC TO LOGIC

Chapter 1 contained extensive discussion of the philosophical goals of Frege's logicist project as well as his strategy of identifying natural numbers with classes of Fregean concepts (functions from objects to truth values) the extensions of which (the sets of objects to which they assign truth) are equinumerous with one another (i.e., can be put in one-to-one correspondence). In addition, his logical axioms and definitions of arithmetically primitive notions were presented, along with some details of how he proved the axioms of arithmetic as theorems of his system. We now turn to Russell's version of the project. By 1910, when he and his coauthor Alfred North Whitehead published the first volume of *Principia Mathematica*, he had been pursuing it for more than a decade.[1] Russell's initial philosophical motivation and conceptual strategy had much in common with Frege's. In particular, his account of natural numbers was strikingly similar to Frege's. Whereas for Frege in the *Foundations of Arithmetic* natural numbers are sets of *concepts* the extensions of which are equinumerous

[1] Volume 1 of *Principia Mathematica* was published in 1910, volume 2 in 1912, and volume 3 in 1913, all by Cambridge University Press.

with one another, for Russell they are sets of equinumerous *sets*. Since for many purposes there is no important difference between a set and the concept that assigns truth to all and only its members, it is common to speak of "the Frege-Russell conception of number"—treating the two formulations as different versions of the same natural idea.

Like Frege, Russell initially sought to anchor our a priori knowledge of arithmetic and higher mathematics in self-evident truths of logic. By doing so, he hoped both to explain how this knowledge is possible, and to justify it by showing mathematical truths to be provable from axioms of logic that are absolutely certain by logical steps that are themselves certain. Of course, success in the project would have other benefits as well—not least of which would be to unify mathematics by treating all its branches as elaborations of the same underlying system, and to answer metaphysical questions about the subject matter of mathematics, including what various kinds of numbers are. In chapter 2, I expressed doubts about whether even a successful derivation of arithmetic from logic would achieve Frege's strong epistemological goals (or his ambition to decisively identify the natural numbers). As we will see, these doubts carry over to Russell.

As for the paradox that defeated Frege's attempted reduction of arithmetic to logic, Russell was, of course, more successful than Frege in framing his reduction to avoid it. In section 1 of chapter 7, I explained how Russell arrived at the paradox by using Cantor's Theorem—that the set of all subsets of a set s can never be put into one-to-one correspondence with s, or any of its subsets—to show that there can be no set of all and only non-self-membered sets. In section 2, I further noted how the hierarchical idea built into Frege's higher-order system of logic could be reshaped to avoid paradox.

The ontology of Frege's system is divided between objects and concepts, the former designated by singular terms, the latter by predicates. Concepts are sorted into a hierarchy of levels. First-level concepts are functions from objects to truth values, second-level concepts are functions from first-level concepts to truth values, and so on. Although every concept has an extension (the set of things to which it assigns *truth*), and although sets count as objects (no matter whether their members are concepts or objects), no concept is an object. Quantification involves predicating an $(n + 1)$-level concept (expressed by the quantifier) of an n-level concept (expressed by the n-level formula to which the quantifier attaches). So first-order quantification (over objects) involves predicating a second-level concept (expressed by the quantifier) of a first-level concept (expressed by a first-order formula that functions as a predicate of objects), second-order quantification (over first-level concepts) involves predicating a third-level concept of a second-level concept, and so on. (See section 4 of chapter 1 for details.) Because of the separation of concepts and their arguments into different levels, it is nonsensical to suppose that a Fregean concept could be predicated of itself—i.e., that it could map itself onto a truth value. Neither the idea that a concept does, nor that it doesn't, map itself onto a truth value can be expressed in the system. So there is no possibility that Frege's logic might commit him to the existence of a universal concept (true of all concepts), or to there being a concept that assigns truth to all and only those concepts that don't assign truths to themselves. However, he could express the first-level concept *being the extension E of a concept that does not assign truth to E*. This, as I showed in section 9 of chapter 2, generates the contradiction in Frege's system.

Suppose, however, we were to modify his system by stipulating that predicates are to designate, not Fregean concepts, but the extensions of those concepts (i.e., the sets of objects assigned truth by the concepts)— *while trading Frege's hierarchy of concepts for a hierarchy of sets*. On this picture, first-level sets are sets of objects (i.e., non-sets), second-level sets are sets of first-level sets, and so on. Quantification involves predicating membership of an n-level set in an $(n + 1)$-level set. So first-order quantification (over objects) involves predicating membership of a first-level set (the extension of the first-order formula to which the quantifier attaches) in a second-level set (the extension of the quantifier), second-order quantification (over first-level sets) involves predicating membership of a second-level set (the extension of the second-order formula to which the quantifier attaches) in a third-level set (the extension of the quantifier), and so on. Now, Russell's paradox will not arise, since we can't even express the idea of a set either being a member of itself, or not being a member of itself.

This is a good place to start the explanation of Russell's reduction. The result will be a system in which the number 1 is the second-level set of single-membered first-level sets, the number 2 is the second-level set of double-membered first-level sets, and so on (where the definitions of these sets don't themselves include numerical concepts like 'single' and 'double'). Though it may sound a bit strange initially, zero will be the second-level set the only member of which is the first-level set that contains no members. The set of natural numbers is then the smallest third-level set of second-level sets that contains zero and is closed under successor (i.e., contains the successor of each of its members). Provided we don't run out of sets, this will be sufficient to prove the axioms of arithmetic in a paradox-free logical system built on a type hierarchy of sets. There will, of course, be complications. However, we will take them in stages.

First, the reduction will be presented in the simplest and most comprehensible form. To this end, an elementary first-order system (in which all quantificational variables are singular terms) will be substituted for Russell's higher-order system (which allows quantificational variables to occupy the positions of predicates). The first-order system will incorporate restrictions based on the hierarchy of sets mentioned above. All singular terms (including quantificational variables) will be indexed to indicate the level of the type hierarchy (individuals, sets of individuals, sets of sets of individuals, etc.) on which their referents are located. Restrictions on predicates will be stated in terms of the indices of the singular terms with which they can meaningfully combine. Doing things this way requires introducing a predicate—treated as a logical symbol—standing for the membership relation between elements of a set and the set itself. The price of this route is that today few, if any, accord the membership predicate this status, viewing it instead as a *mathematical* primitive in an elementary mathematical theory capable of providing the foundation for much of the rest of mathematics. The value of this way of presenting Russell is that it makes fully explicit what is perhaps the most natural way of understanding his reduction—since one very natural way of reading his higher-order quantifiers is to take them to range over sets that are the referents of predicate variables relative to assignments.

This will bring us to the second stage in the reconstruction of his reduction, where I translate the first-order reconstruction into a system of higher-order quantification over sets in the type-theoretical hierarchy. Although this wasn't Russell's own understanding, the interpretation of the quantifiers I will use is the one typically found in textbooks today, so, while the form will be new, the content of the reduction will remain the same. Next, I will explore an aspect of Russell's own interpretation of the quantifiers, according to which they designate not sets, but properties of propositional functions, with higher-order quantifiers ranging over propositional functions at lower levels. On this interpretation, propositional functions (rather than sets) are the elements of the type hierarchy. But what are propositional functions? The most natural answer from our perspective today is that they are functions from objects to old-style Russellian propositions (of the kind he accepted before adopting the multiple relation theory of judgment). As we will see, his famous definition of classes (sets) in *Principia Mathematica* can be taken as eliminating them in favor of propositional functions (so understood). However, although this "elimination" is technically fine, it is, I think, of little philosophical significance. Given propositional functions, we can easily get functions from objects to truth values, which are characteristic functions of sets. Whatever philosophical doubts one might harbor about the relatively well-understood and well-behaved universe of sets won't be quelled by replacing sets with their characteristic functions.

But this is still not the end. Since Russell had adopted the multiple relation theory at the time *Principia Mathematica* was published, the natural interpretation of a *propositional function* as a function from objects to propositions can't (then) have been his. Unfortunately, the alternatives aren't attractive. One might hope that the *facts* about propositional attitudes that he had come to take to be the bearers of truth value could play the role of propositions. But this won't do, since it saddles his brilliant reduction with the manifest problems of his ill-considered multiple relation theory. Another possibility, which conforms to a number of his comments—both contemporaneous and subsequent—is to take propositional functions to be formulas (rather than that which they designate). What this amounts to, and whether or not it offers a reasonable interpretation of Russell's logicist reduction, is a complicated and contentious matter that will be addressed in some detail in section 5.

2. REDUCTION, ARITHMETIC, AND THE SCOPE OF PHILOSOPHICAL ANALYSIS

In developing his theory of descriptions, Russell distinguished logical form from grammatical form and used the distinction to solve philosophical puzzles. His theory of descriptions was widely taken to be a paradigm of analysis, the success of which added impetus to the view that logical analysis was the road to progress in philosophy. This idea was given further support by the logicist reduction in *Principia Mathematica*. As indicated in chapter 1, logicism can be divided into two parts—the reduction of higher mathematics to arithmetic, and the reduction of arithmetic to logic. Russell's main contribution was to the second reduction, the completion of which led many to view mathematics as a branch of logic.

To understand this program, one must understand what a mathematical or logical theory is, and what it means to reduce one such theory to another. One can think of a *theory* as a set of sentences, each of which is a logical consequence of the *axioms* of the theory. The axioms express propositions the theorist accepts without proof. The *theorems* are the totality of statements that are provable from the axioms. Since they are logical consequences of the axioms, they must be true, if the axioms are. The axioms contain the *primitive vocabulary* of the theory, which express concepts with which we are familiar without definition. Sometimes, a theory also contains *definitions* that introduce new terminology defined in terms of its primitives. For example, in many theories there is no primitive symbol for the definite article *the* used in forming singular definite descriptions. Since it is often convenient to have the ability to form such descriptions, the description operator can be introduced by the following definition:

Where Ψ is any (simple) atomic predicate, and Φ is any formula,

$$\Psi \text{ the } x \, \Phi x \cong_{df} \exists x \, \forall y \, [(\Phi y \longleftrightarrow y = x) \, \& \, \Psi x]$$

When the description operator is introduced in this way, some theorems will contain definite descriptions, even though the axioms don't. The theorems are then logical consequences of the axioms *plus* the definitions of the theory—where the latter are either taken to establish stipulated synonyms, or to report preexisting ones.

We now turn to the notion of theoretical reduction. Suppose we have two theories, T1 and T2. To reduce T2 to T1 one must accomplish three technical tasks and one philosophical task. First, one defines the primitive vocabulary of T2 in terms of the vocabulary of T1—i.e., one provides terms appearing in the axioms of T2 with definitions from T1. Second, one provides similar definitions of the defined terms, if any, of T2. Third, one derives the axioms and definitions of T2 from those of T1. Finally, one provides a reason for thinking that T1 is more basic than T2, and hence can be used to give illuminating *analyses* of the concepts of T2. If one succeeds in all of these tasks, one can claim to have analyzed the concepts of T2 using those of T1, and to have given rigorous justifications of the axioms of T2, which had previously been accepted without proof, by proving them from the more basic axioms of T1—making the theorems of T2 theorems of T1. T2 is then seen as an elaboration of what was implicitly present in T1.

The theory we wish to reduce is, of course, arithmetic, which had already been formalized by Dedekind, and widely known from its presentation in Peano (1889). As indicated in section 6 of chapter 1, its axioms and definitions can be stated in several related ways. Here, I will take successor to be a function rather than a two-place relation (as I did there), I will compress two of the earlier axioms into one, and I will state arithmetic as a first-order theory formalized without higher-order quantification, but with a predicate for set membership (taken to be a logical symbol). There are three arithmetical primitives: 'N', which stands for the set of natural numbers; '0', which stands for the first number in the series of natural numbers; and prime— ' —standing for the successor function, which maps a natural number onto the one immediately following it in the series. These terms appear in the axioms and are taken to be understood without definition. To give the theory in this way is, in effect, to presuppose that we know what a natural number is, that we know what zero is, and that we know what it is to go from one number to the next. In addition to the primitives, the axioms contain logical vocabulary common to many theories—quantifiers, variables, and truth-functional connectives. Two further symbols—'=' (for identity) and 'ε' (for set membership)—will here be treated as logically primitive predicates

Axioms of First-order Peano Arithmetic

A1. $0 \, \varepsilon \, N$
   Zero is a natural number.
A2. $\forall x \, (x \, \varepsilon \, N \rightarrow x' \, \varepsilon \, N)$
   The successor of any natural number is a natural number.
A3. $\sim \exists x \, (0 = x')$
   Zero is not the successor of anything.
A4. $\forall x \, \forall y \, [(x \, \varepsilon \, N \, \& \, y \, \varepsilon \, N \, \& \, x' = y') \rightarrow x = y]$
   No two (different) natural numbers have the same successor.

A5. $[F(0) \ \& \ \forall x \ (x \ \varepsilon \ N \rightarrow (Fx \rightarrow Fx'))] \rightarrow \forall x \ (x \ \varepsilon \ N \rightarrow Fx)$

This is an axiom schema, which stands for the infinite set of axioms obtainable by substituting for 'F' any formula in the language of arithmetic that contains free occurrences of the variable 'x'. 'F(0)' stands for the result of replacing all free occurrences of 'x' in the formula replacing 'F' with occurrences of '0'. Informally, it says that zero "is F." Thus, each instance of A5 says that if zero "is F" and if whenever a natural number "is F" then its successor also "is F," then every natural number "is F." Instances of A5 are called *induction axioms*.

Arithmetical Definitions: Addition (+) and Multiplication (*)

D+. $\forall x \ \forall y \ [(x \ \varepsilon \ N \ \& \ y \ \varepsilon \ N) \rightarrow ((x+0) = x \ \& \ (x+y') = (x+y)')]$
For any natural numbers x and y, the sum of x and 0 is x, and the sum of x and the successor of y is the successor of the sum of x and y.

D×. $\forall x \ \forall y \ [(x \ \varepsilon \ N \ \& \ y \ \varepsilon \ N) \rightarrow ((x \times 0) = 0 \ \& \ (x \times y') = (x \times y) + x)]$
For any natural numbers x and y, the result of multiplying x times zero is zero, and the result of multiplying x times the successor of y is the sum of x and the result of multiplying x times y.

In using D+, we first note that adding 0 to x yields x. We then use the second conjunct of the consequent of the definition to tell us that the sum of x and 1 is the successor of x + 0, which is the successor of x. Next we apply the definition again to determine that the sum of x and 2 is the successor of the sum of x and 1. The process can be repeated to determine, for each number y, the result of adding y to x. Since x can be any number, D+ completely determines the sum of every pair of numbers, even though it does not have the familiar form of an explicit definition. This is illustrated by the following example.

Illustration: $3 + 2 = 5$

(i) $(0''' + 0'') = (0''' + 0')'$	From D+, together with A1 and A2, which guarante that $0'''$ and $0''$ are natural numbers.
(ii) $(0''' + 0') = (0''' + 0)'$	From D+, A1, and A2
(iii) $(0''' + 0'') = (0''' + 0)''$	From substitution in (i) of equals for equals on the basis of (ii)
(iv) $(0''' + 0) = 0'''$	D+
(v) $(0''' + 0'') = 0'''''$	From substitution in (iii) on the basis of (iv)

D× works in the same way as D+. Multiplication is defined in terms of repeated addition, which in turn is defined in terms of repeated application of the successor function. All the usual arithmetical results can be proved in this system using A1–A5, D+, and D×. This is the theory to which higher branches of mathematics can be reduced, and which Russell reduces to his system of logic.

3. RUSSELL'S LOGIC AND REDUCTION: FIRST PASS

3.1. The First-Order Set-Theoretic System

Next I turn to the first approximation of the system to which Russell reduced this system of arithmetic. I assume without stating the usual logical principles that allow one to prove straightforward logical truths like $\ulcorner Pv \sim P\urcorner$, $\ulcorner \forall xFx \rightarrow Fa\urcorner$, $\ulcorner \forall x \, \forall y \, (x = y \rightarrow (Fx \leftrightarrow Fy))\urcorner$. In addition to a new primitive symbol 'ε' standing for set membership, the system has special axioms not found in standard systems of logic today. Crucially, the system will incorporate a type theory that stratifies the universe starting with individuals (non-sets), which I will label "level 0," moving to first-level sets (of individuals), which I will label "level 1," second-level sets (of first-level sets), and so on. Corresponding to this hierarchical universe is a hierarchical language, which is a normal first-order language (as indicated in chapter 1) with two modifications. First, variables and names are given subscripts to indicate the level of the thing they name, or range over—e.g., x, x_i, x_{ii}, x_{iii}.[2] Second, these subscripts are used to restrict which formulas are meaningful and which aren't. The restrictions on $\ulcorner x_m \, \varepsilon \, y_n\urcorner$ requires the singular term that appears to the right of 'ε' be indexed for the level immediately following the level for which the singular term that appears to its left is indexed. The restrictions on $\ulcorner x_n = y_m\urcorner$ require the singular terms flanking '=' to carry the same index. Formulas violating these restrictions—e.g., $\ulcorner x_n \, \varepsilon \, y_n\urcorner$ and $\ulcorner x_{ni} = y_n\urcorner$—are declared meaningless.[3]

These restrictions are incorporated in the *axiom schema of comprehension.*

$$\exists y_{ni} \, \forall x_n \, (Fx_n \longleftrightarrow x_n \, \varepsilon \, y_{ni})$$

Instances are obtained by replacing 'Fx_n' with any formula of at most level ni in which 'x_n' has a free occurrence (and 'y_{ni}' does not). (A formula of level m is one containing a subscripted term of level m, but no higher level.)

---

[2] Think of the first of these, namely 'x', as containing the null index, and ranging over non-sets.

[3] I use 'x_n' and 'x_{ni}' as convenient abbreviations for 'x' subscripted by a string of n occurrences 'i' and 'x' subscripted by a string of n + 1 occurrences 'i', respectively.

This axiom schema tells us that for any condition stated on things of an arbitrary level n, there is a set at the next level of all and only those things at level n that satisfy the condition. Note that the formulas '$\sim x \, \varepsilon$ x' and '$\sim x_n \, \varepsilon \, x_n$' can't be substituted for 'Fx_n', but rather are classified as meaningless. Nor can '$\sim x_n \, \varepsilon \, y_{ni}$' be substituted for '$Fx_n$'. Although this formula is meaningful, both 'x_n' and 'y_{ni}' have free occurrences in it, and so we can't obtain an instance from it. Each genuine instance will assert the existence of a set at the level above n of all and only those things of level n that satisfy 'Fx_n'. Call this set '$\underline{y_{ni}}$'.[4] Given any such instance, we know that something of the form

$$\forall x_n \, (Fx_n \longleftrightarrow x_n \, \varepsilon \, \underline{y_{ni}})$$

is true. When we derive consequences from this by erasing the universal quantifier and substituting the name of any arbitrary object of level n for the occurrences of the variable 'x_n', we are barred from using any name for an object at the next level; hence we cannot select '$\underline{y_{ni}}$'. This prevents Russell's paradox from arising.

So long as these restrictions are observed, the axiom schema of comprehension is very natural. To adopt it is to hold that for every meaningful open formula in the language, there is a set of precisely those things that have the property it expresses. To take this to be a logical principle is to take the statement *that x is so-and-so* to come to essentially the same thing as the statement *that x is a member of the set of things that are so-and-so*. Examples of sets asserted to exist by instances of this axiom are as follows:

(i) when the formula replacing 'Fx_n' means *is a natural number less than 29*, the existence of the set of natural numbers less than 29 is asserted;

(ii) when '$x_2 = x_2$' replaces 'Fx_n', the existence of the third-level set of all second-level sets is asserted;

(iii) when '$x \neq x$' replaces 'Fx_n', the existence of the empty first-level set $\emptyset_1$, i.e., the first-level set with no (non-set) members, is asserted.

(iv) when '$\forall z \, (z \, \varepsilon \, x_1 \longleftrightarrow z \neq z)$' replaces '$Fx_n$', the existence of the second-level set whose only member is the first-level set, $\emptyset_1$, with no members is asserted.

The next axiom governing Russell's primitive 'ε' is *the axiom of extensionality*.

$$\forall a_{ni} \, \forall b_{ni} [\forall x_n \, (x_n \, \varepsilon \, a_{ni} \longleftrightarrow x_n \, \varepsilon \, b_{ni}) \rightarrow a_{ni} = b_{ni}]$$

If a and b are sets of a given level with the same members (of the preceding level), then a = b—i.e., no two sets at any level have the same members.

The final special axiom is called *the axiom of infinity*.

$$\emptyset_2 \notin N_3$$

The empty set at the second level is not a member of the set of natural numbers.

---

[4] I use underlined variables as names.

Its purpose is to ensure that enough objects exist to allow the reduction of arithmetic to logic to go through. The reason it is needed, and is stated in this way, will become clear in the course of the reduction.

Finally, I will introduce some defined terms into Russell's system of logic to serve as convenient abbreviations for concepts that will be useful in the reduction. The first definition, of definite descriptions, will provide the basis for the rest.

(i) Definite descriptions

$$\Psi \,(\text{the } z_n \,\Phi(z_n)) \cong_{df} \exists z_n \,\forall w_n \,[(\Phi(w_n) \longleftrightarrow w_n = z_n) \,\&\, \Psi(z_n)]$$

Here, '$\Psi(\ )$' and '$\Phi(\ )$' stand for formulas in which the terms within their brackets appear. The definition tells us that any formula containing an occurrence of a description (represented on the left-hand side) is an abbreviation of the corresponding formula (represented on the right)—subject to the proviso that the description always be given what was called in chapter 8 "narrow scope." This means that when the description occurs in a multi-clause formula Θ, the formula Θ abbreviates is the one gotten from the definition by taking '$\Psi(\ )$' to be the smallest sub-formula of Θ containing the occurrence of the description. The level on the hierarchy of the resulting formula will be determined by the level of the formulas represented by '$\Psi(\ )$' and '$\Phi(\ )$'. They will always be at least of level n. However, the level will be greater if the levels of '$\Psi(\ )$' and '$\Phi(\ )$' are.

(ii) The empty set
$$\varnothing_{ni} \cong_{df} \text{the } x_{ni} : (\forall z_n \,(z_n \notin x_{ni}))$$

(iii) The set the only member of which is w
$$\{w_n\}_{ni} \cong_{df} \text{the } x_{ni} \,[\forall z_n \,(z_n \,\varepsilon\, x_{ni} \longleftrightarrow z_n = w_n)]$$

(iv) The set of all and only the things that "have the property expressed by F"
$$\uparrow z_n \,Fz_n \uparrow_{ni} \cong_{df} \text{the } y_{ni} \,[\forall z_n \,(Fz_n \longleftrightarrow z_n \,\varepsilon\, y_{ni})]$$

(v) The intersection of the sets x and y—i.e., the set of things that are members of both
$$[x_{ni} \cap y_{ni}]_{ni} \cong_{df} \text{the } s_{ni} \,[\forall w_n \,(w_n \,\varepsilon\, s_{ni} \longleftrightarrow (w_n \,\varepsilon\, x_{ni} \,\&\, w_n \,\varepsilon\, y_{ni})]$$

(vi) The union of sets x and y—i.e., the set of things that are members of either one
$$[x_{ni} \cup y_{ni}]_{ni} \cong_{df} \text{the } s_{ni} \,[\forall w_n \,(w_n \,\varepsilon\, s_{ni} \longleftrightarrow (w_n \,\varepsilon\, x_{ni} \,V\, w_n \,\varepsilon\, y_{ni})]$$

(vii) The complement of a set x—the set of all things (of a given level) not in set x
$$\text{Comp}(x_{ni})_{ni} \cong_{df} \text{the } y_{ni} \,[\forall z_n \,(z_n \,\varepsilon\, y_{ni} \longleftrightarrow z_n \notin x_{ni})]$$

3.2. The Reduction of Arithmetic to This System

In order to reduce arithmetic to our logico-set-theoretic system, one must define the arithmetical primitives using terms of the system, and then derive all arithmetical axioms from those definitions, plus axioms of the logic. The trick is coming up with the right definitions. We begin with Russell's definitions of zero and successor.

Definition of Zero

$$0_2 = \{\varnothing_1\}_2$$

Zero is the second-level set the only member of which is the empty set of individuals.

Definition of Successor

$$x_2' = \uparrow y_1 \, [\exists z \, (z \, \varepsilon \, y_1 \, \& \, [(y_1 \cap Comp(\{z\}_1)_1)_1 \, \varepsilon \, x_2])] \uparrow_2$$

The successor of a set x of sets of individuals is the set of all sets y of individuals that contain an individual z which, when eliminated from y, leaves one with a member of x. Otherwise put, the successor of a set x = the set of all sets y that contain a member z such that the intersection of y with the complement of the set the only member of which is z—i.e., with the set containing everything except z—is a member of x.

These definitions interact with one another in the following way:

$$0' = \uparrow y_1 \, [\exists z \, (z \, \varepsilon \, y_1 \, \& \, [(y_1 \cap Comp(\{z\}_1)_1)_1 \, \varepsilon \, \{\varnothing_1\}_2])] \uparrow_2$$

The successor of zero [i.e., the number 1] is the set of all sets y of individuals that contain a member z which, when eliminated from y, leaves one with the empty set of individuals. In other words, it is the set of one-membered sets of individuals; the successor of the successor of zero (the number 2) is the set of two-membered sets of individuals, and so on.

There are three things to notice about this procedure. First, it's not circular. Although 2 turns out to be the set of all *two-membered sets of individuals*, that isn't its definition. It is defined as *the successor of 1*, which in turn is defined as *the successor of zero*. Since *zero* and *successor* are themselves defined without any arithmetical concepts, there is no circle. Second, one can see from the procedure that no two natural numbers m and n (reached via the chain of successors) can share a member in common. If n consists of all and only n-membered sets, while m consists of all and only m-membered sets, then no set can be a member of both m and n, provided that m and n are different numbers. Although I haven't proved this, it turns out to be provable from the axioms of our logical system. Third, as Russell points out, these definitions of the numbers are very natural.

In seeking a definition of number, the first thing to be clear about is what we may call the grammar of our inquiry. Many philosophers, when attempting to define number, are really setting to work to define plurality, which is quite a different thing. *Number* is what is characteristic of numbers, as *man* is what is characteristic of men. A plurality is not an instance of number, but of some particular number. A trio of men, for example, is an instance of the number 3, and the number 3 is an instance of number; but the trio is not an instance of number. This point may seem elementary and scarcely worth mentioning; yet it has proved too subtle for the philosophers, with few exceptions.

A particular number is not identical with any collection of terms having that number: the number 3 is not identical with the trio consisting of Brown, Jones, and Robinson. *The number 3 is something which all trios have in common*, and which distinguishes them from other collections. A number is something that characterizes certain collections, namely, those that have that number.[5]

Russell's point is that just as the property of being red is not identical with any red thing, but rather is something all red things have in common, so the number 3 is not identical with any set of three things, but rather is something that all sets of three things have in common. We could say that the number 3 is the property of having (exactly) three members, though in our present reconstruction we talk directly of sets instead.

We are now ready to define the final arithmetical primitive—'N'—which stands for the set of natural numbers. Since we already have zero and successor, it might seem that we could define it as the set of those sets each of which can be reached by starting with zero and applying successor finitely many times. But that presupposes the notion *finite number,* which is, in effect, the very arithmetical concept we are trying to define. What about saying that *N is the set that contains zero, and is closed under successor—i.e., that contains the successor of each of its members*? This won't work either, because there is no such thing as *the* set satisfying the condition. For example, each of the following sets contains zero and is closed under successor.

Set 1 $\{0, 0', 0'' \ldots\}$

Set 2 $\{0, 0', 0'' \ldots \{\{Bill\}\}$, the set of all sets that contain Bill plus something else, $\ldots\}$

Set 3 $\{0, 0', 0'' \ldots \{\{Bill\}, \{Mary, Ron\}\}$, the union of the successor of $\{\{Bill\}\}$ and the set of all triples containing Mary and Ron, $\ldots\}$

We need some way of enriching the condition used to define 'N' that eliminates all but set 1. We can do this as follows.

The Definition of Natural Number

N = the smallest set containing zero and closed under successor.

---

[5] Bertrand Russell (1919a), pp. 11–12 of the 1993 reprinting, my emphasis.

$$N_3 = \uparrow x_2 \left[\forall y_3 \left((0_2 \; \varepsilon \; y_3 \; \& \; \forall z_2 \left(z_2 \; \varepsilon \; y_3 \rightarrow z'_2 \; \varepsilon \; y_3 \right)) \rightarrow x_2 \; \varepsilon \; y_3 \right) \right] \uparrow_3$$

The set of natural numbers is the third-level set of all and only those second-level sets x which are members of every third-level set y that contains zero and is closed under successor.

This concludes the definition of arithmetical concepts in terms of the concepts of our first approximation of Russell's logical system. All that remains to complete the reduction is to prove the arithmetical axioms from the logical axioms plus these definitions.

The first two axioms follow trivially from the definitions.

A1. $0_2 \; \varepsilon \; N_3$
     Zero is a natural number.

Using the definition of 'N_3', we see that this says that zero is a member of the smallest set containing zero and closed under successor.

A2. $\forall x_2 \left(x_2 \; \varepsilon \; N_3 \rightarrow x'_2 \; \varepsilon \; N_3 \right)$
     The successor of any natural number is a natural number.

Again using the definition of 'N_3', we see that this says that *if x is a member of the smallest set containing zero and closed under successor, then the successor of x is a member of that set too.* This also is trivial—from what it means for a set to be *closed under successor*.

Next consider A3, which says that zero isn't the successor of anything.

A3. $\sim \exists x_2 \left(0_2 = x'_2 \right)$

This can be proved by *reductio ad absurdum*:

    (i) Suppose that for some x_2, zero is the successor of x_2.
   (ii) By the definition of 0_2, this means that $\{\varnothing_1\}_2 = x'_2$.
  (iii) By the definition of successor, we have: for any member y_1 of $\{\varnothing_1\}_2$, there is a member z of y_1 which is such that removing z from y_1 leaves one with a member of x_2.
  (iv) From this it follows that there is a member z of $\varnothing_1$.
   (v) But that is impossible, since $\varnothing_1$ has no members.
  (vi) So, (i) is false; zero is not the successor of anything.

We now skip to axiom schema A5.

A5. $\left[F(0_2) \; \& \; \forall x_2 \left(x_2 \; \varepsilon \; N_3 \rightarrow (Fx_2 \rightarrow Fx'_2) \right) \right] \rightarrow \forall x_2 \left(x_2 \; \varepsilon \; N_3 \rightarrow Fx_2 \right)$

Here '$F(0_2)$' stands for the result of replacing all free occurrences of 'x_2' in the formula that replaces 'Fx_2' with occurrences of '0_2'. Informally, the sentence replacing '$F(0_2)$' says that zero has the property *being F*. So, each instance of A5 says that if zero has that property and if whenever a natural number has it, then its successor also has it, then every natural number has that property.

We prove this for an arbitrary instance of the schema. To do so, we assume the antecedent and try to prove the consequent. The antecedent says that (i) zero is $\mathcal{F}$ and (ii) whenever a natural number is $\mathcal{F}$, then its successor is too. We must show that if this is true, then the consequent must also true—i.e., it must be true that (iii) every natural number is $\mathcal{F}$. We begin by considering *the class that consists of all and only those natural numbers that are $\mathcal{F}$.* The axiom schema of comprehension guarantees that there is such a set. The two clauses of the antecedent tell us that this set contains zero and is closed under successor. Recall that we defined the natural numbers to be members of *every* set that contains zero and is closed under successor. Since *the class of natural numbers that are $\mathcal{F}$* is one such set, every natural number must be a member of it. Thus every natural number is $\mathcal{F}$. In this way we prove each instance of A5.

To complete the reduction, all that needs to be proved is A4.

A4. $\forall x_2 \, \forall y_2 \, [(x_2 \, \varepsilon \, N_3 \, \& \, y_2 \, \varepsilon \, N_3 \, \& \, x'_2 = y'_2) \rightarrow x_2 = y_2]$
    No two (different) natural numbers have the same successor.

To prove this we assume

   (i) x_2 and y_2 are natural numbers; and
  (ii) $x'_2 = y'_2$

and then show that (iii) follows.

  (iii) $x_2 = y_2$

In showing this, we will consider two possibilities that may at first seem strange, but will become clear.

Possibility 1

$x'_2 = y'_2 \neq \varnothing_2$ (i.e., it is not the empty set of sets of individuals)

Possibility 2

$x'_2 = y'_2 = \varnothing_2$

First consider possibility 1. For any member w_1 of x'_2 (i.e., of y'_2), eliminating one of the individuals z that is a member of it gives us a set s_1 of individuals that is a member of x_2 (from the definition of successor). Similarly, for any member w_1 of y'_2 (i.e., x'_2), eliminating one of the individuals z^* that is a member of it gives us a set of individuals s^*_1 that is a member of y_2 (from the definition of successor). Since x'_2 (y'_2) is a number, s_1 is a member of x_2 and y_2, as is s^*_1. (This follows from the fact that when n' is a number, it doesn't matter which member of a member w of n' one eliminates; the result will always be a member of n. So, it doesn't matter which member (z or z^*) of a member of x'_2 (i.e., y'_2) one eliminates; the set one ends up with must be a member of both x_2 and

y_2.[6]) Thus, x_2 and y_2 have a member in common. Since the argument applies to *every* member of x'_2 (i.e., y'_2), x_2 and y_2 will have all their members in common, and so be identical. This is sufficient to prove A4, provided we can exclude possibility 2.

How could $\varnothing_2$ be the successor of anything? Suppose there were only ten individuals available to be used to construct numbers. On Russell's definition, 10_2 = the set of all ten-membered sets of individuals. By definition, its successor, 11_2, is the set of those sets y_1 of individuals that contain a member z which, when eliminated from y_1, leaves one with a ten-membered set. But if there were only ten individuals to be used to construct numbers, then (i) 11_2 would be the empty set $\varnothing_2$ of sets of individuals, and (ii) its successor would be the set of all sets y_1 of individuals that contain a member z which, when removed from y_1, leaves one with a member of $\varnothing_2$. Since $\varnothing_2$ has no members, no y_1 is such that eliminating one of its members leaves one with a member of $\varnothing_2$. So, in this bizarre scenario, $11'_2 = \varnothing_2 = 11_2$, but $11_2 \neq 10_2$ (which, by hypothesis, isn't empty). So we would have $x' = y'$, but not $x = y$, thereby falsifying A4. Thus, if the universe had only 10 individuals (non-sets)—or indeed if it had only a finite number of individuals—to be used in the construction of Russellian numbers, A4 would fail.

It was the need to avoid this result that prompted Russell to posit the axiom of infinity in the initially strange-seeming formulation—$\varnothing_2 \notin N_3$.[7] In Russell's system, this axiom tells us that every second-level set that is itself a member of every third-level set that contains zero and is closed under successor has at least one member—thus guaranteeing sufficiently many individuals to rule out possibility 2 and ensure the provability of A4, without having to take the notion *finitely many* or *infinitely many* as primitive. Indeed, the sense in which the axiom of infinity guarantees *infinitely many individuals* can itself be defined as follows: Call a set x of individuals *finite* iff it is a member of every set that contains the empty set $\varnothing_1$ of individuals and is closed under the operation of taking the union of any member with the singleton set {a}, for each individual a. Call a set of

---

[6] This point is a little tricky. When applied to an *arbitrary* set x, the definition of successor does *not* say that no matter which member z of a member w of x' one eliminates from w, one will always be left with a member of x. It only says that for every member w of x', there is at least one element z that can be removed from w, leaving one with a member of x. So, if we applied the definition of successor to *arbitrary* sets x and y such that x' = y', the definition would not preclude the possibility that (i) eliminating a certain z from a member w of x' (y') might give us a member of x but not of y; while (ii) eliminating a different z* from w might give us a member of y but not of x. These possibilities *are* precluded when x' (i.e., y') is a natural number, as in A4. Although it is easy to see this intuitively, it is something Russell had to prove.

[7] See Russell's discussion of the role of the axiom of infinity in proving A4 on pp. 131–32 of Russell (1919a).

individuals *infinite* iff it is not finite in this sense. This is the sense in which Russell's axiom of infinity posits infinitely many individuals.[8]

With this, "possibility 2" is characterized as impossible and A4 is proved. There is, of course, a price. Whatever may be said for the assumption that there are infinitely many non-sets, it is hardly either a certainty or merely a matter of logic—as Russell recognized. Hence doing "the reduction" this way forced him to give up the strong Fregean epistemological goals he had shared earlier in his career.

3.3. Types, the Axiom of Infinity, and the Need to Avoid Paradox

I have already discussed the connection between the theory of types and the avoidance of Russell's paradox. The need to postulate the axiom of infinity is part of the same package. Depending on the sorts of things one claims there to be infinitely many of, the claim will be either more, or less, tendentious. If sets are included in the infinite array, it is relatively unproblematic to generate them indefinitely—$\varnothing$, $\{\varnothing\}$, $\{\{\varnothing\}\}$, $\{\varnothing\ \{\varnothing\}\}$, etc. The same can be said if we start with n concrete particulars and use them to construct sets. There will then be 2^n sets of such particulars, 2 to the 2^n sets of such sets, and so on. If all these items were available to us in constructing the natural numbers, the axiom of infinity would hardly be problematic, and might well be provable (and so not have to be added as an axiom, logical or otherwise). But they are not available.

Russell discusses this in chapter 8 of *Introduction to Mathematical Philosophy*, published in 1919.

> It would be natural to suppose—as I supposed myself in former days—that, by means of constructions such as we have been considering, the axiom of

---

[8] See Boolos (1994) for explanation. Note in particular the distinction between this notion of an *infinite set* and the notion of a set that is *Dedekind infinite*—i.e., that can be put into one-to-one correspondence with a proper subset of itself. (Since it is trivial that the set of natural numbers is Dedekind infinite, it is obvious that a set is Dedekind infinite if it, or a proper subset of it, can be put into one-to-one correspondence with the set of natural numbers.) Although it is easily proved that all Dedekind-infinite sets are infinite (in the above sense), the converse is not provable in standard ZF set theory (without the axiom of choice). Nor is it provable that the power set of any infinite set (i.e., the set of all and only its subsets) is Dedekind infinite. *However, one can show that the power set of the power set of an infinite set is Dedekind infinite.* Indeed, as Boolos, following Littlewood (1986), points out, Russell can be seen as demonstrating this. Let u be the universal set of individuals. Then each Russellian natural number n is a member of the power set PPu of the power set Pu of u. Each n is (by the infinity of u) nonempty and (by A4) distinct from all other natural numbers. Moreover, PPu is Dedekind infinite, since (i) the function that maps every natural number onto its successor maps the natural numbers one-to-one onto a proper subset of PPu, or, equivalently (ii) the function that assigns each natural number its successor while mapping every other member of PPu onto itself maps PPu one-to-one onto the proper subset of PPu that comes from removing zero (the set whose only member is the empty set of individuals) from PPu. Boolos (1998, p. 261) calls this result "the mathematical core of the theory of natural numbers given in *Principia Mathematica*."

infinity could be *proved*. It may be said: Let us assume that the number of individuals is n, where n may be zero without spoiling our argument; then if we form the complete set of individuals, classes, classes of classes, etc., all taken together, the number of terms in our whole set will be [n + 2-to-the-n + 2-to-the-2-to-the-n . . . *ad inf*] which is [the first countably infinite ordinal]. Thus taking all kinds of objects together, and not confining ourselves to objects of any one type, we shall certainly obtain an infinite class, and shall therefore not need the axiom of infinity.[9]

So, apparently, Russell once thought. However, by the time of "Mathematical Logic as Based on the Theory of Types," published in 1908, he had come to see this reasoning as fallacious. The basic idea is reported in *Introduction to Mathematical Philosophy*.

> The fallacy involved is the fallacy which may be called "confusion of types." . . . Now the theory of types emphatically does not belong to the finished and certain part of our subject. . . . But the need of *some* doctrine of types is less doubtful than the precise form the doctrine should take; and in connection with the axiom of infinity it is particularly easy to see the necessity of some such doctrine.[10]

Russell goes on to defend the doctrine of types as a response to his discovery of the famous paradox when studying Cantor's Theorem in 1901. After describing the paradox and the theory of types as its solution, he turns to its implications for the axiom of infinity. Returning to the earlier argument that we can generate enough things to construct all natural numbers without having to postulate the axiom of infinity, he says that it contains the same fallacy that lies behind Russell's paradox.

> The fallacy consists in the formulation of what we may call "impure" classes, i.e. classes which are not pure as to "type." As we shall see in a later chapter, classes are logical fictions, and a statement which appears to be about a class will only be significant if it is capable of translation into a form in which no mention is made of the class. This places a limitation upon the ways in which what are nominally, though not really, names for classes can occur significantly: a sentence or set of symbols in which such pseudo-names occur in wrong ways is not false, but strictly devoid of meaning. The supposition that a class is, or that it is not, a member of itself is meaningless in just this way. And more generally, to suppose that one class of individuals is a member, or is not a member, of another class of individuals will be to suppose nonsense; and to construct symbolically any class whose members are not all of the same grade in the logical hierarchy is to use symbols in a way which makes them no longer symbolize anything.
>
> Thus if there are n individuals in the world, and 2^n classes of individuals, we cannot form a new class, consisting of both individuals and classes and

[9] Russell (1919a), pp. 134–35.
[10] Ibid., p. 135.

having $n + 2^n$ members. In this way the attempt to escape from the need for the axiom of infinity breaks down.[11]

Russell here combines two important, but separable, points: the theory of types and his view of classes as "logical fictions." The latter will be discussed in section 5 below. For now, it is the connection of the former to the axiom of infinity that is important. Having explained why the needed infinity must concern individuals rather than classes, he goes on to dismiss all attempts to establish its truth by *a priori* means, and then to suggest that we have *no empirical reason* to think that it is true, either. He sums up this dispiriting conclusion as follows:

> From the fact that the infinite is not self-contradictory, but is also not demonstrable logically, we must conclude that nothing can be known *a priori* as to whether the number of things in the world is finite or infinite. The conclusion is, therefore, to adopt a Leibnizian phraseology, that some of the possible worlds are finite, some infinite, and *we have no means of knowing* to which of these two kinds our actual world belongs. The axiom of infinity will be true in some possible worlds and false in others; *whether it is true or false in this world, we cannot tell.*[12]

By "things in the world" (about which who knows how many there are), Russell means "individuals." Up to now I have said nothing about their identity, except that they aren't classes. To understand what Russell takes them to be, it is important to remember that he is speaking in 1919, when he was a logical atomist. Since chapter 12 will be devoted to his version of atomism, the details of logical atomism can be postponed until then. For now, I simply note that the "individuals" of chapter 8 of *Introduction to Mathematical Philosophy* are taken to be the ultimate bearers of properties and relations in the atomic facts that make up the world. It was the number of these things—whether finite or infinite—that Russell was claiming to be unknown (and perhaps unknowable). This is made clear in the final paragraph of the chapter, where, after characterizing them as things that could only "occur as subjects of propositions"—a phrase used in the essentially same sense that "occur as terms in propositions" is used in *The Principles of Mathematics*—he further connects individuals with proper names, logico-linguistic analysis, and ultimate metaphysical simples.

> We shall further define "individuals" or "particulars" as the objects that can be named by proper names. . . . It is, of course, possible that there is an endless regress [of analysis]: that whatever appears as a particular [named by a logically proper name] is really, on closer scrutiny, a class or some kind of complex [denoted by a description]. *If this be the case, the axiom of infinity must of course be true.* But if it is not the case, it must be theoretically possible for

[11] Ibid., p. 137.
[12] Ibid., p. 141, my emphasis.

analysis to reach *ultimate subjects*, and it is these that give the meaning of "particulars" or "individuals." *It is to the number of these that the axiom of infinity is assumed to apply.* If it is true of them, it is true of classes of them, and classes of classes of them, and so on; similarly if it is false of them, it is false throughout this hierarchy. Hence it is natural to enunciate the axiom concerning *them*, rather than concerning any other stage in the hierarchy. *But whether the axiom is true or false, there seems no known method of discovering.*[13]

Russell's conclusion is startling, and raises an obvious question. How valuable can the reduction of arithmetic to the "logic" of *Principia Mathematica* be if it rests on a "logical axiom" the truth or falsity of which cannot be discovered? The question seems to invite the answer, "Of no value at all." But that is too quick. For one thing, the passage represents Russell's perspective on the reduction nine years after it was published. Since the logically atomist position he then accepted is itself far from compelling, there is no obligation for us today to assess the significance of his logicist reduction from that perspective. For another, there are other forms that the reduction may take that don't require Russell's axiom of infinity. Finally, the question just raised about the value of the reduction presupposes that any value it has must be due to its strengthening the *justification* for our knowledge of arithmetic, and through it classical mathematics. In the next section, I will explain why this is not so.

Before doing that, it is necessary to say a word about further problems raised by the theory of types (as I have so far interpreted it)—independent of its interaction with the axiom of infinity. The first involves the fact that the reduction of arithmetic to logic must take place at a certain level of the type hierarchy. The obvious choice is the one we have made, in which the natural numbers are second-level sets, and the set of natural numbers is a third-level set. But the mere fact that we have to select a level at which to identify the natural numbers threatens an attractive feature of the Frege-Russell conception of numbers originally insisted on, in different ways, by both philosophers.

As I mentioned in chapter 1, one of Frege's stock criticisms of earlier accounts of numbers was that absolutely anything can be counted—a fact that contributed to his critique of attempts to identify numbers with marks on paper, ideas in people's minds, physical objects of any kind, or with things existing in time. His own theory avoided this criticism by making the number belonging to F be the extension of the concept *being a concept equal to F* (i.e., having an extension equinumerous with that of F). On this account, concepts at all levels of Frege's hierarchy of concepts have extensions which, being sets, are Fregean objects, and so are entities at the lowest level. So if we have distinct concepts A, B, C, the set {A, B, C} is the extension of the concept *being identical with A, B, or C*. The number

---

[13] Ibid., pp. 142–43, my emphasis.

of this concept, namely three, will contain each concept the extension of which is a trio, no matter on which level of the hierarchy the concept appears. This is what all trios have in common.

If, like Russell, we wished to ignore the difference between a concept and its extension, we might want to put this by saying that *being a member of the number three* is what is common to all trios. But this won't do. When types are introduced into the set-theoretic universe, one loses this pleasing picture of arbitrary trios bearing the same natural relation to the number three. In the type-theoretic reduction, the number three is the set of all trios *of individuals*, which means that only those trios, and no others, are members of the number three. If, as we have been assuming, sets are themselves genuine entities, then since there are many other trios of things that are not individuals, but rather occur elsewhere in the type hierarchy, they must bear quite a different relation to the number three. This threatens, or at the very least complicates, the attractive idea that membership in the number three is something that *all trios* have in common.

Ironically, it is just this idea that Russell touts in a passage from *The Principles of Mathematics* quoted in section 3.2 above and repeated here.

> In seeking a definition of number, the first thing to be clear about is what we may call the grammar of our inquiry. Many philosophers, when attempting to define number, are really setting to work to define plurality, which is quite a different thing. *Number* is what is characteristic of numbers, as *man* is what is characteristic of men. A plurality is not an instance of number, but of some particular number. A trio of men, for example, is an instance of the number 3, and the number 3 is an instance of number; but the trio is not an instance of number. This point may seem elementary and scarcely worth mentioning; yet it has proved too subtle for the philosophers, with few exceptions.
>
> A particular number is not identical with any collection of terms having that number: the number 3 is not identical with the trio consisting of Brown, Jones, and Robinson. The number 3 is something which all trios have in common, and which distinguishes them from other collections. A number is something that characterizes certain collections, namely, those that have that number.[14]

What this passage suggests may have been a central part of Russell's initial, highly natural conception of number. However, once he introduced the type hierarchy of sets, the idea could no longer be put in its most natural form. It is somewhat disconcerting that he here fails to call attention to that point. I suspect that the reason he doesn't is that by 1919, when the passage was written, he had adopted his "no-class theory," according to which classes are mere fictions, rather than genuine entities. What this amounts to, and how he could reject classes while talking freely about his type-theoretic hierarchy of classes in *Principia Mathematica,* will be

[14] Ibid., pp. 11–12.

explained in section 5. For now it is enough to notice that if there are no classes—and hence no numbers—then (i) the question of what *all trios of individuals* have in common won't be answered by citing any class to which they all bear a common relation, and (ii) the question of what *all trios* have in common, *including those that involve classes,* won't arise, and won't ruin whatever the final Russellian answer to the question of what all trios have in common turns out to be.

The second problem with the theory of types (construed set-theoretically), independent of its interaction with the axiom of infinity, is the perplexing parallel it posits between language and reality. Just as it is impossible for a set to be a member of itself, so, the theory maintains, it is *meaningless*, not just false, to say that a set is a member of itself. Just as it is impossible for a constituent at one level of the hierarchy to be identical with something at another level, so, the theory tells us, it is *meaningless* to say that something at one level is, or is not, identical with something at another level. But why should we think that? It certainly doesn't *seem* to be so. In my discussion of the theory, I have repeatedly said things like: "No constituent of one level is identical with any constituent at another level," "No set is a member of itself," and "It is impossible for a set to be a member of itself." But if the theory is correct, all those statements are meaningless. That's hard to accept. To say that no set is identical with any of its members *seems true*; and if it is, doesn't this show the type theory to be false? In explaining the theory, one finds it virtually irresistible to say things which, once one has the theory, are declared to be meaningless. But surely, one is inclined to think, there is something wrong with any theory the strictures of which pronounce the most natural and compelling descriptions of the theory itself to be incoherent.

One response to this might be to claim that the system of subscripts adopted in the theory of types somehow *expresses* or *shows* that which one futilely tries to *say* or *assert* when one utters the words "No set is identical with any of its members." The system shows this because the formation rules for '=' require identical subscripts, whereas those for 'ε' prohibit them. But this too is problematic. Although uses of a sentence S often do show something they don't state, in all such cases one can answer the question "What do they show?" by using another sentence, ⌜They show that S*⌝. However, it is quite perplexing to claim that the use of some sentences show things that are impossible to state in any way at all. This, it would seem, is what Russell needs.[15] In section 5, it will be suggested that he may have taken the constraints on meaningfulness imposed by his type restrictions to be justified by an unusual conception of quantification and its relation to truth that was bound up with his contentious "no-class" theory.

---

[15] These points about "showing" and "stating" will be discussed in more detail in volume 2 in connection with Wittgenstein's doctrine of showing in the *Tractatus*.

3.4. The Philosophical Significance of This Reduction

In section 1, I noted that Russell initially shared Frege's philosophical goals of (i) explaining how our a priori knowledge of arithmetic and, through arithmetic, of higher mathematics, is possible, and (ii) justifying this knowledge by (iii) showing mathematical truths to be provable from indispensable axioms of logic that are absolutely certain. Russell's paradox prevented Frege from achieving these goals by wrecking his reduction. Although Russell's reduction wasn't wrecked, the steps he took to avoid the paradox made these stirring epistemological goals impossible to achieve. With this came a significant weakening of the sense in which he remained a logicist in *Principia Mathematica* and later works.

Logicism, as classically understood, is the view that arithmetic and much of higher mathematics is derivable from pure logic, and so is properly a branch of logic itself. However, as we have already seen, by 1919 Russell had come to view the axiom of infinity as at best an empirical, rather than a logical, truth. This point is further illustrated by another passage from *Introduction to Mathematical Philosophy*.

> We may take the axiom of infinity as an example of a proposition which, though it can be enunciated in logical terms, cannot be asserted by logic to be true. . . . We are left to empirical observation to determine whether there are as many as n individuals in the world. . . . There does not even seem any logical necessity why there should be even one individual—why in fact there should be any world at all.[16]

Nor, it seems, does this represent a change in view from *Principia Mathematica*. As noted in Boolos (1994), there are similar comments in that work without any clear statements that the system to which arithmetic is reduced is to be regarded as purely logical.[17] Although some passages in *Introduction to Mathematical Philosophy* are less cautious,[18] and might seem to suggest that Russell remained a classical logicist, Boolos makes a good case that his considered view was a weaker form of logicism— that all *mathematical concepts* are reducible to *purely logical concepts*, even though the proofs of many mathematical truths require nonlogical existence claims about how many individuals there are.

This retreat, though significant, is not such a bad result—in part because it is extremely doubtful that the original, classical version of logicism is achievable and in part because the final, weaker version contributes to the achievement of goals different from the original aim of *justifying* mathematics, and explaining our knowledge of it. By 1907 Russell had come to appreciate the central difficulty with doing that. *We are more certain of the*

---

[16] Russell (1919a), pp. 202–3.
[17] Boolos (1994), at pp. 268–70 of Boolos (1998).
[18] See, e.g., pp. 24–25, 192, and 194–95.

axioms of arithmetic, and less in the dark about how we can know them to be true, than we are of the axioms of any purported system of logic or set theory to which they might be reduced. As he realized, his own theory of types plus axioms of comprehension and infinity raise more questions, and are subject to greater rational doubt, than the arithmetical system he derives from it. Hence the former can't be used to justify the latter.

This point generalizes far beyond the reduction in *Principia Mathematica*. Although the theory of types provided a convenient way for Russell to avoid his famous paradox, while keeping a version of what is often called "naïve set theory" (defined by his axiom schema of comprehension), this is not the only or, arguably, the best, way of developing a paradox-free theory of sets. Between 1904 and 1922 Ernest Zermelo and Abraham Fraenkel published articles jettisoning the axiom of comprehension and developing set theory in quite a different way—without types or the Russellian axiom of infinity.[19] Rather than trying to incorporate set theory into logic, they developed it as an independent mathematical theory with its own special axioms and its own domain of objects. Very quickly this became the dominant approach in set theory, and it remains so today. The reduction of arithmetic, and through it classical mathematics, to ZF can be achieved in several different ways. Without the pretense of a classical reduction to "pure logic," there is no question of *justifying* our knowledge of arithmetic by reducing it to a somehow more secure, and more highly justified, knowledge of set theory. The axioms of ZF, though powerful and more obvious than Russell's, are themselves less obvious than those of arithmetic. Thus, it would seem, the significance of reductions of arithmetic to other systems must be found elsewhere.

By 1907, Russell had seen this in connection with his own reduction, and had come to view justification as going in the other direction—from the reduced theory to the reducing theory. In that year, he gave a paper, "The Regressive Method of Discovering the Premises of Mathematics," in which he argued that sometimes previously unknown, and unobvious, logical or mathematical truths can be justified by the fact that they provide *explanations* of the known and obvious truths that follow from them.[20] The suggestion is that his unobvious logico-set-theoretic system is justified, at least in part, by the fact that the intrinsically obvious and antecedently justified theory of arithmetic follows from it.

Russell lays down three features of his reduction that contribute to this justification of his underlying system. First, he says, in showing that the arithmetical axioms, and through them the theorems of classical

---

[19] Zermelo (1904, 1908a, 1908b), and Fraenkel (1922). Zermelo (1908b) has its own axiom of infinity, which guarantees the existence of infinite sets. However, there is no theory of types, and the import of the infinity axiom is different from Russell's, and much less problematic.

[20] This paper (cited in the References as Russell 1907) wasn't published until 1973.

mathematics, are derivable from his system, we see how our overall system of mathematical knowledge is (or can be?) organized, and how different parts of that system are related to one another. Second, he notes, the reduction can lead to useful extensions and unifications of mathematical knowledge, such as the extension of our ordinary notion of number to include transfinite numbers. Third, he claims that by illuminating the logical nature of mathematics we can throw light on the philosophical question of what mathematical knowledge amounts to, and how it is achieved.[21] Similar points can be made, arguably with greater force, for reductions of arithmetic to ZF set theory.

Although there is merit in Russell's first two points, the status of the third is less clear. How exactly does his, or any related, reduction help explain what arithmetical knowledge amounts to, and how it is possible? If, as he seems to indicate, we are not in a position to know the axiom of infinity, it would seem to follow that we are not in a position to know the logicized version of arithmetic he uses the axiom to derive. So, if we do know arithmetic as it is ordinarily understood, and indeed know it a priori, it is hard to see how *Russell's reduction* could shed light on this knowledge.

A related point holds even for reductions that don't rely on the problematic axiom of infinity. Suppose that the axioms of arithmetic, along with many theorems derivable from them, are justified and known (a priori) by us to be true. Does the system to which arithmetic is reduced provide an *analysis* of arithmetical statements that explains how this knowledge is possible? In asking this question, let us stipulate that the basic principles of the reducing theory *are known a priori*, and that this knowledge is itself readily explainable. Given all this, we can be sure that *if* arithmetical sentences mean the same as the logical or set-theoretical sentences into which they are translated, then our ability to come to know the propositions expressed by the arithmetical sentences will be readily explainable.

But do arithmetical sentences express the same propositions as their logical or set-theoretic translations? This is the same question I asked about Frege's attempted reduction in section 8 of chapter 2, and the answer here is the same as it was there. It depends on the status of the "definitions" of arithmetical notions in terms of logical or set-theoretic primitives. One can, if one likes, simply *stipulate* that one will mean by various arithmetical symbols precisely that which is expressed by their logical or set-theoretic translations. With this decision, one gets the trivial result that knowledge of the reducing theory includes knowledge of what one calls "arithmetic." But this is unsatisfying. What propositions, we are inclined to ask, did arithmetical sentences express before anyone came up with the reduction? Surely we don't want to deny that mathematicians, philosophers, and ordinary people used such sentences to perform correct

---

[21] See pp. 282–83 of the 1973 printing of the paper.

arithmetical calculations. Presumably, the sentences they used had meanings and expressed propositions that many *knew* to be true. What did *they* know when they knew *that (3 × 3) + (4 × 4) = (5 × 5)*?

There are two reasons to think that the proposition they knew was *not* the same as the proposition expressed by a translation of the sentence into a system of logic or set theory. First, the latter proposition is too complicated. Many people who know *that (3 × 3) + (4 × 4) = (5 × 5)* wouldn't understand a long and complex logical or set-theoretic translation of it, even if it were explained to them. It is implausible to claim that what they have known all along is something it took a mathematical genius to discover. Second, as I have indicated, there are many different ways of reducing arithmetic to systems of logic or set theory. One doesn't have to take zero to be the (second-level) set the only member of which is the (first-level) empty set, or to define successor exactly as Russell did. There are very different ways of defining arithmetical concepts in terms of logical or set-theoretical concepts. Given two such ways, there will typically be two very different translations of an arithmetical sentence like '(3 × 3) + (4 × 4) = (5 × 5)'. When the details are spelled out, it is plausible to suppose that the two translations express different propositions, in which case they can't both express *the* proposition *that (3 × 3) + (4 × 4) = (5 × 5)*. Moreover, there may be no obvious reason to think that one translation is more faithful to our untutored understanding of arithmetical sentences than the other. In such a case, the most reasonable thing to say may be that neither expresses the same proposition as the arithmetical sentence, though both express propositions that are, in a certain sense, equivalent to it.[22]

Though quite plausible, this view presents Russell and others seeking a metaphysically and epistemologically real reduction of numbers to something else with a difficulty. If ordinary arithmetical propositions are merely equivalent to, rather than identical with, their reductive counterparts, in what sense can an explanation of how the latter are known, or knowable, contribute to an explanation of how the former are known, or knowable? The answer to this question is far from clear. One can say, as I did in chapter 2, that (i) if we can know the reducing theory a priori, and (ii) we can also know a priori that the definitions used in the reduction yield statements of the reducing theory that are *equivalent* to statements of the reduced theory, then (iii) we will have shown that the reduced theory *can be known a priori* (via this route), even if this isn't how ordinary people actually know it. However, this is not terribly exciting, since if one were

---

[22] This is the argument of Benacerraf (1965), which is there extended to the claim than no set-theoretic identification of a number—e.g., 3 with the set of triples—can be correct. The argument for this is that for every such identification there is a different, equally good one that arises from another equally good reduction of arithmetic to logic or set theory. Since all these reductions and concomitant identifications can't be correct, and no one is better than any of the others, it is argued that none is correct. In short, no number is identical with any set.

genuinely worried, prior to the reduction, that we don't or can't know arithmetic a priori—or if one were philosophically perplexed about how such knowledge was possible—it is likely that similar worries or perplexities would apply to (i) or (ii) above.

Because of this, it is hard to maintain that even the best of reductions will vindicate the third claim in Russell (1907)—namely that they will throw light on the philosophical question of what mathematical knowledge amounts to, and how it is achieved. However, this does not undermine his other points. Showing arithmetic, and, through it, classical mathematics, to be derivable from a plausible underlying set-theoretic system does indicate how mathematics is (or can be) organized, and how different branches of it are (or can be) related to one another. In addition, a successful reduction can lead to useful extensions and unifications of mathematical knowledge. These are valuable results to which Russell's path-breaking reduction contributed.

3.5. Logicism as Precursor

For Frege and Russell, mathematics was a science, mathematical knowledge was highly informative, and the reduction of classical mathematics to arithmetic, and arithmetic to logic, was originally motivated by a desire to systematize and extend that science, while putting it on the firmest of foundations. Although their reductions, and those they helped to inspire, were looked upon with admiration by later logically and scientifically minded philosophers, their fundamental conceptions of logic and mathematics were not widely shared by their successors. While continuing to view logic and mathematics as a priori, and to be friendly to the idea that the contents of mathematical statements are the same as those of corresponding logical statements, a number of the most important philosophical successors of the two great logicists purchased these threads of continuity with classical logicism at the price of draining mathematical statements of much of their substance and informativeness.

An illustration of this is provided by the renowned logical positivist and philosopher of science Carl Hempel in his summary article "On the Nature of Mathematical Truth," in 1945. Addressing the issue of justification, Hempel writes:

> If therefore mathematics is to be a correct theory of the mathematical concepts in their intended meaning, it is not sufficient for its validation to have shown that the entire system is derivable from the Peano postulates plus suitable definitions; *rather, we have to inquire further whether the Peano postulates are actually true* when the primitives are understood in their customary meaning. This question, of course, can be answered only after the customary meaning of the terms "0", "natural number", and "successor" have been clearly defined.[23]

---

[23] Benacerraf and Putnam (1983), p. 374, my emphasis.

In this passage Hempel indicates that he takes the problem of justifying the arithmetical axioms to require defining the primitive arithmetical terms that appear in them. After saying this, he immediately turns to the Russellian definitions, which he accepts as giving "the customary meaning" of the terms '0', 'natural number', and 'successor'. He stresses the fact that by using these definitions plus the postulates of Russell's system, one can *prove* the arithmetical axioms to be true.[24] This, according to Hempel, solves the problem of justification.

Summing up his take on logicism, he enunciates, without elaboration or apparent justification, a position even stronger and more philosophically ambitious than the classical logicist position from which Russell himself had forthrightly retreated. Hempel says:

> Mathematics is a branch of logic. It can be derived from logic in the following sense:
>
> a. All the concepts of mathematics, i.e. of arithmetic, algebra, and analysis, can be defined in terms of four concepts of pure logic.
> b. All the theorems of mathematics can be deduced from those definitions by means of the principles of logic (including the axioms of infinity and choice).
>
> In this sense it can be said that the propositions of the system of mathematics as here delimited are true by virtue of the definitions of the mathematical concepts involved, or that they make explicit certain characteristics with which we have endowed our mathematical concepts by definition. *The propositions of mathematics have, therefore, the same unquestionable certainty which is typical of such propositions as "All bachelors are unmarried," but they also share the complete lack of empirical content which is associated with that certainty:* The propositions of mathematics are devoid of all factual content; they convey no information whatever on any empirical subject matter.[25]

Not only are mathematical propositions supposed to be "unquestionably certain" because they are analytic, the explanation of how they can be known to be true a priori is supposed to bottom out in the explanation of how we can know trivialities like *All bachelors are unmarried* to be true. The idea, by this time, was that we can know them to be true because they are *true in virtue of meaning*—where *what they mean* is something we surely know. In short, according to Hempel the truths of mathematics are analytic because they can be reduced to logical truths plus definitions, both of which can, transparently, be known to be true merely by understanding them.

Although there are elements in this of the views of Frege and Russell, the overall picture is different. It is true that Frege aimed to show arithmetic

---

[24] In ibid., p. 375, fn. 9, Hempel indicates that by the "customary meaning" of the relevant terms he has in mind what he calls "the logical sense of 'meaning'" rather than "the psychological sense."

[25] Ibid., p. 378, my emphasis.

to be analytic, in the sense of being reducible to logic plus definitions. However, he never claimed that logical truths are themselves true by virtue of meaning, and so—in principle—knowable simply by understanding the linguistic conventions governing the logical vocabulary. Moreover, as we saw in section 8 of chapter 2, the sense in which Frege "defined" arithmetical terms using logical terms in *The Foundations of Arithmetic* was *not* one that satisfied his later criteria for sameness of ordinary meaning, or sense. Russell was even more distant from the Hempelian picture.

By the time Hempel was writing, the logical positivists had something else to work with—namely Rudolf Carnap's account of truth by convention. To apply this idea to logic itself is, very roughly, to view the meanings of logical words as fixed by the intention to endow them with whatever meanings they must have in order to make true the syntactic forms we call "classical logical truths." But if the truth and certainty of logic could successfully be explained in this way, then presumably the truth and certainty of Zermelo-Fraenkel set theory, or of Peano arithmetic itself, could be seen as the direct result of semantic stipulations about its vocabulary—without the necessity of going through a reduction in the style of Frege or Russell. As we will see in the next volume of this series, there are serious objections to Carnap's truth by convention that cast doubt on its application to either logic or mathematics. However, in its heyday it was a powerful force driving scientifically minded philosophers to a view that incorporated certain classically logicist ideas about the foundations of mathematics into an overall picture rather different from that of Frege and Russell. The beginning of this post–Frege-Russell view of logic and mathematics was the *Tractatus* (also to be discussed in the next volume), where Wittgenstein enunciates his view that all of mathematics, and indeed all necessary truths, are nothing more than "tautologies."

4. RUSSELL'S HIGHER-ORDER LOGIC AND REDUCTION: SECOND PASS

The formulation of Russell's reduction in sections 3.1 and 3.2 was designed to highlight its heavily set-theoretical content. To that end, what I characterized as his logico-set-theoretic system was, more or less transparently, a version of naïve set theory. Far from being a system with no subject matter of its own but providing the epistemological bedrock for systematic reasoning about any subject, it is an elementary mathematical theory of a special class of objects—sets. Though capable of providing a kind of foundation for arithmetic and much else in mathematics, its level of certainty is less than arithmetic's, and its epistemological status is not significantly privileged over other areas of mathematics. All of this was underlined, and made easier to see, by formulating the system in a first-order language with a special set-membership predicate.

By contrast, Russell's own formulation made use of higher orders of quantification and employed no such predicate. Though I won't attempt to close the large gap between his formulation and mine, I will try to narrow it a little by translating the first-order system of the previous section, plus the definitions of arithmetical primitives, into a system of higher-order logic incorporating a theory of types. This will not change the content and nature of the reduction. However, expressing it in this slightly more Russellian way will allow me to say a few words about (i) the intermingling of mathematical logic and set theory in the early decades of their development, (ii) the fundamental distinction between first-order logic and second-order logic established decades after *Principia Mathematica*, and (iii) the extent to which substantive set-theoretical concerns remain central parts of the standard model theory of higher-order logic today.

The first step is to move from a first-order language with 'ε' to a second-order language without it. To do this, we add new n-place predicate variables—X, Y, Z, etc.—for arbitrary n. (We could, if we wished, add new n-place function variables too, but I will ignore such quantification here). Syntactically, the predicate variables are just like predicate constants and so may combine with singular terms to form atomic formulas. The new variables combine with '$\exists$' and '$\forall$' to form second-order quantifiers. When $\Phi(X)$ is a formula containing the predicate variable X, $\ulcorner\forall X\,\Phi(X)\urcorner$ is a universal generalization of $\Phi(X)$, and $\ulcorner\exists X\,\Phi(X)\urcorner$ is an existential generalization.[26] The standard textbook treatment of predicate variables takes them to range over sets. In the now standard model theory, a first-order language is interpreted by a model consisting of a set D of individuals that constitute the domain over which the first-order quantifiers range, plus an assignment to each name of an individual in D, an assignment to each n-place function sign of an n-place function from n-tuples of individuals in D to individuals in D, and an assignment to each predicate constant of a set of n-tuples of individuals in D. When second-order quantifiers are added, they range over all and only the subsets of D. If the language contains function signs capable of taking predicates as arguments, these are assigned functions from n-tuples of possible predicate extensions (subsets of D) onto predicate extensions.

Thinking of this as the beginning of our type theory, we characterize second-order quantifiers as ranging over first-level sets (of individuals). Using existential quantification as our illustration, we characterize the difference between first- and second-order quantification as follows:

---

[26] I use 'X', 'Y', 'Z' in the metalanguage as metalinguistic variables ranging over predicate variables 'X', 'Y', 'Z' in the object language. I use '$\Phi(X)$' in the metalanguage as a metalinguistic variable that ranges over formulas of the object language containing X (occurring free in Φ).

First-Order Quantification

'∃x' is a 2nd-level predicate the extension of which is a 2nd-level set $\exists_{S2}$. The members of $\exists_{S2}$ are all and only those 1st-level sets that contain at least one member. So ⌜∃x Φx⌝ is true iff *the 1st-level set of individuals that is the extension of Φx (the individuals of which the formula is true) is a member of $\exists_{S2}$* iff there is at least one individual the assignment of which to 'x' makes Φx true.

Second-Order Quantification

'∃X' is a 3rd-level predicate, the extension of which is a 3rd-level set $\exists_{S3}$; its members are all and only those 2nd-level sets that contain at least one 1st-level set as member. So ⌜∃X (X...)⌝ is true iff *the 2nd-level set that is the extension of (X...)—i.e., the set of 1st-level sets of which the formula is true—is a member of $\exists_{S3}$* iff there is at least one set of 1st-level sets the assignment of which to 'X' makes the formula (X...) true. Example: '∃X(X Aristotle & X Plato & ~X Pericles)' is true iff the 2nd-level set of those 1st-level sets of which Plato and Aristotle are members but Pericles is not has at least one member.

The rules for the corresponding types of universal quantification are exactly analogous.

The language of our type theory will be hierarchical. First-order formulas are at level 1 of the hierarchy. Second-order formulas (of the kind just illustrated) are at level 2. The levels can be continued indefinitely. For all finite $n > 1$, we have n^{th}-order quantification over sets of level $n - 1$. For example, call any pair of first-level sets *equal* iff they have the same members. We may express this relation using the second-level, two-place predicate—'( ) $=_2$ ( )'—which combines with a pair of first-level predicates F and G to form an atomic formula, ⌜F $=_2$ G⌝.[27] The extension of the new predicate is the second-level set of ordered pairs $<s_1, s_1>$, where s_1 is a first-level set (of individuals). Next we replace '$=_2$' with a 2-place, second-level predicate variable Y_2 that ranges over second-level sets. This gives us the formula ⌜F Y_2 G⌝ the extension of which is the third-level set that contains all and only those second-level sets that contain the ordered pair the

---

[27] To reduce clutter, I will not include indices on predicates, or predicate variables, to specify the number of arguments they take, but will take that to be understood. Similarly I will not index either singular term variables (over individuals), or predicate variables over first-level sets. For example, it is to be understood that the unadorned 'x' is assigned entities of type zero as value, and the unadorned 'P' is assigned level-1 sets as values. 'F' and 'G' above are used as metalinguistic variables over first-level predicates/formulas.

first member of which is the set of individuals of which F is true and the second member of which is the set of individuals of which G is true. The extension of the existential quantifier $\lceil \exists Y_2 \rceil$ will then be fourth-level set $\exists_{S4}$ the members of which are those third-level sets that contain at least one second-level set as member. Thus, the quantified sentence $\lceil \exists Y_2 [F \ Y_2 \ G_1] \rceil$ is true iff the third-level set that is the extension of the formula, $\lceil [F_1 \ Y_2 \ G_1] \rceil$, is a member of the set $\exists_{S4}$, *and so is nonempty*. In other words, the quantified sentence will be true iff there is at least one second-level set that contains the ordered pair consisting of the extension of F followed by the extension of G. This is an example of third-order quantification, which is quantification over second-level sets—i.e., sets of sets of individuals. (The order level comes from the level of set designated by the formula that is the argument of the quantifier.) The hierarchy continues in this way for all finite levels.

Next we restate Russell's three axioms in the higher-order system, starting with the axiom schema of comprehension.

Axiom Schema of Comprehension[28]

$$\exists Y_n \ \forall X_{n\text{-}1} \ (F_n (X_{n\text{-}1}) \longleftrightarrow Y_n (X_{n\text{-}1}))$$

This tells us that for any condition on items of level $n - 1$ stated by a formula of at most level n, there is a set of level n of all and only those items at the previous level that satisfy the condition. Instances are obtained by replacing '$F_n (X_{n-1})$' with any formula of level n in which the only variable that has free occurrence is 'X_{n-1}'. (A formula of level n is one containing a subscripted term of level n, but no higher level.) This schema can be thought of as the infinite

---

[28] Here I state a simple schema involving formulas with a single free variable and the sets that are their extensions. This can be extended to corresponding schemata involving formulas in which any finite number m of variables have free occurrences in the formulas. (With ordered n-tuples, thought of as individual elements, the extensions of relational predicates that are guaranteed by comprehension will be sets of these.) A further complication would come into play if we allowed an operator '†' which, when combined with a predicate G of level n, produced a singular term $\lceil †G \rceil$ of level n designating the extension of G, which could then serve as argument for an n-level predicate. For then we could have, for example, $\lceil \exists Y \ \forall x (\exists X \ (x = X \ \& \sim Xx) \longleftrightarrow Yx) \rceil$ as an instance of the axiom schema in which the set being defined would be among the entities from which it was being defined. Russell regarded such definitions as viciously circular, and so excluded them. (Since we are not allowing this transition from a predicate to a singular term naming the predicate's extension, we don't get such an instance anyway). In order to be explicit about the exclusion, Russell himself didn't allow formulas replacing 'F_n' in the schema to contain any free, or bound, occurrences of a predicate variable of level n. However, this created difficulties when it came to defining the set of natural numbers and ensuring its existence through the axiom schema of comprehension. To get around these problems, he introduced a further axiom schema called the axiom schema of reducibility. I won't go into these complications, which are briefly treated on pp. 40–42 of Burgess (2005).

collection of schemata corresponding to the levels of the hierarchy.

$$\exists Y_1 \, \forall x \, (F_1 x \longleftrightarrow Y_1 x)$$
$$\exists Y_2 \, \forall X_1 \, (F_2(X_1) \longleftrightarrow Y_2(X_1))$$
$$\exists Y_3 \, \forall X_2 \, (F_3(X_2) \longleftrightarrow Y_3(X_2))$$

.
.
.

The axioms that are instances of these schemata guarantee the existence of the same sets that our earlier, first-order, version of the schema did—while avoiding Russell's paradox in the same way.

Nevertheless, the higher-order schemata seem to, and to a certain extent do, have a status different from that of the first-order schema of comprehension stated earlier. Looked at from the perspective of the now textbook model theory for first- and higher-order systems (which incorporates standard set theory), it is clear that instances of the first-order schema are *not* logical truths, while instances of the second-order schema are. The former aren't logical truths because there are models in which the predicate 'ε' is assigned a relation that doesn't verify them. By contrast, instances of the schema $\exists Y_1 \forall x (F_1 x \longleftrightarrow Y_1 x)$ are logical truths. Since every model that assigns an interpretation to the formula replacing $F_1 x$ will determine a subset (possibly empty) of the domain D of individuals given by the model, and since the second-order quantifier is interpreted as ranging over all these subsets, the quantified sentence will be true in every model. A similar point can be made for the higher-level schemata encompassed by the new version of the axiom schema of comprehension. Putting aside lingering disputes about whether higher-order logic is really *logic*, this result can be viewed as vindicating the idea that—Russell's axiom of infinity aside—the higher-order system to which arithmetic is to be reduced really is a system of logic, whereas the first-order system of the previous section isn't.

How significant is this? On the one hand, it makes sense of the widespread perception that Russell's logicist reduction was in fact an attempt to ground mathematics in something that is genuinely recognizable as logic. On the other hand, we now know that the differences between first-order logic and second-order logic are profound. Among the striking differences are these:

(i) Whereas first-order logical truth is fully formalizable, second-order logical truth is not—i.e., although every first-order sentence that is true in all interpretations can be proved from the same decidable set of axioms by finitely many applications of the same finitely many purely mechanical rules of inference, it is impossible for any such formalized proof procedure for second-order logic to derive all (and only) the second-order logical truths.

(ii) Whereas any inconsistent set of first-order sentences has a finite subset that is inconsistent, this is not true of second-order sentences.

(iii) Every set of first-order sentences that are jointly satisfiable in a countably infinite model are jointly satisfiable in uncountably infinite models, and conversely.

(iv) There are differences between first- and second-order arithmetic. Second-order Peano arithmetic results from the first-order Peano axioms by substituting the second-order quantified version of the induction axiom $\forall Y[[Y(0) \ \& \ \forall x(Yx \rightarrow Yx')] \rightarrow \forall x(Nx \rightarrow Yx)]$—for the first-order axiom schema of induction $[F(0) \ \& \ \forall x(Fx \rightarrow Fx')] \rightarrow \forall x(Nx \rightarrow Fx)$. Whereas the second-order system is complete (and consistent), no complete consistent first-order recursive axiomatization of arithmetic is possible. So, whereas all arithmetical truths are logical consequences of second-order Peano arithmetic, for every consistent first-order recursive axiomatization, some (in fact infinitely many) first-order arithmetical truths are not logical consequences of it—since for some (in fact infinitely many) such sentences S, neither S nor its negation is a theorem of the first-order system.[29]

(v) Whereas second-order Peano arithmetic is categorical (any two models are isomorphic), no first-order arithmetical theory is categorical; so even those first-order theories that are true of the natural numbers—0, 1, 2, . . . are equally true of progressions that are *not* isomorphic to the natural numbers—0, 1, 2, . . . o*, o**, o***, ... In short, we can specify the natural numbers up to isomorphism using a second-order system, but not a first-order system.

These differences are correlated with the different ontological commitments of first- and second-order theories. While the former are committed to the individuals in the domain of first-order quantification, the latter are also committed to all sets of those things. One particularly graphic illustration of the intermingling of second-order logic with set theory is provided by a highly controversial question in set theory. Are there any sets larger than the set of natural numbers but smaller than the set of all sets of natural numbers (where set S1 is larger than set S2 iff S2 can be mapped one-to-one onto a subset of S1, but S1 can't be mapped one-to-one onto any subset of S2)? The hypothesis that there are no such sets, called "the continuum hypothesis" (CH), has been proven to be independent of the axioms of standard ZF set theory. This means that neither CH nor its negation ~CH is a logical consequence of those axioms. For this reason, there has been no decisive proof of CH or ~CH—and it may turn out that we will never be able to determine which is true. Nevertheless, there

---

[29] Note, I here use 'N' as a predicate the extension of which is the set of natural numbers instead of as a singular term naming that set—which was how I used it in section 3 when reducing arithmetic to a first-order theory employing the predicate 'ε'.

are sentences A and B of second-order logic for which the claim that *A is a second-order logical truth* is provably equivalent to CH and the claim that *B is a second-order logical truth* is provably equivalent to ~CH. On the supposition that either CH is true or ~CH is true, there is a second-order sentence the establishment of which as a logical truth (true in all second-order models) requires the resolution of a set-theoretic mystery that may turn out to be irresolvable. Nothing like this holds for first-order logic.[30]

Some see the differences between first- and second-order logic, and the heavy involvement of the latter with set theory, as a reason for denying that the latter is really logic, and restricting logic proper to first-order systems. The most prominent of those taking this view is W.V.O. Quine, who, in a section of Quine (1986) entitled "Set Theory in Sheep's Clothing," writes:

> [Some philosopher/logicians] have continued to quantify predicate letters, obtaining what they call a higher-order predicate calculus. The values of these variables are in effect sets; and this way of presenting set theory gives it a deceptive resemblance to logic. One is apt to feel that no abrupt addition to the ordinary logic of quantification has been made; just some more quantifiers, governing predicate letters already present. In order to appreciate how deceptive this line can be, consider the hypothesis '$\exists y \forall x (x \, \varepsilon \, y \leftrightarrow Fx)$'. It assumes a set $\{x: Fx\}$, determined by an open sentence in the role of 'Fx'. This [the axiom schema of comprehension] is the central hypothesis of set theory, and the one that has to be restrained in one way or another to avoid the paradoxes. The hypothesis itself falls out of sight in the so-called higher-order predicate calculus. We get '$\exists G \forall x (Gx \leftrightarrow Fx)$', which evidently follows from the genuinely logical triviality '$\forall x (Fx \leftrightarrow Fx)$' by an elementary logical inference. There is no actual risk of paradox as long as the ranges of values of 'x' and 'G' are kept apart, but still a fair bit of set theory has slipped in unheralded.[31]

Though I don't see that the domain of logic must be restricted in the way Quine suggests, there are indeed fundamental differences between the first- and higher-order systems. Very roughly, first-order logic enforces tight epistemological constraints on logical truth and consequence; its interpretations are more or less ontologically uncontentious; and, as a result, its descriptive power is limited. By contrast, higher-order logic encodes weaker epistemological constraints on logical truth and consequence, and—on its textbook model-theoretic interpretation—incorporates enough set theory to generate substantial ontological commitments. As a result, it has much more descriptive power than first-order systems.

---

[30] For discussion about what this does or doesn't show about second-order logic, see chapter 8 of Etchemendy (1990), Gomez-Torrente (1999), and the appendix to chapter 4 of Soames (1999).

[31] Quine (1986), p. 68.

Looking back today on the logicist project, it is important to recognize that since none of the above results were known at the time, it was natural for early logicists to see first-, second-, and higher-order quantification as a seamless continuum, and to think of logic and set theory as tightly intertwined. As Quine puts it:

> Pioneers in modern logic viewed set theory as logic; thus Frege, Peano, and various of their followers, notably Whitehead and Russell. Frege, Whitehead and Russell made a point of reducing mathematics to logic; Frege claimed in 1884 to have proved in this way, contrary to Kant, that the truths of arithmetic are analytic. But the logic capable of encompassing this reduction was logic inclusive of set theory.[32]

It is important to keep this point in mind when assessing the philosophical—as opposed to the technical—import of Frege's and Russell's reductions of arithmetic to logic. Whereas their original epistemological goals are more in line with what we now know about first-order systems, their aim of reducing arithmetic to *logic*, and their practice in attempting to achieve this goal, made higher-order systems the natural choice.

With this we can get back to translating the earlier, first-order formulation of the reduction onto the new higher-order version. Next up are the axioms of extensionality and infinity.[33] They can be stated as follows.

The Axiom of Extensionality

$$\forall X \, \forall Y \, [\forall z \, (X z \longleftrightarrow Yz) \to X = Y]$$
$$\forall X_n \, \forall Y_n [\forall Z_{n-1} \, (X_n(Z_{n-1}) \longleftrightarrow Y_n(Z_{n-1})) \to X_n =_{n+1} Y_n]$$

If a and b are sets of individuals, they are one and the same set iff they have the same members. If a and b are both n-level sets of sets of level n − 1, they are one and the same iff they have the same members.

The Russellian Axiom of Infinity

$$\sim N_3(\varnothing_2)$$

Here, 'N_3' is the third-level predicate the extension of which is the set of all second-level sets that are natural

---

[32] Ibid., pp. 65–66.

[33] Although Russell himself didn't posit axioms of extensionality, he got the effect of such axioms by a complicated route connected with his choice of "propositional functions" (rather than sets) as the real values of higher-order variables. This move to "propositional functions" will be covered in the next section. For a brief discussion of Russell's means of securing the effects of extensionality, see Burgess (2005), pp. 37–40. One minor point: if, like Russell, one defines '$X = Y$' as '$\forall z \, (Xz \longleftrightarrow Yz)$', the (first-level) instances of '$\forall X \, \forall Y \, [\forall z \, (X z \longleftrightarrow Yz) \to X = Y]$' will be theorems anyway, without positing it as an axiom.

numbers. '$\varnothing_2$' is second-level predicate the extension of which is the empty second-level set.

In reading these formulas, one should note that $X_n =_{n+1} Y_n$ is a formula in which a higher-order identity predicate is flanked not by singular terms, but by predicates of the previous level. The identity claim is true iff the extensions of the predicates (relative to an assignment) are the same. It may also be noted that Russell *defines* identity as satisfaction of all the same predicates, which (here) amounts to membership in the same sets. Though one may quarrel with the conceptual priorities implicit in this procedure, it doesn't cause problems so long as we have all the sets we need. However, vexing issues will arise when I discuss the "no-class theory."

The next step is to add higher-order translations of the abbreviatory definitions used in explaining the reduction. As before we start with descriptions.

(i) Definite Descriptions

$$\Psi \text{ (the } x: \Phi x) \cong_{df} \exists x \, \forall w \, [(\Phi(w) \longleftrightarrow w = x) \, \& \, \Psi(x)]$$
$$\Psi \text{ (THE } X_n \, \Phi(X_n)) \cong_{df} \exists X_n \forall W_n [(\Phi(W_n) \longleftrightarrow W_n =_{n+1} X_n) \, \& \, \Psi(X_n)]$$

Again, '$\Psi(\ )$' and '$\Phi(\ )$' stand for formulas in which the terms within their brackets appear. The definition tells us that any formula containing an occurrence of a description (represented on the left-hand side) is an abbreviation of the corresponding formula (represented on the right)—subject to the proviso that the description always be given narrow scope. This means that when the description occurs in a multi-clause formula Θ, the formula Θ abbreviates is the one gotten from the definition by taking '$\Psi(\ )$' to be the smallest sub-formula of Θ containing the occurrence of the description. The level on the hierarchy of the resulting formula will be determined by the level of the formulas represented by '$\Psi(\ )$' and '$\Phi(\ )$'. They will always be at least of level n. However, they may be of level $n + 1$ when the levels of the formulas represented by '$\Psi(\ )$' or '$\Phi(\ )$' are level $n + 1$—e.g., when the description to be eliminated occurs as an argument of a higher predicate in the formula represented by 'Ψ (the x: Φx)'.

Now we turn to the abbreviatory definitions based on definite descriptions.

(ii) Definition of an n-level predicate the extension of which is *the empty set of (n − 1)-level elements*

$$\varnothing_n \cong_{df} \text{THE } X_n: \forall Z_{n-1} \, [\sim X_n(Z_{n-1})]$$

Together (i) and (ii) specify that the formula $\Psi (\varnothing_n)$ is an abbreviation of the formula

$$\exists X_n \forall W_n \, [(\forall Z_{n-1} \sim W_n(Z_{n-1}) \longleftrightarrow W_n =_{n+1} X_n) \, \& \, \Psi(X_n)]$$

which tells us that the formula represented by '$\Psi(X_n)$' is true of the unique empty set of level n.

(iii) Definition of an n-level predicate the extension of which is the set the only member of which is the $(n - 1)$-level element w

$$\{W_{n-1}\}_n \cong_{df} THE\ X_n\ [\forall Z_{n-1}(X_n\ (Z_{n-1}) \longleftrightarrow Z_{n-1} =_n W_{n-1}]$$

(iv) Definition of an n-level predicate the extension of which is the set of $(n - 1)$-level elements of which the formula represented by '$\Psi(Z_{n-1})$' is true.

$$\uparrow Z_{n-1}\ \Psi(Z_{n-1}) \uparrow_n \cong_{df} THE\ X_n\ [\forall Z_{n-1}(\Psi(Z_{n-1}) \longleftrightarrow X_n(Z_{n-1})]$$

(v) Definition of an n-level predicate the extension of which is the intersection of the extensions of a pair of n-level predicates. Here '∩' stands for a function mapping pairs of n-level predicate extensions onto predicate extensions.

$$[X_n \cap Y_n]_n \cong_{df} THE\ Z_n\ [\forall W_{n-1}(Z_n(W_{n-1}) \longleftrightarrow (X_n(W_{n-1})\ \&\ Y_n(W_{n-1})))]$$

(vi) Definition of an n-level predicate the extension of which is the union of the extensions of a pair of n-level predicates. Here '∪' is of the same category as '∩' in (v).

$$[X_n \cup Y_n]_n \cong_{df} THE\ Z_n\ [\forall W_{n-1}(Z_n(W_{n-1}) \longleftrightarrow (X_n(W_{n-1}) \vee Y_n(W_{n-1})))]$$

(vii) Definition of an n-level predicate the extension of which is the complement of the extension of an n-level predicate—i.e. the set of all elements of level $n - 1$ not in that extension.

$$Comp(X_n)_n \cong_{df} THE\ Y_n[\forall Z_{n-1}(Y_n(Z_{n-1}) \longleftrightarrow \sim X_n(Z_{n-1}))]$$

Finally, we state the definitions of zero, successor, and natural number in the new system.

Definition of Zero

$$0_2 =_3 \{\varnothing_1\}_2$$

'0_2' is a second-level predicate the extension of which—namely zero—is the second-level set the only member of which is the empty set of individuals.

Definition of Successor

$$X'_2 =_3 \uparrow Y_1[\exists z(Y_1 z\ \&\ X_2(Y_1 \cap Comp(\{z\}_1)_1)_1]\uparrow_2$$

The successor of a second-level set designated by 'X_2' is the set of all first-level sets that contain an individual which, when removed from them, leaves one with a member of the set designated by 'X_2'. Otherwise put, the successor of the second-level set designated by 'X_2' is the set of all first-level sets available to serve as the extension of 'Y_1' that contain an individual z such that the intersection of the set assigned to 'Y$_1$' with the complement of the set the only member of which is z—i.e., with the set containing everything except z—is a member of the set designated by 'X$_2$'.

These definitions interact to give us definitions of '1', '2', and the other numerals, just as before. The only difference is that these numerals are not singular terms but second-level predicates the extensions of which are the sets that served as referents of the singular-term numerals of the previous reduction. This reflects the fact that what was said by the previous reduction remains in all relevant respects the same; only the packaging is different. This repackaging is completed by the definition of the third-level predicate 'N$_3$', the extension of which is the set of natural numbers.

The Definition of Natural Number

$$N_3 =_4 \uparrow X_2[\forall Y_3((Y_3(0_2) \,\&\, \forall Z_2(Y_3(Z_2) \to Y_3(Z_2'))) \to Y_3 (X_2))]\uparrow_3$$

The set of natural numbers (which is the extension of the predicate 'N$_3$') is the third-level set of all and only second-level sets that are members of every third-level set that contains zero and is closed under successor.

With this the reduction of arithmetic to logic can proceed just as before. The only difference is that the arithmetical definitions and theorems will be repackaged by eliminating the set membership predicate 'ε', and trading singular terms referring to numbers for higher-order predicates the extensions of which are numbers. Other than that, the proofs are essentially the same.

A1. $N_3(0_2)$
   Zero is a natural number.
A2. $\forall X_2 [N(X_2) \to N(X_2')]$
   The successor of any natural number is a natural number.
A3. $\sim \exists X_2 (0_2 =_3 X_2')$
   Zero is not the successor of anything.
A4. $\forall X_2 \forall Y_2 [(N_3(X_2) \,\&\, (N_3(X_2) \,\&\, X_2' = Y_2') \to X_2 = Y_2]$
   No two (different) natural numbers have the same successor.
A5. $[F_3(0_2) \,\&\, \forall X_2 (N_3(X_2) \to (F_3(X_2) \to F_3(X_2')))] \to \forall X_2 (N_3(X_2) \to F_3(X_2))$
   This is an axiom schema that stands for the infinite set of axioms obtainable by substituting for 'F$_3$' any third-level formula in the language that contains free occurrences of the predicate variable 'X$_2$' and only that variable. 'F$_3(0_2)$' stands for the result of replacing all free occurrences of 'X$_2$' in the formula replacing 'F$_3(X_2)$' with occurrences of '0$_2$'. Informally, it says that zero has the property *being* F. Thus, each instance of A5 says that if zero has that property and if whenever a natural number has

that property, its successor does too, then every natural number has the property.

Of course, once we have higher-order quantification it is much more natural to state the induction axiom as A5+—with massive increase in expressive power and loss of formal provability of many of the resulting theorems of the system.

A5+. $\forall Z_3 [Z_3(0_2) \,\&\, \forall X_2(N_3(X_2) \to (Z_3(X_2) \to Z_3(X_2')))] \to \forall X_2(N_3(X_2) \to Z_3(X_2))$

Finally, we have the arithmetical definitions of addition and multiplication.

> Definitions: Addition (+) and Multiplication (×)
>
> D+. $\forall X_2 \,\forall Y_2 \,[(N_3(X_2) \,\&\, N_3(Y_2)) \to ((X_2 + 0_2) =_3 X_2 \,\&\,$
> $(X_2 + Y_2') =_3 (X_2 + Y_2)')]$
>
> Here '+' denotes a two-place function on the extensions of pairs of level 2 predicates that maps them onto second-level sets. For any natural number, the sum of that number and zero is that number, and the sum of that number and the successor of a second number is the successor of the sum of the first and second numbers.
>
> D*. $\forall X_2 \forall Y_2 \,[(N_3(X_2) \,\&\, N_3(Y_2)) \to ((X_2 \times 0_2) =_3 0_2 \,\&\,$
> $(X_2 \times Y_2') =_3 (X_2 \times Y_2) + X_2)]$
>
> Here '×' denotes a two-place function on the extensions of pairs of level 2 predicates that maps them onto second-level sets. For any natural number, the product of that number and zero is zero, and the product of that number and successor of a second number is the sum of the first number and the product of the two.

This completes the reformulation of the reduction originally presented in section 3, this time using a system of higher-order logic. Though the formulation is different, the essential philosophical significance is the same.

5. PROPOSITIONAL FUNCTIONS, SUBSTITUTIONAL QUANTIFICATION, AND THE NO-CLASS THEORY

We now come to a puzzling irony about Russell's reduction in *Principia Mathematica*. On the one hand, his theory of types, his implicit set theory, and his vision of mathematics grounded in logic-cum–set theory strongly influenced logicians and scientifically minded philosophers in the decades to follow. Tarski, Carnap, Hempel, and Quine all saw it as an important achievement, and took lessons from it about the importance of set theory for the development of logic and mathematics.[34] Quine's own approach to set theory owed much to Russell, and when Tarski used the theory of types it was a logical theory based on a stratification of the set-theoretic universe. On the other hand, by the time he and Whitehead wrote *Principia Mathematica*, Russell had long rejected sets, or "classes," which he now regarded as "logical fictions." Unlike the system sketched in the previous section, his higher-order variables were said to range over "propositional functions." Moreover, by this time his view of such functions had become a radically deflationary version of his earlier "realist" view of them as nonlinguistic entities. The result was a thoroughly de-ontologized interpretation of his technical reduction. However, despite the importance that Russell attached to this philosophical interpretation, it had virtually no impact on later mathematicians, logicians, and philosophers—for whom an ontology of sets was relatively unproblematic, and whose preferred method of studying them often came not from a set-theoretic version of Russell's theory of types, but from the axiomatic treatment of ZF set theory.

Although Russell allows himself to use the language of "sets/classes," he explicitly disavows commitment to sets/classes as entities. His general position is sketched in section 2 of chapter 3 of the introduction to *Principia Mathematica*.

> The symbols for classes, like those for descriptions, are, in our system, incomplete symbols: their uses are defined, but they themselves are not assumed to mean anything at all. That is to say, the uses of such symbols are so defined that when the *definiens* is substituted for the *definiendum*, there no longer remains any symbol supposed to represent a class. Thus classes, so far as we introduce them, are merely symbolic or linguistic conveniences, not genuine objects as their members are if they are individuals.[35]

The contextual definition of the usual class notation is given at *20.01 of Russell and Whitehead (2010).

$$F (\uparrow x\ Gx \uparrow) =_{df} \exists H\ [\forall y\ (Hy \leftrightarrow Gy)\ \&\ F(H)]$$

According to this definition, a formula that seems to say that F is true of the (first-level) set of individuals satisfying G is really an abbreviation for a more complex formula that says that F is true of something that is true of all and only the individuals that satisfy G. According to Russell, this something is "a propositional function." Suppose, for the moment, that propositional functions are what we have so far taken them to be—functions

---

[34] Much of the influence of Russell's (ramified) theory of types was filtered through Ramsey (1925), which replaced it with the "simple theory of types" that freed the construction from the Axiom of Reducibility.

[35] Russell and Whitehead (1910), pp. 71–72.

from objects to propositions. On this view, to say that such a function is true of an object is to say that it assigns the object a true proposition, and to say that propositional functions are *extensionally equivalent* is to say they are true of the same things. (Similarly for two properties or for a property and a propositional function.) So whenever G and G* stand for extensionally equivalent properties or propositional functions, $\ulcorner$F ($\uparrow$x: Gx$\uparrow$)$\urcorner$ and $\ulcorner$F ($\uparrow$x: G*x$\uparrow$)$\urcorner$ will, according to the definition, agree in truth value—as they should.

Next consider a propositional function that takes a property or propositional function as argument. Call it *extensional* iff whenever it is true of its argument A, it is true of all arguments extensionally equivalent to A. As Russell notes at *Principia* *20, not all propositional functions are extensional in this sense.

> [the propositional function designated by] 'I believe $\forall$x Φx' is an *intensional* function [and so not extensional] because even if $\forall$x (Φx $\longleftrightarrow$ Ψx), it by no means follows that I believe $\forall$x Ψx provided that I believe $\forall$x Φx.[36]

Suppose that $p_{\Phi x}$ and $p_{\Psi x}$ are different but extensionally equivalent propositional functions, the former mapping an arbitrary individual a onto the proposition *that if a is a human, then a is a human* and the latter mapping a onto the proposition *that if a is a featherless biped, then a is a human*. Now let Y be a first-level predicate variable. Then the propositional function designated by $\ulcorner$I believe $\forall$x Yx$\urcorner$—which maps propositional functions onto propositions expressed by the corresponding belief ascriptions—may assign $p_{\Phi x}$ a true proposition about what I believe, while assigning $p_{\Psi x}$ a false proposition. Thus, the propositional function designated by the belief ascription is *intensional*, rather than extensional. However, since, as Russell plausibly holds, *only* extensional propositional functions are relevant to mathematics, the system in *Principia Mathematica* can be restricted to them. When one does this, the only thing about the proposition assigned by a propositional function to a given argument that matters to the construction is its truth value. This being so, we can reinterpret the entire construction in terms of functions from arguments to truth values (rather than propositions)—*without losing anything essential to the reduction.*[37]

Although the result is pleasing, it is also perplexing. A function from arguments to truth values is *the characteristic function of the set* of things to which it assigns truth. There is no mathematically significant difference between working with sets and working with their characteristic functions; anything done with one can be done with the other. Nor does there seem to be any important ontological or philosophical difference between the two. But then, what can be the point of the contextual definition *20.01 of sets in terms of their characteristic functions? To most of

---

[36] Ibid., p. 187.
[37] This in fact is what is done in Burgess (2005); see pp. 39–40.

the mathematicians, logicians, and philosophers who followed Russell, there seemed to be none. Although they realized that their perspective on the reduction differed from Russell's, they believed that their take on these ontological issues simplified matters without losing anything of significance.

Even if one agrees with this, as I do, one still may wonder why Russell didn't see things that way. The first thing to remember is that by the time *Principia Mathematica* appeared in 1910, he no longer believed that there were any nonlinguistic entities that could play the role of propositions or propositional functions. Since chapter 9 has already covered his rejection of propositions, I won't go into it further. Of course, if there are no propositions, there can be no functions from objects to propositions either. However, there is more to be said about Russell's reasons for rejecting propositional functions as nonlinguistic things.

The story begins in 1903. A proposition in *The Principles of Mathematics* is a structurally complex object "unified" by a relation functioning "as a verb," and thereby (really) relating the concepts or objects occurring in the proposition as terms. Propositional functions are the result of replacing a constituent of a proposition with a variable, the latter being understood in an unusual way. By "a variable," Russell then meant not a linguistic expression, but the most general denoting concept. Denoting concepts were constituents, occurring in term position in propositions, that stand for predication targets, rather than being the targets themselves. For example, he spoke of the denoting concept *any number* as "ambiguously denoting" individual numbers, which are the things said to be odd in the proposition *that any number is odd or even*. A variable was a generalization of this—a concept ambiguously denoting every entity. A propositional function containing such a variable was a kind of degenerate proposition; though not itself a bearer of truth value, it is said to be true or false *for the different values of its variable*.[38]

Although this view is rather obscure, nothing truly significant would change if propositional functions were taken to be genuine functions mapping individuals and properties onto propositions. Russell's view of classes was more unstable. Granting their existence in *The Principles of Mathematics*, he added an appendix in which they form a type hierarchy provisionally adopted as a way of avoiding paradox.[39] This led to difficulties, including some arising from the impossibility of locating the natural numbers at any finite level—since elements at any level can be numbered.[40] Dealing with this while continuing to avoid paradox was a daunting challenge that soon led him to abandon classes altogether. As reported in Klement (2004), for a time he tried different views of propositional

[38] See Russell (1903a), pp. 12, 13, 19–20, and 263.

[39] More will be said about this in section 6.

[40] Russell (1903a), pp. 525–26.

functions without satisfying himself that he could justify taking them as entities while preventing any such function from taking itself as one of its arguments—thereby threatening contradiction.

By contrast, when genuine concepts (universals) like humanity were involved, Russell had no problem recognizing that they could occur both *as concept* and *as term* in the same proposition. For him, 'Humanity is human' was not senseless but false, while 'Concepthood is a concept' is true—the latter expressing a true, and the former a false, proposition. This won't lead to paradox provided one doesn't allow *being a concept that doesn't apply to itself* to be a concept, which, I suspect, was fine with Russell. So, if genuine universals are simple (and relatively few in number), and complexity is dealt with by logical construction, the burden of blocking the paradoxes will fall on the materials used in such constructions (classes or propositional functions). The problem for Russell was that since classes and propositional functions must be virtually unbounded, admitting them as entities seemed to require restricting the range of propositions in which they can occur as terms (i.e., as logical subjects of predication). One might think that such restrictions could be imposed by fiat, but justifying them was problematic. In addition, Russell seemed to think, there must be a level at which all genuine entities can truly be said to be logical subjects. Since this threatened contradiction, by 1906 he had begun exploring ways of treating not just classes but also (nonlinguistic) propositional functions as "logical fictions."[41]

In *Principia Mathematica* he speaks of propositions and propositional functions in a variety of different, and not always consistent, ways. However, most of the time he seems to take propositions to be sentences, and propositional functions to be formulas one gets from sentences by replacing an occurrence of an expression with a free occurrence of a variable (now thought of as an expression). Thus, in *An Inquiry into Truth and Meaning* (1940, p. 192) he says, "In the language of the second-order, variables denote symbols, not what is symbolized," while in *My Philosophical Development* (1959, p. 92) he says, "Whitehead and I thought of a propositional function as an expression." If this really was what the authors meant, and if propositional functions were the values over which their higher-order variables ranged, it would seem that a sentence of the form '∀P ...P...' must mean that *every value of the formula '...P...'* is true.

Language very like this is not hard to find in *Principia Mathematica*. For example, in section 3 of chapter 3 of the introduction, Russell sketches the idea of a hierarchy of notions of truth that apply to the different levels of his type construction. Assuming that truth has already been defined for quantifier-free sentences at the lowest level, he explains first-order quantification as follows:

---

[41] The story of Russell's struggle with propositional functions and classes between 1903 and 1908 is summarized on pp. 16–22 of Klement (2004).

Consider now the proposition $\ulcorner\forall x\ \Phi x\urcorner$. If this has truth of the sort appropriate to it, that will mean that every value of Φx has "first truth" [the lowest level of truth]. Thus if we call the sort of truth that is appropriate to $\ulcorner\forall x\ \Phi x\urcorner$ "second truth," *we may define* $\ulcorner\forall x\ \Phi x\urcorner$ *as meaning* $\ulcorner$*every value for 'Φx' has first truth*$\urcorner$. . . . Similarly, if we denote by $\ulcorner\exists x\ \Phi x\urcorner$ the proposition $\ulcorner\Phi x$ sometimes$\urcorner$, i.e. as we may less accurately express it, $\ulcorner$'Φx' with some value for 'x'$\urcorner$, we find that $\ulcorner\exists x\ \Phi x\urcorner$ has second truth if there is an x with which Φx has first truth; thus *we may define* $\ulcorner\exists x\ \Phi x\urcorner$ *as meaning* $\ulcorner$*some value for 'Φx' has first truth*$\urcorner$.[42]

Here, in addition to assuming that a similar explanation can be given for higher-order quantification, we are to assume that "first-truth" conditions and meanings have been given for quantifier-free sentences at the lowest level.

For atomic sentences, the truth conditions are assumed to involve correspondence with atomic facts that consist of particular individuals standing in n-place relations. For truth-functions of atomic sentences, the identities of the corresponding facts are not specified; this was a problem that continued to worry Russell for years to come. Although he admits, in Russell (1918), the need for both negative and general facts—the existence of which are necessary and sufficient for the truth of negative and quantificational sentences—there is no such recognition in *Principia Mathematica*. Instead he seems to reject general facts, and to give the truth conditions of quantified sentences in terms of the truth of their instances.

Supposing that propositional functions are formulas with free occurrences of variables, we next need to know what *a value* of such a function is. Since Russell insists that such a value doesn't contain the propositional function itself, it is most natural to take the value to be a sentence that results from substituting an individual constant for all free occurrences of the variable in the propositional function. On this interpretation, his above claim about what quantified sentences *mean* takes them to predicate truth of the (closed) sentences that are "values" of the corresponding open formulas that are identified with "propositional functions"; universal generalizations say that each of these "values" is true, while existential generalizations say that some are. Thus, it would seem, quantificational statements are metalinguistic, *even though their quantifier-free instances are not.*

This won't do. First, it would make all arithmetical statements arising from the reduction metalinguistic statements about Russell's logical language, with the result that all arithmetical knowledge would be characterized as knowledge of that language. This surely can't be correct. Second, it would drive an epistemological and metaphysical wedge between quantified statements and their instances. For when quantificational statements are understood in this way and $\ulcorner\Phi n\urcorner$ makes no claim whatever about

---

[42] Russell and Whitehead (1910), p. 42, my emphasis. I have here changed Russell's notation in inessential ways, and used corner quotes to clear up some of the use/mention sloppiness.

language, it will be neither an a priori nor a necessary consequence of ⌜∀x Φx⌝ (if the semantic properties of Φx are neither essential to it nor knowable a priori), while ⌜∃x Φx⌝ will be neither an a priori nor a necessary consequence of ⌜Φn⌝ (on the same assumption). Third, it doesn't fit what Russell says four pages later in *Principia Mathematica* about the relationship between the facts in virtue of which universal generalizations are true and those in which their instances are.

> We use the symbol ⌜∀x Φx⌝ to express the general judgment which asserts all judgments of the form Φx. Then the judgment "all men are mortal" is equivalent to "∀x('x is a man' implies 'x is mortal')"—i.e. (in virtue of the definition of implication) to "∀x (x is not a man or x is mortal)." As we have just seen, the meaning of 'truth' which is applicable to this proposition is not the same as the meaning of 'truth' which is applicable to "x is a man" or to "x is mortal." And generally, in any judgment ⌜∀x Φx⌝ the sense in which this judgment is or may be true is not the same as that in which Φx is or may be true. If Φx is an elementary judgment, it is true when it *points to* a corresponding complex [i.e., to a fact that makes it true]. But ⌜∀x Φx⌝ does not point to a single corresponding complex [i.e., there is no single fact that makes it true]: the corresponding complexes [facts] are as numerous as the possible values of x.[43]

If ⌜∀x Φx⌝ *meant* that all substitution instances of the formula Φx were true (in the appropriate sense of 'truth'), then the condition necessary and sufficient for its truth *would be* the existence of a general fact about language, and not the existence of the multiplicity of nonlinguistic facts corresponding to all its instances (which seems to be what Russell has in mind). Moreover, the metalinguistic judgment expressed by ⌜∀x Φx⌝ would not, as Russell indicates that it does, straightforwardly "assert" all the nonmetalinguistic judgments expressed by its instances. For these reasons, the metalinguistic interpretation of quantification suggested by some of Russell's remarks seems not to have been his consistent and considered view (if indeed he had one).

There is another interpretation that could be given to his remarks. On this interpretation, the quantifiers in his reduction are what are now called "substitutional." When so understood, they don't range over objects of any kind—linguistic or nonlinguistic. Instead they are associated with substitution classes of expressions. Although their *truth conditions* are stated metalinguistically, *their content* is supposed to be nonlinguistic. Thus, they are not subject to the objections just raised against the metalinguistic interpretation of the quantifiers. Using objectual quantifiers over expressions, we can give substitutional *truth conditions* of quantified sentences in the normal way—as Russell does. ⌜∀x Φx⌝ and ⌜∃x Φx⌝ are true, respectively, iff all, or some, of their substitution instances are true, where

---

[43] Ibid., p. 46. Though I have not tried to remove all the use/mention confusions here, I have added corner quotes to make the passage a bit clearer.

the latter are gotten from replacing free occurrences of 'x' in Φx by an expression in the relevant substitution class. This explanation will work, provided that the truth values of the sentences on which the quantified sentences depend are already determined before reaching the quantified sentences, and so do not themselves depend on the truth or falsity of any higher-level substitutionally quantified sentences.[44]

For our purposes, there are three important points to note. First, if one combines the hierarchical restriction inherent in substitutional quantification with Russell's system of higher levels of quantification, strong versions of the type restrictions he needs will fall out from the restrictions on substitutional quantification, without requiring further justification. Second, on the substitutional interpretation, there is no need for what look like "existential" generalizations—i.e., $\ulcorner \exists x\, \Phi x \urcorner$, $\ulcorner \exists P\, \Phi(P) \urcorner$, $\ulcorner \exists P_2\, \Phi(P_2) \urcorner$, etc.—to carry any ontological commitment. They won't—as long as the relevant substitution instances can be true even when the expression replacing the bound variable doesn't designate anything. Third, for this reason, it is tempting to think that no quantificational statements in the hierarchy carry any ontological commitments not already carried by quantifier-free sentences at the lowest level. Since Russell took accepting their truth to commit one only to individuals and properties, it would be natural for him to take himself to be free to characterize classes, numbers, and nonlinguistic propositions and propositional functions as merely "logical fictions," while nevertheless appealing to them when "speaking with the vulgar."

These points have recently been made in Klement (2004). After drawing attention to the previous two passages from *Principia Mathematica* quoted above, he writes:

> Russell seems to endorse a substitutional (or Kripkean), as opposed to an on-tological (or Tarskian), semantics for quantification. . . . The core idea is that a formula involving a *free higher-order variable*, e.g., "$\Phi!a$", has as its substitution instances first-order formulae containing the constant "a" occurring in log-ical subject position . . . one or more times. . . . Just as a proposition involv-ing an individual quantifier is true just in case all its substitution instances are, similarly a proposition involving a higher-order quantifier is as well. So "$\forall\Phi(\Phi!a)$" has "third truth" if and only if all closed substitution instances of "$\Phi!a$" have "second truth." Russell's different notions of truth . . . are derived from the recursive truth definition for his language; ramification [the sys-tem of type restrictions in *Principia Mathematica*] is *required* in order for the truth conditions not to be circular. Russell uses the notation "$\Phi!a$" for a func-tion whose arguments are predicative functions of a, i.e. those not involving quantification over functions; if we allowed impredicative expressions to be substitution instances of "$\Phi!a$", then the conditions under which "$\forall\Phi(\Phi!a)$"

---

[44] For explanation, see Kripke (1976). See Soames (1999), pp. 86–90, for an application of Kripke's main point to an argument given in Tarski (1935).

has third truth could not be defined in terms of second truth alone. This, and not any ontological doctrine, is the heart of the "vicious circle principle" [justifying the type restrictions]. Russell seems to have anticipated Kripke's suggestion . . . that higher-order quantification can be given a substitutional semantics only if the allowable instances of the variables cannot contain expressions involving bound variables of the same order.[45]

Simply put, Klement takes the quantifiers in the construction given in *Principia Mathematica* to be entirely substitutional, and the reduction itself not to be committed to the existence of numbers, sets, nonlinguistic propositions, or nonlinguistic propositional functions. Although normal first-order quantification "over individuals" is itself claimed to be substitutional, Russell is seen as ontologically committed to the referents of the logically proper names in the substitution classes of these quantifiers because their existence is required for the quantifier-free sentences that contain them to be true.[46]

This interpretation of Russell does not, of course, credit him with mastering all of what we now recognize to be the ins and outs of substitutional quantification and its difference from objectual quantification. However, it does claim to capture an important element in his thought, and to develop it more clearly, precisely, and consistently than he himself did. The end result, it is felt, harmonizes and vindicates his central logical and philosophical views—an improvement on the actual Russell, but a modest one, the key elements of which were there all along.

Though I find this interpretation illuminating in some respects, I don't agree with it. Not knowing precisely what Russell was thinking, I don't dispute the idea that his radically deflationist thoughts on ontology, his need for a philosophical justification for his theory of types, and his contention that "the vicious circle principle" underlying his type theory provided a unified treatment of a broad range of logical and semantic paradoxes, may well have contained inchoate substitutional elements of the sort identified by Klement, Landini, and others. However, I don't think that the substitutional reading of *Principia Mathematica* makes good philosophical or mathematical sense on its own, or coheres well with Russell's most important goals and doctrines. If he did, when waxing metatheoretic, sometimes succumb to the substitutional temptation, the mathematical work of the reduction shouldn't be made contingent on it, and he would have done better to resist that temptation in the philosophical and metatheoretic remarks he made about his technical system.

---

[45] Klement (2004), pp. 28–29.

[46] Ibid., p. 28, n 25. Landini (1998) also adopts a substitutional reading of Russell's higher-order quantifiers, but takes the first-order quantifiers over individuals to be objectual (whereas Klement takes the substitutional reading of Russell to incorporate all quantification). An early suggestion that Russell might be read as interpreting quantification substitutionally is explored in Sainsbury (1979).

My reasons are divided into two parts. The first spotlights deleterious effects of the substitutional interpretation on Russell's logicist reduction. The second focuses on disadvantages of the substitutional account for his more general philosophical logic. One issue I will discuss along the way is whether, if higher-order quantification in *Principia Mathematica* is to be interpreted as substitutional, first-order quantification should then be so understood. Or (for defenders of "On Denoting"), since first-order quantification must be objectual, shouldn't higher-order quantification also be?

Suppose, for the moment, that Russell's first-order quantification is substitutional, and so depends on quantifier-free sentences at the first level of his hierarchy. These sentences will include all truth-functional compounds of the atomic sentences (which consist of n-place predicates combined with n occurrences of names). Predicates stand for n-place properties, while names designate individuals. An atomic sentence is true iff its names designate individuals that have the property designated by its predicate. Since Russell's axiom of infinity requires infinitely many individuals (non-sets), a substitutional interpretation of first-order quantification will require *infinitely many names* that can be substituted for individual variables in order to secure all the instances needed to evaluate quantified sentences. On this interpretation, $\ulcorner \forall x\ \Phi x \urcorner$ will be true iff every sentence is true that results from substituting an occurrence of a name associated with 'x' for each occurrence of 'x' in Φx; $\ulcorner \exists x\ \Phi x \urcorner$ is true iff at least one such substitution instance is true.

Second-order quantification occurs at the next level of the hierarchy. Here predicate variables are associated with predicates of the first level. The associated predicates include all simple predicates used to construct atomic sentences, plus complex predicates. For any first-level sentence in which simple predicates occur, we need a complex predicate for each of the ways of abstracting one or more of the predicates via lambda abstraction—as illustrated by expressions like $\lambda F \lambda G[\Phi\ (...F...G)]$. All these predicates, simple and compound, are associated with the predicate variables. So, on the substitutional interpretation, $\ulcorner \forall X_1\ \Phi(X_1) \urcorner$ is true iff every sentence is true that results from substituting an occurrence of a predicate, simple or complex, associated with 'X_1' for each occurrence of 'X_1' in $\Phi(X_1)$; similarly for second-order existential quantification.

Looking at this from the outside (where we continue to allow ourselves to speak of sets), this means that our substitutional construal of second-order quantification parallels ordinary objectual second-order quantification over *those sets that are extensions of first-level predicates of individuals* (including complex predicates). This process is repeated for third-order quantification, except that here complex predicates are the only ones in the substitution class. This level mimics objectual quantification over *those sets that are extensions of second-level predicates, members of which are sets of individuals that are extensions of first-level predicates.* The hierarchy continues uniformly from there on.

Note the diminished expressive power of the substitutional interpretation of higher-order quantification. Whereas the objectual quantifiers range over *all sets at a given level*—both those that are extensions of predicates at that level (of the Russellian logical language) and those that are not—the substitutional quantifier mimics only quantification over the former. If, as is standardly assumed, every sentence and every predicate is a finite sequence of the logical and nonlogical vocabulary, the domain of all sets at a given level will far outstrip the domain of all sets that are the extensions of predicates at that level.[47] As a result, the expressive power of the underlying "logical" theory to which arithmetic is to be reduced is diminished by treating its quantifiers substitutionally. This diminishment affects Russell's derivations.

Recall his definition of *natural number*, patterned on Frege's original idea. The first-order formulation, using an explicit membership predicate, is as follows.

The Definition of Natural Number

N = the smallest set containing zero and closed under successor.

$$N_3 = \ \uparrow x_2 \left[\forall y_3 \left((0_2 \ \varepsilon \ y_3 \ \& \ \forall z_2 \ (z_2 \ \varepsilon \ y_3 \rightarrow z'_2 \ \varepsilon \ y_3)) \rightarrow x_2 \ \varepsilon \ y_3) \right] \uparrow_3$$

The set of natural numbers is the third-level set of all and only those second-level sets x that are members of every third-level set y that contains zero and is closed under successor.

The higher-order formulation is put in the form of a definition of a third-level predicate.

The Definition of Natural Number

$$N_3 =_4 \ \uparrow X_2 \left[\forall Y_3 \left((Y_3(0_2) \ \& \ \forall Z_2 \ (Y_3(Z_2) \rightarrow Y_3(Z_2')) \rightarrow Y_3(X_2)) \right] \uparrow_3$$

The set of natural numbers (which is the extension of the predicate 'N_3') is the third-level set of all and only

---

[47] This can be mitigated by allowing individual formulas to be infinitely long, and interpreting higher-order substitutional quantifications in terms of substitution instances that are infinitely long. This strategy is meticulously developed in Hodes (2012), which shows it to be needed by a substitutional interpretation of higher-order quantifiers in *Principia Mathematic* leading to a ramified theory of types, without classes or nonlinguistic propositions and propositional functions. As Hodes notes, the price of this approach is high, since it renders Russell's logical language incapable of being understood by agents whose cognitive powers are finite. See Gödel (1944) for further discussion.

second-level sets that are members of every third-level set
that contains zero and is closed under successor.

The definition plays a crucial role in Russell's proof of the arithmetical
axiom of mathematical induction, stated below both as a first-order set-
theoretic schema and as a higher-order quantified sentence.

A5. $[F(0_2) \mathbin{\&} \forall x_2 (x_2 \varepsilon N_3 \to (Fx_2 \to Fx'_2))] \to \forall x_2 (x_2 \varepsilon N_3 \to Fx_2)$

Here '$F(0_2)$' stands for the result of replacing all free occurrences of 'x_2'
in the formula that replaces 'Fx_2' with occurrences of '0_2'. Informally,
the sentence replacing '$F(0_2)$' says that zero has the property *being F*. So,
each instance of A5 says that if zero has that property, and if whenever
a natural number has it, then its successor also has it, then every natural
number has that property.

A5+. $\forall Z_3[Z_3(0_2) \mathbin{\&} \forall X_2(N_3(X_2) \to (Z_3(X_2) \to Z_3(X_2')))] \to \forall X_2(N_3(X_2) \to Z_3(X_2))$

Earlier, I sketched the idea behind a proof of A5 by indicating how to
prove an arbitrary instance, which involves assuming the antecedent and
proving the consequent. The antecedent says that zero *is F* and whenever
a natural number *is F*, then its successor is too. Given this, one shows, following Frege (and Russell), that every natural number *is F*. To do so one
considers *the class that consists of all and only those natural numbers that are F*.
The axiom schema of comprehension guarantees that there is such a set.
The two clauses of the antecedent tell us that it contains zero and is closed
under successor. Since the set of natural numbers is *defined* as the set that
contains all and only those sets that contain zero and are closed under
successor, and since we have assumed that *the class of natural numbers that
are F* is one of those, it follows that every natural number must be a member of it, in which case, every natural number is F. Thus we prove A5.

The derivation involves a crucial feature of the definition of 'N'. Expressed in unabbreviated form, 'N' is an open quantified formula containing free occurrences of 'x_2' (or 'X_2'). Understood objectually, the crucial
quantification is over all level-three sets—i.e., sets the members of which
are sets of sets of individuals. Among those sets are, of course, *the set of
natural numbers itself*, and *the set of natural numbers that are F* (used in the
proof of mathematical induction). Suppose we had restricted the quantification used in defining 'N' to ranging over *those level-three sets that are the
extensions of (complex) predicates involving at most quantification over level-
two sets*. In so doing we would have excluded the set of natural numbers
itself, as well as the set of natural numbers that are F, from the range of
quantifiers—*thereby weakening the definition and calling the proof of mathematical induction into question*.

This is what the substitutional interpretation of the quantifiers used in
the reduction mimics. The crucial constraint on the substitutional quantifier leading to this result is one that excludes any expressions in the substitution class associated with a substitutional variable from containing

that variable. (When this constraint is violated, truth cannot be defined for the original quantified sentence.) So when we have a substitutional interpretation of the quantification employed in the definition of 'N' and the statement of mathematical induction, the complex predicates that are substitutable for the third-level predicate variable can't themselves contain such a variable. With this, we lose the simple Fregean way of understanding and proving mathematical induction. Thus, the strongest argument against the substitutional interpretation of quantification in *Principia Mathematica* is that it threatens the reduction there.[48]

To make a long and highly complex story very short, the basic situation seems to be this. The idea behind Russell's definition of number and his reduction of arithmetic to logic was fundamentally the same as Frege's. But to block the set-theoretic paradox, he needed a theory of types. In point of fact, the theory he adopted—called *the ramified theory of types*—was far more complex than the simple type theory I have informally employed (which itself is sufficient to block the paradox). In the ramified theory, each type restricting the arguments a propositional function can take is subdivided into a hierarchy of orders that impose restrictions on variables bound by quantifiers (so that whatever is defined using a quantifier cannot be among what the quantifier ranges over). The effect has often been seen as imposing something like constructability requirements on elements in the hierarchy, so that nothing can be specified at a higher order except in terms of expressions the extensions of which are already fixed at lower orders. Imposing a substitutional constraint on the quantifiers will have this effect. Thus, one who thought of quantification substitutionally and saw it as a way to avoid not only classes, but also nonlinguistic propositions and propositional functions, might well arrive at the ramified theory that Russell in fact employed.[49]

However, one who takes this route weakens the underlying logic-cum–set theory, affecting, among a great many other things, the natural way of thinking about the definition of natural numbers, and of proving the induction axiom. Russell's remedy was to add another axiom, called *the Axiom of Reducibility*, which I have not previously mentioned and will not discuss in any detail. Suffice it to say that the axiom was not historically well received. As Kamareddine, Laan, and Nederpelt put it:

> The validity of the Axiom of Reducibility has been questioned from the moment it was introduced. In the introduction to the second edition of the *Principia*, Whitehead and Russell admit: "This axiom has a purely pragmatic justification; it leads to the desired results, and no others. But clearly it is not the sort of axiom with which we can rest content." (*Principia Mathematic*, xiv)[50]

[48] For fruitful related discussion, see Gödel (1944), pp. 145–46.

[49] Whether or not substitutional quantification is a viable reason to ramify is illuminatingly explored in Hodes (2012).

[50] Kamareddine, Laan, and Nederpelt (2002), p. 233.

The result was a search for a way to eliminate the axiom, and with it the ramified theory of types, in favor of what has been called *the simple theory of types,* which dispenses with the orders within types—and hence with constructability-like requirements that might be secured by a substitutional interpretation of higher-order quantification. Successful solutions along these lines can be found in Chwistek (1924, 1925), Ramsey (1925), and Hilbert and Ackermann (1928). It is through the prism of works such as these that *Principia Mathematica,* rightfully, had its greatest historical influence.

From this (historically victorious) perspective, it is apparent that a substitutional reading of the quantification in *Principia Mathematica* understates its logical power. Even apart from Russell's reduction, the difference between first- and second-order Peano arithmetic is the difference between a formalization in which the axioms include every instance of the first-order *axiom schema [F(0) & ∀x (Fx → Fx')] → ∀x (Nx → Fx)* obtainable by substituting for 'F' a formula in the language of arithmetic that contains free occurrences of the variable 'x', and a formalization that uses the second-order *axiom* of induction *∀Y[[Y(0) & ∀x(Yx → Yx')] → ∀x(Nx → Yx)].* The enormous difference between the logical power of the two systems alluded to in section 4 above is due to a simple fact. Although the extension of every formula replacing 'F' in one of the first-order induction axioms is among the sets over which the second-order variable 'Y' ranges, the sets included in the range of that variable vastly outstrip those definable by first-order formulas. This explanation *depends* on an objectual interpretation of second-order quantification. If the second-order quantifier were read substitutionally (with a substitution class consisting of the formulas that can replace 'F' in the first-order schema), this difference in logical power would be obliterated.

Now that we recognize the power of objectual second-order quantification, and its relevance for arithmetic, the idea of depriving the higher-order system of *Principia Mathematica* of that power should be a nonstarter; we certainly shouldn't do so in order to avoid ontological commitment to sets. Though Russell wasn't in a position to know this in 1910, sets have proven so useful for all sorts of theories—not least of which are model theories for logic and semantics—that giving them up seems virtually out of the question. It is not even clear that we would know how to investigate the differences between first- and second-order logic without sets.[51] To read *Principia Mathematica* in a way that distances him from the progress made in the tradition he helped to create would be to let tenuous and philosophical thoughts about the elimination of classes—which were at best underdeveloped—obscure his positive contribution.

---

[51] Although there are new interpretations of second-order systems that use the notion of plural quantification, and although these interpretations have important uses, it is doubtful that they should be seen as replacing or eliminating set-theoretic interpretations of second-order systems.

Worse, commitment to an imagined world without classes—as well as Fregean concepts and real (nonlinguistic) functions from objects to (non-linguistic) propositions—threatens basic Russellian commitments. Without these abstracta, even first-order quantification must be substitutional, and Russell's ontological commitments will be limited to infinitely many individuals and properties, at the lowest level of the hierarchy.[52] Apart from worries inherent in this idea (to which I will return shortly), there are further worries concerning mathematical theories the ontological commitments of which go beyond those of arithmetic. Since there are uncountably many real numbers, theories of the reals seem to be committed to uncountably many things. If the reals are definable as set-theoretic constructions of the natural numbers, this isn't a problem for the reduction of mathematics to logic, provided that the set-theoretic constructions are real things. However, if there were no natural numbers, no sets, and no nonlinguistic functions to use in these constructions, what would remain is simply not rich enough to provide a foundation for the rest of higher mathematics, which defeats the purpose of Russell's reduction of arithmetic to "logic," quite apart from the fact that this first reduction is itself threatened by the expressive weakness of substitutional quantification.[53]

I now turn to a different set of criticisms of the substitutional interpretation of quantification in *Principia Mathematica*. In addition to being ill-suited for Russell's logicist program, it has other problems, not least of which are the threats it poses to other aspects of his philosophy. The chief of these concerns his signature philosophical achievement—the generalized theory of first-order quantification presented in "On Denoting." The point can be made with any generalized quantifier, including the unrestricted universal quantifier. According to "On Denoting," the proposition *that everything is F* predicates *always assigning a truth when given an object as argument* of the function that maps an argument o onto the proposition that predicates F-hood of o. This quantified proposition isn't equivalent to any collection of propositions, finite or infinite: that o_1 is F, that o_2 is F, ... For any such collection C, it is possible for the general proposition to be false even if all the particular propositions in C are true.[54] (Just imagine possible scenarios in which there are more individuals, of the relevant sort, than are covered by the individuals in C.) Also, knowing that everything is F doesn't guarantee knowing any instance of that claim, though one who knows the general proposition, while also knowing of o, has enough to conclude that o is F.

Russell did not repudiate these thoughts, so congenial to the usual objectual understanding of first-order Frege-Russell quantification, when

[52] Hereafter, I will include properties under the heading 'individuals', which will include both universals and particulars. See Hodes (2012) for discussion.

[53] Gödel (1944) also comments on this.

[54] In this paragraph, I use 'F' as a schematic letter.

writing volume 1 of *Principia Mathematica*. Granted, the passage quoted above—about the "second truth" of quantified sentences being defined in terms of the "first truth" of their quantifier-free instances—can, along with other passages cited by Klement, be read as suggesting a unified substitutional treatment of all quantification in *Principia Mathematica*. Nevertheless, such an interpretation doesn't fit well with passages from *Principia* like the following.

> Our judgment that all men are mortal collects together a number of elementary judgments. It is not, however, composed of these, since (e.g.) *the fact that Socrates is mortal is no part of what we assert, as may be seen by considering the fact that our assertion can be understood by a person who has never heard of Socrates. In order to understand the judgment "all men are mortal," it is not necessary to know what men there are.* We must admit, therefore, as a radically new kind of judgment, such general assertions as "all men are mortal."[55]

On a substitutional interpretation, the truth of 'All men are mortal' should, for Russell, consist in the truth of 'If Socrates is a man, then Socrates is mortal', 'If Plato is a man, then Plato is mortal', etc. Putting this together with the passage from *Principia* leads to an obvious question. How can one who has never encountered the name 'Socrates' or heard of the man it names (and similarly for other men and names) make the judgment, or even understand the sentence 'All men are mortal"?[56]

This question is easily answered, if the quantification is objectual in the usual Frege-Russell sense. On this interpretation, the proposition expressed by the sentence says of a certain (real, nonlinguistic) function f_{mortal}—from arguments to truth (in Frege's case) or from arguments to truths (in Russell's case)—that it *assigns truth (or a truth) to an argument iff that argument is a man.*[57] Although entertaining this proposition, and knowing it to be true, requires acquaintance with f_{mortal} and the property predicated of the function, it does not require acquaintance with any particular individual, much less knowledge of which individuals are men, or even what individuals there are. Hence, the objectual understanding of the quantifier fits Russell's observation in the passage.

A similar point can be made about metalinguistic quantification over expressions. Let S be the sentence *For all names n of men, the sentence ⌈n is mortal⌉ is true.* The proposition expressed by S says of a certain function

[55] Russell and Whitehead (1910), p. 45, my emphasis.

[56] Though Russell puts the point in a way that invites us to understand the claim that all men are mortal as involving the restricted quantifier 'all men', I here treat the example as involving the unrestricted quantifier 'everyone/thing'. The reason for this is to illustrate that his point holds even for the unrestricted form of quantification that he standardly employs in *Principia* (and elsewhere). Once this is seen it is harmless to move back and forth between restricted and unrestricted quantification.

[57] For Frege, f_{mortal} assigns truth to a iff a is mortal; for Russell, f_{mortal} assigns a the proposition that a is mortal, and so assigns a true proposition to a iff a is mortal.

$f_{\text{'is mortal'}}$ that it *assigns truth (or a truth) to an argument iff that argument is the name of a man.*[58] Although entertaining this proposition, and knowing it to be true, requires acquaintance with the metalinguistic function $f_{\text{'is mortal'}}$ and the property predicated of the function, it does not require acquaintance with any particular name, much less knowledge of which expressions are names of men, or of which expressions are names at all. In short, metalinguistic quantification over expressions, being a species of objectual quantification, fits Russell's observation.

The same can't be said for substitutional quantification. It is not enough to be told that on a substitutional interpretation ⌜Everything is F⌝ is true iff each sentence that is a substitution instance of it is. Statements of truth conditions of this sort are too weak to tell us what sentences mean, or what it is to understand them.[59] Until we are told *what is asserted, believed, or known* when one asserts, believes, or knows the proposition the sentence expresses—plus what possible states of the world would make that assertion or belief true—we won't have an account of quantification that bears on Russell's last cited observation.[60] To provide one, he needs a property expressed by the quantifier in ⌜John believes that everyone (everything) is F⌝ that the substitutional interpretation doesn't provide. Moreover, since the belief isn't about a formula (and could be had by an agent ignorant of any formula one might suggest), it is no use looking for a linguistic property.

How should we understand what substitutionally quantified sentences mean, once we have distinguished substitutional quantification from metalinguistic, but objectual, quantification over expressions? We know that the substitutional interpretations of (1a) and (2a) *do not mean* (1b) and (2b).

1a. $\forall x$ (Man x ⊃ Mortal x)
   b. For every name n ⌜Man n ⊃ Mortal n⌝ is a true sentence.
2a. $\exists x$ (Man x & Mortal x)
   b. For some name n ⌜Man n ⊃ Mortal n⌝ is a true sentence.

If (1a) and (2a) did mean (1b) and (2b), and if 'Socrates' was in the substitution class of the variables, then (1c) would be a necessary and a priori

---

[58] For Frege, $f_{\text{'is mortal'}}$ assigns truth to a iff substituting a for 'x' in 'x is mortal' results in a true sentence; for Russell, $f_{\text{'is mortal'}}$ assigns a the proposition that substituting a for 'x' in 'x is mortal' results in a true sentence, and so assigns a true proposition to a iff ⌜a is mortal⌝ is a true sentence.

[59] This is not always seen, because substitutional quantifiers are often introduced by metalinguistic statements of their truth conditions—e.g., ⌜∃x Fx⌝ is true in L iff there is a name n such that ⌜Fn⌝ is true in L. Although this metalinguistic statement of truth conditions is fine, it is not a meaning-preserving analysis of the quantificational claim any more than the innocuous statement *that ⌜P&Q⌝ is true iff P is true and Q is true* is a meaning-preserving analysis. The conjunctive sentence doesn't mean, nor is it used to say, that its sentential conjuncts are true. Similarly, the objectual existential quantifier is often introduced by saying that ⌜∃x Fx⌝ is true iff Fx is true relative to an assignment of some object o to 'x'—despite the fact that the quantified sentence makes no claim whatsoever about the formula Fx.

[60] In this paragraph, F is a metalinguistic variable.

consequence of (1a) but (1d) would not, and (2a) would be such a consequence of (2c), but not of (2d).[61]

　　1c. 'Socrates is a man ⊃ Socrates is mortal' is a true sentence.
　　　d. Socrates is a man ⊃ Socrates is mortal.
　　2c. 'Socrates is a man & is mortal' is a true sentence.
　　　d. Socrates is a man & is mortal.

This is not how substitutional quantification is standardly understood. On the contrary, it is (1d) and that is standardly said to be a consequence of the substitutional interpretation of (1a), and (2d) that is said to be a consequence of the substitutional interpretation of (2a). This suggests that understanding the substitutional interpretations of (1a) and (2a), when 'Socrates' is in the substitution class for the variable, requires understanding the name 'Socrates'—which for Russell requires *being acquainted with the man Socrates*. The same holds for all names in the substitution class. Far from vindicating the observation quoted above from *Principia Mathematica* about the nature of general judgments, this result contradicts it.[62] Thus, if first-order quantification in *Principia* is substitutional, then the account of quantification in *Principia* is inconsistent with Russell's meta-theoretical statements about it there, as well as with the account of quantification in "On Denoting," which underwrites those statements.

　　Although it hardly seems possible for things to get worse for the substitutional interpretation of Russell, they do. As I have indicated, to avoid all commitment to classes, Fregean concepts, and nonlinguistic propositional functions, he would have to treat even first-order quantification as substitutional. But then, since his axiom of infinity will require infinitely many individuals, he will need infinitely many *logically proper names*. For Russell, these are simple terms the meanings of which are their referents— with which we must be acquainted in order to understand the names. It is, to say the least, highly doubtful that anyone's language could contain infinitely many such terms. Surely, they couldn't all be learned as separate lessons, which is how one imagines they would have to be acquired. It is similarly doubtful that anyone could be acquainted, in Russell's highly restrictive sense, with infinitely many individuals.[63] If, as presumably we must, we assume that no one is capable of such understanding and acquaintance, while recognizing that understanding the substitutional quantification employed requires it, we arrive at an interpretation of Russell's system that renders it unintelligible *by his own lights*.[64]

---

[61] I assume that semantic properties of expressions are not both necessary and a priori properties of them.

[62] Hodes (2012) endorses this conclusion in his sections 5 and 6.

[63] By 1910 agents were said to be acquainted only with sense data they were experiencing at the moment plus the universals they had cognized.

[64] A remark in Russell (1919a) shows that he did not think of the quantification employed in his logical system as substitutional. On pp. 200–201 he says, "It is one of the marks of

In response, one might say that a reasonable interpreter should revise some of Russell's restrictive views about names and acquaintance in the service of arriving at a more adequate version of his overall position. I agree, but if one takes this route, there are compelling reasons to include his skepticism about classes and his flirtation with substitutional quantification—which he was not then in any position to fully understand—as prime candidates for revision. The point is reinforced when we bring identity into the mix. The analysis of singular definite descriptions in "On Denoting" tells us that a formula $\ulcorner \Psi$ (the x: Φx)$\urcorner$ containing a description is an abbreviation of the formula $\ulcorner \exists x \forall w \, [(\Phi(w) \longleftrightarrow w = x)$ & $\Psi(x)]\urcorner$ containing the identity predicate. In *Principia Mathematica,* Russell's definition of identity (between individuals) tells us that the formula 'w = x' is an abbreviation of the higher-order formula $\ulcorner \forall \Theta \, (\Theta w \longleftrightarrow \Theta x)\urcorner$. Putting the two together, we have the result that $\ulcorner \Psi$ (the x: Φx)$\urcorner$ is an abbreviation of $\ulcorner \exists x \forall w \, [(\Phi(w) \longleftrightarrow \forall \Theta \, (\Theta w \longleftrightarrow \Theta x)) \, \& \, \Psi(x)]\urcorner$.

This is no problem if the predicate variables range over all subsets of the domain of individuals (or over their characteristic functions). Since these include all sets that contain only a single individual, x and w will be members of the same sets, and so satisfy the same predicates iff they are identical. But if quantifiers are interpreted substitutionally, then (since '=' isn't primitive) there will be no guarantee that for every individual in the domain, there is a first-order formula that is true of it, and nothing else. Indeed, there will be no guarantee that two or more different objects won't satisfy precisely the same first-order formulas, and so be indistinguishable in the system. Suppose there are such individuals. Then, Russell's axiom of infinity (needed for the proof of arithmetical axiom 4) will require not just infinitely many individuals, but *infinitely many individuals distinguished from one another by quantifier-free first-order formulas.* Worse, if distinct individuals x and y are not distinguished by the formal system, then any formula true of x will be true of y—even one that (on the ordinary objectual reading of quantification) says *that x is the only member of a certain set,* or one that says that x, *together with a distinct z,* exhaust the members of a member of the number 2 (the set of pairs of individuals).

---

a proposition of logic [which contains no nonlogical vocabulary] that, given a suitable language, such a proposition [sentence] can be asserted by a person who knows the syntax without knowing a single word of the [nonlogical] vocabulary." Although the remark is true on an objectual understanding of quantification, it is incompatible with treating quantifiers in a "proposition of logic" substitutionally. As correctly noted in section 5 of Hodes (2012), "If a quantifier-prefix in the sentence used to make such an assertion is to be interpreted substitutionally, and a relevant substituend contained an un-understood word, the speaker would not understand a relevant substituend, and so would not understand that quantifier-prefix, and so would not understand the sentence!" The upshot is that a genuinely substitutional interpretation of the quantifiers imposes requirements at variance with Russell's understanding of his own system, and could not have been accepted by him without sacrificing views he took to be central.

How might these problems be avoided? One could add infinitely many primitive predicates of individuals, each applying to a single individual and no two such predicates applying to the same individual. But Russell didn't do that. Nor would he have done so, since it would, in effect, make knowledge of the arithmetical system *derived* from what was supposed to be *logic* dependent on understanding infinitely many primitive predicates of individuals—in violation of his doctrine that one can understand propositions of logic without knowing any nonlogical vocabulary. Thus, in addition to weakening his logicist program, the uniform substitutional interpretation of the hierarchy creates a problem for his definition of identity and conflicts with the standard formulation of his theory of descriptions, which he continued to employ in *Principia*.[65]

In light of all these problems, it is, I think, a mistake to read a uniformly substitutional account of quantification into Russell's logicist program.[66] This is not to deny that some more or less inchoate thoughts of a substitutional sort played a role in his views about how paradoxes are to be avoided, how his type restrictions might be justified, and how classes, nonlinguistic propositions, and nonlinguistic propositional functions might be eliminated. On the contrary, the powerful attraction of eliminating what he saw as problematic entities, his need to see type restrictions as conditions on the very intelligibility of seeming quantification over classes, and his commitment to what he called "the vicious circle principle" as the key to solving a wide range of paradoxes, were powerful motivators pushing him toward a substitutional view of the quantifiers and a ramified theory of types. The problem, as I have argued, is that a reconstruction of his position that systematically treats quantification as genuinely substitutional rather than objectual creates far worse problems than it solves—for both his logicist program and his broader philosophy.

That Russell himself didn't see these problems is due, in part, to the fact that he was not in a position to understand substitutional quantification as fully as we do today. How could he? Prior to the 1960s and 1970s few, if any, philosophers clearly recognized and distinguished substitutional from objectual quantification. What's more, the fundamental metalogical and metamathematical results mentioned above—e.g., distinguishing first- and second-order arithmetic in terms of the power of second-order quantification over sets—were still many years in the future when *Principia Mathematica* was written. It is no shame on Russell that he was not aware of these things. What would be a shame is to saddle *Principia Mathematica* with an interpretation which, if completely and consistently carried through, would obliterate or obscure much of the progress he made there.

---

[65] Russell could, of course, simply have taken identity to be primitive, but it is telling that he didn't, and, in any case, it would scarcely have solved his problems.

[66] For a more recent exploration and defense of the interpretation, see Klement (2010).

The best interpretation is, I think, the one that best coheres with Russell's most important philosophical views, best advances his understanding of the relationship between logic and mathematics, and best explains the impact of his work on those who followed. Such an interpretation should, I believe, dismiss his radical eliminativism about classes and his flirtation with substitutional quantification as regrettable but understandable errors, while treating the quantification in his hierarchy as objectual, ranging over individuals and classes (or nonlinguistic propositional functions). The complex ramified theory of types and the Axiom of Reducibility can then be dropped in favor of the simple theory of types in Ramsey (1925), through which most of the historical influence of Russell's reduction has flowed. I believe that it is this (relatively standard) interpretation that has the best chance of illuminating the strengths and weaknesses of his logicist program, while making intelligible its impact on later philosophers and logicians.

6. PARADOXES, TYPES, AND VICIOUS CIRCLES

At the end of *Principles of Mathematics* (1903, p. 527), Russell presented the following seeming paradox.[67]

> If m be a class of propositions, the proposition "every [member of] m is true" may or may not be itself an m [i.e., a member of m]. But there is a one-one relation of this proposition to m: if n be different from m, "every [member of] n is true" is not the same proposition as "every [member of] m is true." Consider now the whole class of propositions of the form "every [member of] m is true," and having the property of not being members of their respective m's. Let this class be w, and let p be the proposition "every [member of] w is true." If p is a [member of] w, it must possess the defining property of w; but this property demands that p should not be a [member of] w. On the other hand, if p is not a [member of] w, then p does possess the defining property of w, and therefore is a [member of] w. Thus a contradiction appears unavoidable.

In discussing this puzzle, Russell relates it to one mentioned earlier in the work that is avoidable by a simple theory of types. His worry here is that this later apparent paradox is not so avoidable, which prompts him to look for a deeper diagnosis. His final words in the book are:

> It appears that the special contradiction of Chapter x is solved by the doctrine of types, but that there is at least one closely analogous contradiction which is probably not soluable by this doctrine. The totality of all logical

---

[67] The paradoxical argument noted at the end of *Principles of Mathematics* is related to one reported in 1910 in "The Theory of Logical Types" (Russell 1910d) which motivated his search for the theory of types presented in *Principia Mathematica*.

objects, or of all propositions, involves, it would seem, a fundamental logical difficulty. What the complete solution to the difficulty may be, I have not succeeded in discovering; but as it affects the very foundations of reasoning, I earnestly commend the study of it to the attention of all students of logic.[68]

Did this paradox, which Russell realized was not blocked by a simple type theory, influence his later move to the more complicated ramified theory of *Principia Mathematica*? On the one hand Bernard Linsky (2002–3) reports that Russell found a seemingly related paradox in 1907 that led him to a version of a type theory shortly before the publication of *Principia*. On the other hand, André Fuhrmann (2002) argues that already in 1903 Russell had come to view the "propositional paradox" at the end of *Principles of Mathematics* to be fallacious on independent grounds. If so, it presumably didn't played a role in the development of the ramified theory of types. Hodes (2012) strengthens the latter point by extracting two more precisely stated propositional paradoxes from the purported paradox at the end of *Principles*. He argues that despite initial appearances, neither truth nor any other semantic notion plays an essential role in them; moreover, these puzzles are not genuinely paradoxical, since they rely on ancillary principles that are themselves dubious. In short, puzzles like the one at the end of *Principles* do not genuinely motivate a ramified rather than a simple theory of types.

By 1906 Russell had come to view all paradoxes of logic and semantics as resulting from a certain kind of vicious circularity the avoidance of which would also lead to an avoidance of classes by construing apparent quantification over the latter as being ultimately analyzable in terms of conditions on their apparent members (the apparent members of apparent members, etc.).[69] Unfortunately, he never gave a precise statement of his "vicious circle principle." Rather, he contented himself with various informal (not obviously equivalent) statements, illustrated here by a collection of remarks from Russell (1906), (1908), and *Principia Mathematica*.

Whatever involves *all* of a collection must not be one of the collection; or conversely, if, provided a collection had a total, it would have members definable only in terms of that total, then the said collection has no total.[70] Whatever involves an apparent variable must not be among the possible values of that variable.[71] No totality can contain members definable in terms of itself.[72] Given any set of objects such that, if we suppose the set to have a total, it will contain members which presuppose this total, then such a set cannot have a

---

[68] Russell (1903), p. 528.
[69] Russell (1906).
[70] Russell (1908a), p. 63 of the reprinting in Russell (1971).
[71] Russell (1906), p. 198 of the reprinting in Russell (1973); Russell (1908), p. 75 of Russell (1971).
[72] Russell (1906), p. 75 of Russell (1971).

total. By saying that a set has 'no total', we mean, primarily, that no significant statement can be made about 'all of its members'.[73]

These remarks are illuminatingly discussed in Gödel (1944) and Sainsbury (1979). For our purposes, it is enough to observe that the concern
they register goes beyond worries about paradoxes arising from the size,
or exhaustiveness, of totalities of sets, propositions, or properties.

For Russell, denying "a totality" amounts to denying the *intelligibility*
of corresponding quantifiers of the form "all so-and-so." But why? One
might think that all intelligible quantification requires a domain, which is
a totality of some sort.[74] But this is far from obvious. For example, it seems
perfectly *intelligible* to take Zermelo-Fraenkel set theory to be about all
sets, while repudiating any set (totality) of all sets. Similarly, there may be
good reasons for doubting that there is a set (totality) of all propositions, a
set (totality) of all properties, or a property of having every property. But
absent further argument, such doubts don't preclude intelligible quantification over all propositions or properties.

Russell's statements of, and remarks about, the vicious circle principle
have sometimes been read (as they are in Gödel 1944 and Sainsbury 1979)
as reflecting "a constructivist" outlook about mathematics—as if in defining or describing various mathematical totalities we were building them
up from already completed items of the same sort. On this simple but
contentious metaphysical picture of what mathematical entities are, one
shouldn't countenance any entity the definition of which *requires* reference
to a totality of which it is a part—since the entity being "constructed" by
the definition must already be in place for the totality required by the
definition. From this perspective, it may seem that restrictions on definitions arising from the vicious circle principle are nothing more than
good sense. However, even if blanket expressive limitations on definitions
could be extracted from such a picture of mathematical reality, the picture
itself is highly contentious, and hence, it is hardly a plausible candidate
for inclusion in the foundations of mathematics.

Moreover, the spirit of Russell's "no-class theory" and his repudiation of
nonlinguistic propositions and propositional functions is *not* constructivist, but eliminativist. It is the prospect of eliminativism that provides his
most compelling rationale a substitutional account of quantification, and
with it a ramified theory of types, understood as conforming to the vicious
circle principle.[75] However, it also presents him with a dilemma regarding
first-order quantification. On the one hand, failing to extend the substitutional account to quantification over individuals risks losing the desired
ontological eliminativism. For if first-order quantification remains objectual, then, on the usual Frege-Russell story, one will need, as arguments of

[73] Russell and Whitehead (1910), p. 37.
[74] Sainsbury (1979), p. 328, sees Russell as attracted to this idea.
[75] See Hodes (2012).

first-order quantifiers, either classes of individuals, Fregean concepts that map individuals onto truth values (i.e., characteristic functions of classes of individuals), or nonlinguistic propositional functions that map individuals onto nonlinguistic propositions. However, one can't *eliminate* classes, their characteristic functions, and objective propositional functions, while *retaining* some of them. Indeed, there is little *ontological* sense in trying to eliminate all classes, while leaving some objective characteristic or propositional functions in place. Thus, if ontology is the prime motivation for the substitutional interpretation of the quantifiers, either all of Russell's quantifiers should be substitutional or none should be.

On the other hand, the fundamental problems catalogued in the previous section militate against adopting such a uniformly substitutional interpretation of Russell's quantification. In short, there is no good way of getting everything Russell wants. As I have indicated, the best reconstruction is to eschew that substitutional interpretation, the ramified theory of types, and the vicious circle principle.

For the logicist reduction, this means objectual quantification over either Fregean concepts or nonlinguistic Russellian propositional functions. For the paradoxes, it means distinguishing Russell's paradox about classes—which can be dealt with by Ramsey's simple theory of types— from the semantic paradoxes, which, contrary to Russell's view in 1910, require a different solution. Semantic paradoxes are those that crucially involve notions like truth, designation, and application (for predicates). Three of these, cited by Russell, are the liar paradox (which in simplest form involves statements that say of themselves that they are not true), Grelling's paradox concerning the meaningfulness of the predicate 'heterological' (which is defined as a predicate applying to all and only those predicates that do not apply to themselves), and Barry's paradox concerning 'the least integer not nameable in fewer than nineteen syllables'.[76] Russell thought that the proper diagnosis for all of these, along with his paradox about set membership, is that they violated the vicious circle principle.[77] Hence, he thought they all required the same solution. Ramsey disagreed, maintaining that while the simple theory of types is sufficient to block Russell's paradox, the semantic paradoxes require a different treatment.[78] Since each semantic paradox depends on a semantic notion—*truth, designation, application*—which is usually thought to require relativization to a language (*truth in L, designation in L, application in L*), the accepted consensus, following Tarski (1935), is that the solution to the paradoxes depends on distinguishing one's object language from its metalanguage.

[76] The first and third of these semantic paradoxes are cited on pp. 60–61 of Russell and Whitehead (1910). The second is discussed on pp. 80, 97, and 102 of Russell (1903a).

[77] For discussion, see Sainsbury (1979), pp. 308–13.

[78] Ramsey (1925).

CHAPTER 11

∽✎✐∾

Our Knowledge of the External World

1. Russell's Task: To Explain Common Knowledge by Showing It to Be Justifiable
   1.1. The Knowledge to Be Justified and the Analytic Method of Justification
   1.2. Sense Data as Starting Point
   1.3. Logical Constructions
2. Material Objects as Logical Constructions out of Sense Data
   2.1. Informal Presentation and Rationale
   2.2. The Robust System of Private Perspectives
   2.3. The Elimination of Unoccupied Perspectives and Unsensed Sense Data
3. Knowledge, Verification, and Content: Critique of Russell's Rationale
4. Other Minds
   4.1. A Working Hypothesis?
   4.2. How Not to Make Progress

1. RUSSELL'S TASK: TO EXPLAIN COMMON KNOWLEDGE BY SHOWING IT TO BE JUSTIFIABLE

In the spring of 1914, Russell delivered a series of eight Lowell Lectures at Harvard University meant to illustrate the power of his new method of logical and linguistic analysis as the route to progress in philosophy. Fresh off the widely acclaimed success of his theory of denoting phrases presented in "On Denoting" and of his logicist reduction, presented in *Principia Mathematica*, he focused on a variety of topics including causation and free will, infinity, "logic as the essence of philosophy," and the application of mathematical notions of continuous series to spatiotemporal occurrences involving change, motion, and speed. However, the heart of the lectures, and the book that followed, were the two lectures on empirical knowledge—"Lecture 3: On Our Knowledge of the External World," and "Lecture 4: The World of Physics and the World of Sense." The project in these lectures was to explain our scientific and our nonscientific knowledge of the external world. The intended explanation was, of course, not psychological or historical, but philosophical. The aim was to show how most of what we confidently take ourselves to know about the world is capable of being justified—and in fact is justified—in the face of skeptical doubt of the sort familiar since Descartes.

1.1. The Knowledge to Be Justified and the Analytic Method of Justification

Russell begins with a brief description of the scope of the common knowledge to be explained. In lecture 3, that knowledge is said to include

> first, our acquaintance with particular objects of daily life—furniture, towns, houses, other people, and so on. Then there is the extension of such particular knowledge to particular things outside our personal experience, through history and geography, newspapers, etc. And lastly, there is the systematization of all this knowledge of particulars by means of physical science, which derives immense persuasive force from its astonishing power of foretelling the future. We are quite willing to admit that there may be errors of detail in this knowledge, but we believe them to be discoverable and corrigible by the methods which have given rise to our beliefs, and we do not, as practical men, entertain for a moment the hypothesis that the whole edifice may be built on insecure foundations. In the main, therefore . . . we accept this mass of common knowledge as affording data for our philosophical analysis.[1]

In lecture 4, he indentifies the knowledge to be explained and the task of explaining it.

> Among the objections to the reality of objects of sense, there is one which is derived from the apparent difference between matter as it appears in physics and things as they appear in sensation. Men of science, for the most part, are willing to condemn immediate [sense] data as "merely subjective," while yet maintaining the truth of the physics inferred from those data. But such an attitude, though it may be *capable* of justification, obviously stands in need of it; and the only justification possible must be one which exhibits matter as a logical construction from sense data—unless, indeed, there were some wholly *a priori* principle by which unknown entities could be inferred from such as are known. It is therefore necessary to find some way of bridging the gulf between the world of physics and the world of sense. . . . Physics started from the common-sense belief in fairly permanent and fairly rigid bodies—tables and chairs, stones, mountains. . . . This common-sense belief, it should be noticed, is a piece of audacious metaphysical theorizing; objects are not continually present to sensation, and it may be doubted whether they are there when they are not seen or felt. This problem . . . is ignored by common sense, and has therefore hitherto been ignored by physicists. We have thus here a

---

[1] Russell (1914), p. 66. *Our Knowledge of the External World* was originally published in 1914 by Open Court. Russell produced a revised version for Allen and Unwin that appeared in 1926, and another for a Norton volume that appeared in 1929. Except when otherwise indicated, all page references will be to the 1914 edition.

first departure from the immediate data of sensation, though it is a departure merely by way of extension, and was probably made by our savage ancestors in some very remote prehistoric epoch.[2]

The knowledge to be justified includes not only highly abstract, non-observational claims of physical theory, plus claims about ordinary objects existing at distant times or far-off places and claims based on the testimony of others, but also the most ordinary claims about the existence of tables, chairs, stones, and mountains (at moments when they are not perceived). Although Russell believes all these claims *need* justification, he also believes that they *are* capable of being justified. He is convinced that the evidence justifying these claims must come from what he calls *the immediate data of sensation*, which informs us only of the properties of *sensible objects at the moments at which they are perceived*. These objects apparently differ in kind from ordinary physical objects that persist when not present to sensation, which are, Russell thinks, pieces of "audacious metaphysical theorizing."

Finally, and perhaps most significantly, he indicates that the justification we seek for our knowledge of the world can *only* be had by conceiving of matter as *a logical construction from sense data*. This is taken to be the only reasonable alternative to (unreasonably) appealing to an imagined purely *a priori* principle for inferring unknown (unperceived) entities from those that are known (perceived). Although Russell doesn't say in these passages what logical construction is, it turns out to be a method of logico-linguistic analysis. The idea is to give an analysis of what a sentence *must mean* if the claim it is used to express is to be counted as something we are capable of knowing. Just as an enthusiastic logicist might dream of answering the question "How is mathematical knowledge possible?" by analyzing mathematical statements as being nothing more than putatively knowable logical statements, so, Russell hoped, the epistemologist might answer the skeptic about the external world by analyzing empirical statements as putatively knowable statements about sense data. With this ambitious project, philosophy as logico-linguistic analysis jumped from what some would regard as the periphery of the subject to what, since Descartes, many would regard to be its core.

1.2. Sense Data as Starting Point

Russell describes the starting point for reconstructing our empirical knowledge as consisting of "hard data." He says:

> The hardest of hard data are of two sorts: the particular facts of sense, and the general truths of logic. The more we reflect upon . . . exactly what doubt concerning them really means, the more luminously certain do they become.

[2] Russell (1914), pp. 101–2.

Verbal doubt concerning even these is possible, but verbal doubt may occur when what is nominally being doubted is not really our thoughts, and only words are actually present in our minds. Real doubt . . . would, I think, be pathological.[3]

Our data now are primarily the facts of sense (i.e. of *our own* sense-data) and the laws of logic. But even the severest scrutiny will allow some additions. . . . Some facts of memory—especially of recent memory—seem to have the highest degree of certainty. Some introspective facts are as certain as any facts of sense. . . . Certain common beliefs are undoubtedly excluded from hard data. Such is the belief . . . that sensible objects in general persist when we are not perceiving them. Such also is the belief in other people's minds. . . . Belief in what is reported by the testimony of others . . . is of course involved in the doubt as to whether other people have minds at all. Thus the world from which our reconstruction is to begin is very fragmentary. The best we can say for it is that it is slightly more extensive than the world at which Descartes arrived by a similar process, since that world contained nothing except himself and his thoughts.[4]

For Russell, hard data are points of certainty about which doubt would be pathological. He is very strict about what he counts as certain (as well as what would, or wouldn't, be pathological to doubt). Given his standards, I am *not certain* that I have two hands, that I am married to another person, or that I have two children; for me to doubt these things *wouldn't be pathological* in the sense in which he is here speaking. I am also *not certain*, and it would *not be pathological for me to doubt*, that the computer on which I am writing this book, the desk on which it sits, and the wall behind it still exist when I sit back and close my eyes for a moment. In contrast, Russell *would* have me take myself to be certain, as I type, that I am having momentary tactile impressions of hardness, and visual impressions of strings of small black alphabetic shapes separated by spaces appearing against a white background. It would, he thinks, be pathological to doubt, as I have these experiences, that I do touch something hard, or that I do see things that really are small, black, and alphabetic in shape, plus something else—another visual sense datum—that really is white. However, he thinks, the extent of my certainty about even these things is severely limited. I am not certain that they will continue to exist when I am not perceiving them, or that they did exist before I perceived them; to doubt that they will or did is not in the least pathological.

Far from it. At the beginning of lecture 3, Russell (1914, p. 64) says it is "probable" that "the immediate objects of sense [i.e., sense data] depend for their existence upon physiological conditions in ourselves, and that, for example, the coloured surfaces which we see cease to exist when we

---

[3] Ibid., pp. 70–71.
[4] Ibid., pp. 72–73.

shut our eyes." Still, he immediately adds, it would be a mistake to infer from this "that they are dependent upon mind, not real while we see them, or not the sole basis for our knowledge of the external world." On the contrary, his aim is to show that these fleeting entities—the very existence and (one must presume) properties of which probably depend on the state of mind of the observer—constitute *the sole* evidentiary basis on which all our beliefs about the world rest. For this reason, he takes them to be as fully real as anything can be. As for the relation that a sense datum S bears to the mind M that perceives it, Russell appears tacitly to admit that S is, or very well may be, *causally dependent* on M. However, writing in 1914 (pp. 74–75), he denies that S is "logically" or conceptually dependent on M.

In so doing, he was relying on Moore's plausible and influential distinction—presented in "The Refutation of Idealism" in 1903—between sensation as the cognitive act of perceiving or experiencing something and sensation as that which one perceives or experiences. Russell makes this distinction himself in the following passage.

> Now it is necessary here first of all to distinguish between (1) our sensation, which is a mental event consisting in our being aware of a sensible object, and (2) the sensible object of which we are aware in sensation. When I speak of the sensible object, it must be understood that I do not mean such a thing as a table, which is both visible and tangible, [and] can be seen by many people at once, and is more or less permanent. What I mean is just that patch of colour which is momentarily seen when we look at the table, or just that particular hardness which is felt when we press it, or just that particular sound which is heard when we rap it. Each of these I call a sensible object, and our awareness of it I call a sensation.[5]

Moore's example was the experience of perceiving something blue versus, as he there put it, "the blue" one perceives or experiences. The experience is that of the mind standing in a certain cognitive relation to the thing perceived. Although having this experience is clearly something mental, it doesn't follow that the thing experienced is mental. Indeed Moore in 1903—and Russell in 1914—denied that the perceived sense datum was literally part of the mind that perceived it. For this reason, both then agreed that it is *conceivable* that the sense datum might exist unperceived. However, if one assimilates the perception-like experiences one has when one dreams, hallucinates, sees afterimages, or "sees double" to normal cases of seeing shapes, colors, and the like—as Russell did in 1914—there will be strong pressure to think that although it is *conceivable* that all these objects of perception might exist unperceived, in fact they probably don't. This was his position in 1914.

[5] Ibid., p. 76. Russell adds on pp. 84–85: "A patch of colour, even if it exists only when it is seen, is still something quite different from the seeing of it; the seeing of it is mental, but the patch of color is not."

By 1926, when he (slightly) revised the book for a second edition, he had changed his mind about this, saying:

> According to some authors—among whom I was *formerly* included—it is necessary to distinguish between a sensation, *which is a mental event*, and its object, which is a patch of colour or a noise or what not. If this distinction is made, the object of the sensation is called a "sense datum." . . . *Nothing in the problems to be discussed in this book depends upon the question whether this distinction is valid or not.* . . . For reasons explained . . . [elsewhere] . . . I have come to regard the distinction as *not valid*, and to consider the sense-datum *identical* with the sensation.[6]

The upshot of this change of mind for our discussion is that the central arguments of *Our Knowledge of the External World* do not require choosing between the claims (i) that it is impossible for sense data to exist unperceived, (ii) that there are, in actual fact, no unperceived sense data, but there could have been, (iii) that there are probably no unperceived sense data, and (iv) that we have no way of knowing whether there are, or are not, unperceived sense data. In short, neither the existence of unperceived sense data, nor denial of such existence, is required by Russell's project.[7] The data on which his reconstruction of our knowledge of the external world depends include only statements about objects of sense—things capable of being seen, heard, touched, or felt—that presently exist and are being perceived, or have, in the not too distant past, existed and been perceived, and now are remembered. It is data of this sort about which Russell (1914, p. 73) asks, "Can the existence of anything other than our own hard data be inferred from the existence of those data?"

What more can be said about the hard data of sense that provide the justification for all empirical knowledge? They are, Russell thinks, statements about objects of *immediate* perception—the things *directly* seen, heard, touched, or felt.[8] But what are these things? They are, it would seem, things that have precisely the observational properties they are perceived to have. If I seem to be touching something hard, then the tactile datum I touch is hard. If I am having a visual experience as of something

---

[6] Russell (1926), p. 83, my emphasis. Two things changed between the 1914 and the 1926 editions of *OKEW*: (i) Russell gave up the distinction between sensation and sense datum, and (ii) he saw that this made *no difference* to his overall argument. This assessment is confirmed by his remark in the preface to the 1929 Norton edition (p. xi) that "the only philosophical change in the present edition [as compared with the original 1914 edition] is the abandonment of the distinction between sensations and sense-data, which I now agree with the American realists in regarding as illusory."

[7] This point is missed in Griffin (2005) and Pincock (2005–6), both of which are discussed in Soames (2005d).

[8] Think of *directly seeing* x as seeing x without seeing it by virtue of seeing something else. When one sees an actor in a movie, a politician on TV, or a photo of a friend, one sees the actor, the politician, or the friend indirectly, in virtue of seeing the movie, the TV screen, or the photo. Although sense data are, for Russell, seen directly, whether or not material objects are depends on our analysis of them.

small, black, and alphabetic in shape, then I am seeing a visual sense datum that has these properties. This is so no matter whether I am awake or asleep, hallucinating, seeing double, experiencing an afterimage, or perceiving normally.

Russell broaches this issue in a remarkable passage comparing dreams with waking experience.

> The first thing to realize is that there are no such things as "illusions of sense." Objects of sense, even when they occur in dreams, are the most indubitably real objects known to us. What, then, makes us call them unreal in dreams? Merely the unusual nature of their connection with other objects of sense. I dream that I am in America, but I wake up and find myself in England, without those intervening days on the Atlantic which, alas! are inseparably connected with a "real" visit to America. Objects of sense are called "real" when they have the kind of connection with other objects of sense which experience has led us to regard as normal; when they fail in this, they are called "illusions." But what is illusory is only the inferences to which they give rise; in themselves, they are every bit as real as the objects of waking life. And conversely, the sensible objects of waking life must not be expected to have any more intrinsic reality than those of dreams.[9]

Two points are worth emphasizing. First, Russell is not saying merely that the cognitive experiences we have when dreaming and those we have when we are awake are equally things that exist. He is saying that in both cases we perceive—e.g., see—real things. When we seem to be seeing something, there is something we really see—no matter whether we are dreaming, hallucinating, or perceiving naturally. Second, he does not characterize illusions as cases in which we see, or otherwise perceive, something as having a certain property that it really doesn't have. Rather, he says, "what is illusory is only the inferences to which they [the real objects of sense] give rise." Presumably he means that when we perceive something as being a certain way—and so really do perceive a datum that is that way—this experience sometimes causes us to draw a further inference that turns out to be false. The "illusion" is, in effect, a false prediction inferred from (or caused by) the accurate perception of a sense datum. As he puts it, the inference involves "the kind of connection" the sense datum we have perceived has "with other objects of sense" that we know from past experience normally precede or follow a sense datum of the sort we have just perceived. This suggests that the "illusion" amounts to a false claim about sense data—past or future—other than the sense datum we perceived. About the perceived sense datum itself, there is no error.

Russell continues:

> Accepting the indubitable momentary reality of objects of sense, the next thing to notice is the confusion underlying objections derived from their

[9] Russell (1914), pp. 85–86.

changeableness. As we walk round the table, its aspect changes; but it is thought impossible to maintain either that the table changes, or that its various aspects can all "really exist at the same place."[10]

In speaking of changes in *the aspects of the table*, he is clearly speaking of changes in *the appearance of the table*—which presumably involves changes in things like the color, size, and shape it is perceived as having. When the color, shape, or size of the table appear to change, we don't say that the table has changed, or that it simultaneously has different colors, shapes, and sizes. Instead, Russell seems to suggest, it is the table-type sense data we see from moment to moment that change. We first see a table-type sense datum with one property, and then see a table-type sense datum with a different property. In these cases it isn't the "aspects"—i.e., appearances—of the original sense datum that have changed; rather, one sense datum has been replaced with another. But if change in appearance is always a change in sense data seen, then sense data are, in effect, appearances—which don't themselves have further appearances. When it appears to one as if one is seeing, hearing, touching, or feeling something that has observational property P, one is seeing, hearing, touching, or feeling something that really does have P. Russell continues in this vein, closing the passage with a comment about a case in which what is seen is commonly described to be an image.

> If we press one eyeball, we shall see two tables; but it is thought preposterous to maintain that there are "really" two tables. Such arguments, however, seem to involve the assumption that there can be something more real than objects of sense. If we see two tables, then there *are* two visual tables.[11]

Note, he doesn't say that there are "two tables." He says there are "two *visual* tables," by which he means that we see two table-images. This, he maintains, is what is really given in perception.

So far we know three things about the objects that Russell takes to be immediately perceived: (i) they are things that we cannot know to exist unperceived, and that probably do not so exist, (ii) they are things that have whatever observable properties they are perceived to have, and (iii) knowledge of them is the sole source of evidence capable of justifying knowledge of the external world. Further conclusions are suggested by the following passage, which contrasts what can truly be said of material objects with what can truly be said of sense data.

> [By a sensible object of which we are aware in sensation] I do *not* mean such a thing as a table, *which is both visible and tangible*, [and] *can be seen by many people at once*, and is more or less permanent. What I mean is just that patch of

colour which is momentarily seen when we look at the table, or just that particular hardness which is felt when we press it, or just that particular sound which is heard when we rap it.[12]

It is hard to read this passage without taking the contrast between the table and the sense data perceived in connection with it as indicating (iv) that a sense datum can be perceived by only a single mind (at any one time), and (v) that no sense datum can be perceived by more than one sense modality—e.g., no sense datum that is the object of a visual experience can be the object of a tactile experience, and vice versa—and (vi) that sense data have only momentary existence.[13]

The privacy of sense data is already suggested by Russell's insistence that dream images and double images have precisely the same status as what is seen in ordinary perception. Since surely no one else does, will, or perhaps even could, see the two images of a pencil that I just saw when I pressed on my eye, the same thing should follow for all other objects of immediate perception—with which these images are on a par. A similar conclusion is suggested by Russell's admission that "the immediate objects of sense depend for their existence upon physiological conditions in ourselves,"[14] and by his treatment of these objects as having precisely the properties they are perceived to have. If two people both dream or hallucinate that there are rats running across the floor, which one perceives as white and the other perceives as pink, the sense data they perceive must be different; and if whenever a difference in (immediate) perception guarantees that different things are perceived, the conclusion that the objects of immediate perception are inherently private can hardly be avoided.

Russell (1914, p. 87) builds this into his model for explaining empirical knowledge when he stipulates the following:

Each mind sees at each moment an immensely complex three-dimensional world [of sense data]; but there is absolutely nothing which is seen by two minds simultaneously. When we say that two people see the same thing, we always find that, owing to differences of point of view, there are differences, however slight, between their immediate sensible objects.

It is quite natural that he should assume this. Surely it is no part of one's "hard data" that one can ever *know* that anyone else perceives the very same momentary datum that one presently perceives. Thus, the evidentiary base for Russell's reconstruction must treat the sense data perceived by different agents as if they were different.

---

[12] Ibid., p. 76, my emphasis.
[13] Russell (1914) says more in support of (v) at pp. 78, and 80–81, to be discussed below.
[14] Ibid., p. 64.

1.3. Logical Constructions

I now return to Russell's statement that "the only justification possible [for our empirical knowledge, including that provided by physical science] must be one which exhibits matter as a logical construction from sense data."[15] The idea is summed up in a slogan: *Material objects are logical constructions out of sense data.* Although this might sound like a doctrine about how material objects are constituted, it isn't. Rather, it is a linguistic doctrine about the meanings of sentences of a certain kind. According to the doctrine, sentences that appear to be about material objects are really about sense data and nothing more. Before I spell out what this meant for Russell, I will illustrate the idea with some simpler examples of the type of analysis he had in mind.

Among the simplest such cases are statements about "the average child." Consider, for example, sentence (1).

1. The average child between the ages of 6 and 18 has had 4.7 cavities.

Looking at the grammatical structure of this sentence, one might take it to be about some one person, the average child between the ages 6 and 18, and to say that this child has had 4.7 cavities. But we all know this is not what the sentence really means; it means something roughly along the lines of (2).

2. The number of children between the ages of 6 and 18 multiplied by 4.7 equals the number of cavities they have had.

Sentence (2) talks about the cavities of individual children, but it doesn't single out any individual as the average child (between 6 and 18); nor does it attribute the property *having had 4.7 cavities* to anyone. Philosophers in the decades after *Our Knowledge of the External World* expressed this by saying that the average child is a *logical construction* out of individual children. By this, they meant that all statements which might, on the basis of their grammatical structure, appear to be about the average child are really statements with complex logical forms about individual children. Thus, if we were to count all the things in the universe, we would have to count each child, but once we had done that, there would be no other "average child" remaining to be counted.

A less obvious example of what some would view as the same thing is provided by statements about nations.

3. Great Britain devalued the pound.

Here we have a sentence which, by its grammatical form, looks to be about a certain nation. What is a nation? Some might answer that a nation consists of a group of people who live in a certain place and engage in certain

[15] Ibid., p. 101.

patterns of thought and behavior, some of which involve conformity to a set of laws, including those that constitute a monetary system. Is there anything more to a nation than this? If one were counting the entities in the universe, one would have to count people, places, physical objects, and perhaps even thoughts, actions, and laws. But when one had done that, would there be any further entities—nations—left over to count? Some philosophers would say *no*; and some of these would further say that when we talk about nations we are really just talking about people, places, physical objects, and the complex patterns of thought and behavior they engage in. For example, these philosophers might say, what appear to be statements about Great Britain are just rough shorthand ways of making statements about the thoughts and activities of people living on a large island in the Atlantic off the west coast of Europe. On this view, the meaning of each sentence that appears on the surface to be about "the country Great Britain" is given by a set of more complex sentences about people living at a certain time and place. A philosopher taking this position would say that nations are logical constructions out of people and places.

There is, of course, a big difference between statements "about the average child" and statements "about nations." Typically, it is pretty clear what statement or statements about individual children a statement about the average child is short for—which means that average-child statements typically have more or less transparent analyses. This is not true of statements about nations. Though some might claim it to be conceptually possible, no one would dream of attempting a precise analysis of the statements made by utterances of sentences like (3) or (4), solely in terms of more basic statements about people and places.

4. Great Britain was once the world's dominant power.

Despite this, some philosophers have felt that nations must be logical constructions out of people and places, because there is nothing other than people and places for nation-statements to be about.

2. MATERIAL OBJECTS AS LOGICAL CONSTRUCTIONS OUT OF SENSE DATA

2.1. Informal Presentation and Rationale

With this in mind, I return to Russell's idea that our knowledge of material objects can be genuine, and capable of justification, only if they are logical constructions out of sense data. On this view, statements that appear to be "about material objects" must, on analysis, be understood really to be about sense data and nothing more. So, if we were counting the entities in the world, we would have to count each individual sense datum and each perceiver—but after these had been counted there would be no material objects left over to count. By avoiding the claim that material-object statements are about entities the existence of which is merely inferred from the sense data they supposedly cause, the proponent of this view hopes to remove a source of skepticism about the truth of such statements, and to provide an analysis that explains how they can be known. Since knowing the truth of a material-object statement simply requires knowing about sense data, no unsupported inference to other entities with which we are not directly acquainted can undermine the justification needed for knowledge.

Russell illustrates what he has in mind in a passage in which he describes what one comes to know when one walks around a table, viewing it from different positions.

> A table viewed from one place presents a different appearance from that which it presents from another place. This is the language of common sense, but this language already assumes that there is a real table of which we see the appearances. Let us try to state what is known in terms of sensible objects alone, without any element of hypothesis. We find that as we walk round the table, we perceive a series of gradually changing visible objects. But in speaking of "walking round the table," we have still retained the hypothesis that there is a single table connected with all the appearances. What we ought to say is that, while we have those muscular and other sensations which make us say we are walking, our visual sensations change in a continuous way, so that, for example, a striking patch of colour is not suddenly replaced by something wholly different, but is replaced by an insensible gradation of slightly different colours with slightly different shapes. *This is what we really know by experience, when we have freed our mind from the assumption of permanent "things" with changing appearances. What is really known is a correlation of muscular and other bodily sensations with changes in visual sensations.*[16]

Here, Russell provides background for what will be his striking doctrine—that material objects are logical constructions out of sense data. The background for the doctrine consists in (i) his conviction that we do use "material-object statements" to express genuine knowledge, plus (ii) the view, sketched in the passage, that the knowledge so expressed is simply that certain types of sense data are correlated with other types of sense data. Insofar as ordinary sentences "about material objects" express knowledge, the statements they are used to make are about sense data and nothing more.

What, then, might an analysis look like of the knowledge (5) is used to express?

5. I see a table.

Part of the analysis is certainly something of the sort indicated by (5a).

___

[16] Ibid., p. 77, my emphasis.

> 5a. I see a certain kind of table-like sense datum (with such-and-such shape and size).

Of course, this is too vague. What does a visual sense datum have to be like to count as table-like? But even apart from this vagueness, (5a) couldn't be the whole of the analysis. After all, we must distinguish seeing a table from dreaming or hallucinating a table, as well as from merely seeing an image of a table. If (5a) gave the whole content of (5), it would be impossible to make these distinctions. Thus, the analysis of (5) must also include clauses of the sort indicated by (5b) and (5c).

> 5b. If I were to have the sensations called "walking toward the table"—i.e., if I were to have the "muscular" sensations called "walking" at the same time that I had a sequence of gradually changing, and steadily larger, visual "table-like" sense data—then, ultimately, I would experience tactile sense data of pressure and hardness.
> c. If I were to have the sensations called "walking around the table," then my visual sense data would gradually change in a certain continuous way.

This isn't all. There are many different ways of perceptually verifying (5). Assuming that there is no special reason to include some of these in the analysis, while excluding others, a proponent of the view that material objects are logical constructions out of sense data is under pressure to include a clause in the analysis of (5) for every sense experience that would contribute to verifying it. But then, what looks on the surface like a very simple statement of English may end up having an enormously long and complex analysis.

The passage that immediately follows the one last quoted gives some sense of the complexities involved. The problem in the passage concerns making sense of perceiving something—e.g., a table—as blue, not because it is blue, but because one is wearing blue spectacles. That is how we would describe the case in everyday material-object talk. Russell's challenge is to describe it, and related cases, solely in terms of sense data. He sets up the problem as follows:

> Let us take the case of the blue spectacles. . . . The frame of the spectacles is of course visible, but the blue glass, if it is clean, is not visible. The blueness, which we say is in the glass, appears as being in the objects seen through the glass. The glass itself is known by means of the sense of touch. In order to know that it is between us and the objects seen through it, we must know how to correlate *the space of touch* with *the space of sight*. . . .When it [the correlation] has been accomplished, it becomes possible to attach a meaning to the statement that the blue glass, which we can touch, is between us and the object seen, as we say, "through" it. But we have still not reduced our statement completely to what is actually given in sense. We have fallen into the assumption that the object of which we are conscious when we touch the blue spectacles still exists after we have ceased to touch them. . . . If we are to account for

the blue appearance of objects other than the spectacles, when seen through them, it might seem as if we must assume that the spectacles still exist when we are not touching them. . . . It may be questioned, however, whether this assumption is actually unavoidable. . . . We may say that the object of which we become aware when we touch the spectacles continues to have effects afterwards, though perhaps it no longer exists.[17]

Think of the problem Russell here confronts as that of giving an analysis of the "knowledge content" of a claim ordinarily expressed using sentence (6).

> 6. I am seeing a table that appears blue because I am seeing it through blue spectacles.

On the basis of what we have been given so far, it might seem that the sense-data analysis of this content would have to include (i) the analysis of (5) (which is the first clause of (6)), (ii) the claim that the table-type sense data I see are blue, and (iii) the claim that I have experienced a hard sense datum in a position in my "touch space" that is correlated in a certain way with my "sight space." Daunting as it would be to fill out (i–iii), Russell clearly sees that doing so wouldn't be enough.

He identifies the problem, in the next passage.

It may be said that our hypothesis is useless in the case when the blue glass is never touched at all. How, in that case, are we to account for the blue appearance of objects? And more generally, what are we to make of the *hypothetical* [i.e., counterfactual] sensations of touch which we associate with untouched visible objects, *which we know would be verified if we chose, though in fact we do not verify them?*[18]

Note the counterfactual language—*what would be so-and-so, if conditions were such-and-such.* Russell here uses such language to show that (iii) above cannot be part of the analysis because (6) can be true when (iii) isn't; instead, a (potentially) counterfactual claim is needed—*if I were to have the experiences called "putting my finger in a certain place," then I would touch something hard (have a tactile experience of a hard sense datum).*

Russell takes this to be the solution to his problem. First, he addresses the general question "What are we to make of the *hypothetical* sensations of touch which we associate with untouched visible objects, which we know would be verified if we chose, though we do not verify them?" He says:

Experience has taught us that where we see certain kinds of coloured surfaces we can, by touch, obtain certain expected sensations of hardness or softness, tactile shape, and so on. [*Note the assumption that tactile shape is not the same as visual shape because sense modalities acquaint us with different sensible objects.*]

---

[17] Ibid., pp. 77–79, my emphasis.
[18] Ibid., pp. 79–80, my emphasis.

This leads us to believe that what is seen is usually tangible, and that it has, whether we touch it or not, the hardness or softness which we should expect to feel if we touched it. *But the mere fact that we are able to infer what our tactile sensations would be shows that it is not logically necessary to assume tactile qualities before they are felt.* All that is really known is that the visual appearance in question, together with touch, will lead to certain sensations [or rather *would* lead to them], which can necessarily be determined in terms of the visual appearance, since otherwise they could not be inferred from it.[19]

The lesson here is quite general; analyses of material-object statements must standardly include (potentially) counterfactual claims about *what sense data would occur, if specified conditions were met*—rather than categorical claims about what sense data actually occur. The key point for Russell is that the need to include these statements is no cause for worry, because their truth is inductively inferable from correlations of sense data that have been observed in the past.

The final step is to apply this lesson directly to the blue spectacles.

We can now give a statement of the experienced facts concerning the blue spectacles, which will supply an interpretation of common-sense beliefs *without assuming anything beyond the existence of sensible objects at the times when they are sensible.* By experience of the correlation of touch and sight sensations, we become able to associate a certain place in touch-space with a certain corresponding place in sight-space. Sometimes, namely in the case of transparent things, we find that there is a tangible object in a touch-place without there being any visible object in the corresponding sight-place. But in such a case as that of the blue spectacles, we find that whatever object is visible beyond the empty sight-place in the same line of sight has a different colour from what it has when there is no tangible object in the intervening touch-place; and as we move the tangible object in touch-space, the blue patch moves in sight-space. If now we find a blue patch moving in this way in sight-space, when we have no sensible experience of an intervening tangible object, we nevertheless infer that, *if we put our hand at a certain place in touch-space, we should [i.e., would] experience a certain touch-sensation.* If we are to avoid non-sensible objects, *this must be taken as the whole of our meaning* when we say that the blue spectacles are in a certain place, though we have not touched them, and have only seen other things rendered blue by their interposition.[20]

Here we see that the analysis of material-object statements—like (6) involving the blue spectacles—must include (potentially) counterfactual statements of what sensations would occur if various conditions were fulfilled.[21] These (potential) counterfactuals are taken to be epistemically

[19] Ibid., p. 80, my emphasis.
[20] Ibid., pp. 80–81, my emphasis.
[21] This point, which seems transparently obvious from the text, is made in Soames (2006a) in reply to Sainsbury (2006), where it is, inexplicably, denied.

unproblematic by virtue of being inductively supported by past correlations of sense data of the relevant sort. Roughly put, for any sense data the occurrence of which under the specified conditions would be expected in order to verify the material-object statement under analysis, the analysis should include a (potentially) counterfactual statement to the effect that those sense data would occur if the conditions were satisfied. Since there will typically be enormously many of these, the analysis of even the simplest material-object statement can be expected to be enormously complex.

Russell himself never indicated that he thought otherwise, or that he had arrived at a complete analysis of any particular material-object statement. He seems to have realized that no matter how many clauses he might produce, there would always be many more with an equal claim to being part of the analysis. He also knew that clauses like those I have used—e.g., (5a–c), with their vague talk of sense data of a certain sort or type—are themselves sketchy and not fully specified. But this didn't deter him, or later philosophers who were influenced by him. Rather, they adopted for material-object statements an extreme version of the attitude I mentioned earlier about nation statements. Even though it isn't clear how to map statements about nations onto equivalent statements that make precise and definite claims only about people and places, some have felt that talk about nations must somehow be so reducible because there are no other entities for nation statements to be about. For a number of philosophers, including Russell between 1914 and 1926, material-object statements were similar. Even though it is, for all practical purposes, *impossible* to give even approximate translations of material-object statements into epistemically equivalent statements about sense data, these philosophers felt that talk "about material objects" must reduce to talk about sense data, if material-object statements are to express any genuine empirical knowledge.

The following passage gives a good indication of why Russell felt this way.

> I think it may be laid down quite generally that, *in so far* as physics or common sense is verifiable, it must be capable of interpretation in terms of actual sense-data alone. The reason for this is simple. Verification consists always in the occurrence of an expected sense-datum. . . . Now if an expected sense-datum constitutes a verification, what was asserted must have been about sense-data; or, at any rate, if part of what was asserted was not about sense-data, then only the other part has been verified.[22]

If we ignore his final qualification for now (he doesn't make serious use of it), then the content of the passage may be expressed by the following principles.

7. Verification always consists in the occurrence of sense data.
8. If the occurrence of sense data constitutes verification of a statement S, then S must be about sense data.

---

[22] Russell (1914), pp. 81–82.

Russell's reasoning can be reconstructed more or less as follows: From (7) and (8) it follows that insofar as ordinary statements of common sense, and also statements about physics, are verifiable, they must be about sense data. Since we know these statements to be true, they must be verifiable; indeed, it is by verifying them that we come to know them. Thus, the statements of both physics and common sense must be about sense data. Although I take this little argument to be deeply misguided, I will defer raising difficulties for it until later. The next step is to look more closely at Russell's overall model for reducing material-object statements to sense-data statements.

2.2. The Robust System of Private Perspectives

About two-thirds of the way through lecture 3, Russell notes a certain problem with his informal discussion to that point. The problem is making sense of the notion of the table being in the same place, as one walks around it. Bodily movement changes one's perspective, and hence the three-dimensional array of visual sense data one perceives. For each perspective, we can determine the spatial relations in which the sense data seen there stand to one another. But we need to do more than this to explicate talk of seeing the same table from different perspectives, without presupposing in our explication the existence of enduring material objects located in physical space. Somehow, Russell realizes, we must find a way to use the materials provided by multiple spatial arrays of (visual) sense data seen from individual perspectives to *construct* a conception of space within which the individual spaces of particular perspectives can themselves be located.

Upon reaching this point he announces:

> We will now make a new start. . . . Instead of inquiring what is the minimum of assumption by which we can explain the world of sense, we will, in order to have a model hypothesis . . . construct one possible (not necessary) explanation of the facts. It may perhaps then be possible to pare away what is superfluous in our hypothesis, leaving a residue which may be regarded as the abstract answer to our problem.[23]

The final point is one to bear in mind. The framework Russell is about to introduce is provisional; it will contain more robust assumptions than are, in his opinion, necessary. In the end they will be pared away. He describes the framework as follows:

> [I]magine that each mind looks out upon the world . . . from a point of view peculiar to itself. . . . Each mind sees at each moment an immensely complex three-dimensional world; but there is absolutely nothing which is seen by two minds simultaneously. . . . The three-dimensional world seen by one

---

[23] Ibid., p. 87.

mind therefore contains no place in common with that seen by another, for places can only be constituted by the things in or around them. *Hence we may suppose . . . that each [world] exists entire exactly as it is perceived, and might be exactly as it is even if it were not perceived. We may further suppose that there are an infinite number of such worlds which are in fact unperceived.* If two men are sitting in a room, two somewhat similar worlds are perceived by them; if a third man enters and sits between them, a third world, intermediate between the two previous worlds, begins to be perceived. . . . The system consisting of all views of the universe perceived and unperceived, I shall call the system of "perspectives."[24]

This framework is designed to aid us in constructing a space in which the sense data perceived from one perspective can be related to sense data perceived from other perspectives. For example, starting with the perception "of the table" from an initial perspective, we want to identify certain further perceptions of the table as seen from perspectives that are "closer to the table," and certain other perceptions of the table as seen from perspectives that are "farther from the table." Similarly for sense data one perceives as one moves "in one direction from the table" versus those that one perceives as one moves "in the opposite direction from the table." Although the complications involved in the construction of such a space are enormous, the fundamental idea is simple. Look at something in your immediate environment—e.g., an orange. Notice how its visible appearance changes ever so slightly as you move slightly to the right, to the left, toward, or away from it. Complications aside, the general rule of thumb is that slight movements result in slight changes of appearance, with movements in different directions resulting in changes of different, but related, sorts.

That, of course, is how we describe our visual perceptions using the language of common sense. For Russell the trick is to invert the order of explanation. To do this, one takes the sense data perceivable from different perspectives as fundamental, along with the properties of those sense data and the similarities they bear to other sense data from the same or different perspectives. From this foundation, one *defines* objects, their locations, and the locations of different perspectives (in relation to one another). On this picture, "movement" toward or away from an object is *not* what *causes* one to have sense data of a systematically related sort. Rather, talk about "movement" and "location" is itself nothing more than shorthand for complicated talk about systematic relations of similarity and difference of perceived, and perceivable, sense data.

Here is the (rough) idea. For a certain perspective (position) Pn to be "closer to the orange" than another perspective (position) Px (along the same line of sight) is just for there to be a (linear) sequence of perspectives

[24] Ibid., pp. 87–88, my emphasis.

(positions) with the following characteristics: (i) the sequence starts with P1, in which the orange-like visual sense datum is of maximal size (taking up one's entire visual field), (ii) the next perspective (position) is P2 in which the visual datum of the orange is just the tiniest bit smaller (and in all other respects indiscernible or virtually indiscernible from the sense datum seen from P1), (iii) each succeeding perspective (position) bears the same relation to its predecessor as P2 does to P1, and (iv) Pn comes earlier in the sequence than Px. Next, construct a similar series by starting at a point "P1-L" (which is ever so slightly different in "the left way" from P1) and generating another (linear) sequence of points "farther and farther away from the orange." Do the same "all the way around the orange (on the same plane)" until one arrives at the original perspective P1 again. Repeat all this in ways that constitute rotating the planes to get a three-dimensional space. Don't worry about the stupefying complexity of the task, or even the difficulties here being held in abeyance; Russell didn't. The construction I imagine is very crude, as is Russell's, who only gestures at what might ultimately be involved. The point is that the orange—or more properly "the visual orange," since that is all we have so far—is a collection of sense data present in a vast array of occupied and unoccupied perspectives, each of which has a position with respect to each other perspective and to the orange itself, which is located in the part of the constructed space that is bounded by all the P1-perspectives of the above construction.

In painting this picture, I have, of course, made use of a vast multitude of unoccupied perspectives and unperceived sense data. Russell notes this aspect of the view in his summary overview.

> Two men are sometimes found to perceive very similar perspectives. . . . Thus it is possible, sometimes, to establish a correlation by similarity between a great many of the things of one perspective, and a great many of the things of another. In case the similarity is very great, we say the points of view of the two perspectives are near together in space; but this space in which they are near together is totally different from the spaces inside the two perspectives. It is a relation between the perspectives, and is not in either of them. . . . *Between two perceived perspectives which are similar, we can imagine a whole series of other perspectives, some at least unperceived, and such that between any two, however similar, there are others still more similar. In this way the space which consists of relations between perspectives can be rendered continuous, and (if we choose) three-dimensional.*

> We can now define the momentary common-sense "thing". . . . By similarity of neighbouring perspectives, many objects [sense data] in the one can be correlated with objects in the other, namely with similar objects. Given an object [sense datum] in one perspective, form the system of all the objects correlated with it in all the perspectives; that system may by identified with the momentary

common-sense "thing." Thus an aspect of a "thing" is a member of the system of aspects which *is* the "thing" at the moment. . . . All the aspects of the thing are real, whereas the thing is a mere logical construction.[25]

Details aside, the framework incorporates large, so far undischarged, assumptions concerning the existence of, and one's knowledge about, (i) vast numbers of unoccupied perspectives and unperceived sense data, and (ii) minds other than one's own occupying perspectives that one does not, and perceiving sense data that one does not perceive. Since the point of Russell's reconstruction is to explain how the knowledge one expresses using ordinary material-object statements can be justified, any reliance on assumptions that may themselves be difficult to justify poses a direct threat to the project. Thus, we will need to keep an eye on (i) and (ii) as the project progresses.

2.3. The Elimination of Unoccupied Perspectives and Unsensed Sense Data

In lecture 4, Russell extends his reconstruction of our empirical knowledge to include the statements of physical science. One of his points is that the same habits of mind that lead us to think of ourselves as located in a world of ordinary, relatively stable, middle-sized objects that cause the fleeting and fragmentary sense data we experience has been at work in physical science since its inception.

The belief in indestructible "things" very early took the form of atomism. The underlying motive in atomism was not, I think, any empirical success in interpreting phenomena, but rather an instinctive belief that beneath all the changes of the sensible world there must be something permanent and unchanging. This belief was, no doubt, fostered and nourished by its practical successes, culminating in the conservation of mass; but it was not produced by these successes. On the contrary, they were produced by it. Philosophical writers on physics sometimes speak as though the conservation of something or other were essential to the possibility of science, but this, I believe, is an entirely erroneous opinion. If the *a priori* belief in permanence had not existed, the same laws which are now formulated in terms of this belief might just as well have been formulated without it. *Why should we suppose that, when ice melts, the water which replaces it is the same thing in a new form?* Merely because this supposition enables us to state the phenomena in a way which is consonant with our prejudices. *What we really know is that, under certain conditions of temperature, the appearance we call ice is replaced by the appearance we call water. We can give laws according to which the one appearance will be succeeded by*

[25] Ibid., pp. 88–89, my emphasis for "Between two perceived perspectives. . . ."

the other, but there is no reason except prejudice for regarding both as appearances of the same substance.[26]

Russell's point is not, of course, that no empirical knowledge is expressed by well-supported physical laws, but that the knowledge they are used to express is mixed with unjustifiable philosophical beliefs, owing to their usual formulation in terms of permanent or quasi-permanent things underlying appearances. The task of his reconstruction is, as he indicates, to root these out.

> The above extrusion of permanent things affords an example of the maxim which inspires all scientific philosophizing, namely "Occam's razor": *Entities are not to be multiplied without necessity.* In other words, in dealing with any subject-matter, find out what entities are undeniably involved, and state everything in terms of these entities. Very often the resulting statement is more complicated and difficult than one which, like common sense and most philosophy, assumes hypothetical entities whose existence there is no good reason to believe in. We find it easier to imagine a wall-paper with changing colours [with the passage of time] than to think merely of the series of colours; but it is a mistake to suppose that what is easy and natural in thought is what is most free from unwarrantable assumptions, as the case of "things" very aptly illustrates.[27]

Although one can understand Russell's desire to rid physics of "unwarrantable" assumptions, it is very hard to imagine physics getting along without the assumption that matter exists when it is not perceived. Since physics encompasses the entire universe throughout eons in which there have been no observers, nearly everything it tells us is about matter that is, or was, unperceived. Of course, Russell realizes this, but he also believes that to conceptualize physics in the usual way is to render it unverifiable— and hence not capable of being known. Since his task is to lay bare the genuine knowledge we possess, while disentangling it from unwarranted and unverifiable assumptions, he needs a way of extracting the empirical content of physical theory that explains how the claims it makes can be verified.

He addresses this point in the following passage.

> We have been considering . . . the question of the *verifiability* of physics. . . . For a proposition to be verifiable, it is not enough that it should be true, but it must also be such as we can *discover* to be true. Thus, verifiability depends on our capacity for acquiring knowledge, and not only upon the objective truth. In physics, as ordinarily set forth, there is much that is unverifiable: there are hypothesis as to (α) how things would appear to a spectator in a place where, as it happens, there is no spectator, (β) how things would

[26] Ibid., pp. 104–5, my emphasis.
[27] Ibid., p. 107.

appear at times when, in fact, they are not appearing to anyone; (γ) things which never appear at all. All these are introduced to simplify the statement of the causal laws, but none of them forms an integral part of what is *known* in physics.[28]

Note the qualifying phrase in the passage, "In physics, *as ordinarily set forth. . . .*" By this, I take it, Russell means "In physics, *understood as incorporating the assumption of enduring matter and material objects, whether perceived or not.*" In physics, so understood, statements are made about the properties such things have even when they are not perceived, including statements about those among them that are never perceived. He maintains that these statements are not *known* to be true, and seems to suggest that they are not verifiable, and so are *unknowable*.

This is another version of what he has been saying all along, which is why he is determined to *reconstruct* the genuine knowledge we use the statements of physics to express in a way that excludes these unknowable elements. But how can he succeed? After all, the Leibnizian framework used for his reconstruction itself makes heavy use of the properties of unobserved sense data in unoccupied perspectives. Aren't statements about them unknowable, while being indispensable to Russell's logical constructions? When using that framework to provide logical constructions of the "enduring things" given to us by unreconstructed physics, he identifies each such thing with a totality of sense data many, if not most, of which are unperceived. In the vast number of cases provided by physics these totalities will consist *exclusively* of unperceived sense data. How then can the purified statements of physics provided by Russell's theory of logical constructions themselves be verifiable, and hence knowable?

Russell addresses this worry in the next passage, which I will present interspersed with commentary.

If physics is to consist wholly of propositions known to be true, or at least capable of being proved or disproved, the three types of hypothetical entities we have just enumerated must all be capable of being logical functions of sense data.[29]

Russell's project requires the reconstructed propositions of physics, not to be known, not even to always be knowable, but to be *capable of being "proved," and so known, or "disproved," and so known not to be true*. In short, he demands a construction that shows the statements of physics to be *verifiable*—in the sense of capable of being confirmed or disconfirmed by evidence. What does it mean to say that a proposition p is *verifiable* in his sense? Presumably, that there are specifiable conditions which, should they occur, would yield evidence confirming or disconfirming p. Russell

---

[28] Ibid., pp. 110–11.
[29] Ibid., p. 111.

apparently thinks that (unanalyzed) statements about enduring but un-observed material things are not verifiable in this sense. Is the same true of statements about unobserved sense data in unoccupied Leibnizian perspectives?

He answers:

[L]et us recall the hypothetical Leibnizian universe of Lecture III. In that universe, we had a number of perspectives, two of which never had any en-tity in common, but often contained entities which could be sufficiently cor-related to be regarded as belonging to the same thing. We will call one of these an "actual" private world when there is an actual spectator to which it appears, and "ideal" when it is merely constructed on principles of continu-ity. A physical thing consists, at each instant, of the whole set of its aspects at that instant, in all the different worlds; thus a momentary state of a thing is a whole set of aspects. An "ideal" appearance will be an aspect merely cal-culated, but not actually perceived by a spectator. An "ideal" state of a thing will be a state at a moment when all its appearances are ideal. An ideal thing will be one whose states at all times are ideal. *Ideal appearances, states, and things, since they are calculated, must be functions of actual appearances, states, and things; in fact, ultimately, they must be functions of actual appearances [sense data]. Thus it is unnecessary, for the enunciation of the laws of physics, to assign any reality to ideal elements: it is enough to accept them as logical constructions, provided we have means of knowing how to determine when they become actual.*[30]

Here Russell makes good on his earlier declaration of intent to remove unnecessary and unsupported assumptions from his Leibnizian system of perspectives used to reconstruct our empirical knowledge. No longer will he consider unperceived sense data in unoccupied perspectives to be real elements of the system used to provide logical constructions of material objects. This brings his treatment of unperceived sense data in the system of perspectives into line with his statement that unperceived sense data probably don't, and are not assumed to, exist—made in lecture 3 of the 1914 version of *Our Knowledge of the External World*—and with his stronger statement that sense data are nothing more than the experiences of per-ceivers (which makes it impossible for them to exist on their own)—made in the very slightly revised 1926 version of chapter 3.

That much is clear.[31] It is less clear what we should make of Russell's talk of "ideal appearances" (unperceived sense data) being "functions of," "logical constructions out of," or merely "calculated from" "actual appear-ances" (perceived sense data). Although there is an interpretation of the passage that makes sense, and advances Russell's goal, it is not obvious from his brief remarks that he clearly separated it from other, indefensible,

---

[30] Ibid., pp. 111–12, my emphasis.
[31] This point is made in Soames (2005d) and Soames (2006a) in response to misinterpre-tations in Griffin (2005), Pincock (2005–6), and Sainsbury (2006).

positions. The interpretation that moves the discussion forward construes talk of unperceived sense data (in unoccupied perspectives) as shorthand for talk about what sense data *would be* perceived, *if those perspectives were occupied.* On this view, unperceived sense data from unoccupied perspectives are *logical constructions* out of perceived sense data from occupied perspectives.

There is, however, no eliminating (potentially) counterfactual claims about what sense data *would be perceived, if certain perspectives were occupied* (i.e., if certain conditions were fulfilled). Fortunately, they don't need to be eliminated, since they are "calculated from"—i.e., based upon—past observations of what really occurred. For example, I now know that *if I were to hold an American silver dollar in front of me and let it go, unsupported, it would fall to the floor.* I know this because I have abundant evidence that things of this type left unsupported very near the surface of the earth have, in past cases I have observed, fallen to the floor; indeed they have never in my experience done otherwise. Since evidence of this sort is (arguably) all that is required in order for me to know the (potentially) counterfactual statement to be true, there is no need to maintain that the *content* of that statement is identical to the content of the conjunction of the evidential claims that support it. Surely it isn't. Nor does that conjunction logically or conceptually entail the (potentially) counterfactual statement—since there is no *contradiction* or *incoherence* in denying the latter while affirming the former. All of this is consistent with the fact that my knowledge of the former provides me with knowledge of the latter.

Applying this lesson to Russell, we arrive at the following position: insofar as material-object statements from both physics and everyday life express propositions capable of being known to be true, or known to be untrue, *the contents of these statements are wholly definable in terms of categorical statements about sense data that have been perceived in the past, as well as those that are presently being perceived, plus (potentially) counterfactual statements about what sense data would be perceived, if certain conditions were, or had been, fulfilled (leading to certain unoccupied perspectives being occupied).* Although the truth or falsity of complex claims of this sort are not always known, they are often knowable solely on the basis of knowing enough about sense data actually perceived, now or in the past. I have, to be sure, articulated this position more clearly and unequivocally than Russell does in the passages from which I have extracted it. Nevertheless, I believe it captures the spirit of his position—as partially indicated by the following remark.

> I think it may be laid down quite generally that, *in so far* as physics or common sense is verifiable, it must be capable of interpretation in terms of actual sense data alone.[32]

---

[32] Russell (1914), p. 81.

3. KNOWLEDGE, VERIFICATION, AND CONTENT: CRITIQUE OF RUSSELL'S RATIONALE

The passage just quoted continues.

> The reason is simple. Verification consists always in the occurrence of an expected sense-datum. . . . Now if an expected sense-datum constitutes verification, what was asserted must have been about sense-data; or, at any rate, if part of what was asserted was not about sense data, then only the other part has been verified.[33]

As I indicated at the end of section 2.1, we can, simplifying a bit, take Russell's project to be guided by principles (7) and (8).

7. Verification always consists in the occurrence of sense data.
8. If the occurrence of sense data constitutes verification of a statement S, then S must be about sense data.

From these principles, it follows that insofar as ordinary statements of common sense and physics are verifiable, they must be about sense data. Since we know many of these statements to be true, they must be verifiable; indeed, it is by verifying them that we come to know them. Thus, the statements of both physics and common sense must be about sense data. That, I believe, is Russell's reasoning.

However, neither (7) nor (8) is obviously correct. For example, consider (9), which differs from (8) only in being more general.

9. If occurrences of x verify a statement S, then S must be about x's.

Putting aside Russell's project, one may find it worthwhile to test the independent plausibility of this principle. One kind of case involves theoretical statements in physics—e.g., statements about tiny subatomic particles, or massive black holes. Although we don't directly observe these things, we posit their existence because they help explain things we do observe. Many observations we are interested in are recorded by complex measuring instruments. So, the way we verify some statements about subatomic particles and black holes is by taking readings from instruments. If (9) were true, this would mean that our statements about subatomic particles and black holes are really about instrument readings. However, they certainly don't seem to be. Doesn't this tell against (9)? Or again, suppose we are trying to figure out whether in the distant past a certain person x murdered someone y. Since x and y are now long gone, all we can do to verify the claim that x murdered y is to consult the surviving historical records. If (9) were correct, then the claim that x murdered y would be a claim about actual and counterfactual observations of those records. But that doesn't seem right; the claim seems to be about x and y themselves.

[33] Ibid., p. 81.

Considerations like these provide *prima facie* reasons to reject (9), and to maintain that *what a statement is about* can't always be identified with *the observations one could make to verify it.* But if (9) is rejected, one must ask, what, if anything, makes (8), which is a special case of (9), any more acceptable? This question threatens Russell's project.

Of course, the argument could also be run the other way. If, like Russell, one is convinced that (8) is correct, one might accept (9) too, together with the corollary that statements about subatomic particles and black holes are (to the extent they are knowable) just abbreviations of complex statements about instrument readings, and the related corollary that statements about the distant past are (to the extent they are knowable) just abbreviations of statements about observations we make of presently existing historical records. The point of my questioning of (8) and (9) is not that it leaves Russell with no reply. The point is simply that the fundamental, unargued premises driving his sweeping reanalysis of physics and common sense are not antecedently obvious, and so require defense. Thus, he can't legitimately expect his revisionary conception of empirical knowledge to be accepted without defending them.

Why did Russell accept (8)? Although he doesn't say in any detail, his acceptance appears to stem from an overly simple general conception of how knowledge arises. The picture includes principles like the following:

(i) The foundation of all empirical knowledge (about the world) consists of sense data statements—e.g., *I am now seeing, or have seen in the not too distant past, a circular red patch.* These are the statements of which we can be most certain. Provided that we have the right sort of experiences, it would be pathological to doubt them.

(ii) All other empirical knowledge is built from, and justified by, these foundational statements in certain fixed ways. Two main ways are deduction and simple enumerative induction—*this A is B, that A is B, ... so (defeasibly) All A's are B's.*

If one thinks of deduction as *logical deduction*, and induction as simply enumerative in this way, one will naturally expect the conclusions they license to be conclusions about sense data when one's premises are sense-data statements. On this picture, any knowledge reached by induction or deduction from truths about sense data alone must itself be confined to sense data.

That said, I believe Russell would also recognize another way of building up empirical knowledge—something one might call *the method of hypothesis.* This method consists of formulating a hypothesis and deducing observational consequences from it (together with further observational statements). If these consequences are true in enough cases, one may characterize the hypothesis as confirmed. When the confirmation is strong and systematic enough, we may even come to *know* the hypothesis to be true.

This method of arriving at knowledge should be familiar from the physical sciences. However, I believe that Russell's conception of what it involves was limited, and to a certain extent misrepresented its power. He would, I suspect, have claimed that if the observable consequences one deduces from the hypothesis (together with further, independent observational claims) are sense-data statements, then the hypothesis itself must be a sense data statement. Actually, he foresees two possibilities. Either the hypothesis is solely about sense data, in which case he would say that it is verifiable and hence a possible object of knowledge, or the hypothesis is partially about sense data and partially about something else, in which case he would hold that the part about something else must be unverifiable and unknowable. On this view, the only knowledge that the method of hypothesis can provide is knowledge of sense data. Since the only other ways of obtaining empirical knowledge he seems to recognize are induction and deduction from sense data statements, he concludes that the only knowledge one can have of the world is knowledge of sense data. Agreeing with Moore that we do know various material-object statements to be true, he thinks that material-object statements *must* be analyzable into sense data statements. Hence, he thinks, material objects are logical constructions out of sense data.

One of the questionable aspects of this reasoning is the claim that if one can *deduce* observational consequences about observable objects from a hypothesis H, then H must be about those observable objects. What conception of deduction would justify this claim? Well, *logical deduction* in a purely formal system of logic would. If P is a substantive, noncontradictory premise containing certain nonlogical vocabulary, and Q is a substantive, nonnecessary conclusion containing only nonlogical vocabulary that does not appear in P—e.g., if Q is made up of observational predicates that are applied to observable objects on the basis of ordinary perceptual experience, whereas P contains no such predicates—then Q will not be a *logical consequence* of P, and so will not be *logically deducible* from P without appealing to definitions of at least some of the vocabulary of P in terms of the vocabulary of Q. Think of Russell's mathematical model. We can deduce claims about sets from claims about numbers because numbers are definable in terms of sets. With this model in mind, one might well think that a hypothesis H from which one could deduce an observational claim $(O_1 \supset O_2)$ must itself either contain the observational vocabulary of O_1 and O_2, or contain vocabulary that is definable in terms of that vocabulary. Either way, if this were so, H might justifiably be said to be about observational objects.

But this conception of deduction is quite narrow. As I pointed out in chapter 4—when discussing Moore's flawed use of the concepts *analyticity, entailment,* and *logical consequence* in attempting to show that claims about goodness can't be derived from other claims—there are conceptual relations between concepts, even when those concepts are not definable in terms of one another. Because of this, there are cases in which Q is a necessary and a priori, but not a logical, consequence of P, as well as being knowable by virtue of knowing P—even though P and Q are contingent, the nonlogical vocabulary of Q differs completely from that of P, and the two are not related by any definitions. Corresponding to such cases, there are truth-guaranteeing deductions for which it is not ruled out that observational predictions might be deduced from a hypothesis that itself contains no observational vocabulary and is not *about* observable objects in any direct sense. This means that we can't rule out coming to know a hypothesis to be true by having observational evidence that confirms it, even though the hypothesis is not overtly about the evidence.

Beyond this, there is a further related problem with the reasoning behind Russell's conception of verifiable statements as limited to those solely about sense data. A hypothesis H may consist of a set of statements, or of a single complex statement with many clauses. In many such cases, the observational consequences deducible from H can be derived only by appeal to many or even all parts of H, whether they be clauses or separate statements. In such cases—when it takes many or all parts of a hypothesis working together, so to speak, to entail its observational predictions— there may be no way to divide up those predictions and assign each to one part of the hypothesis as opposed to others. Since, in this sort of case, many or all parts of the hypothesis are needed to derive the predictions, if those predictions are discovered by observation to be true, they may be taken to confirm *the whole hypothesis*—or at least all the parts, observational and non-observational alike, that together conspire to generate the predictions. Thus, Russell's restriction, which tacitly assumes that the observational predictions of a hypothesis can always be traced solely to its observational parts, cannot be supported.[34] Taken together, these two

---

[34] This criticism of the idea that one can always assign observational consequences to discrete parts of a hypothesis is a version of what has come to be known as "the Quine-Duhem point." Compare with the discussion of Quine (1951, pp. 38–41): "This is *radical reductionism*. Every meaningful statement is held to be translatable into a statement about immediate experience. . . . Radical reductionism, conceived now with statements as units, set itself the task of specifying a sense-datum language and showing how to translate the rest of significant discourse, statement by statement, into it. . . . The dogma of reductionism survives in the supposition that each statement, taken in isolation from its fellows, can admit of confirmation or infirmation [disconfirmation] at all. My counter suggestion . . . is that our statements about the external world face the tribunal of sense not individually, but only as a corporate body" (at this point Duhem (1906) is cited). The key points about confirmation are (i) that what is confirmed by evidence is a whole set of statements, and (ii) that one cannot correlate individual statements, one by one, with evidence supporting or undermining them. It is interesting to note that although Quine's point corrects the shortcoming I have noted in Russell, Quine himself, in 1951, was still thinking of the evidence supporting empirical theories as true sense data statements, and of the content/meaning of *entire theories* as given by the true sense data statements that would support them. Russell would have added the qualification "to the extent that those theories are knowable."

problems—the narrowness of the conception of *deduction* and the assumption that the observable consequences of a hypothesis can be separated out and traced to discrete parts of the hypothesis—undermine his argument that insofar as the claims made by material-object statements are knowable, these claims must be analyzable into sense data statements.

4. OTHER MINDS

4.1. A Working Hypothesis?

At the time he wrote *Our Knowledge of the External World*, Russell saw the view that material objects are logical constructions out of sense data as providing an answer, perhaps the only possible answer, to the question *Granted that we have knowledge expressed by material-object statements, how is this knowledge possible?* If material objects are simply logical constructions out of sense data, then the knowledge expressed by material-object statements is nothing more than knowledge of categorical and hypothetical (including potentially counterfactual) statements about sense data. Since such knowledge seemed to be relatively unproblematic, Russell saw his view as a solution to a central part of the philosophical problem regarding knowledge of the external world.

However, there was a serious difficulty, of which he was fully aware, with this basic strategy. Our knowledge of the external world includes not only knowledge of material objects, but also knowledge of other people. Still, Russell was *not* willing to say that other people are merely logical constructions out of one's own sense data. To say this would be to claim that when I say that you exist, all I am really saying is something about my own sense data. To his credit, this is something he was sensible enough not to accept.

> When we see our friend drop a weight upon his toe, and hear him say—what we should say in similar circumstances, the phenomena *can* no doubt be explained without assuming that he is anything but a series of shapes and noises seen and heard by us, but practically no man is so infected with philosophy as not to be quite certain that his friend has felt the same kind of pain as he himself would feel.[35]

Here Russell indicates that he will not attempt to analyze statements about other people in terms of statements about his own sense data. But then, how can he explain our knowledge of other people?

He briefly considers one traditional philosophical argument—the argument from analogy. The argument goes more or less as follows: (i) I notice that there is a correlation between things that happen to my body

[35] Russell (1914), p. 82.

and certain experiences I have. For example, if I prick my finger with a needle, I feel pain. (ii) I also notice that there are other bodies like mine, and that some of the same things that happen to my body happen to those bodies. (iii) When a finger of another body is pricked with a needle, I don't feel pain. But since I have observed a correlation between my body and my experiences, I postulate that the same correlation holds for other bodies. (iv) Consequently, I conclude that when a finger of another body is pricked with a needle, that event is accompanied by someone else's experience of pain. But to say that someone else experiences pain is to say that other people/minds exist. (v) I *know* that they exist, because I *know* that the correlation between bodily events and mental events holds in my own case, and I *know*, on the basis of the argument from analogy, that it holds for other people too.

Russell didn't entirely dismiss this argument, but he wasn't very happy with it, and didn't believe he could place much weight on it. Two difficulties stand out. First, at best the argument is a matter of induction from a single case. One finds an instance of a correlation between events involving one's body and one's feeling of pain. One then observes thousands of other bodies, and on the basis of one observed correlation posits that the same correlation holds for all those cases. But why is this any more reasonable than thinking either that since one doesn't feel pain oneself in cases involving other bodies, there really is no pain in those cases, or that, since one has no way of knowing whether there are other minds that feel pain, one simply has no basis for determining whether the correlation holds in those cases? Nothing in the argument from analogy answers this question. Since the question is just another way of expressing the original difficulty—*How does one know that there are other people?*—the argument can hardly be regarded as successful.

The second objection, in the context of Russell's project, starts with the observation that in its usual form the argument from analogy takes it for granted that there are real, enduring material objects, in the form of human bodies. But if, like Russell, one takes bodies to be logical constructions out of sense data, the argument from analogy takes a bizarre twist. I can more or less understand what it would be for the same correlation to exist between *other bodies* and *their experiences* as exists between *my body* and *my experience—provided that bodies are taken for granted and not analyzed away.* But if they are not taken for granted, but instead analyzed in terms of sense data, what I am asked to accept becomes very problematic. If bodies are logical constructions out of sense data, then they must be logical constructions out of *someone's* sense data. Since at this stage of the argument Russell is trying to establish the existence of other minds, he can't assume other minds in the analysis of material-objects statements. With this in mind, imagine that I am trying to employ Russell's argument myself. It appears that my only recourse is to regard material objects as logical constructions out of *my* sense data. But then the argument from analogy would have me saying that the same correlation that exists between *my experiences* and certain of *my* sense data (used to analyze statements about my body) also exists between the experiences of *other minds* and certain other sense data of *mine* (those that I use to analyze statements about other bodies). That's strange. How can one suppose that I am connected with my sense data in the same way that other minds are connected with *my* sense data? If we eliminate the assumption that there really are other bodies from the argument from analogy and try to state it making use only of one's own private sense data, the argument becomes utterly unreasonable.

Thus, it is good that Russell doesn't put much credence in it.

> The hypothesis that other people have minds must, I think, be allowed to be not susceptible of any very strong support from the analogical argument. At the same time, it is a hypothesis which systematizes a vast body of facts and never leads to any consequences which there is reason to think false. There is therefore nothing to be said against its truth, and good reason to use it as a working hypothesis. When once it is admitted, it enables us to extend our knowledge of the sensible world by testimony, and thus leads to the system of private worlds which we assumed in our hypothetical construction. In actual fact, whatever we may try to think as philosophers, we cannot help believing in the minds of other people, so that the question whether our belief is justified has a merely speculative interest. And if it is justified, then there is no further difficulty of principle in that vast extension of our knowledge, beyond our own private data, which we find in science and common sense.[36]

In this passage Russell indicates that we should accept the claim that there are other people as a *working hypothesis*. He seems to be thinking along the following lines: We begin with the problem of explaining how we know there are material objects and other minds. We can't satisfactorily explain or justify our knowledge of the latter. But if we grant that there are other people, we can explain and justify our knowledge of material objects; we can know that there are material objects because they are logical constructions out of our own sense data and those of others, where sense data are things we can all know about. By reducing the problem of explaining our knowledge of the external world to the problem of explaining our knowledge of other minds, we have cut the problem in half. Russell seemed to think this was progress.

4.2. How Not to Make Progress

For my own part, I can see no such progress. On the contrary, I believe Russell makes the problem worse. Consider the analysis of a simple material-object statement.

10. There is a table in the classroom.

---

[36] Ibid., p. 96.

Presumably the analysis can't be given solely in terms of my sense data—as is shown by the fact that if I assertively utter (10), and you assertively utter (11),

11. There is no table in the classroom.

what you say is logically incompatible with what I say; it is logically impossible for what I say and what you say to be jointly true. However, if you were to make a statement solely about your sense data, it would not be logically incompatible with any statement solely about my sense data. Thus, the statements that you and I make when we utter sentences like (10) and (11) can't both be analyzed into statements that are solely about the private sense data of the speaker. And if they can't both be so analyzed, then surely neither one can be analyzed as being about a single person's sense data.

Although Russell implicitly recognizes this, he doesn't recognize its implications. If material objects are to be logical constructions out of sense data, they must be logical constructions out of everyone's sense data. On this view, (10) is analyzed into a series of statements of the sort illustrated by (10a) and (10b).

10a. Anyone in such-and-such position ("in the classroom") satisfying such-and-such condition ("looking in the right place") (at this time) would have visual sense data of such-and-such type.
  b. Anyone undergoing such-and-such changes ("walking toward the table") would end up having tactile sensations of hardness and pressure of so-and-so type.

But surely, if Russell can't explain how we know other people exist, then he can't explain our alleged knowledge of what everyone else's sense data would be like under all relevant conditions. For this reason, his analysis of material objects as logical constructions out of everyone's sense data doesn't solve the problem it was designed to solve.

In fact, it makes the problem worse. At least I can be sure, pre-theoretically, that I know that there are material objects. But I am far from sure that I know what everyone else's private sense experiences would be like under all imaginable conditions. Perhaps, it will be suggested, reports made by other agents of seeing something "red," "round," and the like will help. Although the suggestion is natural, Russell is in no position to take advantage of it. When, in everyday life, I observe agents applying these predicates *to enduring material things we both perceive*, I can check their use against mine to determine whether they mean what I do by the terms. If I notice that, systematically and over time, they tend to apply the observational predicates to more or less the same things I do, then I have some reason to suppose that we mean the same thing. Even in cases in which I notice large discrepancies in our use, I may be able to test various hypotheses about what they mean. Once I have satisfied myself about their meanings, I may be able to come to some estimate about the reliability of their testimony in cases of various types. All this is needed, if Russell's "working hypothesis" is going to do any good.

The problem is that he can't appeal to any of this. If all we ever perceived were things private to ourselves, no method of the sort just sketched would be available. How then could one ever interpret the "testimony" one took oneself to receive from one's mysterious fellows? If we were, truly, in the position described by Russell's "working hypothesis," we would have no way of understanding, let alone any basis for relying on, whatever, if anything, others were "telling" us. Thus, to analyze knowledge of material objects in terms of alleged knowledge of other people's private sense experience is *not* to reduce a complicated type of knowledge to something more tractable; it is to replace a challenging philosophical problem with an intractable one.

Since this is the opposite of progress, the most reasonable alternative is to reject the analysis of material objects as logical constructions out of sense data. So it seems to me, at any rate. Needless to say, this was not how Russell and a number of later philosophers saw the matter. Despite what appear to be crippling difficulties with the view that material objects are logical constructions out of sense data, it continued to exercise a strong influence on philosophers of an empiricist bent—including Rudolf Carnap and Willard Van Orman Quine—for more than three decades.

CHAPTER 12

༄ৎ ཨ ৎ

The Philosophy of Logical Atomism

1. Towards a Comprehensive Philosophical System
2. Methodology, Facts, and Propositions
3. Linguistic Simples, Metaphysical Simples, and the Language/World Parallel
4. Molecular Propositions, General Propositions, and the Facts Corresponding to Them
5. Existence
6. The Multiple Relation Theory of Judgment Revisited
7. Descriptions and Incomplete Symbols
8. No Class: The Theory of Types and the Purported Elimination of Classes
9. Russell's Unholy Trinity: Analysis, Science, and Revisionary Metaphysics

1. TOWARDS A COMPREHENSIVE PHILOSOPHICAL SYSTEM

As we have seen, Russell's mature philosophical development began with an intense focus on issues in logic, language, and the philosophy of mathematics illustrated in *The Principles of Mathematics* (1903) and "On Denoting" (1905). The issues raised there led to deeper and broader concerns with the nature of truth, falsity, facts, judgments, and propositions found in "On the Nature of Truth" (1906), "On the Nature of Truth and Falsity" (1910), chapter 12 of *The Problems of Philosophy* (1912), and *Theory of Knowledge* (1913). At the same time, he waded more deeply into epistemology and the philosophy of mind with his increasingly radical doctrine of acquaintance, and correspondingly stark distinction between knowledge by acquaintance and knowledge by description, illustrated in "Knowledge by Acquaintance and Knowledge by Description" (1910) and chapter 5 of *The Problems of Philosophy*. This was also the time at which his logicist project came to fruition in "The Regressive Method of Discovering the Premises of Mathematics" (1907), "Mathematical Logic as Based on the Theory of Types" (1908), and *Principia Mathematica* (1910, 1912, 1913). By this point, Russell's views about "analysis" as an all-purpose philosophical method had taken shape, and were being applied to a variety of philosophical problems.

Two broad tendencies, yoked together, were now discernible. The first was an ambitious analytic reductionism, by which he sought to avoid ontological commitment to entities thought to be problematic. Just as he took his theory of descriptions, and his analysis of ordinary names as disguised descriptions, to provide the treatment of negative existentials needed to finally put to rest his earlier broadly Meinongian ontology, so he took his multiple relation analysis of judgment to eliminate propositions, and his reduction of natural numbers to classes to dispense with an independent category of abstract objects. But that was only the beginning. His more radical view of classes themselves as "logical fictions" advanced a strikingly minimalist metaphysical agenda, present from *Principia Mathematica* onward. In *Our Knowledge of the External World,* he took a giant step of a similar sort in the service of avowedly epistemological concerns. It was there that Russell renounced commitment to physical objects as independently existing substances—characterizing them instead as "logical constructions" out of the objects of immediate sense perception. By this time his view of reality had been stripped of all abstract objects except "universals"—i.e., properties and relations—and all particulars except for individual selves (themselves to be eliminated in *The Philosophy of Logical Atomism)* and the fleeting, private objects of their immediate perception.

In all of this, we see the second broadly methodological tendency, which linked his evolving metaphysical minimalism with an ambitious search for secure epistemological foundations. Russell's epistemological practice, explicit in *Our Knowledge of the External World* but present throughout, consisted of two distinguishable sub-tasks. The first was to isolate a domain of putative pre-theoretic knowledge, which though revisable at the margins was, rightly, taken to be, on the whole, beyond serious doubt. In the case of logicism, this domain was our knowledge of arithmetic and other branches of mathematics; in the case of the external world, it was our knowledge of physical science, and of the truth of most ordinary judgments about "physical objects." The second sub-task was to identify a minimal set of underlying notions to be used in formulating a set of primitive judgments or axioms, plus definitions from which the overwhelming majority of the pre-theoretic claims taken as data could be analyzed/derived. In order for the strategy to be judged successful, Russell did not require the underlying axioms or definitions to be self-evidently obvious. It was enough that they be capable of explaining how the pre-theoretic claims under analysis could be true, and known by us to be so—while allowing us to avoid puzzles and paradoxes generated by the gratuitous postulation of entities the nature and existence of which we have no way of knowing.

I have already questioned several aspects of Russell's use of this method in earlier chapters. Among the questionable elements central to his emerging system are:

(i) the analysis of ordinary names as disguised definite descriptions—the difficulties with which are easier to see today (with the benefit of Saul

Kripke's distinction between rigid and non-rigid designators) than they were in Russell's time;

(ii) the treatment of the meanings of genuine (logically proper) names and predicates as transparent to the agent—which forces Russell to take the constituents of atomic sentences to designate only sense data and universals, since those are the only things an agent who contemplates them (allegedly) can't be mistaken about;

(iii) the restriction of the objects about which we bear the attitudes of direct knowledge, belief, and assertion to entities with which we are *immediately acquainted* in Russell's restrictive sense—which prevents him from recognizing the truth of many attitude ascriptions in which definite descriptions occurring in content clauses of attitude verbs have primary occurrence;

(iv) the elimination of propositions by the flawed multiple relation theory of judgment—which cripples his account of the attitudes and threatens his elegant analysis of sentences containing denoting phrases as predicating higher-order properties of propositional functions;

(v) the post-*Principia* reconstrual of propositional functions as formulas and the problematic elimination of classes using either metalinguistic quantification over such formulas or substitutional quantification specified in terms of them;

(vi) the treatment of physical objects as logical constructions out of one's own momentary sense data plus the unknowable sense data of other, unknowable, agents; and

(vii) the insistence that *existence* is a property of "propositional functions," and the related failure to capture the actual, present truth of certain modal or temporal claims about things that could, did, or will exist but don't actually exist now.

These elements—along with his theory of descriptions and a new discussion of facts corresponding to different types of fully analyzed sentences— are among those used in the eight lectures given in 1918, published as *The Philosophy of Logical Atomism,* to construct his version of that view.[1] Although Russell's method goes by the innocent-sounding sounding name "analysis," the resulting system is as radically revisionary as the great

---

[1] Wittgenstein's version of logical atomism did not appear in print in English until the *Tractatus Logico-Philosophicus* was published in 1922. Although Russell hadn't been in contact with his former pupil in the four years prior to the lectures, he was familiar with, and had been heavily influenced by, Wittgenstein's pre–World War I views on many of the topics that would be covered in the *Tractatus.* The crucial document through which this influence was expressed was Wittgenstein's 1913 "Notes on Logic," translated and transcribed by Russell (working with Costello) in early 1914, when Russell was preparing lectures at Harvard. "Notes on Logic" is reprinted as Appendices A and B of Michael Potter (2009), the main text of which is a thorough commentary on it (including its influence on Russell). I postpone discussion of Wittgenstein's (quite different) system of atomism until vol. 2.

metaphysical systems of old—a point implicitly acknowledged in one of his typically apt remarks:

> the point of philosophy is to start with something so simple as not to seem worth stating [the domain of pre-theoretic knowledge under analysis], and to end with something so paradoxical that no one will believe [the conception of reality deemed to underlie and explain the pre-theoretic "data"].[2]

2. METHODOLOGY, FACTS, AND PROPOSITIONS

Russell begins in lecture 1 by sketching his methodology. The aim is to outline the structure of a world we are capable of knowing, based on the ideas (i) that most of what we are given by the empirical and deductive sciences, and by the most fundamental judgments of common sense, is true and capable of being known, (ii) that although we are justifiably confident of this, we do not know the precise content of these truths, and (iii) that the job of analysis is to elucidate this content, thereby explaining how we do, or at least could come to, know it. He warns that we can't anticipate the end result of analysis in advance, and admonishes us not to dismiss what may seem to be highly revisionary characterizations of the knowable content of empirical and a priori claims, and of the sources of our knowledge of those claims. Granting this, we should, however, ask for clarification. Is the task to explain what justifies the vast pre-theoretic knowledge we already have, or is it to articulate what our evidence really justifies, and hence *what we could come to know, if we adopted a frankly revisionary view of the world*? Although Russell seems to lean toward the first conception of the task, his discussion is equivocal.

These points are prefigured early in the lecture when he says:

> It is a rather curious fact in philosophy that the data which are undeniable to start with are always rather vague and ambiguous. You can . . . say: 'There are a number of people in this room at the moment.' That is obviously in some sense undeniable. But when you . . . try to define what a room is, and what it is for a person to be in a room, how you are going to distinguish one person from another, and so forth, you find that *you really do not know what you meant*. That is a rather singular fact, *that everything you are really sure of right off is something you do not know the meaning of, and the moment you get a precise statement you will not be sure whether it is true or false,* at least right off. The process of sound philosophizing . . . consists mainly in passing from those obvious, vague, ambiguous things, that we feel quite sure of, to something precise, clear, definite, which by reflection and analysis *we find is involved in the vague thing that we start from*, and is . . . the real truth from which the vague thing is a sort of shadow. . . . Everything is vague to a degree you do not realize till

[2] Russell (1918–19), at p. 53 of the reprinted version, Russell (1985).

you have tried to make it precise, and everything precise is so remote from everything we normally think, that you cannot suppose for a moment that it is what we really mean when we say what we think.[3]

The overall drift is clear: Russell's "analyses" of pre-theoretic truths are going to be surprising and counterintuitive. Nevertheless, he suggests, they are merely the result of making clear, precise, and definite what was originally unclear, imprecise, and ambiguous. But his illustration is less helpful than he imagines. His example—'There are a number of people in the room'—is neither ambiguous nor unclear. It doesn't semantically express multiple propositions—*that there are exactly two people in the room, that there are exactly three, exactly four, etc.*—only one of which is "the real truth" that the speaker knows and meant. The sentence doesn't express any of those more specific propositions, and the speaker can know the proposition it is used to express without knowing any of them. The remark may well be vague—in the sense that it may be unclear what counts as "a number of people" in the context in which Russell uses it. But in that context—lecturing to an audience—there is no need to set a precise borderline in order to know that the remark is true. Russell knew what he *really meant*, which was inconsequentially vague—with nothing more precise standing behind it.

The same points hold for whatever vagueness there is in the concepts *room, person,* and *person in the room.* Two quite different things commonly go by the name 'vagueness' in philosophy. One applies to claims that are insufficiently informative for the inquiry at hand. Russell's example isn't vague in this way. The other applies to remarks involving concepts for which the range of all possible things to which they clearly apply is separated from the range to which they clearly do not apply by a seemingly ineliminable range of "borderline cases" for which application or non-application is both unclear and resistant to clarification. Although Russell's remark is vague in this way, this doesn't show that he doesn't, or we don't, know what he meant. A speaker can intend to assert something that he knows to be vague in this sense. This had better be so, since many of Russell's "analyses" are themselves vague.

For all these reasons, Russell's illustration is unfortunate. The true justification for the method of analysis that leads him to his system of logical atomism is *not* to replace vagueness and unclarity with precision and clarity; it is to uncover what is genuinely knowable in our experience, and to discard what isn't. It is an open question whether, and to what extent, what emerges as knowable will match what we somehow already *really* mean and know, or is a *replacement* for what we mean and wrongly take ourselves to know.

Having delivered his methodological preamble, Russell turns to facts and propositions.

---

[3] Ibid., pp. 37–38, my emphasis.

The first truism to which I wish to draw your attention . . . is that the world contains *facts* [independent of us], and that there are also *beliefs*, which have reference to facts, and by reference to facts are either true or false. . . . When I speak of a fact . . . I mean the kind of thing that makes a proposition true or false.[4]

For Russell facts are constituents of reality that make beliefs and propositions true or false. One might think from this passage that making beliefs and propositions true come to the same thing, since a belief is true when the proposition believed is true. But Russell gave up this view when he adopted the multiple relation theory of judgment, to which he remains tenuously committed in *The Philosophy of Logical Atomism*. During this period, he took "a belief" to be a kind of fact—the holding of the belief relation between a believer and the constituents of the belief. For a belief to be true is for these constituents to be united into an independent fact by the one or more among them that "functions as a verb." Propositions are not *what is believed*; there is no such thing as "what is believed" in the ordinary sense of that term. Instead, propositions are sentences.

A proposition, one may say, is a sentence in the indicative, a sentence asserting something, not questioning or commanding or wishing. It may also be a sentence of that sort preceded by the word 'that' [i.e., a clause]. For example, 'That Socrates is alive', 'That two and two are four', 'That two and two are five', anything of that sort will be a proposition. A proposition is just a symbol. It is a complex symbol in the sense that it has parts which are also symbols.[5]

Russell spends most of the rest of lecture 1 describing the relationship between sentences and facts. Just as the former are complex symbols made up of simpler symbols, the latter are complex constituents of reality made up of "logical atoms." As he puts it:

[W]hen I speak of a fact I do not mean a particular existing thing, such as Socrates or the rain or the sun. . . . What I call a fact is the sort of thing that is expressed by a whole sentence, not by a single name like 'Socrates'. . . . We express a fact, for example, when we say that a certain thing has a certain property, or that it has a certain relation to another thing, but the thing that has the property or the relation is not what I call 'a fact'.[6]

Although propositions (i.e., sentences and clauses of a certain sort) are true or false, Russell tells us that "a fact cannot be either true or false."[7] However, since he recognizes beliefs to be true or false, while continuing to regard them as a species of fact, this can't be quite right. Rather, he takes facts to be neither true nor false, except for those which, like beliefs,

---

[4] Ibid., p. 40.
[5] Ibid., pp. 44–45.
[6] Ibid., p. 41.
[7] Ibid., p. 43.

involve an agent's standing in a relation designated by an attitude verb to the constituents of the attitude.

Russell's final point in lecture 1 is that language parallels reality. He tells us that *linguistically simple symbols*—logically proper names—name *metaphysically simple constituents of reality*, while linguistically complex symbols—sentences-cum-propositions—stand for (but do not name) facts, the constituents of which are metaphysically simple. Since this is only the first of eight lectures, the examples he uses to illustrate the point come from ordinary English, rather than the imagined ideal logical language to be reached at the end of analysis. Nevertheless, his remarks are revealing.

> As to what one means by 'meaning', I will give a few illustrations. For instance, the word 'Socrates', you will say [if you take it to genuinely function as a name], means a certain man; the word 'mortal' means a certain quality [property]; and the sentence 'Socrates is mortal' means a certain fact. But these three sorts of meaning are entirely distinct. . . . A name would be a proper symbol for a person; a sentence (or a proposition) is the proper symbol for a fact.[8]

In the end, 'Socrates' will be treated as a disguised definite description involving non-ontologically-committing (metalinguistic or substitutional) quantification. As a result, the truth or falsity of (ordinary language) sentences containing 'Socrates' will be seen as determined by the truth values of atomic sentences of the ideal language, which themselves contain genuine logically proper names of particular sense experiences and the momentary objects of those experiences (the sense data perceived), plus n-place predicates standing for various qualities of, and relations holding between, entities of these kinds. Once this level is reached, the meanings of linguistically simple names will be metaphysically simple constituents of reality—just as 'Socrates' is imagined (prior to analysis) to be a name of an independent substance. Facts, which are linguistically complex, can never be named.[9]

Russell's defense of this claim rests heavily on the contention that the expressions—namely sentences (and clauses)—that "mean" facts come in pairs, corresponding in two different ways to each fact, whereas names and their objects do not have this duality.

> *[P]ropositions are not names for facts* . . . [since] there are *two* propositions corresponding to each fact. Suppose it is a fact that Socrates is dead. You have two propositions: 'Socrates is dead' and 'Socrates is not dead' . . . corresponding to the same fact; there is one fact in the world which makes one true and one false. . . . There are two different relations . . . that a proposition may have

---

[8] Ibid., p. 46.

[9] In this, and in much of what Russell says about facts and the relations they bear to sentences, Russell was following Wittgenstein (1914–16). See in particular chapter 14 of Potter (2009).

to a fact: the one the relation that you may call being true to the fact, and the other being false to the fact . . . whereas in the case of a name, there is only one relation that it can have to what it names. A name can just name a particular, or, if it does not, it is not a name at all, it is a noise. It cannot be a name without having just that one particular relation of naming a certain thing, whereas a proposition does not cease to be a proposition if it is false. It has two ways, of being true and being false, which together correspond to the property of being a name. Just as a word may be a name or be not a name but just a meaningless noise, so a phrase which is apparently a proposition may be either true or false, or may be meaningless, but the true and false belong together as against the meaningless. . . . You must not run away with the idea that you can name facts. . . . You cannot name them at all.[10]

It seems that for Russell, (i) expresses a crucial similarity between names and propositions, while (ii) expresses a crucial difference.

(i) Just as a purported name is meaningful, and hence a genuine (logically proper) name iff there is an object it designates, so a sentence or clause (of a certain type) is meaningful, and hence a genuine proposition iff there is a fact to which it is true, or to which it is false.

(ii) Whereas the meaning of a name is what it designates, the meaning of a sentence that qualifies as a proposition is *not* the fact to which it is true, or to which it is false.

Although Russell clearly accepts (i), he nowhere explicitly comments on (ii). In fact, he seems to suggest otherwise, both when he says (p. 45), "When I speak of a symbol [simple or complex] I simply mean something that 'means' something else," and when he says (p. 46), "'Socrates is mortal' means a certain fact." Surely, one is inclined to think, if 'Socrates is mortal' means a certain fact, then the fact it means is the fact that Socrates is mortal. What fact does 'Socrates isn't mortal' mean? It would seem, in light of Russell's duality, that it must be the fact that makes the sentence false—which is the very same fact that makes 'Socrates is mortal' true. However, it would be absurd to maintain that 'Socrates is mortal' and 'Socrates isn't mortal' *mean the same thing*, and so are *synonymous*. This absurdity can be blocked by distinguishing *having the same meaning* from *having the same sense*, which is what Wittgenstein did in *Notes on Logic*. There, he says, "the meaning of a proposition is the fact which actually corresponds to it" and "in my theory p has the same meaning as not-p but opposite sense"—which, of course, applies to the Socrates examples too.[11] Here, Russell seems to be taking over Wittgenstein's usage, without going to the trouble of explaining his special use of *'means'* and *'meaning'*.[12]

---

[10] Ibid., pp 46–47.
[11] Wittgenstein (1914–16), pp. 94–95.
[12] Thanks again to my referees.

Could Russell say that two true sentences *have the same sense, and so are synonymous* iff they are made true by the same fact, and that two false sentences *are similarly synonymous* iff they are made false by the same fact? Not really, though the full explanation of why he can't won't come until later. For now it is enough to note that the suggestion won't work because he recognizes (a) pairs of non-synonymous true sentences—e.g., 'Snow is white or grass is red' and 'Snow is white'—that are made true by exactly the same fact, and (b) pairs of non-synonymous false sentences—e.g., 'Snow is white and Socrates isn't dead' and 'Socrates isn't dead'—that are made false by the same fact. Nor do more complicated formulations fare any better.

The lesson here is that although Russell sometimes talks about "the meanings of sentences," he clearly has in mind something quite different from what we ordinarily have in mind when talking about sentence meaning. There is nothing in his ontology that plays the role of sentence meaning, as ordinarily understood. Instead, we should interpret him as dispensing with ordinary *sentence meanings* in favor of truth and falsity makers, and characterizing a sentence as *meaningful* iff there are conditions under which it is true or false—where truth and falsity is a matter of correspondence, of two different sorts, with facts.

Russell ends the lecture with another important, but difficult to interpret, point. After saying that you cannot name a fact, he adds:

> The only thing you can do is to assert it, or deny it, or desire it, or will it, or wish it, or question it, but all those are things involving the whole proposition. *You can never put the sort of thing that makes a proposition to be true or false in the position of a logical subject.* You can only have it there as something to be asserted or denied or something of that sort, but not something to be named.[13]

The key point is paradoxical: *one can never put a fact in the position of a logical subject*—by which Russell means that one can never meaningfully predicate any property of a fact, or any relation as holding among facts. To do so, one would have to name facts with either logically proper names or variables relative to assignments, thereby making facts subjects of predication in atomic sentences of the ideal language. This, Russell maintains, is impossible, since, as he will tell us later, only unstructured atomic simples can be referents of logically proper names; and facts aren't simples. But whatever the source of his doctrine, it is hard to see how it could be true.[14] Haven't we been faithfully following him in saying things about facts, and hence in predicating properties and relations of them, throughout our discussion of lecture 1? It is not as if facts are logical fictions that disappear on analysis, rendering our discourse only ostensibly about them, but

---

[13] Ibid., p. 47, my emphasis.

[14] Again, Russell appears to be following Wittgenstein, who says in "Notes on Logic" that "facts cannot be *named*." See p. 284, Appendix A, of Potter (2009).

really about something else. On the contrary, Russell tells us that facts are ultimate constituents of reality. Isn't that telling us something *about facts*?

The examples he gives in the passage of what we can do with facts—namely to assert, deny, desire, or question them—don't help. For one thing, his multiple relation theory of judgment makes no room for entities that are asserted, denied, desired, or questioned. Nor does it help that he holds that for any suitably related pair of assertions—e.g., to the effect that snow is white or that snow is not white (which are, respectively, the fact that an agent asserts that snow is white and the fact that an agent asserts that snow is not white)—there is a single fact (in this case, the fact that snow is white) that makes one of the assertions true and one false. Since this thesis itself predicates something of facts, it violates the stricture that one can never put facts "in the position of a logical subject." This is, of course, a version of the problem that leads Wittgenstein in the *Tractatus* to advocate kicking away a ladder once one has climbed it. Unlike Russell, Wittgenstein at least makes a point of explicitly noting it.

3. LINGUISTIC SIMPLES, METAPHYSICAL SIMPLES, AND THE LANGUAGE/WORLD PARALLEL

In chapters 2–5, Russell presents his conception of a *logically perfect language* as an ideal tool for describing reality. Although it is a version of the formal language of "On Denoting" and *Principia Mathematica,* the use to which it is put in *The Philosophy of Logical Atomism* is more ambitious. Its atomic sentences each consist of a predicate followed by one or more logically proper names—e.g., 'Ra' (a is red), or 'Lab' (a is to the left of b). These linguistically simple elements—predicates and logically proper names—stand for the most basic constituents of reality. Predicates stand for simple, unanalyzable properties and relations; names stand for the metaphysically simple objects. When they are true, atomic sentences stand for the simplest complex constituents of realty, which are facts consisting of objects named by logically proper names bearing the properties, and standing in the relations, designated by predicates. Why, one might wonder, should such a parallel between linguistic and metaphysical simplicity be assumed?

It is natural, though not inevitable, to assume, as Russell did, that there are simple elements of language—expressions the meanings of which are simply the things they stand for, independent of the meanings of other expressions. But why assume that all *objects* are decomposable into basic particulars that cannot further be broken down into simpler constituents, or that, if there are such basic particulars, they, and only they, can be named? Russell's reason comes from his epistemology. According to his doctrine of acquaintance, the only propositions we are capable of entertaining, and hence the only thoughts we are capable of having, are those the constituents of which we are directly acquainted with in a way that precludes significant error. It is a corollary of this doctrine that we can't be mistaken about what we mean by a logically proper name. Since the meaning of such a name is its referent, he concludes that the only things one can name are one's own sense experiences, the private objects perceived in those experiences, and other items of one's conscious awareness. That these were taken to be metaphysically simple is understandable.

It is more difficult to understand how Russell could have imagined reality to be exhausted by facts about these things. After all, his distinction between knowledge by acquaintance and knowledge by description was designed to accommodate things one can use descriptions to think about that one isn't, and can't be, directly acquainted with. On the face of it, this leaves it open that reality might contain objects over and above the epistemically available metaphysical simples named by logically proper names, some of which may be metaphysical simples of a quite different kind, while others may be objects that are metaphysically complex. Genuine material objects are a case in point. To be sure, one might wonder how one could be justified in believing in them. In *Our Knowledge of the External World,* Russell tried to circumvent this question by arguing that material objects are logical constructions out of actual and hypothetical sense data (of oneself and others). Continuing to stand by this view, he took material objects (as ordinarily conceived) to have been analyzed away—thus removing a class of objects that are neither metaphysically simple, nor knowable a priori to be composed out of simples.

In chapter 11, I explained why I take this treatment of material objects to be flawed. The problem raised here is deeper, reaching the limits of what Russell is in a position to regard as intelligible. In "On Denoting" he explained how we use descriptions to think and talk about things with which we are not acquainted. Sentences containing descriptions involve quantification. On the analysis given there, ⌜∃x Fx⌝ expresses the proposition that predicates *being sometimes true* of a function that assigns an object o the (nonlinguistic) proposition that predicates *F-hood* of o; similarly for sentences containing the universal quantifier. By 1918, however, nonlinguistic propositions and propositional functions had been eliminated in favor of sentences and formulas. This presented a challenge for the analysis of quantification. Is all quantification now to be understood metalinguistically?

In chapter 10, I distinguished between objectual (metalinguistic) quantification over expressions, and non-objectual substitutional quantification. With the latter, there is no domain of objects over which the quantifiers range, and the truth conditions of quantified sentences are defined directly in terms of the truth or falsity of sentences that result from substituting members of the substitution classes associated with variables for the variables themselves. Although Russell doesn't clearly distinguish these two options in *Principia Mathematica* or elsewhere, the metalinguistic option is not very attractive for his purposes. If all quantification were metalinguistic, then all quantificational thought would be thought *about language*. Since this is extremely implausible, a substitutional interpretation of the quantifiers may seem preferable. In chapter 10 I noted that Landini and Klement have plausibly argued that the restrictions in Russell's type theory fall out naturally from those independently required by substitutional quantification. The crucial point here is that when quantification is interpreted substitutionally, his analysis of sentences that seem to be about classes in terms of quantification involving propositional functions doesn't introduce any new ontological commitments. Since this is the heart of his infamous "no-class" theory, which remains fully in force in *The Philosophy of Logical Atomism*, the idea that he may have been operating with an inchoate substitutional theory in *Principia Mathematica* carries over to *The Philosophy of Logical Atomism*.

In chapter 10, I noted serious problems for Russell's philosophical logic if his quantification is given a unified substitutional interpretation.[15] Here I extend that discussion by noting a crippling difficulty made evident by the parameters of his logical atomism. Think about the claims made by sentences containing descriptions. As I have noted, in giving up non-linguistic propositions, Russell replaces talk of sentence meaning in the ordinary sense with explanations of the meaningfulness of sentences in terms of their truth conditions. As a result, the meaningfulness of sentences containing substitutionally quantified sentences must be explained in terms of the meaningfulness, and truth conditions, of the sentences that are their substitution instances. If all quantification in the language of a given agent is substitutional, this means that the meaningfulness of all quantified sentences is explained in terms of the meaningfulness, and truth conditions, of atomic sentences of the logically perfect language that underlies the agent's ordinary spoken language. Since the concrete particulars that are "logical subjects" of these underlying sentences are items private to the agent him- or herself (of which various properties and relations are predicated), there seems to be no way for Russell to accommodate an agent's thought about any other concrete particulars—*including other agents or their sense data*. This problem goes far beyond the difficulty of explaining how the agent can *know* about other agents and their sense data. The problem is that there seems to be no way for an agent to *express* any claim about concrete particulars other than those that momentarily occur in his or her stream of consciousness, in which case there will be no way for the agent to *entertain any intelligible thought* about other things. One can scarcely imagine a worse result.

---

[15] As noted there, Russell gives no indication that first-order quantification is to be construed objectually while higher-order quantification is to be interpreted substitutionally. On the contrary, his discussions indicate that he had a unified treatment in mind. As I explained, this suggests the deeply flawed view that all quantification may be substitutional.

Since Russell saves most of his discussion of quantification for later lectures, I will revisit this difficulty then. However, the problem appears to be inescapable. The "no-class theory"—which he here extends to all abstract objects other than simple properties and relations—is central to his logical atomism.[16] Without substitutional quantification, the no-class theory is, arguably, indefensible. But, as we have just seen, the combination of a unified treatment of all quantification as substitutional with Russell's restrictive epistemology of acquaintance, and his conception of the metaphysical simples capable of occurring as logical subjects of atomic sentences of an agent's underlying ideal language, leads to unacceptable solipsistic limits on intelligibility. This, of course, was not Russell's intention. The best means of avoiding such a *reductio* is to explicitly endorse objectual, not substitutional, first-order quantification. Whether or not this would require giving up the "no-class theory" is a question that would then have to be faced.

Having indicated Russell's problematic conception of the relationship between linguistically simple names and metaphysically simple objects, I turn to his conception of linguistically simple (unanalyzable) predicates and the simple properties and relations they stand for. As before, the mark of the simple is epistemological. Russell begins with an account of linguistic simplicity and complexity.

> You can understand a proposition when you understand the words of which it is composed even though you never heard the proposition before. That seems a very humble property, but it is a property which marks it as complex and distinguishes it from words whose meaning is simple. . . . Take the word 'red' for example. . . . You cannot understand the meaning of the word 'red' except through seeing red things. There is no other way in which it can be done. It is no use to learn languages, or to look up dictionaries. None of these things will help you understand the meaning of the word 'red'. . . . All analysis is only possible in regard to what is complex, and it always depends, in the last analysis, upon direct acquaintance with the objects which are the meanings of certain simple symbols.[17]

---

[16] An example of the heavy analytic and ontological use to which he puts the no-class theory is found in the following passage from lecture 2 (Russell 1985, p. 52, my emphasis):

'Piccadilly', on the face of it, is the name for a certain portion of the earth's surface, and I suppose, if you wanted to define it, you would have to define it as a series of classes of material entities, namely those which, at various times, occupy that portion of the earth's surface. So that you would find that the logical status of Piccadilly is bound up with the logical status of series and classes, and if you are going to hold Piccadilly as real, you must hold that series of classes are real. . . . As you know, *I believe that series and classes are of the nature of logical fictions: therefore that thesis, if it can be maintained, will dissolve Piccadilly into a fiction.* Exactly the same remarks will apply to other instances: Rumania, Twelfth Night, and Socrates . . . for the sake of argument, one might identify Socrates with the series of his experiences. *He would really be a series of classes. . . . Therefore he becomes very like Piccadilly.*

[17] Ibid., pp. 53–54.

"Red' is a simple predicate, whereas 'square' is not, because the latter can be learned by being told that a square is a rectangle with equal sides, while the former can only be learned by direct acquaintance with things that are red. The idea appears to be that direct acquaintance with particulars that are red provides one with direct acquaintance with the property *being red* that they share. Russell sums up:

> Those objects [which here include properties and relations as well as particulars] which it is impossible to symbolize otherwise than by simple symbols may be called 'simple', while those which can be symbolized by a combination of symbols may be called 'complex'.[18]

It may be objected that Russell's dichotomy—between notions like *square* that are fully analyzable and those like *red* that (according to him) are simple and can be learned only by acquaintance with their instances—isn't exhaustive. Aren't there notions—perhaps like *knowledge* and *truth,* or like those applying to moves and pieces in a game—which are neither fully analyzable into simpler notions, nor masterable simply by acquaintance with their instances—but rather are members of a family of related notions, mastery of which requires recognition of conceptual connections holding among them? Although there seem to be many such notions, they don't fit into the rigid conception of analysis to which Russell adheres in *The Philosophy of Logical Atomism.*

For him, complex properties or relations are fully analyzable into simple properties and relations, which serve as meanings of the simple predicates of the underlying logically perfect language of an agent. These include properties and relations with which the agent can be directly acquainted only by virtue of being directly acquainted with the concrete particulars that are their instances. According to Russell, *being red* is such a property. Perhaps properties of such properties—like *being a color*—with which an agent may become directly acquainted through being acquainted with its instances—like *being red, being green,* etc.—also qualify as simple. Are there other simple properties and relations for which an agent's epistemic access is *not* ultimately grounded in direct awareness of the momentary private concrete particulars of his or her immediate consciousness? If not, it would appear that the expressive power of the resulting system will be highly restricted. As far as I can tell, Russell doesn't definitively pronounce on the matter, but it is hard to see how, on his conception, there could be simple properties and relations beyond those of the sort I have indicated.

This does *not* mean that instances of the simple properties and relations with which an agent is acquainted truly apply only to the momentary concrete particulars he or she immediately perceives (plus properties of such properties and relations). I may have no way of knowing whether any of the private objects of your immediate perception exemplify the same

[18] Ibid., p. 54.

shade of red that some of the private objects of my immediate perception do. However—supposing that I can make sense of the notions of other agents and their private objects of perception—there is nothing in Russell that rules out the possibility that some of the objects of your immediate perception are red in the same sense that some of mine are. By the same token, there is no guarantee that we both mean precisely the same property by 'red'—even if the predicate is common to our underlying logically perfect languages. On the contrary, Russell suggests that it is commonplace for different agents to mean something at least somewhat different by some of their words—though one might wonder how, given his strictures, he can know this.[19]

I have spoken throughout of metaphysically simple particulars, properties, and relations. This can be misleading. According to Russell, all particulars, properties, and relations are simple. Everything that appears to be complex is a "logical fiction" that disappears on analysis. The only exception to this are facts, which, Russell tells us, can't be named or made into "logical subjects." Nevertheless, he does (somehow) manage to communicate many things to us about them, e.g., that atomic sentences—which consist of n-place predicates plus n logically proper names—are made true by atomic facts—which are complexes of constituents each of which consist of the holding of an n-place property by n particulars. He sums up the range of atomic facts as follows:

> The simplest imaginable facts are those which consist in the possession of a quality by some particular thing. Such facts, say, as 'This is white'. . . . The next simplest would be those in which you have a relation between two facts [he must mean 'particulars'], such as: 'This is to the left of that.' Next you come to those where you have a triadic relation between three particulars. (An instance which Royce gives is 'A gives B to C.') . . . So you get relations which require as their minimum three terms . . . and those which require four terms . . . and so on. There you have a whole infinite hierarchy of facts—facts in which you have a thing and a quality, two things and a relation, three things and a relation, four things and a relation, and so on. The whole hierarchy constitutes what I call *atomic* facts, and they are the simplest sort of fact. . . . The propositions expressing them are what I call *atomic propositions*.[20]

Though most of this is straightforward, one point is puzzling. Russell may seem to be suggesting that since there is an infinite hierarchy of atomic facts, there is an infinite number of atomic propositions expressing them—i.e., meaningful atomic sentences each constituent of which is a simple symbol. Indeed, it would appear that he may require infinitely many simple unanalyzable relational predicates, the learning of each of which can only be a discrete, individual lesson. Surely no individual agent could

[19] Ibid., p. 56.
[20] Ibid., pp. 59–60.

master, and come to understand, all these predicates and the atomic propositions in which they occur. If this is so, it would appear that the ideal "logically perfect language" is too perfect for any agent to master.

A different puzzle arises involving restrictions on Russellian names used by an agent. We already know that the concrete particulars designated by an agent's use of a name are restricted to items in the agent's stream of consciousness. We also know that the meaning of any genuine name is one of these momentary items. As Russell notes, this makes naming rather peculiar.

> The only kind of word that is theoretically capable of standing for a particular is a proper name. . . . [Y]ou cannot ever talk about a particular except by means of a proper name. You cannot use general words except by way of description. . . . An atomic proposition is one which does mention actual particulars. . . . A name, in the narrow logical sense of a word whose meaning is a particular, can only be applied to a particular with which the speaker is acquainted. . . . That makes it very difficult to get any instance of a name. . . . The only words one does use as words in the logical sense [of a name] are words like 'this' or 'that'. One can use 'this' as a name to stand for a particular with which one is acquainted *at the moment*. We say, 'This is white'. If you assert that 'This is white', meaning the [particular denoted by] 'this' that you see, you are using 'this' as a proper name. But if you try to apprehend the proposition that I am expressing when I say 'This is white', you cannot do it. If you mean this piece of chalk as a physical object, then you are not using a proper name. It is only when you use 'this' quite strictly to stand for an actual [private] object of sense, that it is really a proper name. . . . [Thus] *it seldom means the same thing two moments running and does not mean the same thing to the speaker and to the hearer.*[21]

The linguistic, epistemic, and metaphysical consequences of this view are stunning.

The linguistic consequences include (i) and (ii):

(i) All atomic sentences about concrete particulars in an agent's "ideal" underlying language, including all truth-functional compounds of such sentences, mean something different from the sentences of the language of any other agent, and are, in principle, intelligible only to the original agent and that agent alone.

(ii) If all first-order quantification over concrete particulars is substitutional, the results of (i) carry over to all sentences containing such quantification.

Were it not for the possibility—which, as far as I can tell, is not ruled out by Russell—that some simple properties and relations might themselves be bearers of logically proper names, and hence be capable as serving as arguments of other simple properties and relations in some atomic

---

[21] Ibid., pp 61–63, my emphasis.

propositions, (i) and (ii) would entail that every sentence of the "logically perfect" Russellian language of an agent means something different from the sentences of any other agent's language, and is, in principle, unintelligible to any other agent. However, the impact of this limitation on the inherent privacy of the agent's "logically perfect" language is minimal, since Russell never makes systematic use of it. The class of sentences capable of meaning the same thing in the languages of different agents is highly restricted, and even if the meaning of a sentence (about simple properties and relations) remains the same from one agent to another, the agents themselves are in no position to know that it does.

A more significant exception to inherent linguistic privacy could be carved out by taking first-order quantification to be objectual, despite the threat this would pose to Russell's no-class theory, to which he remains passionately committed and of which he makes extensive use. In addition, he would either have to reinstate the nonlinguistic propositions and propositional functions used to explain objectual quantification in "On Denoting," or provide a new interpretation that does not explain the meaningfulness of quantified sentences in terms of the meaningfulness of quantifier-free sentences in the logically perfect language of the agent. Needless to say, he makes no constructive suggestion of what this might amount to.

The epistemic consequences corresponding to (i) and (ii) are, first, that all thoughts an agent is capable of having about concrete particulars using atomic sentences, and truth-functional compounds of such, are about things with which the agent is acquainted *at the present moment*; and second, that if, in addition, all first-order quantification over such particulars is substitutional, then all thoughts an agent is capable of having by using quantified sentences to *describe* concrete particulars are limited to those that name or describe those with which he is acquainted *at the present moment*.[22] Assuming, as I am sure Russell does, that every thought an agent is capable of having is one the agent is, in principle, capable of expressing, we arrive at the incredible conclusion that the only concrete particulars an agent can even conceive are private contents of the agent's own consciousness of which he or she is presently aware.

As before, the full force of this grotesque conclusion could be avoided by trading first-order substitutional quantification for ordinary objectual quantification. The aim, of course, would be to allow quantification over concrete particulars with which the agent was or will be acquainted, plus some with which the agent will never be acquainted—like other agents

---

[22] Asked in the question period at the end of lecture 2 to specify the length of the present moment—during which one can keep the referent of one's use of 'this' fixed—he responds (ibid., p. 65): "You can keep 'this' going for about a minute or two. I made that dot and talked about it for some little time. I mean, it varies often. If you argue quickly, you can get some little way before it is finished. I think things [concrete particulars with which one is acquainted] last for a finite time, a matter of some seconds or minutes or whatever it may happen to be."

and the concrete particulars of their past, present, and future acquaintance. Apart from the difficulties noted above, doing this would require explaining how it is both that such quantified claims are intelligible and that some such claims can be known by us to be true. Desirable though such a revision may be, it is not clear how much of Russell's logical atomism would survive it.

I have indicated that the metaphysics of logical atomism includes present conscious experiences and their momentary objects. In light of Russell's postulated parallel between language and the world, it is not clear that there is room to posit other concrete particulars beyond these. In addition to concrete particulars, there are, of course, properties and relations. All such items are metaphysically simple. Beyond this, atomic facts are complex constituents of reality. In later lectures he adds certain further facts over and above these. As far as I can see, there is no room for anything other than these metaphysical simples plus facts in his ontology.

Strictly speaking, there isn't even room for the facts. On the assumption that one's ontology is limited to things of which one is capable of saying *that there are, or exist, such things*, Russell's atomist ontology can't include facts—since they can neither be named nor quantified over. Like Wittgenstein, whom he largely follows in these lectures, Russell can't resist asserting much that is excluded by his own doctrines. The same is true of his talk of the conscious experience of other agents, or of his own past or future experience—if first-order quantification is substitutional (while if such quantification isn't substitutional, it is unclear why other agents and their sense data should have preference over other "transcendent" objects.) It would seem, to paraphrase his illustrious former student, that the limits of his world are the limits of his present self.

To this incredible picture, Russell adds the following metaphysical view.

> Particulars have this peculiarity, among the sort of objects that you have to take account of in an inventory of the world, *that each of them stands entirely alone and is completely self-subsistent*. It has the sort of self-subsistence that used to belong to substance, except that it usually only persists through a very short time. That is to say, *each particular that there is in the world does not in any way logically depend upon any other particular. Each one might happen to be the whole universe; it is merely an empirical fact that this is not the case.* There is no reason why you should not have a universe consisting of one particular and nothing else. That is a peculiarity of a particular. In the same way, in order to understand a name for a particular, the one thing necessary is to be acquainted with that particular. When you are acquainted with that particular, you have a full, adequate, and complete understanding of the name, and no further information is required.[23]

[23] Ibid., p. 63, my emphasis.

There is much hinted at in this brief passage. First, notice the way in which *logical* independence is linked with *modal or metaphysical* independence. Does Russell think that each concrete particular is *logically* independent of all others because each *could* exist in splendid isolation from all others, or is it the other way around? Although he may think both, it is the latter that is most noteworthy here. What reason is there to think that each such particular could exist all by itself? Let n be a logically proper name of a concrete particular o. Since ⌜∼∀x x = n⌝ isn't a logical truth, it is *logically possible* for o to be the only existing concrete particular. The implicit (unargued) suggestion is that all logical possibility is modal or metaphysical possibility—in which case, it will follow that it is *metaphysically possible* for o to be the only existing concrete particular. Since the converse inference is likely to seem even more plausible, I suspect that Russell implicitly takes modal necessity/possibility and logical necessity/possibility to coincide.[24]

Next notice his implicit assertion that for any concrete particular o, the claim that o isn't the only existing thing is "empirical," and hence *can be known only a posteriori.* Why would that be? Well, if all a priori truths are logically necessary, then the fact that ⌜∼∀x x = n⌝ isn't logically necessary shows that it can't be known a priori. For one who shares Russell's grand vision of analysis, this reduction of epistemic modality to logical modality is well-nigh irresistible. It is a central aim of logical atomism to replace unanalyzed terms, predicates, and sentences-cum-propositions—which may stand in conceptual relations to one another—with logically proper names, simple unanalyzable predicates, and fully analyzed propositions. When this aim is achieved, the conceptual properties of, and relations holding among, unanalyzed expressions and sentences are traced to genuinely logical properties of, and relations holding among, fully analyzed propositions of the agent's logically perfect underlying language. To take a simple example, it is knowable a priori that all squares are rectangles because the unanalyzed sentence *all squares are rectangles* is reduced, on analysis, to the fully analyzed proposition *all rectangles with equal sides are rectangles,* which is *logically necessary*—and hence knowable a priori. The idea that analyses with similar results can be carried through whenever we encounter conceptual or modal dependencies in unanalyzed language is a driving force behind logical atomism. In this way, Russell is led down a path that makes a reduction of epistemic and metaphysical modalities to logical ones seem plausible.

---

[24] Not that he explicitly says so. On the contrary, his use of normally modal terms like "possible" and "necessary" is decidedly idiosyncratic. However, it is hard for anyone to get along without sometimes implicitly invoking metaphysically modal notions—as he did in using (potentially) counterfactual conditionals in his informal discussion of the reduction in *Our Knowledge of the External World,* and as he does here in discussing possible states that the universe could be, or have been, in.

Given all this, one can understand his thinking in the previous passage. Nevertheless, the conclusion that he reaches—namely, that each of his momentary metaphysical simples could have been the only existing thing in the universe—isn't credible. Could it have been the case that the entire universe consisted of a single sensation—say my olfactory sensation as of a hot apple pie baking in the oven—with no other sensation, no agent to have the sensation, and indeed no other concrete particulars of any sort? Surely not—even though there is no contradiction-revealing analysis of $\ulcorner \forall x \ x = n \urcorner$ where n is a logically proper name of that sensation. This suggests that the implicit reduction of the epistemic and metaphysical modalities to logical modalities inherent in logical atomism is badly off track.

That, of course, is not how Russell viewed the matter. There is, however, a final difficulty involving the nature of sensation that he was, I think, implicitly aware of. In the first edition of *Our Knowledge of the External World*, in 1914, he distinguished the private object of immediate sense perception (the thing perceived) from the perception of that object (the conscious experience of perceiving it)—even though he was inclined to think that the former never outlasts the latter. In the second edition, in 1926, he identified the two. Up to now in discussing *The Philosophy of Logical Atomism* (1918), I have stuck with his 1914 view—while counting *the experience* and *that of which it is an experience* as different metaphysical simples. This is extremely implausible, if one insists that each simple concrete particular could exist on its own in splendid isolation. One who retains the isolation thesis must either (i) maintain that the *experience of perceiving, e.g., a yellow image*, and *the yellow image perceived* are identical (as Russell was prepared to admit in 1926), or (ii) resist the identification while insisting that a pure perceptual experience *that isn't an experience of anything* could exist entirely on its own in a universe devoid of everything else, or (iii) dismiss the perceptual experience as a "logical fiction" and try to get by with things perceived without perceptual experiences. For me, the implausibility of each of these options is a further argument that Russell has painted himself into a corner. This issue arises again in the last few pages of *The Philosophy of Logical Atomism*.

4. MOLECULAR PROPOSITIONS, GENERAL PROPOSITIONS, AND THE FACTS CORRESPONDING TO THEM

In addition to atomic sentences (propositions), Russell's logically perfect language also contains sentences (propositions) constructed using truth-functional operators. If S is a sentence of the language, so is its negation $\ulcorner \sim S \urcorner$; and if R is also a sentence, so is the conjunction $\ulcorner S \ \& \ R \urcorner$, the disjunction $\ulcorner S \lor R \urcorner$, the conditional $\ulcorner S \rightarrow R \urcorner$, and the biconditional $\ulcorner S \leftrightarrow R \urcorner$. Russell calls these *molecular sentences*. What relationship do they bear to facts? True atomic sentences (positively) correspond to atomic facts. Do true molecular sentences (positively) correspond to molecular facts? Are negation, conjunction, disjunction, and the like somehow "in the world" (as constituents of facts)?

Russell's answer is complex. He takes conjunction and disjunction to be easy cases. ⌜S & R⌝ is true iff there is a fact that makes S true and a fact that makes R true, which together make the conjunction true. Since correspondence to these two facts is enough to explain the truth of the conjunction, no further conjunctive fact is needed, and '&' needn't stand for anything in the world. He makes a similar point about disjunction. ⌜R ∨ S⌝ is true iff either there is a fact that makes R true, or there is a fact that makes S true. Since correspondence to one or both of these facts is sufficient to explain the truth of the disjunction, '∨' doesn't stand for anything in the world, and no disjunctive fact is needed.

But negation was another story. Russell's remarks on conjunction and disjunction suggest that he was guided by something like the following principle.

The Correspondence Principle

For any true sentence S, there is a set F of facts such that correspondence of S with one or more of the members of F is responsible for the truth of S.

Although this principle is compatible with the lack of conjunctive and disjunctive facts, it arguably requires negative facts. The truth of ⌜∼ S⌝ can't be due to correspondence with a fact that makes S true, for there is no such fact. What other fact could it correspond to? Though Russell considered various possibilities, in the end he could see no plausible alternative to admitting negative facts. The worry, of course, is that the constituents of a negative fact—e.g., *that Desdemona doesn't love Cassio*—must include Desdemona, Cassio, and loving, plus some real-world counterpart of 'not'. What could it be, and how, even if there were a real-world negator, could the loving relation (or anything else) unite the constituents into a single fact, which has to be a unified entity? Since Desdemona doesn't love Cassio, she is not related by *loving* to Cassio, which is how Russell used to reason when worrying about his old nemesis—the unity of the proposition. In effect, what he has done is recreate his nemesis in a new form.[25]

He did, of course, recognize this worry, remarking in lecture 3:

One has a certain repugnance to negative facts, the same sort of feeling that makes you wish not to have a fact '*p* or *q*' going about the world [*which Russell*

---

[25] Where molecular sentences are concerned—which can all be put in conjunctive normal form (i.e., transformed into conjunctions of disjunctions, the disjuncts of which are either atomic sentences or negations of such)—the only negative facts Russell needs are those corresponding to negations of false atomic sentences.

earlier explains would amount to positing a real-world disjunctive element desig-nated by 'or']. You have the feeling that there are only positive facts, and that negative propositions have somehow or other got to be expressions of pos-itive facts. When I was lecturing on this subject at Harvard, I argued that there are negative facts, and it nearly produced a riot; the class would not hear of there being negative facts at all. But I am still inclined to think that there are.[26]

Responding to this worry, he considers a counterproposal which claims that

when we assert 'not-*p*' we are really asserting that there is some proposition *q* which is true and is incompatible with *p*. . . . That is [the] suggested definition:

'not-*p*' means 'There is a proposition q which is true and incompatible with *p*.'[27]

Russell brings two main objections against this view. First, in taking *in-compatibility* as primitive, the view is committed to taking the relation to be unanalyzable, which is implausible. Second, the proposed interpreta-tion of negation involves positing propositions as metaphysically simple constituents of reality, which they clearly are not. Russell says:

[I]f you are going to take incompatibility as a fundamental fact, you have got, in explaining negatives, to take as your fundamental fact something involv-ing propositions as opposed to facts. *It is quite clear that propositions are not what you might call 'real'. If you were taking an inventory of the world, propositions would not come in. Facts would, beliefs, wishes, wills would, but propositions would not. They do not have being independently.*[28]

Here, he appears to be saying that there are no such things as propositions—which makes perfect sense if he here means the nonlinguistic entities he once called "propositions," and makes some sense, even if he is here continuing with his new official definition of them as sentences. Being meaningful sentences, propositions are *complex* linguistic objects. Since facts are the only complex constituents of reality that he recognizes, he must hold that if sentences themselves are not facts, then, strictly speak-ing, there are no propositions/sentences. Surely, however, the linguisti-cally *simple* constituents from which they are constructed should count as real—which is a reminder that he has not explicitly said that they are. Correcting for this omission, we can make a further point against the at-tempted analysis of negation in terms of incompatibility; contrary to what it suggests, when one asserts that Socrates is not alive, one is *not* asserting anything about expressions.

[26] Ibid., p.74.
[27] Ibid., p. 76.
[28] Ibid., p. 77, my emphasis.

So Russell had ample reason to reject the proposed analysis of negation in terms of incompatibility. This being so, and seeing no other alternative, he acquiesced in accepting negative facts. He needn't have. Though avoiding them would have required replacing the Correspondence Principle with something else, doing so would not have threatened the leading ideas of his atomist project.

Here, it is helpful to revisit his discussion of disjunction and other truth functions.

> I do not think any difficulties will arise from the supposition that the truth or falsehood of this proposition '*p* or *q*' does not depend upon a single objective fact which is disjunctive but depends on the two facts one of which corresponds to *p* and the other to *q*. . . . Generally speaking, as regards to things that you make up out of two propositions, *the whole of what is necessary in order to know their meaning is to know under what circumstances they are true, given the truth or falsehood of p and the truth or falsehood of q.* This is perfectly obvious. You have as a schema, for '*p* or *q*', using '*TT*' for '*p* and *q* are both true' [and] '*TF*' for '*p* is true and *q* is false', etc.
>
> TT TF FT FF
> T   T   T   F
>
> where the bottom line states the truth or the falsehood of '*p* or *q*'. You must not look about the real world for an object which you can call 'or', and say, 'Now, look at this. This is "or".' There is no such thing . . . the meaning of disjunction will be entirely explained by the above schema.[29]

Earlier, I pointed out that Russell's rejection of independent meanings expressed by sentences, and his embrace of facts that make sentences true or false, implicitly brought with it an embryonic truth-conditional conception of meaning and meaningfulness. The emerging view is that for a sentence to be meaningful is for there to be facts that make it true, or facts that make it false. This in turn suggests that to know the meaning of a sentence is to know what would have to be a fact in order for the sentence to be true, and what would have to be a fact in order for a sentence to be false.

Although this is consistent with what Russell says about conjunction and disjunction, adhering to it pushes one to negative facts. However, it is possible to reformulate the truth-conditional idea in a way that avoids this. We may say:

(i) Atomic sentences/propositions are true iff there is an atomic fact that makes them true; they are false iff no fact makes them true.

(ii) When the truth or falsity of P and Q have already been explained by their correspondence, or lack of correspondence, with facts, (a) their conjunction is true iff both conjuncts are, (b) their disjunction is true

---

[29] Ibid., p. 72, my emphasis.

iff at least one of the disjuncts is, and (c) their negations are true iff the propositions they negate are not true (i.e., iff they are false).

Finally, we add:

(iii) A proposition is meaningful iff there are conditions under which it is true or false.
(iv) Knowing the meaning of a proposition requires knowing the conditions under which it is true (and those under which it is false).

Under this reformulation, negative facts are not needed.

Although this is desirable, a word of caution is needed. Russell says:

Generally speaking, as regards to things that you make up out of two propositions, *the whole of what is necessary in order to know their meaning is to know under what circumstances they are true, given the truth or falsehood of p and the truth or falsehood of q.*[30]

It is natural to take this as a universally quantified statement in which its singular term variables 'p' and 'q' range over sentences (propositions). So understood, one of its instances is (1).

1. The whole of what is necessary in order to know the meaning of a molecular proposition the constituents of which are 'Snow is white' and 'Grass is green' is to know under what conditions the molecular proposition is true, given the truth or falsehood of 'Snow is white' and the truth or falsehood of 'Grass is green'.
   This in turn misleadingly suggests (2) and (3).

2. To know the meaning of 'Snow is white' & 'grass is green' is to know that it is true iff 'Snow is white' is true and 'Grass is green' is true; to know the meaning of 'Snow is white ∨ grass is green' is to know it is true iff 'Snow is white' is true or 'Grass is green' is true; and to know the meaning of '~ Snow is white' is to know that it is true iff 'Snow is white' is not true (i.e., is false).

3. More generally, to know the meaning of a conjunction is to know that it is true iff both conjuncts are true, to know the meaning of a disjunction is to know that it is true iff at least one disjunct is true, and to know the meaning of a negation is to know that it is true iff the sentence negated is not true (i.e., is false).

Obviously, these claims are false because they don't require knowing the meanings of the conjoined, disjoined, or negated sentences. Nor are they fixed simply by adding this as a stated requirement, without saying *what it is to know the meanings of those sentences.*

For atomic sentences, it would be tempting to put it as I did above— one knows the meaning of such a sentence iff one knows what *would*

---

[30] Ibid., p. 72, my emphasis.

make it true (false). However, there are two problems with this. First, it requires a formulation in terms of (potentially) counterfactual conditionals—which Russell does not explicitly acknowledge. Second, even the (potentially) counterfactual formulation is not enough—since knowing conditions that are counterfactually equivalent to the claim made by a sentence is arguably not sufficient for knowing what claim the sentence does make. Given these difficulties, Russell was simply not in a position to give a plausible theory of what sentences mean or what it is to understand them.

His primary task in lectures 3 and 5 was to give a theory of truth. This can be done by adopting all instances of the axiom schema (4) that result from replacing 'S' by an atomic sentence/proposition of the logically perfect language, and then using the truth-table rules in (5) to assign truth or falsity to molecular sentences/propositions. [31]

> 4. 'S' is true iff it corresponds to the fact that S.
> 5. ⌐~P⌐ is true iff P is not true; ⌐P & Q⌐ is true iff P is true and Q is true; ⌐P ∨ Q⌐ is true iff P is true or Q is true.

From these, one can derive, for each molecular sentence (proposition), a specification of what atomic facts are required in order for it to be true. Hence, *if* what Russell is after is *simply* an explanation of the truth or falsity of any molecular sentence (proposition) given an inventory of all atomic facts, he doesn't need negative facts.

What about general propositions—quantified sentences—which Russell deals with in lecture 5? Since his remarks about existence are so contentious, I will here deal only with general propositions (involving the universal quantifier), and reserve the discussion of existence to section 5. He sets out his analysis of the general proposition (sentence) 'All Greeks are men' as follows:

> Now when you come to ask what really is asserted in a general proposition, such as 'All Greeks are men' for instance, you find that what is asserted is the truth of all values of what I call a propositional function. A *propositional function* is simply *any expression containing an undetermined constituent, or several undetermined constituents, and becoming a proposition as soon as the undetermined constituents are determined.* If I say 'x is a man' or 'n is a number', that is a propositional function; so is any formula of algebra, say $(x + y)(x - y) = x^2 - y^2$. A propositional function is nothing, but like most of the things one wants to talk about in logic, it does not lose its importance through that fact. The only thing that you can really do with a propositional function is assert either that it is always true, or that it is sometimes true, or that it is never true. If you take 'If x is a man, x is mortal', that is always true.[32]

---

[31] Note that 'S' is a schematic letter; 'P' and 'Q' are metalinguistic variables.
[32] *The Philosophy of Logical Atomism*, p. 96 of Russell (1985); emphasis in the original.

Propositional functions are explicitly identified with formulas, which makes sense if propositions are to be sentences. However, the claim that *what one asserts* when one asserts that all Greeks are men is that the formula 'If x is Greek, then x is a man' is *always true* (i.e., every sentence gotten from that formula by replacing 'x' with a name is true) is clearly false. When one asserts that all Greeks are men, one doesn't assert anything about expressions, formulas, or sentences.

There are two ways of rectifying this difficulty, one modest and one ambitious. The modest route is to give up claims about what one *means* or *asserts* when one asserts a universally quantified statement, and to restrict oneself to extending one's theory of truth to cover such statements. If we take (4) and (5) to be in place—as components of a modified Russellian truth theory—all we need to add is (6).

6. $\ulcorner \forall x\ (\ldots x \ldots)\urcorner$ is true iff the propositional function '$\ldots x \ldots$' is such that for every object o, '$\ldots x \ldots$' is true when 'x' is taken as a name of o.

For example, when F and G are predicates of the logically perfect language that express the properties *being F* and *being G,* the general sentence/ proposition $\ulcorner \forall x\ (Fx \to Gx)\urcorner$ is equivalent to $\ulcorner \forall x\ (\sim Fx \lor Gx)\urcorner$, which is true iff for every object o either there is no atomic fact *o's being F*, or there is an atomic fact *o's being G* along with the fact *o's being F*. In this way, we explain the truth or falsity of the universal generalization in terms of the existence or nonexistence of atomic facts of the specified types.

True, the explanation itself employs quantifiers. But this is no more objectionable than Russell's own use of conjunction in explaining the truth of a conjunctive proposition as being due to *both* the existence of a fact corresponding to the first conjunct *and* the existence of a fact corresponding to the second conjunct, or his use of disjunction in explaining the truth of a disjunctive proposition as being due to *either* the existence of a fact corresponding to the first disjunct *or* the existence of a fact corresponding to the second disjunct. Since in none of these cases (involving conjunction, disjunction, or quantification) are we trying to give an *analysis* of the *meanings* of the relevant sentences, there is nothing amiss in this procedure.

The approach just illustrated with $\ulcorner \forall x\ (Fx \to Gx)\urcorner$ generalizes, providing explanations of the truth or falsity of all universally quantified sentences. Since existentially quantified sentences are, for Russell, definable using the universal quantifier plus negation, the truth or falsity of all molecular, and all quantified, statements of his logically perfect language can be explained in terms of the existence or nonexistence of atomic facts of specified kinds. Thus, when one confines oneself to giving a theory of truth for his system, atomic facts are the only facts one needs.

The more ambitious way of rectifying Russell's problem is to embrace this account of truth as correspondence, while adding a theory of the content of quantified claims. This could be done by reverting to the theory first given in "On Denoting." On that view, the content of the claim that all Greeks are men is that the propositional function that assigns to any object o the nonlinguistic proposition *that if o is Greek, then o is a man* assigns a true proposition to every object. Since this account doesn't wrongly identify the quantified assertion as being about language, it escapes the objection to Russell's own discussion.[33] The problem, of course, is that by 1918 Russell had given up on nonlinguistic propositions and propositional functions. Hence, his original account of quantificational content was no longer available.

Even if it were, he might have harbored atomist worries about it. To admit nonlinguistic propositions would be to recognize atomic propositions in which a property or relation is predicated of one or more particulars, as well as facts consisting of those particulars having that property, or standing in that relation, corresponding to the true ones. Since, on this model, propositions expressed by quantified sentences predicate properties of propositional functions, an atomist might think that their truth *should require* facts that mirror them. If so, the truth of the proposition *that pf is always true* would require the fact *pf's being always true*—which, in turn, would seem to put *pf* in the role of a metaphysically simple entity which, according to Russell, could have been the only thing in the universe. It is not easy to imagine him being happy with this result.

Nor will it help to treat his seemingly confused metalinguistic remarks about quantification (in the passage last quoted) as clumsy attempts to state a genuinely substitutional view. Supposing that no name fails to have a referent and that every metaphysical simple is named, we could, of course, produce a substitutional version of (6) as part of a Russellian theory of truth that avoids general (and negative) facts.

> 6$_S$. $\ulcorner \forall x (\ldots x \ldots) \urcorner$ is true iff all sentences $\ulcorner \ldots n \ldots \urcorner$ that result from replacing free occurrences of 'x' in '...x...' by names in the substitution class associated with 'x' are true.

As with (6), the result of combining (6$_S$) with (4) and (5) results in a theory in which the truth or falsity of every general and molecular sentence/proposition is explained in terms of the existence or nonexistence of atomic facts of specified types. However, *the content* of a universally quantified sentence understood substitutionally can't be identified with the sum of the contents of each of its instances. Since there is no other plausible account available, this modest rectification of Russell's apparent problem can't be extended to an ambitious one (that specifies what is asserted by utterances of a quantified sentence).

Even this conclusion is too generous. For one thing, the right-hand side of (6$_S$) contains objectual quantification over sentences and names. If one

---

[33] By substituting complex properties for propositional functions, one could, in principle, put the analysis in a form that some might find more plausible. On this construal, the content of the assertion is *the property of being a man if one is Greek is universally instantiated.*

is going to allow objectual quantification in any case (by including (6_S) in one's theory), why go substitutional in the first place? For another, the needed assumption—that every metaphysical simple is named by a proper name in the logically perfect language of the agent—can't be accepted. Implausible on any conception of metaphysical simples, the assumption becomes impossible on Russell's narrowly empiricist view. For him, (i) one can name only items with which one is acquainted, (ii) one is never acquainted with the private objects of immediate perception of anyone else, and (iii) the metaphysically simple particulars in the universe include many such objects. Under these assumptions, the substitutional interpretation of quantified sentences of the language of an agent is far too restrictive.

Having shown how Russell could have employed (4–6) to avoid negative and general facts in constructing a modest theory of truth—while staying silent about the meanings of negative and universally quantified sentences, and the contents of assertive utterances of them—I now turn to his stated reasons for positing general facts.

> We have such propositions as 'All men are mortal' and 'Some men are Greeks'. But you have not only such *propositions*; you have also such *facts*, and that, of course, is where you get back to the inventory of the world: that, in addition to particular facts, which I have been talking about in previous lectures, there are also general facts and existence-facts, that is to say, there are not merely *propositions* of that sort but also *facts* of that sort. That is rather an important point to realize. You cannot ever arrive at a general fact by inference from particular facts, however numerous. . . . Suppose, for example, that you wish to prove in that way that 'All men are mortal', you are supposed to proceed by complete induction, and say 'A is a man that is mortal', 'B is a man that is mortal', 'C is a man that is mortal', and so on until you finish. You will not be able, in that way, to arrive at the proposition 'All men are mortal', unless you know when you have finished. That is to say that, in order to arrive by this road at the general proposition 'All men are mortal', you must already have the general proposition 'All men are among those I have enumerated'. You never can arrive at a general proposition by inference from particular propositions alone. You will always have to have at least one general proposition in your premises.[34]

There are several points suggested here. In the discussion immediately following the passage, Russell draws a conclusion about knowledge. Taking it for granted that we do know some general truths, he concludes that there must be knowledge of general propositions that isn't based on logical, deductive inference from non-general propositions. This conclusion in turn is based on the elementary point that no universal generalization $\ulcorner \forall x\ (Ax \to Bx) \urcorner$ is a logical consequence of any set *Inst* of its instances— $\ulcorner An \to Bn \urcorner$, $\ulcorner An' \to Bn' \urcorner$, etc. No matter how large *Inst* may be—even if it contains an instance for each actual thing x of which A is true—it will still

---

[34] Russell (1985), p. 101.

be *logically possible* for there to be more things of which A is true. Since it is logically possible that B might *not* be true of some of these things, it is logically possible for all the sentences in *Inst* to be true, while ⌜∀x (Ax → Bx)⌝ is false. Thus the universal generalization is *not* a logical consequence of the set of individual sentences that are its instances.

Corresponding to this logical point is an ontological one. Suppose that for each thing x of which A is actually true, there is a true sentence ⌜An → Bn⌝ in *Inst*, in which n refers to x. Suppose further that there is a set of facts F that includes the facts *o's being 𝒜* and *o's being ℬ* for each o of which A is true. If, as we have seen, it is *logically possible* for there to be still more things of which A is true, then it is natural to think that there *could have been* more things of which A is true than there actually are. Supposing that B could have failed to be true of some of these, we get the result that there is a possible state of the world—a way the universe could have been—in which all the facts in F continue to obtain, yet ⌜∀x (Ax → Bx)⌝ is untrue.

Russell took this possibility to show that there must be general facts that are not reducible to particular facts. Why? Earlier, I speculated that his willingness to posit negative facts, while avoiding conjunctive and disjunctive facts, may have stemmed from his tacit acceptance of what I called his "Correspondence Principle."

The Correspondence Principle

For any true sentence S, there is a set F of facts such that correspondence of S with one or more of the members of F is responsible for the truth of S.

His willingness to posit general facts can be explained by adding the following corollary.

Corollary to the Correspondence Principle

Correspondence to members in F is responsible for the truth of S only if it would be impossible for the members of F to exist without S being true.

However, had he not accepted these principles, he could have given a theory of truth while positing only atomic facts. The fact that universal generalizations are not logical, a priori, or metaphysically necessary consequences of their instances doesn't undermine the explanation of the actual truth of universally quantified sentences in terms of the actual existence or nonexistence of atomic facts of specified kinds. Consider again the example of a true universal generalization ⌜∀x (Fx → Gx)⌝. According to my modified version of Russell's theory, it is true because for *every object* o either there is no atomic fact *o's being 𝓕*, or there is an atomic fact *o's being 𝒢* along with *o's being 𝓕*. Hence, Russell could have explained the truth of all propositions of his logical language entirely in terms of the existence or nonexistence of atomic facts of specified types.

That he didn't see a way of doing this cost him more than just a bloated ontology. Though Russell took general facts to be needed, he had no analysis of what they were.

> I do not profess to know what the right analysis of general facts is. . . . I am sure that, although the convenient technical treatment is by means of propositional functions, that is not the whole of the right analysis. Beyond that I cannot go.[35]

This sad passage is a tacit admission of the enormous price he paid for abandoning genuine (nonlinguistic) propositions and propositional functions, due to his inability to solve the problem of the unity of the proposition. It doesn't matter that he lacks an analysis of general facts; they aren't really needed anyway. What matters is that he lost the insight in "On Denoting"—which brilliantly tells us what we say/assert through the use of generalized quantifiers. Had he not lost it, he would not have had to wander through the hall of mirrors that is his multiple relation theory of judgment, his flirtation with substitutional quantification, and his historically inconsequential "no-class" theory. Here, in his atomist phase, he would not have been (unintentionally) threatened by an implicitly solipsistic doctrine of intelligibility. Instead, he could have embraced entertainable thoughts that are descriptively about things with which one can't, on his view, be acquainted. And, if he insisted on positing general facts, he could have identified them with the having of properties by propositional functions.

Not having an analysis of general facts was not the only thing about them that worried Russell. In addition, he correctly saw them as threatening his doctrine that there are no molecular facts.

> There is one point about whether there are molecular facts. I think I mentioned, when I was saying that I did not think there were disjunctive facts, that a certain difficulty does arise in regard to general facts. Take 'All men are mortal'. That means . . . that '"x is a man" implies "x is a mortal" is always true' is a fact. [*Russell uses 'implies' for the relation that the antecedent of a true material conditional bears to the consequent.*] It is perhaps a little difficult to see how that can be true if one is going to say that '"Socrates is a man" implies "Socrates is mortal"' is not itself a fact, which is what I suggested when I was discussing disjunctive facts. I do not feel sure you could not get around that difficulty. I only suggest it as a point which should be considered when one is denying that there are molecular facts, since if it cannot be got round, we shall have to admit molecular facts.[36]

• Better, perhaps, to get along without either general or molecular facts.

---

[35] Ibid., p. 103.
[36] Ibid., pp. 103–4.

5. EXISTENCE

In chapter 2 of volume 1, I criticized Frege's view that existence is a property of concepts, not objects. Russell opens himself to similar criticism in the following passages of lecture 5.

> When you take any propositional function and assert of it that . . . it is sometimes true, that gives you the fundamental meaning of 'existence'. You may express it by saying that there is at least one value of x for which the propositional function is true. Take 'x is a man'. There is at least one value for x for which this is true. That is what one means by saying that 'There are men', or that 'Men exist'. Existence is essentially a property of a propositional function. It means that the propositional function is true in at least one instance. . . . It will be out of this notion of sometimes . . . that we get the notion of existence.[37]

> Exactly the same applies to existence . . . the actual things [particulars] that there are in the world do not exist, or, at least, that is putting it too strongly, because that is utter nonsense. To say that they do not exist is strictly nonsense, but to say that they do exist is also utter nonsense. It is of propositional functions that you can assert or deny existence.[38]

Russell suggests that *existence* is a property of propositional functions, not other objects. In admitting that it is a property, he is tacitly admitting that it is, or can be, expressed by the predicate 'exist'. This leads him into trouble, since for any property p and predicate P that expresses p, and for any entity o, p is a property of o iff p is *true of* o iff ⌜Px⌝ is *true* relative to an assignment of o to x—i.e., iff ⌜Px⌝ is *true* when 'x' is treated as a name of o. For example, since honesty, kindness, and intelligence are properties of Susan but not Sam, they are *true of* Susan but not Sam, with the result that the sentences 'Susan is honest/kind/intelligent' are *true*, while the sentences 'Sam is honest/kind/ intelligent' are *not*. Applying the same reasoning to Russell's claim that existence is a property only of propositional functions yields the absurd result that propositional functions are the only things that exist.

How did Russell go astray? Consider the examples in (7).

    7a. A member of that species exists.
      b. There exists a member of that species.

As (8) and (9) illustrate, the variation between (7a) and (7b) is common, with 'there' functioning as a mere filler in the (b)-versions.

    8a. A mouse is in the bathtub.
      b. There is a mouse in the bathtub.
    9a. An event that shocked the nation occurred on December 7, 1941.
      b. There occurred on December 7, 1941 an event that shocked the nation.

---

[37] Ibid., pp. 98–99, my emphasis.
[38] Ibid., p. 99, my emphasis.

Not noticing examples like these, Russell took (7b) as the basic form and symbolized 'there exists' as '∃x' and 'a member of that species' as 'x is a member of that species'. As a result, (7c) was assigned as the logical form of (7a,b).

7c. ∃x (x is a member of that species).

Continuing to read the quantified formula as *there exists a member of that species,* Russell insisted that what (7c) says is that a certain propositional function (expressed by the matrix formula) *is sometimes true.* Next comes the fundamental error. Thinking that (7c) (and hence (7a,b)) predicate *being sometimes true* of something, and also that to assertively utter these sentences is to say or assert that a member of that species *exists,* one slips all too easily into thinking that the property *being sometimes true,* which is predicated in (7), is the property *existence,* expressed by 'exists'. This is a mistake. Not only does it lead to the absurd conclusion that *only propositional functions exist*; it leads to the further conclusion that *only some propositional functions exist*—those that are "sometimes true". From this it follows that every propositional function is true of some objects, and hence that there can, on Russell's own analysis, be no true negative existentials.

The easiest way for Russell to avoid this plunge back into the Meinongian jungle is to deny that there is a property, *existence,* expressed by the word 'exists'. [39] In so doing, he could retain his analysis of negative existentials, according to which to say that men exist but carnivorous cows don't is to say that the function that assigns to o the proposition that o is a man *is sometimes true,* while the function that assigns the proposition that o is carnivorous and o is a cow *is never true.* On this view, ⌜n exists⌝ and ⌜n doesn't exist⌝ are neither true nor false, but rather are uninterpretable nonsense for any singular term n—no matter what n designates. This is what Russell was trying, not entirely successfully, to get at with his remark:

> If you say that 'Men exist and Socrates is a man, therefore Socrates exists', that is exactly the same sort of fallacy as it would be if you said 'Men are numerous, Socrates is a man, therefore Socrates is numerous', *because existence is a predicate of a propositional function....* When you say of a propositional function that it is numerous, you will mean that there are several values of *x* that will satisfy it.... If *x, y,* and *z* all satisfy a propositional function, you

[39] Writing at the same time that Russell was presenting *The Philosophy of Logical Atomism,* Moore avoids the error described in the previous paragraph, maintaining that 'real' and 'unreal' in 'Lions are real/unreal' "do not in this usage stand for any conceptions [properties] at all" and that "the only conceptions [properties] that occur in the proposition "Lions are real" are ... (i) the conception [property] of being a lion, and (2) the conception [property] of belonging to [being true of] something, and perfectly obviously 'real' does not stand for either of these" (Moore 1917–18, p. 212 of the reprinting in Moore 1922a). Moore extends the point to 'exists' in an illuminating discussion of the confusion F. H. Bradley falls into in *Appearance and Reality* (1893) in trying to maintain the existence of things like Time *as appearances* while denying their supposed *reality.*

may say that [it] is numerous, but *x, y,* and *z* severally are not numerous. Exactly the same applies to existence, that is to say that the actual things [particulars] that there are in the world do not exist, or, at least, that is putting it too strongly, because that is utter nonsense. To say that they do not exist is strictly nonsense, but to say that they do exist is also utter nonsense. *It is of propositional functions that you can assert or deny existence.*[40]

Russell slips when he says that 'Men exist and Socrates is a man, therefore Socrates exists' is fallacious "because existence is a predicate of a propositional function." He could have said that the argument is fallacious because (i) the grammatical predicate 'exists' doesn't express any property, but rather serves to signal that the clause in which it occurs is to be understood as predicating *being sometimes true* of a propositional function, *when the clause is properly transformable into an existentially quantified logical form,* and (ii) the clause 'Socrates exists' is not so transformable. Understood in this way, Russell's position is merely wrong, rather than patently absurd.

In section 4.3 of chapter 8, I argued that once his illuminating treatment of unrestricted quantifiers in "On Denoting" is extended to all generalized quantifiers—including descriptions like 'the teacher of Plato'—we need a genuine existence predicate to give the logical form (10b) of (10a).[41]

10a. It is not the case that the teacher of Plato exists.
  b. ~[the x: x taught Plato] x exists

I then used the logical form (11b) of (11a) to show that quantifiers must sometimes range over (presently) nonexisting things (of which the tensed formula '~x exists' is true).

11a. The teacher of Plato is dead and so doesn't exist.
  b. [the x: x taught Plato] (x is dead, and so ~x exists)

These sentences are true iff the propositional function that assigns to an object o the proposition *that o is dead and o doesn't exist* is true of an individual who is unique in having taught Plato. This requires genuine propositions predicating existence of objects (e.g., Socrates), propositional functions assigning such propositions to objects, and quantifiers ranging over things that don't (presently) exist. Similar examples showing that the particular quantifiers ⌜∃x: Φx⌝ and '∃x' do not always carry existential import (because the domain of objects over which they range is not always restricted to presently existing individuals) is provided by (12a) and (12b).

12a. Some great philosophers no longer exist.
    [∃x: x is a great philosopher] (x existed & ~x exists)
  b. Some individuals don't exist but once did.
    ∃x (~x exists but x existed)

---

[40] Russell (1985), p. 99, my emphasis.
[41] See also section 1 of chapter 2.

Once this is seen, there is no bar to treating 'Socrates' as a genuine name—rather than a disguised description—and truly predicating the property *nonexistence* of him.

In drawing these lessons, nothing essential depends on the fact that my examples involve talk about the past. Both the future and the merely possible will do just as well. Suppose, for example, that I have all the materials to build a doghouse, plus a blueprint indicating how each of the materials will be used. Having studied the blueprint and materials, I know exactly what I intend to create. Since I have identified it uniquely, I can refer to it, predicate properties of it, and even name it. After I do, I can truly say "Although Lilly-Pad doesn't exist yet, it soon will, and tomorrow my dog will move into it." Since this remark is true, I must now be able to refer to the object, and truly predicate properties of it, even though it doesn't yet exist. I can also quantify over it, by saying "The name 'Lilly-Pad' refers to something I plan to build." So, present nonexistence is no bar to either naming or quantification.

Nothing of significance changes if Lilly-Pad never exists because I don't follow through on the plan, despite the fact that I could do so. In such a case, the fact that Lilly-Pad's existence is merely possible doesn't prevent me from referring to, naming, or quantifying over it—by saying "The name 'Lilly-Pad' refers to something I could have constructed, but didn't."[42] Since reference to an entity requires one to identify it uniquely, whereas quantification over it doesn't, reference to possible but nonexistent objects is harder than quantification over them. Because we are in no position to uniquely identify many merely possible objects, we can't name them. But this doesn't prevent us from quantifying over them.

In sum, there is good reason to believe (i) that 'exists' is a genuine predicate, (ii) that it expresses the property *existence*, (iii) that the property *being sometimes true* expressed by the particular quantifier is neither identical nor coextensive with *existence,* (iv) that many objects exemplify *existence*, but some do not, and (v) that it is possible to quantify over, and name, things that don't exist. It remains to examine Russell's further comments on existence and existence statements in light of the grounds offered for these conclusions.

I left off, after discussing the last passage quoted from lecture 5, restating Russell's view so as to deny (i) and (ii), while making it consistent with (iii) above. Here is the passage that immediately follows the one last quoted.

> If I say 'The things that there are in the world exist', that is a perfectly correct statement, because I am there saying something about a certain class of things; I say it in the same sense in which I say 'Men exist'. But I must not go

---

[42] Nonexistence is also no bar to having properties. Lilly-Pad has the properties *being something I will build, or could have built,* even though it doesn't (actually) exist. For further discussion, see section 1 of chapter 2. For more far-reaching cases, see Salmon (1987).

on to 'This is a thing in the world, and therefore it exists'. It is there that the fallacy comes in, and it is simply . . . a fallacy of transferring to the individual that satisfies a propositional function a predicate which only applies to a propositional function.[43]

The error in the passage is clear. The logical form of (13a) is (13b).

13a. Some men exist.
   b. [∃x: x is a man] x exists.

Although an assertive utterance of (13a) does indeed predicate something of a propositional function pf—namely that it is sometimes true—the fact that pf assigns to o the proposition that predicates existence of o ensures that pf's being sometimes true guarantees that some object instantiates *existence*. There is no fallacy.

Russell continues the passage by giving an argument for his position.

> You can see this in various ways. For instance, you sometimes know the truth of an existence proposition without knowing any instance of it. You know that there are people in Timbuktu, but I doubt if any of you could give me an instance of one. Therefore you clearly can know existence propositions without knowing any individual that makes them true. Existence propositions do not say anything about the actual individual but only about a class or function.[44]

This is no argument. For one thing, the claim that existence propositions don't say anything about an individual is false even on Russell's own account—as is shown by his analysis of '∃x (x = Saul Kripke)'. Perhaps he thought that if 'exists' were a genuine predicate, there would be no quantified existence claims the truth of which could be known without knowing the truth of any instances. But, as the logical forms suggested above for the sentences in (10–13) have shown, there is no problem with formulating quantified existence claims in which 'exists' functions as a genuine predicate expressing a property predicated of objects. Many such existence claims can be known to be true even if none of their instances are known to be true. Since this is not true of all existence claims, the last sentence in that passage just quoted is a non sequitur.

In answering a question at the end of lecture 5, Russell gives another ineffective argument against the idea that 'exist' is a genuine predicate expressing a property of individuals.

> There is no sort of point in a predicate which could not conceivably be false. I mean, it is perfectly clear that, if there were such a thing as this existence of individuals that we talk of, *it would be absolutely impossible for it not to apply*, and that is a characteristic of a mistake.[45]

---

[43] Russell (1985), pp. 99–100.
[44] Ibid., p. 100.
[45] Ibid., p. 108, my emphasis.

Here again, Russell has gone astray. His thought is that if existence were a predicate, then it would be impossible for it *not to apply to everything*. But surely, he thinks, a predicate that was guaranteed to apply to everything would be one that it would not make sense to predicate of anything, or indeed to put to any useful purpose. But this is incorrect. First, since Socrates no longer exists, and since Lilly-Pad never existed and never will, the predicate 'exist' doesn't apply to Socrates or Lilly-Pad. Consequently, some things are *not* in the extension of 'exist', which means that the predicate *doesn't apply to everything*. Second, even if one thought that at each world-state 'exists' applies to "everything," uses of it could still be informative in some modal contexts provided that its extension changes from world-state to world-state.

Russell's final argument is given at the beginning of lecture 6.

> If you take such a proposition as 'Romulus existed', probably most of us think that Romulus did not exist. It is obviously a perfectly significant statement, whether true or false, to say that Romulus existed. If Romulus himself entered into our statement, it would be plain that the statement that he did not exist would be nonsense, because you cannot have a constituent of a proposition which is nothing at all. . . . You see therefore . . . that 'Romulus' is not really a name but a sort of truncated description. . . . If it were really a name, the question of existence could not arise, *because a name has got to name something or it is not a name.*[46]

Note the last claim. There is a sense in which it is plausible, and might even be true. That is the sense paraphraseable by (14a) and formally representable by (14b).

14a. For an expression n, n is a name only if something is named by n.

  b. $\forall$n (n is a name → $\exists$x (n names x))

There is nothing obviously objectionable here as long as '$\exists$x' is read 'for some x', rather than 'there exists an x', and the clause of which it is a constituent is understood as predicating the property *assigns a true proposition to at least one object*, rather than the property *assigns a true proposition to at least one existing object*. Since I have argued that uses of particular quantifiers sometimes require this understanding, there is a natural way of taking Russell's claim to be true, while denying that it makes his point. To be sure, he would not accept this reading—because he assumes (with no compelling argument) both (i) that the particular quantifier must be existential and (ii) that any name used by an agent must designate an object the existence and nature of which the agent can't possibly be mistaken about. Having already been noted on several occasions, the difficulties caused by (ii) require no further critical comment here.

The final point to notice is that Russell's discussion of propositions involving the particular quantifier assumes the standard "On Denoting"

---

[46] Ibid., pp. 109–10, my emphasis.

analysis throughout. All such propositions are seen as predicating *being true of some (existing) object* of one or another "propositional function." What he seems not to have noticed is that it is one thing to embrace this analysis when propositional functions are genuine functions from objects to nonlinguistic propositions; it is quite another to do so after insisting that propositional functions are formulas of a particular "logically perfect" language. Read literally, Russell's discussion commits him to the obviously false view that all quantified propositions make metalinguistic claims about words. The fact that he nowhere notices this, or says anything about how to avoid this absurd conclusion, is compelling evidence that by 1918 he had become deeply confused about quantification. Nor would it help to read his remarks about quantification substitutionally. In addition to the manifest problems for atomism noted earlier that are created by such an interpretation, it is inconsistent with his repeated insistence that existential claims *predicate properties that only propositional functions can have.* On the substitutional interpretation, nothing is predicated, or asserted, of the formulas to which quantifiers are attached. At this stage of his career, Russell was neither a consistent substitutionalist nor a consistent objectualist. Oblivious to the differences between the two, he was simply confused.

6. THE MULTIPLE RELATION THEORY OF JUDGMENT REVISITED

The title of lecture 4 is "Propositions and Facts with More than One Verb: Beliefs, etc." The question at issue is the nature of facts that correspond to true sentences like those illustrated in (15).

15a. Othello *believes* that Desdemona *loves* Cassio.
  b. Othello *doesn't want* Desdemona to *love* Cassio.

In each case, the sentence contains a "propositional attitude verb" plus a verb in the complement clause. At one time Russell took the propositional attitude verb to express a relation between an agent and a nonlinguistic proposition expressed by the complement clause. As we have seen, by 1910 he had given up that view for want of an explanation of how there could be false propositions, like the one expressed by the embedded clauses in these examples. The problem for which he could not find a solution was to explain the representational unity of a complex the constituents of which were Desdemona, Cassio, and the relation of loving, when Desdemona does *not* in fact stand in that relation to Cassio. As I explained in chapter 9, his solution was to reanalyze propositional attitude verbs as expressing relations between agents and belief-desire (etc.) constituents—e.g., between Othello and the constituents Desdemona, Cassio, and loving. On this view, the logical forms of (15a,b) are (16a,b), and the facts to which they correspond are (a) Othello's standing in the (4-place) belief relation to Desdemona, Cassio, and loving and (b) Othello's not standing in the (4-place) desire relation to the same trio.

16a. Believes (Othello, Desdemona, Cassio, loving)
  b. ~ Want (Othello, Desdemona, Cassio, loving)

The view on offer in *The Philosophy of Logical Atomism* is an incompletely conceptualized variant of this view. It is like the earlier multiple relation theory (i) in rejecting both nonlinguistic propositions and the analysis of propositional attitude verbs as expressing two-place relations between an agent and something believed, desired, etc., (ii) in taking facts corresponding to true propositional-attitude sentences to involve *arbitrarily many arguments* standing in various relations, and (iii) in taking belief-facts to be *beliefs*, which are themselves bearers of truth or falsity. However, the new view differs from the earlier view in maintaining that the facts in question contain two "verbs" *functioning as verbs*. The following four brief passages encompass everything positive that Russell has to say about this new view.

> [T]he facts that occur when one believes or wishes or wills have a different logical form from the atomic facts containing a single verb. . . . Take any sort of proposition, say 'I believe Socrates is mortal'. Suppose that that belief does actually occur. The statement that it occurs is a statement of fact. You have there two verbs. . . . You will perceive that it is not only the proposition that has the two verbs, but also the fact, which is expressed by the proposition, has two constituents corresponding to verbs.[47]

> Suppose I take 'A believes that B loves C'. 'Othello believes that Desdemona loves Cassio'. There you have a false belief. *You have this odd state of affairs that the verb 'loves' occurs in that proposition and seems to occur as relating Desdemona to Cassio whereas in fact it does not do so, but yet it does occur as a verb.* I mean that when A believes that B loves C, you have to have a verb in the place where 'loves' occurs. You cannot put a substantive in its place. *Therefore it is clear that the subordinate verb . . . is functioning as a verb, and seems to be relating two terms, but as a matter of fact does not when a judgment happens to be false. That is what constitutes the puzzle about the nature of belief.*[48]

> There are really two main things that one wants to notice in this matter. . . . The *first* is the impossibility of treating the proposition believed as an independent entity, entering as a unit into the occurrence of the belief, and the *other* is the impossibility of putting the subordinate verb on a level with its terms as an object term in the belief. That is a point in which I think that the theory of judgment which I set forth once . . . was a little unduly simple, because I did then treat the object verb . . . as if one could put 'loves' on a level with Desdemona and Cassio as a term for the relation 'believe'.[49]

[47] Ibid., pp. 80–81.
[48] Ibid., pp. 89–90, my emphasis.
[49] Ibid., pp. 91–92.

But a belief is true or false . . . so that you do have facts in the world that are true or false. I said a while back that there was no distinction of true and false among facts, but as regards the special class of facts that we call 'beliefs', there is, in th[e] sense that a belief which occurs may be true or false, though it is equally a fact in either case.[50]

This multiple-verbs version of the original multiple relation theory— the need for which Russell attributes to Wittgenstein's objection to the original theory (discussed in section 6 of chapter 9)—shares all the problems with the original theory identified in chapter 9, plus the further problem of not explaining what the mysterious subordinate "verbs" are, or what it is for something to "function as a verb" in one of his special facts-with-truth-values.[51] Nevertheless, there are three closely related respects in which the multiple-verbs version of the theory can be seen as moving in the right direction. First, since the semantic function of an n-place predicate (verb) in a true or false sentence or sentential clause is to truly or falsely *predicate* an n-place property of n things, the new theory's insistence on constituents of beliefs *functioning as verbs* can naturally be interpreted as an insistence that belief always involve a property *being predicated (by the agent) of the other constituents of the belief.* Second, this understanding of the multiple-verbs theory provides a transparent explanation for the ill-formedness of any purported logical form, like (17), which fails to provide anything that can be predicated of other things.

17. *Believes (Othello, Desdemona, Cassio)

Third, the need to specify what is predicated of what is made evident by examples like (18a), which fails to specify which of the three relevant constituents is predicated of the other two.

18a. Judges (Sam, difference, identity, similarity)
  b. Sam judges that difference is similar to identity.
  c. Sam judges that difference is identical to similarity.
  d. Sam judges that identity is different from similarity.

This problem is solved by specifying which constituent is "functioning as a verb."

Though I suspect that Russell was sensitive to these points, he didn't view them in quite this way, and could hardly have done so without allowing nonlinguistic propositions back into his ontology. On the view

---

[50] Ibid., p. 93.

[51] Roughly half of lecture 4 is devoted to recapitulating his reasons for rejecting his early theory of nonlinguistic propositions, and entertaining a variant of behaviorism about propositional attitudes that he could not (at that time) bring himself to accept, despite what he took to be its connection with a view to which he was becoming increasingly attracted— neutral monism.

of verbs and predication I have just suggested, for Sam to judge *that difference is similar to identity* is for him to predicate *similarity* of difference and identity, and to bear something like the relation of affirming or endorsing to the result of his predication. For Mary to judge *that it is not the case that difference is similar to identity* is for her to predicate *not being true* of the thing that Sam affirmed, and for her to endorse the result of her predication. What are these *results of predications*, which may themselves be the targets of further predications? They are propositions thought of along the lines of cognitive acts or event types of the sort discussed in section 5 of chapter 9. They are abstract, nonlinguistic entities the existence of which does not require agents to entertain them (i.e., to perform or produce instances of them), but the intentionality of which is explained by the fact that for them to be entertained is for *agents* to predicate properties of things, and hence to represent those things as being certain ways.[52]

As the following passage obliquely suggests, it was precisely this unusual combination of properties that Russell could not envision that prevented him from using the multiple-verbs version of the multiple relation theory of judgment to reconstitute, and naturalize, propositions in this way.

> To suppose that in the actual world of nature there is a whole set of [nonlinguistic] false propositions going about is to my mind monstrous. I cannot bring myself to suppose it. I cannot believe that they are there in the sense in which facts are there. There seems to me to be something about the fact that 'Today is Tuesday' on a different level of reality from the supposition that 'Today is Wednesday'. I do not mean the occurrence in the future of a state of mind in which you think it is Wednesday, but I am talking about the theory that there is something quite logical, *something not involving mind in any way;* and such a thing as that I do not think you can take a false proposition to be.[53]

Unable to conceive of nonlinguistic propositions the intentionality of which is explained via the intentionality of the cognitive processes of (possible) agents who entertain them, Russell had no way of dealing with the manifest problems of the original multiple relation theory, or of demystifying what was, at bottom, a genuine but insufficiently articulated insight about the special role played by "subordinate verbs" in facts about cognitive attitudes. For this reason, it shouldn't be surprising that the theory of judgment in *The Philosophy of Logical Atomism* was the last gasp of this ill-fated theory, which he abandoned shortly after finishing the lectures.

---

[52] For further explanation, see the final section of chapter 12 of Soames (2014c).
[53] Russell (1985), p. 88, my emphasis.

7. DESCRIPTIONS AND INCOMPLETE SYMBOLS

In lecture 6, Russell reiterates his theory of names and descriptions. Although he doesn't break new ground, he does amplify his familiar analyses of existence statements, logically proper names, ordinary names, singular definite descriptions, and "incomplete symbols." He begins with existence claims. Speaking of such statements as 'I exist', 'God exists', and 'Homer existed', he says that the usual treatment of them in metaphysics rests on "a simple logical mistake." He continues:

> One way of examining a proposition of that sort is to ask yourself what would happen if it were false. If you take such a proposition as 'Romulus existed', probably most of us think that Romulus did not exist. It is obviously a perfectly significant statement, whether true or false, to say that Romulus existed. *If Romulus himself entered into our statement, it would be plain that the statement that he did not exist would be nonsense, because you cannot have a constituent of a proposition which is nothing at all.* . . . That [i.e., that the statement is nonsense] is obviously not the case, and the first conclusion one draws is that, although it looks as if Romulus were a constituent of that proposition, that is really a mistake. Romulus does not occur in the proposition 'Romulus did not exist'.[54]

Although the view is familiar, its expression here is complicated by the choice of a mythical character—Romulus—as exemplar, and by the seeming vacillation between taking "propositions" to be meaningful sentences and taking them to be nonlinguistic entities expressed by such sentences. The special features of fictional characters and the statements we make about them were discussed in section 4.4 of chapter 7, and won't be repeated here. Since Russell was oblivious to these features, we may treat the example as if it involved an ordinary, rather than a fictional, name. As for his talk about propositions, the question of whether Romulus, Socrates, or Lilly-Pad "can be a constituent of a proposition" is not, on the face of it, a question about whether they can be constituents of a *sentence*—which, by this time, was his official view of what a proposition was. Rather, his talk of constituency invites one to take propositions to be nonlinguistic contents expressed by sentences. On the other hand, his claim that if Romulus were a constituent of the proposition that Romulus does not exist, then *the proposition* would be nonsense, is naturally understood as the claim that *the sentence* 'Romulus does not exist' would be meaningless. One can straighten this out in either of two ways. Reverting to nonlinguistic propositions, one may interpret Russell as asserting that if 'Romulus', 'Socrates', and 'Lilly-Pad' were names, then they would fail to introduce constituents into propositions expressed by sentences containing them—with the result that no (existing) propositions would be expressed, and no true or false proposition would be asserted by uttering

[54] Ibid., pp. 109–10, my emphasis.

such sentences. Alternatively, one might understand him as asserting that if these ordinary names functioned as genuine names, then sentences containing them would be meaningless, rather than true or false.

Either way, the chief problem with the view is that it fails to distinguish *referring to something that doesn't exist* from *failing to refer*. As I have previously observed, the fact that neither Socrates nor Lilly-Pad exists doesn't prevent us from referring to them. On the contrary, referring to things that don't exist now, but either did or will exist is commonplace. Since nothing of significance changes when we speak of certain individuals that could have existed, but never have or will exist, reference to them is no more problematic. Russell provides no compelling argument to the contrary.

He continues with his positive analysis of 'Romulus does not exist'.

> Suppose you try to make out what you do mean by that proposition [sentence]. You can take, say, all the things that Livy has to say about Romulus, all properties he ascribes to him, including the only one most of you probably remember, namely, the fact that he was called 'Romulus'. *You can put all this together, and make a propositional function saying 'x has such and such properties', the properties being those you find enumerated in Livy.* There you have a propositional function, and when you say that Romulus did not exist, *you are simply saying that the propositional function is never true . . . that there is no value of x that makes it true.* You see, therefore, that this proposition . . . *does introduce a propositional function, because the name 'Romulus' is not really a name but a sort of truncated description.* . . . If it were really a name, the question of existence could not arise, because a name has got to name something or it is not a name, and if there is no such person as Romulus, there cannot be a name of a person who is not there.[55]

Living in a post-Kripkean world, we know that this purely descriptive analysis of names can't be correct. A further independent error is derivable from Russell's claim that one who says that Romulus did not exist is "simply saying that the propositional function is never true." Substituting a description for 'Romulus', one might well characterize what one says when assertively uttering ⌜D does not exist⌝ in this way. Or, rather, one might do so, *if one accepted the quantificational analysis of descriptions in "On Denoting," in which propositional functions are functions from objects to nonlinguistic propositions.* However, no such characterization—of *what is said* by uttering ⌜D does not exist⌝—is available to one who either (a) revises the theory in "On Denoting" by taking propositional functions to be formulas of a particular language (about which it is clear one is not making any assertion), or (b) replaces that theory with a substitutional analysis of quantification (according to which no assertion about either formulas or nonlinguistic propositional functions is made). Russell, who must be

---

[55] Ibid., p. 110, my emphasis.

doing one or the other, while trying to retain his "On Denoting" account of what is said, is illegitimately trying to have it both ways.

After reprising his theory of descriptions, he turns to the question of the "constituents" of propositions in which a definite description occurs, and to the facts correspondence with which makes them true.

> Now the next point that I want to make clear is that when a description . . . occurs in a proposition, *there is no constituent of that proposition corresponding to that description as a whole.* In the true analysis of the proposition, the description is broken up and disappears. That is to say, when I say 'Scott is the author of *Waverley*' it is a wrong analysis of that to suppose that you have there three constituents, 'Scott', 'is', and 'the author of *Waverley*'. . . . 'The author of *Waverley*' is not a constituent of the proposition at all. . . . The first and most obvious reason is that you can have significant propositions denying the existence of 'the so-and-so'. 'The unicorn does not exist.' 'The greatest finite number does not exist.' Propositions of that sort are perfectly significant, perfectly sober, true, decent propositions, *and that could not possibly be the case if the unicorn were a constituent of the proposition, because plainly it could not be a constituent as long as there were not any unicorns. Because the constituents of a proposition, of course, are the same as the constituents of the corresponding facts*, and since it is a fact that the unicorn does not exist, *it is perfectly clear that the unicorn is not a constituent of that fact*, because if there were any fact of which the unicorn was a constituent, there would be a unicorn, and it would not be true that it did not exist.[56]

None of the points Russell makes is "perfectly clear," even after one disentangles the seeming vacillation between linguistic and nonlinguistic propositions, and clarifies the relationship between constituents of "propositions" and constituents of facts. Let us follow the official line that propositions are sentences. The claim that a definite description D is not constituent of a proposition in which D occurs can then be taken to be a way of saying that when D is a grammatical constituent of a sentence S, neither D nor anything corresponding to D is a constituent of the formula that is the logical form of S.

Russell's reasons for taking this reformulated claim to be true are those given in "On Denoting." In addition to the argument for his quantificational analysis of English definite descriptions over competing analyses that treat them as complex singular terms, he tries to show that complex singular terms are *impossible* in any language. As I explained in section 2 of chapter 8 (and elaborated in section 5 of chapter 9), his argument hinged on the alleged impossibility of distinguishing a proposition in which a given property is predicated of the meaning of such a term from the proposition in which that property is predicated of the individual designated by the term. Although I maintained that the argument was unsound, I

---

[56] Ibid., pp. 116–17, my emphasis.

tried to show that the way in which he conceived of nonlinguistic propositions gave it considerable persuasive force. What remains of that force,
now that nonlinguistic propositions have been repudiated?

In answering this question, we let 'ιx' stand for a function f_ι that takes
a Russellian propositional function p_F as argument and assigns as value
the unique object to which p_F assigns a true proposition, and otherwise is
undefined. We stipulate that 'ιx' combines with a formula F(x), standing
for p_F, to form a complex singular term $\ulcorner \iota x\ Fx\urcorner$ that designates the value of
f_ι at p_F. Invoking Russell's own earlier conception of nonlinguistic propositions, we characterize the proposition expressed by $\ulcorner[\iota x\ F]$ is so-and-so$\urcorner$
as consisting of the property *being so-and-so*, plus the meaning of $\ulcorner \iota x\ Fx\urcorner$,
which is the complex in which f_ι is combined with its argument p_F. One
who entertains this proposition cognizes both functions, and predicates
being so-and-so of whatever results from applying the former to the latter.
The proposition is true iff the function assigns the argument an object that
is so-and-so. The problem on which Russell's purported impossibility argument rested was that we have no way of distinguishing this proposition
from the proposition that predicates *being so-and-so* of the complex consisting of f_ι and p_F. Since this was intolerable, he concluded that definite
descriptions cannot be complex singular terms, and do not introduce constituents into the propositions expressed by sentences containing them.

When nonlinguistic propositions are given up, this argument disappears. Now, for a description to be a constituent of the proposition expressed by S is simply for it—the description itself—to be a constituent of
the formula that is the logical form of S. The logical form (19a) can simply
be characterized as true iff the formula Fx is true of exactly one object,
which in turn is an object of which G is true.

19a. G (ιx Fx)

Since no entity is posited as the meaning of the description, and no nonlinguistic proposition is posited in which *being G* is predicated of such a
meaning, there is no pair of distinct propositions that we are unable to
discriminate. Hence, there is no impossibility result. Could one object
that although the truth conditions provided for (19a) are correct, they are
no substitute for a statement of the meaning of the sentence $\ulcorner$The F is G$\urcorner$?
Perhaps. However, Russell is in no position to do so, since the same objection could be raised against the statement of the truth conditions (but not
the meaning) of his preferred logical form (19b).

19b. $\exists x \forall y\ ((Fy \longleftrightarrow x = y)\ \&\ Gx)$

One could, of course, go metalinguistic, and claim that (19a) *means* that
the unique object of which the propositional function—i.e., formula—Fx
is true, is G. Though not a good account of meaning (since such claims
are not standardly about formulas), it is no worse than a metalinguistic
account of the meaning of Russell's (19b). Dispensing with such incorrect

claims about meaning, one might interpret *The Philosophy of Logical Atomism* as eschewing the task of explicitly stating what individual sentences mean, while nevertheless stating their truth conditions, and specifying the facts to which true sentences correspond. But then *one cannot rely on the impossibility argument in "On Denoting"* to support the thesis that "it could not possibly be the case that" descriptions occur as constituents of propositions (i.e., of logical forms).

Does Russell have another persuasive argument for this claim? Recall his remark:

> *Because the constituents of a proposition, of course, are the same as the constituents of the corresponding facts,* and since it is a fact that the unicorn does not exist, *it is perfectly clear that the unicorn is not a constituent of that fact,* because if there were any fact of which the unicorn was a constituent, there would be a unicorn, and it would not be true that it did not exist.

This is wrong on two counts. First, now that propositions are formulas, their constituents, which are symbols, are *not* constituents of the facts to which they correspond. Second, there is nothing to stop nonexistent objects from occurring as constituents of facts. Although Socrates is dead, and so no longer exists, he was the teacher of Plato. Hence, 'The teacher of Plato doesn't exist' is true, which we may express by saying "It is a fact that the teacher of Plato doesn't exist." If one supposes that a negative existential statement is made true by the fact to which it corresponds, one may conclude that the fact in question is the fact that *Socrates* doesn't exist (or is nonexistent). (Similar points could be made about merely possible objects like Lilly-Pad.) In general, one may maintain that a "proposition" ⌜The F is G⌝ is true iff there is a fact that consists of o's *being G*, where o is unique in instantiating *being F*. I do not say that this view is forced on Russell—only that his rejection of nonlinguistic propositions robs him of what he would otherwise have regarded as a central and compelling component of his argument against it. He appears not to have noticed this.

Another of his doctrines about existence claims is undone when one recognizes existence as a genuine property of objects, expressed by the predicate 'exists'.

> When I say 'the author of *Waverley* exists', I mean that there is an entity c such that 'x wrote *Waverley*' is true when x is c, and is false when x is not c. 'The author of *Waverley*' as a constituent has quite disappeared there, so that when I say 'The author of *Waverley* exists' *I am not saying anything about the author of Waverley.* . . . I have now defined what I mean by saying that a thing described exists. I have still to explain what I mean by saying that a thing described has a certain property. Supposing you want to say 'The author of *Waverley* was human', that will be represented thus: '("x wrote *Waverley*" is equivalent to "x is c" whatever x may be, and c is human) is possible with respect to c [i.e., is true for some c]'. . . . You will observe that what we gave before as the meaning of 'The author of *Waverley* exists' is part of the proposition. . . . If I

say the author of *Waverley* was human, or a poet, or a Scotsman, or *whatever I say about the author of Waverly* . . . always this statement of his existence is part of the proposition. In that sense all these propositions that I make *about the author of Waverley* imply that the author of *Waverley* exists.[57]

Notice the asymmetry: when I say that the author of *Waverley* exists, I don't say anything *about* the author of *Waverley;* but when I say that the author of *Waverley* is human, I do say something *about* the author of *Waverley*. This asymmetry is closely related to Russell's distinction between knowledge by acquaintance and knowledge by description, introduced in the second paragraph of "On Denoting"[58] (quoted in chapter 8, section 1.1, above).

Putting all this together, we see that Russell is committed to a contrast between knowing that the $\mathcal{F}$ is G and knowing that the $\mathcal{F}$ exists. According to him, the former is a case of *knowing by description* that a certain object (which is identical with any object iff that object is $\mathcal{F}$) is G, whereas the latter is *not* a case of *knowing anything by description*. This asymmetry, implicit from "On Denoting" onwards, is made explicit in the above passage from *The Philosophy of Logical Atomism*. The implausible asymmetry disappears if one avoids Russell's mistake, and recognizes existence as the property it really is.

It is striking how intensely he is committed to this mistake.

It is of the utmost importance to realize that 'the so-and-so' does not occur in the analysis of propositions in whose verbal expression it occurs . . . [and] that when I say 'The author of *Waverley* is human', that is not a proposition of the same form as 'Scott is human'. It does not contain a constituent 'the author of *Waverley*'. *The importance of that is very great for many reasons, and one of them is the question of existence.* As I pointed out to you last time, there is a vast amount of philosophy that rests upon the notion that existence is, so to speak, a property that you can attribute to things, and the things that exist have the property of existence and the things that do not exist do not. That is rubbish, whether you take kinds of things, or individual things described. . . . It is only where a propositional function comes in that existence may be significantly asserted. You can assert 'The so-and-so exists', meaning that there is just one c which has those properties [associated with 'so-and-so'], but when you get hold of a c that has them, you cannot say of this c that it exists, because that is nonsense. . . . So the individuals that there are in the world do not exist, or rather it is nonsense to say that they exist and nonsense to say that they do not exist.[59]

In addition to disagreeing with Russell about existence, I also disagree with him about the consequences of our disagreement. They are not,

[57] Ibid., p. 118–19, my emphasis.
[58] Russell (1905d), pp. 479–80.
[59] Russell (1985), p. 121, my emphasis.

as far as I can see, nearly as far-reaching as he suggests. A great deal of metaphysics may remain the same, no matter which side of this issue one takes.

However, there is something of much greater metaphysical and general philosophical significance for which Russell's discussion of existence and descriptions is a seductive, though misleading, introduction. This is his doctrine of incomplete symbols, which he describes at the end of lecture 6.

> The sort of things that are like these descriptions in that they occur in words in a proposition but are not in actual fact constituents of the proposition rightly analyzed, things of that sort I call 'incomplete symbols'. There are a great many sorts of incomplete symbols in logic, and they are sources of a great deal of confusion and false philosophy. . . . There are a great many other sorts of incomplete symbols besides descriptions. These are classes, . . . relations taken in extension [essentially classes of ordered pairs], and so on. Such aggregations of symbols are really the same thing as what I call 'logical fictions', and they embrace practically all the familiar objects of daily life: tables, chairs, Piccadilly, Socrates, and so on. Most of them are either classes, or series, or series of classes. In any case they are incomplete symbols, i.e. they are aggregations that only have a meaning in use and do not have any meaning in themselves.[60]

Definite descriptions are the paradigm cases of incomplete symbols for Russell. They are grammatical constituents of sentences that disappear on analysis, and so do not occur in the logical forms of those sentences. Right or wrong, this idea is straightforward, and readily comprehensible. Much more difficult is the claim that certain *things*—classes, tables, Socrates, and Piccadilly—*are incomplete symbols*. Roughly put, what Russell means is that although ordinary, unanalyzed sentences appear to contain many grammatical constituents that refer to, or quantify over, these things, no such constituents occur in the logical forms of these sentences.

The conclusion he draws is that these sentences don't really represent the world as containing any of these things; hence the truth of these sentences doesn't require the existence of such things. In saying that these things are "logical fictions," he seems to be saying that they don't really exist—that there are no such things. However, that is too simple. Since he admits the truth of 'There is a smallest class containing zero and closed under successor', 'There are tables and chairs in some Cambridge rooms', 'Piccadilly is a district of London', and 'Socrates existed centuries ago', he must deny 'There are no classes', 'There are no tables and chairs', 'There is no such thing as the district Piccadilly,' and 'Socrates never existed'. So, what is the ontological import of his ambitious doctrine of incomplete symbols? Russell addresses this question in the next lecture.

[60] Ibid., p. 122.

8. NO CLASS: THE THEORY OF TYPES AND THE PURPORTED ELIMINATION OF CLASSES

In Lecture 7 Russell informally sketches his "no-class theory." After presenting his paradox concerning the class of all classes that are not members of themselves, he states his diagnosis of the problem and its solution:

> The contradiction is extremely interesting. . . . I think it is clear that you can only get around it by observing that the whole question whether a class is or is not a member of itself is nonsense. . . . *That has to do with the fact that classes . . . are incomplete symbols in the same sense in which the descriptions are*: you are talking nonsense when you ask yourself whether a class is or is not a member of itself, because in any full statement of what is meant by a proposition which seems to be about a class, you will find that the class is not mentioned at all and that there is nothing about a class in that statement. *It is absolutely necessary, if a statement about a class is to be significant and not pure nonsense, that it should be capable of being translated into a form in which it does not mention the class at all.*[61]

This idea, which is central to Russell's thought, can easily be misunderstood. First, whereas descriptions are expressions, classes are not; so the two cannot be *incomplete symbols* in the same sense. One might think that this defect is mere sloppiness that can easily be fixed. Surely, what Russell means is that expressions that purport to refer to, or quantify over, classes are incomplete symbols in the sense in which descriptions are: neither occur as constituents of the logical forms of sentences. This is what leads him to say that any meaningful statement S that appears to be about a class must be translatable into a statement—the logical form of S—in which no class is designated or quantified over.

In *Principia Mathematica* Russell adopts the following contextual definition of singular terms purportedly designating classes:

CLASS $F (\uparrow x: Gx \uparrow) =_{df} \exists H [\forall y (Hy \longleftrightarrow Gy) \& F(H)]$

As with singular definite descriptions, the definition can be seen as eliminating what appear to be singular terms from sentences, and replacing them with more complicated constructions in the logical forms of those sentences. In this way, class terms are treated similarly to descriptions. However, problems arise when we try to clarify what the class-term definition tells us. According to it, a formula that seems to say that F is true of *the class of individuals satisfying G* is really an abbreviation of a more complex formula that says that F is true of *something that is true of all and only the individuals that satisfy G*. This something is a propositional function; so a claim that appears to say that the class of things that satisfy G has the property *being F* really says that some propositional function that is true of the same

[61] Ibid., p. 132, my emphasis.

things as the propositional function f_G has that property. Thus, it seems, classes are reduced to, or replaced by, propositional functions.

But what are propositional functions, and which of their properties are needed in *Principia Mathematica*? Let us begin by thinking of them in Russell's original, nonlinguistic way—as genuine functions. As noted in chapter 10, propositional functions that assign true propositions to the same objects are *extensionally equivalent*, and in Russell's reconstruction of mathematics, all propositional functions that take propositional functions as arguments are *extensional*—i.e., whenever they are true of a function g, they are true of all propositional functions extensionally equivalent to g. As a result, Russell's logicist reduction doesn't distinguish among extensionally equivalent propositional functions: any theorem with a constituent c that designates g is true iff any corresponding sentence is true in which a constituent c' has been substituted for c, where c' designates a propositional function extensionally equivalent to g. Because of this, one can substitute quantification over functions from objects to truth values for quantification over propositional functions. To do this is simply to replace quantification over classes, with quantification over their characteristic functions. Since there are no significant mathematical or philosophical advantages in this, the elimination of classes comes to nothing when propositions and quantification over them are interpreted in this way.

Not surprisingly, this was not Russell's interpretation. Already at the time of *Principia Mathematica*, but certainly in *The Philosophy of Logical Atomism*, he thought of propositional functions simply as formulas. With this understanding, the most straightforward reading of his class-term definition tells us that a formula that seems to predicate *being F* of the class of individuals that have the property *being G* is really an abbreviation for a more complex formula that says that *being F* is true of some formula that is extensionally equivalent to the formula Gx. However, as noted in chapter 10, this is implausible. First, it would make all arithmetical statements arising from Russell's logicist reduction metalinguistic statements that make claims *about his logical language*, with the result that arithmetical knowledge is nothing more than knowledge of the properties of formulas of that language. Second, it would drive an epistemological and metaphysical wedge between quantified statements and their instances. For, when quantificational statements are understood in this way and $\ulcorner \Phi n \urcorner$ makes no claim about language, it will be neither an a priori nor a necessary consequence of $\ulcorner \forall x\ \Phi x \urcorner$ (if the semantic properties of Φx are neither essential to it nor knowable a priori), while $\ulcorner \exists x\ \Phi x \urcorner$ will be neither an a priori nor a necessary consequence of $\ulcorner \Phi n \urcorner$ (on the same assumption). Equally important, this way of replacing classes in Russell's reduction does nothing to block the class-theoretic paradoxes with which he was concerned.

The problem underlying those paradoxes was, he thought, an instance of a more general problem that is also exhibited by the liar paradox, about which he says:

The man who says "I am lying" is really asserting 'There is a proposition which I am asserting, and which is false'. . . . In order to get out [of] the contradiction you have to take that whole assertion of his as one of the propositions to which his assertion applies. . . . Therefore you have to suppose that you have a certain totality, viz., that of propositions, but that *the totality contains members which can only be defined in terms of itself.* Because when you say, 'There is a proposition which I am asserting, and which is false', that is a statement whose meaning can only be got by reference to the totality of propositions. . . . Therefore it presupposes that the totality of propositions is spread out before you and that some one, though you do not say which, is being asserted falsely. It is quite clear that you get a *vicious circle* if you first suppose that this totality of propositions is spread out before you . . . and that yet when you have gone on to say 'Some one out of this totality is being asserted falsely', that assertion is itself one of the totality you were to pick out from. That is exactly what you have in the paradox of the liar.[62]

The solution to this violation of the vicious circle principle was, Russell thought, to break up the range of application of the term 'proposition' into an infinite hierarchy of levels or orders that can be used to state restrictions on the intelligibility of uses of sentences involving the notion of a proposition. According to this idea,

we have got to divide propositions up into sets, and can make statements about all propositions in a given set, but those propositions will not themselves be members of the set. . . . If you try to say 'All propositions are either true or false', without qualification, you are uttering nonsense, because if it were not nonsense it would have to be itself a proposition and one of those included in its own scope. . . . You have to cut propositions up into different types, and you can start with atomic propositions or, if you like, propositions that do not refer to sets of propositions at all. Then you will take next those that refer to sets of propositions of that sort that you had first. Those that refer to sets of propositions of the first type, you may call the second type, and so on. If you apply that to a person who says 'I am lying', you will find that the contradiction has disappeared, because he will have to say what type of liar he is. If he says 'I am asserting a false proposition of the first type', as a matter of fact that statement, since it refers to the totality of propositions of the first type, is of the second type. Hence it is not true that he is asserting a false proposition of the first type, and he remains a liar.[63]

Though one can understand the appeal of Russell's idea, one should not underestimate its drawbacks. The claim that one can make no unrestricted generalizations about propositions—that they are all true or false, that they all predicate something of something, that each is self-identical, and

---

[62] Ibid., pp. 133–34, my emphasis.
[63] Ibid., 134–35.

that every proposition occurs somewhere in Russell's hierarchy—is hard to accept. Even Russell, who gestures at such a hierarchy, has a hard time. What does he mean when he says, "we have got to divide propositions up into sets, and can make statements about all propositions in a set"? He means that we have to divide *all the propositions there are* into sets, and for *absolutely any set of propositions* we can make statements about all its members by asserting *some proposition outside the set*. The problem is not an aberration: one cannot describe the kind of hierarchy he imagines without breaking the restrictions on intelligibility it was constructed to define.

Having come this far, Russell next applies the same line of reasoning to the paradoxes about classes.

> You can lay it down that a totality of any sort cannot be a member of itself. That applies to what we were saying about classes. For instance, the totality of classes in the world cannot be a class in the same sense in which they are. So we shall have to distinguish a hierarchy of classes of particulars: that will be the first type of classes. Then we will go on to classes whose members are classes of the first type: that will be the second type . . . and so on. *Never is it possible for a class of one type either to be or not to be identical with a class of another type.*[64]

The virtues and vices of this proposed solution to the paradox about non-self-membered classes parallel those of Russell's solution of the liar. In each case, paradox is blocked by restrictions on the intelligibility of claims about items in a hierarchy constructed for that purpose. The cost is that too many claims are characterized as meaningless, including some needed to describe the hierarchy itself.

However, at this point we get something new.

> I have been talking, for brevity's sake, as if there really were all these different sorts of things. Of course, that is nonsense. There are particulars, but when one comes to classes, and classes of classes, and classes of classes of classes, one is talking of logical fictions.[65]

Why should that be? Think of the parallel with propositions, thought of as meaningful sentences. Construct a hierarchy starting at level 0 with particulars to serve as subjects of propositions. At level 1 we have propositions all of whose subjects are of level 0. At level 2, we have propositions whose subjects are propositions of level 1, and so on. Sentences that seem to require propositions to appear at more than one level, or that appear to predicate relations holding among propositions at different levels, are labeled meaningless. Whatever one may think of such a construction, nothing in it supports the claim that propositions—i.e., meaningful sentences—are *logical fictions*. On the contrary, there are propositions galore. Why then does Russell speak this way about classes?

[64] Ibid., p. 135, my emphasis.
[65] Ibid., p. 136.

His answer is equivocal.

When I say there are no such things [as classes, classes of classes, etc.], that again is not correct. It is not significant to say 'There are such things', in the same sense of the words 'there are' in which you can say 'There are particulars.' If I say 'There are particulars' and 'There are classes', the two phrases 'there are' will have to have different meanings in those two propositions, and if they have suitable different meanings, both propositions may be true. If, on the other hand, the words 'there are' are used in the same sense in both, then one at least of those statements must be nonsense.[66]

Why should 'there are' be ambiguous in this way? Doesn't it always express the property *being a propositional function that is true of at least one of its arguments?* And aren't the arguments of some propositional functions restricted to particulars, while the arguments of others are restricted to classes, to classes of classes, and so on? If so, shouldn't 'there are' be univocal? Suppose, however, we acquiesce in Russell's denial that it is. For now, let us stipulate that when we use 'there are' to quantify over particulars, it expresses the property *is a propositional function that is true of at least one particular,* and that when we use it to quantify over classes, it expresses the property *is a propositional function that is true of at least one class* (and so on). In itself this does nothing to justify speaking of classes, but not particulars, as "logical fictions," or to lessen our ontological commitment to any of them. Hence, we still have nothing to support Russell's eliminativist point.

He comes closer to the point when, continuing the above passage, he says:

The question then arises, what is the sense in which one can say 'There are classes', or in other words, what do you mean by a statement in which a class appears to come in? First of all, what are the sort of things you would like to say about classes? They are just the same as the sort of things you want to say about propositional functions. You want to say of a propositional function that it is sometimes true. That is the same thing as saying of a class that it has members. All the things you want to say about classes are the same as the things you want to say about propositional functions.[67]

These remarks fit his contextual definition CLASS. Both suggest an ontology of classes is to be replaced by an ontology of propositional functions. In endorsing the suggestion, he notes a certain disanalogy between classes and propositional functions: whereas classes are identical when extensionally equivalent (i.e., when they have the same members), extensionally equivalent propositional functions may differ. Nevertheless, this difference can be accommodated. He says:

any statement about a propositional function which will remain true or remain false . . . when you substitute for it another formally [i.e., extensionally]

[66] Ibid., p. 136.
[67] Ibid., p. 136.

equivalent propositional function, may be regarded as being about the class which is associated with the propositional function. I want you to take the words *may be regarded* strictly. I am using them instead of *is*, because *is* would be untrue. 'Extensional' statements about functions . . . remain true when you substitute any other formally equivalent function, and these are the ones that may be regarded as being about the class. If you have any statement that is about a function which is not extensional, you can always derive from it a somewhat similar statement which is extensional, viz., there is a function formally equivalent to the one in question about which the statement in question is true. The statement, which is manufactured out of the one you started with, will be extensional. It will always be equally true or equally false of any two formally equivalent functions, and this derived extensionally equivalent statement may be regarded as being the corresponding statement about the associated class. So when I say that 'The class of men has so-and-so many members' . . . that will be derived from the statement that 'x is human' is satisfied by so-and-so many values of *x*, and in order to get it into the extensional form, one will put it in this way, that 'There is a function formally equivalent to "*x* is human", which is true for so and so many values of *x*'.[68]

This is Russell's explanation of CLASS in *The Philosophy of Logical Atomism*.

Unfortunately, he stops there. On the face of it, all we have is a translation of talk about classes (arranged in a hierarchy to avoid paradox) into talk about formulas (arranged in a hierarchy). Everything he says here is most straightforwardly read as taking higher-order quantification to be objectual quantification over formulas, despite the fact that such an interpretation carries with it severe shortcomings. Although these defects can be avoided by trading metalinguistic quantification for quantification over functions from objects to truth values, the resulting "reduction" of classes to their characteristic functions is of no metaphysical significance. To make matters worse, neither of these ways of understanding the quantifiers explains or justifies the severe and counterintuitive intelligibility restrictions required by Russell's type hierarchy.

In chapter 10, this fact led me to consider a substitutional interpretation of the higher-order quantifier in CLASS, and of those throughout *Principia Mathematica*. Since the objections raised against taking them to be objectual quantifiers ranging over formulas don't apply to the substitutional interpretation, and since, as we saw, the needed type restrictions fall out of those required independently by higher-order substitutional quantifiers, a case can be made that a substitutional interpretation of higher-order quantification is needed for Russell's discussion of the no-class theory in *The Philosophy of Logical Atomism*. On this interpretation, the quantifiers in class-statements do *not* range over anything, and sentences containing them do *not* make any statements about "functions" of any sort—linguistic or nonlinguistic. Since the truth conditions of such

---

[68] Ibid., pp. 136–37.

sentences are defined solely in terms of those of their instances, they carry no ontological commitments beyond the entities—Russellian particulars—to which one is committed by accepting the instances. Since classes are never among these, a substitutional construal of class-statements is quite naturally and appropriately described as one that treats classes as "logical fictions."

Despite these reasons for reading of Russell's discussion substitutionally, there are compelling reasons against doing so. First, as an exegetical matter, the interpretation can be adopted only if it is admitted that he ran together, and didn't clearly distinguish between, objectual quantification over formulas (presupposed by his ubiquitous talk of quantified statements predicating properties of propositional functions, linguistically construed) and substitutional quantification involving variables the substituends of which are expressions (presupposed by his ambitious talk of eliminating classes). Second, as I argued in chapter 10, the objections to a substitutional interpretation of quantification in *Principia Mathematica* are crippling to both Russell's logicist program and his broader philosophical logic. Finally, there are the disastrous consequences listed in sections 3 and 4 above that would result from adopting a substitutional interpretation of all quantification (including first-order) needed outside of mathematics in *The Philosophy of Logical Atomism*.

Nor is it promising to attempt to avoid those consequences by stipulating that first-order quantification over particulars of all sorts (linguistic and nonlinguistic) is genuinely objectual, whereas higher-order quantification is substitutional. For one thing, a proper account of objectual first-order quantification will itself require either classes, their objective characteristic functions, or nonlinguistic propositional attitudes (and propositions), hence ruining Russell's program of eliminating all such things from his ontology. For another, much of the attraction of the substitutional interpretation is the prospect of explaining the severe type restrictions Russell needs as being *inherent* in the nature of quantification itself. Once objectual quantification is admitted, the question of whether the expressive drawbacks inherent in Russell's restrictions require a different approach to the paradoxes reappears as a question about whether the logicist reduction could better be pursued with higher-order objectual quantification. For all these reasons it is both understandable and just that Russell's ontologically ambitious "no-class theory" soon fell into obscurity and failed to exert substantial influence on the development of the foundations of mathematics that occurred in the 1920s, the 1930s, and beyond.

9. RUSSELL'S UNHOLY TRINITY: ANALYSIS, SCIENCE, AND REVISIONARY METAPHYSICS

Having explained what he took to be the triumph of his elimination of classes, and thereby of numbers, Russell initiates the final lecture in his series with a noteworthy summary of his conception of the role of logico-linguistic analysis in philosophy.

> I come now to the last lecture of this course, and I propose briefly to point out a few of the morals that are to be gathered from what has gone before, in the way of suggesting the bearing of the doctrines that I have been advocating upon various problems of metaphysics. I have dealt hitherto upon what one may call philosophical grammar. . . . I think the importance of philosophical grammar is very much greater than it is generally thought to be. *I think that practically all traditional metaphysics is filled with mistakes due to bad grammar, and that almost all the traditional problems of metaphysics and traditional results—supposed results—of metaphysics are due to a failure to make the kind of distinctions in what we may call philosophical grammar with which we have been concerned.*[69]

For Russell, logical and linguistic analysis had shown itself to be the most powerful weapon in the philosopher's arsenal. Nevertheless, the problems of philosophy were not themselves taken to be linguistic problems, or rather mere pseudo-problems upon which linguistic confusion had bestowed a false legitimacy. On the contrary, for Russell the traditional problems of metaphysics and epistemology raise genuine, though perplexing, questions about reality and our knowledge of it. The dissolution of logico-linguistic confusion was merely his method for answering these questions and thereby arriving at philosophical truth—by which he meant, not anything sublime or ultimately indemonstrable, but truth supported by evidence and reason in the way in which scientific truth is so supported.

Indeed, for him, philosophy is the leading edge of science.

> I believe the only difference between science and philosophy is that science is what you more or less know and philosophy is what you do not know. Philosophy is that part of science which at present people choose to have opinions about, but which they have no knowledge about. Therefore every advance in knowledge robs philosophy of some problems which formerly it had, and if there is any truth, if there is any value in the kind of procedure of mathematical logic, it will follow that a number of problems which had belonged to philosophy will have ceased to belong to philosophy and will belong to science.[70]

It is, for me, impossible not to admire this insightful and uplifting statement about the nature of philosophy—which contrasts so sharply with the conception articulated in the other great work of logical atomism, Wittgenstein's *Tractatus*. Unfortunately, the same cannot be said of the view of reality and our knowledge of it that emerges in Russell's version of logical atomism. The view advanced by Russell is both a classical metaphysical system of the traditional (empiricist) sort, and a theory of the

---

[69] Ibid., p. 141, my emphasis.
[70] Ibid., p. 154.

world almost as far from science and common sense as what one gets in McTaggart (1921,1927).

Russell's final lecture is devoted to sketching this worldview. He begins with his conception of a reality without classes or numbers.

> If you think that 1, 2, 3, and 4, and the rest of the numbers, are in any sense entities, if you think that there are objects, having those names, in the realm of being, you have at once a very considerable apparatus for your metaphysics to deal with. . . . When you say, e.g., that 2 and 2 are 4, you suppose in that case that you are making a proposition of which the number 2 and the number 4 are constituents, and that has all sorts of consequences . . . upon your general metaphysical outlook. If there has been any truth in the doctrines that we have been considering, all numbers are, as it were, fictions at two removes, fictions of fictions. Therefore you do not have, as part of the ultimate constituents of your world, those queer entities that you are inclined to call numbers.[71]

Though such a view is not widely credited today, something not entirely unlike it would soon be adopted (and defended well into the 1950s) by logical positivists such as Rudolf Carnap. According to the coming view, mathematics is true by convention; hence what look like genuine existence claims involving abstract objects are really ontologically innocent (because such statements are guaranteed to be true by their meanings alone).[72] Though this was not Russell's view, his view shared with the view that would follow the attractive feature that, if it were correct, knowledge of arithmetical and other mathematical statements would not require special epistemic access to any domain of entities not required for ordinary empirical knowledge.

Achieving this and related epistemological goals was central to Russell's metaphysical reductionism. In the opening pages of the lecture, he states his aim as that of identifying the smallest set of primitive concepts, incorporated into the smallest number of basic propositions, in terms of which most of what we take ourselves to know in science and everyday life can be explained. Applying this idea to physics, he says:

> You find, if you read the words of physicists, that they reduce matter down to . . . very tiny bits of matter that are still just like matter in the fact that they persist through time, and that they travel through space. . . . Things of that sort, I say, are not the ultimate constituents of matter in any metaphysical sense. . . . *Those things are all of them . . . logical fictions. . . . It is possible that there may be all these things that the physicist talks about in actual reality, but it is impossible that we should have any reason whatsoever for supposing that there are.*[73]

---

[71] Ibid., pp. 141–42.
[72] See in particular Carnap (1956) and Soames (2009e).
[73] Russell (1985), pp. 143–44, my emphasis.

Although this sounds startling out of context—*Nothing moves through time and space?*—it is simply a recapitulation of the view for which Russell argues in chapters 3 and 4 of *Our Knowledge of the External World*, which I explained and criticized in the previous chapter. As I indicated there, he maintains that the only knowledge we use either material-object statements drawn from everyday life or those given in physical science to express is *knowledge of our own private sense data and the private sense data of others.* The task he envisions (but of course only sketches) in that earlier work is that of translating all material-object statements into other statements (logical forms of the originals) in which only agents and their sense data are explicitly mentioned. It is only in this way, he thinks, that one can capture what science really teaches us, along with what we report when we talk about things like tables, chairs, desks, or human bodies. Although he seems to believe that it is *possible* to engage in meaningful speculation about epistemically inaccessible entities beyond our sense data, he also believes that it is *impossible* to provide any empirical justification for such speculative claims.

Applying the same idea to objects encountered in everyday life, he claims that all we really know when we observe changes in something like a desk over time is not anything about an object that really persists through time; rather, what we know is simply that certain momentary appearances have occurred that have been related to each other in certain ways.

> [I]n all cases where you seem to have a continuous entity persisting through changes, what you have to do is to ask yourself what makes you consider the successive appearances as belonging to one thing. . . . What I can know is that there are a certain series of appearances linked together, and the series of those appearances I shall define as being a desk. In that way the desk is reduced to being a logical fiction, because a series is [due to the no-class "result"] a logical fiction. *In that way all the ordinary objects of daily life are extruded from the world of what there is, and in their place as what there is you find a number of passing particulars of the kind that one is immediately conscious of in sense.*[74]

The immediate objects of sensation—images, impressions, and the like—though fleeting, are fully real. These are the particulars of which the universe truly consists.

> Speaking of fleeting sense data, I think it is very important to remove out of one's instincts any disposition to believe that the real is the permanent. There had been a metaphysical prejudice always that if a thing is really real, it has to last either forever or for a fairly decent length of time. That to my mind is an entire mistake. The things that are really real last a very short time. Again I am not denying that there *may* be things that last forever, or for thousands

---

[74] Ibid., pp. 145–46, my emphasis.

of years: I only say that those are not within our experience, and that the real things that we know by experience last for a very short time, one tenth or half a second. . . . Phantoms and hallucinations are among those, among the ultimate constituents of the world. The things that we call real, like tables and chairs are systems, series of classes of particulars, and the particulars are the real things, the particulars being sense data when they happen to be given to you. A table or chair will be a series of classes of particulars, and therefore a logical fiction.[75]

All of this is as it was in *Our Knowledge of the External World*.

The new element in Russell's metaphysics is his treatment of human agents. As pointed out in chapter 11, it was the status of these agents that presented the most egregious problem for the empiricist reduction proposed in his earlier work. Although the logical construction of material objects out of sense data requires claims about the sense data of others, as well as one's own sense data, our knowledge of others and their sense data is more problematic than, and in fact dependent upon, prior knowledge both of their bodies and of their linguistic and nonlinguistic interaction with material objects and with us. Since there is no way to square this circle, I argued that the reduction in *Our Knowledge of the External World* couldn't possibly succeed, and indeed made the explanation of our knowledge of the world harder, not easier, to explain. Whether or not the same objection applies here is a bit less clear, due to the new account of human agents. In *Our Knowledge of the External World* other minds are theoretical posits, the justification of which derives from their (alleged) fruitfulness in allowing us to explain our knowledge of material objects. In *The Philosophy of Logical Atomism,* other minds along with oneself are, incredibly, said to be theoretical fictions—which for Russell means *that there are no such things*!

Russell reaches this result through a series of steps. The first is that what leads us to recognize other people is not their individual egos, or seats of consciousness.

Take a person. What is it that makes you say when you meet your friend Jones, 'Why, this is Jones'? *It is clearly not the persistence of a metaphysical entity inside Jones somewhere*, because even if there be such an entity, it certainly is not what you see . . . it certainly is something that you are not acquainted with. . . . Therefore plainly there is something in the empirical appearances which he presents to you, something in their relations one to another, which enables you to collect all these together and say, *'These are what I call the appearances of one person'*, and that something . . . *is not the persistence of a metaphysical subject. . . . Therefore Jones is not constituted as he is known by a sort of pin-point ego that is underlying his appearances*.[76]

[75] Ibid., p. 147.
[76] Ibid., 148–49, my emphasis.

Russell's reasoning here is quite remarkable. How do we recognize one of our friends? Not, of course, by perceiving a metaphysical ego living inside the human body we see. Rather, we discern who it is by recognizing features of that body and its actions that we have observed before. But, since this truism presupposes that we are in epistemic contact with other bodies, both animate and inanimate, it is *not* grist for Russell's mill. On the contrary, it illustrates my critical point that our knowledge of others depends on knowledge of other human bodies and their activities.

Since Russell can't admit this, he has to frame the discussion in another way. He says that we recognize our friend Jones "by the appearances *he* presents" to us. But this still presupposes a human being who causes my visual and other experiences. What Russell must mean is that I come to have certain sense data private to me, similar to those I have had on other occasions, and which we may call "Jones-data." For Russell, it is their similarity that makes them what he calls "appearances of one and the same person." Since it is this similarity in past and present sense data of mine—and not the presence of a metaphysical ego called 'Jones'—that leads me to say I am in the presence of someone I know, Russell concludes that Jones is *not*, insofar as he is known to me, *constituted* by any metaphysical self, or seat of consciousness.

Having given this argument, Russell must now answer the question, "*What then does constitute Jones?*" But he can't. Since the argument against Jones as metaphysical ego can be reproduced with equal force to "show" that Jones isn't constituted by anything other than similarities holding among certain of my private sense data, Russell can't both embrace the argument and answer the question. Surely Jones isn't constituted by *my* private data—i.e., by all the sense data in *my experience* that bear the *are-both-appearances-of-the-same-person relation* to one another. That would exclude the private sense data of others from contributing to the constitution of Jones; worse, it would exclude *Jones's own sense data* from contributing to the constitution of Jones himself. Clearly, Russell needs to start again without, in so doing, presupposing Jones or any other agents as particular entities.

His attempt to do so comes in the following continuation of the above passage.

[Y]ou have got to find some correlations among the appearances which are of the sort that make you put all those appearances together and say, they are the appearances of one person. *Those are different when it is other people and when it is yourself.* When it is yourself you . . . have not only what you look like, you have also your thoughts and memories and all your organic sensations. . . . *So you can collect a whole set of experiences into one string as all belonging to you*, and similarly other people's experiences can be collected together as all belonging to them *by relations that are actually observable and without assuming the existence of the persistent ego* . . . the mere fact that you can know that two experiences belong to the same person proves that there is such an empirical relation. . . . *Let us call the relation R. . . . [W]hen two experiences have to each other the relation R, then they are said to be experiences of the same person. . . . The person who has a given experience x will be the class of all those experiences which are 'experiences of the same person' as the one who experiences x. . . .* [T]wo events are co-personal when there is between them a certain relation *R,* namely that which makes us say that they are experiences of the same person. *You can define the person who has a certain experience as being those experiences that are co-personal with the experience. . . . Therefore we shall say that a person is a certain series of experiences.*[77]

With this passage, the confusing dialectic of Russell's discussion is to some extent clarified. Having earlier dismissed a certain metaphysical ego as constituting Jones by observing that it is not any such thing that allows *me* to recognize him as the same man I have seen on different occasions, Russell seemed to invite the suggestion that what constitutes Jones is a relation of similarity—dubbed "being appearances of one person"—that holds between some of *my* past perceptions and some of *my* present ones. However, that can't be right, because no experiences *of mine* could possibly constitute Jones. Now Russell can be read as indicating that Jones is constituted very much as I am. Each of us is a series of experiences that bear a similarity relation dubbed *"being experiences of the same person."* Of course series are *logical fictions* for Russell, so no persons *really* exist. The only particulars that really exist are the experiences. Some—call them "M-experiences"—are "mine," and others—call them "J-experiences"—are "Jones's." All M experiences bear the relation *being experiences-of-one-person* to one another, and to nothing else, while all J-experiences bear the relation *being experiences-of-one-person* to one another, and to nothing else. So, when I say that *I exist,* all I am really saying is that these M-experiences exist. The same goes for Jones: when he says that *he exists,* all he is saying is that certain J-experiences do.

That is the view. The first thing to notice is that if, as Russell says, momentary experiences are the only particulars, then either *no particulars—i.e., no experiences—themselves perceive or experience anything,* or some experiences themselves perceive or experience things. Since the latter seems to make no sense—the event that is one's seeing yellow doesn't itself see anything—it is not surprising that Russell never suggests it. So perhaps we are to suppose that no particular ever perceives or experiences anything. One way of putting this is to say that perceiving and experiencing are *logical fictions.* Although some unanalyzed sentences that *appear* to attribute such cognitive activities to agents are *true,* what these sentences really express is *not* about agents, or about anything perceiving or experiencing anything. Rather, the claims made by these sentences

[77] Ibid., 149–50, my emphasis.

are solely about the properties of, and relations holding among, real particulars—which are "unexperienced experiences" and "unperceived perceptions."

That, at least, is how one might put it, if one follows Russell in describing particulars as "experiences." Probably one shouldn't. Verbs like 'perceive' and 'experience' take two arguments, and so express two-place relations between *a perceiver or experiencer* and *that which is perceived or experienced.* Therefore, one with Russell's concern for proper philosophical grammar shouldn't use nominal forms of these verbs to describe his metaphysical particulars. How they are to be described is certainly harder to say, and may well be impossible. In addition to being momentary, his particulars are in a certain sense private—which must mean that the crucial relation R previously described as "*being experiences-of-one-person*" is an equivalence relation, which divides all past, present, and future momentary particulars in the universe into separate, non-intersecting equivalence classes (corresponding to different "agents"). Of course, even that isn't right, since Russell insists that classes are *fictions.* Still, it provides a rough idea of what he seems to be getting at.

This, I believe, is roughly the picture that lies behind Russell's inconclusive discussion of neutral monism in the last few pages of *The Philosophy of Logical Atomism.* The basic idea is that all particulars are momentary (ultimately unperceived) sense data arranged into two different systems of classes—those that constitute "agents," and those that constitute the things—like tables, chairs, human bodies, etc.—that we pre-theoretically (but ultimately misleadingly) describe agents as "perceiving."[78] The system is said to be *monistic* because the ultimate constituents of reality are all of a single type; they are all said to be "sense data"—as if, with the loss of ultimate perceivers, we understood what that meant. It is called "neutral" because the logical fictions known as "agents" and those known as "physical objects" are in the end mere constructions of the same "sense data." Though very much attracted to this system, Russell here expresses doubts that he does not attempt to resolve. Nevertheless, it is as good a picture as any of where he ends up in this work.

What can one say by way of evaluation of his system? The first point to note is how thoroughly revisionary it is of the pre-philosophical conception of ourselves and the world of natural science and ordinary life. More revisionary, I should think, than Berkeley's, Russell's revisionism may surpass McTaggart's dreamlike conception of Reality as an eternal, unchanging community of human souls. If one had been under the misconception that the new tradition in analytic philosophy had left such

---

[78] Since the discussion is brief, Russell does not explore whether "there are unperceived physical objects"—i.e., whether there are systems of particulars bearing the relevant "physical-object" similarity relations to one another that are *not* among the particulars that constitute any agent.

extravagant metaphysical speculation behind, studying *The Philosophy of Logical Atomism* should convince one otherwise.

Being so revisionary, Russell's system is threatened by a problem endemic to such systems. Highly revisionary systems tend to destroy the arguments and observations that motivated them. Russell's was motivated by the desire to explain and justify our knowledge of mathematics and the external world. In chapter 10, I raised critical questions about the success of his logicist reduction in accomplishing this task for our mathematical knowledge. In chapter 11, I raised similar critical questions about the attempted reduction of our knowledge of material objects to knowledge of our own sense data, and that of others. Those objections seem to carry over with a vengeance to *The Philosophy of Logical Atomism*, which attempts to build upon *Principia Mathematica* and *Our Knowledge of the External World*.

However, because the new system is so radical, this critical assessment must be qualified. According to Russell's articulation of the system, the ultimate constituents of reality seem to include no words or sentences, no material objects, no cognitive agents, no thoughts, no events in which one perceives or experiences things, and nothing that moves through space or lasts for more than a moment of time. Instead, the ultimate constituents of reality appear to be discrete, isolated clusters of momentary instantiations of yellowness, hardness, loudness, and the like, where the elements of each cluster bear an unexplainable primitive relation to other items in the cluster, but never bear this relation to those of other clusters. To the extent that we can understand what the new system allows us to say about ourselves, our beliefs, our perceptions, our evidence, and our knowledge, the objections raised against Russell's earlier, partial characterizations of the system seem to carry over. But it is hard to be sure, since he never provides clear instructions for how we are to translate the ordinary thought and talk used to motivate and argue for his final system into the purified language he imagines being used to express it.

This leaves us in a quandary. In order to state the problems his system was designed to solve, we must take it for granted that we speak truly when we say, as he did, that we perceive this or that item, with these or those properties, that such data is, as he earlier indicated, private to ourselves, that our evidence for the truth of material-object statements, as well as for statements about other people and the contents of their perceptions, consists entirely of that which is given to us in our own perception, and so on. But once we have arrived at his ultimate view, it is hard to see what to make of these claims that constituted his starting point, let alone to take them for granted or to use them to explain what was to be explained. We don't know what to make of them because we haven't been told how to express them in fully analyzed statements about Russell's newly identified ultimate particulars. We don't even know that the reasoning that led him to this final view can be stated, let alone accepted, by one who adopts it.

LOOKING AHEAD

The main contributions of Frege, Moore, Russell, and others during the early years of the analytic tradition were (i) the invention of modern symbolic logic, (ii) the use of it in building the foundations of mathematics, (iii) the application of ideas drawn from the early development of logic (including its informal semantics) to natural language, (iv) the attempt to develop logico-linguistic analysis into an all-purpose tool for solving broad philosophical problems, (v) the replacement of Idealism by a new approach based on "analysis" as the center of philosophical attention, (vi) the elevation of science and common sense and the de-emphasis of religion as touchstones for philosophers , and (vii) the autonomy of ethics wrought by Moore's dubious, but highly influential, analysis of 'good'. Although these were large and important changes, they had not yet brought about a substantial change in philosophers' conception of the fundamental aims of their discipline. As I pointed out in the Preface, Frege, Moore, and Russell continued to adhere to more or less traditional understandings of the aims of philosophy. However, by the end of the second decade of the twentieth century, they had brought analytic philosophy to the brink of a fundamental change, which occurred with the publication in English of Wittgenstein's *Tractatus Logico-Philosophicus* in 1922. It was this work, more than any other, that ushered in the era that viewed philosophical problems as linguistic problems to be solved by linguistic means.

For this reason, volume 2 of *The Analytic Tradition in Philosophy* will begin with chapters on the metaphysics of the *Tractatus*, the theories of meaning, truth, logic and the modalities (both metaphysical and epistemic) that it contains, and, most importantly, the Tractarian test of intelligibility and its consequences for philosophy. This will be followed by chapters on the development, led by Rudolf Carnap and other members of the Vienna Circle, of a new logicized version of traditional scientific positivism. To this I will add discussions of the revolutionary advances in logic made by Gödel, Tarski, and Church, as well as the birth of semantics as a well-defined field of study in the work of Tarski and Carnap. Further chapters will discuss the then central philosophical notions of analyticity, necessity, and apriority, as well as the rise and fall of the empiricist criterion of meaning. Emotivism and its critics, plus the related battles between metaethics and normative ethics, will round out the picture.

Looking one step beyond to volume 3, I plan to discuss the struggle for modal logic involving, among others, C. I. Lewis, Ruth Barcan Marcus, Rudolf Carnap, and the young Saul Kripke. I will then take up Quine's extensive critiques of necessity, quantified modal logic, analyticity, and related "dogmas" of empiricism. Special attention will be paid to his attempt to save verificationism by making it holistic, which plays an important, but often neglected, role in properly understanding the epic Quine-Carnap debate over analyticity and ontology in the 1950s. The volume will close with extensive critical discussions of Quine's theses of indeterminacy of translation and ontological relativity, as well as his radical semantic eliminativism.

Later volumes will deal with the second half of the twentieth century.

REFERENCES

Allard, James. 2003. "Idealism in Britain and the United States." In Baldwin 2003, 43–59.

Angelelli, I., ed. 1967. *Begriffsschrift und andere Aufsätze*. Hildesheim: Olm.

Ayer, A. J., ed. 1959. *Logical Positivism*. New York and London: The Free Press.

———. 1971. *Moore and Russell, The Analytical Heritage*. Cambridge, MA: Harvard University Press.

Baldwin, J. Mark, ed. 1902. *Dictionary of Philosophy and Psychology,* vol. 2. London: Macmillan.

Baldwin, Thomas. 1990. *G. E. Moore*. London: Routledge.

———. 2003. *The Cambridge History of Philosophy 1870–1945*. Cambridge: Cambridge University Press.

Barwise, Jon, and John Perry. 1983. *Situations and Attitudes*. Cambridge, MA: MIT Press.

Beaney, Michael. 1996. *Making Sense*. London: Duckworth.

Benacerraf, Paul. 1965. "What Numbers Could Not Be." *Philosophical Review.* 74: 47–73.

Benacerraf, Paul, and Hilary Putnam. 1983. *The Philosophy of Mathematics*, 2nd ed. Cambridge: Cambridge University Press.

Black, Max. 1964. *A Companion to Wittgenstein's Tractatus*. Cambridge: Cambridge University Press.

Bradley, F. H. 1893. *Appearance and Reality*. London: Swan Sonnenschein; New York: Macmillan.

Boer, Stephen, and William Lycan. 1986. *Knowing Who*. Cambridge, MA: MIT Press.

Boolos, George. 1994. "The Advantages of Honest Toil over Theft." In Alexander George, ed., *Mathematics and Mind,* Oxford: Oxford University Press, 27–44; reprinted in Boolos 1998, 261–74.

———. 1998. *Logic, Logic, Logic*. Cambridge, MA: Harvard University Press.

Bowman, Brian. 2012. *Linguistic Understanding and Semantic Theory,* unpublished dissertation, University of Southern Calfornia.

Burgess, John. 2005. *Fixing Frege*. Princeton, NJ: Princeton University Press.

Byrne, Alex. 2001. "Intentionalism Defended." *Philosophical Review* 110: 199–240.

Byrne, Alex, and Judith Thomson, eds. 2006. *Content and Modality*. Oxford: Oxford University Press.

Carnap, Rudolf. 1928. *Der logische Aufbau der Welt,* Leipzig: Felix Meiner Verlag; English translation by Rolf A. George: *The Logical Structure of the World; Pseudo-problems in Philosophy*, Berkeley: University of California Press, 1967.

———. 1956. "Empiricism, Semantics, and Ontology." In *Meaning and Necessity*. 2nd ed., Chicago and London: University of Chicago Press; originally published in *Revue Internationale de Philosophie* 4: 20–40.

Cartwright, Richard 1987a. "A Neglected Theory of Truth." In Cartwright, *Philosophical Essays*, Cambridge, MA: MIT Press, 71–93.

——. 1987b. "On the Origins of Russell's Theory of Descriptions." In Cartwright, *Philosophical Essays*, Cambridge, MA: MIT Press, 95–133.

Chwistek, Leon. 1924. "The Theory of Constructive Types, Part I." *Annales de la Societé Polonaise de Mathematique , vol. 2 (for 1923), 9–48.*

——, 1925. *"The Theory of Constructive Types, Part II." Annales de la Societé Polonaise de Mathematique . vol. 3 (for 1924), 92–141.*

Coffa, J. Alberto. 1991. *The Semantic Tradition from Kant to Carnap.* Cambridge: Cambridge University Press.

Currie, Gregory. 1982. *Frege.* Brighton: Harvester Press.

Davies, Martin. 2000. "Externalism and Armchair Knowledge." In Paul Boghossian, and Christopher Peacocke, eds., *New Essays on the A Priori*, Oxford: Oxford University Press, 384–414.

Dejnozka, Jan. 1981. "Frege on Identity." *International Studies in Philosophy* 13: 31–41.

——. 1996. *The Ontology of the Analytic Tradition in Philosophy and Its Origins: Realism and Identity in Frege, Russell, Wittgenstein, and Quine* Lanham, MD: Littlefield Adams.

Devitt, Michael. 1981. "Devitt's Distinction." In Peter French, Theodore Uehling, Jr., and Howard Wettstein, eds., *Midwest Studies in Philosophy VI*, Minneapolis: University of Minnesota Press, 511–24.

Donnellan, Keith. 1966. "Reference and Definite Descriptions." *Philosophical Review* 75: 281–304.

——. 1978. "Speaker Reference, Descriptions, and Anaphora." In Peter Cole, ed., *Syntax and Semantics, vol. 9: Pragmatics*, New York: Academic Press, 47–68; reprinted in French, Uehling, and Wettstein 1979.

Duhem, Pierre. 1906. *La Théorie physique: son objet et sa structure.* Paris: Gauthier-Villars.

Dummett, Michael, ed. 1973. *Frege's Philosophy of Language.* London: Duckworth.

Etchemendy, John. 1990. *The Concept of Logical Consequence.* Cambridge, MA: Harvard University Press.

Fara, Delia Graff. 2001. "Descriptions as Predicates." *Philosophical Studies* 102: 1–42.

Fine, Kit. 2007. *Semantic Relationism.* Oxford: Blackwell.

Finlay, Stephen. Forthcoming. *Confusion of Tongues.*

Fraenkel, Abraham. 1922. "The Notion 'Definite' and the Independence of the Axiom of Choice," trans. by Beverly Woodward. In Van Heijenoort 1967, 284–89.

Frege, Gottlob. 1874. *Rechnungsmethoden, die sich auf eine Erweiterung des Grossenbegriffes grunden* [Methods of Calculation, based on an extension of the Concept of Magnitude]. In Angelelli 1967, 50–84.

——. 1879. *Begriffsschrift*, trans. by S. Bauer-Mengelberg, in Van Heijenoort 1967, 1–82; selections trans. by Michael Beaney in Frege 1997, 47–78.

——. 1880–81. "Booles rechnende Logik und die Begriffsschrift," trans. by Peter Long and Roger White as "Boole's Logical Calculus and Concept-Script." In Frege 1979, 9–46.

——. 1882. "Booles logische Formelsprache und meine Begriffsschrift," trans. by Peter Long and Roger White as "Boole's Logical Formula-language and my Concept-script." In Frege 1979, 47–52.

——. 1884. *Die Grundlagen der Arithmetik*, Breslau: Verlag von Wilhelm Koebner 1884. Translated in Frege 1950; selections trans. by Michael Beaney in Frege 1997, 84–129.

———. 1885. "Über formale Theorien der Arithmetik," *Jenaische Zeitschrift für Natur-wissenschaft*, 19, 94–104; trans. as "On Formal Theories of Arithmetic." In Kluge 1971, 141–53.

———. 1879–91. "Logik," trans. by Peter Long and Roger White as "Logic." In Frege 1979, 1–8.

———. 1891a. "Function und Begriff." Address given to the *Jenaische Gesellschaft für Medicin und Naturwissenschaft*, January 9, 1891, Jena; trans. as "Function and Concept" by Peter Geach, in Geach and Black 1970, 21–41, also in Frege 1997, 131–48.

———. 1891b. "Letter to Husserl," trans. by Hans Kaal, in Frege 1997, 149–50.

———. 1892a. "On Concept and Object," first published in the *Vierteljahrsschrift für wissenschaftliche Philosophie* 16: 192–205; trans. by Peter Geach, in Geach and Black 1970, 42–55, also in Frege 1997, 181–93.

———. 1892b. "Über Sinn and Bedeutung," *Zeitschrift für Philosophie und philoso-phische Kritik*, C, 1892; trans. as "On Sense and Reference," by Max Black, in Geach and Black 1970, 56–78, also in Frege 1997, 151–80.

———. 1892c. "Letter to Russell," trans. by Hans Kaal, in Frege 1997, 254.

———. 1892d. "Ausfuhrung über Sinn und Bedeutung," trans. by Peter Long and Roger White as "Comments on Sense and Reference." In Frege 1979, 118–25, also in Frege 1997, 172–80.

———. 1893, 1903. *Grundgesetze der Arithmetik*, vol. 1 1893, vol. 2 1903, Jena; trans. as *The Basic Laws of Arithmetic*, by M. Furth, ed., Berkeley and Los Angeles: University of California Press, 1964; selections trans. Michael Beaney in Frege 1997, 194–223, 258–89.

———. 1896. "Über die Begriffsschrift des Herrn Peano und meine eigene." *Bericht über die Verhandlungen der Königlich Sachsischen Gesellschaft der Wissenschaften zu Leipzig Mathematisch-Physische Klasse* 48: 361–78. Translated as Frege 1969.

———. 1897. "Logik," trans. by Peter Long and Roger White as "Logic." In Frege 1979, 126–51.

———. 1899–1906. "Über euklidische Geometrie," trans. by Peter Long and Roger White as "On Euclidean Geometry." In Frege 1979, 167–69.

———. 1906. "17 Kernsatze zur Logik," trans. by Peter Long and Roger White as "17 Key Sentences on Logic." In Frege 1979, 174–75.

———. 1914. "Logik in der Mathematik," trans. by Peter Long and Roger White as "Logic in Mathematics." In Frege 1979, 203–50.

———. 1918a. "Der Gedanke," *Beitrage zur Philosophie des deutschen Idealismus* 1 (1918): 58–77; translated as "The Thought" by A. and M. Quinton, in *Mind* 65 (1956): 289–311; as "Thought" by Peter Geach and R. H. Stoothoff in Geach 1977, 1–30; also in Frege 1997, 325–45.

———. 1918b. "Die Verneinung," *Beitrage zur Philosophie des deutschen Idealismus*, 1, 1918, 143–57; "Negation," trans. by Peter Geach, in Geach 1977, 31–53, also in Frege 1997, 346–61.

———. 1919. "Notes for Ludwig Darmstaedter," reprinted in Frege 1997).

———. 1923. "Gedankengehfuge." *Beitrage zur Philosophie des deutschen Idealismus* 3: 36–51; trans. as "Compound Thoughts" by Peter Geach in Geach 1977, 55–77.

———. 1950. *The Foundations of Arithmetic,* trans. by J. L. Austin. Oxford: Blackwell. Translation of Frege 1884.

———. 1964. *The Basic Laws of Arithmetic*, trans. from *Grundgesetze der Arithmetik* by M. Furth. Berkeley and Los Angeles: University of California Press.

———. 1969. "On Herr Peano's Begriffsschrift and My Own." *Australasian Journal of Philosophy* 47: 1–14. Translation of Frege 1896.

———. 1979. *Posthumous Writings,* trans. Peter Long and Roger White, ed. Hans Hermes, Friedrich Kambartel, and Friedrich Kaulbach. Chicago: University of Chicago Press.

———. 1997. *The Frege Reader.* Ed. and trans. Michael Beaney. Oxford: Blackwell.

French, Peter, Theodore Uehling, Jr., and Howard Wettstein, eds. 1979. *Contemporary Perspectives in the Philosophy of Language.* Minneapolis: University of Minnesota Press.

Fuhrmann, André. 2002. "Russell's Way Out of the Paradox of Propositions," *History and Philosophy of Logic* 23: 197–213.

Geach, Peter. 1956. "Good and Evil," *Analysis,* 17, 32–42; reprinted in *Theories of Ethics,* Philippa Foot, ed. (Oxford: Oxford University Press), 1967.

———. 1977. *Logical Investigations.* Oxford: Blackwell.

Geach, Peter, and Black, Max, eds. 1970. *Translations from the Philosophical Writings of Gottlob Frege.* Oxford: Blackwell.

Gödel, Kurt. 1930. "Die Vollstandigkeit der Axiome des logischen Funktionenkalkuls." *Monatshefte für Mathematik und Physik* 37: 349–60; trans. as "The Completeness of the Axioms of the Functional Calculus of Logic," by S. Bauer-Mengelberg, in Van Heijenoort 1967, 582–91.

———. 1931. "Über formal unentscheidbare Satze der Principia mathematica und verwandter Systeme I." *Monatshefte für Mathematik und Physik* 38: 173–98; trans. as "On Formally Undecidable Propositions of 'Principia Mathematica' and Related Systems I," by Jean Van Heijenoort, in Van Heijenoort 1967, 596–616.

———. 1944. "Russell's Mathematical Logic." In Schilpp 1944, 125–53.

Gomez-Torrente, Mario. 1999. "Logical Truth and Tarskian Logical Truth." *Synthèse* 117: 375–403.

Griffin, Nicholas. 1985. "Russell's Multiple Relation Theory of Judgment." *Philosophical Studies* 47: 213–47.

———. 1985/86. "Wittgenstein's Criticism of Russell's Theory of Judgment." *Russell* 5: 132–45.

———. 1991. "Was Russell Shot or Did He Fall?" *Dialogue* 30: 549–53.

———. 2003a. *The Cambridge Companion to Bertrand Russell,* Cambridge: Cambridge University Press.

———. 2003b. "Russell's Philosophical Background." In Griffin 2003a, 84–107.

———. 2005. "Review of *Philosophical Analysis in the Twentieth Century.*" *Philosophy in Review* 25: 140–43.

Hanks, Peter. 2007. "How Wittgenstein Defeated Russell's Multiple Relation Theory of Judgment." *Synthèse* 154: 121–46.

Hempel, Carl. 1945. "On the Nature of Mathematical Truth." *American Mathematical Monthly* 52: 543–56; reprinted in Benacerraf and Putnam 1983.

Hilbert D., and Ackermann, W. 1928. *Grundzuge der theoretischen Logik,* 1st ed. Vol. 27 in *Die Grundlehren der Mathematischen Wissenschaften in Einzeldarstellungen,* Berlin: Springer-Verlag.

Hodes, Harold. 1990. "Where do Natural Numbers Come From?" *Synthèse* 84: 347–407.

———. 2012. "Why Ramify?" Unpublished manuscript.

Hylton, Peter. 1984. "The Nature of Propositions and the Revolt Against Idealism." In R. Rorty, J. B. Schneewind, and Q. Skinner, eds., *Philosophy in History,* Cambridge: Cambridge University Press, 375–97.

———. 1990. *Russell, Idealism, and the Emergence of Analytic Philosophy.* Oxford: Oxford University Press.

James, William. 1907. *Pragmatism*. New York: Longmans, Green, and Co.; reprinted in 1965, Cleveland and New York: The World Publishing Co.

———. 1909. *The Meaning of Truth*. New York: Longmans, Green, and Co.; reprinted in 1975, Cambridge, MA: Harvard University Press.

Joachim, Harold H. 1906. *The Nature of Truth*. Oxford: Oxford University Press.

Kamareddine, Fairouz, Twan Laan, and Rob Nederpelt. 2002. "Types in Logic and Mathematics before 1940." *Bulletin of Symbolic Logic* 8: 185–245.

Kant, Immanuel. 1781, 1787. *Critique of Pure Reason*, trans. by Norman Kemp Smith. London: Macmillan, 1929.

Kaplan, David. 1968–69. "Quantifying In." *Synthèse* 19: 178–214.

———. 1978. "Dthat." In Peter Cole, ed., *Syntax and Semantics, vol. 9: Pragmatics*, New York: Academic Press, 221–43.

———. 1989. "Demonstratives." In Joseph Almog, John Perry, and Howard Wettstein, eds., *Themes from Kaplan*, New York: Oxford University Press, 481–563.

King, Jeffrey, Scott Soames, and Jeffrey Speaks. 2014. *New Thinking about Propositions*. Oxford: Oxford University Press.

Klement, Kevin. 2004. "Putting Form before Function: Logical Grammar in Frege, Russell, and Wittgenstein." *Philosophers' Imprint* <*www.philosophersimprint.org /004002/*> 4, 2: August 2.

———. 2010. "The Functions of Russell's No Class Theory." *Review of Symbolic Logic* 3: 633–64.

Kluge, E.H.W. 1971. *On the Foundations of Geometry and Formal Theories of Arithmetic*. New Haven, CT: Yale University Press.

Kneale, William and Martha Kneale. 1962. *The Development of Logic*. Oxford: Clarendon Press.

Kremer, Michael. 2008. "Soames on Russell's Logic: A Reply." *Philosophical Studies* 39: 209–12.

Kripke, Saul. 1972. "Naming and Necessity." In Donald Davidson and Gilbert Harman, eds., *Semantics of Natural Languages*, Dordrecht: Reidel, 253–355. Reissued as *Naming and Necessity*, Cambridge, MA: Harvard University Press, 1980.

———. 1976. "Does Substitutional Quantification Rest on a Mistake?" In G. Evans and J. McDowell, *Truth and Meaning*, Oxford: Oxford University Press, 325–419.

———. 1977. "Speaker Reference and Semantic Reference." In *Midwest Studies in Philosophy, II: Studies in the Philosophy of Language*, 255–76; reprinted in French, Uehling, and Wettstein 1979, 6–27.

———. 1979. "A Puzzle about Belief." In Avishi Margalit, ed., *Meaning and Use*, Dordrecht: Reidel, 239–83.

———. 2005. "Russell's Notion of Scope." *Mind* 114: 1005–37.

———. 2008. "Frege's Theory of Sense and Reference." *Theoria* 74: 181–218.

Landini, Gregory. 1991. "A New Interpretation of Russell's Multiple-Relation Theory of Judgment." *History and Philosophy of Logic* 21: 37–69.

———. 1998. *Russell's Hidden Substitutional Theory*. Oxford: Oxford University Press.

Lewis, David. 1979. "Attitudes *De Dicto* and *De Se*." *Philosophical Review* 88: 513–43.

———. 1989. "Dispositional Theories of Value." *Proceedings of the Aristotelian Society* supplementary vol. 63: 113–37.

Linnebo, Øystein. 2003. "Plural Quantification Exposed." *Noûs* **37**: 71–92.

———. 2010. "Plural Quantification." In *Stanford Encyclopedia of Philosophy*, Winter 2010 ed., Edward N. Zalta, ed., URL = <http://plato.stanford.edu/archives /win2010/entries/plural-quant/>.

Linsky, Bernard. 2002–3. "The Substitutional Paradox in Russell's 1907 Letter to Hawtry." *Russell: The Journal of Russell Studies,* The Bertrand Russell Research Center, McMaster University, n.s. 22: 151–60.

Littlewood, J. E. 1986. *Littlewood's Miscellany*. Cambridge: Cambridge University Press.

MacColl, Hugh. 1905. "Symbolic Reasoning." *Mind* 14: 74–81.

McTaggart, J.M.E. 1901. *Studies in Hegalian Cosmology*, Cambridge, Cambridge University Press.

———. 1921. *The Nature of Existence,* vol. 1. Cambridge: Cambridge University Press.

———. 1927. *The Nature of Existence,* vol. 2. Cambridge: Cambridge University Press.

Merricks, Trenton. 2007. *Truth and Ontology*. Oxford: Clarendon Press.

Mill, John Stuart. 1843. *A System of Logic*; reprinted London: Longmans, 1961.

Moore, G. E. 1898. "Freedom." *Mind* 7: 179–204.

———. 1899. "The Nature of Judgement." *Mind* 8: 176–93.

———. 1901–2. "Mr. McTaggart's Studies in Hegelian Cosmology." *Proceedings of the Aristotelian Society* 2: 177–212.

———. 1902a. "Truth and Falsity." In Baldwin 1902, 716–18.

———. 1902b. "Change." In Baldwin 1902, 171–73.

———. 1902c. "Relative and Absolute." In Baldwin 1902, 443–46.

———. 1903a. "The Refutation of Idealism." *Mind* 12: 433–53; reprinted in Moore 1922a, 1–30.

———. 1903b. *Principia Ethica*. Cambridge: Cambridge University Press.

———. 1903–4. "Kant's Idealism." *Proceedings of the Aristotelian Society* 4: 177–214.

———. 1907–8. "Professor James' 'Pragmatism.'<~?~thinspace>" *Proceedings of the Aristotelian Society* 8: 33–77; reprinted in Moore 1922a, 97–146.

———. 1909. "Hume's Philosophy." *New Quarterly*: November 1909; reprinted in Moore 1922a, 147–67.

———. 1912. *Ethics*. London, Oxford, New York: Oxford University Press.

———. 1917–18. "The Conception of Reality." *Proceedings of the Aristotelian Society*; reprinted in Moore 1922a, 197–219.

———. 1919–20. "External and Internal Relations." *Proceedings of the Aristotelian Society*, reprinted in Moore 1922a, 276–309.

———. 1922a. *Philosophical Studies*. London: Routledge and Kegan Paul; reprinted 1968, Totowa, NJ: Littlefield and Adams.

———. 1922b. "The Conception of Intrinsic Value." In Moore 1922a, 253–75.

———. 1925. "A Defense of Common Sense." In J. H. Muirhead, ed., *Contemporary British Philosophy*, 2nd Series, New York: Macmillan; reprinted in Moore 1958, 32–59.

———. 1939. "Proof of an External World." *Proceedings of the British Academy*, vol. 25; reprinted in Moore 1958.

———. 1942. "Autobiography." In Schilpp 1942, 3–39.

———. 1953. *Some Main Problems of Philosophy*. London: George Allen and Unwin.

———. 1958. *Philosophical Papers*. London: George Allen and Unwin; reprinted in 1962, New York: Collier Books, 1962.

———. 1993. *Principia Ethica*, revised ed., with previously unpublished preface for planned 2nd ed., edited with an introduction by Thomas Baldwin. Cambridge: Cambridge University Press.

Morris, Thomas V. 1984. *Understanding Identity Statements*. Aberdeen: Aberdeen University Press.

Neale, Stephen. 1990. *Descriptions*. Cambridge, MA: MIT Press.

Nozick, Robert. 1974. *Anarchy, State, and Utopia*. New York: Basic Books.

Partee, Barbara. 1972. "Opacity, Coreference and Pronouns." In Donald Davidson and Gilbert Harman, eds., *Semantics of Natural Language*. Dordrecht: Reidel, 415–41.

Peano, Giuseppe. 1889. *Arithmetices principia, novo methodo exposita* (The Principles of Arithmetic, Presented by a New Method). Torino: Bocco; reprinted in Van Heijenoort 1967, 83–97.

Pears, David. 1977. "The Relation between Wittgenstein's Picture Theory of Propositions and Russell's Theories of Judgment." *Philosophical Review* 86: 177–96.

———. 1978. "Wittgenstein's Picture Theory and Russell's *Theory of Knowledge*. In H. Berghel, A. Hubner, and E. Kohler, eds., *Wittgenstein, The Vienna Circle, and Critical Rationalism: The Proceedings of the 3rd International Wittgenstein Symposium*, Vienna: Holder-Pichler-Tempsky, 101–7.

———. 1989. "Russell's 1913 *Theory of Knowledge* Manuscript." In C. S. Savage and C. A. Anderson, eds., *Rereading Russell: Essays on Bertrand Russell's Metaphysics and Epistemology*, Minnesota Studies in Philosophy of Science, 12, Minneapolis: University of Minnesota Press, 169–82.

Perry, John. 1977. "Frege on Demonstratives." *Philosophical Review* 86: 474–97.

———. 1979. "The Essential Indexical." *Noûs* 13: 3–21.

———. 2006. "Stalnaker and Indexical Belief." In Byrne and Thomson 2006, 204–21.

Pigden, Charles. 1990. "Geach on 'Good'<~?~THINSPACE>" *Philosophical Quarterly* 40: 129–54.

———. 2007a. "Russell's Moral Philosophy." In *Stanford Online Encyclopedia of Philosophy*, http://plato.stanford.edu/entries/russell-moral/,

———. 2007b. "Desiring to Desire: Russell, Lewis and G.E. Moore." In Susana Nuccatelli and Gary Seay, eds., *Themes from G. E. Moore: New Essays in Epistemology and Ethics*, Oxford: Oxford University Press, 244–69.

Pincock, Christopher. 2005–6. "Review of S. Soames, *Philosophical Analysis in the Twentieth Century.*" *Russell* 25: 167–71.

———. 2008. "Russell's Last (and Best) Multiple-Relation Theory of Judgment." *Mind* 117: 107–39.

Potter, Michael. 2009. *Wittgenstein's Notes on Logic*. Oxford: Oxford University Press.

Pryor, James. 2000. "The Skeptic and the Dogmatist." *Noûs* 34: 517–49.

———. 2004. "What's Wrong with Moore's Argument?" *Philosophical Issues* 14: 349–77.

Putnam, Hilary. 1970. "Is Semantics Possible?" *Metaphilosophy* 1: 187–201.

———. 1973. "Explanation and Reference." In G. Pearce and P. Maynard, eds., *Conceptual Change*, Dordrecht: Reidel, 199–221.

———. 1975. "The Meaning of 'Meaning.'" In K. Gunderson, ed., *Language, Mind, and Knowledge*, Minnesota Studies in the Philosophy of Science, vol. 7, Minneapolis: University of Minnesota Press, 131–93.

Quine, W.V.O. 1951. "Two Dogmas of Empiricism." *Philosophical Review* 60: 20–43; reprinted in *From a Logical Point of View*, 2nd ed., Cambridge, MA: Harvard University Press, 1980.

———. 1955. "On Frege's Way Out." *Mind* 64: 145–59.

———. 1986. *Philosophy of Logic*, 2nd ed. Cambridge, MA: Harvard University Press.

Ramsey, F. P. 1925. "The Foundations of Mathematics." *Proceedings of the London Mathematical Society* 25: 338–84; reprinted in R. B. Braithwaith, ed., *The Foundations of Mathematics*, London: Paul, Trench, Tubner, 1931.

Rayo, Augustine. 2002. "Frege's Unofficial Arithmetic." *Journal of Symbolic Logic* 67: 1623–38.

———. 2007. "Plurals." *Philosophical Compass* 2: 411–27.

Rawls, John. 1971. *A Theory of Justice*. Cambridge, MA: Harvard University Press.

Reiber, Stephen. 1992. "Understanding Synonyms without Knowing That They are Synonymous." *Analysis* 52: 224–28.

Resnik, Michael. 1980. *Frege and the Philosophy of Mathematics*. Ithaca, NY, and London: Cornell University Press.

Richard, Mark. 1993. "Articulated Terms." *Philosophical Perspectives* 7: 207–30.

Rosen, Gideon. 1994. "What Is Constructive Empiricism?" *Philosophical Studies* 74: 143–78.

Ross, W. D. 1930. *The Right and the Good*. Oxford: Clarendon Press.

Russell, Bertrand. 1893. "On the Foundations of Ethics"; originally published in Russell 1983, 206–11; reprinted in Russell 1999, 31–36.

———. 1894. "Cleopatra or Maggie Tulliver?"; originally published in Russell 1983, 90–98; reprinted in Russell 1999, 57–67.

———. 1896. *German Social Democracy*. London: Longmans, Green & Co.

———. 1897a. *An Essay on the Foundations of Geometry*. Cambridge: Cambridge University Press.

———. 1897b. "Is Ethics a Branch of Empirical Psychology?" In Russell 1983, 99–104, and Russell 1999, 71–78.

———. 1897c. "Seems Madam? Nay, It Is." Originally published in Russell 1957, 94–103; reprinted in Russell 1983, 105–11, and Russell 1999, 79–86.

———. 1900. *A Critical Exposition of the Philosophy of Leibniz*. Cambridge: Cambridge University Press.

———. 1902. "Letter to Frege," trans. by Hans Kaal. In Frege 1997, 153.

———. 1903a. *Principles of Mathematics*. New York: Norton.

———. 1903b. "On the Meaning and Denotation of Phrases"; first published in Russell 1994, 283–96.

———. 1903c. "Points about Denoting"; first published in Russell 1994, 305–13.

———. 1903d. "On Meaning and Denotation"; first published in Russell 1994, 314–58.

———. 1904a. "Meinong's Theory of Complexes and Assumptions." *Mind* 13: 204–19, 336–34, 509–24; reprinted in Russell 1973, 21–76.

———. 1904b. "Review of *Principia Ethica.*" *Independent Review* 2: 328–33; reprinted as "The Meaning of Good" in Russell 1994, 571–75, and in Russell 1999, 95–104.

———. 1905a. "The Existential Import of Propositions." *Mind* 14: 398–401; reprinted in Russell 1973, 98–102 .

———. 1905b. "Review of Meinong et al., *Untersuchungen zur Gegenstandstheorie und Psychologie.*" *Mind* 14: 503–8; reprinted in Russell 1994, 595–606.

———. 1905c. "On Fundamentals"; first published in Russell 1994, 359–413.

———. 1905d. "On Denoting." *Mind* 14: 479–93.

———. 1906. "On Insolubilia and Their Solution by Symbolic Logic"; originally published as "Les Paradoxes de la Logique," *Revue de Metaphysicque et de Morale* 14: 627–50; English version published in Bertrand Russell 1973, 190–214.

———. 1906–7. "On the Nature of Truth." *Proceedings of the Aristotelian Society*, New Series, 7: 28–49.

———. 1907. "The Regressive Method of Discovering the Premises of Mathematics." Published posthumously in Russell 1973, 272–83.

——. 1908a. "Mathematical Logic as Based on the Theory of Types." *American Journal of Mathematics* 30: 222–62; reprinted in Van Heijenoort 1967, 150–82, and in Russell 1971, 59–102.

——. 1908b). "Transatlantic 'Truth,'" *Albany Review* 2: 393–410; reprinted as "William James's Conception of Truth." In Russell 1910c, 112–30.

——. 1909. "Pragmatism." *Edinburgh Review* 109: 363–88; reprinted in Russell 1910c, 79–111.

——. 1910a. "The Monistic Theory of Truth," published in Russell 1910c, 131–46; originally appeared as the first two sections of Russell 1906–7.

——. 1910b. "On the Nature of Truth and Falsehood." In Russell 1910c, 147–59.

——. 1910c. *Philosophical Essays*. London: Allen and Unwin.

——. 1910d. "The Theory of Logical Types." *Revue de Métaphysique et de la Morale* 18: 263–301; English translation by Russell reprinted in Russell 1973, 215–52.

——. 1910–11. "Knowledge by Acquaintance and Knowledge by Description." *Proceedings of the Aristotelian Society* 11: 108–28.

——. 1912. *The Problems of Philosophy*. London: Williams and Norgate; New York: Henry Holt and Company; repr. New York and Oxford: Oxford University Press, 1997.

——. 1913. *Theory of Knowledge*. Originally published as Russell 1984.

——. 1914. *Our Knowledge of the External World*. Chicago and London: Open Court. Revised as Russell 1926.

——. 1918–19. "The Philosophy of Logical Atomism." *Monist* 5, 28: 495–527; *Monist* 5, 29: 32–63, 190–222, 345–80; reprinted Russell 1985.

——. 1919a. *Introduction to Mathematical Philosophy*. London: George Allen and Unwin; reprinted New York: Dover Publications, 1993.

——. 1919b. "On Propositions: What They Are and How They Mean." *Proceedings of the Aristotelian Society,* supplementary volume 2: 1–43.

——. 1924. "Logical Atomism." In *Contemporary British Philosophy*, First Series, London: George Allen & Unwin, and New York: Macmillan Co.; reprinted in Russell 1985, 157–81.

——. 1926. *Our Knowledge of the External World*, 2nd, rev. ed. London: Allen and Unwin.

——. 1940. *An Inquiry into Meaning and Truth*. London: Allen and Unwin.

——. 1944. "My Mental Development." In Schilpp 1944, 3–20.

——. 1957. Edwards, ed., *Why I Am Not a Christian*. Allen and Unwin.

——. 1959. *My Philosophical Development*. London: Routledge.

——. 1961. *Fact and Fiction*. London: Allen and Unwin; reprinted with a new introduction by Slater, 1994, London: Routledge.

——. 1962. Letter to Professor van Heijenoort. In van Heijenoort 1967, 127.

——. 1971. Robert C. Marsh, ed., *Logic and Knowledge*. New York: Macmillan.

——. 1973. *Essays in Analysis*, ed. Douglas Lackey. New York: George Braziller.

——. 1983. *The Collected Papers of Bertrand Russell, Vol. 1, Cambridge Essays 1888–1889*, ed. K. Blackwell, A. Brink, N. Griffin, R. Rempel, and J. Slater. London: Allen and Unwin.

——. 1984. *The Collected Papers of Bertrand Russell,* vol. 7, ed. K. Blackwell and E. Eames. London: George Allen and Unwin.

——. 1985. *The Philosophy of Logical Atomism*. Peru, IL: Open Court Publishing, with an introduction by David Pears.

———. 1989. "*Russell's Theory of Knowledge* Manuscript." In C. W. Savage and C. A. Anderson, eds., Minnesota Studies in the Philosophy of Science, 12, Minneapolis: University of Minnesota Press, 169–82.

———. 1994. *The Collected Papers of Bertrand Russell, Vol. 4, Foundations of Logic*, ed. Alasdair Urquhart and Albert C. Lewis. London: Routledge.

———. 1999. *Russell on Ethics*, ed. Charles Pigden. London and New York: Routledge.

———. 2002. *The Selected Letters of Bertrand Russell: The Private Years, 1884–1914*, ed. N. Griffin. London: Routledge.

Russell, Bertrand, and Alfred North Whitehead. 1910. *Principia Mathematica*, vol. 1. Cambridge: Cambridge University Press.

———. 1912. *Principia Mathematica*, vol. 2. Cambridge: Cambridge University Press.

———. 1913. *Principia Mathematica*, vol. 3. Cambridge: Cambridge University Press.

Ryle, Gilbert. 1970. "G. E. Moore's 'The Nature of Judgment.'" In Alice Ambrose and Morris Lazerowitz, eds., *G. E. Moore: Essays in Retrospect*. London: George Allen and Unwin, 90–98.

Sainsbury, Mark. 1979. *Russell*. London: Routledge.

———. 2006. "Review of Scott Soames, *Philosophical Analysis in the Twentieth Century, Vol. 1*." *Philosophical Studies* 129: 637–43.

Salmon, Nathan. 1981. *Reference and Essence*. Princeton, NJ: Princeton University Press.

———. 1982. "Assertion and Incomplete Descriptions" *Philosophical Studies* 42: 37–45.

———. 1986. *Frege's Puzzle*. Cambridge, MA: MIT Press.

———. 1987. "Existence." In James Tomberlin, ed., *Philosophical Perspectives* 1: 49–108.

———. 1989. "How to Become a Millian Heir." *Noûs* 23: 211–20.

———. 1990. "A Millian Heir Rejects the Wages of *Sinn*." In C. A. Anderson and J. Owens, eds., *Propositional Attitudes: The Role of Content in Logic, Language, and Mind*, Stanford, CA: CSLI, 215–47.

———. 1998. "Nonexistence." *Noûs* 32: 277–319.

———. 2002. "Demonstrating and Necessity." *Philosophical Review* 111: 497–537.

———. 2005. "On Designating." *Mind* 114: 1069–1133.

Salmon, Nathan, and Scott Soames. 1988. *Propositions and Attitudes*. Oxford: Oxford University Press.

Scanlon, Thomas. 1998. *What We Owe to Each Other*. Cambridge, MA: Harvard University Press.

Schilpp, P. A., ed. 1942. *The Philosophy of G. E. Moore*. Evanston, IL: Northwestern.

———, ed. 1944. *The Philosophy of Bertrand Russell*. Library of the Living Philosophers. La Salle, IL: Open Court.

Shultz, Bart. 2004. *Henry Sidgwick: The Eye of the Universe*. Cambridge: Cambridge University Press.

Sidgwick, Henry. 1874. *Methods of Ethics*. London: Macmillan.

———. 1907. *Methods of Ethics*. 7th ed. London: Macmillan.

Soames, Scott. 1979. "A Projection Problem for Speaker Presuppositions." *Linguistic Inquiry* 10: 623–66; reprinted in Soames 2009a.

———. 1982. "How Presuppositions Are Inherited: A Solution to the Projection Problem." *Linguistic Inquiry* 12: 483–545.

———. 1986a. "Incomplete Definite Descriptions." *Notre Dame Journal of Formal Logic* 27: 349–375.

———. 1986b. "Substitutivity." In J. J. Thomson, ed., *On Being and Saying: Essays for Richard L. Cartwright*, Cambridge, MA: MIT Press, 99–132.

———. 1987. "Direct Reference, Propositional Attitudes, and Semantic Content." *Philosophical Topics* 14: 47–87; reprinted in Soames 2009b.

———. 1988. Review of Stephen E. Boer and William G. Lycan, *Knowing Who*. *Journal of Symbolic Logic* 53: 657–59.

———. 1989a. "Presupposition." In D. Gabbay and F. Guenthner, eds., *Handbook of Philosophical Logic*, vol. 4: *Topics in the Philosophy of Language*, Dordrecht: Reidel, 553–616; reprinted in Soames 2009a.

———. 1989b. "Semantics and Semantic Competence." In James Tomberlin, ed., *Philosophy of Mind and Action Theory*, Philosophical Perspectives 3, Atascadero, CA: Ridgeview, 575–96; reprinted in Soames 2009a.

———. 1994. "Donnellan's Referential/Attributive Distinction." *Philosophical Studies* 73: 149–68; reprinted in Soames 2009a.

———. 1999. *Understanding Truth*. New York: Oxford University Press.

———. 2002. *Beyond Rigidity*. New York: Oxford University Press.

———. 2003a. "Understanding Deflationism." In John Hawthorne and Dean Zimmerman, eds., *Philosophical Perspectives* 17: 369–83; reprinted in Soames 2009b.

———. 2003b. "Higher-Order Vagueness for Partially Defined Predicates." In J. C. Beall, ed., *Liars and Heaps: New Essays on Paradox*. Oxford: Oxford University Press, 128–50; reprinted in Soames 2009b.

———. 2003c. *Philosophical Analysis in the Twentieth Century*, vol. 1. Princeton and Oxford: Princeton University Press.

———. 2003d. *Philosophical Analysis in the Twentieth Century*, vol. 2. Princeton and Oxford: Princeton University Press.

———. 2005a. "Naming and Asserting." In Zoltan Szabo, ed., *Semantics vs. Pragmatics*. New York: Oxford University Press, 356–82; reprinted in Soames 2009b.

———. 2005b. "Why Incomplete Descriptions Do Not Defeat Russell's Theory of Descriptions." *Teorema* 24: 7–30; reprinted in Soames 2009a.

———. 2005c. *Reference and Description*. Princeton and Oxford: Princeton University Press.

———. 2005d. "Reply to Pincock." *Russell* 25: 9–14.

———. 2006a. "What Is History For?" *Philosophical Studies* 129: 645–65.

———. 2006b. "The Philosophical Significance of the Kripkean Necessary Aposteriori." *Philosophical Issues* 16: 288–309; reprinted in Soames 2009b.

———. 2007a. "What Are Natural Kinds?" *Philosophical Topics* 35: 329–42.

———. 2007b. "Actually." In Mark Kalderon, ed., *Proceedings of the Aristotelian Society*, supplementary volume 81: 251–77, reprinted in Soames 2009a.

———. 2008a. "Truthmakers?" *Philosophical Books* 49: 317–27.

———. 2008b. "No Class: Russell on Contextual Definition and the Elimination of Sets." *Philosophical Studies* 39: 213–18.

———. 2009a. *Philosophical Essays*, vol. 1. Princeton, NJ: Princeton University Press.

———. 2009b. *Philosophical Essays*, vol. 2. Princeton, NJ: Princeton University Press.

———. 2009c. "The Possibility of Partial Definition." In Soames 2009b, 362–81; Also published in *Cuts and Clouds*, R. Dietz and S. Moruzzi, eds., Oxford: Oxford University Press, 46–62.

——. 2009d. "The Gap between Meaning and Assertion: Why What We Literally Say Often Differs from What Our Words Literally Mean." In Soames 2009a, 278–97.

——. 2009e. "Ontology, Analyticity, and Meaning: The Quine-Carnap Dispute." In David Chalmers, David Manley, and Ryan Wasserman, eds., *Metametaphysics*, New York: Oxford University Press, 424–443.

——. 2010a. *Philosophy of Language,* Princeton, NJ: Princeton University Press.

——. 2010b. *What Is Meaning?* Princeton, NJ: Princeton University Press.

——. 2010c. "True At." *Analysis* 71: 124–33.

——. 2012a. "Propositions." In Delia Fara Graff and Gillian Russell, eds., *Companion to the Philosophy of Language*, New York: Routledge, 201–20.

——. 2012b. "Two Versions of Millianism." In Michael O'Rourke, *Reference and Referring: Philosophical Topics*, vol. 10, Cambridge, MA: MIT Press, 83–118; reprinted in Soames 2014b.

——. 2014a. "A Puzzle about the Frege/Russell Analysis of Quantification, in Soames 2014b.

——. 2014b. *Analytic Philosophy in America and Other Historical and Contemporary Essays,* Princeton, NJ: Princeton University Press.

——. 2014c. "Why the Possible-World's Conception of Propositions Can't Be Correct," "Propositions as Cognitive Event Types," "Critique of Two Views: Propositions as Properties and Propositions as Facts," and "Clarifying and Improving the Cognitive Theory to Meet its Explanatory Burden," chapters 3, 6, 9, and 12 of King, Soames, and Speaks 2014.

——. Forthcoming. *Rethinking Language, Mind, and Meaning.* Princeton, NJ: Princeton University Press.

Somerville, Stephen. 1980. "Wittgenstein to Russell (July 1913). 'I Am Very Sorry to Hear . . . My Objection Paralyses You.'<~?~thinspace>" In R. Haller and W. Grassl, eds., *Language, Logic, and Philosophy: Proceedings of the 4ᵗʰ International Wittgenstein Symposium,* Vienna: Holder-Pichler-Tempsky, 182–88.

Speaks, Jeff. 2014. "Representational Entities and Representational Acts." Chapter 8 of King, Soames, and Speaks 2014.

Stalnaker, Robert. 1972. "Pragmatics." In Donald Davidson and Gilbert Harman, eds., *Semantics of Natural Language*, Dordrecht: Reidel, 380–97.

——. 2006. "Responses." In Byrne and Thomson 2006, 285–89 (response to Perry).

——. 2008. *Our Knowledge of the Internal World.* Oxford: Oxford University Press.

Stanley, Jason. 2000. "Context and Logical Form." *Linguistics and Philosophy* 23: 391–434.

——. 2002. "Making It Articulated." *Mind and Language* 17: 149–68.

Stanley, Jason, and Szabo, Zoltan Gendler. 2000. "Quantifier Domain Restriction." *Mind and Language* 15: 219–61.

Stevens, Graham. 2003. "Re-examining Russell's Paralysis: Ramified Type-Theory and Wittgenstein's Objection to Russell's Theory of Judgment." *Russell* 23: 5–26.

——. 2005. *The Russellian Origins of Analytical Philosophy: Bertrand Russell and the Unity of the Proposition.* New York: Routledge.

Stevenson, Charles. 1937. "The Emotive Meaning of Ethical Terms." *Mind 46: 14–31; reprinted in Ayer 1959.*

Stove, David. 1991. *The Plato Cult and Other Philosophical Follies.* Oxford: Blackwell.

Strawson, Peter. 1950. "On Referring." *Mind* 59: 320–44.

Stroll, Avrum. 1967. "Identity." In Paul Edwards, ed., *Encyclopedia of Philosophy,* vol. 4, 123–124.

Tarski, Alfred. 1935. "Der Wahrheitsbegriff in den formalisierten Sprachen." *Studia Philosophica* 1: 261–405; trans. as "The Concept of Truth in Formalized Languages" in Woodger 1956, 152–278.

Thau, Michael, and Caplan, Ben. 2000. "What's Puzzling Gottlob Frege?" *Canadian Journal of Philosophy* 31: 159–200.

Thomson, Judith Jarvis. 1992. "On Some Ways in Which a Thing Can Be Good." *Social Philosophy and Policy* 9: 96–117.

———. 2003. "The Legacy of *Principia*." *Southwestern Journal of Philosophy* 41: 62–82.

———. 2008. *Normativity*. Chicago and La Salle, IL: Open Court.

Van Fraassen, Bas. 1980. *The Scientific Image*. Oxford: Clarendon Press.

Van Heijenoort, Jean, ed. 1967. *From Frege to Gödel*. Cambridge, MA: Harvard University Press.

Weiss, B. 1995. "On the Demise of Russell's Multiple Relation Theory of Judgment." *Theoria* 61: 262–82.

Wettstein, Howard. 1981. "Demonstrative Reference and Definite Descriptions." *Philosophical Studies* 40: 241–57.

Williamson, Timothy. 2008. *The Philosophy of Philosophy*. Malden MA and Oxford: Wiley-Blackwell.

Wittgenstein, Ludwig. 1914–16. *Notebooks. 1914–1916*, ed. G. H. Von Wright and G.E.M. Anscombe, trans. by G.E.M. Anscombe. New York: Harper, originally published 1961; this volume contains the Harry T. Costello version of Wittgenstein's "Notes on Logic," *Journal of Philosophy* 54 (1957): 230–44.

———. 1922. *Tractatus Logico-Philosophicus*, trans. by C. K. Ogden. London: Routledge and Kegan Paul; reprinted in 1999 by Dover Publications.

———. 1961. *Tractatus Logico-Philosophicus*, trans. by D. Pears and B. McGuinness. London: Routledge, 1961.

———. 1995. *Ludwig Wittgenstein: Cambridge Letters*, B. McGuinness and G. H. von Wright, eds. New York: Harper.

Wright, Crispin. 1985. "Facts and Certainty." *Proceedings of the British Academy* 71: 429–72.

———. 2000. "Cogency and Question-Begging: Some Reflections on McKinsey's Paradox and Putnam's Proof." *Philosophical Issues* 10: 140–63.

———. 2002. "(Anti-) Sceptics Simple and Subtle: Moore and McDowell." *Philosophy and Phenomenological Research* 65: 330–48.

———. 2003. "Some Reflections on the Acquisition of Warrant by Inference." In Susana Nuccetelli, ed., *New Essays on Semantic Externalism and Self-Knowledge*, Cambridge, MA: MIT Press, 57–77.

———. 2004. "Warrant for Nothing (and Foundations for Free)." *Aristotelian Society Supplement* 78: 167–212.

Yourgrau, Palle. 1982. "Frege, Perry, and Demonstratives." *Canadian Journal of Philosophy* 12: 725–52.

———. 1986–87. "The Path Back to Frege." *Proceedings of the Aristotelian Society* 87: 169–210.

Zermelo, Ernst. 1904. "Proof That Every Set Can Be Well Ordered," trans. by S. Bauer-Mengelberg. In Van Heijenoort 1967, 139–41.

———. 1908a. "A New Proof of the Possibility of a Well-Ordering," trans. by S. Bauer-Mengelberg. In Van Heijenoort 1967, 183–98.

———. 1908b. "Investigations of the Foundations of Set Theory I," trans. by S. Bauer-Mengelberg. In Van Heijenoort 1967, 199–215.

INDEX

∽−◯−⌒

Absolute Idealism, 133, 149–53, 264, 266–69, 420
Absolute Spirit, 267
Ackermann, W., 524
acquaintance: and denoting, 410; in Frege's logic, 96–100, 107–11, 368–69; knowledge about vs., 329; knowledge by, 330–31, 363, 379, 578; with objects, 322, 378; with propositions, 453; Russell's notion of, 303, 362–63, 399, 410, 577–78
addition, defined, 57–58, 479, 511
afterimages, 213, 228–29, 238
agents' cognitive operations, and propositions, 309–10, 313–15, 365–66, 451–52, 462–63, 465, 471–72
ambiguity, 210–11, 372–73, 375, 402, 418–19
analytic implication, 186
analyticity, 87, 177–78, 184–93
analytic obviousness, 188–90, 196–98, 244
analytic philosophy: founders of, 134; Frege and, 4, 260; Moore and, 206, 259–60; not an integrated philosophical system, 431–32
analytic truths, 13, 22n14, 41–42, 87, 118–19, 156–60, 177–78
anaphora, 100
ancestral of a relation, 52–53
Anglo-Hegelians, 421
a posteriori truths, 41–42, 162, 586
Apostles Society, 200–201, 267–68
appearance: Idealist conception of, 266–67; perception of, 167, 169, 212–14, 238, 542, 546, 549, 555, 557, 624–27; reality in relation to, 135–36, 149, 151, 153, 209–11, 214, 227–28, 267, 268
Appearance Principle, 238
a priori truths, 13, 32, 35 41–44, 87–88, 115–20, 149, 156, 158, 177–78, 185–88, 190, 192, 196, 244–45, 424, 474, 490, 494, 496–99, 517, 527, 528, 562, 571, 578, 586, 616
Aristotle, 20
arithmetic: as analytic, 13, 42, 499–500; axioms of, 24–28, 53–56, 478–79, 510–11;

definitions in, 22, 34, 37, 38, 42, 45–48, 50–53, 57, 58, 115–19, 479, 483–85, 487, 492, 496–500, 509–11, 521–23; derived from logic, 4, 13, 27–30, 53–59, 114–20, 128, 273–78, 473–80, 482–88, 500–11 (see also logicism); and empiricism, 33–40; formal theories of, 27–29; geometry compared to, 41–45; justification of, 115–20, 494–95, 499; Mill on, 33–38; operations of, 56–58, 479–80, 511
ascriptions. See attitude ascriptions; self-ascription
assertion, 69, 71, 75–76, 78–79, 83, 106, 109–10, 113, 115, 309–15, 399, 402, 404–9, 432, 434, 437, 449–50, 526–27, 570, 577
atomic facts, 490, 516, 582, 585, 590
atomic propositions, 290, 582–83, 594, 617
atomic sentences, 14, 23, 339, 348, 516, 520, 570, 574, 576, 577, 579–80, 582–84, 587, 588, 590–92
atomism, 554. See also logical atomism
attitude ascriptions, 18–20, 96–106, 109–10, 112–13, 137–38, 142–43, 281–82, 368–69, 373–78, 390, 399, 438–47, 449–50, 460
attitudes, complex propositions and, 452–56
author of *Waverly* examples, 324, 359–60, 374–78, 396n, 398–99, 612–13
"average child," 544
axiom of extensionality, 481, 507
axiom of infinity, 481–82, 487–93, 495–96, 507–8, 520, 528–29
axiom of internal relations, 415–20
Axiom of Reducibility, 512, 523–24, 531
axioms, defined, 477
axiom schema of comprehension, 121–22, 480–81, 486, 495, 503–4, 506, 522
axiom schemas, 27
Axiom V, 54–56, 58–59, 123–26, 272
Axiom V', 125–28
Ayer, A. J., 144

Baldwin, James Mark, *Dictionary of Philosophy and Psychology*, 150

barren tautology argument, 203–4
Barry's paradox, 534
Beaney, Michael, 13
being: existence and, 280–81, 382–84; Frege's third realm of, 98, 369; Russell on, 280–82, 284–88, 303–7, 382–89, 395–98. *See also* ontology, Russell's
being always true, 68, 331–34, 394–95
beliefs: elevated credence and provisional acceptance vs., 426; process of forming and maintaining, 423–25; Russell's conception of, 440–50; truth/falsity and, 438; utility not a factor in, 427–28
Benacerraf, Paul, 497n
Bentham, Jeremy, 173
Berkeley, George, 152, 209, 628
Boole, George, 23
Boolos, George, 488n, 494
Bradley, F. H., 133, 137–47, 150, 264, 267–68, 414, 416, 420, 421
brain in a vat example, 235–36, 239–40
Burgess, John, 58, 59, 126, 503n, 507n33, 513n37
Byrne, Alex, 165–66

Cantor, George, 28–29, 121, 269–70
Cantor's Theorem, 121, 269–70, 474, 489
Carnap, Rudolf, 4, 32, 130, 500, 511, 567, 623, 631, 632
Cartwright, Richard, 143–44, 289n, 290n, 318n, 322n82
Church, Alonzo, 631
Chwistek, Leon, 524
classes: comprehension for, 54, 112–22, 126, 271–74, 480–81, 486, 495, 503–4, 506, 522; extensionality of, 54, 276, 481, 507; hierarchy of, 129, 475, 492, 618; as logical fictions, 489–90, 492, 511–31, 533–34, 614, 618–19, 621 (*see also* no-class theory); one-to-one correspondence of, 49–51, 55, 121, 269, 473–74, 488n, 505; propositional functions and, 278–79, 476, 512–14. *See also* extensions of concepts
class-theoretic paradoxes, 120–23, 270–72, 474–75, 481, 488–93, 495, 504, 506, 514, 519, 523, 530, 533, 534, 615–18
cognitive operations. *See* agents' cognitive operations, and propositions
cognitive value, 87–89, 91
coherence theory of truth, 415
common sense: characteristics of, 208, 221–23; as epistemological ground, 220–25; and existence, 208; Idealism vs., 163; Moore's philosophy and, 134, 163,

207–25; and perception, 209–15; philosophy in conflict with, 149, 155, 171, 207–9, 219–25; and worldly knowledge, 219–21, 225–37
compactness, of logical system, 24n
completeness: of a formal theory, 29; of a logical system, 24
complex singular terms, 350–60, 461–64
comprehension, axiom schema of, 121–29, 481, 503–4
comprehension for classes. *See* classes, comprehension for
concept comprehension, 53, 271
concept extensionality, 54
concepts: as constituents of propositions, 138–40, 284, 287; definability of, 175–76; denoting concepts, 288–303; existence and, 60–64, 140–41, 598–604; extensions of, 49–50, 54, 123, 125; in Frege's philosophy, 7–10, 17, 70–77, 271–78; hierarchy of levels, 25–26, 129, 274–76, 474–75; horse as instance of, 71, 175–76; Moore on, 138–40, 147–49; numbers and, 45–46, 49–50, 272–76; and objects, 70–76; as part of mind-independent reality, 8, 138, 147; in Russell's philosophy, 287–303
concept script, 4, 21n, 27
conjunctive propositions, 453–54
consciousness, 152, 161–71, 281–82
consequentialism, 173–74, 252–57
consistency of a logical system, 22–23
constructivism, 533
Context Principle, 46–47
contingency, 149, 417–19, 585–87
continuum hypothesis, 505
contradiction, in Idealist beliefs, 158–61
correspondence theories of truth, 84–85, 137, 139, 141–42, 145, 434, 438, 588, 596
counterfactuals, in Russell's analysis of perceptual knowledge, 548–50, 558
Currie, Gregory, 33, 47, 88

Davidson, Donald, 20
Davies, Martin, 232
decision procedures, 23
Dedekind, Richard, 54, 114, 478
Dedekind infinity, 488n
deduction, knowledge and, 561–62
definite description operator, 10, 22, 356–57, 455, 462, 477
definite descriptions: in Frege's philosophy of language, 12, 88–89, 95–96; in higher-order logic, 508; incomplete, 401, 403–4, 407–9; as incomplete symbols, 345, 354,

357, 370, 391, 512, 614, 615; names as, 319–20, 386, 395–96; Russell's critique of definite descriptions as singular terms, 350–70, 460–64; Russell's critique of Frege on, 346–50; in Russell's logic, 482, 529; in Russell's 1903 theory, 301–5, 308–9, 323. *See also* singular definite descriptions

definition: analytic/synthetic distinction and, 177–79; of arithmetical primitives, 116–19, 496, 500; of concepts, 175–76; of "good," 174–94, 199, 201, 203–4, 243–44, 252; inductive definitions, 57; Moore on, 174–75; recursive definitions, 57; in a theory, 477

democracy, 430

denoting, theory of. *See* theory of denoting

denoting concepts, 288–303, 307, 322–27, 514

denoting phrases, 329, 331–36, 346, 350–55, 390–95, 410

Descartes, René, 226–27,

descriptions: attributive and referential uses of, 402–3; knowledge by, 330–31, 363, 379, 578, 613. *See also* theory of descriptions

descriptivism about names, 398–400

desire, and goodness, 181–84, 193, 197, 201–2, 204

Dewey, John, 421, 423–24, 428

direct predication, 463

Direct Realism, 238

direct reference theories, 183

disjunctive propositions, 453–54

Donnellan, Keith, 402–5, 407–8

double images, 213–14, 228–29, 238, 542, 543

dream images, 541, 543

Duality of Practical Reason, 265–67

Dummett, Michael, 126

duty, 172–73, 196, 247, 249, 253–57, 265–67

eliminativism, 531, 533–34, 632

emotivism, 205, 243, 249, 259, 631

empiricism, mathematics and, 33–38

enlightened self-interest, 265–67

entailment, 184, 185–94, 244, 561

entity occurrences, 324

entity positions, 325

epistemology: common sense as ground for, 220–25; Frege and, 29–32, 98–99, 115, 129, 369–70; logic and, 29–32, 115, 129; Moore and, 206–41; Moore's moral, 242–48, 257–59; Russell and, 361–64,

389–90, 410–11, 535–67, 569, 571, 623–25; and skepticism, 226–28, 235–37. *See also* knowledge

equinumerousness, 49–50

error theory, 205

esse is *percipi* (to be is to be perceived), 155–71, 229

ethics: Absolute Idealism and, 266–68; critique of Idealist, 153; evidence in, 173–94, 174n, 199; generalizations in, 199–200; justification in, 198–200, 245–46; kinds of questions in, 172; kinds of statements in, 173; mathematics compared to, 197–98; Moore and, 134, 172–205, 242–60; objectivity in, 257–59; Russell and, 200–205, 254n14, 265–68; science of, 243; self-evidence in, 194–200, 245–46; subjectivism and, 257–59. *See also* goodness

Euclidean geometry, 21n, 41–45, 44n48, 114, 128

event types, existence of, 456–59, 607

evolution, 430

excluded middle, law of, 370–73

existence: being and, 139, 280–81, 284–87, 303–7, 382–89; commonsense view of, 208–11; as a concept, 60–62, 140–41, 147–48, 598–604; of event types, 456–59; of fictional characters, 306–7; Frege on, 60–64; as a predicate, 61, 63–64; Russell on, 280–81, 284–87, 303–7, 382–89, 395–400, 598–604, 608–14; of sense data, 208–11, truth not dependent on, 458–59. *See also* *esse* is *percipi* (to be is to be perceived)

existential quantification, 25–26, 60–64, 395–97

experience, critique of Idealist conception of, 161–71

extended analyticity, 189–93

extended entailment, 189–93

extensional equivalence of propositional functions, 277, 513; and classes, 278, 619–20; and Russell's reduction 513, 616

extensionality for classes, 54, 619

extensions of concepts, 49, 50, 52, 54, 55, 56, 58, 59n, 115, 121, 123, 125, 269, 271–76, 473, 475, 491. *See also* classes

external world, knowledge of, 215–21, 225–37, 535–67, 623–27

facts: atomic, 490, 516, 582, 585, 587, 590, 592–97, 605; general, 516–17, 595–97; molecular, 588, 597; in multiple relation theory, 438–44, 446–47, 450, 465, 471–72; negative, 588–92, 596; not logical subjects,

facts (*continued*)
576, 582; and pragmatist theory of truth/
belief, 424; Russell and, 573–77; sentences
and, 573–74; true propositions and, 142–
47, 435–36, 438–44
the False, 8, 16, 18, 56, 77–82, 126
false beliefs, 438–43
fictional/legendary characters, 306–7,
319–21, 386, 398
first-order predicate calculus, 24–27
first-order quantification, 26–27, 502, 520,
525–28, 533–34
first-order set-theoretic system, 478–82, 500
formalism, and mathematics, 40–41
Fraenkel, Abraham, 495
freedom, 135–37
Frege, Gottlob, 138, 141; *Basic Laws of Arithmetic*, 4, 31, 32, 38–39, 42, 53, 58, 124n;
Begriffsschrift (*Concept Script*), 4, 20, 21n,
23, 30–31, 52–53, 69, 70, 86, 92–93, 122;
birth and education of, 3; and Cantor's
Theorem, 269–71; "Comments on Sense
and Reference," 16n5, 17n8; "Concept and
Object," 61, 68, 70–77, 272; on concepts,
7–10, 25–26, 271–78; contributions of, 4,
130; epistemology of, 29–32, 33, 37, 41,
98–99, 115, 129, 369–70; on existence,
60–64; *The Foundations of Arithmetic*, 4, 31,
33–53, 61, 114–15, 212, 269, 500; "Function and Concept," 4; hierarchy: of concepts, 25–26, 129, 271, 272n14, 274–76; of
senses and referents, 19–20, 96–100, 368–
70; and indexicality, 106–14; influence of,
3–4, 129–30, 260; and Kant, 41–45; logic,
20–33, 115; and logicism, 53–59, 120–29,
273–76, 473–75; "Negation," 66–67; and
nontransparent thoughts, 100–106; "On
Sense and Reference," 4, 11–14, 69, 77, 81,
86–96, 104; overview of, 3–5; philosophical goals of, 4, 130, 494; philosophy of
language, 5–20, 60–114, 118, 276–77; philosophy of mathematics, 33–59, 114–30;
on propositions, 146; Russell's criticisms
of, 346–50, 367–70; Russell's paradox and,
120–29, 271–76; "Thought," 4, 104, 106–9;
and time, 106–14; on truth, 77–86
Fregean thoughts: 16–19, 70–75; first-
person, 104–5, 108, 110–14; individuation or sameness of, 65–68, 73, 78–79,
104–5, 109, 117; and meaning, 16, 17,
107–14; in the philosophy of mathematics, 117–19; Russellian propositions
compared to, 277; and sentences, 16n7;
transparency of, 73, 87, 98, 100–106, 110;

and truth, 77–86; unsaturated senses as
components of, 74
Frege-Russell conception of numbers, 474,
491
Frege's puzzle, 11–14, 86–96, 396, 398–99
Fuhrmann, André, 532
function-argument expressions, 356–57
functions, 7–10, 17, 20

Geach, Peter, 126n85, 247–51
general facts, 471–72, 516–17, 595–97
generalizations, in ethics, 177, 199–200, 246
generalized quantifiers, 295, 329, 392–94,
410, 597, 600
general propositions, 35, 592–93, 595
geometry, 21n, 41–45, 128, 263, 264, 268;
non-Euclidean, 43–45, 44n48
Gödel, Kurt, 24, 26–27, 29, 130, 521n,
523n48, 525n53, 533, 631
good: defining, 174–94, 199, 201, 203–4,
243–44, 252; emotivism and, 243–44; incompleteness of, 251–52; meaning of, 176;
predicative vs. attributive uses of, 247–52;
self-evident propositions concerning,
194–99; unprovability of, 174–99
grammar, 72, 76, 283–84, 345, 359–60, 384,
417–18, 484, 622, 628
Gray's Elegy argument, 350–70, 391, 460–64
Green, T. H., 421
Grelling's paradox, 534

hallucinations, 164–65, 171, 212–14, 238, 625,
Hanks, Peter, 468–70
hard data, 537–38, 540–41, 543
Hegel, G.W.F., 151, 413; cosmology of, 133,
150, 152
Hempel, Carl, 498–500, 511
higher-order logic, 500–511
higher-order quantification, 25, 476, 478,
507, 511, 516, 518–22, 524, 579n, 620, 621
Hilbert, David, 40n37, 361, 524
Hodes, Harold, 275n, 521n, 532, 533n75
horse, as a concept, 71, 175–76
Hume, David, 48–50, 138, 215–20, 235, 236,
246, 430
Hume's Principle, 49–50, 59n
Husserl, Edmund, 4, 93n46
hypothesis, method of, 560–62

Idealism: Moore and, 133–35, 224; Moore's
critique of, 149–53, 417–19; refutation
of, 154–71, 210, 214, 281; Russell and,
264, 266–69, 413–20; Russell's critique of,
414–20; and time, 152–53, 210

identity: denoting concepts and, 302; objects and criteria of, 48–50; as relation between objects, 86–96; Russell on, 302, 373–79, 396, 529; substitutivity of, 373–79. *See also* personal identity
identity predicate, 22
immortality, 151–52, 267
incomplete descriptions, 400–9
incompleteness: of formal theories, 29, 32; of the good, 247–62; of some senses and referents, 70, 75–76, 272, 274; of tensed and indexical sentences, 106–8
incomplete symbols, 391–94, 445–47, 512, 608, 614–15. *See also* definite descriptions: as incomplete symbols
indefinability of "good," 174–94, 199, 203–4, 243–44, 252
indefinite descriptions, 335–36
indexicality, 106–14, 185, 405n
indirect predication, 366, 463
indirect sense, 19–20, 78, 96–100, 368–69
individualist approach to philosophy, 399, 410–12
induction: and arithmetic, 33–38; enumerative, 560–61, 595, mathematical, 27–29, 52, 55, 522–23; pragmatism and, 421, 429, 430
induction axioms, 479, 505, 511
inductive definitions, 57
inference rules, 20–21
infinite sets, 269–70, 488n, 495n19
infinities, countable vs. uncountable, 269–70
infinity. *See* axiom of infinity
Intentionalism, 165
intentionality, of propositions, 282, 309–18, 365, 433–43, 451–52, 607
internal relations, 415–20
interpretation and propositions, 437
intuitions, Kantian, 42–44, 48

James, William, 421–30
Joachim, Harold H., 414
justification: of arithmetic, 115–20, 129, 474, 494; in ethics, 198–200, 245–47; logic and, 30–32; preservation of, 30

Kamareddine, Fairouz, 523
Kant, Immanuel: and existence, 61; on external world, 225–28; Frege's critique of mathematical theories of, 41–45; Moore's critique of, 134–37
Kaplan, David, 102, 104, 111, 130
Klement, Kevin, 277n 514, 515n, 518–19, 526, 530n66, 579

knowledge: commonsense view of, 221–25; of external world, 215–37, 535–67, 623–27; perception and, 211–21; requiring explanation, 536–37; of sense data, 211–14, 559–63; and verification, 559–63; without evidence, 31–32, 176–77. *See also* epistemology
knowledge by acquaintance, 329–31, 362–63, 378–79, 388–90, 399, 568, 578
knowledge by description, 330–31, 363, 379, 386–90, 568, 578, 613
knowledge of, 100–2, 326–27, 354, 367–68, 427
knowledge that, 327, 354
Kripke, Saul, 96–99, 107, 109–14, 130, 162, 193n, 362n, 380n, 399nn, 400n64, 403–4, 411, 518n, 569–70, 609, 632

Laan, Twan, 523
Landini, Greg, 465n, 467n77, 519, 579
language: Frege's philosophy of, 4–20, 118; of logic, 5–11; of logical form, 336–45; logically perfect, 81, 104n54, 105n, 339, 577, 579, 583–84, 587, 604; of mathematics, 5–11; reality in relation to, 574, 577–87; representational view of, 7; in Russell's logical atomism, 577–87; Russell's philosophy of, 276–412
law of noncontradiction, 158
law of the excluded middle, 370–73
Leibniz, Gottfried Wilhelm, 264, 557
Lewis, C. I., 632
Lewis, David, 113
liar paradox, 534, 616–17
linguistic simples, 577–87
Linsky, Bernard, 532
Locke, John, 138
logic: arithmetic derived from, 4, 13, 27–30, 45–59, 114–29, 472–534 (*see also* logicism); axioms of, 52–54; epistemology and, 29–32, 115, 129, 494–95; first-order vs. second-order, 504–7; foundations of, 31–32; Frege's conception of, 115; Frege's contributions to, 5–11, 20–33, 115, 130; higher-order, 500–511; language of, 5–11; mathematics grounded in, 4, 58–59, 114–20, 393–94, 494–98 (*see also* logicism); metaphysics in relation to, 115; Russell's contributions to, 120–29, 336–41, 473–534; semantics in relation to, 69–70, 115
logical atomism, 464, 568–629; facts and propositions in, 573–77, 587–97; and individuals, 490–91; logical and linguistic simples in, 577–87; methodology of,

logical atomism (*continued*)
571–72; and the multiple relation theory, 604–8; as a philosophical system, 621–29
logical consequence, 22, 27
logical constructions, 537, 544–58, 561, 563–67
logical forms: grammatical vs., 340–45, 384–86, 417–18; and logical laws, 370–79; in Russell's multiple relation theory, 464–65; of sentences containing generalized quantifiers, 392–93
logical laws, 31–32, 38–39
logically perfect language, 81, 339, 577, 579, 581–84, 587, 592–95, 604
logically proper names, 322, 329, 351, 354, 358, 360, 375–78, 387–90, 396, 398–99, 460–61, 519–28, 574, 574–78, 608
logical scope, 372–73, 418
logical subjects, 300n, 311–13, 515, 518, 576–82
logical truth, 22, 22n14, 27
logical types, 129, 467. *See also* types, Russell's theory of
logical vocabulary, 22, 478, 500, 521
logicism: Frege's, 53–59, 120–29, 473–75; higher-order logic and, 500–511; philosophical significance of, 494–98, 507; Russell's, 473–534; strategy for, 473–77; successors of, 498–500, 511–12, 531; weaker form of, 494. *See also* logic: arithmetic derived from; logic: mathematics grounded in
Lowell Lectures, Harvard University (1914), 535

MacColl, Hugh, 320–21
Marcus, Ruth Barcan, 632
material conditionals, 7–8
material objects: existence of, 208–9, 214–20, 225–37; as logical constructions, 544–58, 565–67, 578; sense data and, 211–20, 237–41, 480, 542–58, 561, 563–67
mathematical induction, 27–29, 52, 55–56, 58, 522–23
mathematics: ethics compared to, 197–98; formalism and, 40–41; Frege's philosophy of, 33–57, 114–20; Kant's views on, 41–45; language of, 5–11, 476–78, 480; logic as ground of, 4, 29–32, 114–20 (*see also* logicism); a priori truths in, 115–20; psychologism and, 38–40; Russell's philosophy of, 269–79, 473–80, 493–500; as a science, 498. *See also* arithmetic; philosophy of mathematics

McTaggart, J.M.E., 133, 135, 149–53, 263, 264, 266–68, 421, 623, 628
meaning: and assertion, 405–9; denoting phrases and, 334, 350–57; in isolation, 334, 345, 354, 370, 390–95; and "knowledge of," 327, 363–64; propositions and, 277, 283, 317–18, 357–61, 365–67; transparency of, 87, 100–6, 182–83, 363; truth-conditional conception of, 590–91. *See also* sense
Meinong, Alexius, 307, 345–46, 349, 381, 443, 457, 569, 599
memory, 153n39, 239
mental images, 45–46, 48, 111, 152, 164–69, 209–10, 212–15, 239, 539–43, 547, 587, 624
mentioning, 304–6
metalinguistic quantification over expressions, 516–17, 526–27, 574, 578–79, 594, 604, 611, 616, 620
metaphysical simples, 490, 577–87, 594–95
metaphysics: grammar and, 622; logic in relation to, 115; Moore and, 134–37, 139, 147–71; Russell and, 285–87, 292, 303–7, 512–14, 545–58, 567–69, 577–87, 622–29. *See also* reality
method of hypothesis, 560–62
Mill, John Stuart, 33–38, 138, 173, 240, 264, 430
models/interpretations, 22
model theory, 115, 501, 504, 506, 524
modes of presentation, 12, 16–18, 72, 78, 91–96, 98–99, 102–4, 367–68
modus ponens, 21
molecular facts, 588, 597
molecular sentences, 587–88, 592–94
monism, 267, 414–20, 606n51, 628
Montague, Richard, 130
Moore, G. E.: birth, education, and career of, 133–34; and common sense, 171, 207–25; critical and analytical approach of, 150, 154–55, 259–60; critique of Bradley by, 137–47; critique of Kant by, 134–37; "A Defense of Common Sense," 221–25; epistemology of, 206–41; and ethics, 134, 172–205, 242–60; *Ethics*, 256; "External and Internal Relations," 417; "Freedom," 133; and Idealism, 133–35, 154–71, 224, 417–19; influence of, 134, 154, 194, 199, 225, 241–43, 245, 259–60, 281, 435, 539; influences on, 133, 200–205; "Kant's Idealism," 134; later vs. early views of, 134, 137, 149, 154; metaphysics of, 147–49; moral epistemology of, 242–47; "Mr.

McTaggart's Studies in Hegelian Cosmology," 133, 150; "The Nature of Judgment," 133, 138–41, 149n; on perception, 161–71, 211–15, 237–41, 281; *Philosophical Papers*, 134; on philosophy, 206–11; *Principia Ethica*, 134, 147, 172, 184–85, 193–95, 197, 200–205, 243, 253, 255–56, 259–60; "Proof of an External World," 225–37; on propositions, 137–47, 279–80, 434–37; "The Refutation of Idealism," 134, 154, 539; "Relative and Absolute," 134; Russell and, 133, 154, 200–205, 435; *Some Main Problems of Philosophy*, 134, 206–21; "Truth and Falsity," 133; on truth and propositions, 137–47

multiple relation theory of judgment, 367, 438–60, 464–72, 573, 604–7

multiplication, defined, 58, 479, 511

naïve set theory, 495, 500

names: competence with, 362; as descriptions, 386, 395–96, 398–400; of fictional/legendary characters, 306–7, 319–20, 386, 398; in Frege's philosophy, 8, 12–13, 70–71, 104–5, 367–68; meaning of, 575; as rigid designators, 400; in Russell's philosophy, 303–6, 314, 319–22, 362–63, 386–87, 395–400, 528–29, 574–75, 583. *See also* logically proper names; ordinary proper names

naturalism, and mathematics, 33–38

naturalistic fallacy, 252–54

natural language: description vs. improvement of, 81, 105n; formal language in relation to, 15; Frege's interest in, 81, 350; Frege's semantic framework and, 63; indexicals in, 110; reference failure in, 18, 80–81; Russell's interest in, 283, 350, 393–94, 400, 410

natural numbers, 45–53, 275–76, 473–74, 483–85, 509–10, 521

necessary a posteriori, 162

Nederpelt, Rob, 523

negation, 15, 67, 448–49, 469, 588

negative existentials, 303–9, 381–89, 395–400

negative facts, 588–92

neutral monism, 606n51, 628

no-class theory, 492–93, 533, 579–80, 580n, 584, 597, 615–21. *See also* classes: as logical fictions

noncognitivism, 243–44, 247, 249, 259

non-denoting occurrences of denoting concepts, 318–19, 322, 324–25

nonlogical vocabulary, 22, 157, 185–86, 521, 529n, 530, 561–62

nonnaturalism, 249

number: concepts and, 45–46, 272–75; empiricist theories of, 35–38; Frege's definition of, 45–53, 119, 272, 491–92; natural numbers, 51–53, 275–76, 473–75, 483–85, 510–11, 521–22; objects and, 46–50, 272–75; Russell's definition of, 473–75, 483–85, 491–93, 510–11, 521–22

objectivity, in ethics, 257–59

objects: concepts and, 9, 70–76, 272; criteria of identity for, 48–50; knowledge of, 378–79; as logical constructions, 545–58; mind-dependent vs. mind-independent, 227–29; numbers as 46–50; as possibilities of sensation. *See also* material objects

objectual quantification, 517, 519–22, 524–27, 534, 578–79, 584, 594–95, 620–21

Occam's razor, 555

occurrence, primary vs. secondary, 372–77

one-to-one correspondence, 49

ontology, Russell's, 278, 292, 297–307, 318–21. *See also* being; reality

open-question test for definability, 181–84, 191–94, 203–5, 243–44, 422–23

ordinary proper names, 12, 272, 362, 386, 389, 395, 398–400

ordinary sense, 19–20, 96–100, 368

other minds, 378–79, 563–67, 625–27

pain, 165–66, 228–29, 266, 563–64

particular quantification, 60–64

Peano, Giuseppe, 54, 114, 478, 507

Peano arithmetic, 54–58, 114, 120, 478–79, 498, 500, 505, 524

Peirce, Charles Sanders, 20n11, 421, 428

perception: appearance and, 209–15; counterfactuals in the analysis of, 548–558; critique of Idealist conception of, 161–71; perception and knowledge, 215–21, 237–41; Russellian propositions and, 279–80; and sense data, 211–14, 238–39, 537–54. *See also* esse is *percipi* (to be is to be perceived)

permanent possibilities of sensation, 240–41

Perry, John, 111n66, 112, 403n70

personal identity, 153n39

philosophy: common sense in conflict with, 149, 155, 171, 207–11, 219–25; Frege's goals in, 4, 494; Moore on, 206–11; philosophy of life vs. epistemology, metaphysics, and logic, 428–32; problems of,

philosophy (*continued*)
    622, 631; Russell's goals in, 494, 568–71;
    science in relation to, 622
Pigden, Charles, 200n22, 201, 203–4, 205n,
    252n8, 264–66
Pincock, Christopher, 465n, 468, 471,
    540n7, 557n31
Platonism, 17, 98
power set, 28–29, 121, 269–70, 488n
pragmatism, 421–32
predicate (verb), 313–18, 365–67, 451–56,
    460–64
predicate calculus, 20, 23–27, 506; first-
    order, 24–27; second-order, 24–27
predicates, 5, 24–25, 337, 577, 580–82
predication: direct and indirect, 463; truth
    and, 77–86; and unity of propositions,
    314–16, 437
predication targets, 311, 353, 361, 363, 365–
    66, 370, 434, 454, 457, 460–63, 514
pre-philosophical thought, 41, 149, 155,
    171, 207, 224, 246, 537–38
pre-theoretic knowledge, 37, 119, 163, 246,
    566, 569, 571–72
primitive vocabulary, 477
private perspectives, 551–58
probability, 35
problem of the unity of the proposition,
    146, 282, 309–18, 365, 433–37, 444, 449,
    588, 597
proof procedure, 20–24
proper names. *See* logically proper names;
    names; ordinary proper names
propositional attitudes, 47, 100–6, 108–14,
    372–80, 390, 441, 450–56, 604–5, 606n51
propositional calculus, 20, 23
propositional functions, 276–78, 322,
    330–36, 332n4, 338, 340–42, 345, 356, 370,
    385, 391–95, 397, 409–11, 448, 454–55,
    468, 476, 507n33, 512–16, 518–19, 521n,
    523, 528, 530–34, 578–79, 584, 592–94,
    597–600, 602, 604, 609, 611, 613, 615–16,
    619–21
propositions; attempt to eliminate, 438–50,
    464–72, 514–31, 533–34, 578–79, 584, 589,
    594–95, 597, 610–14, 617–18; cognitive
    theory of, 365–67, 451–64; intentionality
    of, 282, 309, 311–18; Moore on, 137–47,
    279–80, 434–37 ; paradoxes involving,
    532; place of, in cognitive architecture,
    459; Russell and, 277, 279–85, 310–18,
    338–41, 434–39, 573–77; structure and
    constituents of, 284–85, 310–18, 338–41,
    365–67, 452–56, 462–64; truth and,

137–47, 433–36, 438; unity of, 16, 146,
    309–18, 365–67, 432–37, 439, 468–69, 471,
    597; visualization of, 460–61, 463–64
psychologism, 38–40
Putnam, Hilary, 411

quantification: first-order, 25–27, 331–36,
    340–41, 502, 520, 525–28, 533–34; in
    Frege's logic, 20, 25–27, 60–70, 75–77;
    higher-order, 25–26, 475, 502–3, 520–21;
    logic of, 10; metalinguistic, 515–17,
    526–27; nth-order, 26, 502; objectual, 517,
    519–22, 524–27, 534, 578–80, 584, 594–95,
    604, 620–21; plural, 298–99, 524n; Rus-
    sell's early theory of, 288–306, in Russell's
    logic, , 328–36, 390–95; second-order,
    26–27, 502, 520; substitutional, 517–31,
    533–34, 573–74, 578–80, 584–85, 594–95,
    597, 604, 609, 620–21
quantifiers, 390–91. *See also* generalized
    quantifiers
Quine, W.V.O., 126, 506–7, 511–12, 567, 632
Quine-Duhem point, 562n

ramified theory of types, 512n34, 521n,
    523–24, 530, 531, 533–34
Ramsey, F. P., 512n34, 524, 531, 534
Rayo, Augustine, 275n, 298n54
Realism: direct, 238, metaphysical, 147–49;
    scientific, 427
reality: appearance in relation to, 135–36,
    209–10, 214, 268; Idealist conception of,
    151–53, 266–67; language in relation to,
    574, 577–87; Moore on, 134–37, 147–49;
    Russell on, 628–29. *See also* metaphysics;
    ontology, Russell's
reasoning, laws of, 38–39
recursive definitions, 57
reference: failures of, 14–15, 18, 80–82, 347–
    350, 457, 609; and identity, 86–96; sense
    in relation to, 11–13, 16–20, 70–72, 86–96
relations, in Idealist philosophy, 415–20
representation, 282, 309–10, 314, 316–18,
    450–54
restricted quantifiers, 336
rightness, 172–73, 207, 243, 246, 253–59
rigid designation, 97–98, 111, 114, 369, 400,
    570
Ross, David, 199, 254–56
Royce, Josiah, 421, 582
Russell, Bertrand, 20, 28, 59, 61, 99, 130;
    Cantor's influence on, 269–71; corre-
    spondence between Frege and, 122, 124;
    A Critical Exposition of the Philosophy of

Leibniz, 263–64; education of, 264; epistemology of, 361–64, 389–90, 410–12, 535–67, 623–25; *An Essay on the Foundations of Geometry*, 263; and ethics, 200–205, 254n14, 265–68; "The Existential Import of Propositions," 318; on Frege's character, 129; Frege's influence on, 3, 129; *German Social Democracy*, 263; and Idealism, 264, 266–69, 413–20; influence of, 124–25, 134, 328, 409–12, 524, 531, 567; *An Inquiry into Truth and Meaning*, 515; introduction of, to philosophy, 263–69; *Introduction to Mathematical Philosophy*, 488–91, 494; "Is Ethics a Branch of Empirical Psychology?," 201; "Knowledge by Acquaintance and Knowledge by Description," 363, 386, 388–90, 568; "Lecture 3: On Our Knowledge of the External World," 535; "Lecture 4: The World of Physics and the World of Sense," 535; and logic, 120–29, 370–89, 488n, 494; and logical atomism, 568–629; logicism of, 473–534; "Mathematical Logic as Based on the Theory of Types," 489, 568; metaphysics of, 284–87, 292, 303–7, 395–98, 568–69, 585–86, 622–29; "The Monistic Theory of Truth," 414, 417; Moore and, 133, 137–38, 142, 147, 154, 200–205, 279–81, 309; multiple relation theory of, 367, 440–50, 464–72, 604–7; "My Mental Development," 264–65; *My Philosophical Development*, 515; "On Denoting," 99, 318, 320, 322, 326, 328–412, 460–64, 525, 528, 529, 535, 568, 577, 578, 584, 594, 597, 600, 603, 609–10, 612, 613; "On Fundamentals," 318, 322–27, 363, 378; "On Meaning and Denotation," 318; "On the Meaning and Denotation of Phrases," 318; "On the Nature of Truth," 414, 568; "On the Nature of Truth and Falsity," 568; "On Truth and Falsehood," 366–67; *Our Knowledge of the External World*, 427, 535–567, 569, 578, 586n, 587, 624, 625, 629; philosophical goals of, 494–98, 568–71; philosophy of language, 276–412; *The Philosophy of Logical Atomism*, 569–629; philosophy of mathematics, 269–79, 473–534; "Points about Denoting," 318; "Pragmatism," 421, 429; and pragmatism, 421–32; *Principia Mathematica*, 129, 263, 273, 278, 308, 473, 476, 477, 488n, 491, 492, 494–95, 511–20, 523–30, 532–33, 535, 568–69, 577–79, 615–16, 620–21, 629; *The Principles of Mathematics*, 121, 147, 263, 273, 277–78, 283, 285, 288, 292, 296, 303–4, 306–7, 318, 321–22, 326, 327, 331, 332n4, 345–46, 353, 354, 365, 367, 382–83, 490, 492, 514, 531–32, 568; *The Problems of Philosophy*, 147, 318, 438, 568; "The Regressive Method of Discovering the Premises of Mathematics," 495, 568; religious background, 264–65; "Review of Meinong et al., *Untersuchungen zur Gegenstandstheorie und Psychologie*," 318; revisionism of, 571–72, 628–29; *Theory of Knowledge*, 449n59, 464, 466, 472, 568; "Transatlantic 'Truth'," 421, 422; on truth and propositions, 137–47, 309–18, 338–39, 364–67, 414–43, 460–64; "William James's Conception of Truth," 421; Wittgenstein and, 464, 466–70, 472, 570n, 574n9, 575, 576n14, 577, 585, 606, 622

Russell's paradox, 120–29, 271–76, 474–75, 488–89, 494, 495, 534, 615

Ryle, Gilbert, 149n

Sainsbury, Mark, 519n46, 533, 534n77, 549n21, 557n31

Salmon, Nathan, 62n, 64n6, 88n34, 91n40, 107n59, 112n69, 114, 193n15, 307n61, 321n81, 326n, 352, 360n33, 378n, 380n, 398n, 399n60, 400n63, 403n71, 456n, 601n

saturated expressions, 8

saturated senses, 70

Schiller, F.C.S., 421, 423–24, 428–29

science: and knowledge of external world, 536, 554–58; philosophy in relation to, 622; and reductionism, 623; verifiability of, 555–57

second-order arithmetic, 28–30, 505, 524, 530

second-order predicate calculus, 24–27, 29, 32, 275n, 501, 504–6, 524

second-order quantification, 26–27, 474–75, 501–2, 520, 524

self, transcendental, 135. *See also* personal identity

self-ascription, 113

self-evidence, 21n, 31–33, 45, 115–16, 119, 126, 129, 156–58, 171, 184, 187, 190, 195–200, 245–46, 257, 474, 569

semantic paradoxes, 534

semantics: Frege's vs. Russell's, 276–77; logic in relation to, 69–70, 115; sense and, 105n

sensation: as cognitive act vs. object of perception, 159, 162–66, 169, 539–40; commonsense view of, 209–10; critique of Idealist conception of, 159–71 sense: hierarchy of, 19–20, 96–100, 368–70; and identity, 86–96; indirect sense, 19–20, 96–100; ordinary sense, 96–100; reference in relation to, 11–13, 16–20, 70–72, 86–96

sense data: and material objects, 211–21, 237–41, 538–58, 561; in Moore's epistemology, 211–27, 238–41; in Russell's epistemology, 537–63; unsensed, 554–58; verification and, 559–63

sentences: and facts, 573–74; in Frege's philosophy of language, 6–11; in Russell's language of logical forms, 337–38; senses and referents of, 18; and thoughts, 16n7; truth values and, 16, 18

sentence types, existence of, 458

sets, hierarchy of, 475. See also classes

set theory, 128, 130, 480–82, 495, 500–501, 504–7, 511–12, 523, 533. See also infinite sets; power sets

Sidgwick, Henry, 133, 200–201, 204, 264, 265–67

simples, linguistic, 577–87

simples, metaphysical, 577–87

simple theory of types, 524, 531–32, 534

singular definite descriptions, 336, 343–45, 400–401, 410

skepticism: beliefs underlying, 224; and epistemology, 226–28, 235–37; and ethics, 244; about external world, 226–28, 230–31, 234–37; grounds of, 235; pragmatism and, 429–30

solipsism, 579–80

soundness of a logical system, 23

spirituality, of the universe, 151, 154–56

Stevens, Graham, 468, 470n, 472

Stevenson, Charles, 259

Stout, G. F., 134, 264

Strawson, Peter, 400–402, 408

subjectivism, in ethics, 257–59

substitutional quantification, 517–31, 533–34, 574, 578–80, 584–85, 594–95, 597, 604, 609, 620–21

substitutivity of identity, 373–79

successor, 51–52, 54–55, 483, 509–10

synthetic truths, 41–44, 128, 156–58, 174n, 177–80, 195, 254

Tarski, Alfred, 22, 130, 336, 511–12, 534, 631

tautology, 23

tense, 107

term-accessible positions, 288–90, 324, 325

term occurrences, 324

terms, 5–6, 284–87, 337

"the," 62, 302–3, 308, 341–45, 356–57, 477

theorems, defined, 477

theoretical reduction, 477–78

theory, defined, 477

theory of denoting, 318–412; foundational issues in, 409–12; logical puzzles pertaining to, 370–89; problems, challenges, and refinements in, 389–409; Russell's critiques concerning, 324–27, 345–70; Russell's early, 288–303; Russell's new, 328–45

theory of descriptions, 328–412, 609–11

things, 287, 553–54, 557

third realm of being, 98, 369

"this," 386–87, 583–84

time: in Frege's semantics, 106–14; Idealist conception of, 152–53, 210; unreality of, 134–35

transcendental self, 135

transitive closure, 52

transparency: of meaning, 87, 182–83, 363; of thoughts, 73, 100–106, 363

the True, 7, 8, 18, 61–62, 64–68, 77–82

truth: being always true, 333, 394–95; coherence theory of, 415; by convention, 500; correspondence theories of, 84–85, 137, 139, 141–42, 145, 434–35, 438, 588, 596; definability of, 84–86; Frege on, 77–86; laws of, 30; logic and, 30; Moore on, 137–47; necessary truths, 140; not dependent on existence, 458; pragmatism and, 421–28, 430; and propositions, 137–47, 277–80, 310–18, 433–34, 438–39, 452–53, 456, 458, 459; Russell on, 280, 338–39, 414–43, 456, 592–94; as simple, unanalyzable property, 140, 142, 435; thoughts and, 82–83. See also logical truths

truth bearers, 77–86, 137, 277, 279–80, 310–18, 438–43, 452–53, 456, 458, 459

truth conditions, 7, 576

truth preservation, 30

truth values: absence of, 15; assignment of, 7; sentences and, 16, 18, 79–82; use of term, 79–80

types, Russell's theory of, 273–74, 467–68, 488–93, 501–12, 518, 523–24, 531

understanding, 361–64

unity of the proposition, 146, 309–18, 365–67, 432–37, 439, 468–69, 471, 597

Universal Being, 286–87, 304–5

universal quantification, 26, 65, 68–69, 502

universal set, 121, 126, 128, 270–71, 292

unsaturated expressions, 8

unsaturated senses, 70–76, 146

utilitarianism, 173, 254, 265–66

vagueness, 572

Van Fraassen, Bas, 427

verbs, in propositions, 310–12, 472, 604–7

verification: in science, 555–57; and sense data, 559–63

vicious circle principle, 519, 530, 532–34, 617

Vienna Circle, 631

Ward, James, 134, 264

Whitehead, Alfred North, 264, 507, 515; *Principia Mathematica*, 129, 263, 308, 473, 512, 523

Wittgenstein, Ludwig: and facts and truth, 145; Frege's influence on, 4; influence of, 134; and logical atomism, 570n, 622; "Notes on Logic," 467, 468, 570n, 575; Russell and, 464, 466–70, 472, 570n, 585; *Tractatus Logico-Philosophicus*, 145, 464, 467, 500, 577, 622, 631

yacht example, 379–80

yellow: definability of, 175–77, 179–81; as a property, 247–48; sensation of, 159–61

Yourgrau, Palle, 99

Zermelo, Ernest, 495

zero, 50, 56, 483, 509

ZF set theory, 488n, 495, 496, 500, 505, 512, 533